Comprehensive Clinical Psychology

Comprehensive Clinical Psychology

Editors-in-Chief
Alan S. Bellack
The University of Maryland at Baltimore, MD, USA
Michel Hersen
Pacific University, Forest Grove, OR, USA

Volume 10
SOCIOCULTURAL AND INDIVIDUAL DIFFERENCES

Volume Editor
Cynthia D. Belar
University of Florida Health Sciences Center, Gainesville, FL, USA

1998
AN IMPRINT OF ELSEVIER SCIENCE
AMSTERDAM—LAUSANNE—NEW YORK—OXFORD—SHANNON—SINGAPORE—TOKYO

Elsevier Science Ltd., The Boulevard, Langford Lane, Kidlington, Oxford, OX5 1GB, UK

First edition 1998

Library of Congress Cataloging-in-Publication Data
Comprehensive clinical psychology / editors-in-chief. Alan S. Bellack, Michel Hersen. —1st ed.
p. cm.
Includes indexes.
Contents: v. 1. Foundations / volume editor, C. Eugene Walker — v. 2. Professional issues / volume editor, Arthur N. Wiens — v. 3. Research and Methods / volume editor, Nina R. Schooler — v. 4. Assessment / volume editor, Cecil R. Reynolds — v. 5. Children & adolescents / volume editor, Thomas Ollendick — v. 6. Adults / volume editor, Paul Salkovskis — v. 7. Clinical geropsychology / volume editor, Barry Edelstein — v. 8. Health psychology / volume editors, Derek W. Johnston and Marie Jonhston — v. 9. Applications in diverse populations / volume editor, Nirbhay N. Singh — v. 10. Sociocultural and individual differences / volume editor, Cynthia D. Belar — v. 11. Indexes.
1. Clinical psychology. I. Bellack, Alan S. II. Hersen, Michel.
[DNLM: 1. Psychology, Clinical. WM 105 C737 1998]
RC467.C597 1998
616.89--dc21
DNLM/DLC
for Library of Congress 97-50185
CIP

British Library Cataloguing in Publication Data
A catalogue record for this book is available from the British Library.

ISBN 0-08-042707-3 (set : alk. paper)
ISBN 0-08-043149-6 (Volume 10)

∞™ The paper used in this publication meets the minimum requirements of the American National Standard for Information Sciences—Permanence of Paper for Printed Library Materials, ANSI Z39.48–1984.

Typeset by Bibliocraft, Dundee, UK.
Printed and bound in Great Britain by BPC Wheatons Ltd., Exeter, UK.

Contents

Introduction to *Comprehensive Clinical Psychology* vii

Honorary International Editorial Advisory Board xiii

Preface xv

Contributors to Volume 10 xix

Volume Editors xxi

Section I: Foundations

1 Introduction to Diversity in Clinical Psychology 1
H. C. TRIANDIS, *University of Illinois, Urbana, IL, USA*

2 Cross-cultural Psychopathology 35
F. M. CHEUNG, *The Chinese University of Hong Kong, Hong Kong*

3 Cultural Bias in Testing of Intelligence and Personality 53
C. R. REYNOLDS, *Texas A&M University, College Station, TX, USA*

4 Cross-cultural Clinical Interventions 93
J. E. LEWIS, *Nova Southeastern University, Fort Lauderdale, FL, USA*

5 Cultural Competence Training in Clinical Psychology: Assessment, Clinical Intervention, and Research 127
F. G. CASTRO, *Arizona State University, Tempe, AZ, USA*

Section II: Special Topics

6 Reconstructing Race, Rethinking Ethnicity 141
M. P. P. ROOT, *University of Washington, Seattle, WA, USA*

7 The Psychology of Gender and Health 161
R. M. EISLER, *Virginia Polytechnic Institute and State University, Blacksburg, VA, USA*

8 A Cultural Perspective on Families Across the Life Cycle: Patterns, Assessment, and Intervention Outline 173
N. J. KASLOW and K. A. WOOD, *Emory University School of Medicine, Atlanta, GA, USA*, and M. R. LOUNDY, *Georgia State University, Atlanta, GA, USA*

9 Sexual Orientation 207
B. GREENE, *St. John's University, Jamaica, NY, USA*

10 Diversity Matters: Religion and the Practice of Clinical Psychology 233
D. W. PREUSSLER, R. E. BUTMAN, and S. L. JONES, *Wheaton College, IL, USA*

11 Mental Health in Rural Society 255
M. MURRAY, *Memorial University of Newfoundland, St. John's, NF, Canada*, D. S. HARGROVE, *University of Mississippi, MS, USA*, and M. BLANK, *University of Virginia, Charlottesville, VA, USA*

Section III: International Perspectives

12 Objective Personality Assessment: Computer-based Minnesota Multiphasic Personality Inventory-2 Interpretation in International Clinical Settings 277
J. N. BUTCHER, *University of Minnesota, Minneapolis, MN, USA*, E. BERAH and P. MIACH, *Monash Medical Centre, Clayton, Vic, Australia*, B. ELLERTSEN, *University of Bergen, Norway*, L. JEEYOUNG, *Samsung Group, Jeongdun-Maul, Sungnam-City, South Korea*, E. NEZAMI, *USC/IPR, Los Angeles, CA, USA*, P. PANCHERI, *5a Cattedra di Clinica Psichiatrica, Rome, Italy*, J. DERKSEN, *University of Nijmegen, The Netherlands*, and M. ALMAGOR, *University of Haifa, Israel*

13 Mental Health in the Arab World 313
M. DWAIRY, *Nova Southeastern University, Oakland Park, FL, USA*

14 Perspectives from Lithuania 325
D. GAILIENĖ, *University of Vilnius, Lithuania*

15 From a Monocultural Identity to Diversity Identity: A Psychological Model for Diversity Management in South African Organizations 335
K. LETLAKA-RENNERT, *Johannesburg, South Africa*, and W. P. RENNERT, *University of the Witwatersrand, Johannesburg, South Africa*

16 Clinical Psychology in Asia: A Taiwanese Perspective 343
S.-H. CHEN, *National Taiwan University, Taipei, Taiwan* and E. K. EMORY, *Emory University, Atlanta, GA, USA*

17 Clinical Psychology in Aotearoa/New Zealand: Indigenous Perspectives 349
T. M. MOEKE-PICKERING, M. K. PAEWAI, A. TURANGI-JOSEPH, and A. M. L. HERBERT, *University of Waikato, Hamilton, New Zealand*

18 Perspectives from Sub-Sahara Africa 357
P. K. ESSANDOH, *Jersey City State College, NJ, USA*

Subject Index 365

Introduction to *Comprehensive Clinical Psychology*

Co-Editors-in-Chief

Alan S. Bellack and Michel Hersen

Background

Clinical psychology is a relatively new field. While its roots can be traced back to at least the late nineteenth century, its evolution as a distinct academic discipline and profession dates only to the Second World War. The first 20 years of this postwar period saw steady, albeit nonspectacular, growth. Based substantially in the United States and Europe during this period, the study of clinical psychology developed as an alternative to medical school and psychiatry for many students interested in clinical service careers or the scientific study of human behavior. Postgraduate training was conducted exclusively in large university psychology departments within a strict scientist–practitioner model. The total number of Ph.D. candidates admitted to graduate school programs each year was relatively small; there were fewer than 50 accredited programs in the United States during much of this period, each admitting only 5–10 students. The number of new Ph.D.'s produced each year was substantially less, as many students failed to complete the rigorous scientific requirements of these elite programs. Career opportunities were similarly delimited, due in no small part to restraints on clinical practice imposed by psychiatrists and other physicians. The dominant form of psychotherapy was psychoanalysis, and psychologists were either excluded from psychoanalytic institutes or trained only as lay analysts who were proscribed from clinical practice. Few jurisdictions awarded licenses for independent practice, and psychologists generally were not reimbursed for their activities unless they worked under the direction of a physician. A sizable minority of clinical psychologists followed their mentors into university positions, teaching and conducting research. The majority, who were more interested in clinical service, opted for work in large psychiatric or Veterans Administration hospitals, where the modal activity was psychological testing; verbal psychotherapy was provided at the discretion of medical supervisors. A gradually increasing number of psychologists elected to be in private practice, where there was a greater professional autonomy. Medical hegemony over services for psychiatric disorders was even greater in Europe and Latin America.

The last 30 years has witnessed a massive change in the profession, stimulated by a number of scientific, clinical, and economic factors. Psychoanalysis gradually fell out of favor due to a dearth of data on its effectiveness and a desire for shorter term treatments that were not the primary purview of psychiatrists. First, client-centered therapy and then behavior therapy emerged as brief, highly effective alternatives. The former was entirely a product of clinical psychology, and was the intellectual and technical forebear of the current mandate for empirical evaluation of psychotherapies.

Carl Rogers, his colleagues, and students were the first to demonstrate the feasibility of careful, objective evaluation of the therapy process as well as outcome. While behavior therapy owes much of its legacy to psychiatrists such as Joseph Wolpe, it was substantially a product of academic psychologists searching for an approach with a strong scientific underpinning (in this case learning theory) that could be subjected to rigorous scientific scrutiny. Early behavior therapy emerged simultaneously in the UK and the US: in the UK psychologists such as Hans Eysenck based their work on Pavlov and classical conditioning, while in the US researchers were following Skinner and operant conditioning theories. The two schools merged with cognitive therapy, developed largely by Beck and Ellis through the 1960s, when the limitations of behavior therapy in isolation became apparent, particulary with depressed patients, and cognitive-behavior therapy is now widely practised.

Behavior therapy and cognitive-behavior therapy have not only proven themselves to be effective with a broad array of disorders, they have since been shown to be very successful alternatives to pharmacotherapy as well. Notably, behavior therapy was able to produce significant changes in populations that had previously been warehoused as untreatable, including people with physical and developmental disabilities and schizophrenia. Many of the most important contributions to the behavior therapies came from the UK, The Netherlands, South Africa, Australia, and Scandinavia, providing a tremendous stimulus for the development of clinical psychology globally. The availability of cost-effective, scientifically sound nonmedical treatments has decreased the medical monopoly of psychiatric/mental health services around the world and fostered the evolution of clinical psychology as a legally sanctioned helping profession, as well as a prestigious scientific discipline.

Scientific advances in our understanding of the brain and the role of psychosocial factors in physical health and illness have led to the development of two other rapidly growing subspecialties of clinical psychology: neuropsychology and health psychology. Novel assessment and treatment technologies in these two areas have created professional opportunities for clinical psychologists in medical schools, general medical hospitals, and other nonpsychiatric settings. Clinical psychologists can now be found conducting research and providing services in departments of neurology and neurosurgery, medicine, cardiac surgery, pediatrics, anesthesiology, oncology, and other medical specialty areas, as well as in the traditional psychiatric settings. They increasingly serve as directors of governmental agencies and service facilities. They comprise a large percentage of research grant recipients in the US, Canada, and the UK, and sit on prestigious government and foundation review boards. In fact the field has earned sufficient public recognition that it now has the somewhat dubious distinction of having clinical psychologists as lead characters on television shows and in cinema.

Stimulated, in part, by these exciting developments in scientific progress and clinical creativity, the field has grown geometrically in the past two decades. Psychology is now the second leading undergraduate major in the US and is increasingly popular elsewhere in the world as well. There are now more than 175 doctoral programs in the United States, each admitting many more students per annum than the 5–10 that has been typical of traditional scientist–practitioner Ph.D. programs over the past 25 years. Some of these schools have entering classes as large as 200 per year. Moreover, along with the professional school movement, which began in the 1970s, a new degree, the Psy.D. (or Doctorate in Psychology), is regularly being offered as an alternative to the Ph.D. Basically a professional rather than an academic degree, the Psy.D. is reflective of the local practitioner–scientist model rather than the scientist–practitioner.

Yet another trend in the field is the proliferation of master's level psychologists, specifically trained to carry out some of the more mundane functions formerly implemented by doctoral level psychologists. Indeed, each year in the United States alone 10 000 new master's level psychologists graduate from university programs. The financial and programmatic implication of such large numbers is obvious.

Statistics are not readily available about the size of the profession in all regions of the globe, but anecdotal evidence supports the hypothesis that the field is growing worldwide. As previously indicated, behavioral and cognitive-behavioral therapies owe a substantial debt to scientists and clinicians from Europe, Australia, and South Africa. There are now enough cognitive-behavior therapists to support national societies in most Western European countries, as well as Asia, Australia, and Latin America. Many of the most important developments in the psychosocial treatment of severe and persistent mental illness in the last decade have come from the United Kingdom, Australia, Switzerland, and Germany. Psychologists in Scandinavia, the United Kingdom, and the Netherlands have played a central role in the development of cognitive-behavioral treatments for anxiety and depression, and there have also been notable contributions from these regions to health psychology. As the hold of psychoanalytic therapies on psychiatric treatment in Europe continues its inevitable decline, there will be increasing opportunities for clinical psychologists to provide shorter term behavioral and cognitive-behavioral treatments. In addition, exciting developments are also emerging from Japan, China, and other countries in the Pacific rim. It seems likely that the global influence of regional approaches and thinking will lead to a more multicultural and universal psychology than has been the case in the past.

The scientific and clinical literatures have burgeoned along with the number of clinical psychologists in the world. This has been an era of rapid growth of knowledge and increasing specialization. General topics, such as psychological assessment, clinical child psychology, and psychotherapy, that used to merit only one or two graduate courses to establish expertise, have expanded and are subdivided to the extent that circumscribed specialty areas, such as neuropsychology, geropsychology, behavioral pediatrics, or cognitive-behavior therapy for depression can each require postdoctoral training. Consequently, hundreds of undergraduate, graduate, and professional level texts are published each year. Specialty journals abound. Where a few key generalist journals such as the *Journal of Consulting and Clinical Psychology* used to represent the entire field, each subdiscipline now has multiple journals, and there are both national journals (e.g., the *British Journal of Clinical Psychology*, the *British Journal of Health Psychology*, the *Australian Journal of Cognitive and Behavioral Therapy*) and journals representing specific populations or disorders (e.g., *Addictive Behaviors*, *Journal of Family Violence*, *Journal of Clinical Geropsychology*), or domains of practice (e.g., *Journal of Clinical Psychology in Medical Setting*). Specialization has made it difficult for professionals to keep abreast of developments within their immediate areas of expertise, and impossible for them to be conversant with the literature in other areas. Moreover, given the plethora of choices, it is also virtually impossible for either students or professionals to know where to find the most accurate, up-to-date information in most areas.

The combination of a large and increasing number of students and professionals, and rapidly growing scientific and clinical literature, makes this a particularly appropriate time for *Comprehensive Clinical Psychology*. This multivolume work encompasses the entire field, and represents a single source of information on the scientific status of clinical psychology and its subspecialties, on theory, and on clinical techniques. The work covers the history of the field, and current thinking about training, professional standards and practices, and sociocultural factors in mental health and illness.

Genesis of Comprehensive Clinical Psychology

Following preliminary conceptual discussions between Elsevier Science and Alan S. Bellack at several international conferences in 1994, Michel Hersen was asked to join as Co-Editor-in-Chief. The first official planning meeting for the project took place in June 1995. In addition to Elsevier Science staff, Alan S. Bellack and Michel Hersen invited Tom Ollendick, Nina Schooler, and Warren Tryon to serve as consultants. At that meeting, the philosophical and international scope of the project was agreed upon and established, with the scientific underpinnings of the field identified as the model. The objective here was to ensure that chapters reflect our core knowledge and that the material stand the test of time.

At that meeting, we also underscored that since clinical psychology was now an international discipline, the work should reflect contributions at the cross-cultural level, with chapters solicited from eminent psychologists worldwide. Although it was acknowledged that the United States was in the forefront of the field, the work could not simply represent the American perspective but to the extent possible would represent diversity at its best. Consistent with the international perspective, at the initial planning meeting, the importance of having an Honorary International Editorial Advisory Board comprised of international representatives was acknowledged, and the 10 specific volumes to comprise *Comprehensive Clinical Psychology* were identified. Preliminary outlines for each volume were developed and volumes editors were considered.

The international perspective was to be reflected at a tripartite level. First, diversity among editors and contributors for their respective volumes was selected as a goal. Second, chapters in each volume were designed to reflect diversity by providing the reader with worldwide examples, not simply the Anglo-Saxon view. Of course, where basic facts and principles were the same, there was no need to present regional diversity. Third, and related to the first two parts, the Honorary International Editorial Advisory Board provided us with an international perspective on overall organization and specifics for the individual volumes.

Between June and October 1995, Alan S. Bellack and Michel Hersen, in consultation with Elsevier Science, invited the ten volume editors to assume their positions, and a meeting of the Editors-in-Chief, the ten volume editors (C. Eugene Walker, Arthur N. Wiens, Nina R. Schooler, Cecil R. Reynolds, Thomas Ollendick, Paul Salkovskis, Barry Edelstein, Marie Johnston and Derek W. Johnston, Nirbhay N. Singh, and Cynthia D. Belar), and Elsevier Science staff was convened in October of that year. At that meeting, each of the volume editors presented his or her conception of the relevant volume, and the nature of coverage and particular contributors was discussed at length. Most of all the philosophical underpinnings of the work were stressed so as to insure intervolume consistency.

Subsequent to the October 1995 meeting, the enormous work to bring this project to fruition began, with potential authors invited to contribute, manuscripts reviewed, and then edited. Were it not for the wonders of electronic communication, a project of this scope would not have been possible, especially given the international aspects involved. A lengthy series of checks and balances was instituted to guarantee the quality and excellence of each contribution. The volume editor first approved each contributor's chapter outline, followed by editing and approval of the text. This process frequently required several revisions. The Co-Editor-in-Chief then reviewed each chapter for scope, level, and overlap, but only after the volume editor had first verified the accuracy of references cited. After the Co-Editor-in-Chief's labors, the manuscript was reviewed by Elsevier staff for format, writing style, reference checking, and other technical issues.

Aims and Scope

The final organization and contents of the work evolved over a series of discussions between the Editors-in-Chief, the volume editors, and Elsevier Science. It was comparatively easy to select the primary domains that needed to be covered: history, treatment, assessment, research, training, and professional issues. It was also comparatively easy to identify the first two-thirds, or so, of specific topics that required chapter-length coverage: treatment of the primary *DSM/ICD* disorders, basic research strategies, standard assessment techniques, etc. However, organizing the vast set of requisite topics into coherent volumes, determining which topics warranted independent chapters, and assigning page limits to individual chapters proved to be daunting. Two broad organizational themes immediately suggested themselves: a focus on core themes or techniques across populations vs. integrated coverage of populations. For example, the former would have entailed volumes on treatment modalities, such as behavior therapy, as they are applied to children and adults, while the latter would call for separate volumes on children and adults that covered diverse approaches. To complicate matters, some topics, such as Research Methods and Professional Issues, do not lend themselves to breakdown by population, and others, such as Behavioral Medicine, do not lend themselves to a breakdown by themes or techniques. Volume length was also an important factor, making some content-based solutions less practical than others. For example, we determined that treatment should receive more attention than assessment; a strict population-based solution would have led to separate short volumes on assessment of adults and children. Ultimately, we opted for an organizational structure that balanced practical considerations with our collective prediction about how the individual volumes would be used. While it was different earlier in the development of the field, we believe that the current trend is for people to be more organized around populations than techniques. Hence, more people are likely to pick up and cross-reference a single volume on children or the elderly than a volume on Behavior Therapy. Our strategy for identifying chapter length topics and associated page limits is more difficult to explain. Once again, we relied on our collective judgement, honed by negotiation. In rough order, priority was given to topics that had established empirical literatures, that were deemed to be "important," that had broad interest, and that were likely to be at least as important in the next decade. Page limits were determined substantially by estimates of the first two criteria. We began with an overall target for the entire work and minimums and maximums for volumes, and then worked backwards to divide up the allotted pages among the chapters designated for each volume. Given that no scheme will please everyone, we are confident that the organization of the work adequately reflects the field now and in the foreseeable future.

Under the careful aegis of the outstanding group of experts comprising the Honorary International Editorial Advisory Board, 10 leading international scholars were selected to edit the 10 specific volumes.

Volume 1 (*Foundations*), edited by C. Eugene Walker, provides a complete overview of the basic foundations of clinical psychology, with special emphasis on the relationship between clinical psychology and other fields of science. Beginning with a brief history of clinical psychology, as well as a look at its current scientific status, this informative volume covers such topics as the biological bases of clinical psychology, elucidating research in genetics, psychobiology, psychopharmacology, and the use of animal models in human mental health problems; clinical psychology in the behavioral sciences, including anthropology, epidemiology, sociology, and research psychology; and the major systems and theories that are used in clinical psychology. The volume also describes various techniques for library research and information retrieval in psychology.

Volume 2 (*Professional Issues*), edited by Arthur W. Wiens, focuses on the professional, legal, and ethical issues that are relevant to clinical psychology. The volume addresses the various educational and training programs available, such as doctoral study, internship training, and postdoctoral residency programs, and reviews the accreditation of these programs. Also highlighted are the various international government guidelines for registration, certification, and licensing, including a discussion of the advantages of specialty recognition and practice certificates. The volume concludes with a look at ethical and legal guidelines in the management of clinical psychology practices, national healthcare policies, and advocacy efforts for government support for practitioners.

Volume 3 (*Research and Methods*), edited by Nina R. Schooler, explores the function of research in clinical psychology. The volume begins with an in-depth look at research approaches, including the use of descriptive studies, single case designs, observational methods, and other methods of analysis. The volume goes on to explore a broad range of topics that have been the focus of research, such as test development and validation, personality assessment, clinical interventions, and service evaluations and outcomes. Finally, various statistical techniques are reviewed, including descriptive and inferential statistics, factor analysis, and sampling and generalizability.

Volume 4 (*Assessment*), edited by Cecil R. Reynolds, provides valuable information on the development and role of assessment in clinical practice, analyzing such topics as psychometrics; taxonomic, functional, and actuarial approaches to diagnosis; and specific instruments, techniques, and procedures. Chapters also review the range of assessment techniques and procedures used in clinical practice, with emphasis on intelligence, neuropsychological, personality, projective, computer-assisted, therapeutic, and forensic assessment. The volume concludes with a review of legal guidelines and regulations in the use of psychological testing.

Volume 5 (*Children & Adolescents: Clinical Formulation & Treatment*), edited by Thomas Ollendick, draws on the experience and research of leading scientists and clinicians from Australia, Canada, Israel, the United Kingdom, and the United States to present state-of-the-art information on all aspects of child psychology and psychiatry, with special attention given to the psychopathology, assessment, treatment, and prevention of childhood behavioral disorders. The volume highlights the developmental-contextual framework used in the clinical formulation of these disorders, as well as process and outcome issues in treatment. Various theoretical perspectives are also reviewed, including applied behavior analysis, family systems therapy, play therapy, and pharmacologic therapy. In the final section, all of the major childhood disorders found in the *DSM* and *ICD* are described, with information on their prevalence, etiology, assessment, and treatment. This section also analyzes the empirical status of the various therapies used for treatment of childhood disorders.

Volume 6 (*Adults: Clinical Formulation & Treatment*), edited by Paul Salkovskis, provides valuable insights into the basis of the psychological theories and interventions used for behavioral and emotional problems and reviews how to integrate clinical skills with these theories. Various treatment approaches are addressed, such as cognitive therapy, family therapy, and Humanistic/Rogerian/Gestalt approaches, as well as the issues related to treatments, including stress management, arousal reduction methods, suicidal behavior, and specific issues in working with groups. The final section details specific problem areas and disorders, ranging from such universally recognized problems as gambling and substance abuse to more specific disorders such as post-traumatic stress, depression, obsessive-compulsive, and the various phobias. Each chapter in the volume emphasizes approaches that have an empirical basis.

Volume 7 (*Clinical Geropsychology*), edited by Barry Edelstein, addresses the emerging field of clinical psychology in the aging population. The volume begins with a review of this area of research, presenting important epidemiological information. The volume then offers a detailed look at issues that range from analyzing physiological and cognitive aspects to cognitive changes and specific neurological disorders common among older adults. Specific topics covered include sexuality, bereavement, anxiety, substance abuse, and schizophrenia. Each chapter presents a summary of clinical research and its practical application. Voids in the knowledge base are also noted, along with recommendations for the direction of future investigations. The volume also addresses management problems, such as incontinence, wandering, and aggressive behavior, and reviews the various mental healthcare systems available in different countries.

Volume 8 (*Health Psychology*), edited by Derek W. Johnston and Marie Johnston, provides a comprehensive overview of the development and application of clinical health psychology. Beginning with a discussion of training, assessment, and measurement issues, this volume analyzes the key behaviors that either affect or are related to health. Topics covered include stress and disease, the experience of illness, and behavior that can affect the neuroendocrine, cardiovascular, and immune systems. The volume also provides a detailed analysis of specific clinical problems and their psychological aspects and interventions. These include cancer, diabetes, epilepsy, disfigurement, and smoking.

Volume 9 (*Applications in Diverse Populations*), edited by Nirbhay N. Singh, covers the broad spectrum of diverse issues that clinical psychologists typically face in their work. Four sections outline the various psychological aspects found in different populations, as well as methods for assessment, diagnostic information, and interventions useful with these different groups. Section I focuses on select child, adolescent, and adult populations, including those with developmental disorders, learning disabilities, and mental retardation. Section II is devoted to various types of families and their issues, including families of individuals with HIV or AIDS, families of alcoholics, and families of children with serious emotional disturbances. Section III covers victims of violence and abuse, including child sexual abuse. Section IV examines perpetrators of violence and abuse, including sex offenders and issues of domestic violence.

Volume 10 (*Sociocultural and Individual Differences*), edited by Cynthia D. Belar, covers cross-cultural psychopathology and interventions. Chapters examine such select topics as gender, sexual orientation, socioeconomic status, religions, and training for clinical psychologists. The volume also provides valuable insights into the use of clinical psychology in different parts of the world, as well as personality assessment across international settings.

Given the scope and detail of *Comprehensive Clinical Psychology*, Volume 11 is devoted to: (i) a Name Index, (ii) a Subject Index, (iii) a List of Contributors, and (iv) a list of the Contents of All Volumes. The Name Index is an accumulation of all the authors who are cited in text in the reference sections throughout the entire work. The Subject Index, consisting of more than 40 000 entries, is a consolidation of all the individual volume subject indexes. It is presented in word-by-word alphabetical sequence with a maximum of three levels of heading. Terminology in the index is based on standard internationally recognized sources. Cross-references are provided to assist the user to locate preferred terms and terms of related interest.

Acknowledgments

To produce a tome of this magnitude requires an enormous number of individuals with unique talents working in concert. To begin with, we applaud the herculean efforts of our driving force and friend at Elsevier Science, Barbara Barrett. We also gratefully acknowledge the efforts of two other publishing editors at Elsevier Science, Susan Hanscom and David Hoole, who provided guidance and encouragement along the way. We are particularly thankful for the exceptionally hard work of Angela Greenwell and her staff in Oxford, who made sure that all tasks were implemented reasonably on time and who orchestrated the day-to-day management of this huge undertaking. Next, we thank our eminent volume editors, who had the difficult job of soliciting, tracking, and editing manuscripts for their respective volumes. Similarly, we thank the Honorary International Editorial Advisory Board for their excellent input in developing the outline for the work and suggestions as to potential international contributors. Of course, we owe a great deal to the individual contributors who agreed to share their expertise with us in a timely fashion. Finally, we are most appreciative of our own editorial assistants, Sonia McQuarters and Burt G. Bolton, who repeatedly have provided us with the kind of support that makes all of this a possibility.

HONORARY INTERNATIONAL EDITORIAL ADVISORY BOARD

Preface

Although psychology began as a science of individual differences, some would argue that it became a science of means, medians, and modes based on a predominantly Eurocentric world view. Nevertheless, it is well accepted that research and practice in clinical psychology are dependent upon an understanding of sociocultural and individual differences, and during the last several decades multiculturalism has become a potent force in all psychology.

In the United States, multiculturalism has become institutionalized through mechanisms such as accreditation criteria for professional psychology training programs and the development of guidelines for psychological practice with culturally diverse populations. (American Psychological Association, 1991, 1996). In fact, Bernal and Castro (1994) conclude from their review of United States governmental and professional policy documents that "it is unethical for scientists who are inadequately prepared to address theory, method, and interpretation of findings in scientific work on minority populations to conduct research on them" (p. 797). Hall (1997) warns of "cultural malpractice" by professional psychologists who are poorly trained in issues of diversity. Without culturally competent services, clients may be misdiagnosed, mistreated, or prematurely terminate treatment. Without culturally competent researchers, the development of new knowledge will be limited at best. At worst we will be misled by inaccurate knowledge that has potential for significant negative consequences. From an international perspective, psychology as a discipline will cease to be relevant without continued attention to individual differences.

To detail each and every important sociocultural and individual difference in clinical psychology would require a voluminous book series in and of itself. For example, McGoldrick, Giordano, and Pearce (1996) published an excellent text on ethnicity and family therapy, yet in 700-plus pages detailing 47 different family groups, they could only address one factor (ethnicity) as it was embedded within one culture (the United States). Thus the approach taken for this volume of *Comprehensive Clinical Psychology* has been to address broad issues of many aspects of diversity, with descriptions of specific populations used for illustrative purposes only. The goal is to be comprehensive about major issues in theory, research, and practice, without an attempt to be exhaustive in scope. Scholars with expertise in issues of human diversity from throughout the world have contributed chapters that are allocated to one of three sections: Section I, Foundations; Section II, Special Topics; and Section III, International Perspectives.

Section I, Foundations (Chapters 1–5), addresses important foundations for our understanding of sociocultural and individual differences.

Harry Triandis (Chapter 1, Introduction to Diversity in Clinical Psychology) focuses on the importance of sociocultural issues for clinical psychology. The main purpose of this chapter is to provide the conceptual underpinnings of culture and world views, as well as detail related to research methodologies. Triandis defines basic terms in the area, and critiques a number of methodologies for the study of world views while providing criteria for good cross-cultural research.

In Chapter 2 (Cross-cultural Psychopathology), Fannie Cheung describes how the Anglo-American ethnocentric approach to psychopathology has dominated clinical psychology. She examines the role of cultural factors in the etiology, presentation, and interpretation of psychopathology, and then focuses on the growth of cross-cultural psychopathology. She advocates for a combined emic–etic approach, asserting that utilization of such an approach will also facilitate bringing culture into the mainstream of clinical psychology.

Cecil Reynolds (Chapter 3, Cultural Bias in Testing of Intelligence and Personality) examines cultural bias as a fundamental issue in psychological assessment. He details sources of bias and discusses methodologic issues of related research, while highlighting the synergistic relationship between test use and pure psychometrics.

John Lewis (Chapter 4, Cross-cultural Clinical Interventions) reviews research on proximal and distal variables in cross-cultural counseling. He then examines the clinical intervention process, with a focus on effective intercultural communication and the importance of proxemics, kinesics, and paralinguistics.

Lewis also examines the long-standing debate regarding therapist–client match, and then details methodologic issues in treatment outcome research that must be addressed for the field to progress.

Completing Section I is Chapter 5 by Felipe Castro (Cultural Competence Training in Clinical Psychology: Assessment, Clinical Intervention, and Research). Castro highlights the importance of training clinical psychologists for cultural competence. He presents a three-factor model that operationalizes the development of cultural competence in assessment, intervention, and research activities. Castro also addresses the implications for clinical training programs, and articulates the need for a commitment to life-long learning if professional psychologists are to achieve cultural competence.

Section II, Special Topics (Chapters 6–11), focuses on a selection of major features in sociocultural and individual differences. Maria Root (Chapter 6, Reconstructing Race, Rethinking Ethnicity) addresses the concepts of race and ethnicity, and their differentiation. She then describes processes of identity development and summarizes current racial and ethnic identity models. Root proposes that the field utilize an ecological identity model that considers not only race, but also gender, regional history of race relations, generation, and class, which in her model includes inherited influences (e.g., language, values, sexual orientation, and phenotype) as well as traits (e.g., talents, coping skills).

Richard Eisler (Chapter 7, The Psychology of Gender and Health) provides a review of gender differences in both somatic and mental health problems. He concludes that differences found are related to an interaction of biological differences with psychosocial factors. To further elucidate these relationships, Eisler examines the literature on gender role stress, and gender differences in coping with stress, self-disclosure, help-seeking, and social support among other topics.

Nadine Kaslow and her colleagues (Chapter 8, A Cultural Perspective on Families Across the Life Cycle: Patterns, Assessment, and Intervention Outline) articulate a cultural perspective of families, noting implications for the conduct of culturally sensitive clinical interventions. The close attention to family life cycle stages is an important contribution to our understanding of the culture-relatedness of developmental issues.

In Chapter 9 (Sexual Orientation), Beverly Greene reviews research and practice related to sexual orientation. In describing historical changes in diagnostic nomenclature, she reports the depathologizing of gay and lesbian sexual orientations and describes the diversity within the community itself.

Although often ignored when addressing individual differences, religious diversity and its implication for practice is addressed by Stanton Jones and his colleagues in Chapter 10 (Diversity Matters: Religion and the Practice of Clinical Psychology). These authors address the heterogeneity of world religions, describing important dimensions on which religions vary. They also articulate the philosophical and empirical bases for consideration of religious diversity in clinical care, providing numerous examples of how practice could benefit from such awareness.

Finally, as an example of dwelling-related sources of individual differences, Michael Murray and his colleagues (Chapter 11, Mental Health in Rural Society) address the structure of rural society, with its related health and mental health issues. These authors also describe the roles of psychologists in rural communities, highlighting the special training required and ethical issues encountered.

Section III, International Perspectives (Chapters 12–18), presents a sampling of international perspectives and is thus the most diverse of all sections in this volume. James Butcher has organized Chapter 12 (Objective Personality Assessment: Computer-based Minnesota Multiphasic Personality Inventory-2 Interpretation in International Clinical Settings) to describe the use of perhaps the most widely employed and internationally adapted personality measure, the MMPI. The authors report an empirical evaluation of computer-based reports on Australian, French, Norwegian, and American patients, and describe clinical case examples from The Netherlands, Italy, Korea, Iran, and Israel.

Other chapters address mental health issues in various countries, including the impact of sociopolitical forces on the development of psychology as a discipline itself. For example, Marwan Dwairy (Chapter 13, Mental Health in the Arab World) describes the cultural background of Arabs living in some 21 countries. He details important psychocultural features, and then discusses implications for clinical assessment and treatment, presenting clear evidence of the inappropriateness of Eurocentric models for many presenting problems.

Danutė Gailienė (Chapter 14, Perspectives from Lithuania) describes the development of clinical psychology in Lithuania as inextricably related to that country's sociopolitical history. Gailienė highlights the impact of Soviet domination, perestroika, and the achievement of Lithuanian independence upon psychology education and training and the development of professional practice.

In Chapter 15 (From a Monocultural Identity to Diversity Identity: A Psychological Model for Diversity Management in South African Organizations), Kedibone Letlaka-Rennert and Wolfgang Rennert describe sociopolitical changes in South Africa that have had significant impact on the evolution of psychology. As their country moves from cultural exclusion and oppression to become a "rainbow nation," psychologists' roles are shifting from support of apartheid to an active role in diversity management and social transformation.

Eugene Emory and Sue-Huei Chen (Chapter 16, Clinical Psychology in Asia: A Taiwanese Perspective) provide a Taiwanese perspective on mental health issues and psychology. They examine the impact of collectivism on psychopathology and describe features of Asian culture related to the types of clinical services needed and offered.

In Chapter 17 (Clinical Psychology in Aotearoa/New Zealand: Indigenous Perspectives), Taima Moeke-Pickering and her colleagues examine bicultural developments in psychology in response to the needs of the Maori. This chapter provides an indigenous perspective of psychology as a discipline with respect to theory, research, and service development.

Finally, in Chapter 18 (Perspectives from Sub-Sahara Africa), Pius Essandoh describes sociocultural factors in psychological health in sub-Sahara Africa. He highlights the importance of beliefs related to spirituality, kinship, and life-span development as well as the need for a mental health system that is pluralistic rather than monocultural.

In its entirety, this volume provides a comprehensive, but not exhaustive, overview of sociocultural and individual differences in clinical psychology. The reader is encouraged to focus on the conceptual frameworks presented, the methodologic issues involved, and the training model suggested in preparing for his or her own diversity competence for research, teaching, and practice in clinical psychology. This volume is also culturally biased. For example, the value of diversity as a core principle in psychology is promoted throughout the book, and authors consistently portray cultural groups as equals, presenting a multicultural perspective as superior to racist, imperialistic, or xenophobic viewpoints of human diversity. Indeed the editor did not seek authors representing these latter perspectives. However, as Fowers and Richardson (1996) have so eloquently articulated, the values of multiculturalism are themselves culturally based, rooted in Euro-American moral and political traditions that have evolved to respect human dignity and rights. Ironically, the universalization of multiculturalism represents the imposition of these values of tolerance and respect on groups who might hold racist or ethnocentric views, or have different values regarding human life and suffering. We must recognize that multiculturalism itself has moral roots in Euro-American culture.

Acknowledgments

The greatest source of inspiration for participation in this project came from my graduate students in clinical psychology at the University of Florida. It was their thirst for knowledge and craving for experience with diversity that led me to develop a special course on the topic for our curriculum. The systematic review of relevant literature for that course resulted in my recognition of the need for an integrated text on the subject. Other major contributors to this effort have been Michel Hersen and Angela Greenwell, who provided unfailing good judgment and help in pulling this volume together. I would also like to acknowledge the ongoing support provided by my husband, Jean-Louis Monfraix.

Dedication

To Herbert and Glennie Belar.

References

American Psychological Association (1991). *Guidelines for providers of psychological services to ethnic, linguistic, and culturally diverse populations*. Washington, DC: Author.

American Psychological Association (1996). *Guidelines and principles for accreditation of programs in professional psychology*. Washington, DC: Author.

Bernal, M. E., & Castro, F. G. (1994). Are clinical psychologists prepared for service and research with ethnic minorities? *American Psychologist, 49,* 797–805.

Fowers, B. J., & Richardson, F. C. (1996). Why is multiculturalism good? *American Psychologist, 51,* 609–621.

Hall, C. C. (1997). Cultural malpractice: The growing obsolescence of psychology with the changing US population. *American Psychologist, 52,* 642–651.

McGoldrick, M., Giordano, J., & Pearce, J. K. (Eds.) (1996). *Ethnicity and family therapy* (2nd ed.). New York: Guilford Press.

Contributors to Volume 10

Dr. M. Almagor
Department of Psychology, University of Haifa, Haifa, Israel 31905

Dr. E. Berah
Monash Medical Centre, Adult Psychiatry, 246 Clayton Road, Clayton, Victoria 3168, Australia

Dr. M. Blank
Southeastern Rural Mental Health Research Center, University of Virginia, Charlottesville, VA 22901, USA

Dr. J. N. Butcher
Department of Psychology, University of Minnesota, Elliott Hall, 75 East River Road, Minneapolis, MN 55455-0344, USA

Dr. R. E. Butman
Department of Psychology, Wheaton College, 501 E. College, Wheaton, IL 60187-5593, USA

Professor F. G. Castro
Hispanic Research Center, Arizona State University, PO Box 872702, Tempe, AZ 85287-2702, USA

Dr. S.-H. Chen
Department of Psychology, National Taiwan University, Taipei 10764, Taiwan

Professor F. M. Cheung
Department of Psychology, The Chinese University of Hong Kong, Shatin, N. T., Hong Kong

Dr. J. Derksen
University of Nijmegen, 6523 LW Nijmegen, The Netherlands

Dr. M. Dwairy
PO Box 2123, Nazareth 16000, Israel

Dr. R. M. Eisler
Department of Psychology, Virginia Polytechnic Institute and State University, 4088A Derring Hall, Blacksburg, VA 24061-0436, USA

Dr. B. Ellertsen
Department of Clinical Neuropsychology, University of Bergen, Arstadveien 21, N-5009 Bergen, Norway

Dr. E. K. Emory
Department of Psychology, Emory University, Atlanta, GA, USA

Dr. P. K. Essandoh
Psychology Department, Jersey City State College, 2039 Kennedy Memorial Boulevard, Jersey City, NJ 07305, USA

Dr. D. Gailienė
University of Vilnius, Tvaidenio 27, 2004 Vilnius, Lithuania

Professor B. Greene
Department of Psychology, St. John's University, 8000 Utopia Parkway, Jamaica, NY 11439, USA
26 St. John's Place No. 3, Brooklyn, NY 11217, USA

Dr. D. S. Hargrove
Department of Psychology, University of Mississippi, Mississippi 38677, USA

Dr. A. M. L. Herbert
Psychology Department, University of Waikato, Private Bag 3105, Hamilton, New Zealand

Dr. L. Jeeyoung
Samsung Group, 802-501 Hanjin A.P.T., Jeongdun-Maul, 193 Jeongja-Dong, Boondang-Gu, Sungnam-City, Kyanggi-Do, South Korea

Professor S. L. Jones
Provost's Office, Wheaton College, 501 E. College, Wheaton, IL 60187-5593, USA

Dr. N. J. Kaslow
Department of Psychiatry and Behavioral Sciences, Emory University School of Medicine, Grady Health System, 80 Butler Street Southeast, Atlanta, GA 30335, USA

Dr. K. Letlaka-Rennert
Hay Management Consultants, PO Box 78400, Sandton 2146, Johannesburg, South Africa

Dr. J. E. Lewis
Center for Psychological Studies, Nova Southeastern University, 3301 College Avenue, Fort Lauderdale, FL 33314, USA

Ms. M. R. Loundy
Department of Counseling and Psychological Services, Georgia State University, Atlanta, GA, USA

Dr. P. Miach
Monash Medical Centre, Adult Psychiatry, 246 Clayton Road, Clayton, Victoria 3168, Australia

Dr. T. M. Moeke-Pickcring
Psychology Department, University of Waikato, Private Bag 3105, Hamilton, New Zealand

Dr. M. Murray
Division of Community Health, Faculty of Medicine, The Health Sciences Centre, Memorial University of Newfoundland, St. John's, NF, Canada A1B 3V6

Dr. E. Nezami
USC/IPR, 1540 Alcazar Chp 208A, Los Angeles, CA 90033, USA

Dr. M. K. Paewai
Psychology Department, University of Waikato, Private Bag 3105, Hamilton, New Zealand

Dr. P. Pancheri
5a Cattedra di Clinica Psichiatrica, 36, Viale Dell' Università, 00185 Rome, Italy

Dr. D. W. Preussler
Department of Psychology, Wheaton College, 501 E. College, Wheaton, IL 60187-5593, USA

Dr. W. P. Rennert
Chris Hani Baragwanath Hospital, University of the Witwatersrand, PO Bertsham 2013, Johannesburg, South Africa

Professor C. R. Reynolds
Department of Educational Psychology, Texas A&M University, College Station, TX 77843-4225, USA

Dr. M. P. P. Root
Department of American Ethnic Studies, University of Washington, Box 354380, Seattle, WA 98112, USA

Professor H. C. Triandis
Department of Psychology, University of Illinois at Urbana-Champaign, 603 East Daniel Street, Champaign, IL 61820, USA

Dr. A. Turangi-Joseph
Psychology Department, University of Waikato, Private Bag 3105, Hamilton, New Zealand

Dr. K. A. Wood
Department of Psychiatry and Behavioral Sciences, Emory University School of Medicine, Grady Health System, 80 Butler Street Southeast, Atlanta, GA 30335, USA

Volume Editors

Volume 1: Foundations
Professor C. Eugene Walker, *University of Oklahoma Health Sciences Center, Oklahoma City, OK, USA*

Volume 2: Professional Issues
Professor Arthur N. Wiens, *Oregon Health Sciences University, Portland, OR, USA*

Volume 3: Research and Methods
Professor Nina R. Schooler, *Hillside Hospital, Glen Oaks, NY, USA*

Volume 4: Assessment
Professor Cecil R. Reynolds, *Texas A&M University, College Station, TX, USA*

Volume 5: Children & Adolescents: Clinical Formulation & Treatment
Professor Thomas Ollendick, *Virginia Tech, Blacksburg, VA, USA*

Volume 6: Adults: Clinical Formulation & Treatment
Professor Paul Salkovskis, *University of Oxford, Warneford Hospital, UK*

Volume 7: Clinical Geropsychology
Professor Barry Edelstein, *West Virginia University, Morgantown, WV, USA*

Volume 8: Health Psychology
Professor Derek W. Johnston and Professor Marie Johnston, *University of St. Andrews, UK*

Volume 9: Applications in Diverse Populations
Dr Nirbhay N. Singh, *Virginia Commonwealth University, Richmond, VA, USA*

Volume 10: Sociocultural and Individual Differences
Professor Cynthia D. Belar, *University of Florida Health Sciences Center, Gainesville, FL, USA*

Volume 11: Indexes

10.01 Introduction to Diversity in Clinical Psychology

HARRY C. TRIANDIS
University of Illinois, Urbana, IL, USA

10.01.1 INTRODUCTION 2

10.01.2 DEFINITIONS 2

10.01.2.1 Culture 2
10.01.2.2 Cultural Syndromes 3
10.01.2.3 Identity 3
10.01.2.4 Acculturation 3
10.01.2.5 Ecology 4
10.01.2.6 Psychological Processes 4
10.01.2.7 Cultural Distance 4
10.01.2.8 Culture Shock 4
10.01.2.9 Ethnocentrism 4
10.01.2.10 Racism 4
10.01.2.11 Prejudice 5
10.01.2.12 Emic and Etic Aspects of Culture 5
10.01.2.13 An Integrative Example of These Definitions 5

10.01.3 WORLD VIEWS 6

10.01.3.1 Cultural Complexity 6
10.01.3.2 Tightness–Looseness 6
10.01.3.3 Collectivism 7
10.01.3.4 Individualism 7
10.01.3.5 Horizontality 7
10.01.3.6 Verticality 7
10.01.3.7 Active–Passive 7
10.01.3.8 Honor 8
10.01.3.9 Universalism–Particularism 8
10.01.3.10 Diffuseness–Specificity 8
10.01.3.11 Ascription–Achievement 8
10.01.3.12 Instrumental–Expressive 8
10.01.3.13 Value Orientations 8
10.01.3.14 Dionysian vs. Apollonian Cultures 9

10.01.4 METHODOLOGIES FOR THE STUDY OF WORLD VIEWS 9

10.01.4.1 Some General Strategies 11
10.01.4.2 Good Theory Can Eliminate Some Rival Hypotheses 12
10.01.4.3 Methods that Can Establish Measurement Equivalence Across Cultures 12
10.01.4.4 Emics and Etics in Cross-cultural Research 12
10.01.4.5 How to Use Emic Measurements of Etic Constructs 14
10.01.4.5.1 General recommendations 15
10.01.4.6 Examples of Multimethod Measurements 15
10.01.4.6.1 Ethnographic work 15
10.01.4.6.2 Establishing shared cognitions 16
10.01.4.6.3 Conclusions 17

10.01.4.7 Translations 18
10.01.4.8 Ethics of Cross-cultural Studies 19
10.01.4.9 Ethnocentric and Androcentric Bias of Researchers 19
10.01.4.10 Summary of Criteria of Good Cross-cultural Research 20
10.01.5 ACCULTURATION 20
10.01.6 IDENTITIES OF AFRICAN- AND EUROPEAN-AMERICANS AS AN EXAMPLE OF THE IDENTITIES OF CLINICIANS AND CLIENTS 21
10.01.7 METHODS FOR THE DEVELOPMENT OF AN UNDERSTANDING OF THE CULTURE OF THE CLIENT 23
10.01.7.1 Methods of Culture Learning 24
10.01.7.1.1 Culture-general vs. culture-specific training 25
10.01.7.1.2 Self-insight 26
10.01.7.1.3 Experiential training 26
10.01.7.1.4 Exposure to many local cultures 26
10.01.7.1.5 Field trips 26
10.01.7.1.6 Culture assimilators or intercultural sensitizers 26
10.01.7.1.7 Behavior modification cross-cultural training 29
10.01.7.1.8 Some summary points about training 29
10.01.8 FUTURE DIRECTIONS 30
10.01.9 SUMMARY AND CONCLUSIONS 30
10.01.10 REFERENCES 30

10.01.1 INTRODUCTION

Clinical psychologists deal with many kinds of diversity. While diversity due to culture may be the most imporant kind that affects their work, it is useful to remember that diversity in social class, sexual orientation, gender definitions, disabilities, political perspectives, esthetic preferences, religion, and the definition of what is "true" may also affect their practice.

Diversity may be defined as the condition of interacting with another person who is perceived to be "different." It is a condition which is increasingly more frequent, since most societies are multicultural and a number of factors favor interactions among the cultures. In the US the clients of clinical psychologists are becoming more different from the white middle-class which was the usual clientele of these professionals a few years ago.

It is impossible to deal with all the aspects of diversity in one chapter, so the focus will be on culture. However, some of the other kinds of diversity (e.g., in religion or social class) do interact with cultural differences, and some of the experience which clinicians have acquired in dealing with these other kinds of diversity may prove useful in dealing with cultural diversity.

This chapter will begin with definitions of concepts such as culture, and the relevance of ethnocentrism, prejudice, and racism in making judgments about the behavior of other humans. It will also examine the terminology for dealing with what is culture-common (etic) and culture-specific (emic). Section 10.01.3 will describe some of the diversity of world views and values, and will examine methodologies which can provide reliable information concerning such world views. The focus will be on helping clinicians discriminate reliable from unreliable cross-cultural studies, so that they can begin developing a body of knowledge about cultural differences. Then, the chapter will examine the relationship of acculturation to varieties of cultural identity (in both the majority and minority culture). Finally, it will describe methods and procedures that clinicians can use to develop more detailed understandings of other cultures, and to improve the effectiveness of their behavior when interacting with diverse clients.

10.01.2 DEFINITIONS

10.01.2.1 Culture

Culture is to society what memory is to individuals (Kluckhohn, 1954, p. 967). It includes all the things which have "worked" in the history of an interacting group of humans, and have become unstated assumptions, standard operating procedures, standards of perceiving, judging, deciding, and acting. Cultural anthropologists (e.g., Kroeber & Kluckhohn, 1952) have developed more than 100 definitions of "culture," such as that culture is the human-made part of the environment (Herskovits, 1955). Such a definition is too broad, but it does have the advantage that we can ask: Is this particular element human-made? For instance, is this belief human-made? Then it is an aspect of culture. The Herskovits' definition can become more useful if we distinguish material culture (tools, roads, houses) from subjective culture (categorizations, beliefs, attitudes, self-definitions, role definitions, norms, values (Triandis, 1972).

Most contemporary anthropologists (e.g., Shweder & Levine, 1984) agree that culture is a system of *shared* meanings. Hence my favorite definition:

> Culture is a set of human-made objective and subjective elements that in the past have increased the probability of survival and resulted in satisfactions for the participants in an ecological niche, and thus became *shared* among those who could communicate with each other because they had a common language and they lived in the same time period and place. (Triandis, 1994, p. 22)

Note that this definition, in addition to focusing on what is shared, specifies that a common language is important, and communication can take place because people live in the same time period and geographic region. Thus, in principle, people who live next door to each other but speak different languages (say, in Los Angeles, Hispanics and Thais), or during different time periods (say, in Los Angeles in 1950 and in 1996), or in different geographic regions (say, in Texas and New York) may have different cultures. Physicians have their own language in the hospital, and thus physicians-on-the-job may constitute a culture, by this definition. According to this definition the number of cultures is enormous.

Humans regardless of culture have many common attributes. All humans have language, food habits, art, myths, religious practices, family structures, economic systems, "truth," government, war, kinship, shelter, training systems, hygiene, and incest taboos (Brown, 1991). However, note that these categories are extremely broad. Take an easy one to think about: food habits. What people eat, when, where, with whom, and to what effect are clearly diverse. If we are to pay attention to that level of detail, it is obvious that the diversity of cultures is enormous.

10.01.2.2 Cultural Syndromes

Shared patterns of beliefs, attitudes, self-definitions, norms, roles, and values are sometimes organized around a common theme. When they are and found among members of a culture, they constitute a cultural syndrome. The logic of shared elements of subjective culture allows us to identify such syndromes (Triandis, 1996). For example, we can examine the response distributions obtained from samples in a particular culture, and if an arbitrary 90% of the participants give a response on the same side of the neutral point, on a nine-point scale that measures an element of subjective culture, then that element is an aspect of the cultural syndrome. Another method (see Triandis, Bontempo, Leung, & Hui, 1990) is to form (say 50) triads of representatives of each culture, and ask them to reach a group agreement on an element of subjective culture, for example, "Do you agree that widows should not eat chicken?" Agreement in less than 60 seconds, among say 90% of the triads, would indicate that the belief is widely shared, and thus it is an element of the culture syndrome. In sum, both the time to reach agreement and the percentage of triads which reach agreement can be used as criteria for determining the presence of an element of a cultural syndrome. When the cultural elements, identified by such procedures, which represent attitudes, beliefs, norms, role-definitions, self-definitions, and values are interrelated, we have defined empirically the cultural syndrome.

10.01.2.3 Identity

People make statements that include the words "me," "mine," "myself," "I," and the like. All these statements taken together constitute the *self*. An important aspect of the self concerns statements about belonging to some group. For example "I am a Korean" specifies a Korean identity. "I am a bridge-player" is also an identity. Brewer (1991) has argued that each individual experiences forces toward differentiation from groups as well as assimilation to groups. These opposing forces are in equilibrium at the point of "optimal distinctiveness" which is characteristic of each person. This point is determined by cultural norms, individual socialization, and recent experiences with the group. For instance, in traditional cultures, which tend to be collectivist, the forces of assimilation are stronger than the forces of differentiation, and thus the optimal distinctiveness point is closer to the group than in modern cultures.

10.01.2.4 Acculturation

Some individuals, especially in multicultural cities, are exposed to numerous cultures simultaneously. They may use more than one identity, for example, "I am Mexican" and "I am American." The more elements of one culture are attached to an identity (e.g., Since I am Mexican I speak Spanish most of the time), the more influential is that identity in determining behavior. An individual may be more or less bicultural, include elements from both cultures in an identity, assimilated, include mostly elements of another culture in an identity, separated, that is, even though the individual lives in an environment which includes many cultures the identity is separate and distinct and monocultural, or alienated, may reject all cultures.

10.01.2.5 Ecology

Ecology refers to where people live. It consists of objects, resources, the geography of the environment, and the ways of making a living and surviving in that environment. Ecology provides schedules of reinforcement (Skinner, 1981), which shape both the elements of subjective culture and the behavior of those who live in these ecologies. Thus, culture emerges from the ecology.

10.01.2.6 Psychological Processes

Clinicians are, of course, focusing on psychological processes, such as personality, behavior patterns, and the beliefs, attitudes, and values of their clients. It is obvious from the above definitions that culture influences many of these psychological processes. Poor clinical analyses occur when the clinician and the client come from different cultures, because the very same behavior may have different meanings in the two cultural systems and very frequently these meanings influence important judgments, such as diagnoses.

Take one simple example: in collectivist cultures, such as those found in the Far East, communications that are unclear and indirect which save someone's face are expected and are very common. In individualistic cultures, such as in the West, people are expected to provide "straight talk" and not "beat around the bush." Similarly, a lie is morally reprehensible in the West much more than in the East. Authenticity (Trilling, 1972) is valued in the West, and that includes "telling it as it is" and telling the truth. Thus, the same behavior can be interpreted differently in the two kinds of cultures. Indirect communications may be seen as "tactful and polite" and a lie can be seen as saving face in the East, while the same behaviors may be seen as "confused and confusing" and reprehensible in the West. The interpretation is an aspect of an integrated conceptual system, and is often so compelling that it is difficult for either party to easily use the other's way of thinking.

10.01.2.7 Cultural Distance

Cultural distance is an important concept in understanding diversity, and the way it affects human relationships. Cultural distance can reflect differences in (i) language (e.g., language families, such as the client speaks a tonal language and the clinician an Indo-European language), (ii) family structure (say, monogamous vs. polygamous marriages can create distance), (iii) religions (e.g., animist and Christian religions), (iv) wealth and life style (e.g., the difference between a wealthy jetsetter and a member of a culture of hunters and gatherers), (v) values (e.g., the difference between conservative, very traditional values and self-actualizing, hedonistic values).

10.01.2.8 Culture Shock

Triandis and Gelfand (1994) presented a model that links cultural distance and culture shock (Oberg, 1960). The larger the cultural distance the larger the culture shock. The model posits that cultural distance leads to low perceived similarity. When people perceive each other as dissimilar and are also in contact, the relationship is tense, and punishing, resulting in distortions such as extreme stereotypes, inaccurate attributions (e.g., clinician and client attribute different causes to the same behavior), which lower the sense of control (ability to act so as to obtain positive outcomes from relationships). A low sense of control results in culture shock. The model also includes other variables, which need not concern us here.

10.01.2.9 Ethnocentrism

Most humans are ethnocentric (Brewer & Campbell, 1976; Campbell & Levine, 1968; Triandis, 1994). Ethnocentrism follows from the fact that most humans are only exposed to their own culture. Only humans who live in multicultural environments, or have traveled extensively, are moderately ethnocentric. The extent our culture influences our perceptions of the behavior of others is large and subtle. We are usually not aware of our ethnocentrism. Those who have been exposed to other cultures learn to appreciate aspects of these cultures which are not included in their own cultures, and thus become less ethnocentric. Clinicians must control their ethnocentrism by learning to appreciate other cultures. Yet that is especially difficult when the cultural distance between their culture and the client's culture is large. In that case it may be best to admit that they are not able to help the client, and it is desirable to find colleagues whose cultural distance is smaller and who might be able to help the client.

10.01.2.10 Racism

Racism is a special case of ethnocentrism, where the standards of one's own racial group are used to judge other racial groups.

10.01.2.11 Prejudice

Prejudice is judgment of the attributes and behavior of members of another culture on the basis of negative preconceived ideas and inaccurate stereotypes. Such judgments are usually associated with negative emotional reactions toward members of the other culture, as well as with self-instructions to keep some social distance from the members of the other culture (rejection of positive and endorsement of negative behavioral intentions toward the members of the other culture). People who are very ethnocentric tend to be prejudiced. Even people who score as nonprejudiced on attitude scales, when responding to ethnic stimuli tachistoscopically, so that they do not have the opportunity to "control" their prejudice, show themselves to use unfavorable stereotypes. In short, the unprejudiced have learned to control their prejudice and not show it to researchers, but the negative stereotypes are nevertheless present in their cognitive system (Devine, 1989).

10.01.2.12 Emic and Etic Aspects of Culture

Phon*etics* deals with sounds which occur in all languages. Phon*emics* deals with sounds which occur in only one language. This led the linguist Pike (1967) to coin the words *etics* and *emics* to refer to the culture-general and culture-specific elements of culture. *Etics* reflect constructs which apply to phenomena that occur in all cultures. *Emics* are constructs which occur in only one culture.

For example, in all cultures ingroup members (family, tribe, co-workers, co-religionists) are treated better than outgroup members (enemies, strangers, outsiders). That is an etic. However, there are also emic patterns. For example, when Hispanics and non-Hispanics were presented with several hundred situations and asked if they expected people in such a situation to use positive (e.g., admire, respect, support) or negative (e.g., criticize, dominate, fight with) behaviors, there was a response pattern which was called the "*simpatia* cultural script" (Triandis, Marin, Lisansky, & Betancourt, 1984) that emerged when the Hispanic responses were compared to the non-Hispanic responses to the same situations. Specifically, Hispanics compared to non-Hispanics expected more positive behaviors and fewer negative behaviors in a wide range of situations. They expected people to try to be *simpatico*, that is, to be nice and pleasant, even in situations where non-Hispanics expected neutral or negative behaviors. This is similar, but not identical, to the greater importance of face in collectivist than in individualistic cultures that has been discussed by East Asian social scientists (e.g., Ting-Toomey, 1988). The simpatia cultural script is an emic.

In other words, when dealing with ingroup members or even acquaintances, Hispanics tend to be more positive in their behaviors than non-Hispanics. The practical significance of this pattern is that, relative to non-Hispanics, Hispanics will expect a clinician to be more positive in situations that ordinarily will be ambiguous or call for somewhat negative behaviors. For instance, criticism or other negative behaviors may be more upsetting to Hispanics than to non-Hispanics.

For another example of an emic motif, consider the *amae* pattern found in Japan (Doi, 1986). Japanese often presume that they may depend on others, the way a child depends on a parent. Mutual dependence is an emic aspect of that culture.

The significance of the emic and etic distinction is that it alerts us to which specific cultures may have idiosyncratic ways of cutting the pie of experience. If we use only etics, we miss some of that information and do not identify many cultural differences (Marin & Marin, 1991).

There are ways to combine emics and etics (see Triandis, 1992), making our measurements culture-sensitive but also equivalent across cultures. These techniques will be discussed in Section 10.01.4.5. Many techniques specific to cultural studies have been identified (see Triandis & Berry, 1980). Some of these use methods (e.g., Szalay, 1970; Szalay & Deese, 1978) such as word association which are also used by some clinical psychologists.

10.01.2.13 An Integrative Example of These Definitions

The ethnocentrism mentioned above is an etic. It is accentuated by two other phenomena, which are also probable etics: (i) we have a tendency toward *naive realism* which limits our capacity to appreciate the extent to which our construals are subjective (Robinson, Keltner, Ward, & Ross, 1995); and (ii) we have a tendency toward *false consensus*, which is to think that other humans agree with our positions more than is true, and disagree with our position less than is true (Krueger & Clement, 1994).

In short, we tend to think that the way we see the world is both valid and universal. Our culture provides the "lenses" for seeing the world in a particular way and that way of seeing is so obvious that it is not questioned.

Consider this example. In Orissa, India, most of the population believes that widows must not eat chicken (Shweder, Mahapatra, & Miller, 1990). When asked if this behavior should be universal they say: "Of course. It is a great sin for widows to eat chicken." When told that Americans do not believe this, they look down upon Americans, and explain this "moral deficiency" by noting that America is a young country which has not yet reached the level of moral maturity found in India.

Now, consider what happens when Illinois participants are asked whether widows must not eat chicken. They say that this belief is silly. When asked if this rule should be universal, they object vehemently. When told that people in Orissa, India, strongly believe that widows must not eat chicken, they look down upon these Indians, and point out that they are not sufficiently developed to have "correct views."

Do you see the ethnocentrism in *both* perspectives? The Indian view stems from the basic assumption that people are interdependent. Married individuals are supposed to be linked to each other for ever. For a widow to eat chicken is a sin because they believe that eating chicken makes one sexually aroused, and such arousal will result in the widow having sexual relations with someone, and thus breaking the eternal bond with her husband. Note that cultures often have sets of beliefs which are supportive of each other.

Now consider the American view. The basic assumption is consistent with American individualism (Triandis, 1995) which assumes that people are autonomous entities. Widows can do their own thing. If Indians have an idea that is different from the American idea, it is because they are not sufficiently developed!

Thus, both cultures conclude that their views are superior and the views of the other culture are inferior. Ethnocentrism leads to prejudice, and attempts to impose the subjective culture of one's own culture on other cultural groups.

This is not the place to debate the merits of individualism and collectivism. Hofstede (1980) linked these concepts with many ecological variables. Triandis (1995) has suggested that individualism is associated with high levels of achievement, creativity, self-actualization, and democracy, but also with high levels of crime, divorce, and child abuse. Collectivism is associated with high levels of social support, cooperation, interpersonal sensitivity, and pleasantness in social relationships, but also with extreme conformity, low creativity, and ethnic cleansing. In short, both cultural patterns have both positive and negative elements, and it is natural for most people from all types of cultures to prefer their cultures. As scientists we can examine the links of ecology, culture, and social pathology, but preferences for social pathology are matters of taste, not scientific judgment!

10.01.3 WORLD VIEWS

Many cultural syndromes have been identified thus far. The exact number of syndromes is not known, but a guess is that a score may be sufficient to describe the most important cultural differences. Here we present some of the most important syndromes.

10.01.3.1 Cultural Complexity

Simple cultures such as hunters and gatherers have few roles, simple social structures, few levels of social and political stratification, simple religious beliefs, simple understandings of the nature of the world, few domains of esthetic activity, and simple methods of economic exchange (e.g., barter). Specific simple cultures may be very complex in one domain, such as people may have an extensive knowledge of the history of their ancestors, as is found among Australian aborigines, but in most domains they are simple. Many attributes of culture are associated with cultural simplicity. For example, simple cultures are characterized by small communities (often bands of 50 individuals), the use of barter, walking as the only means of transportation, and so on.

Complex cultures, such as information societies, have many roles, for example, a quarter of a million occupations in the *Dictionary of Occupational Titles*, complex social structures, for example, General Motors, complex social and political stratification (e.g., federal, state, and local governments), a multiplicity of religious beliefs, a complex understanding of the nature of the world, for example, modern science, multiple types of esthetic activities, and numerous methods of economic exchange, such as, money, bonds, stock, certificates of deposit, etc. They include mostly urban social patterns. Again, in one domain there might be considerable simplicity, such as a family structure that consists of only a mother and her children, but on the whole there is complexity in most domains.

In complex cultures subjective cultures also tend to be more complex, for example, one finds large vocabularies (100 000+ terms in English) and complex ways of classifying experience, as well as complex beliefs.

10.01.3.2 Tightness–Looseness

Some cultures have (i) many rules, norms, and detailed specifications about how one is to act, and (ii) members who react quite strongly (e.g., criticize or even kill those who deviate from the norms) to minor deviations from the rules, norms, and "proper behavior" (Triandis, 1989, 1994). Such cultures are called "tight." Other cultures are loose, that is, have few rules, norms, and do not specify how one is to behave in very many situations, and when a person deviates from these few rules, norms, or conceptions about proper behavior, people tolerate such deviations.

Tight cultures provide criticism and severe sanctions (e.g., 50 lashes) for deviation; loose cultures criticize only major deviations and provide mild sanctions (e.g., a fine) for most deviations.

Tightness and looseness are domain specific. For example, a culture may be very tight about the use of time, but be rather loose about the way one chooses friends. For example, the US, in 1996, is very tight about writing bad checks and rather loose about who one lives with. However, across domains, tight cultures tend to be tight, and loose cultures tend to be loose.

Japan is an example of a tight culture, and Thailand an example of a loose culture. The US is fairly loose. For example, one extreme incident that occurred in Japan in 1990 was that a teacher killed a student who was two minutes late for class. Japanese opinion was divided about this teacher, most arguing that he was "deranged" even though they understood his efforts to impose discipline. However, some psychopathology is an extreme expression of a cultural norm (Draguns, 1990)!

Rural Thailand is loose. An employee may come to work, or not come to work, and no explanations are offered (Phillips, 1965). After living in Thailand for several months, Phillips (1965) had difficulty understanding "the mystifying American capacity to conform to the expectations of others" (p. 204).

10.01.3.3 Collectivism

The collectivism syndrome has been studied more extensively than most of the other syndromes (Kim, Triandis, Choi, Kagitcibasi, & Yoon, 1994; Markus & Kitayama, 1991; Triandis, 1990, 1995). It has received a central position in most reviews of cultural differences in social behavior (e.g., M. Bond & Smith, 1996). Triandis (1994) has speculated that maximum collectivism occurs in simple tight cultures, such as theocracies. He also argued (Triandis, 1995) that in collectivist cultures individuals define themselves as aspects of groups (i.e., I am a member of ...), place the goals of their collectives ahead of their personal goals, behave under the influence of norms and roles imposed by their groups, and relate to ingroup members by paying attention to the needs of others rather than to their own needs. Many East Asian societies are collectivist, as are many traditional societies in Africa and Latin America. In the US, Hispanics and Asians tend to be collectivists.

10.01.3.4 Individualism

Triandis (1994) speculated that this pattern is maximal in complex, loose cultures, and is characterized (Triandis, 1995) by individualists perceiving themselves as autonomous from their groups, giving priority to their personal rather than to their ingroup's goals, behaving according to their attitudes and feelings of enjoyment, and dealing with members of their ingroups by paying attention to the "profit" and "loss" incurred from the relationship, as specified by exchange theory (Thibaut & Kelley, 1959). Many Western societies are individualistic, especially the US, Australia, and Britain.

10.01.3.5 Horizontality

Cultures that are egalitarian, such as the Eskimos, and tend to emphasize tit-for-tat, one person one vote and the like are horizontal. In such cultures, people do not share or distribute resources according to need, contributions (equity), or status, but equally. There is little social stratification; most people carry out most of the tasks of the society.

10.01.3.6 Verticality

The cultural pattern of verticality emphasizes hierarchy. It is similar to Hofstede's (1980) "power distance," a cultural pattern in which people at the top of the power hierarchy seem to be very distant from people at the bottom of the hierarchy. Resources are divided according to status. There is much deference for those who have status. High levels of stratification are present.

10.01.3.7 Active–Passive

This syndrome was described by Diaz-Guerrero (1979) when he compared US and Mexican data. Those who are active, such as Americans, thrive on competition, action, and emphasize self-fulfillment. They try to change the world, rather than change themselves to fit into the world. Those who are passive, are cooperative, emphasize the experience of being, and tend to change themselves to fit into situations.

10.01.3.8 Honor

Honor is a narrow syndrome, found in environments in which property is mobile, and thus individuals develop attitudes, values, and behaviors that are designed to scare others, so as to ensure that their property is not taken away from them. For example, cattle are more easily stolen than agricultural property, so that people in cattle cultures are fierce, aggressive, hypersensitive to affronts, stress defense of one's honor, and socialize their children to react to challenges more than occurs in agricultural societies (Cohen & Nisbett, 1994; Nisbett & Cohen, 1996). Several kinds of studies support the view that the American South is high on this cultural syndrome. Cohen, Nisbett, Bowdle, and Schwartz (1996) reported three experiments where University of Michigan students from the North or South of the US were insulted by a confederate. They reported that Southerners were more likely to think that their masculine reputation was threatened, became more upset (as shown by the rise of cortisol levels), became more physiologically primed for aggression (as shown by testosterone levels), were more cognitively primed for aggression, and more likely to engage in aggressive and dominant behavior than students from the North. Cohen (1996) showed that this cultural syndrome was reflected in social policies. An analysis of laws relating to guns, defense of self and home, corporal punishment, capital punishment, and attitudes toward foreign policy issues showed greater approval of violence in the South than in the North.

While the Nisbett and Cohen research focuses on the higher levels of honor found in the American South than the North, extreme emphasis on honor can be found also in most of the Mediterranean societies, for example, Corsica, the Serbs. Campbell's (1964) ethnography of a culture of Northern Greece (the Karakatzanoi) provides details of this syndrome.

10.01.3.9 Universalism–Particularism

Parsons and Shils (1951) contrasted cultures where people categorize other people on the basis of universal criteria, and cultures in which people categorize other people by taking into account their particular characteristics and the unique situation within which they are interacting with them.

10.01.3.10 Diffuseness–Specificity

Parsons and Shils (1951) contrasted cultures in which people respond in a diffuse, holistic manner (e.g., I do not like your report implies I do not like you) with cultures where people respond with specificity.

10.01.3.11 Ascription–Achievement

Parsons and Shils (1951) discussed cultures in which people judge others primarily on the basis of ascribed attributes (e.g., sex, race, family membership) with those which use achieved attributes (e.g., has received this award).

10.01.3.12 Instrumental–Expressive

Parsons and Shils (1951) contrasted cultures in which most interaction has instrumental purposes (get task done) with cultures in which most interactions are expressive (friendship, enjoyment).

10.01.3.13 Value Orientations

Kluckhohn and Strodtbeck (1961) identified several value orientations which may well be the bases of additional cultural syndromes. Specifically, they identified societies where innate human nature is assumed to be (i) evil, neutral, or good; (ii) mutable or immutable. When human nature is assumed to be evil, many rules are introduced to control people and make them behave appropriately; when it is assumed to be good there is a tendency towards minimal government; when it is assumed to be mutable institutions are created (e.g. educational systems) which can change them in the appropriate direction, but when they are assumed to be immutable there is little support for such institutions.

(iii) Humans are assumed to be subjugated to nature, in harmony with nature, or allowed to master nature. In cultures which emphasize mastery over nature, beliefs, attitudes, values, and behaviors favor changes of the environment. Where harmony is emphasized, there is more concern about not changing the environment (e.g., the "greens" of the world). When subjugation is emphasized there are many beliefs, attitudes, and behavior showing reverence for nature (e.g., in many Native American cultures).

(iv) Varieties of time orientation, such as emphases on the past, present, or future. Time orientation also differs because some societies use linear time (e.g., the West) and others use circular time (e.g. the ancient Mayans). Monochronic use of time (i.e., people can carry out only one conversation at a time) or polychronic use of time (i.e., people can carry out several conversations at the same time) are also important cultural differences in the use of time.

(v) The emphasis is on doing, being (the experience), or becoming (growing, changing, improving). For example, in doing cultures, such as the US, a person's worth is measured by a record of accomplishments, income, previous actions. In cultures which emphasize experiences, a person's worth depends on the experiences that the person has had. In cultures which emphasize becoming, the focus is in how much and how fast the person is changing.

10.01.3.14 Dionysian vs. Apollonian Cultures

Again this is a narrow syndrome focused on the way people are expected to deal with emotions. In Dionysian cultures they are taught to express emotions. Loud speech is expected. Beliefs that one should state a view by using extreme language are common (e.g., as found among some Arabs), and attitudes such as the positive evaluation of touching, kissing, close positioning of the bodies, looking into the eye, and other behaviors are often associated with this pattern.

The Apollonian pattern requires people to control their emotions (e.g., East Asians), to stand far from others, not touch, not look into the eye. Corresponding beliefs, attitudes, and values support these behaviors. For example, it is impolite, and an indication of low social class, to speak loudly. Related to the above pattern is: high contact vs. low contact cultures, which reflects high or low level of voice, eye contact, frequency of gestures, touching, distance between the bodies. Interrelationships of the syndromes. Since the concept of cultural syndromes is relatively new, there has not been much research on their number or a clear indication of how many syndromes there are or how they are interrelated.

In addition, there will be emic patterns, which will characterize each individual culture. To identify cultural syndromes it is necessary to do research, based on the fact that syndromes reflect shared psychological processes (see Triandis, 1996) to see exactly what cultural elements are to be included in each cultural syndrome. We need to develop reliable and valid methods for the measurement of cultural syndromes, and then correlate these measurements to discover how the syndromes are related to each other.

10.01.4 METHODOLOGIES FOR THE STUDY OF WORLD VIEWS

The general perspective of this section is not to teach the reader how to do cross-cultural research, but how to tell the difference between a "good" and a "bad" study. I assume that clinicians read the literature, but the literature includes many "bad" studies. The most common error is to take an instrument that has been developed with middle-class mainstream undergraduates and use it with some ethnic group that is quite different from the standardization sample, without any attempt to check the reliability and construct validity of the instrument in this new sample.

Those wishing to do cross-cultural studies can consult a more advanced text. The most complete one is the volume by Triandis and Berry (1980). A shorter volume is by Lonner and Berry (1986). Special issues concerning the equivalence of cross-cultural measurement, and the unstated assumptions that are made by people who collect cross-cultural data are discussed in Hui and Triandis (1985).

Good cross-cultural research is like ordinary social research, only more difficult because of the complexity of the issues of translation, equivalence of measurement, and the like. Those who want to do such research should become familiar with the writings of Campbell (1988), as well as the publications mentioned above.

A central issue in cross-cultural research is whether we have a "real" cultural difference or an "apparent" difference due to an artifact or a "rival hypothesis." For example, it may be that people in one culture respond to a particular method of data collection differently from the way people in another culture respond to it. In such a case we do not have a substantive finding but rather a finding that is best explained by the way people react to the method of data collection. Or, it may be that we have an apparent "race" effect, but careful examination would reveal that it is a "social class" effect.

To establish a "real" cultural difference we need to eliminate all plausible "rival hypotheses" (Malpass & Poortinga, 1986) that may account for the observed difference.

Consider the following specific case. We tested two samples and found a difference in their level of anxiety. What are some of the plausible rival hypotheses?

(i) Anxiety may mean different things in the two cultures. The perceived antecedents of anxiety may be different. For example, in one culture it may be seen as caused by the prospect of lack of food and in the other by the possibility of downsizing the corporations most people work for.

To eliminate this rival hypothesis one needs to study the meaning of constructs, in the relevant cultures, independently of their measurement. For example, one can ask samples of participants from the various cultures: What makes you anxious? When you are anxious, what happens after that? Content analyses of the responses to such questions obtained in the relevant cultures can reveal both similarities and differences in the meaning of the construct. Associations of events with anxiety, semantic differential judgments involving the words "Fear," "Anxiety," and their synonyms, can result in an understanding of the these similarities and differences in the meaning of the concept.

More generally, when we compare two cultures we are comparing entities that differ in a myriad of ways. The conclusion that the difference reflects a particular variable (e.g., anxiety) requires that we "control" all the interactions of anxiety with other plausible variables. Furthermore, we need to sort out which aspect of culture is the relevant one. For example, in a comparison of African-Americans and White-Americans, we need to distinguish a difference due to race/color, *per se*, from differences due to nutrition, social class, neighborhood, historical influences, and so on. If all the observed differences are due to social class, it is scientifically irresponsible to report them as due to race. If both social class and race are relevant, one must report that fact also.

Since any two cultures differ in many ways, it becomes apparent that a two-culture comparison will have almost no scientific value, since in science we want to find relationships among well-defined, clear, reliably measured variables. Suppose we want to check the relationship of nutrition to anxiety. Ideally (assuming we have the funds), we should try to include a large sample of cultures in our study that differ in measurable ways on the nutrition variable. Ideally, the cultures that we select should differ in many ways, except that they should be ranked on one clear variable, nutrition. Then the countless other variables will not be systematically associated with nutrition, and we will be able to say something reliable about the relationship of nutrition to anxiety (Leung, 1989).

Campbell (1988) makes a valid point: the comparison of any two cultures is essentially useless (except for preliminary, hypotheses-generating work). This point requires us to study many cultures (a minimum of two "high" and two "low" on the variable of interest). The more cultures we can include in our analyses, the better. Furthermore, we must select cultures which are similar on the variable of interest but very different on all other variables, because of the phenomenon of cultural diffusion. It is well known that cultural elements are copied in adjacent cultures. If there is a lot of diffusion we do not have two independent cases, but actually only one case.

In addition, we must replicate the study with many different methods, since each method has its own meaning in each culture, but it is unlikely that an unsound hypothesis will be supported with very different methods. It is especially important to replicate the study with both nonreactive (e.g., participant observations) and more reliable (but usually reactive) methods, such as tests or questionnaires.

In sum, one must be skeptical about the equivalence of the meaning of concepts. For example, Diener (personal communication) asked samples in different parts of the world whether they were "happy." One respondent in India said: "I do not know; ask my husband."

In what follows I will identify some of the more obvious additional rival hypotheses which may produce an "apparent" difference when a "real" difference is not present.

(ii) The instructions may not be understood the same way. This is especially likely if the members of one culture have much less experience with a method or task than the members of the other. Related to this variable is the extent the two populations are familiar with the measurement method. For example, multiple choice tests are widely used in the US and a measure which uses such a format can give US subjects an advantage over a population from a country where such tests are not used.

A special test which measures the "understanding of the instructions" should be used routinely to eliminate this rival hypothesis. Familiarity with the measurement format and content has to be equated. This can be done by using formats which are equally familiar (and contents which have been pretested to be equally familiar) in the two cultures.

(iii) The level of motivation to respond to the particular method of the two samples may be different. Americans are likely to be motivated if an experimenter tells them that their "anxiety" will be measured to give an accurate response. They may want to know "their score" and how it compares to the scores of their peers. But in other cultures, where "anxiety" is perceived as a private matter not to be revealed to outsiders, or where it is mandatory to lie to outsiders, or where anxiety is conceived as something shameful, there may be strong motivation to give an inaccurate answer.

Independent measurements of the levels of motivation should be used to eliminate this rival hypothesis.

(iv) The reactions to the experimenter may be different. For example, in some cultures it is against the norms to cooperate with "outsiders." In some cultures it is mandatory to "lie" to outsiders or trick them! In such cultures villagers compete among themselves in telling lies about their culture, and later discuss among themselves what lies they told and laugh at the researcher for having believed their lies. To overcome such difficulties it is necessary to use several researchers, some "insiders," and some "outsiders" to obtain some estimate of the importance of this factor.

(v) The meaning of the test situation is not always the same. For example, in some studies (Bond & Yang, 1982; Bond & Cheung, 1984; Yang & Bond, 1980) the language of the instructions influenced the results. When instructions were given to Hong Kong subjects in Mandarin, Cantonese, or English, the results differed. Apparently, the language of the instructions suggested to the subjects who was interested in the results of the study—the Beijing authorities, the Hong Kong authorities, or the British colonial authorities.

(vi) Response sets differ across cultures (Hui & Triandis, 1989; Triandis, 1972). For example, in some cultures if one is "sincere" one gives a strong answer (e.g., "I strongly agree."), but if one is not sincere, one might use the middle of a Likert scale. In Japan it is arrogant to use an extreme response, and it is appropriate (modest, polite) to use the middle of the scale ("perhaps I agree with it"). In some cultures people only answer the questions which they are absolutely sure of; in others, they answer all the questions.

Marin, Gamba, and Marin (1992) found that Hispanics in the US, relative to non-Hispanics, are more likely to use extreme responses (e.g., I strongly agree) and to show acquiescence (agree with every question). The more acculturated (spent a lot of time in the US, are comfortable when using English) the Hispanics are to the US, the less they do that. In some cultures people are expected to agree when asked questions; in others they are expected to disagree when asked questions by "outsiders."

(vii) The samples, in the relevant cultures, may not have been strictly equivalent. For example, there might have been differences in social class, age, sex, religion, or some other demographic attributes which are the "real" cause of the difference, yet the difference is attributed to language/culture. One should analyze the data separately for each demographic category. Furthermore, the two populations under study may not be stable over time (e.g., sampling in 1960 and assuming that the results apply in 1999 may well be an error). When a population is heterogeneous, sampling in one area and hoping that the results are valid in another area (e.g., sampling in New York and assuming that the results apply to the whole of the US) may be misleading. For that reason, ideally, one should obtain samples in different parts of a country, and from different occupational, sex, and age groups, and check the consistency of the findings across these samples.

(viii) The ethical acceptability of the method may not have been the same in the various cultures. For example, in some cultures some samples (e.g., women) are not supposed to have an opinion, let alone an opinion which is different from their husband's. If one asks about that opinion, people can become embarrassed or angry because the experimenter "dared" to ask such a question. Pretests are needed in which samples are asked after the pretest "what did you think about this method?" It is useful to use a set of scales (such as good vs. bad, active vs. passive, strong vs. weak) for the subjects to rate the test situation itself (was the test situation pleasant or unpleasant?) One of these scales could be moral vs. immoral. If the study appears moral in one culture and immoral in the other, it would be necessary to investigate the matter further, before collecting much data.

It is clear from the above that there are many ways in which a difference may appear. A difference is easy to obtain across cultures, but the question is: Is the difference a substantive finding, or is the apparent difference due to something which is indirectly associated with the measurement? We can never be sure that we "controlled" all rival hypotheses, so any conclusions about cultural differences must remain tentative.

The discussion presented above does not mean that we must reject all forms of measurement. One can control statistically variables which are correlated with the dependent variable of interest. For example, if there is a response set, one way to control it is to "standardize" the data statistically. One method is to standardize the data obtained from a single participant (within participant standardization), thus eliminating individual differences, but focusing of cultural differences. If one is interested in individual differences, the best strategy is to measure them within culture, not across cultures.

10.01.4.1 Some General Strategies

When studying a phenomenon across cultures it is highly desirable to work with local social scientists who understand their culture. Such scientists are likely to insist that culture-specific aspects of the phenomenon be included in the study. Measurement can be made sensitive to the cultural context. Interpretation of the results can be much more sound when the perspectives of many cultures are used during data interpretations.

In addition, it is necessary to use more than one method because each method has a different meaning in each culture. If the results of several different methods converge, it is unlikely that the same bias accounts for all the results.

One must also do separate "construct validations" within each culture. In a construct validation, one has a theory and tests the theory. If the data hang together the way the theory predicts, then both the theory and the measurements of the constructs must be valid.

Suppose you have a theory which predicts that there are certain "antecedents" of anxiety in every environment and certain "consequences." If you measure anxiety with different methods in each culture and you find that the correlations between your measures of anxiety and the several antecedents and consequences specified by your theory are approximately the same in all cultures, then you have validated your measures in those cultures. If the patterns of correlations are similar, and if certain statistical tests (discussed by Irvine & Carroll, 1980) indicate that the measures are equivalent, then you can compare the results across the cultures.

10.01.4.2 Good Theory Can Eliminate Some Rival Hypotheses

If one has a well-developed theory that makes several predictions, and the theory is supported by *the* data, some of the rival hypotheses become less plausible (Malpass, 1977). Suppose my theory predicts that in a collectivist culture people will be low in anxiety when they are with members of their ingroups and higher in anxiety when they are far away from their ingroups. In an individualistic culture my theory predicts no difference when the individual is tested when with or away from members of the ingroup.

Suppose I collected data in rural China and rural America and I found what I predicted. In that case many of the rival hypotheses—different definitions of the constructs, different levels of motivation, response sets—become less plausible.

This does not mean we should not worry about rival hypotheses when we have good theory. Clearly, if the theory and a rival hypothesis make the same predictions, we cannot use the theory to eliminate that rival hypothesis. But in many cases the theory and the rival hypothesis will make different predictions and then if the data support the theory that is reassuring.

The main point to remember from this discussion is that cultural comparisons which indicate a cultural difference require a lot of work, checking, elimination of rival hypotheses, multimethod measurements, and the like, before the presence of cultural difference becomes plausible. As a sophisticated consumer of cross-cultural research, the reader should be looking for evidence that this extra work, checking, and elimination of rival hypotheses was actually undertaken by the researcher.

10.01.4.3 Methods that Can Establish Measurement Equivalence Across Cultures

Several methods may be used to establish cross-cultural equivalence.

(i) Suppose one has measured several variables in each culture and submits the correlations among these variables to a factor analysis. If the same factor structure appears in each culture (e.g., Tucker coefficients of 0.90 + for each factor) that is one indication that the variables have the same meaning in the relevant cultures.

(ii) Item response theory (Hulin, Drasgow, & Parsons, 1983) provides a statistical procedure which indicates if a particular item has the same meaning in two or more cultures. The procedure is based on the similarity in the way people respond to that item and to all the other items.

(iii) Psychophysical methods allow some physical variable (e.g., distance between physical objects) to be linked to a psychological variable (how do you feel about social entities) (for an example, see Triandis, McCusker, & Hui, 1990).

10.01.4.4 Emics and Etics in Cross-cultural Research

I introduced above the idea of etic (universal) and emic (culture specific) cultural elements. Here I will elaborate on the meaning of these constructs and explain how they might be used in the measurement of constructs.

Emics, roughly speaking, are ideas, behaviors, items, and concepts, which are culture-specific. Etics, roughly speaking, are ideas, behaviors, items, and concepts which are culture-general—that is, universal.

Emic concepts are especially useful in communicating within a culture, where one word can sometimes be used to convey a very complex idea. For example, a geographer who has studied the inhabitants of the Tierra del Fuego in the Southern tip of South America, told me that they have a word, *mamihlapinatapei*, which means "looking at each other hoping that either one will offer to do something that both desire but are unwilling to be the first to do."

One can almost see the scenario when boy meets girl and they mamihlapinatapei! One learns quite a bit about that culture by knowing the definition of this word. Similarly, by learning particular words, we get to know more about a culture.

Emic concepts are essential for understanding a culture. However, since they are unique to the particular culture, they are not useful for cross-cultural comparisons.

Let us consider an analogy, the comparison of apples and oranges. Apples and oranges have some common attributes, such as size, weight, price, and availability. They also have some unique attributes, such as unique flavor and aroma. Clearly, if we are going to understand what an orange is, we need to know about orange flavor. But we can not compare apples and oranges on orange flavor, except to say that apples do not have it. On the other hand, if we want to talk about price, we can compare apples and oranges. If we want to compare price to size or weight we can certainly do that, too. So, we can have a "theory" of size–weight–price relationships and see if it holds as well for apples as it does for oranges, and we can even extend it to other fruits. Emics are like apple or orangeflavor; etics are like size, weight, and price. So, for certain purposes, such as comparisons, we must use etic concepts; for other purposes, such as getting a real "taste" of the culture, we must use emic concepts.

More formally, emics are studied within the system in one culture, and their structure is discovered within the system. Etics are studied outside the system, in more than one culture, and their structure is theoretical. To develop "scientific" generalizations about relationships among variables, we must use etics. However, if we are going to "understand" a culture we must use emics.

Many anthropologists work with emics and think that etics are silly. They would say: "you do not know about apples by just knowing about their price, weight, and size." Psychologists want to make generalizations about people, so they do not want to get into the details of a single culture. Cross-cultural psychologists try to both understand and compare cultures. They work with both emics and etics.

The important point is to find convergence between different methods of understanding reality. I do not agree with the view expounded by some "deconstruction" humanists, or even some who pretend to be scientists, who argue that nature is constructed, not discovered—that truth is made, not found (e.g., Haraway, 1991). I think that this is an extreme position which is not science, since it cannot be discomfirmed. On the other hand, I do grant that our subjective responses to reality are often constructed. I am a realist, so I do not believe that women are less good as Chief Executive Officers (CEOs), just because that is the male-dominated "construction" and conventional wisdom of current CEOs. But I would agree with this view if someone showed me a convincing study, with hard criteria, which indicated that this view is correct.

"Constructionism" can result too easily in an image of reality which is found in only one person's mind. It might be good literature, but it is terrible science. The essence of science is a conversation between scientists and nature. It requires probing with multiple methods, to replicate important findings, and establish convergence between observations and measurements. If such convergence is broad, that is, includes humanistic "findings" as well as findings obtained through scientific methods, we can be much more certain that we have identified an important phenomenon than if we have only one person's argument or a single set of findings obtained in one place, with only one method. An important distinction between the humanistic and the scientific method is the contrast between the subjective and the objective. If the humanistic insight is to be taken seriously it has to converge at some point with other evidence; it cannot remain entirely subjective.

If we take a construct generated in our culture and use it in another culture, we may have a pseudoetic (false etic) construct. We must get empirical evidence that the construct operates the same way in the other culture, that is, it is a true etic, before we use it to compare the cultures. Remember the discussion about construct validity above? That is what needs to be done to establish a true etic. Then we have to make sure that this etic construct is measured in ways that are culturally sensitive. That often requires the use of local terms and ideas. In short, we must use both etic constructs and emic ways to measure them. That is why cross-cultural psychologists advocate the use of *both* emics and etics (Berry, Poortinga, Segall, & Dasen, 1992; Triandis, 1972, 1992).

One advantage of such a strategy is that one can obtain more sensitive information about the relevant cultures, which implies that one can obtain more cultural differences if one uses both emics and etics in the design of cross-cultural studies. In one study (Triandis & Marin, 1983), samples of Hispanics and non-Hispanics responded to either a questionnaire based on ideas generated in previous studies with American samples (pseudoetic) or a questionnaire which used ideas obtained from focus groups (informal discussion groups which generated items to be used in the questionnaire) of Hispanics and non-Hispanics. The latter questionnaire included both emic items which were spontaneously generated only by the Hispanic focus groups and etic items which were generated by both the Hispanic and non-Hispanic focus groups. Since the questionnaires in that study had 600 questions, one could get six cultural differences by chance (at the 0.01 level of significance). The number obtained by the pseudoetic questionnaire was 14 and the number obtained by the emic plus etic questionnaire was 50. In other words, one can miss a lot of subtle information about the way cultures differ if one does not use emics.

The importance of emics cannot be overestimated. There are emic concepts that are extremely difficult to understand by people who use an etic framework.

Consider this example: What is a geisha? Most Westerners are likely to freely associate "prostitute" with that concept, and as a result they will be quite wrong. A 500+ page ethnography about geishas (Dalby, 1983) shows that the closest association to "geisha" should be "jester." Just like the jester in a king's court had the function of diverting the king and his guests, so a geisha has as her chief function entertaining the clients of an establishment. Most geishas spend their time reciting poetry, singing, dancing, and serving their clients while they eat and drink.

Furthermore, there are many kinds of geishas, and only a minority are actual prostitutes (yujo). Most do other things, including greeting people at the door or playing musical instruments. The most highly sought geishas are older, more experienced, and thus able to act more appropriately. President Ford, the first US President to visit post-war Japan, had dinner with several geishas as part of his touring experience. The most beautiful were placed next to him; but the ones who did most of the entertaining were the older, more experienced ones. Of course, without knowledge of Japanese, President Ford may not have been able to appreciate the entertainment.

The contrast between "geisha" and "wife," in terms of the free associations of these words among Japanese males, is instructive. The former is seen as sexy, artistic, witty, and economically self-sufficient; the latter as sober, humdrum, serious, and economically dependent. The former is likely to be well read, know the latest poems and songs; the latter is likely to talk about the problems of the children.

Now that you have a glimpse of the meaning of geisha, do you see that it is a culturally specific role, that corresponds to an emic Japanese term, and the Western view that she is a "prostitute" is a pseudoetic, and becomes a true etic only when it uses the idea of "jester?" The general point is that using our own emic terms to understand other cultures will generally result in misunderstandings. We need to obtain etic terms which correspond to the emics.

10.01.4.5 How to Use Emic Measurements of Etic Constructs

Any theoretical construct of some generality in psychology is likely to have both etic and emic aspects. For example, the concept of "social distance" makes sense in every culture, and even among animals where territoriality is a well-established phenomenon. You allow some people to come close while you keep others away from you. The original concept, developed by Bogardus (1925), was operationalized by asking people if they would like to "marry," "live in the same neighborhood," "exclude from the country," etc. certain groups of people. It was found that Americans, in the 1920s, showed little social distance toward Western Europeans, especially those who came from the UK, and much social distance toward "Negroes," "Turks," and "Jews."

While the social distance concept is etic, the way it is operationalized can vary with culture. In India, the idea of "ritual pollution" results in social distance, and while a person may not mind living in the same neighborhood with a member of the lower castes, especially if that person is a servant, one can mind very much if that person "touches my earthenware." Thus, in India, social distance is indexed differently. Touching earthenware is an Indian emic; social distance is a theoretical concept, an etic.

Let me give you an example of how to use emic items to measure etic constructs. In a study I did a long time ago (Triandis & Triandis, 1962) I asked focus groups to generate items which measure social distance in Athens, Greece, and in Champaign, Illinois. I obtained at least 100 ideas from each sample. I then subjected the items to Thurstone scaling, which eliminates items which are ambiguous in each culture, and provides scale values for each item on an equal interval scale. I found that some items were etic, for example, "I would accept this person as an intimate friend" had a scale value of 11.1 in the US, and "I would accept this person as a best friend" had a scale value of 13.5 in Greece. But "I would accept this person as a roommate" was an American emic, with a scale value of 29.5. "I would accept this person as a member of my *parea*" was a Greek emic, with a scale value of 31.1. *Parea* means, roughly, regularly-meeting peer group. Thus, these two items mean more or less the same thing, but the American item does not make sense in Greece, and the Greek item does not make sense in the US. The method allows for culture-sensitive measurement, since Greeks rarely live in residential quarters in college, and thus rarely have roommates, while Americans are used to that concept. On the other hand, Greeks do have regular-meeting peers and a term for that. "I would accept this person as my family's friend" had a scale value of 40.9 in the US and 24.0 in Greece, indicating that while that item makes sense in both cultures it implies much less social distance in Greece than in the US. It apparently was more significant to be a friend of the family in Greece (a collectivist culture at that time, where the family was the most important social group) than in the US. Similarly, "I would rent a room from this person" implied less social distance in Greece (42.8) than in the US (57.5). On the other hand, "I would exclude this person from my country" had about the same meaning (95 in US, 82.6 in Greece).

Thurstone scaling uses judges to obtain the scale values of the items. The judges examine each item and place it on an 11-point scale, according to how much social distance is implied when a person agrees with that item. About 30 judges seem to be sufficient for each culture. The distributions of the 30 judgments concerning each item are examined. When these distributions are broad or bimodal, the item is rejected because it is ambiguous, or does not measure the quality of interest. These judgments are then treated statistically to obtain the scale values for each item. In this case the top and bottom of the scale were called 100 and zero for easy comprehension.

When the actual people are studied, the items of the social distance scale are presented to them in a scrambled order. They are asked to pick three statements which best represent how they would act toward a particular stimulus person, for example, a "50-year-old unskilled Chinese laborer." The respondent's social distance is the average social distance value of the three items which were endorsed. One can generate stimuli systematically, by varying, for instance, the age, nationality, and occupation (or whatever one is interested in studying) of the stimulus person and then obtain the social distance each respondent feels toward that stimulus combination. This allows the researcher to do analyses of variance that show the relative importance of the attributes, such as age, nationality, and occupation, as determinants of the social distance judgments. Note that the data come from the scale values of the statements that have been generated and standardized in each culture separately. So, the fact that the statements have different scale values in different cultures does not produce a problem. They are emic values, but the construct is etic, allowing cross-cultural comparison.

The same strategy can be used with most concepts and any attitude. Concepts may have a universal meaning that most researchers understand the same way, yet they must be operationalized and measured differently in each culture, because behavior has different meanings in each culture (Triandis, Vassiliou, & Nassiakou, 1968). Those interested in a more detailed discussion of this approach may find Triandis (1992) useful.

10.01.4.5.1 General recommendations

In summary, for good cross-cultural work we must start with the theoretical construct and discuss it with local informants to see how it is best operationalized. It is then useful to use "focus groups," that is, small groups that do some brainstorming, and come up with around 100 ideas about how to measure the construct. While these ideas will probably be different in each culture, the chances are that some of them will be generated in both cultures.

Next, we should take each of these 100 ideas and "scale them" separately in each culture. This means local standardization of the items. The technique developed by Thurstone (1931) (see, Edwards, 1957, Chapter 5) seems most helpful, but other scaling strategies may also be useful. With this method a small set of 15 or so scaled items can be identified in each culture that have been locally standardized but link to the etic continuum under study.

This method provides excellent locally standardized and equivalent equal-interval scales in the two cultures. Then the 15 items are scrambled and presented to the subjects under study in each culture with the instructions: "Pick three of the following 15 items which describe your most likely behaviors toward (the social category of interest)."

10.01.4.6 Examples of Multimethod Measurements

We have already emphasized the desirability of using multimethod measurements in cross-cultural studies. The following list of methods suggests the range of possibilities.

10.01.4.6.1 Ethnographic work

This is based on observations, with some questioning of informants and occasionally an experiment or survey (see Goodenough, 1980, for details). In such work an anthropologist spends one or two years among a group of people as a participant observer. After learning the local language, the scientist becomes a member of the culture, and often assumes one of the existing roles within the culture (e.g., the chief's son). After that, observations can be done informally or formally (see Longabaugh, 1980, for details) using video tapes or films which are later coded by several coders to establish inter-rater reliability.

10.01.4.6.2 Establishing shared cognitions

This approach includes the measurement of a psychological construct with several methods in each culture, and checking if the measurements converge. However, it is important to be able to distinguish a psychological from a demographic or cultural construct. Culture consists of shared elements. When we measure a psychological construct we do not know if it is shared so it may or may not be part of culture.

Triandis, Bontempo, Leung, and Hui (1990) have developed a method which allows a researcher to sort the personal, demographic, and cultural constructs. The basic idea is to have triads (three respondents) hear a question and answer it while the time it takes for them to agree on the answer is measured. Cultural elements do not require debate. For example, if you ask three Americans whether "fairness" is important or unimportant in everyday life, they are likely to supply a "Yes" in less than two seconds, and over 90% of the triads which are tested will agree. But if you ask: Is "fame" important or unimportant, they engage in a debate. Being famous is not a widely shared element of American culture; some want to be famous and others do not. For those who want to be famous this is a personal construct.

Using these two criteria (length of time to respond, percent of the triads who agree), the researchers can pick those elements of the culture which are widely shared.

This study was done in Hong Kong and Illinois as a demonstration of what can be done to measure cultural elements. The same could be done with demographic elements (men vs. women, old vs. young, rich vs. poor) by assembling appropriate triads and measuring how much time it takes for them to agree on how to answer a question, and what percentages of the triads do agree. Also, this study was limited to "values," but it could be done with any element of subjective culture.

Unfortunately, this method is participant-intensive. To have 50 triads, which is not an especially large number for a somewhat heterogeneous culture, 150 people are needed in each culture.

It is possible to compare the data of this method with the results obtained by questioning one person at a time with other methods. If the results are similar, one has evidence about the convergent validity of both methods. The Hong Kong/Illinois study did that and convergent validity was obtained.

Another strategy which takes seriously the fact that culture consists of shared elements is to examine the distributions of the responses of people from each culture to any psychological measure. If an arbitrary 90% of the respondents give the same answer, that is a cultural element. Clearly, the identification of cultural elements is important in studying cultures, but is of little interest when the focus is on individual differences. The two strategies are quite different. When studying individual differences we should do it within culture.

Interviews and surveys are often used (Pareek & Rao, 1980). Some of these are informal and allow for questions to be asked as the interview proceeds, while others follow a rigid schedule. These interviews can be based on limited or representative samples of the culture.

One might also use tests (Irvine & Carroll, 1980), attitude scales, personality scales, projective tests (Holtzman, 1980), and psychophysical tests.

Experiments can be done in more than one culture, but they present special difficulties (see Brown & Secrest, 1980; Ciborowski, 1980). For example, it is extremely difficult to ensure that the same degree of manipulation of the independent variables has been used in each culture.

However, some interesting results can be obtained when the same experimental procedure is used in each culture. Strodtbeck (1951) provides an interesting example. He examined whether culture is related to the probability that the wife or the husband will "win" an argument. He tested 10 husband-wife pairs in each of three cultures: Navajos (where the custom was for the husband to live with his wife's relatives, and hence one might expect husbands to have less power), Texans, and Mormons (where traditional male supremacy was used). The study began by asking each spouse a number of questions separately. The researcher noted on which questions the spouses disagreed. He then put them together and tape-recorded their interactions while they discussed their answers to the questions and attempted to reconcile their differences. If the couple finally agreed with the husband's original position, that indicated husband dominance; if the couple finally agreed with the wife's original position, it indicated wife dominance. The results were as follows:

Number of decisions "won" by	Husband	Wife
Navajos	34	46
Texans	39	33
Mormons	42	29

The hypothesis was supported. Culture predicts who wins, with the Navajo more likely to agree with the wife and the Mormons with the husband.

Finally, I will mention two methods which can obtain data from texts or other kinds of published materials:

(i) Content analyses (see Brislin, 1980) of children's stories, newspaper stories, myths, formal and informal communications, speeches, or movies produced in several cultures have been used to measure attitudes, motives, opinions, values, and other attributes. For example, one rates the materials on two variables and sees if the ratings are correlated.

(ii) The human relations area files (Barry, 1980) is a very useful data set. It consists of photocopies of much of the world's ethnographic record classified alphabetically according to the content of each paragraph. Thus, for instance, a researcher who is interested in checking if the "age of weaning" of a child is related to "level of anxiety" in the culture's adult population would look in the files under "weaning" and would find the ages of weaning which were reported by ethnographers who had studied several cultures. Similarly, this researcher would find some categories which might index the extent adults in the culture are high or low in anxiety. Then the researcher would either plot the data, or use correlations or chi-squares to check the relationship of age of weaning to anxiety.

Of course, ethnographies do not include every type of information, so it may be that there is no information relevant to anxiety in a particular culture. The result is "missing data."

In these analyses the number of cultures is the number of observations on the basis of which the correlation is computed, or N cultures are classified as "high" or "low" on each of the variables to compute the chi-square test. In other words, one can establish an association between two variables, based on holocultural data (all cultures on which there is information; see, Naroll, Michik, & Naroll, 1980 for details).

10.01.4.6.3 Conclusions

It is ideal to test a hypothesis with as many of these methods as feasible. Some of these methods are "operant" in the sense that the researcher provides a minimal stimulus and the subjects provide many responses (operate on the stimulus as they see fit when responding). For example, sentence completion or projective techniques, ethnographies and the human relations area files, observations, unobtrusive measures (see Bochner, 1980, for details), and content analyses are operant techniques. In most cases the researcher does nothing to stimulate the production of the data. In some cases a minimal stimulus, such as "Please write 20 statements which begin with the words '*I am*,'" is provided.

By contrast, experiments, surveys, and interviews are "respondent" methods; the subject is responding to stimuli presented by the researcher.

Respondent methods are more obtrusive, and they are more likely to be distorted by reactivity. The respondents are more likely to distort their answers, so they will appear to be socially desirable people to the researcher, their peers, the authorities in their culture, or from the point of view of their culture's ideal. In short, respondent methods are more likely to result in cultural differences due to the method. However, it is easier to "control" artifacts, when using respondent methods because the study can be replicated under a variety of conditions.

Operant methods are generally less reliable. Many observations or responses are obtained and it is not clear which ones are the most important. Operant methods also have a high "dross rate" (irrelevant information is a high proportion of the total information obtained). Furthermore, the observer may be biased and only see or hear what is consistent with a hypothesis.

Both kinds of methods should be used at different points in the research sequence. At the initial stages of the research, when one knows little about the culture, lacks good hypotheses, and is dealing with respondents who are not familiar with social science methodologies, it is best to use operant methods. Such methods are especially good when investigating complex relationships. These relationships can be kept in mind while making additional observations. However, since these methods are not sufficiently reliable, and are difficult to check for reliability and validity, one should not reach definitive conclusions by using only these methods. Rather, it is best to refine existing hypotheses, develop new ones, and keep an open mind about the culture while using them.

At a later stage in the research process when more is known about the culture, the hypotheses are more likely to be supported and then it might be possible to design experiments, questionnaires, and interview schedules which are appropriate for the problem. It also helps if the participants are familiar with the researcher's methods, since they may then be more likely to give the same meaning as the researcher to the testing situation.

In other words, no method is perfect; each method has both advantages and disadvantages. The sophisticated consumer of cross-cultural research will give more weight to findings which have been supported by more than one method, particularly if the methods were very different.

Separate tests of hypotheses within cultures and between cultures, and with more than one method, increase the confidence in any finding.

However, we must not assume that a test at the between cultures level will necessarily give the same results as a test at the within cultures level. For example, consider the variable "degree of industrialization" and correlate it with the variable "probability that a worker will vote for the communist party." In India and the US, there is a greater probability of a communist vote in a highly industrialized voting district than in a less industrial one. In other words, within countries there is a positive relationship between the variables of interest. But when we compare the two countries we see a negative relationship between these two variables. In the US there is a higher level of industrialization and also a low probability that anyone will vote for the communist party; in India, there is less industrialization, but a relatively high probability that a worker will vote for the communists. In short, there is a reversal of the sign of the relationship between the two variables when we study the phenomenon across vs. within cultures.

This means that while we should do our analyses at both the between and within cultures levels, we need not become discouraged when these results are inconsistent. Of course, consistency boosts our confidence that the relationship is robust. There are examples (see Rohner, 1986; Schwartz, 1994) in which a hypothesis has been tested at both levels and was supported consistently.

10.01.4.7 Translations

It is ideal to gather the data in each culture independently by using the same procedures but without translation of specific items. This view is supported by the realization that translation is at best approximate.

There are some hilarious examples of poor translation that suggest how difficult it is to translate. For example, outside a Hong Kong tailor shop: "Ladies may have a fit upstairs." In a Greek tailor shop: "Order your suits here; because of a big rush we will execute customers in strict rotation." An Italian laundry: "Ladies, leave your clothes here and spend the afternoon having a good time." In a Japanese hotel: "You are invited to take advantage of the chambermaid." A Norwegian cocktail lounge: "Ladies are requested not to have children in the bar." At the office of an Italian physician: "Specialist in women and other diseases." A Japanese hotel air conditioner: "Cools and Heats: If you want just condition of warm in your room, please control yourself."

In short, one can make the case that translation should be avoided. But that is not always practical, so a word about translation is necessary.

Translation of single words is unwise. It is extremely difficult to establish exact equivalence in meaning for single words. Only if the study focuses on the meaning of single words and uses several methods to tap that meaning is translation of single words acceptable.

The greater the context of a text, idea, or concept, the more likely it is that it can be translated properly. If one expresses an idea in more than one way, translation has a chance of reaching linguistic equivalence. Thus, it is helpful to introduce redundancy, synonyms, and context.

Brislin (1980) provides many useful suggestions on how to maximize linguistic equivalence. A good approximation to the ideal translation uses the Werner and Campbell (1970) method of double translation with decentering. This method is based on the realization that there are many ways to say the same thing, and careful adjustments to the original language of the research project may not produce any difficulties for the research but may facilitate the translation.

For example, the researcher starts with an English text (E), and asks a bilingual to translate it into Japanese (J). Then, he/she asks another bilingual to translate it back into English to obtain E′. A comparison of E and E′ indicates where problems may exist. If the discrepancies of E and E′ are significant, the researcher can "decenter" the text by producing a new text (E″ which is satisfactory for the purposes of the research, but is closer to E′ than to E). Such a text is likely to translate into Japanese more easily, since E′ was an English version of a Japanese text. The process of translation, back-translation, and decentering continues until two English texts emerge that are more or less identical.

Back translation seems like a good way to obtain linguistic equivalence but it has problems. First, many words in languages of the same language family (e.g., Indo-European languages cover a wide area from India to Europe to the Americas) have the same roots but different meanings. For example, in the Latin-based languages, the term *sympatique* or *simpatico* means "pleasant or agreeable person." In English *sympathetic* means "someone who feels like the other person does." Clearly, the meanings are not the same. Yet, bilinguals are apt to translate it and back-translate it into the original language when in fact the translation is not correct.

Second, skilled bilinguals are good at imagining what the original text might have looked like. So, suppose a Japanese text is being translated, the interpreter may be able to guess what the original E or E′ was and produce an E″ which is just like it. The researcher would be reassured, but the translation is imperfect. In short, while back-translation is desirable, it does not guarantee linguistic equivalence.

One technique which is useful, continuing with our example of English and Japanese, is administration of both the English and Japanese version of a questionnaire to a sample of Japanese bilinguals. In such a case one can compare the responses of the same person when answering in the two languages. This can provide a check on the translation, since the same answer would indicate good translation. However, even this technique is problematic because bilinguals have a tendency to present themselves in a more socially desirable way to "outsiders" than to "insiders" (Marin, Triandis, Betancourt, & Kashima, 1983). Thus, it is likely that a Japanese bilingual will present a more favorable set of answers when answering in English than when answering in Japanese.

In sum, to be safe do not translate. Basically, you can carry out the same data gathering operations in each culture, and the only text that needs to be translated is the instructions, which usually have a good deal of context. Then, standardization is done separately in each culture. Comparison of distributions, computation of Tucker coefficients of the factor structures that emerge from the correlations of the variables of the study, item response theory checks, etc. can be done to establish equivalence before any comparisons are made.

Finally, studies which report a large number of cultural similarities, and show the cultural differences as being embedded in these similarities, are more dependable than studies which do not report similarities. If all the data from one culture is different from all the data from another, it is very likely that the tasks were not communicated adequately from one culture to another, and the cultural differences are due to some artifact.

10.01.4.8 Ethics of Cross-cultural Studies

The sophisticated consumer of cross-cultural research will want to see that the research has been carried out ethically. Good research is ethical. Unfortunately, not all researchers carry out their work ethically. Some study what is easy to study, and as a result we know a lot more about the disadvantaged than the advantaged segments of most cultures. When two groups are in conflict and a researcher offers to study the conflict, the weak are more likely than the strong to accept the study. The powerful do not submit to research very easily; that means our picture of the powerful members of a culture may be distorted.

Some researchers do not provide their subjects "informed consent." Ethical research requires that the participants are able to avoid participation in studies they consider unethical or disadvantageous to them. But in many nonliterate societies the concept of "research" is nonexistent, and it is impossible for the prospective participants to provide meaningful informed consent.

With most operant methods the chances are that people will not be exposed to stress or risks. But with respondent methods some risks can be significant. If risks beyond those of ordinary life are involved in a research method it is essential that the risks be explained to the individuals, and they should have the opportunity to decline participation. This, of course, produces other problems, such as distorted samples consisting mostly of volunteers. Nevertheless, if risk is involved the subjects must be informed.

Since risk is perceived differently in each culture, it is important to bring research collaborators into the decision-making process at the earliest points of a project. If a method which appears risk free in one culture is not risk free in another, the method may have to be changed. There are many ways to collect data, so it does not follow that because we changed the method we cannot test an important theory.

There are special problems of research collaboration across cultures that are discussed in detail by Tapp, Kelman, Triandis, Wrightsman, and Coelho (1974). For example, research collaborators may be harmed by collaborating with someone from a culture that is politically taboo in their country. It is generally believed that researchers must leave something of value in the culture they studied to avoid "intellectual colonialism." What is of value will, of course, vary with culture but it can be information, procedures, material goods, or payments.

10.01.4.9 Ethnocentric and Androcentric Bias of Researchers

Most cross-cultural researchers are Western men; we all have difficulties in escaping our ethnocentric (my culture is the standard of comparison) and androcentric (my gender offers the only valid perspective on an issue) biases. We can try to control such biases, but the choices of problems, theories, and methods are likely to reflect such biases. For example, we cannot be sure that we have controlled such biases when we evaluate whether or not gender inequalities are similar or different across cultures. Thus, when evaluating cross-cultural research it is wise to ask whether such biases may have colored the reported findings, interpretations, and conclusions. A useful way to overcome such biases is to collaborate with researchers from other cultures and the other sex.

10.01.4.10 Summary of Criteria of Good Cross-cultural Research

(i) Does the study include many similarities across the cultures and are cultural differences embedded in the similarities?

(ii) Did the study use multimethod procedures that converged (Fiske, 1986; Fiske & Shweder, 1986)?

(iii) Did the study use tests both within (psychological level) and between (cultural level) cultures? Were the results consistent, or when inconsistent theoretically meaningful?

(iv) Were rival hypotheses checked and eliminated?

(v) Did the study use etic constructs measured emically, that is, with emic items generated in each culture to tap the etic constructs. Ideally, researchers should generate items from both men and women (Harding, 1987; Nielson, 1990; Reinharz, 1992), as well as from all important groups that make the culture heterogeneous (e.g., social class, religion, language, age, family structure). Were measurements standardized independently in each culture?

(vi) Was the study conducted ethically?

(vii) Did the researchers make an effort to control ethnocentric and androcentric biases?

10.01.5 ACCULTURATION

The discussion above assumed that cultures are isolated entities. However, in fact, they are in constant interaction. Individuals are often influenced by many cultures.

When two cultures come in contact with each other, individuals have the tendency to adopt some of the attributes of members of the other culture (accommodation), and sometimes they are so enthusiastic in adopting elements of the other culture that they overshoot. For example, individuals who come from a culture which uses time flexibly, for example, Mexico, may become superpunctual in a culture where "time is money."

However, migrants who are rejected sometimes react to the culture contact by emphasizing their own culture (ethnic affirmation). For example, they may become even more flexible about their use of time, and advocate that one should not own a watch, or bother to be on time, because that reduces one's freedom and makes a person like an automaton.

A complication is that in some domains people show accommodation or overshooting, and in other domains they show ethnic affirmation. Triandis, Kashima, Shimada, and Villareal (1986) hypothesized that if newcomers in the US are accepted they will show accommodation or overshooting, but if they are rejected they will show ethnic affirmation. In addition, accommodation and overshooting are more likely on visible traits, such as clothing, and ethnic affirmation is more likely on subjective traits, such as beliefs, stereotypes, or values.

A socio-political issue of great importance, when two cultures meet, is whether individuals should adopt or reject the other culture, and also try to maintain or reject their own culture. Berry (1990) identified four outcomes of the acculturation process: he used the terminology integration for the situation when the individual adopts the other culture while maintaining his/her own culture; assimilation for the situation when the individual adopts the other culture and rejects his/her own culture, separation for the situation where the individuals maintain their own culture and reject the other culture, and marginalization for the situation where both cultures are rejected.

Given that in the US, integration, as used in the press, means something different from Berry's integration, it may be best to call that condition biculturalism. In any case, Berry, Kim, Power, Young, and Bujaki (1989) found that people who adopt the integration or biculturalism solution to the acculturation situation, and secondarily the assimilation pattern, are better adjusted, both physically and in terms of their mental health, than those who use the other two acculturation patterns.

If we note that learning about another culture is similar to learning another language, we can see the advantages of knowing about more than one culture. Segalowitz (1980) identified many cognitive advantages associated with bilingualism, for example, cognitive flexibility, creativity. Similarly, a multicultural person has more than one way of interpreting reality. However, as Lambert (1992) has noted, bilingualism can be both negative and positive. It is negative when in the process of learning another language one forgets one's own language; it is positive when one is actually comfortable in both languages. Similarly, Triandis (1976a) has argued that multiculturalism can be both negative (assimilation) and positive (biculturalism). Adjustment is likely to be superior when positive multiculturalism is present.

Social identity (Tajfel, 1982) is strongly linked with the processes reflected in acculturation. An interesting example is provided by Rhee, Uleman, Lee, and Roman (1995). They asked Korean and American participants to complete 20 statements that started with "I am ... " They coded the responses into nine categories, one of which was "pure traits." Previous work (e.g., Triandis et al., 1990) had found that in collectivist cultures the content of the responses to the 20 statements is more social than in individualistic cultures. Clearly, pure traits is an individualistic category. European-Americans gave pure trait responses 29% of the time, Koreans did so only 12% of the time.

Asian-Americans were classified according to whether when completing "I am ..." sentences they had identified their ethnicity "never," "once," or "twice." Those who never mentioned their ethnicity gave 39% pure trait responses—a case of overshooting the European-American norm. They must have been the assimilated Asian-Americans. Those who identified their ethnicity once (e.g., I am Asian or I am Korean-American) averaged 25%, almost the same as the European-Americans. Those who identified their ethnicity twice averaged 17%, which is very similar to the 12% of the Koreans in Korea. In short, those with a strong Asian-American identity responded like the Koreans.

The implications for clinical work of the observation that biculturalism is best is that far from pressuring clients to discard their culture, clinicians should urge them to maintain parts of their culture as well as to acquire those aspects of the mainstream's culture which will help their economic advancement. That may at times seem difficult to achieve. However, there are opportunities for "cultural synergy" (Adler, 1991). Adler argues that when one culture solves a problem one way and the other culture solves it in a different way, rather than become frozen in the opposing ways to solve the problem, one should seek creative solutions which are acceptable to both cultures. In short, rather than the parochial "our way is the only way," or the ethnocentric "our way is the best way," there should be the synergistic, that is, the "creative combinations of our way and their way may be the best way" (p. 107).

To achieve synergy one needs to understand the point of view of each culture first. Second, one needs to explore and understand the cultural assumptions which underpin the particular beliefs. Then one can create new alternatives which are based on, but are not limited to, the cultures involved. For example, in the clash of collectivist and individualist perspectives, one might find a perspective which is compatible with both sets of assumptions. In our previous example about widows not eating chicken, one could serve a food which is not perceived as having the attributes of increasing sexual desire (as seen in Orissa) and is interesting and desirable (as seen in the US). The next step is to check if the solution fits the assumptions of both cultures. One must discuss the solution with members of each culture to make sure that the solution is acceptable.

10.01.6 IDENTITIES OF AFRICAN- AND EUROPEAN-AMERICANS AS AN EXAMPLE OF THE IDENTITIES OF CLINICIANS AND CLIENTS

The US includes 125 ethnic groups with nontrivial numbers (Thernstrom, 1980). Thus, a clinical psychologist is likely to encounter clients from many ethnic groups. Of course, a lot will depend on location. There are more Albanians or Zairians in one city than another. Also, fortunately, there are similarities among cultures. Anthropologists identify "cultural regions" within which there is considerable cultural similarity. Generally speaking, Africa South of the Sahara is one region; the cultures around the Mediterranean, including most of Europe, have much in common; the cultures of East Asia, South Asia, and the Pacific Islands have similarities. Native Americans (of course, they include tribes in South, Central, as well as North America) are among the most diverse cultures. For example, according to the criterion of social structure, they belong to five cultural regions (Burton, Moore, Whiting, & Romney, 1996). Clearly, clinicians cannot be expected to know much about all 125 cultures, or even about most of the cultural regions. However, there are some ethnic groups which are sufficiently common to require such knowledge. African-Americans are by far the most important, both because of their numbers and the long history of cross-cultural contact between them and the European cultures.

Each pair of cultures has a unique history of contact. For example, African- and European-Americans have had a history of contact which is not the same as the history of Asian-Americans with African-Americans. It is important to realize that the history of contact is an important factor in the kinds of identity which each group develops, and the kinds of "contact models" which each group generates.

Carter (1995) argues that people in the US develop a racial identity which affects their thoughts, feelings, and behaviors. Any valid psychotherapeutic process in this country must include race. He believes that this identity is important even in White–White interactions because so much of the content of social behavior in the US reflects inter-racial experiences in school, work, dating, neighborhood, or public policy.

Carter (1995) also argues that each ethnic group (Native Americans, Asian-Americans, Hispanics, African-Americans) goes through a series of stages in developing an ethnic identity which is bound to enter into the clinician–client relationship. Ethnic identity reflects how the individuals think about their own group as well as how they view the relationship between their group and the other ethnic groups.

Ethnic identity, of course, also reflects the kinds of acculturation patterns which are operating, as discussed above.

Carter's (1995) discussion of Black racial identity specifies four stages, each of which includes two levels. I will only describe the four stages.

Stage 1 is the pre-encounter stage during which there is dependency on White society for self-definition and approval. Racial identity attitudes towards Blackness are negative and White culture and society are seen as the ideal. There is an idealization of whites: much anxiety, low self-esteem, and a weak ego (in Loevinger's, 1976, 1979, sense). Most Blacks in this stage have higher than average incomes and do not report that they experience discrimination in the workplace. The client in this stage prefers a white counselor.

Stage 2, the encounter stage, begins when the individual has a personal and challenging racial experience. It includes confusion, emotions which are bitter, hurt, angry; there is high anxiety, low psychological well-being, high depression, and preference for a Black counselor.

Stage 3, the immersion stage, is characterized by positive feelings toward Blacks and idealization of Black culture, while having intense negative feelings toward Whites and White culture. The emotions include rage and depression. Individuals have low self-esteem and low self-actualization tendencies, are characterized by emotional dependence, but people in this stage have a strong ego in Loevinger's sense. This stage is most common among those of low education, who are separatists with Afro-centric values and anti-White/system attitudes.

Stage 4 is internalization. Here individuals realize that both Blacks and Whites have both strengths and weaknesses. Black identity is experienced as positive, important, and a valued aspect of the self. Individuals in this stage respect Whites and tolerate differences between Whites and Blacks. The emotions are self-confidence and security. At the most developed level of this stage there is individual activity to promote the welfare of Black people.

Carter (1995) describes five stages of White racial identity: stage 1, contact, includes persons who are unaware of others in racial terms, and deny the importance of race. However, they experience discomfort with unfamiliar people and situations. They are characterized by low anxiety, poor self-image, dependence, and are immature interpersonally. Such people have Euro-American values, but support organizations that promote equity.

In Stage 2, disintegration, people become aware of social norms and pressures associated with cross-racial interactions, see negative reactions by Whites to inter-racial associations, and attempt to find some balance between human decency and external pressures to be negative toward Blacks. Typical emotions are anger and guilt. They are still interpersonally immature, prefer a White counselor, are confused by Blacks, have Euro-American values, and may have negative views of racial issues in the workplace.

Stage 3 is reintegration. People at this stage are fearful, angry and hostile toward Blacks. They are anti-Black and pro-White, and see Blacks stereotypically. Individuals idealize Whiteness, devalue other races, and are anti-Black. Their emotions include fear and anger. They feel high anxiety and hold racist views; they have Euro-American values and negative views of the racial issues in the workplace.

Stage 4 is called pseudo-independence. At this stage people understand that there are similarities and differences between the races and accept the differences. However, these people understand the differences only intellectually, and remain emotionally distant from Blacks. They may be interpersonally mature, may accept inter-racial dating, may be comfortable in cross-racial settings, but nevertheless prefer White company.

Stage 5, autonomy, is the most accepting and flexible of the White racial identities. People at this stage accept race as a positive part of the self, are calm, secure, self-confident, mature interpersonally, self-actualized, inner-directed, support racial integration, have balanced views of inter-racial relations, and positive racial views of the workplace.

Carter's theory is that if the therapist (Black or White) and client (Black or White) are at equivalent levels of racial identity development, there will be little improvement in the client's condition. Even worse, if the therapist is at a lower stage than the client, there can be regression. Only when the therapist is at a higher stage than the client will there be progress in psychotherapy. Thus, he argues that racial identity is crucial in understanding the therapeutic relationship. In fact, it is not race as such but racial identity that is most important in understanding the course of psychotherapy.

Therapists who are not aware of the proper way of understanding Black behavior may misinterpret as pathological behaviors which are normal in the other culture, or clients might feel anxious for not being what the dominant culture expects them to be. Thus, Carter (1995) advocates that racial identity must be incorporated in clinical training and practice and he criticizes models of intercultural training which do not explicitly deal with racial identity. The second part of his book reports empirical studies which support some of these arguments.

This theory may have merit, but perhaps Carter (1995) overemphasizes the importance of race, and also does not seem to take seriously the importance of the situation. There is at least one study which suggests that identity may switch rather readily. Sussman and Rosenfeld (1982) asked Venezuelan and Japanese bilingual students to place their chairs anywhere in an empty room and chat for 10 minutes in either their own language or in English. The researchers measured the distance between the chairs. They found that when these students spoke in their own languages the Venezuelans placed their chairs close to each other and the Japanese placed them far from each other. But when these participants spoke in English there were no cultural differences. This study would suggest that the situation (speaking in own language or in English) determined the participants' identity and behavior. It would seem that any theory about the way racial identity influences behavior should take the situation into account.

10.01.7 METHODS FOR THE DEVELOPMENT OF AN UNDERSTANDING OF THE CULTURE OF THE CLIENT

Analysis of the subjective culture of the clients (Triandis, 1972) requires examination of the way clients categorize experience, the meaning of key terms, associations, beliefs, evaluations, expectations, norms, role definitions, self-definitions, ideals, and values (see Triandis, 1994, Chapter 4). This is often done most easily by reading ethnographies about the client's culture, or empirical studies which have measured these cultural elements.

All 125 or so of the American ethnic groups (Thernstrom, 1980) are quite heterogeneous, so that any statement made about them must be used very carefully. For example, Hispanics are quite different depending on whether they have come from Cuba, Mexico, South America, or Puerto Rico. Social class differences, the relative influence of African or Native American cultures, the genetic mixture of European- and Native-American populations, and factors reflecting the history of the relationship between the ethnic group and the mainstream populations of the US, have influenced the kind of culture that has emerged.

A major difference between Asian- and Hispanic-Americans, on the one hand, and European-Americans, on the other, is that the former are more collectivist than the latter. Many of the attributes of these two kinds of cultural patterns (see Triandis, 1995, for details) are reflected in the greater emphasis on politeness, being a nice person, saving face (Ting-Toomey, 1988), and the like which are associated with collectivism and increasingly neglected among extreme individualists. Asian-Americans are also said to be less assertive than European-Americans (e.g., Zane, Sue, Hu, & Kwon, 1991). An excellent comparison of Chinese and Americans can be found in Hsu (1981).

Hispanics have been found to be rather collectivist (Marin & Triandis, 1985), especially familist (see Triandis, 1994, p. 247 for references), concerned with smooth interpersonal relationships (Triandis et al., 1984), interpersonal connections, and personalistic relationships (dealing with each person differently). They are especially concerned with "respect," "dignity," "loyalty," and "cooperation" (Albert, 1996).

African-Americans value expression in movement, sound, and the visual modalities more than European-Americans. Expression as personal style and movement, and the use of a "cool pose" (Majors & Mancini-Billson, 1992), as well as different patterns of communication in both language (Landis, McGrew, Day, Savage, & Saral, 1976) and paralinguistically, require that for effective interaction with African-Americans, European-Americans must learn a good deal about the African-American subcultures. Some analysts have argued that African-Americans when compared to European-Americans are more spiritual, higher in harmony with nature, more present oriented, use time more flexibly, emphasize oral expressions, movement, surprise, improvisation (see jazz), rejection of routine, have an identity that is defined by expression, style, and spontaneous activity, are more gregarious, flexible, easygoing, affectively driven, and high in affect (Boykin, 1983; Jones,1986, 1988).

The largest differences between European- and African-Americans have been found among those African-Americans who have never had a job (Triandis, 1976b). While those with jobs often have a very positive self-concept and a subjective culture that is not very different from the subjective culture of mainstream Americans, those who have never had a job often have neutral self-concepts; they accept the conditions of the ghettos (e.g., high crime rates) as natural, have strong antiestablishment attitudes, and see little connection between what one does and what one gets. They can be characterized as having "ecosystem distrust," that is, they do not trust people in their environment, and see events in their environment as unpredictable.

Some of these perceptions may reflect the realities of life in segregated ghettos. For example, if discrimination prevents people from getting a job, not seeing a link between finishing school and a job may actually be a veridical judgment rather than an aspect of ecosystem distrust. It may be the case that people in those environments are untrustworthy. What is striking, however, is that the great distrust is uncovered across the board, in the way they rate stimuli like mother, father, teachers, Black women, Black professionals, Black men, and so forth (Triandis, 1976b, p. 123).

When clinicians interact with ethnics, such as those described above, they may well experience "culture shock" (Oberg, 1960). Culture shock is a consequence of not having as much control (Langer, 1983) over the social environment as one is used to having. If the way clinicians usually approach their clients does not result in anticipated changes, the clinicians may feel that they have lost control of their clients. To regain control clinicians need to put themselves into the shoes of their clients (Brislin, 1993). That means learning to make "isomorphic attributions" (Triandis, 1975). That is, when they explain the behavior of their clients, they must use approximately the same causal attributions as their clients use to explain their own behavior.

10.01.7.1 Methods of Culture Learning

There are numerous ways clinicians can learn about another culture: they can spend time with members of the other culture; they can read about them; they can ask people who have worked with members of the other culture to describe that culture. Each of these methods can be effective, but each has limitations.

One of the major problems in culture learning is convincing the clinician that culture training is worthwhile. After all the clinician is busy, and culture learning is like learning another language. Can the time it takes to learn about the other culture be justified?

Also, most people are ethnocentric and feel that others must learn about their culture rather than they should learn about other cultures. After all, if clients are going to be successful in American culture they must learn how to negotiate situations within that culture, that is, learn the culture of the clinician. So why should the clinician bother to learn their culture?

Many clinicians also feel that they already know enough. Thus, very little cross-cultural learning is likely to take place.

However, if one is to do a good job with a client from another culture it is important to learn as much as possible about that culture. Changing a behavior which is central to the other culture can do more harm than good. For example, clients from collectivist cultures often appear to be too dependent on their families. A clinician may be tempted to make them more autonomous. Yet that is likely to upset many beliefs, feelings, and behavioral patterns if it is attempted too quickly and while the client is still young. Changing a client without understanding that behaviors which appear pathological are normal in the client's culture is extremely dangerous.

Qureshi (1989) has written a whole book about misdiagnoses which are likely when the health provider and the client come from different cultures. For example, if the clinician does not know that in Pakistan it is inappropriate to say "I do not know," or in India it is rare that one says "thank you," major misunderstandings might occur. If the clinician does not know that in the Eastern Mediterranean there is often a culture of honor (Campbell, 1964), and many people show an "Othelo syndrome" which consists of excessive concern about the chastity of spouse, jealousy, and delusions that the wife is unfaithful, he might interpret "normal behavior" as abnormal. Differences in gestures, such as using the gesture that in the US says "no" to say "yes," as in Bulgaria and Southern India, can cause serious problems for interaction. Culture-linked diets can result in misinterpretations. Differences in what is normal social structure (e.g., equality or inequality of roles), conceptions of beauty (e.g., fat is beautiful in some cultures), taboos (what parts of the body can a clinician not touch), conceptions about what it means to be "sick" and what one is supposed to do about it (e.g., go to a shaman or take a drink which contains mercury that is supposed to be a therapy for impotence), beliefs about the proper behavior after a birth, marriage, death, and bereavement can also result in misunderstandings.

Psychopathology often is an exaggeration or caricature of normal culture (Draguns, 1988). It may reflect culture-linked myths, religious beliefs, political views, esthetic standards, economic conditions which are unknown to the clinician, and result in misunderstandings. It often reflects the basic personality which is most frequent in the culture, social representations found in that culture, the inability to deal with specific environments, the values of the culture, specific forms of the self, methods of self-control, and culture-linked lifestyles. Even highly educated samples may use indigenous methods of dealing with illness. For example, Cook (1994) asked university level samples of Chinese, Indian, and Anglo-Canadians about their beliefs. Three kinds of methods of dealing with 16 illnesses were provided: (i) biomedical (e.g., consult a physician), (ii) psychosocial (e.g., use a remedy recommended by the family), and (iii) indigenous (consult a religious leader). There were highly significant differences among the three cultural groups in the extent of endorsement of the indigenous and psychosocial beliefs, but their endorsement of the biomedical methods was equivalent. For example, the Chinese indicated that in many cases they would not go beyond the family for help. Issues of "face" are linked with going for help outside the family in Chinese culture. There is also much more somatization of psychological problems in that culture.

There are many forms of cross-cultural training. Here I will describe them briefly. Landis and Bhagat (1996) have provided a Handbook which discusses them in detail.

10.01.7.1.1 Culture-general vs. culture-specific training

There are many topics relevant to understanding other cultures that are not specific to any culture. These include:

(i) Know that we are all ethnocentric. Try to catch yourself when you are ethnocentric.

(ii) Know that the attributions that clients will make about their own behavior are likely to be different from the attributions which you will make about their behavior. Look for discrepancies in these attributions.

(iii) Learn to sort what is personal from what is ethnic. When clients react to you they are often seeing you as a "representative" of your own ethnic group. They may be hostile, not because they do not like you, but because they do not like your ethnic group, which may have dominated their ethnic group. Also, people may be reacting to a cultural trait (e.g., they may not like professionals who wear white coats) rather than to a personal trait.

(iv) Learn that it is most difficult to act correctly in an environment where the situation looks just as it does in your own culture, but where the required behavior is very different. Most cross-cultural errors occur in such situations. You are in a situation called psychotherapy and have tendencies to behave as that situation specifies, not taking into account the special attributes of the client that may require some different behaviors.

(v) Learn how to initiate conversations which will teach you about the client's culture. For instance, ask questions like these: What do you think has caused your problem? When did it start? Who is likely to be involved in causing your problem? Why do you think it started when it did? What do you think your problem is doing to you? How does it do that? How severe is your difficulty? Will it have a short or a long course? What kinds of treatment do you think you should receive? What are the most important results which you hope to receive from this treatment? What are the chief side effects which your difficulty has caused you? What do you fear most about your condition?

From such questions the clinician can construct the client's "cultural model of the problem." Especially important is to obtain clear definitions of the meaning of terms, associations between terms and other terms, and the perceived antecedents and perceived consequences of the clients "problem." For instance, one can ask "In your culture, most people experience what conditions which result in the kind of problem you are having?" "In your culture, people who have the condition you are having experience what kinds of consequences?"

The cultural model that is identified may be quite different from any model encountered in the clinician's culture. To place it in context, it may be useful to inquire about religious beliefs, myths, norms, values, and the like which may have influenced the definition of the problem and the expected outcomes of the treatment.

(vi) Learn to see a positive aspect in every one of the client's cultural traits.

(vii) Learn to suspend judgment, to live with ambiguity, to categorize broadly (e.g., while the client's response is different from the typical response of most clients, it is not that different).

(viii) Learn how people react when they are confronted by differences in attitudes and values: they are likely to (a) ignore the difference; (b) bolster their position (I am obviously correct and you are stupid; they are likely to find additional arguments to strengthen their own position, or get social support from others who agree with them); (c) differentiate—it is okay for people in the other culture to do it that way, and for us to do it our way; and (d) transcend—both are correct under some conditions; our way is best under conditions X and their way is best under conditions Y. Once you know these four ways of reacting to what is different, try to suppress the first two and use the last one more frequently.

10.01.7.1.2 Self-insight

The emphasis in this kind of training is the development of an understanding of how culture affects one's behavior. This technique uses an actor to behave in the opposite way from the way which is prescribed by the culture of the trainee. For example, in training Americans, the actor behaves like a "contrast-American" (Stewart, 1966).

Topics include the American emphasis on material goals vs. stress on spiritual goals (e.g., as in India), the emphasis on achievement vs. ascribed status based on family prestige; Americans see competition as desirable, whereas in many cultures it is undesirable; Westerners in general emphasize planning, while traditional cultures emphasize fate; Westerners also place reliance on self, while in high power cultures reliance on superiors is more likely. Similarly, in low power distance cultures, the emphasis is on equality, while status differences are most important in high power distance cultures. Other contrasts: the belief that knowledge through observation is superior to knowledge received from authorities; the belief that thoughts cannot influence events vs. the belief that they can do so.

The actor interacts with the trainee and the session is videotaped. The trainer then spends time with the trainee going over the tape and explaining how the trainee's behavior is determined by culture.

This method is good because the trainee learns about his/her own culture. However, the trainee does not learn anything specific about another particular culture.

10.01.7.1.3 Experiential training

Experiential training involves bringing the trainees into contact with members of the host culture in situations where they can make mistakes which will not hurt long-term relationships.

For example, in the early 1960s, the Peace Corps used an exact replica of a South Pacific village (no electricity, no movies, no running water, etc.) in a valley on the Big Island of Hawaii (Brislin, 1993). Trainees spent several weeks learning the languages and customs of such villages while interacting with trainers from South Pacific cultures. Many trainees exposed to the rigors of that environment decided to drop out, saving the Peace Corps the expense of early repatriation and the embarrassment of failure on the job.

This method, however, is expensive, and depends on trial and error learning, which is slow. Nevertheless, it produces results if the training organization can spend the money and the trainees have the time.

10.01.7.1.4 Exposure to many local cultures

It is assumed that the more experience trainees have had in entering, learning about, and leaving cultures, the better equipped they will be to deal with new cultures. This type of training was developed by the late psychiatrist Wedge. It encourages the trainees to join different urban subcultures, such as the police, the fire department, unions, top management of corporations, school boards, religious groups, political groups, pickpockets, prostitutes, and so on. Each of these groups has a unique culture, and the skills required to join it should be valuable. One has to learn how to scout, enter, explore, terminate, evaluate the new skills and transfer them to the next culture. The trainer helps the trainee get in and out of each subculture, and discusses the experiences of the trainees once a week in review sessions where each trainee's problems in getting in and out of each culture are examined.

This method has a number of practical difficulties. It is difficult for a trainee to get into some of these groups (e.g., in one case, when a trainee wanted to join some stevedores they attacked him with a knife), and while there is much to be said for the process skills which one acquires, trainees do not learn much content about the host culture.

10.01.7.1.5 Field trips

The clinician may visit the culture of the client for some weeks to become familiar with the environment. This method teaches very little in depth about the local culture.

10.01.7.1.6 Culture assimilators or intercultural sensitizers

The introduction to this section mentioned the importance of learning to make isomorphic attributions (Triandis, 1975). In order to train people to make isomorphic attributions this technique was developed and validated (e.g., Fiedler, Mitchell, & Triandis, 1971) and found to work. It is the only cross-cultural training method that has been evaluated so far, with random assignment of trainees to experimental and control groups and has been shown to be effective (Albert, 1983). This does not mean that the other methods do not work; it only means that rigorous studies have not yet been reported.

The culture assimilator is a programmed learning approach to cultural training. It consists of a set of 100–200 critical incidents, that is, scenarios where people from two cultures interact. Each episode is followed by four or five explanations of why the member of the other culture has acted in a specific way. The trainee selects one of the explanations and is asked to turn to another page (or computer screen) where feedback is provided concerning the chosen explanation.

Let us look at a simple example. Suppose you are teaching a clinical psychologist to understand the behavior of a lower class Hispanic. If the psychologist understands the Hispanic's viewpoint, this is considered successful training.

Episode: A Hispanic lower class client looks down when spoken to.

Question: Why did the client look down?

Attributions:

(i) He was distracted. Turn to page 50.

(ii) He was fearful. Turn to page 51.

(iii) He was respectful. Turn to page 52.

(iv) He was hostile. Turn to page 53.

When trainees turn to pages 50, 51, or 53, they find negative feedback, along lines such as these: "No, this is incorrect; try another explanation." When the trainees turn to page 52, they get feedback such as: "Excellent! That is correct. When we presented this question to a sample of 80 Hispanics and 95 non-Hispanics, 85% of the Hispanics considered this answer to be the correct one, and only 36% of the non-Hispanic thought that this was correct."

Note that the construction of assimilator training is culture-specific. It requires the use of samples of people from the two cultures who study the episode and the attributions and select the attribution they consider to be correct. Thus, the training is validated as it is being constructed.

In addition, the feedback gives the percentages of samples who agree or disagree with each answer. This avoids teaching stereotypes. Instead, one learns that judgments about why people acted in a given way are probabilistic, and the probabilities differ across cultures.

Of course, in constructing assimilators it is necessary to have many more episodes than will be used in the final training, because some will not discriminate the two samples of subjects, and thus must be discarded.

Construction of the episodes is based on interviews with people who have wide experience in the two relevant cultures, or on research which has identified differences in the subjective culture of the two relevant samples. Any item of cultural difference can be included. For example, if the trainer wants to teach what it means to be *simpatico* she would have one correct option and several incorrect ones and let the trainee pick options and get feedback.

In training persons from an individualistic culture such as the US to go to a collectivist culture such as the Far East, one might include a variety of items such as:

(i) Differences in norms, such as do not bring a present of a certain color.

(ii) Differences in roles, such as the almost sacred parent–child role in some collectivist cultures (so that if one's spouse disagrees with one's parents, it is obligatory to take the side of one's parents in such a dispute).

(iii) Differences in the way behaviors can express intentions, so that "no" must be expressed most indirectly, and in a very subtle way, for instance during a visit by serving two substances (e.g., tea and bananas) which are usually not served together.

(iv) Differences in self-concepts, for example, collectivist selves are more likely to be appendages of groups than to be autonomous.

(v) Differences in what behaviors are valued, for example, that in collectivist cultures people use a modest introduction of their lecture, such as "what I have to tell you is not very important;" or they may say "I thank you for spending your valuable time with me." In individualist cultures they are more likely to present a self-assured front.

(vi) Differences in the kinds of associations which people make, for instance, in collectivist cultures people are more likely to associate the word "progress" with national rather than with personal progress.

(vii) Differences in the kinds of differentiations (sensitivity to hierarchies based on minor cues) which people typically make, for example, in collectivist cultures there will be more differentiations on the vertical axes than on the horizontal axes of social relationships.

(viii) Differences in the important determinants of behavior—in collectivist cultures behavior is more likely to reflect norms than attitudes.

(ix) Differences in the kinds of reinforcements which people expect for particular behaviors in particular situations—in collectivist cultures one is supposed to give a gift in many situations in which in individualist cultures one would pay.

Triandis, Brislin, and Hui (1988) advised individualists to pay attention to group attributes more than they do in their own culture, to learn more about the ingroups and outgroups of collectivists and to expect sharp differences in behavior when the collectivist interacts with members of such groups, to expect more harmony within the ingroup, for example, no criticism of high status people, than is typical of their own culture. They also suggested that trainees should cultivate long-term relationships, be modest when presenting a lecture, stress equality and need when distributing resources, and give more gifts than is customary in their own culture.

Construction of a typical assimilator begins with 200 or so episodes extracted from discussions with people who know both cultures, or by analyzing relevant ethnographies to identify a set of four or five attributions for each episode. Then the episodes and the attributions are presented to samples from the trainee's and the host's culture, and differences in the response patterns are examined. Those episodes which do not produce significant chi-squares are discarded. Then the assimilator is printed in a book or placed in a computer.

Administration can be done with each trainee working through the book or computer program alone, or the trainer may select some of the more interesting episodes and present them for discussion. Trainees may also role play the content of some of the episodes.

In principle, this method can be expanded for use with an interactive disk technology, so that trainees see videotaped actors performing the episode and participate by pushing buttons that indicate what responses they think are appropriate. Feedback from the computer in the form of praise or criticism can make this task most interesting.

In evaluations of this kind of training, trainees were assigned randomly to two groups: they received or did not receive the training (e.g., Weldon, Carlston, Rissman, Slobobin, and Triandis, 1975). Such studies have shown that trained people learn to make isomorphic attributions, they expand the range of explanations they give for specific behaviors, they become less ethnocentric, and develop more accurate expectations concerning appropriate behavior.

Assimilator training increases cognitive complexity. Cognitive complexity makes it possible to consider the subjective culture of the other cultural group as "valid" and thus lessens prejudice (Gardiner, 1972).

However, culture assimilator training does not strongly increase liking for the other group or reduce social distance toward it. Liking depends on the number of pleasant experiences one has shared with the other group. Just knowing how the other group thinks does not change emotions.

Stephan and Stephan (1984) used a culture assimilator to increase "knowledge of Chicano culture" among Anglo students in New Mexico. This study indicated that Anglo students' attitudes toward Chicanos in the Southwest of the US are related to three factors: (i) how much they know about Chicano culture, (ii) how much contact they have with Chicanos, and (iii) their parents' attitudes toward Chicanos. Contact with Chicanos was determined by the attitudes of their friends toward Chicanos. Finally, contact increased knowledge of Chicano culture, and the assimilator training boosted that knowledge a bit more, so that those who were trained had more positive attitudes than those who were not. The Stephans concluded their study as follows:

> Simple intergroup contact, such as the contact that typically occurs in desegregated schools, is not likely to improve intergroup relations. However, specially designed educational programs, designed to reduce ignorance of the outgroup, do appear to improve intergroup relations. (p. 249)

Social distance often depends on the norms of our own group. If our own group urges us to get along with the other group, we are more likely to do so than if it opposes such friendliness. As in the Stephans' study, when the friends favor contact, there is likely to be an improvement in relationships.

For these reasons culture assimilator training is only one component of cross-cultural training. It is not sufficient by itself. It needs to be supplemented with other methods, such as the self-insight method which is likely to increase the motivation of the trainees to learn about the other culture, and experiential training which can change emotions. Also, the norms of social interaction between the two cultures need to be changed to modify social distance.

Another limitation of assimilator training is that it does not change behavior. It is one thing to know how one is supposed to behave, and quite another to behave correctly. To achieve the latter goal one needs to have behavior modification training.

The development of assimilators is time-consuming. It is obvious that any one clinician cannot afford to develop an assimilator for particular clients. However, a group of clinicians, such as the APA's Division 12, could undertake the development of relevant assimilators.

In addition to assimilators which focus on a specific culture, there is a general assimilator (Brislin, Cushner, Cherrie, & Yong, 1986). It deals with the fact that it is natural and to be expected to: (i) feel anxious abroad, (ii) experience disconfirmed expectancies, (iii) be unable to feel that one belongs to the local culture, (iv) experience ambiguity about what one should do, and (v) be exposed to local prejudices. It teaches that one must learn to control one's own prejudices.

The general assimilator also teaches trainees to expect differences in the way people view: (i) work, (ii) the relationship of work and social interaction, (iii) time, (iv) space, (v) language, (vi) roles, (vii) groups, (viii) rituals, (ix) hierarchies, and (x) values.

It also helps the trainees to understand differences in: (i) categorization, (ii) differentiation (e.g., some people know more about some subjects than you do), (iii) the importance of the ingroup–outgroup distinction (e.g., between collectivists and individualists), (iv) learning styles (not everyone learns best the same way), and (v) attributions (how to make isomorphic attributions).

The general assimilator has been successfully evaluated (Cushner, 1989). Twenty-eight trained adolescents from the Pacific Rim visiting New Zealand were better adjusted than 22 control adolescents hosted by New Zealanders. The trained adolescents completed a number of tasks measuring cross-cultural sensitivity better than the control subjects.

A final point about assimilators: clinicians who have been warned that there will be problems when interacting with members of a specific culture are more likely to be able to deal with these problems than naive clinicians. This phenomenon is parallel to findings with hospital preoperative patients: those who were told that they will feel quite uncomfortable after an operation dealt better with the post-operative pain than those who had been told nothing. In general, the more the training creates realistic expectations about events, the better.

10.01.7.1.7 Behavior modification cross-cultural training

Behavior modification techniques require that people be rewarded for desirable behaviors and be made to do an incompatible behavior whenever they have the urge or tendency to do an undesirable behavior. For example, in Latin America it is customary among friends to give an *abrazo*, a kind of embrace with the arms. Also, holding hands, touching, and other behaviors between good friends of the same sex are common. Yet North Americans have to be trained to carry out such behaviors. If they behave as is expected by the Latinos they will be liked better when interacting with Latinos than if they behave as they do at home. If they do not behave as expected the locals will think of them as cold and undemonstrative "Gringos." But North Americans who behave this way without proper training will feel that they are behaving inappropriately.

Conversely, some behaviors have to be eliminated. For example, in some cultures (e.g., Greece), to show the palm of your open hand is an insult. It is called a "moutza" and reflects utmost contempt. However, many people are in the habit of greeting others by waving an open hand. For these people to stop doing this requires some training. Most people wave without thinking. A trainer must catch them in the act, and tell them not to open their hand. Self-correction after such acts can change the habit, so that the person waves with the palm closed and turned toward themself.

Especially difficult is to change habits such as nodding to say "no" and shaking the head to say "yes" (Bulgaria, Southern India). Here one needs a lot of practice to get over well-established habits.

10.01.7.1.8 Some summary points about training

Cross-cultural training can be effective. Black and Mendelhall (1990) reviewed 29 studies that measured effectiveness. They found that all the studies that measured how people felt about the training had positive results, all the studies which measured effective interpersonal relationships found improvements, all the studies which measured changes in perception found them, and all research which tried to reduce culture shock succeeded in doing so. Two-thirds of the studies which measured performance obtained improved performance.

In general these effects were found in field studies but not in laboratory studies. This may be due to the limited time one can use in the laboratory. A few hours of training are not enough to produce major changes. Furthermore, field studies involve volunteers who are motivated to succeed. If we tried to train the general public perhaps we would not have positive results. No matter how good the training or the trainer, if the trainees do not wish to change, they will not. Nevertheless, the studies with control groups and longitudinal designs reviewed by Black and Mendelhall (1990) show some impressive results which should encourage more cross-cultural training. A meta-analysis which statistically combines the results from many studies has also found that cross-cultural training is effective (Deshpande & Viswesvaran, 1992).

The scientific understanding of how culture affects social behavior and the use of this understanding to improve relationships across cultures has just begun, but it is a promising area of activity.

10.01.8 FUTURE DIRECTIONS

Future research should determine how many cultural syndromes are needed for an adequate understanding of cultural differences. Learning about these cultural syndromes should allow clinicians to improve their understanding of the cultures of their clients.

10.01.9 SUMMARY AND CONCLUSIONS

Culture penetrates our judgments and behaviors in subtle often uncontrollable ways. Becoming familiar with the extent culture shapes our perceptions, standards, and standard operating procedures can be useful. The aim of this chapter was to increase the sensitivity of the readers to the concepts which may help clinicians control the cultural dimensions of their interaction with their clients. It examined the major ways in which cultures differ and explored the attributes of methodologically sound studies which can determine precisely how cultures differ. It then reviewed ways in which clinicians can learn about the culture of their clients.

10.01.10 REFERENCES

Adler, N. (1991). *International dimensions of organizational behavior*. Boston: PWS-Kent Publishing.

Albert, R. D. (1983) The intercultural sensitizer or culture assimilator: A cognitive approach. In D. Landis & R. W. Brislin (Eds.), *Handbook of intercultural training* (Vol. 2, pp. 186–217). New York: Pergamon.

Albert, R. D. (1996). A framework and model for understanding Latin American and Latino/Hispanic cultural patterns. In D. Landis & R. S. Bhagat (Eds.), *Handbook of intercultural training* (2nd ed., pp. 327–348). Thousand Oaks, CA: Sage.

Barry, H. (1980). Description and uses of the Human Relations Area Files. In H. C. Triandis & J. W. Berry (Eds.), *Handbook of cross-cultural psychology* (Vol. 2, pp. 445–478). Boston: Allyn and Bacon.

Berry, J. W. (1990). The psychology of acculturation. In *Nebraska Symposium on Motivation, 1989* (pp. 201–234). Lincoln, NE: University of Nebraska Press.

Berry, J. W., Kim, U., Power, S., Young, M., & Bujaki, M. (1989). Acculturation attitudes in plural societies. *Applied Psychology, 38*, 185–206.

Berry, J. W., Poortinga, Y., Segall, M., & Dasen, P. (1992). *Cross-cultural psychology*. New York: Cambridge University Press.

Black, J. S., & Mendenhall, M. (1990). Cross-cultural training effectiveness: A review and theoretical framework for future research. *Academy of Management Review, 15*, 113–136.

Bochner, S. (1980). Unobtrusive methods in cross-cultural experimentation. In H. C. Triandis & J. W. Berry (Eds.), *Handbook of cross-cultural psychology* (Vol. 2, pp. 319–388). Boston: Allyn and Bacon.

Bogardus, E. S. (1925). Measuring social distance. *Journal of Applied Sociology, 9*, 299–308.

Bond, M. H., & Cheung, M. (1984). Experimenter language choice and ethnic affirmation by Chinese trilinguals in Hong Kong. *International Journal of Intercultural Relations, 8*, 347–356.

Bond, M., & Smith, P. B. (1996). Cross-cultural social and organizational psychology. *Annual Review of Psychology, 47*, 205–235.

Bond, M., & Young, K. S (1982). Ethnic affirmation vs cross-cultural accommodation: The variable impact of questionnaire language on Chinese bilinguals in Hong Kong. *Journal of Cross-Cultural Psychology, 13*, 169–185.

Bond, R., & Smith, P. B. (1996). Culture and conformity: A meta-analysis of studies using Asch's (1952b, 1956) line judgment task. *Psychological Bulletin, 119*, 111–137.

Boykin, A. W. (1983). The academic performance of Afro-American children. In J. Spence (Ed.), *Achievement and achievement motives* (pp. 328–371) New York: Freeman.

Brewer, M. B. (1991). The social self: On being the same and different at the same time. *Personality and Social Psychology Bulletin, 17*, 475–485.

Brewer, M., & Campbell, D. T. (1976). *Ethnocentrism and intergroup attitudes: East African evidence*. New York: Halsted/Wiley.

Brislin, R. W. (1980). Translation and content analysis of oral and written materials. In H. C. Triandis & J. W. Berry (Eds.), *Handbook of cross-cultural psychology* (Vol. 2, pp. 389–444). Boston: Allyn and Bacon.

Brislin, R. (1993). *Understanding cultures influence on behavior*. Fort Worth, TX: Harcourt Brace Jovanovich.

Brislin, R., Cushner, K., Cherrie, C., & Yong, M. (1986). *Intercultural interactions: A practical guide*. Beverly Hills, CA: Sage.

Brown, D. E. (1991). *Human universals*. Philadelphia: Temple University Press.

Brown, E. D., & Secrest, L. (1980). Experiments in cross-cultural research. In H. C. Triandis & J. W. Berry (Eds.), *Handbook of cross-cultural psychology* (Vol. 2, pp. 297–318). Boston: Allyn & Bacon.

Burton, M. L., Moore, C. C., Whiting, J. W. M., & Romney, A. K. (1996). Regions based on social structure. *Current Anthroplogy, 37*, 87–123.

Campbell, D. T. (1988). *Methodology and epistemology for social science*. Chicago: University of Chicago Press.

Campbell, D. T., & Levine, R. (1968). Ethnocentrism and intergroup relations. In R. P. Abelson et al. (Eds.), *Theories of cognitive consistency: A sourcebook* (pp. 551–564). Chicago: Rand McNally.

Campbell, J. K. (1964). *Honor, family and patronage*. Oxford: Clarendon Press.

Carter, R. T. (1995). *The influence of race and racial identity in psychotherapy: Toward a racially inclusive model*. New York: Wiley.

Ciborowski, T. (1980). The role of context, skill and transfer in cross-cultural experimentation. In H. C. Triandis & J. W. Berry (Eds.), *Handbook of cross-cultural psychology* (Vol. 2, pp. 279–296). Boston: Allyn & Bacon.

Cohen, D. (1996). Law, social policy, and violence: The impact of regional cultures. *Journal of Personality and Social Psychology, 70*, 961–978.

Cohen, D., & Nisbett, R. E. (1994). Self-protection and the culture of honor: Explaining Southern violence. *Personality and Social Psychology Bulletin, 20*, 551–567.

Cohen, D., Nisbett, R. E., Bowdle, B. F., & Schwartz, N. (1996). *Journal of Personality and Social Psychology, 70*, 945–960.

Cook, P. (1994). Chronic illness beliefs and the role of social networks among Chinese, Indian, and Angloceltic Canadians. *Journal of Cross-Cultural Psychology, 25*, 452–465.

Cushner, K. (1989) Assessing the impact of a culture-general assimilator. *International Journal of Intercultural Relations, 13,* 125–146.

Dalby, L. C. (1983). *Geisha.* Berkeley, CA: University of California Press.

Deshpande, S. P., & Viswesvaran, C. (1992). Is cross-cultural training of expatriate managers effective: A meta analysis. *International Journal of Intercultural Relations, 16,* 295–310.

Devine, P. G. (1989). Stereotypes and prejudice: The automatic and control components. *Journal of Personality and Social Psychology, 56,* 5–18.

Diaz-Guerrero, R. (1979). The development of coping style. *Human Development, 22,* 320–331.

Doi, T. (1986). *The anatomy of conformity: The individual versus society.* Tokyo: Kadansha.

Draguns, J. (1988). Personality and culture: Are they relevant for the enhancement of quality of mental life? In P. R. Dasen, J. W. Berry, & N. Sartorius (Eds.), *Health and cross-cultural psychology* (pp. 141–161). Newbury Park, CA: Sage.

Draguns, J. (1990). Normal and abnormal behavior in cross-cultural perspective: Specifying the nature of their relationship. In J. Berman (Ed.), *Nebraska symposium on motivation, 1989* (pp. 235–278). Lincoln, NE: University of Nebraska Press.

Edwards, A. L. (1957). *Techniques of attitude scale construction.* New York: Appleton-Century-Crofts.

Fiedler, F. E., Mitchell, T., & Triandis, H. C. (1971). The culture assimilator: An approach to cross-cultural training. *Journal of Applied Psychology, 55,* 95–102.

Fiske, D. W. (1986). Specificity of method and knowledge in social science. In D. W. Fiske & R. A. Shweder (Eds.), *Metatheory in social science* (pp. 61–82). Chicago: University of Chicago Press.

Fiske, D. W., & Shweder, R. A. (1986). *Metatheory in social science.* Chicago: University of Chicago press.

Gardiner, G. S. (1972). Complexity training and prejudice reduction. *Journal of Applied Social Psychology, 2,* 326–342.

Goodenough, W. H. (1980). Ethnographic field techniques. In H. C. Triandis & J. W. Berry (Eds.), *Handbook of cross-cultural psychology* (Vol. 2, pp. 29–56). Boston: Allyn & Bacon.

Haraway, D. J. (1991). *Simians, cyborgs, and women.* New York: Routledge.

Harding, S. (1987) (Ed.). *Feminism and methodology.* Bloomington, IN: Indian University Press.

Herskovits, M. J. (1955). *Cultural anthropology.* New York: Knopf.

Hofstede, G. (1980). *Culture's consequences.* Beverly Hills, CA: Sage.

Holtzman, W. H. (1980). Projective techniques. In H. C. Triandis & J. W. Berry (Eds.), *Handbook of cross-cultural psychology* (Vol. 2, pp. 245–278). Boston: Allyn & Bacon.

Hsu, F. L. K. (1981). *Americans and Chinese: Passage to differences.* Honolulu, HW: University of Hawaii Press.

Hui, C. H., & Triandis, H. C. (1985). Measurement in cross-cultural psychology: A review and comparison of strategies. *Journal of Cross-Cultural Psychology, 16,* 131–152.

Hui, C. H., & Triandis, H. C. (1989). Effects of culture and response format on extreme response style. *Journal of Cross-Cultural Psychology, 20,* 296–309.

Hulin, C. L., Drasgow, F., & Parsons, C. K. (1983). *Item response theory: Applications to psychological measurement.* Homewood, IL: Irwin.

Irvine, S., & Carroll, W. K. (1980). Testing and assessment across cultures: Issues in methodology and theory. In H. C. Triandis & J. W. Berry (Eds.), *Handbook of cross-cultural psychology* (Vol. 2, pp. 181–244). Boston: Allyn & Bacon.

Jones, J. M. (1986). Racism: A cultural analysis. In J. F. Dovidio & S. L. Gaertner (Eds.), *Prejudice, discrimination and racism.* Orlando, FL: Academic Press.

Jones, J. M. (1988). Racism in black and white. In P. A. Katz & D. A. Taylor (Eds.), *Eliminating racism* (pp. 117–135). New York: Plenum.

Kim, U., Triandis, H. C., Choi, S. Kagitcibasi, C., & Yoon, G. (1994). *Individualism and collectivism: Theory, method and applications.* Thousand Oaks, CA: Sage.

Kluckhohn, C. (1954). Culture and behavior. In G. Lindzey (Ed.), *Handbook of social psychology* (Vol. 2, pp. 921–976). Cambridge, MA: Addison-Wesley.

Kluckhohn, F., & Strodtbeck, F. (1961). *Variations in value orientations.* Evanston, IL: Row Peterson.

Kroeber, A. L., & Kluckhohn, C. (1952). *Culture: A critical review of concepts and definitions* (Vol. 147, No. 1). Cambridge, MA: Peabody Museum.

Kruger, J., & Clement, R. W. (1994). The truly false consensus effect: An ineradicable egocentric bias in social perception. *Journal of Personality and Social Psychology, 67,* 596–610.

Lambert, W. E. (1992). Challenging established views on social issues: The power and limitations of research. *American Psychologist, 47,* 533–542.

Landis, D., & Brislin, R. (1983). *Handbook of intercultural training* (in 3 vols). New York: Pergamon.

Landis, D., & Bhagat, R. S. (1996). *Handbook of intercultural training* (2nd ed.). Thousand Oaks, CA: Sage.

Landis, D., McGrew, P., Day, H., Savage, J., & Saral, T. (1976). Word meaning in black and white. In H. C. Triandis (Ed.), *Variations in black and white perceptions of the social environment* (pp. 45–80). Urbana, IL: University of Illinois Press.

Langer, E. J. (1983). *The psychology of control.* Beverly Hills, CA: Sage.

Leung, K. (1989). Cross-cultural differences: Individual-level vs. cultural level analysis. *International Journal of Psychology, 24,* 703–719.

Loevinger, J. (1976). *Ego development.* San Francisco: Jossey-Bass.

Loevinger, J. (1979). The idea of the ego. *Counseling Psychologist, 8,* 3–5.

Longabaugh, R. (1980). The systematic observation of behavior in naturalistic settings. In H. C. Triandis & J. W. Berry (Eds.), *Handbook of cross-cultural psychology* (Vol. 2, pp. 57–126). Boston: Allyn & Bacon.

Lonher, W., & Berry, J. (1986). *Field methods in cross-cultural research.* Beverly Hills, CA: Sage.

Malpass, R. S. (1977). Theory and method in cross-cultural psychology. *American Psychologist, 32,* 1069–1079.

Malpass, R. S., & Poortinga, Y. H. (1986). Strategies for design and analysis. In W. J. Lonner & J. W. Berry (Eds.), *Field methods in cross-cultural research* (pp. 47–84). Beverly Hills, CA: Sage.

Majors, R., & Mancini-Billson, J. (1992). *Cool pose.* New York: Lexington Books.

Marin, G., & Marin, B. V. (1991). *Research with Hispanic populations.* Newbury Park, CA: Sage.

Marin, G., Gamba, R. J., & Marin, B. V. (1992). Extreme response style and acquiescence among Hispanics. *Journal of Cross-Cultural Psychology, 23,* 498–509.

Marin, G., & Triandis, H. C. (1985). Allocentrism as an important characteristic of the behavior of Latin Americans and Hispanics. In R. Diaz-Guerrero (Ed.), *Cross-cultural and national studies in social psychology* (pp. 85–104). Amsterdam: North-Holland.

Marin, G., Triandis, H. C., Betancourt, H., & Kashima, Y. (1983). Ethnic affirmation versus social desirability: Explaining discrepancies in bilinguals' responses to a questionnaire. *Journal of Cross-Cultural Psychology, 14,* 173–186.

Markus, H., & Kitayama, S. (1991). Culture and self:

Implications for cognition, emotion and motivation. *Psychological Review, 98,* 224–253.
McClelland, D. C. (1980). Motive dispositions: The merits of operant and respondent measures. In L. Wheeler (Ed.), *Review of personality and social psychology* (pp. 10–41). Beverly Hills, CA: Sage.
Naroll, R., Michik, G. L., & Naroll, F. (1980). Holocultural research methods. In H. C. Triandis & J. W. Berry (Eds.), *Handbook of cross-cultural psychology* (Vol. 2, pp. 479–522). Boston: Allyn & Bacon.
Nielsen, J. (1990). *Feminist research methods.* Boulder, CO: Westview Press.
Nisbett, R. E., & Cohen, D. (1996). *The culture of honor.* Boulder, CO: Westview Press.
Oberg, K. (1960). Culture shock: Adjustment to new cultural environments. *Practical Anthropology, 7,* 177–182.
Pareek, U., & Rao, T. V. (1980). Cross-cultural surveys and interviewing. In H. C. Triandis & J. W. Berry (Eds.), *Handbook of cross-cultural psychology* (Vol. 2, pp. 127–180). Boston: Allyn & Bacon.
Parsons, T. & Shils, E. A. (1951). *Toward a general theory of action.* Cambridge, MA: Harvard University Press.
Pike, K. L. (1967). *Language in relation to a unified theory of the structure of human behavior.* The Hague: Mouton.
Phillips, H. P. (1965). *Thai peasant personality: The patterning of interpersonal behavior in the village of Bang Chan.* Berkeley, CA: University of California Press.
Qureshi, B. (1989). *Transcultural medicine: Dealing with patients from different cultures* (2nd ed.). Dordrecht: Kluwer.
Reinharz, S. (1992). *Feminist methods in social research.* New York: Oxford University Press
Rhee, E., Uleman, J. S., Lee, H. K., & Roman, R. J. (1995). Spontaneous self-descriptions and ethnic identities in individualistic and collectivist cultures. *Journal of Personality and Social Psychology, 69,* 142–152.
Robinson, R. J., Keltner, D., Ward, A., & Ross, L. (1995). Actual versus assumed differences in construal: "Naive realism" in intergroup perception and conflict. *Journal of Personality and Social Psychology, 68,* 404–417.
Rohner, R. P. (1986). *The warmth dimension: Foundations of parental acceptance-rejection theory.* Newbury Park, CA: Sage.
Schwartz, S. H. (1994). Beyond individualism/collectivism: New cultural dimensions of values. In U. Kim, H. C. Triandis, C. Kagitcibasi, S.-C. Choi, & G. Yoon (Eds.), *Individualism and collectivism: Theory, method and applications* (pp. 85–122). Thousand Oaks, CA: Sage.
Segalowitz, N. S. (1980). Issues in the cross-cultural study of bilingual development. In H. C. Triandis & A. Heron (Eds.), *Handbook of cross-cultural psychology: developmental* (Vol. 4, pp. 55–92). Boston: Allyn & Bacon.
Shweder, R. A., Mahapatra, M. & Miller, J. G. (1990). Culture and moral development. In J. W. Stigler, R. A. Shweder, & G. Herdt (Eds.), *Cultural psychology* (pp. 130–204). New York: Cambridge University Press.
Shweder, R. A., & LeVine, R. (1984). *Culture theory.* Chicago: University of Chicago Press.
Skinner, B. F. (1981). Selection by consequences. *Science, 213,* 501–504.
Sussman, N. M., & Rosenfeld, H. M. (1982). Influence of culture, language, and sex on conversational distance. *Journal of Personality and Social Psychology, 42,* 66–74
Stephan, W. G., & Stephan, C. W. (1984). The role of ignorance in intergroup relations. In N. Miller & M. B. Brewer (Eds.), *Desegregation: Groups in contact* (pp. 229–256). New York: Academic Press.
Strodtbeck, F. (1951). Husband–wife interaction over revealed differences. *American Sociological Review, 16,* 468–473.
Stewart, E. (1966). The simulation of cultural differences. *Journal of Communication, 16,* 291–304.
Szalay, L. B. (1970). *A communication dictionary of cultural meanings.* Washington, DC: American Institutes for Research.
Szalay, L. B. (1985). Psychocultural findings. In H. W. Sinaiko, P. M. Curran, B. T. King, & J. M. Schneider (Eds.), *Hispanic subpopulations and Naval service.* Technical Report SI/MRAS/TR-11. Washington, DC: Office of Naval Research.
Szalay, L. B., & Deese, J. (1978). *Subjective meaning and culture: An assessment through word associations.* New York: Wiley.
Tajfel, H. (1982). *Social identity and intergroup relations.* New York: Cambridge University Press.
Tapp, J. L., Kelman, H. C., Triandis, H. C., Wrightsman, L., & Coelho, G. (1974). Continuing concerns in cross-cultural ethics: A report. *International Journal of Psychology, 9,* 231–249.
Thernstrom. S. (1980). *Harvard encyclopedia of American ethnic groups.* Cambridge, MA: Harvard University Press.
Thurstone, L. L. (1931). The measurement of social attitudes. *Journal of Abnormal and Social Psychology, 26,* 249–269.
Ting-Toomey, S. (1988). A face-negotiation theory. In Y. Kim & W. Gudykunst (Eds.), *Theories of intercultural communication.* Newbury Park, CA: Sage.
Thibaut, J., & Kelley, H. (1959). *The social psychology of groups.* New York: Wiley
Triandis, H. C. (1972). *The analysis of subjective culture.* New York: Wiley.
Triandis, H. C. (1975). Cultural training, cognitive complexity, and interpersonal attitudes. In R. W. Brislin, S. Bochner, & W. J. Lonner (Eds.), *Cross-cultural perspectives on learning* (pp. 39–77). Beverly Hills, CA: Sage.
Triandis, H. C. (1976a). The future of pluralism. *Journal of Social Issues, 32,* 179–208.
Triandis, H. C. (1976b). *Variations in black and white perceptions of the social environment.* Urbana, IL: University of Illinois Press.
Triandis, H. C. (1989). Self and social behavior in differing cultural contexts. *Psychological Review, 96,* 269–289.
Triandis, H. C. (1990). Cross-cultural studies of individualism and collectivism. In J. Berman (Ed.), *Nebraska symposium on motivation, 1989* (pp. 41–133). Lincoln, NE: University of Nebraska Press.
Triandis, H. C. (1992). Cross-cultural research in social psychology. In D. Granberg & G. Sarup (Eds.), *Social judgment and intergroup relations: Essays in honor of Muzafer Sherif* (pp. 229–244). New York: Springer.
Triandis, H. C. (1994). *Culture and social behavior.* New York: McGraw-Hill.
Triandis, H. C. (1995). *Individualism and collectivism.* Boulder, CO: Westview Press.
Triandis, H. C. (1996). The psychological measurement of cultural syndromes. *American Psychologist, 51,* 407–415.
Triandis, H. C., & Berry J. W. (1980). *Handbook of cross-cultural psychology* (Vol. 2). Boston: Allyn and Bacon.
Triandis, H. C., Bontempo, R., Leung, K., & Hui, C. H. (1990). A method for determining cultural, demographic, and personal constructs. *Journal of Cross-Cultural Psychology, 21,* 302–318.
Triandis, H. C., Brislin, R. & Hui, C. H. (1988). Cross-cultural training across the individualism–collectivism divide. *International Journal of Intercultural Relations, 12, 269–289.*
Triandis, H. C., & Gelfand, M. (in press). Converging measurement of horizontal and vertical individualism and collectivism. *Journal of Personality and Social Psychology.*
Triandis, H. C., Kashima, Y., Shimada, E., & Villareal, M.

(1986). Acculturation indices as a means of confirming cultural differences. *International Journal of Psychology, 21,* 43–70.
Triandis & Marin (1983).
Triandis, H. C., Marin, G. Lisansky, J., & Betancourt, H. (1984). *Simpatia* as a cultural script of Hispanics. *Journal of Personality and Social Psychology, 47,* 1363–1375.
Triandis, H. C., McCusker, C., & Hui, C. H. (1990). Multimethod probes of individualism and collectivism. *Journal of Personality and Social Psychology, 59,* 1006–1020.
Triandis, H. C., & Triandis, L. M. (1962). A cross-cultural study of social distance. *Psychological Monographs, 76*(21) (Whole issue of No. 540).
Triandis, H. C., Vassiliou, V., & Nassiakou, M. (1968). Three cross-cultural studies of subjective culture. *Journal of Personality and Social Psychology, Monograph Suppl. 8,* No, 4, 1–42.
Trilling, L. (1972). *Sincerity and authenticity.* London: Oxford University Press.
Weldon, D. E., Carlston, D. E., Rissman, A. K., Slobodin, L., & Triandis, H. C. (1975). A laboratory test of effects of culture assimilator training. *Journal of Personality and Social Psychology, 32,* 300–310.
Werner, O., & Campbell, D. T. (1970). Translation, working through interpreters and the problem of decentering. In R. Naroll & R. Cohen (Eds.), *A handbook of method in cultural anthropology* (pp. 398–422). New York: American Museum of Natural History.
Yang, K-S., & Bond, M. H. (1980). Ethnic affirmation by Chinese bilinguals. *Journal of Cross-Cultural Psychology, 11,* 411–425.
Zane, N. W., Sue, S., Hu, L., & Kwon, J.-H. (1991). Asian-American assertion: A social learning analysis of cultural differences. *Journal of Counseling Psychology, 38,* 63–70.

10.02 Cross-cultural Psychopathology

FANNY M. CHEUNG
The Chinese University of Hong Kong, Hong Kong

10.02.1 INTRODUCTION 35
10.02.2 ETHNOCENTRIC APPROACH OF CLINCIAL PSYCHOLOGY 36
10.02.3 CULTURE-BOUND SYNDROMES 37
10.02.4 KORO 38
10.02.5 ALTERNATIVE VIEWS ON CBS 38
10.02.6 TRANSFORMATION OF NEURASTHENIA 39
10.02.7 ILLNESS EXPERIENCE 41
10.02.8 SOMATIZATION AS A CATEGORY FALLACY 41
10.02.9 SOMATIZATION AS ILLNESS EXPERIENCE 42
10.02.10 CULTURE AND PSYCHOPATHOLOGY 44
10.02.10.1 Role of Culture in Psychopathology 44
10.02.10.1.1 Culture-produced stress 44
10.02.10.1.2 Culture-related problems 44
10.02.10.1.3 Culture-inherited vulnerability 45
10.02.10.1.4 Cultural contribution to choice of psychopathology 45
10.02.10.2 Cultural Explanations 45
10.02.11 CROSS-CULTURAL PSYCHOPATHOLOGY 45
10.02.11.1 Universalist vs. Relativist Approaches 45
10.02.11.2 Recent Research on Cross-cultural Psychopathology 47
10.02.11.3 Future Directions 48
10.02.12 SUMMARY 48
10.02.13 REFERENCES 48

10.02.1 INTRODUCTION

While psychopathology is embedded in the wider cultural context, theories of clinical psychology have generally been ethnocentric in nature. Cross-cultural studies in psychopathology often started with the assumption of the universality of these theories and attempted to compare the similarities and differences between cultural groups on aspects of these theories. Earlier interests in culture-specific aspects of psychopathology were related to peripheral curiosities about bizarre phenomena in exotic cultures. Because of their peripheral status, culture-bound syndromes were identified without much systematic research into the cultural dynamics of these syndromes. While they may have clinical meaning to the specific cultures, there is little relevance to the mainline theories. In this chapter, some of the culture-bound syndromes are demystified. The roles played by cultural factors in the presentation and interpretation of psychopathology are examined. Recent research is incorporating the universalist and relativist approaches of cross-cultural psychology and bringing cultural dimensions of psychopathology into the mainstream.

10.02.2 ETHNOCENTRIC APPROACH OF CLINCIAL PSYCHOLOGY

Clinical psychology has always considered itself to be a scientific field and has placed a strong emphasis on research (Routh, 1994). The major content areas of research include psychopathology, assessment, and intervention. Despite the empirical orientation of psychology, a major deficiency in the prominent models of psychopathology is the lack of cross-cultural awareness in both theory and research. The ethnocentric approach in Anglo-American clinical psychology may be reflected in the emphasis on the individual or the intrapsychic self, be it the biological paradigm, the psychoanalytic paradigm, the learning paradigm, the cognitive paradigm, or the phenomenological paradigm. In none of these models is the wider cultural context considered to be an important factor in understanding the cause, course, and consequences of psychopathology.

Lewis-Fernandez and Kleinman (1994) pointed out three culture-bound assumptions which biased the professional concepts of mental health and illness in North America. The first is the "egocentricity of the self" which is seen as "a self-contained, autonomous entity, characterized by a unique configuration of internal attributes that determine behavior" (p. 67). The focus on the self, individual experience, and internal attributes of personality in understanding psychopathology misses the sociocentric ideology and interpersonal contexts which most of the rest of the world espouses.

The second culture-bound assumption is the philosophical roots of mind–body dualism, which leads to the division of psychopathology into the organic disorders and psychological problems. This dualistic professional model would misinterpret the cultural expressions of patients in most parts of the world who experience human suffering as simultaneous mind and body distress. The integrated somatopsychological idioms of expressions are often viewed as a reflection of a lack of introspection or psychological-mindedness.

The third culture-bound assumption that biases professional concepts is the view that culture is "an arbitrary superimposition on a knowable biological reality" (p. 67). This assumption views culture as "epiphenomenal." Cultural beliefs about disease categories, illness experiences, and healing practices of people in other cultures are reduced to the status of misinformed or superstitious obstacles in the diagnosis, treatment, and outcome of real diseases which are based on an invariant reality of biology.

These culture-bound assumptions result in an ethnocentric psychology based on "culturally specific ways of viewing individuals and their personality development," "diagnostic categories of personality disorder that ignore the fundamental influence of social context and cultural norms on human behavior," and "a psychiatric nosology that claims to be universal but does not take seriously the great cross-cultural diversity of somatic and psychological symptoms" (Lewis-Fernandez & Kleinman, 1994, p. 67).

The lack of a cross-cultural perspective in clinical psychology cannot be explained purely on the grounds of the limited diversity of the ethnic backgrounds of trained clinical psychologists. The ethnic backgrounds of clinical psychologists in the USA have diversified in the past two decades and the population of clinical psychologists in different parts of the world has vastly expanded. The little research found in cross-cultural clinical psychology has focused mainly on applicability of Western or Caucasian middle-class models of treatment or assessment procedures.

In contrast, since the 1960s the field of psychiatry has developed a substantial, albeit peripheral, interest in cultural psychiatry, raising sensitivity to cultural aspects of psychopathology and treatment. It has been pointed out that modern psychiatry was "moulded by specifically Western philosophical and scientific traditions" and should overcome the "inertia of ethnocentricism" (Lin, 1982, p. 235). Large-scale international collaborative research in psychopathology and diagnosis is evident in the activities of international psychiatric organizations and publications of cultural psychiatry. For example, a sociocultural lexicon for psychiatry (Mental Health Division, WHO, in press) will be published to accompany the tenth revision of the *International Classification of Diseases* (*ICD-10*; World Health Organization, 1992). Global collaborative research projects have been set up to compare the etiology, symptomatology and treatment of specific psychiatric disorders such as schizophrenia (World Health Organization, 1973, 1975, 1979, 1991).

Within American psychiatry, there are attempts to make the role of cultural analysis more of a mainstream than a secondary activity. Where the *Diagnostic and statistical manual of mental disorder* (*3rd ed.*) (*DSM-III* American

Psychiatric Association, 1980) has been criticized for ignoring cultural diversity, efforts have been made to represent cultural concerns in *DSM-IV* (American Psychiatric Association, 1994; Good, 1996). A Group on Culture and Diagnosis consisting of anthropologists and cross-cultural psychiatrists was formed to advise the *DSM-IV* Task Force on how to make culture more central to *DSM-IV*. One of the specific aims of the Group was "to devise a mechanism that would facilitate the application of a cultural perspective to the process of clinical interviewing and diagnostic formulation in psychiatry" (Lewis-Fernandez, 1996, p. 133). The Group on Culture and Diagnosis proposed an outline for cultural formulation to supplement multiaxial diagnostic assessment in a multicultural environment. As summarized by Lewis-Fernandez:

> the cultural formulation provides a systematic review of the individual's cultural background, the role of the cultural context in the expression and evaluation of symptoms and dysfunction, and the effect that cultural differences may have on the relationship between the individual and the clinician. (p. 137)

Eventually, however, only an edited and shortened version of this outline was included as an appendix instead of the central text of *DSM-IV*. Nevertheless, compared with previous editions, cultural concerns are represented in a much more significant manner in the text of *DSM-IV* and are included in the introduction, in the context of particular categories, as well as in a glossary of cultural terms (Good, 1996).

No such systematic approach to mainstream cultural analysis is found in the field of clinical psychology. Therefore, reference to the knowledge base developed in cultural psychiatry is needed to review research in cross-cultural psychopathology and culture-bound syndromes.

10.02.3 CULTURE-BOUND SYNDROMES

The interest in culture-bound syndromes (CBS) in cultural psychiatry in itself illustrates a process of transformation in the approach to cultural dimensions of psychopathology. Fascination with CBS has its sources in the "bizarre characteristics of the behavior displayed" (Hughes, 1985). Originating from the voyeuristic interest on folk illnesses in "exotic" cultures, CBS are now included in the glossary of cultural terms in *DSM-IV*. The study of culture-bound syndromes has gained respectability from the scholarly works of pioneers such as Yap who alleged that:

> It has long been known that there are, in certain cultural groups, peculiar aberrations of behavior which are regarded by themselves as abnormal. Over the years a number of terms taken from indigenous languages have crept into the psychiatric literature to denote these conditions, but many of them do not point to novel or distinct forms of disorder unknown elsewhere. Some are simply generic terms for "mental disorders" without definite meaning, others refer only to healing rituals, and still others to supernatural notions of disease causation. ... To avoid stagnation in this field, it is essential to apply the concepts of clinical psychopathology to the analysis of these disorders, to integrate them into recognized classifications of disease if possible, or to broaden the classification if necessary. (1974, p. 86)

Initial interests in CBS have given rise to a host of "folk" taxonomies from different cultures (Simons & Hughes, 1985). More common CBS include the following:

(i) *Latah*. Originating from Malaysia and Indonesia, *Latah* refers to the exaggerated startle response followed by odd behaviors. The afflicted person typically responds to a frightening stimulus with an exaggerated startle or jump, sometimes throwing or dropping a held object, uttering some improper word, or matching the words or movements of people nearby (Simons, 1985, p. 43). The pattern is a highly stereotypic, culturally labeled state which, though contravening the social norm, is differentiated from insanity.

(ii) *Amok*. *Amok* refers to the sudden mass assault taxon indigenous to Malayo-Indonesians, but may find parallel instances of indiscriminate homicide in other parts of the world. It is defined as "an acute outburst of unrestrained violence associated with homicidal attack, preceded by a period of brooding, and ending with exhaustion and amnesia" (Carr, 1985, p. 199). It is believed to have originated from the cultural training for warfare of the early Javanese and Malays which was intended to terrify the enemy into believing that they could expect no mercy and could save themselves only by flight.

(iii) *Pibloktoq*. The term is also labeled as arctic hysteria, polar hysteria, or transitional madness, referring to a group of hysterical symptoms among the Polar Eskimo of Greenland brought on by the depressing or monotonous effects of the Arctic's winter climate. The syndrome is composed of a series of reactive patterns with different combinations of the features in different cases. Disturbance of consciousness during the seizure and amnesia for the attack are the central clinical features. Some frequent behavioral symptoms are tearing off of clothing resulting in nudity, glossolalia, fleeing, and running across or rolling in snow. Gussow (1985) suggested that *Pibloktoq* is a reaction of "the basic Eskimo personality" to "situations of unusually intense, but culturally typical stress" (p. 282).

(iv) *Susto*. Illness arising from spirit separating from the body due to fright is widespread in one form or another in Latin America. The folk interpretation of *Susto* is based on the belief that a person comprises spiritual and organic elements. The spiritual element may be detachable from the host organism under unsettling experiences that disturb the equilibrium or when the unsettled spiritual element is seized and controlled by the spirits of the natural environment. The situation results in loss of appetite, weight, and strength; restlessness in sleep; listlessness when awake; and depression and introversion. "For recovery, the captured spirit must be retrieved from its captor, ransomed in the folk treatment process, and 'led back' to be reincorporated into the victim's body" (Rubel, O'Nell, & Collado, 1985, p. 334).

Most of the initial interest in CBS has surrounded the description of these phenomena. According to Prince and Tcheng-Laroche's (1987) definition of CBS, the culturally distinct meaning of the illness for individuals and cultures affects the occurrence of signs and symptoms of diseases in some cultures but not in others. The difference in occurrence depends on the psychosocial features of those cultures. CBSs have also been called culture-reactive syndromes, which suggests that the psychopathology is deemed to be rooted in social environmental forces and/or situations. The signs and symptoms reflect an attempt by the patients to adapt to major problems in their lives.

In the following section, one of the more popular syndromes in the literature, *Koro*, will be discussed in greater detail to illustrate how the cultural context of CBS affects their manifestation.

10.02.4 KORO

Koro arises from the belief about the retraction of the sexual organs (including penis, breast, nipples) into the body which leads to eventual death. Koro was believed to originate from the Malay word *koro* which means "shrink." An alternative source is from the word *kura* which means a tortoise. The "head of the tortoise" is often used as an expression for the penis by the Malays as well as the Chinese (Edwards, 1985). A similar condition is also found among Chinese under the name of Suoyang, another native terminology for genital retraction complaints. The syndrome was considered an emic or locally defined construct unique to these cultures with culture-specific etiologies.

Cultural meanings have been offered to explain individual and mass episodes of Koro. For example, Bartholomew (1994) argued that Koro is "a rational attempt at problem-solving that involves conformity dynamics, perceptual fallibility, and the local acceptance of koro-associated folk realities" (p. 46). Gwee (1985) offers the interpretation that Koro is an "acute hysterical panic reaction, brought on by auto- or hetero-suggestion and conditioning by the cultural background" (p. 159). The indigenous ethnographic literature describes Koro attacks as "unpredictable, but [they] usually appear after a shock which made the patient anxious or frightened, after performing strenuous manual labor or no labor at all, or as a result of immoderate nocturnal partying" (Edwards, 1985, p. 171). The etiology is attributed to nonconformity with community norms in the cultural context of competitiveness. In Chinese societies, these fears are associated with beliefs about sexual activities. Suoyang appears as "a product of intra- and inter-personal violations of medico-sexual regulations" (Edwards, p. 183).

Originally believed to be indigenous to Southeast Asia, Koro has also been detected in Africa, South Asia, and North America since the late 1970s (Chowdhury, 1996; Fishbain, Barsky, & Goldberg, 1989; Holden, 1987). Attempts have been made to fit Koro into the *etic* or externally defined psychiatric nosology, including acute hysterical panic reaction, anxiety states, depersonalization, conversion disorder, or atypical somatoform disorder (Simons & Hughes, 1985). Hughes (1985) justified the application of conventional diagnostic concepts to culture-bound phenomena in that they provided "the basis for more informed judgment regarding the ontological status and (eventually) etiology of the culture-bound syndromes" (p. 21). He went on to point out that a culturally informed use of the conventional diagnostic categories required knowing the culture of the person being evaluated to make a valid assessment of the behaviors, as well as being skeptical of the implicit values and assumptions underlying these categories. He warned that these categories should be tested against the observed primary behavior patterns and not be taken for granted.

10.02.5 ALTERNATIVE VIEWS ON CBS

In a reversed direction in the search for culture-bound syndromes, some Western-based syndromes such as anorexia nervosa, obesity, or even adolescence have been postulated as Western cases of CBS (Hill & Fortenberry, 1992; Prince, 1985; Ritenbaugh, 1982; Swartz, 1985). It was argued that anorexia nervosa fits the criteria of CBS, namely, that "the syndrome cannot be understood apart from its specific cultural or subcultural context," that "the etiology summarizes and symbolizes core meanings and behavioral norms of that culture," that "diagnosis relies on culture-specific technology as well as ideology," and that "successful treatment is accomplished only by participants in that culture" (Swartz, p. 725). Notwithstanding the need for empirical evidence to demonstrate that anorexia nervosa is indeed restricted to Western cultures, such an encapsulated direction to search for CBS misses the conceptual advances provided by CBS research in understanding the contextual nature of all forms of psychopathology.

Prince and Tcheng-Laroche 1987) justifiably pointed out that Western diagnostic classification systems, including both *ICD* and *DSM*, are based on psychiatric conceptualization of Western medical science. Western medical models are based on universal theories of disease. CBS, on the other hand, do not fit well into these universal models. According to Prince and Tcheng-Laroche, the inherent emic–etic diversity and semantic specificities of the CBS hinder their incorporation into prototype approaches. Instead, they suggested that the descriptive classification consisting of inventories of signs and symptoms based on the meaning of illness both for individuals and for cultures rather than the etiological classification would be more practical for clinical use.

"Culture-bound" syndromes are now generally viewed as "culture-related" syndromes (Mental Health Division, WHO, in press). While these syndromes have been found with differing incidence or prevalence rates across societies, they are considered to be more "overdetermined" or "related" to certain cultures than they are "bound" to those cultures. These culture-related syndromes serve to illustrate both the "core elements" of a psychiatric disorder, as well as "those elements that can be modified by individual psychology, social context, and culture." By examining how cultural contexts affect the conceptualization and manifestation of these syndromes, we not only expand our knowledge of aberrant phenomena unfamiliar to Western models of psychopathology, but also gain a better understanding of the cultural contexts of the conventional models of psychopathology themselves. For example, neurasthenia, once classified as a form of neurosis in Western psychiatric nosology, has assumed the identity of a culture-related syndrome in Chinese societies. The transplantation and transformation of neurasthenia as a disease entity outside Western societies provides an apt illustration of the pathoplasticity of culture-related syndromes.

10.02.6 TRANSFORMATION OF NEURASTHENIA

Neurasthenia as a diagnostic category has a vicissitudinary career in Western psychiatry. Coined by the American neurologist George Beard (1869) to describe the exhaustion of the nervous system, it was found to be common among patients attending general practitioners in the early 1990s. It was, however, ignored as a diagnostic category until being classified among the neuroses in *DSM-II* (American Psychiatric Association, 1968) as a condition characterized by weakness, fatigue, lack of stamina, and exhaustion, as distinguished from hysterical neurosis, anxiety neurosis, and depressive neurosis. Literally, it connotes a condition of "weak nerves" in which the sufferer is "thought to be easily overwhelmed by the ordinary stresses of life, with resultant symptoms of somatization, anxiety, and depression" (Mental Health Division, WHO, in press). It was subsequently dropped from the later revisions of the *DSM* but is still retained in *ICD-10* (World Health Organization, 1992). Because of the somatic focus of the symptoms, it is common for patients complaining of neurasthenia to be diagnosed by physicians for some physical dysfunctions. The vagueness of the nosology, however, does not fit in with the increasing emphasis on objectivity and functionality in the American classification system. Despite its American origin, neurasthenia has become a nondisease in America (Kleinman, 1982).

On the other hand, neurasthenia is now the most widely utilized psychiatric diagnosis in China (Mental Health Division, WHO, in press), and is a popular folk nomenclature in Chinese societies and Japan (Lin, 1989). Literally translated as shenjing shuairuo (weakness of the nervous system), this Western term was believed to be "imported" into China via Japan in the early 1990s (Lin). Popular books on Chinese folk medicine published in the past few decades have included neurasthenia as a condition that could benefit from traditional medical treatment, as if it were an indigenous form of disorder. The term is also commonly used among traditional doctors, physicians, psychiatrists, and lay persons to refer to a range of neurotic, psychosomatic, and psychotic disorders (Cheung, 1989; Lee & Wong, 1995). Etiology and treatment of neurasthenia are also elaborated using lay concepts of mental health and Chinese folk medicine. Cheung (1989) suggested that the term's

> ambiguity as well as the overlap with other psychoneurotic disorders may be reasons leading to the rare use of this diagnosis in Western psychiatry ... [but] due to its popularity among the lay public that new life has been injected into this imported medical term. Neurasthenia has been incorporated into Chinese folk medicine, and a set of beliefs has grown up around the original definitions of the disease outlined by George Beard in 1880. (pp. 235–236)

Cheung proposed two possible reasons to explain the popularity of neurasthenia as a diagnostic term among the Chinese. First, neurasthenia provides an acceptable paradigm of health and medicine. From its original Western definitions, neurasthenia has been "indigenized" and incorporated into the paradigm of traditional Chinese folk medicine which is based on a holistic concept of health and illness. Neurasthenia as a multidimensional illness provides a conceptualization in terms of both psychological and somatic symptoms and contexts. Among Chinese patients, somatic symptoms form an important part of the phenomenology of psychiatric illness. The illness experience of neurasthenia in the form of what Kleinman (1982) described as a "socially and culturally shaped type of somatization" may be affected by the patients" course of help-seeking. The somatic symptoms legitimize the sick role whereby the patient can get sympathy and attention from medical professionals and yet not be rejected or stigmatized.

The second reason is the use of the term neurasthenia as a euphemism by psychiatrists and the lay public alike to destigmatize psychiatric disorders. As many as 30% of Chinese psychiatric patients describe themselves as suffering from neurasthenia when presenting themselves to psychiatric clinics (Kleinman, 1982; Wong & Chan, 1984). The distinction between neurasthenia and other forms of psychiatric disorders may stem from its detachment from the notion of insanity and the stigma of madness. Neurasthenia is attributed to somatic depletion, overwork, irregular lifestyle, and extended intellectual activities. It is an acceptable pretext for seeking help for a variety of conditions including psychological symptoms such as overworry, irritability, and memory difficulties, which when presented on their own accord, may be considered inappropriate or insufficient cause for medical consultation.

Even during the early days of the Great Leap Forward and the Cultural Revolution in the People's Republic of China between the 1950s and 1960s, the problem of neurasthenia as a form of mental illness was readily accepted, whereas other Western theories of psychopathology were deemed mentalistic and therefore inconsistent with the communist ideology. The concept of neurasthenia in the People's Republic of China was originally based on the Pavlovian theory of neurophysiology (Chin & Chin, 1969) during the era of Sino-Soviet cooperation when Soviet neuropsychology had a strong influence on Chinese psychology. Neurasthenia is attributed to "tension in the higher nervous system in excess of its capacity, thus causing a weakening in the functioning capacity of the brain tissues and a lack of balance or confusion in nervous activity" (p. 70). Serious disturbances occur in the activity of the nervous system relating to work, study, society, and family. Its "politically correct" etiology and manifestation allowed the disease entity to survive the Cultural Revolution during which other forms of Western diagnoses tended to be denied (Cheung, 1989). Cadres and professionals were spontaneous in their admission of the high prevalence of neurasthenia especially among their peers since they regarded neurasthenia as the outcome of overwork and not as a form of mental illness.

The manifestation of neurasthenia as an illness has also undergone changes within Chinese societies. Earlier studies in China and Hong Kong (Kleinman, 1982; Wong & Chan, 1984) showed that the presenting complaints of neurasthenic patients were predominantly somatic, especially weakness, fatigue, insufficiency of *qi* (vital energy), poor appetite, backache, and weak limbs. A more recent study with young university students (Lee & Wong, 1995) found a more psychological construal of neurasthenia. Moreover, there is a disparity between lay and professional definitions of neurasthenia. According to Beard's (1869) or the *ICD-10*'s (World Health Organization, 1992) definition, fatigue is considered a core symptom of neurasthenia but is infrequently reported in Taiwan or Hong Kong (Lee & Wong, 1995; Rin & Huang, 1989). The de-emphasis on fatigue distinguishes the Chinese experience from the Western condition of chronic fatigue syndrome which may be considered as a contemporary form of "revived" neurasthenia in the West (Abbey & Garfinkel, 1991). Such a disparity points to the importance of examining cross-cultural differences not only in disease entities, but also in the conceptualization of the illness experience.

10.02.7 ILLNESS EXPERIENCE

Medical sociologists and cultural psychiatrists have distinguished between illness and disease (Mechanic, 1982). Kleinman (1988a) makes the distinction succinctly by referring to illness as "the patient's perception, experience, expression, and pattern of coping with symptoms" and to disease as "the way practitioners recast illness in terms of their theoretical models of pathology" (p. 7). The illness experience is a culturally shaped phenomenon that is interpreted by the patients and their families resulting in a particular course of action. These interpretations are mediated by language, illness beliefs, personal significance of suffering, and learned illness behavior.

The experiences of distress are multifaceted. The distressed persons choose their form of expression according to their own sensitivity to those facets that make sense to them or that conform to their understanding. Folk understanding of psychological distress seldom conforms to the professional classification of disorders, especially in cultures where formalized mental health services are not popular or are inaccessible. Thus, these expressions are necessarily selective, being bound by the personal and cultural repertoire of distress idioms. The repertoire of coping and illness behavior is similarly acquired in the sociocultural context. The illness experience encompasses not only the phenomenology of the individual which focuses on the intrapsychic dimension, but also on the interaction of the person with significant members and aspects of the environment. These social and cultural dimensions form an integral part of the dynamics involved in the process of illness.

A psychiatric diagnosis, on the other hand, is a professional's interpretation of the person's experience which becomes formalized as signs of particular disease states in a static medical model. These diagnostic categories are often reified as real entities by the professionals who try to fit the reported experiences into one of the categories. Through exposure, patients learn to report what the professionals expect of them. However, when the diagnostic categories developed in one culture are projected onto patients in another culture, their validity needs to be established. Mental health professionals who are mostly trained in Western medical models have often imposed these categories in non-Western cultures even when they lack folk coherence. Some of these categories may be more valid or relevant than others, whereas there is strong evidence that psychiatric diagnoses such as organic brain disorders and schizophrenia are valid worldwide (Kleinman, 1988a; World Health Organization, 1973, 1979), other diagnoses such as dysthymic disorder or anorexia nervosa are questioned as examples of "category fallacy" which lack cross-cultural validity. When the culturally imposed categories are found to differ from the illness experience found within the culture, ethnocentric professionals tend to interpret the discrepancy as a problem of the individual or the culture, instead of questioning the relevance of the category itself.

10.02.8 SOMATIZATION AS A CATEGORY FALLACY

The problem of category fallacy can be illustrated by the way in which mental health professionals from Western cultures initially interpreted the tendency among Chinese psychiatric patients to somatize their psychological distress. In the wake of early interest in cultural psychiatry, a number of studies on the patterns of symptom presentation among Chinese psychiatric patients noted that these patients tend to somatize their problems and delay psychiatric treatment (Kleinman, 1977; Lin, 1982; Lin, Tardiff, Donetz, & Goresky, 1978; Marsella, Kinzie, & Gorson, 1973; Tseng, 1975). Somatization has been emphasized as the cultural feature of neurotic disorders, especially depression, among the Chinese. Various aspects of the Chinese culture were then put forth to explain the somatization tendency (Cheung, 1982, 1985, 1995; Cheung & Lau, 1982).

One group of cultural explanations attributes the somatization tendency to denial, suppression, or repression of emotions. The typical Chinese is described as being reserved in expressing feelings and prone to avoiding open display of emotions, especially negative ones. Another group of explanations argues that the use of concrete physical terms in expressing one's distress demonstrates that the Chinese language lacks an adequate vocabulary to express emotions explicitly. So physical metaphors or terms related to body organs are used to represent affective states. The third group of explanations is based on the assumption of mind–body dualism as the standard of epistemology, so that the lack of distinction between psychological and somatic systems among the Chinese was likened to the simple, undifferentiated, and concrete level of thinking among primitive cultures.

These cultural assumptions have been challenged both on the grounds of cultural specificity as well as interpretation. It has been questioned whether somatization is indeed specific to the Chinese as originally claimed. Even so, the explanations for this culturally related observation need further scrutiny. Cheung (1982, 1985) criticized these cultural attributions as *post hoc* explanations based on cultural generalizations without empirical verification. In an extensive review of the literature, Singer (1975) argued that in the first place, the phenomenon of somatization is not exclusive to Chinese patients, but is also commonly found among less educated and lower social-class patients in Western countries. Kleinman (1986) later reckoned that somatization is also very common in the West although the fact may be ignored or de-emphasized there. Cheng (1989) compared survey results on the symptomatology of minor psychiatric morbidity in Taiwan and in Britain and found the rates of somatic symptoms for both countries to be comparable.

There is also evidence to show that although somatic complaints are the dominant features in Chinese patients' symptom presentation, psychological symptoms are by no means suppressed or repressed. Cheung, Lau, and Waldmann (1980–81) found that while depressed patients reported mostly somatic complaints to the medical doctor in general practice, they were very ready to admit to having a range of psychological and emotional symptoms when directly asked by the practitioner. Subsequent studies with psychiatric patients attending psychiatric services for the first time also revealed that psychological symptoms were frequently reported along with somatic complaints (Cheung, Lau, & Wong, 1984). Studies with the general population and with university students in Hong Kong also confirm that psychological problems were commonly reported (Cheung, 1982; Cheung, Lee, & Chan, 1983). However, psychological problems may not be readily reported to the medical practitioner. Instead, the Chinese would turn to their friends and family members for help if they perceive their problems to be psychological in nature.

One of the problems of these early discussions on the somatization tendency suffered from variations in the definitions of the term used. Somatization may be referred to as a psychiatric disorder, various patterns of illness behavior, forms of help-seeking related to bodily symptoms, or a combination of these concepts. Based on the formistic and mechanistic model of biomedicine (Schwartz, 1982), somatic presentation of distress is assumed to be due to an underlying psychological problem masked by the somatic presentation of symptoms often equated with somatization. Somatization, thus, is presumed to be pathological with maladaptive consequences. In the formistic world view, a person is categorized as either sick or well. In the mechanistic world view, a specific cause is linked to a single effect. These approaches ignore the contextual nature of illness involving both the organism and the environment, in which there may be interaction among multiple causes in the organism and the environment.

The focus on somatization as a pathological disorder misses the opportunity to understand in a systemic way the various patterns of illness behavior among Chinese patients, including their subjective experience, problem presentation, communication, and form of help-seeking.

10.02.9 SOMATIZATION AS ILLNESS EXPERIENCE

While studies of Chinese patients in Chinese societies have consistently found that somatic complaints are the dominant features in their descriptions of discomfort, it is also noted that psychological symptoms are readily reported by both clinical and nonclinical samples, especially if directly asked (Cheng, 1988, 1995; Cheung, 1982, 1987; Cheung et al., 1980–81, 1984). An attempt to understand the phenomenon of somatization among the Chinese should take into account the phenomenology of discomfort and suffering, the process of communication, ways of coping and help-seeking, and the patient–doctor relationship.

In his recent works, Kleinman (1986, 1988b) has provided an insightful perspective to understand somatization as human suffering contextualized in the personal, interpersonal, and cultural meanings of illness. He proposed that a "dialectical relationship exists between symptoms and society" (p. 2). The examination of how social factors produce the connection between neurasthenia-depression and pain which may be perceived as the cause of *disease* provides the illustration as to the way "culture shapes the strategic interpretation and negotiated experience of *illness*" (p. 2). As an idiom of distress, somatization is an illustration of the ethnography of the suffering experience. While the narrative of human suffering is not confined to bodily sensations, this mode of expression is highlighted in the medical context especially in non-Western cultures.

The meaning of bodily symptoms for the Chinese has been examined in terms of the Chinese language and traditional Chinese medical practice (Cheng, 1989; Ots, 1990; Tung, 1994). In traditional Chinese medicine, emotional problems are associated with different body organs. Dysharmonic emotions are pathogenic etiological factors which produce somatic dysfunctions, which, in turn, should be treated by harmonizing bodily functions (Ots, 1990). Tung also illustrated that the Chinese use body-related verbal expressions in an all-embracing fashion to express personal and social aspects of human concerns. Body-related words form expressions that are idioms of human conditions. These forms of expression are indigenous and often expressed in local dialects that escape the attention of Western-trained psychiatrists (Cheng, 1989). On the other hand, psychiatrists who try to fit the patients" expressions into their professional taxonomy would miss the rich information that accompanies the patients' expressions.

As illustrated earlier, the use of the term neurasthenia provides culturally legitimized somatic idioms to sidestep the Western framework of mental diseases which are highly stigmatized. However, somatic idioms are more than just euphemistic substitutes for Western diagnostic labels. They encompass schema to make sense of life problems and to direct courses of action. Illness meanings are physiological as well as social. According to Kleinman (1986), "the lived experience of social reality mediated by the body ... is the symbolic bridge, the socio-somatic reticulum that ties failure to headaches, anger to dizziness, loss and demoralization to fatigue" (p. 146).

Zheng, Xu, and Shen 1986) analyzed the styles of verbal expression of emotional and physical experiences of depressed patients and normal controls in China. Both emotional and physical expressions are used as narratives of human suffering, depending on the nature of the experience. For example, a purely psychological verbal style with words such as "unhappy" and "worried" was used to describe abstract emotional states such as indecisiveness, self-pity, guilt, or helplessness. Purely somatic expressions such as "heart beating" would be used for the concrete emotional state of fear. The neutral mode including both psychological and somatic features (e.g., "uncomfortable inside the heart" or "cannot use my brain") was used to express anxiety. For depression, both the somatic and the neutral modes were frequently used. In the expression of suicidal ideation, however, the person was often unable or unwilling to choose an expression, which the authors labeled as the deficient expressive style. The somatic style in expressing emotions among the Chinese patients in this study, however, was not related to symptom manifestation as reported on a symptom checklist.

Cheung (1995) pointed out that "somatization as an idiom of distress is contextualized in a process of communication" (p. 163). This process includes both the discourse between Chinese patients and doctors as well as other interpersonal interactions. Cheung and Lau (1982) showed that situational variations elicited different expectations and behaviors from patients who behave according to what they believe is expected of them in the situation. When Chinese psychiatric patients perceived their consultation to be medical in nature, such as attending a psychiatric clinic, they reported their physical as well as psychological symptoms. On the other hand, when they perceived their consultation to be related to a judicial nature, such as being referred to the psychiatrist at the correctional services by the judge, prisoners would recount the events leading to their arrest instead of presenting their symptoms.

Studies based on experiences of psychiatric patients may be biased by the self-selection of people who have chosen to consult psychiatric services, leading to the conclusion that Chinese patients tend to somatize their psychological problems. To understand the illness experience of the Chinese people, their coping approaches and the course of help-seeking prior to the psychological consultation need to be included. Studies of the patterns of help-seeking among different ethnic groups have shown that non-Caucasian patients generally delay seeking psychiatric treatment and approach other indigenous resources instead, at least initially (Cheung, 1987; Cheung et al., 1984; Lin et al., 1978). In Hong Kong, psychiatric consultation may be delayed by as long as 30 years after the initial onset of symptoms if they were perceived to be purely psychological in nature (Cheung, 1987). The Chinese prefer to endure their suffering, rely on themselves, or seek help from their friends or family for psychological problems. They would be more likely to seek medical attention for physical symptoms which would be perceived as illness needing medical attention (Cheung et al., 1983, 1984). The first medical consultation is predominantly with the general practitioner. Owing to the unfamiliarity with mental health services, the patients generally do not make a distinction among medical and mental health specialties which are more demarcations defined by the professionals.

The dominant role played by the general practitioner in directing psychiatric patients to mental health services has been highlighted by Goldberg and Huxley (1980). They showed that even in developed countries, only a small minority of psychologically disturbed persons reached psychiatric services. Many psychiatric illnesses passed unrecognized by general practitioners who prolonged medical attention on the physical complaints. Cheung (1991) likened the function of the general practitioner to that of "a roundabout where routes may converge and be redirected. When most travelers were unfamiliar with the direct route to recovery, the roundabout was the hub they would return to before embarking on alternative treatment paths" (p. 67). The patients' initial conceptualization of the causes and severity of their illness would direct their coping and help-seeking behavior. They would only seek medical attention if the problem is perceived to be somatic and serious. Once they embark on the medical course, the experience of medical consultation, in turn, would have shaped the patients' interpretation of their suffering. Patients who finally arrived at the psychiatric clinic are likely to have traveled through detours of medical consultation which focus their attention on their somatic complaints. They would be likely to present to the mental health professional, to them another medical doctor, that which they deemed as expected and appropriate (Cheung, 1987).

The reconceptualization of somatization in terms of the individual's culturally embedded illness experience and narratives of suffering advances the theoretical understanding from that of a category fallacy to a useful framework to interpret the phenomena. Psychopathology is after all a scientific attempt to organize and explain the observed phenomena systematically. Recognition of cross-cultural diversities poses new challenges to the traditional ethnocentric ideologies that have encapsulated Western theories of psychopathology and approaches to clinical psychology.

10.02.10 CULTURE AND PSYCHOPATHOLOGY

The role of culture in counseling and psychotherapy has received more attention from psychologists than the role of culture in the area of psychopathology (Leong, 1986; Pedersen, 1983, 1987, 1990, 1991; Pederson & Marsella, 1982; Pedersen, Draguns, Lonner, & Trimble, 1981; Sue, D. W., 1977, 1978, 1989, 1990, 1991; Sue, Arredondo, & McDavis, 1992; Sue & Kirk, 1975; Sue & Sue, 1977, 1990; Sue & Zane, 1987; Vontress, 1974). Culture has gained the status of a generic theory to explain counseling relationships in general, and not just for understanding exotic people. Pedersen (1991) proposed *multiculturalism* as a "fourth force" in counseling, complementary to psychodynamic, behavioral, and humanistic explanations of human behavior. The multicultural perspective "combines the extremes of universalism and relativism by explaining behavior both in terms of those culturally learned perspectives that are unique to a particular culture and in the search for common-ground universals that are shared across cultures" (p. 6). While acknowledging the pervasive nature of multiculturalism in complex modern society, Pedersen's theory is focused only on counseling approaches.

A few attempts have been made to apply specific psychological theories to mental health issues among ethnic subgroups in the USA. For example, S. Sue (1977) and Zane, Sue, Hu, and Kwon (1991) examined cultural differences in learned helplessness and assertion among Asian-Americans using a social learning analysis. Specific interest has been directed to the identity development of ethnic minority groups and how minority identity development may affect mental health problems (Sue, 1989). These efforts result in better understanding of the cultural diversities and cultural differences among specific ethnic groups. There is much less written on the general role of culture in psychopathology or abnormal psychology.

10.02.10.1 Role of Culture in Psychopathology

Tseng and McDermott (1981) gave a more comprehensive introduction to the role of culture in psychiatry. Culture affects psychopathology in many ways, including producing stress, creating specific problems, predisposing vulnerability, and contributing to the choice of psychopathology (pp. 14–24).

10.02.10.1.1 Culture-produced stress

Stress may be created by culturally formed anxiety or culturally demanding performance. Cultural attitudes and beliefs prescribe expectations and standards which if not met would produce mental and emotional stresses. Many societies have established taboos, rules, or rites which, if contravened, would create anxieties. Individuals living in cultures that believe spells can cause death would become ill or even die if they think that they are under a spell. Similarly, cultural demands of individuals cause stress to those who are unable to meet those demands. For example, many cultures demand that a woman produce a male child. The woman would be blamed and would feel guilty if she continued to produce only girls. She would face a loss of status or the threat of replacement by another woman. These demands produce fear, anxiety, and shame.

10.02.10.1.2 Culture-related problems

Specific problems may be created by a culturally determined limitation in behavior range, cultural changes, changing roles, and loss of source of support, as well as sociocultural discrimination. Within a cultural setting where rules are excessive, but the behavior range allowed is very limited, individuals who are not prepared for these restrictions would encounter problems. Similarly, rapid cultural changes may result in a confused value system to individuals who are used to a stable and traditional culture. Changing roles for women, for example, while improving women's social status and sense of independence, may also render them more vulnerable to loneliness and depression when the protection and support women previously obtained from their families have diminished. Sociocultural groups who face discrimination within a society suffer scorn, isolation, and disadvantage, resulting in stress and deficits.

10.02.10.1.3 Culture-inherited vulnerability

Vulnerability to stress may be predisposed by culturally prescribed child-rearing practices which influence the child's personality. In some cultures, parents emphasize independence and early decision making. This push toward independence may put undue pressure on the young person who needs a longer period of dependency. In other cultures, intimate dependency on mothers is extended for a much longer time. This dependency is extended into adult relationships as well which may lead to later problems in socialization with others.

10.02.10.1.4 Cultural contribution to choice of psychopathology

Culture plays a part in how its vulnerabilities find expression by influencing model solutions to problems that may themselves be pathological. The form of psychopathology found in a culture tends to be linked with the stresses within that culture. For example, excessive self-depreciation, a result of compliance to strong external control, may become a cause for depression. There is also a suggestion that low social cohesion in a community is related to the frequency of depression.

10.02.10.2 Cultural Explanations

Once psychological disorders are detected, culture also plays a role in labeling these disorders based on its concepts of mental illness. These labels describe the observed behavior, attribute causes, provide explanations, and convey social acceptance or rejection of the afflicted. Explanations of the nature and cause of mentally disturbed behaviors are grouped into four categories by Tseng and McDermott (1981, pp. 29–33):

(i) *Supernatural explanations*. The disturbance is explained as resulting from spirit possession, soul loss, divine wrath, sorcery, or violation of taboo.

(ii) *Natural explanations*. Illness, misfortune, and unhappiness are related to the underlying principles of the universe which govern all nature. Disharmony of the natural elements within the human body, incompatibility with natural principles in the environment, and noxious factors in the environment upset the natural principles and cause physical and mental disturbance.

(iii) *Physical-medical explanations*. The reasons for illness are viewed as physical or physiological originating from the individual. The causes may be physical-physiognomy problems (such as facial features, body build), physiological imbalance or insufficiency (such as badly balanced diet, excessive sexual activity), or disease.

(iv) *Sociopsychological explanations*. Mental disorder is seen as a psychological reaction to the stress of internal or external maladjustment.

Tseng and McDermott, however, did not make any distinction between the professional or "authoritative" explanations of abnormal behaviors and the folk conceptualizations and attributions of the experience of distress in these categories. In non-Western cultures that have not adopted Western models of medicine and psychology, explanatory models are often based on folk concepts. In cross-cultural comparisons of explanatory models, there may be biases when Western professional models of psychiatric classification are compared with local folk concepts of distress.

10.02.11 CROSS-CULTURAL PSYCHOPATHOLOGY

10.02.11.1 Universalist vs. Relativist Approaches

Cross-cultural psychopathology is premised on two competing orientations. The biological approach assumes that the cultural invariance of mental disorders, that is, the same disorders are prevalent in all cultures (Fernando, 1988, p. 60). In this approach, the "universalist" would use the psychiatric classification system developed in the West as a basis of identifying disorders in other parts of the world. The social-anthropological approach, on the other hand, emphasizes the cultural relativity of psychopathology, with each culture having its own disorders. Culture plays an important role in determining the behavior, thinking, and emotions of the individuals resulting in different forms of mental disorders. The "relativist" looks at illness as a part of the total cultural context deriving its meaning from the specific culture.

The two orientations have led to different research directions in cross-cultural psychopathology. The universalist or etic orientation has focused on cross-cultural comparisons in the rates of major psychiatric disorders, based on classification systems developed in the West. These studies have made use of population surveys with results showing a range of rates of major mental disorders in different countries (cf. Kleinman, 1988a, pp. 34–41, or Draguns, 1985, 1986, 1989 for a review of the findings). However, it has been noted that a narrower range of rates is found when diagnostic criteria are standardized and more homogenous samples of cases are used. International studies have been carried out to compare the prevalence and symptomatology of common psychiatric diseases such as schizophrenia (Sartorius et al., 1986; World Health Organization, 1973, 1979) or depression (Jablensky, Sartorius, Gulbinat, & Ernberg, 1981; World Health Organization, 1983). These studies identified core syndromes of the disorders. For example, across the nine research sites which represented both developed and developing countries, the core syndrome of schizophrenia included "restricted affect, poor insight, thinking aloud, poor rapport, incoherent speech, unrealistic information, and bizarre and/or nihilistic delusions" (Draguns, 1989, p. 242). The more modest project on depression involving four countries (World Health Organization, 1983) also identified a small number of symptoms such as vegetative symptoms which were present in most of the countries. On the other hand, the experience of guilt is much less universal in the symptomatology of depression.

Similar to psychiatric epidemiological studies comparing specific disorders, cross-cultural assessment studies have applied the major assessment instruments developed in the West to other cultures and identified cross-cultural similarities and differences. For example, one personality test that has been translated and tried out in the most number of countries is the Minnesota Multiphasic Personality Inventory (MMPI; Butcher & Clark, 1979; Butcher & Pancheri, 1976; Butcher & Spielberger; 1985, Hathaway & McKinley, 1967). These studies confirmed the clinical utility of the MMPI in other countries although cultural differences are identified and cultural adaptations may have to be made (e.g., Cheung & Song, 1989; Cheung, Song, & Butcher, 1991; Cheung, Song, & Zhang, 1996; Cheung, Zhao, & Wu, 1992).

The relativist or emic orientation has focused on culture-specific phenomena, such as culture-bound syndromes discussed in an earlier section. Research based on in-depth studies within a single culture provides a rich source of information about the phenomena. However, as pointed out earlier, attributions to cultural phenomena were often based on *post hoc* and generalized assumptions about the culture involved without elaboration on the functional relationship between cultural processes and psychopathology.

The shortcoming of the universalist approach lies in its ethnocentricism which assumes that the Western culture is more developed and superior. Cross-cultural differences are interpreted as a reflection of cultural underdevelopment, as in the early days of psychiatry when non-Western cultures were often referred to as "primitive" and "savages" (Fernando, 1988, p. 60). It is assumed that diagnostic categories developed in a Western cultural setting are applicable universally. Standardized research methods are developed to establish reliable diagnoses across cultures in Western terms. However, the cross-cultural validity of the disease as an illness or a phenomenon in those other cultures may not be established (Fernando).

Similarly, the universalist approach to assessment may lead to misleading clinical interpretations. For example, in the application of the MMPI to the Chinese people, several clinical scales, including the Depression scale and the Schizophrenia scale, were found to be consistently elevated even among normal samples when the American norms were used (Cheung, 1995; Cheung, Song, & Zhang, 1996). Both in Hong Kong and the People's Republic of China, the mean T-scores for normal adults on these two scales usually approach the clinical cut-off point used in the USA, although the mean scores for clinical samples are even higher. If cultural universality is assumed, there would be a danger of overinterpreting clinical pathology in the normal Chinese population.

The relativist approach, on the other hand, may not get beyond describing culture-bound syndromes and constructing intracultural explanations, thereby not contributing much to cross-cultural psychopathology. By assuming cultural specificity, no comparison can be made between cultural units. Without a cross-cultural framework, the notion of culture, however, becomes irrelevant. The determination of the cultural unit itself is also a subject of controversy. Cultural groups are usually operationally defined in terms of race, ethnicity, geographic location, or religion, assuming cultural similarity among members of the same groups. Subcultural groups further complicate the assumption of cultural similarity.

An alternative approach to get out of the impasse created by these two extreme positions is to reconstruct cross-cultural psychopathology from the basic units of clinical psychology: observation of the phenomenological experience of individuals from their cultural contexts, description of these expressions and manifestations on the basis of the individuals' perspectives, prescription of labels which are culturally relevant or meaningful based on indigenous and cross-cultural studies, selection of appropriate treatment alternatives, and prediction of outcome. While the world is becoming more multicultural, this contextualized analysis may become a "universal" approach.

10.02.11.2 Recent Research on Cross-cultural Psychopathology

Recent research on cross-cultural differences in psychopathology has attempted to explain the similarities and differences in terms of the cultural contexts. For example, while a pancultural nucleus of symptoms was found for schizophrenia and depression, a variety of cultural transformations was also identified. Draguns (1989) proposed a range of possible relations between culture and the manifestations of the disorders. These include:

(i) magnification or exaggeration—a culturally characteristic behavior being caricatured and reduced to absurdity;

(ii) violation of cultural norms—doing what is not culturally permissible;

(iii) cultural differences in values affecting the characteristic modes of expressing psychopathology—symptom choice and expression being conceptualized as social transactions.

However, there are few studies that examine the functional relationship between cultural characteristics and cross-cultural differences in psychopathology. Draguns (1989) attempted to apply Hofstede's (1980) worldwide study of work-related values to manifestations of abnormal behavior across cultures. In Hofstede's original study, which involved employees from over 40 nationalities, four cultural dimensions were found to be capable of accounting for most of the cultural differences. These four dimensions were individualism/collectivism, uncertainty avoidance, power distance, and masculinity/femininity. Hofstede (1983) had linked the dimension of individualism/collectivism to the distinction made earlier by Benedict (1946) between "guilt" (individualist) and "shame" (collectivist) cultures. However, the relationship between this value dimension and psychopathology involves a more subtle process. Rather than assuming that patients from some Asian cultures do not experience guilt, cultural differences may be found more in the way that guilt is expressed. In individualistic cultures, guilt may be expressed in absolute and abstract terms involving self-accusation and condemnation. In collectivistic cultures, guilt may be expressed in more concrete and interpersonal modes.

To date, there are few studies on cross-cultural psychopathology using the other three dimensions from Hofstede's study. Draguns (1989) further noted that psychopathology varied across cultures even when there was no substantial difference on Hofstede's four dimensions. He pointed to the need for more multicultural studies involving both normal and abnormal samples in order to formulate the functional relationship between cultural characteristics and psychopathology.

The series of studies on somatization among the Chinese described in earlier sections also illustrates how cross-cultural differences in the expression of symptomatology could be understood in terms of the culturally relevant cognitive schema and interpersonal contexts. Through these cultural studies, important dimensions that have not been examined in North American and Western European theories could be incorporated to increase the cultural sensitivity of these theories. This cultural sensitivity is becoming more important not only because ethnic and cultural pluralism is becoming more prevalent in many societies. What are thought to be indigenous categories can in fact be extended to explain the complexity of human personality and psychopathology within and across cultures.

One example of this combined emic-etic approach is the development of the Chinese Personality Assessment Inventory (CPAI; Cheung, Leung, Fan, et al., 1996) which integrated Western methods of personality assessment with folk concepts of personality in the Chinese culture. In addition to etic personality constructs, emic constructs which were not covered in translated personality inventories were included in the CPAI. Scales were developed for personality characteristics such as harmony, relationship orientation, face, modernization, and thrift, which are salient constructs for person descriptions among the Chinese. These scales were loaded on a factor labeled Chinese Tradition. The Chinese Tradition factor was found to be a relevant predictor of mental health measures especially for Chinese males. It enhanced life satisfaction and prevented the acting out of antisocial behavior particularly when the stress level was high (Cheung & Gan, 1996). The Chinese Tradition factor was also found to be culturally distinct from the five-factor structure of personality which is currently accepted as a universal model of personality (Cheung, Leung,

Law, & Zhang, 1996). These emic constructs may introduce new dimensions of the personality structure to Western models of personality and psychopathology.

10.02.11.3 Future Directions

As Lewis-Fernandez and Kleinman (1994) concluded, "we might very well come across local indigenous categories, such as face and favor, that can be used to reformulate our leading models of personality formation and their relationship to psychopathology" (p. 70). The study of cross-cultural psychopathology is expanding beyond the exotic frontier into the mainstream of psychology.

Research in cross-cultural psychopathology, as in other fields of cross-cultural psychology, is incorporating the combined emic–etic approach. There is an increasing recognition that "culture-bound" syndromes may not be unique to a specific culture. Instead, culture-related phenomena such as neurasthenia and somatization help to illustrate the dynamics of cultural forces affecting illness behavior in different societies.

Psychopathology is manifested in a cultural context, and should be interpreted via a contextualized analysis. Cross-cultural psychopathology research can help to identify convergent and divergent dimensions in explaining normal and abnormal behaviors across cultures, enhancing our awareness as researchers and practitioners of the cultural context of our analyses. As our global community becomes more multicultural, the dialectic process of synthesizing new observations and constructs from other cultural contexts poses a challenge to clinical psychologists to recognize culture as an integral part of their theoretical framework.

10.02.12 SUMMARY

Clinical psychology has suffered from an ethnocentric approach blinded by culture-bound assumptions. Early research in cross-cultural psychopathology was borrowed from cultural psychiatry which has focused its interest on the identification of culture-bound syndromes. In this chapter, an alternative approach to study the interplay of cultural dynamics in the manifestation of these "culture-bound syndromes" is illustrated through the discussion of Koro, neurasthenia, and somatization. The transplantation and transformation of neurasthenia from a Western diagnostic category to a culture-related syndrome in Chinese societies demonstrate the fluidity of diagnostic labels in incorporating cultural meanings. By reexamining somatization as an illness experience and narratives of suffering, a more useful framework for studying the relationship between culture and psychopathology is also identified.

Culture affects psychopathology by producing stress, creating specific problems, predisposing vulnerability, and selecting the form of psychopathology. It also provides folk explanations of the nature and cause of aberrant behavior. Earlier research methods have adopted either the emic or the etic approach. The emic approach focused on the relativistic aspects of culture such as culture-bound syndromes. The etic approach, on the other hand, assumes that Western-based constructs are applicable in other cultures and attempts to replicate these constructs in cross-cultural studies. Recent studies attempt to incorporate the emic–etic approaches. For example, the development of an emic–etic instrument such as the CPAI has introduced new dimensions of the personality structure to Western models of psychopathology. Other work such as that by Draguns (1989) are uses multicultural studies to formulate functional relationships between cultural characteristics and psychopathology. These new developments have pointed to the importance of the interpersonal dimension in psychopathology which has often been neglected in Western models of psychopathology. Future directions for study in cross-cultural psychopathology need to bring culture from its marginal status into the mainstream of clinical psychology.

10.02.13 REFERENCES

Abbey, S. E., & Garfinkel, P. E. (1991). Neurasthenia and chronic fatigue syndrome: The role of culture in the making of a diagnosis. *American Journal of Psychiatry, 148,* 1638–1646.

American Psychiatric Association (1968). *Diagnostic and statistical manual of disorders* (2nd ed.). Washington, DC: Author.

American Psychiatric Association (1980). *Diagnostic and statistical manual of mental disorders* (3rd ed.). Washington, DC: Author.

American Psychiatric Association (1994) *Diagnostic and statistical manual of mental disorders* (4th ed.). Washington, DC: Author.

Bartholomew, R. E. (1994). The social psychology of "epidemic" koro. *International Journal of Social Psychiatry, 40,* 46–60.

Beard, G. M. (1869). Neurasthenia, or nervous exhaustion. *Boston Medical and Surgical Journal, 3,* 217–221.

Benedict, R. (1946). *The chrysanthemum and the sword.* Boston: Houghton Mifflin.

Butcher, J. N., & Clark, L. A. (1979). Recent trends in cross-cultural MMPI research and application. In J. N. Butcher (Ed.), *New developments in the use of the MMPI* (pp. 69–111). Minneapolis, MN: University of Minnesota Press.

Butcher, J. N., & Pancheri, P. (1976). *A handbook of cross-national MMPI research.* Minneapolis, MN: University of Minnesota Press.

Butcher, J. N., & Spielberger, C. D. (Eds.) (1985). *Advances in personality assessment* (Vol. 4). Hillsdale, NJ: Erlbaum.

Carr, J. E. (1985). Ethno-behaviorism and the culture-bound syndromes: The case of *Amok*. In R. C.. Simons & C. C.. Hughes (Eds.), *The culture-bound syndromes: Folk illnesses of psychiatric and anthropological interest* (pp. 199–223). Dordrecht, The Netherlands: Reidel.

Cheng, T. A. (1988). A community study of minor psychiatric morbidity. *Psychological Medicine, 18,* 697–708.

Cheng, T. A. (1989). Symptomatology of minor psychiatric morbidity: A cross-cultural comparison. *Psychological Medicine, 19,* 697–708.

Cheng, T. A. (1995). Neuroses in Taiwan: Findings from a community survey. In T. Y. Lin, W. S. Tseng, & E. K. Yeh (Eds.), *Chinese societies and mental health* (pp. 167–175). Hong Kong: Oxford University Press.

Cheung, F. M. (1982). Psychological symptoms among Chinese in urban Hong Kong. *Social Science and Medicine, 16,* 1339–1344.

Cheung, F. M. (1985). An overview of psychopathology in Hong Kong with special reference to somatic presentation. In W. S. Tseng & D. Y. H. Wu (Eds.), *Chinese culture and mental health* (pp. 287–304). Orlando, FL: Academic Press.

Cheung, F. M. (1987). Conceptualization of psychiatric illness and help-seeking behavior among Chinese. *Culture, Medicine, and Psychiatry,* 11, 97–106.

Cheung, F. M. (1989). The indigenization of neurasthenia in Hong Kong. *Culture, Medicine, and Psychiatry, 13,* 227–241.

Cheung, F. M. (1991). Health psychology in Chinese societies in Asia. In M. A. Jensen & J. Weinman (Eds.), *The International development of health psychology* (pp. 63–74). Chur, Switzerland: Harwood.

Cheung, F. M. (1995). Facts and myths about somatization among the Chinese. In T. Y. Lin, W. S. Tseng, & E. K. Yeh (Eds.), *Chinese societies and mental health* (pp. 156–166). Hong Kong: Oxford University Press.

Cheung, F. M., & Gan, Z. Q. (1996). Personality traits as predictors of mental health in Chinese: Cultural and gender issues. Unpublished manuscript.

Cheung, F. M., & Lau, B. W. K. (1982). Situational variations in help-seeking behavior among Chinese patients. *Comprehensive Psychiatry, 23,* 252–262.

Cheung, F. M., Lau, B. W. K., & Waldmann, E. (1980–81). Somatization among Chinese depressives in general practice. *International Journal of Psychiatry in Medicine, 10,* 361–374.

Cheung, F. M., Lau, B. W. K., & Wong, S. W. (1984). Paths to psychiatric care in Hong Kong. *Culture, Medicine, and Psychiatry, 8,* 207–228.

Cheung, F. M., Lee, S. Y., & Chan, Y. Y. (1983). Variations in problem conceptualizations and intended solutions among Hong Kong students. *Culture, Medicine, and Psychiatry, 7,* 263–278.

Cheung, F. M., Leung, K., Fan, R. M., Song, W. Z., Zhang, J. X., & Zhang, J. P. (1996). Development of the Chinese Personality Assessment Inventory. *Journal of Cross-Cultural Psychology, 27,* 181–199.

Cheung, F. M., Leung, K., Law, J. S., & Zhang, J. X. (1996, August). Indigenous Chinese personality constructs. Paper presented at the 26th International Congress of Psychology, Montreal, Canada.

Cheung, F. M., & Song, W. Z. (1989). A review on the clinical applications of the Chinese MMPI. *Psychological Assessment: A Journal of Consulting and Clinical Psychology, 1,* 230–237.

Cheung, F. M., Song, W. Z., & Butcher, J. N. (1991). An infrequency scale for the Chinese MMPI. *Psychological Assessment: A Journal of Consulting and Clinical Psychology, 3,* 648–653.

Cheung, F. M., Song, W. Z., & Zhang, J. X. (1996). The Chinese MMPI-2: Research and applications in Hong Kong and the People's Republic of China. In J. N. Butcher (Ed.), *International adaptations of the MMPI-2: A handbook of research and applications* (pp. 137–161). Minneapolis MN: University of Minnesota Press.

Cheung, F. M., Zhao, J. C., & Wu, C. Y. (1992). Chinese MMPI profiles among neurotic patients. *Psychological Assessment: A Journal of Consulting and Clinical Psychology, 4,* 214–218.

Chin, R., & Chin, A. S. (1969). *Psychological research in communist China: 1949–66.* Cambridge, MA: MIT Press.

Chowdhury, A. N. (1996). The definition and classification of Koro. *Culture, Medicine, and Psychiatry, 20,* 41–65.

Draguns, J. G. (1985). Psychological disorders across cultures. In P. Pedersen (Ed.), *Handbook of cross-cultural counseling and therapy* (pp. 55–62). Westport, CT: Greenwood.

Draguns, J. G. (1986). Culture and psychopathology: What is known about their relationship? *Australian Journal of Psychology, 38,* 329–338.

Draguns, J. G. (1989). Normal and abnormal behavior in cross-cultural perspective: Specifying the nature of their relationship. In J. J. Berman (Ed.), *Nebraska Symposium on Motivation 1989,* (Vol. 37, pp. 235–277). Lincoln, NE: University of Nebraska Press.

Edwards, J. G. (1985). Indigenous Koro, a genital retraction syndrome of insular Southeast Asia: A critical review. In T. C. Simons & C. C. Hughes (Eds.), *The culture-bound syndromes: Folk illnesses of psychiatric and anthropological interest* (pp. 169–192). Dordrecht, The Netherlands: Reidel.

Fernando, S. (1988). *Race and culture in psychiatry.* London: Croom Helm.

Fishbain, D. A., Barsky, S., & Goldberg, M. (1989). "Koro" (genital retraction syndrome): Psychotherapeutic interventions. *American Journal of Psychotherapy, 43,* 87–91.

Goldberg, D., & Huxley, P. (1980). *Mental illness in the community: The pathway to psychiatric care.* London: Tavistock.

Good, B. J. (1996). Culture and DSM-IV: Diagnosis, knowledge and power. *Culture, Medicine, and Psychiatry, 20,* 127–132.

Gussow, Z. (1985). *Pibloktoq* (hysteria) among the Polar Eskimo: An ethnopsychiatrc study. In R. C. Simons & C. C. Hughes (Eds.), *The culture-bound syndromes: Folk illnesses of psychiatric and anthropological interest* (pp. 271–287). Dordrecht, The Netherlands: Reidel.

Gwee, A. L. (1985). Koro—A cultural disease. In T. C. Simons & C. C.. Hughes (Eds.) *The culture-bound syndromes: Folk illnesses of psychiatric and anthropological interest* (pp. 155–160). Dordrecht, The Netherlands: Reidel.

Hathaway, S. R., & McKinley, J. C. (1967). *The Minnesota Multiphasic Personality Inventory Manual.* New York: Psychological Corporation.

Hill, R. F., & Fortenberry, J. D. (1992). Adolescence as a culture-bound syndrome. *Social Science and Medicine, 35,* 73–80.

Hofstede, G. (1980). *Culture's consequences: International differences in work-related values.* Beverly Hills, CA: Sage.

Hofstede, G. (1983). The cultural relativity of organizational practices and theories. *Journal of International Business Studies, 14,* 75–89.

Holden, T. J. (1987). Koro syndrome associated with alcohol-induced systemic disease in a Zulu. *British Journal of Psychiatry, 151,* 695–697.

Hughes, C. C. (1985). Culture-bound or construct-bound: The syndromes and DSM-III. In T. C. Simons & C. C. Hughes (Eds.), *The culture-bound syndromes: Folk illnesses of psychiatric and anthropological interest* (pp. 3–24). Dordrecht, The Netherlands: Reidel.

Jablensky, A., Sartorius, N., Gulbinat, W., & Ernberg, G. (1981). Characteristics of depressive patients contacting psychiatric services in four cultures. *Acta Psychiatrica Scandinavia, 68,* 367–383.

Kleinman, A. (1977). Depression, somatization and the "new cross-cultural psychiatry." *Social Science and Medicine, 11,* 3–10.

Kleinman, A. (1982). Neurasthenia and depression: A study of somatization and culture in China. *Culture, Medicine and Psychiatry, 6,* 117–190.

Kleinman, A. (1986). *Social origins of distress and disease: Neurasthenia, depression and pain in modern China.* New Haven, CT: Yale University Press.

Kleinman, A. (1988a). *Rethinking psychiatry: From cultural category to personal experience.* New York: The Free Press.

Kleinman, A. (1988b). *The illness narratives: Suffering, healing, and the human condition.* New York: Basic Books.

Lee, S., & Wong, K. C. (1995). Rethinking neurasthenia: The illness concepts of Shejing Shuairuo among Chinese undergraduates in Hong Kong. *Culture, Medicine, and Psychiatry, 19,* 91–111.

Leong, F. T. L. (1986). Counseling and psychotherapy with Asian-Americans: Review of the literature. *Journal of Counseling Psychology, 33,* 196–206.

Lewis-Fernandez, R. (1996). Cultural formulation of psychiatric diagnosis. *Culture, Medicine, and Psychiatry, 20,* 133–144.

Lewis-Fernandez, R., & Kleinman, A. (1994). Culture, personality, and psychopathology. *Journal of Abnormal Psychology, 103,* 67–71.

Lin, T. Y. (1982). Culture and psychiatry: A Chinese perspective. *Australian and New Zealand Journal of Psychiatry, 16,* 235–245.

Lin, T. Y. (1989). Neurasthenia revisited: Its place in modern psychiatry. *Culture, Medicine, and Psychiatry, 13,* 105–129.

Lin, T. Y., Tardiff, K., Donetz, G., & Goresky, W. (1978). Ethnicity and patterns of help-seeking. *Culture, Medicine, and Psychiatry, 2,* 3–13.

Marsella, A. J., Kinzie, D., & Gorson, P. (1973). Ethnic variation in the expression of depression. *Journal of Cross-cultural Psychology, 4,* 435–358.

Mechanic, D. (ed.) (1982). *Symptoms, illness behavior and help seeking.* New York: Prodist.

Mental Health Division, WHO (in press). *A sociocultural lexicon for psychiatry.* Geneva, Switzerland: World Health Organization.

Ots, T. (1990). The angry liver, the anxious heart and the melancholy spleen: The phenomenology of perceptions in Chinese culture. *Culture, Medicine, and Psychiatry, 14,* 21–58.

Pederson, P. P. (1983). The cultural complexity of counseling. *International Journal for the Advancement of Counselling, 6,* 177–192.

Pedersen, P. P. (1987). Ten frequent assumptions of cultural bias in counselling. *Journal of Multicultural Counseling and Development, 15,* 16–24.

Pedersen, P. P. (1990). The multicultural perspective as a fourth force in counseling. *Journal of Mental Health Counseling, 12,* 93–95.

Pedersen, P. P. (1991). Multiculturalism as a generic approach to counseling. *Journal of Counseling and Development, 70,* 6–12.

Pedersen, P. P., Draguns, J. G., Lonner, W. J., & Trimble, J. E. (Eds.) (1981). *Counseling across cultures* (Rev. and expanded ed.). Hawaii: East-West Center, University of Hawaii.

Pedersen, P. P. & Marsella, A. J. (1982). The ethical crisis for cross-cultural counseling and therapy. *Professional Psychology: Research and Practice, 13,* 492–500.

Prince, R. (1985). The concept of culture-bound syndromes: Anorexia nervosa and brain-fag. *Social Science and Medicine, 21,* 197–203.

Prince, R., & Tcheng-Laroche, F. (1987). Culture-bound syndromes and international disease classification. *Culture, Medicine, and Psychiatry, 11,* 3–20.

Rin, H., & Huang, M. G. (1989). Neurasthenia as nosological dilemma. *Culture, Medicine, and Psychiatry, 13,* 215–226.

Ritenbaugh, C. (1982). Obesity as a culture-bound syndrome. *Culture, Medicine, and Psychiatry, 6,* 347–361.

Routh, D. K. (1994). *Clinical psychology since 1917: Science, practice, and organization.* New York: Plenum.

Rubel, A. J., O'Nell, C. W., & Collado, R. (1985). The folk illness called *Susto.* In R. C. Simons & C. C. Hughes (Eds.), *The culture-bound syndromes: Folk illnesses of psychiatric and anthropological interest* (pp. 33–350). Dordrecht, The Netherlands: Reidel.

Sartorius, N., Jablensky, A., Korten, A., Ernberg, G., Anker, M., Cooper, J. E., & Day, R. (1986). Early manifestation and first contact incidence of schizophrenia: A preliminary report on the initial evaluation phase of the WHO Collaborative Study on Determinants of Outcome of Severe Mental Disorders. *Psychological Medicine, 16,* 909–928.

Schwartz, G. E. (1982). Testing the biopsychosocial model: The ultimate challenge facing behavioral medicine? *Journal of Consulting and Clinical Psychology, 50,* 1040–1053.

Simons, R. C. (1985). The resolution of the *Latah* paradox. In R. C. Simons & C. C. Hughes (Eds.), *The culture-bound syndromes: Folk illnesses of psychiatric and anthropological interest* (pp. 43–62). Dordrecht, The Netherlands: Reidel.

Simons, R. C. & Hughes, C. C. (Eds.) (1985). *The culture-bound syndromes: Folk illnesses of psychiatric and anthropological interest.* Dordrecht, The Netherlands: Reidel.

Singer, K. (1975). Depressive disorders from a transcultural perspective. *Social Science and Medicine, 9,* 289–301.

Sue, D. W. (1977). Counseling the cu.turally different: A conceptual analysis. *Personnel and Guidance Journal, 55,* 422–425.

Sue, D. W. (1978). Eliminating cultural oppression in counseling: Toward a general theory. *Journal of Counseling Psychology, 25,* 419–428.

Sue, D. W. (1989). Racial/cultural identity development among Asian-Americans: Counseling theory implications. *Asian-American Psychological Association Journal, 13,* 80–86.

Sue, D. W. (1990). Culture-specific strategies in counseling: A conceptual framework. *Professional Psychology: Research and Practice, 21,* 424–433.

Sue, D. W. (1991). A model for cultural diversity training. *Journal of Counseling and Development, 70,* 99–105.

Sue, D. W., Arredondo, P., & McDavis, R. J. (1992). Multicultural counseling competencies and standards: A call to the profession. *Journal of Multicultural Counseling and Development, 20,* 64–88.

Sue, D. W., & Kirk, B. A. (1975). Asian-Americans: Use of counseling and psychiatric services on a college campus. *Journal of Counseling Psychology, 22,* 84–86.

Sue, D. W., & Sue, D. (1977). Barriers to effective cross-cultural counseling. *Journal of Counseling Psychology, 24,* 420–429.

Sue, D. W., & Sue, D. (1990). *Counseling the culturally different: Theory and practice* (2nd ed.). New York: Wiley.

Sue, S. (1977). Psychological theory and implications for Asian Americans. *Personnel and Guidance Journal, 55,* 381–389.

Sue, S., & Zane, N. (1987). The role of culture and cultural techniques in psychotherapy: A critique and reformulation. *American Psychologist, 42,* 37–45.

Swartz, L. (1985). Anorexia nervosa as a culture-bound syndrome. *Social Science and Medicine, 20,* 725–730.

Tseng, W. S. (1975). The nature of somatic complaints among psychiatric patients: The Chinese case. *Comprehensive Psychiatry, 16,* 237–245.

Tseng, W. S., & McDermott, J. F., Jr. (1981). *Culture, mind and therapy: An introduction to cultural psychiatry.* New York: Brunner/Mazel.

Tung, M. P. M. (1994). Symbolic meanings of the body in Chinese culture and "somatization." *Culture, Medicine, and Psychiatry, 18,* 483–492.

Vontress, C. E. (1974). Barriers in cross-cultural counseling. *Counseling and Values, 18,* 160–165.

Wong, C. K., & Chan, T. S. C. (1984). Somatic symptoms among Chinese psychiatric patients. *Hong Kong Journal of Mental Health, 13,* 5–21.

World Health Organization (1973). *Report of the international pilot study of schizophrenia.* Geneva, Switzerland: Author.

World Health Organization (1975). *Schizophrenia, a multinational study: A summary of the initial evaluation phase of the international pilot study of schizophrenia.* Geneva, Switzerland: Author.

World Health Organization (1979). *Schizophrenia: An international follow-up study.* Chichester, UK: Wiley.

World Health Organization (1983). *Depressive disorders in different cultures: Report of the WHO collaborative study of standardized assessment of depressive disorders.* Geneva, Switzerland: Author.

World Health Organization (1991). *Evaluation on methods for treatment of mental disorders: Report of a WHO scientific group on the treatment of psychiatric disorders.* Geneva, Switzerland: Author.

World Health Organization (1992). *The ICD-10 classification of mental and behavioral disorders: Clinical descriptions and diagnostic guidelines.* Geneva, Switzerland: Author.

Yap, P. M. (1974). *Comparative psychiatry: A theoretical framework.* Toronto, Canada: University of Toronto Press.

Zane, N. W., Sue, S., Hu, L. T., & Kwon, J. H. (1991). Asian-American assertion: A social learning analysis of cultural differences. *Journal of Counseling Psychology, 38,* 63–70.

Zheng, Y. P., Xu, L. Y., & Shen, Q. J. (1986). Styles of verbal expression of emotional and physical experiences: A study of depressed patients and normal controls in China. *Culture, Medicine, and Psychiatry, 10,* 231–243.

10.03
Cultural Bias in Testing of Intelligence and Personality

CECIL R. REYNOLDS
Texas A&M University, College Station, TX, USA

10.03.1 INTRODUCTION	53
10.03.2 THE CONTROVERSY OVER BIAS IN PSYCHOLOGICAL TESTING: WHAT IT IS AND WHAT IT IS NOT	54
10.03.3 THE NATURE OF PSYCHOLOGICAL TESTING ADDS TO THE CONTROVERSY	57
10.03.4 WHAT ARE POSSIBLE SOURCES OF BIAS?	59
10.03.5 MEAN SCORE DIFFERENCES AS TEST BIAS	60
10.03.5.1 Culture-free Tests, Culture Loading, and Culture Bias	61
10.03.5.2 The Question of Labeling Effects	62
10.03.6 THE PROBLEM OF DEFINITION	64
10.03.7 RESEARCH STRATEGIES AND RESULTS	65
10.03.7.1 Bias in Content Validity	65
10.03.7.2 Bias in Construct Validity	72
10.03.7.3 Bias in Predictive or Criterion-related Validity	77
10.03.8 CROSS-CULTURAL TESTING WHEN TRANSLATION IS REQUIRED	85
10.03.9 SUMMARY AND FUTURE DIRECTIONS	85
10.03.10 REFERENCES	86

10.03.1 INTRODUCTION

The issues of bias in psychological testing have been a source of intense and recurring social controversy throughout the history of mental measurement. In England, the issue was raised by Burt (1921) early in the twentieth century. The first investigations into cultural bias, however, can be traced to Binet, originating around 1910 in France (Binet & Simon, 1916) and to Stern (1914) shortly therafter. In the USA, discussions pertaining to test bias are frequently accompanied by emotionally laden polemics decrying the use of mental tests with any minority group member, since ethnic minorities have not been exposed to the cultural and environmental circumstances and values of the so-called White middle class. Intertwined within the general issue of bias in tests has been the more specific question of whether intelligence tests should be used for educational purposes. Although scientific and societal discussion pertaining to differences among groups on measures of cognitive or intellectual functioning in no way fully encompasses the broader topic of bias in mental measurement, there is little doubt that the so-called "IQ controversy" has received the lion's share of public scrutiny over the years. It has been the subject of numerous publications in the more popular press (see Gould, 1981;

Herrnstein & Murray, 1994; or Jensen, 1980, chap. 1), and court actions and legislation have addressed the use of IQ tests within schools and industry.

From Binet to Jensen, many professionals have addressed the problem, with varying and inconsistent outcomes. Unlike the pervasive and polemical nature–nuture argument, the bias issue was until the 1970s largely restricted to the professional literature, except for a few early discussions in the popular press (e.g., Freeman, 1923; Lippmann, 1923a, 1923b). Of some interest is the fact that one of the psychologists who initially raised the question was the then-young Cyril Burt (1921), who even in the 1920s was concerned about the extent to which environmental and motivational factors affected performance on intelligence tests. Within the last 30 years, however, the questions of cultural test bias have burst forth as major contemporary problems far beyond the bounds of scholarly academic debate in psychology. The debate over bias has raged in both the professional and the popular press for multiple decades (e.g., Fine, 1975). Entangled in the larger issues of individual liberties, civil rights, and social justice, the bias issue has become a focal point for psychologists, sociologists, politicians, and the public. Increasingly, the issues have become political and legal ones, as reflected in numerous court cases and passage in the state of New York and consideration elsewhere of what is popularly known as "truth-in-testing" legislation. The magnitude—and the uncertainty—of the controversy and its outcome is shown in two highly publicized US Federal district court cases. The judiciary's answer to the question "Are the tests used for pupil assignment to classes for the educably mentally retarded biased against cultural and ethnic minorities?" initially was "Yes" in California (Larry P. et al. v. Wilson Riles et al., 1979) and "No" in Illinois (PASE v. Hannon et al., 1980), although the Larry P. finding has now been overturned, giving a consistent nature to court findings in the USA.

Unfortunately, we are all prisoners of our language. The word bias has several meanings, not all of which are kept distinct. In relation to the present issue, bias as "partiality towards a point of view or prejudice" and bias as "a statistical term referring to a constant error of a measure in one specific direction as opposed to random error" frequently become coalesced. If the latter meaning did not drag along the excess baggage of the former, the issue of bias in mental testing would be far less controversial and emotional than it is. However, as indicated in the *Oxford English Dictionary*, bias as partiality or prejudice can be traced at least to the sixteenth century and clearly antedates the statistical meaning. Nevertheless, the discussion of bias in psychological testing as a scientific issue should concern only the statistical meaning, whether or not there is systematic error in the measurement of a psychological attribute as a function of membership in one or another cultural or racial subgroup (Reynolds, 1982b). This definition, defined more technically as required later, will be followed throughout this chapter.

10.03.2 THE CONTROVERSY OVER BIAS IN PSYCHOLOGICAL TESTING: WHAT IT IS AND WHAT IT IS NOT

Systematic group differences on standardized intelligence and aptitude tests occur as a function of socioeconomic level, race or ethnic background, and other demographic variables throughout the various countries of the world. Black–White differences on IQ measures in the USA have received extensive investigation since the 1930s. The preponderance of these studies have been reviewed by Shuey (1966), Tyler (1965), Jensen (1980), and Willerman (1979). Results have not changed fundamentally in the last century. Although the results occasionally differ slightly, depending on the age groups under consideration, random samples of Blacks and Whites in the USA show a mean score difference of about one standard deviation, with the mean score of the Whites consistently exceeding that of the Black groups. The differences have persisted at relatively constant levels for quite some time and under a variety of methods of investigation. The exception to this is the reduction of the Black–White IQ difference on the Kaufman Assessment Battery for Children (K-ABC; Kaufman & Kaufman, 1983) to about 0.5 standard deviations on the intelligence portion of the scale, a controversial and poorly understood finding (see Kamphaus & Reynolds, 1987, for a discussion). These findings are consistent only for the US Black population, however, and other, quite diverse findings appear for African and other Black populations (e.g., see Jensen, 1980).

When a number of demographic variables are taken into account (most notably socioeconomic status), the size of the mean Black–White difference in the USA reduces to 0.5–0.7 standard deviations (e.g. Jensen, 1980; Kaufman, 1973; Kaufman & Kaufman, 1973; Reynolds & Gutkin, 1981), but remains robust in its appearance. All studies of racial and ethnic group differences on ability tests do not show higher levels of performance by Whites. Although not nearly as thoroughly researched as Black–White groups, Oriental groups have been shown to perform consistently as well as, or better than, White groups (Pintner, 1931; Tyler, 1965; Willerman, 1979). Depending on the specific aspect of intelligence under investigation, other racial and ethnic groups show performance at or above the performance level of White groups. There has been argument over whether any racial differences in intelligence are real or even researchable (e.g., Schoenfeld, 1974), but the reliability across studies is very high, and the existence of the differences is now generally accepted. It should always be kept in mind, however, that the overlap among the distributions of intelligence test scores for the different races is much greater than the degree of differences among the various groups. There is always more within-group variability than between-group variability in performance on psychological tests. The differences are nevertheless real ones and are unquestionably complex (e.g., Reynolds & Jensen, 1983).

The issue at hand is the explanation of those group differences. It should be emphasized that both the lower scores of some groups and the higher scores of others need to be explained, although not necessarily, of course, in the same way. The problem was clearly stated by Eells in his classic study of cultural differences:

> Do the higher test scores of the children from high socioeconomic backgrounds reflect genuine superiority in inherited, or genetic, equipment? Or do the high scores result from a superior environment which has brought about real superiority of the child's "intelligence"? Or do they reflect a bias in the test materials and not any important differences in the children at all? (Eells, Davis, Havighurst, Herrick, & Tyler, 1951, p. 4).

Eells et al. also concisely summarized the cultural-test-bias hypothesis as it applied to differences in socioeconomic status (SES):

> If (a) the children from different social-status levels have different kinds of experiences and have experiences with different types of material, and if (b) the intelligence tests contain a disproportionate amount of material drawn from the cultural experiences with which pupils from the higher social-status levels are more familiar, one would expect (c) that children from the higher social-status levels are more familiar, one would expect (d) that children from the higher social-status levels would show higher IQs than those from the lower levels. This argument tends to conclude that the observed differences in pupil IQs are artifacts dependent upon the specific content of the test items and do not reflect accurately any important underlying ability in the pupils. (Eells et al., 1951 p. 4)

Eells was aware that his descriptions were oversimplifications and that it was unlikely that all of the observed group differences could be explained by any one of the three factors alone. Loehlin, Lindzey, and Spuhler (1975) concluded that all three factors were probably involved in racial differences in intelligence as have a myriad of other researchers (e.g., Bouchard & Segal, 1985; Flynn, 1991). In its present, more complex form, the cultural test bias hypothesis considers other factors than culture-loaded items, as will be seen below. But the basics of Eell's summary of the cultural-test-bias hypothesis still hold: group differences stem from characteristics of the test or from aspects of test administration. Because mental tests are based largely on middle-class White values and knowledge, they are more valid for those groups and are biased against other groups to the extent that these groups deviate from those values and knowledge bases.

This position has been reframed slightly over the years, principally by Mercer (e.g., 1979) and reinforced by Helms (1994), who argue the lower scores of ethnic minorities on aptitude measures can be traced to the Anglocentrism (degree of adherence to White, middle-class value systems of USA families) of aptitude measures. Mercer (1979) developed an entire system of assessments designed to provide complex demographic corrections to IQs obtained by ethnic minorities that had the effect of equating these groups on mean scores. (This system, known as the SOMPA, had quite a bit of popularity for several years but is rarely used today because of its conceptual and psychometric inadequacies.) Lonner (1985) discusses similar issues under the rubric of cultural isomorphism in testing and assessment. Helms (1994) makes similar criticisms of ability tests, rejects most psychometric research on these issues, and posits (quite similar to Mercer's position) it is the Eurocentric nature of aptitude tests that produces artifactual differences in mean levels of performance across ethnic lines, focusing especially on the performance of Black Americans. In all of those conceptual models, which are essentially contemporaneous even with arguments of Burt as early as 1921, ethnic and other group differences in mean levels of performance on aptitude measures are seen to result from flawed psychometric methodology and not from actual differences in aptitude (see also Harrington, 1975, 1976). As described below, this hypothesis reduces to one of differential validity, the hypothesis of differential validity for mental tests being that tests measure intelligence more accurately, and make valid predictions about the level of intellectual functioning for individuals from the groups on which the tests are mainly based than for those from other groups. Artifactually low scores on an aptitude test could lead to denial of employment or in schools to pupil misassignment to educational programs and unfair denial of admission to college, graduate school, or other programs or occupations in which such test scores are an important decision-making component. This is the issue over which most legal cases have been fought in the USA.

Further, there would be dramatic implications for whole areas of psychological research and practice if the cultural-test-bias hypothesis is correct. The principal research of the twentieth century in the psychology of human differences would have to be dismissed as confounded and largely artifactual because much of the work is based on standard psychometric theory and testing technology. The result would be major upheavals in the practice of applied psychology, as the foundations of clinical, school, counseling, and industrial psychology are strongly tied to the basic academic field of individual differences. The issue, then, is crucial not only to the science of psychology but to practice (Lonner, 1985; Reynolds, 1980c).

On the other hand, if the cultural-test-bias hypothesis is incorrect, then group differences are not attributable to the tests and must be due to one of the other factors mentioned by Eells et al. (1951) or to some combination of them. That group differences in test scores reflect real group differences in ability should be admitted as a possibility, and one that calls for scientific study.

The controversy over test bias should not be confused with that over the etiology of any obtained group differences in test scores (see Reynolds & Kaiser, 1990, for a review) other than to rule bias in or out as an explanation. Unfortunately, it has often been inferred that measured differences themselves indicate genetic differences, and therefore the genetically based intellectual inferiority of some groups. Jensen has himself consistently argued since 1969 that mental tests measure, to a greater or lesser extent, the intellectual factor *g* which has a large genetic component, and that group differences in mental test scores may then reflect group differences in *g*. Unless one reads Jensen's statements carefully, it is easy to overlook the many qualifications that he makes regarding these differences and conclusions.

But, in fact, Jensen's or anyone else's position on the genetic basis of actual group differences should be seen as irrelevant to the issue of test bias. However controversial, etiology is a separate issue. It would be tragic to accept the cultual test bias hypothesis as true if it is, in fact, false. In that case, measured differences would be seen as not real, and children, for example, might be denied access to the educational environment best suited to them, and job applicants may end up in occupations for which they are ill-suited or for which others are more qualified. Further, research on the basis of any group differences would be stifled, as would the implementation of programs designed to remediate any deficiencies. The most advantageous position for the true White racist and bigot would be to favour the test bias hypothesis! Acceptance of that hypothesis inappropriately would eventually result in inappropriate pupil assignment, less adaptive education for some groups, and less implementation of long-range programs to raise intellectual performance. Inappropriate confirmation of the test bias hypothesis would appear to maintain, not break down, the poverty cycle (Birch & Gussow, 1970).

The controversy is also not over the blatantly inappropriate administration and use of mental tests. The administration of a test developed and published in English to an individual for whom English is a second language and whose English language skills are poor is inexcusable, regardless of any bias in the tests themselves. It is just as inexcusable to translate the test into the examinee's first or dominant language and assume the validity of the results. Translating a test from its original language is a wholly inadequate process and creates many problems of reliability and validity. Instead, a test must be redeveloped, preferably following the steps outlined and discussed by Hambleton and Kanjee (1995). It is of obvious importance that tests be administered by skilled and sensitive professionals who are aware of the factors that may artifactually lower an individual's test scores. Considering the use of tests to assign pupils to special education classes or other programs, a question needs to be asked: What would one use instead? Teacher recommendations are notoriously less reliable and less valid than standardized test scores, which increases the probability of bias occurring. For college admissions, this question was asked long ago and the use of grades and subjective letters of recommendation and interviews found to be unreliable and biased. This research in the early 1900s led to the formation of the College Entrance Examination Board and the Scholastic Achievement Test (SAT).

The controversy over the use of mental tests is further complicated by the fact that resolution of the cultural test bias question in either direction will not resolve the problem of the role of nonintellective factors that may influence the test scores of individuals from any ethnic group. Regardless of any group differences, it is individuals who are tested and whose scores may or may not be accurate. Similarly, it is individuals who are assigned to classes, chosen for universities, placed in jobs or vocations, and who are accepted or rejected. As indicated by Wechsler (1975) and others, nonintellective factors, informational content, and emotional–motivational conditions may be reflected in performance on mental tests. The extent to which these factors influence individual as opposed to group performance is difficult to determine. Perhaps with more sophisticated multivariate designs, we will be better able to identify individuals with characteristics that are likely to have an adverse effect on their performance on mental tests. Basically, outside the major thrust of the issue of bias against groups, potential bias against individuals is a serious problem itself, and merits research and analysis. Sternberg (1980), also concerned about individual performance, observed a still true matter: research on bias has concentrated on status variables such as ethnicity rather than on functional variables such as cognitive styles and motivations.

10.03.3 THE NATURE OF PSYCHOLOGICAL TESTING ADDS TO THE CONTROVERSY

The question of bias in mental testing arises largely because of the nature of psychological processes and the measurement of those processes (Reynolds & Brown, 1984). Psychological processes, by definition internal and not directly subject to observation or measurement, must be inferred from behavior. Theoretically, in the classic discussion by MacCorquodale and Meehl (1948), a psychological process has the status of an "intervening variable" if it is used only as a component of a system that has no properties beyond those that operationally define it, but it has the status of a "hypothetical construct" if it is thought actually to exist with properties beyond the defining ones. A historical example of a hypothetical construct is gene, which had meaning beyond its use to describe the cross-generational transmission of characteristics. Intelligence, from its treatment in the professional literature, has the status of a hypothetical construct as does personality.

As even beginning psychology students know, it is difficult to determine one-to-one relationships between observable events in the environment, the behavior of an organism, and hypothesized underlying mediational processes. Many classic controversies over theories of learning have revolved around constructs such as expectancy, habit, and inhibition (e.g., Goldstein, Krantz, & Rains, 1965; Hilgard & Bower, 1975; Kimble, 1961). Disputes among different camps in learning have been polemical and of long duration. Indeed, there are still disputes about the nature and the number of processes such as emotion and motivation (e.g., Bolles, 1975; Mandler, 1975). One of the major areas of disagreement has been over the measurement of psychological processes. It should be expected that intelligence, as one of the most complex of psychological processes, involves definitional and measurement disputes that prove difficult to resolve.

Assessment of intelligence and personality, like that of many other psychological processes in humans, is accomplished by standard psychometric procedures that are the focus of the bias issue. These procedures, described in detail in general assessment texts (e.g., Anastasi, 1982; Linn, 1989), are only briefly summarized here in relation to the issue of bias. Problems specific to validity are discussed in Section 10.03.7.

Similar procedures are used in the development of any standardized psychological test. First, a large number of items are developed that for theoretical or practical reasons are thought to measure the construct of interest. Through a series of statistical steps, those items that best measure the construct in a unitary manner are selected for inclusion in the final test battery. The test is then administered to a sample, which should be chosen to represent all aspects of the population on whom the test will be used. Normative scales based on the scores of the standardization sample then serve as the reference for the interpretation of scores of individuals tested thereafter. Thus, as has been pointed out numerous times, an individual's score is meaningful only relative to this normative base and is a relative, not an absolute, measure. Charges of bias frequently arise from the position that the test is more appropriate for the groups heavily represented in the standardization sample. Whether bias does, in fact, result from this procedure is a specific question to be addressed empirically.

As has also been frequently pointed out, there are few charges of bias of any kind relating to physical measures that are on absolute scales, whether interval or ratio. Group differences in height, as an extreme example, are not attributed by anyone we know of to any kind of cultural test bias or specific methods of measuring height. There is no question concerning the validity of measures of the height or weight of anyone in any culture. Nor is there any question about one's ability to make cross-cultural comparisons of these absolute measures (which variables, such as height, are clearly subject to genetic by environmental interactions).

The whole issue of cultural bias arises because of the procedures involved in psychological testing. Psychological tests measure traits that are not directly observable, that are subject to differences in definition, and that are measurable only on a relative scale. From this perspective, the question of cultural bias in mental testing is a subset—obviously of major importance—of the problems of uncertainty and of possible bias in psychological testing generally. Bias may exist not only in mental tests but in other types of psychological test, including personality, vocational, and psychopathological tests. Making the problem of bias in mental testing even more complex is the fact that not all mental tests are of the same quality. Like Orwell's pigs, some may be more equal than others. There is a tendency for critics and defenders alike to overgeneralize across tests, lumping virtually all tests together under the heading "mental tests" or "intelligence tests." As reflected in the *Mental measurements yearbook* (e.g., Buros, 1978), professional opinions of mental tests vary considerably, and some of the most used tests are not well respected by psychometricians. Thus, unfortunately, the question of bias must eventually be answered on a virtually test-by-test basis.

In 1969, the Association of Black Psychologists (ABP), a USA-based professional association, adopted the following official policy on educational and psychological testing:

> The Association of Black Psychologists fully supports those parents who have chosen to defend their rights by refusing to allow their children and themselves to be subjected to achievement, intelligence, aptitude and performance tests which have been and are being used to A. Label Black people as uneducable. B. Place Black children in "special" classes and schools. C. Perpetuate inferior education in Blacks. D. Assign Black children to educational tracts. E. Deny Black students higher educational opportunities. F. Destroy positive growth and development of Black people. (quoted in Reynolds, 1982a, p. 179)

Since 1968, the ABP has sought continuously a moratorium on the use of all psychological and educational tests with the culturally different (Samuda, 1975, and Williams, Dotson, Dow, & Williams, 1980, have provided a more detailed history of these efforts). The ABP, an organizational leader in protesting test bias for all ethnic groups, carried its call for a moratorium to other professional organizations in psychology and education. In direct response to the ABP call, the Board of Directors of the American Psychological Association (APA) requested its Board of Scientific Affairs to appoint a group to study the use of psychological and educational tests with disadvantaged students. The committee report (Cleary, Humphreys, Kendrick, & Wesman, 1975) was subsequently published in the official journal of the APA, *American Psychologist*.

Subsequent to the ABP's policy statement, other groups adopted policy statements on testing. These groups included the National Association for the Advancement of Colored People (NAACP), the National Education Association (NEA), the National Association of Elementary School Principals (NAESP), the American Personnel and Guidance Association (APGA), and others (Committee on Testing, 1974; Williams et al., 1980). The APGA called for the Association for Measurement and Evaluation in Guidance (AMEG), a sister organization, to develop and disseminate a position paper stating the limitations of group intelligence tests particularly and generally of standardized psychological, educational, and employment testing for low socioeconomic and underprivileged and non-White individuals in educational, business, and industrial environments.

The APGA also resolved that, if no progress was made in clarifying and correcting the current testing of minorities, it would also call for a moratorium, but only on the use of group intelligence tests with these groups.

The NAACP adopted a more detailed resolution and joined in the call for a moratorium on standardized testing of minority groups at its annual meeting in 1974. The text of the NAACP resolution was:

> Whereas a disproportionately large number of Black students are being misplaced in special education classes and denied admissions to higher educational opportunities,
>
> Whereas students who fail to show a high verbal or numerical ability, score low on the Scholastic Achievement Test (SAT), the Law School Admissions Test (LSAT), the Graduate Record Examination (GRE), etc., and are routinely excluded from college and graduate or professional education,
>
> Be it resolved that the NAACP demands a moratorium on standardized testing whenever such tests have not been corrected for cultural bias and directs its units to use all administrative and legal remedies to prevent the violation of students" constitutional rights through the misuse of tests, and
>
> Be it further resolved that the NAACP calls upon the Association of Black Psychologists to assert leadership in aiding the College Entrance Examination Board to develop standardized tests which have been corrected for cultural bias and which fairly measure the amount of knowledge retained by students regardless of his or her individual background.
>
> Be it finally resolved that the NAACP directs its units to use all administrative remedies in the event of violation of students' constitutional rights

> through the misuse of tests and directs National Office staff to use its influence to bring the CEEB and ABP together to revise such tests.

Also in 1974, the Committee on Testing of the ABP issued a position paper on the testing of Blacks that described their intent as well as their position:

> (1) To encourage, support and to bring action against *all* institutions, organizations and agencies who continue to use present psychometric instruments in the psychological assessment of Black people;
> (2) To continue efforts to bring about a cessation of the use of standard psychometric instruments on Black people until culturally specific tests are made available;
> (3) To establish a national policy that in effect gives Black folk and other minorities the right to demand that psychological assessment be administered, interpreted, and supervised by competent psychological assessors of their own ethnic background;
> (4) To work toward and encourage efforts to remove from the records of all Black students and Black employees that data obtained from performance on past and currently used standard psychometric, achievement, employment, general aptitude and mental ability tests;
> (5) To establish a national policy that demands the appropriate proportional representation of competent Black psychologists on all committees and agencies responsible for the evaluation and selection of tests used in the assessment of Black folk;
> (6) To establish a national policy that demands that all persons engaged in the evaluation, selection and placement of Black folks undergo extensive training so they may better relate to the Black experience;
> (7) To demand that all Black students improperly diagnosed and placed into special education classes be returned to regular class programs;
> (8) To encourage and support all suits against any public or private agency for the exclusion, improper classification and the denial of advancement opportunities to Black people based on performance tests.

It should be noted that the statements by these organizations have assumed that present tests are biased, and that what is needed is the removal of that assumed bias. These assumptions continue in the work of Helms (e.g., 1992), Mercer (1979), Padilla and Medina (1996), and others (e.g., Guilford Press, 1997).

10.03.4 WHAT ARE POSSIBLE SOURCES OF BIAS?

Many potentially legitimate objections to the use of educational and psychological tests with minorities have been raised by Black and other minority psychologists. Unfortunately, these objections are frequently stated as facts on rational rather than empirical grounds (e.g., Council for Exceptional Children, 1978; Chambers, Barron, & Sprecher, 1980; Dana, 1996; Helms, 1992; Hilliard, 1979). The most frequently stated problems fall into one of the following categories:

(i) *Inappropriate content.* Black and other minorities have not been exposed to the material involved in the test questions or other stimulus materials. The tests are geared primarily toward the majority class homes, vocabulary, and values. Different value systems among cultures may lead to cognitively equivalent answers scored as incorrect based on prejudicial value judgments, not on differences in ability.

(ii) *Inappropriate standardization samples.* Ethnic minorities are underrepresented in standardization samples used in the collection of normative reference data. Population proportionate sampling with stratification by ethnicity is the herald for standardization samples for tests and is done to enhance the accuracy of parameter estimation for scaling purposes. As such, although presented proportionately, ethnic minorities may appear in test standardization samples in small absolute numbers. This may bias item selection (e.g., Harrington, 1975, 1976) and fails to have any impact of significance on the tests themselves from these ethnic groups. In earlier years, it was not unusual for standardization samples to be all White (e.g., the 1937 Binet and 1949 WISC).

(iii) *Examiner and language bias.* Since most psychologists in the USA are White and speak only standard English, they may intimidate Black and other ethnic minorities. They are also unable accurately to communicate with minority children—to the point of being insensitive to ethnic pronunciation of words on the test. Lower test scores for minorities, then, may reflect only this intimidation and difficulty in the communication process or motivational differences (Zigler & Butterfield, 1967), not lower ability. In other countries, professionals such as psychologists tend to be from the dominant culture and similar issues appear.

(iv) *Inequitable social consequences.* As a result of bias in educational and psychological tests, minority group members, already at a disadvantage in the educational and vocational markets because of past discrimination and thought unable to learn, are disproportionately relegated to dead-end educational tracks. Labeling effects also fall under this category.

(v) *Measurement of different constructs.* Related to (i), this position asserts that the tests measure different attributes when used with children from other than the majority culture of a country, the culture on which the tests are largely based, and thus do not measure minority intelligence or personality validly.

(vi) *Differential predictive validity.* Although tests may accurately predict a variety of outcomes for members of a majority culture within a population, they do not predict successfully any relevant behavior for cultural minority group members Further, there are objections to use of the standard criteria against which tests are validated with minority cultural groups. For example, in the USA, scholastic or academic attainment levels in White middle-class schools are themselves considered by a variety of Black psychologists to be biased as criteria (e.g., see discussion in Reynolds, 1982a, pp. 179–180).

(vii) *Minority and majority aptitude and personality are qualitatively distinct.* Championed by Helms (e.g., 1992), this position would lead to the conclusion that ethnic minorities and the majority culture are so different as to require different conceptualizations of ability and personality. Helms (1982), for example, argues the potential existence of a "White *g*" factor that is separate from an "African *g*" factor (p. 1090) that would necessitate separate tests for these groups.

Contrary to the situation of the late 1960s and 1970s, when the current controversies resurfaced after some decades of simmering, research now exists that examines the above areas of potential bias in assessment. Except for the still unresolved issue of labeling effects, the least amount of research is available on the long-term social consequences of testing, although some limited data are available (e.g., Lambert, 1979). Both of these problems are aspects of testing in general and are not limited to minorities. The problem of the social consequences of educational tracking is frequently lumped with the issue of test bias. Those issues, however, are separate. Educational tracking and special education should be treated as problems of education, not assessment. These are going to become more heavily contested areas for psychologists in the future, however, as the revision of the *Joint Technical Standards for Educational and Psychological Tests and Manuals* now underway is likely to add the issue of consequential validity to considerations in test use, reflecting concerns by minority groups within the USA over the consequences of test use with ethnic minorities. Educational tracking as a result of test performance is a prominent problem for ethnic minorities in many countries applying such competitive schooling practices.

The call by Helms (1992) and earlier by Williams (1974) for separate tests for minority groups within the USA deserves comment and raises an interesting set of legal and conceptual issues. The concept of separate but equal programs, facilities, and the like was protested vehemently by minorities for many years and ultimately rejected by the US Supreme Court. It is of interest that some minority scholars would now seek "separate but equal" tests. This could lead to arguments that if the cognitive structures of various ethnic groups are so different as to require distinct tests of intelligence and personality for accurate assessment, then schooling, job training, mental health interventions, and the like might also need to be different—an argument long attacked and rejected by many minority scholars and spokespersons.

10.03.5 MEAN SCORE DIFFERENCES AS TEST BIAS

A popular lay view, and one promoted in the popular media, has been that differences in mean levels of scoring on cognitive, achievement, or personality tests among groups constitute bias in tests; however, such differences alone clearly are not evidence of test bias. A number of writers in the professional literature have taken this position as well (e.g., Adebimpe, Gigandet, & Harris, 1979; Alley & Foster, 1978; Chinn, 1979; Guilford Press, 1997; Hillard, 1979; Jackson, 1975; Mercer, 1976; Padilla, 1988; Williams, 1974; Wright & Isenstein, 1977). Those who support this definition of test bias correctly state there is no valid *a priori* scientific reason to believe that intellectual or other cognitive performance levels should differ across race. It is the inference that tests demonstrating such differences are inherently biased because there can in reality be no differences that is fallacious. Just as there is no *a priori* basis for deciding that differences exist, there is no *a priori* basis for deciding that differences do not exist. From the standpoint of the objective methods of science, *a priori* or premature acceptance of either hypothesis ('differences exist" vs. "differences do not exist") is untenable. As stated by Thorndike (1971), "The presence (or absence) of differences in mean score between groups, or of differences in variability, tells us nothing directly about fairness" (p. 64). Some adherents to the "mean score differences as bias" viewpoint also require that the distribution of test scores in each population or subgroup be identical before one can assume that the test is fair: "Regardless of the purpose of a test or its validity for that purpose, a test should result in distributions that are statistically equivalent across the groups tested in order for it to be considered nondiscriminatory for those groups" (Alley & Foster, 1978,

p. 2). Portraying a test as biased regardless of its purpose or validy is psychometrically naive. Mean score differences and unequivalent distributions have been the most uniformly rejected of all criteria examined by sophisticated psychometricians involved in investigating the problems of bias in assessment. Ethnic group differences in mental test scores are among the best-documented phenomena in psychology, and they have persisted over time at relatively constant levels (Reynolds & Gutkin, 1980a, 1981).

Jensen (1980) has discussed the "mean score differences as bias" position in terms of the egalitarian fallacy. The egalitarian fallacy contends that all human populations are in fact identical on all mental traits or abilities. Any differences with regard to any aspect of the distribution of mental test scores indicates that something is wrong with the test itself. Such an assumption is totally scientifically unwarranted. There are simply too many examples of specific abilities and even sensory capacities that have been shown to differ unmistakably across human populations. The result of the egalitarian assumption, then, is to remove the investigation of population differences in ability from the realm of scientific inquiry. Logically followed, this fallacy leads to other untenable conclusions as well. Torrance (1980), an adherent of the cultural bias hypothesis, pointed out that disadvantaged Black children in the USA occasionally earn higher scores on creativity tests—and therefore, have more creative ability—than many White children because their environment has forced them to learn to "make do" with less and with simpler objects. The egalitarian assumption would hold that this is not true, but rather that the content of creativity tests is biased against White or high SES children.

The attachment of minorities to the "mean score differences as bias" definition is probably related to the nature–nurture controversy at some level, and has been difficult for even databased, minority research scientists to abandon (e.g., Dana, 1993). Certainly data reflecting racial differences on various aptitude measures have been interpreted to indicate support for a hypothesis of genetic differences in intelligence and to imply that one race is superior to another. However, as discussed previously, the so-called nature–nurture issue is not an inextricable component of bias investigation. Assertions as to the relative impact of genetic factors on group ability levels step into a new arena of scientific inquiry, with differing bodies of knowledge and methods of research. Suffice it to say that in the arena of bias investigation, mean differences on aptitude, achievement, or personality measures among selected groups are not evidence *per se* that the measures are biased.

10.03.5.1 Culture-free Tests, Culture Loading, and Culture Bias

A third area of bias investigation that has been confusing in both the professional (e.g., Alley & Foster, 1978; Chinn, 1979) and the lay literature has been the interpretation of culture loading and culture bias. A test can be culture loaded without being culturally biased. Culture loading refers to the degree of cultural specificity present in the test or individual items of the test. Certainly, the greater the cultural specificity of a test item, the greater the likelihood of the item being biased when it is used with individuals from other cultures. The test item "Who was the first president of the United States?" is a culture-loaded item. However, the item is general enough to be considered useful with school-aged children attending school since first grade in the USA. The cultural specificity of the item is too great, however, to allow the item to be used on an aptitude measure of 10-year-old children from other countries. Virtually all tests in current use are bound in some way by their cultural specificity. Culture loading must be viewed on a continuum from general (defining a culture in a broad, liberal sense) to specific (defining a culture in narrow, highly distinctive terms).

A variety of attempts have been made to develop a "culture-free" (sometimes referred to as "culture-fair") intelligence test (e.g., Cattell, 1979). However, the reliability and validity of these tests are uniformly inadequate from a psychometric perspective (Anastasi, 1982; Ebel, 1979). The difficulty in developing a culture-free measure of intelligence lies in the test being irrelevant to intellectual behavior within the culture under study. Intelligent behavior is defined within human society in large part on the basis of behavior judged to be of value to the survival and improvement of the culture and the individuals within the culture. A test that is "culture-blind," then, cannot be expected to predict intelligent behavior within a variety of cultural settings. Once a test has been developed within a culture (a culture-loaded test), its generalizability to other cultures or subcultures within the dominant societal framework becomes a matter for empirical investigation, and tests should not be used cross-culturally without demonstrative evidence for the validity of inferences to be drawn from such tests. The same holds true for personality tests and other techniques designed to assess affective disorders.

Although there exists a universality to certain psychopathological disorders (e.g., schizophrenia, bipolar disorder) in both taxonomy and manifestation, the existence of certain disorders independent of a cultural context can be questioned readily (e.g., dependent personality disorder) and the symptoms or manifestations of other disorders may well vary across cultures as they do across age (e.g., depression, anxiety disorders).

Jensen (1980) admonishes that when one is investigating the psychometric properties of culture-loaded tests across differing societies or cultures, one cannot assume that simple inspection of the content will determine which tests or items are biased against those cultures or societies not represented in the tests or item content. Tests or items that exhibit characteristics of being culturally loaded cannot be determined to be biased with any degree of certainty unless objective statistical inspection is completed. Jensen refers to the mistaken notion that anyone can judge tests and/or items as being "culturally unfair" on superficial inspection as the "culture-bound fallacy." The issue of item bias is revisited in some detail in Section 10.03.7.1.

10.03.5.2 The Question of Labeling Effects

The relative impact of placing a label on a person's behavior or developmental status has also been a hotly discussed issue within the field of psychometrics in general and bias investigation in particular. The issue undoubtedly has been a by-product of the practice of using intellectual measures for the determination of mental retardation. Although the question of labeling effects is a viable and important one, it requires consideration in bias research only in much the same way as does the ongoing debate surrounding the nature–nurture question. As the concept of consequential validity grows, this issue will likewise grow in importance. However, there are some important considerations regarding bias in referral for services, diagnosis, and labeling, which no interested student of the diagnostic process in psychology can afford to ignore.

Rosenthal is the researcher most closely associated with the influence of labeling upon teachers' and parents' perceptions of a child's ability and potential. Even though his early studies had many methodological and statistical difficulties, labeling effects have been shown in some subsequent experimental studies (e.g., Critchley, 1979; Foster & Ysseldyke, 1976; Jacobs, 1978), but not in others (e.g., MacMillan, Jones, & Aloia, 1974; McCoy, 1976). However, these studies have generally been of a short-term nature, and have usually been conducted under quite artificial circumstances. Typically, participants are asked to rate the behavior or degree of pathology of a child seen on videotape. Categorical labels for the child are systematically varied while the observed behaviors remain constant. The demand characteristics of such a design are substantial. Long-term effects of labeling and diagnoses resulting in special education placement or mental health treatment in real-life situations have been examined less vigorously. For example, comparisons of the effects of formal diagnostic labels with the informal, often cursory, personal labeling process that occurs between teachers and children over the course of a school year, and that is subsequently passed on to the next grade via the teachers' lounge (Dworkin & Dworkin, 1979), need to be made. Although Reynolds (1982b) called for this research in past decades, this important question has not been addressed. The strict behaviorist position (Ross, 1974, 1976) also contends that formal diagnostic procedures are unnecessary and potentially harmful because of labeling effects. However, whether or not the application of formal labels has detrimental effects remains an open question now, much as it did at the conclusion of a monumental effort to address these important questions throughout the USA in the mid-1970s (Hobbs, 1975).

Even without the application of formal, codified labels by psychologists or psychiatrists, the mental labeling, classification, and appraisal of individuals by people with whom they come into contact are common, constant occurrences (Reynolds, 1979a). Auerbach (1971) found that adults often interpret early learning difficulties of children as primarily emotional disturbances, unrelated to learning problems. According to Bower (1974), children who start the first grade below the mean age of their classmates and are below average in the development of school readiness skills or have behaviour problems are more likely to be regarded as emotionally disturbed by school staff and are more likely to be referred to residential placement than their peers. The American Psychological Association (1970) acknowledges that such constant appraisal of individuals occurs at the informal level, and in an official position statement takes the stance that specialized, standardized psychological techniques have been developed to supersede our informal, often casual approach to the appraisal of others. The specialized psychological techniques available to the trained examiner add validity and utility to the results of such appraisals. The quantification of behaviour permits systematic comparisons of individuals' characteristics with those of a selected reference or norm group. It is not unreasonable to anticipate that the informal labeling of children so often indulged in by teachers and parents is substantially more harmful than accurate psychoeducational diagnostics intended to accrue beneficial activity toward the child. Should noncategorical funding for services to exceptional children become a reality (Gutkin & Tieger, 1979), or should the use of normative assessment ultimately be banned, the informal labeling process will continue and in all likelihood will exacerbate children's problems.

From the standpoint of cultural test bias issues, the question of labeling persons or not labeling persons is moot. Cultural test bias is concerned with the accuracy of such labels across some nominal grouping system (typically, race, sex, and SES have been the variables of interest). It is a question of whether race, sex, or any other demographic variable of interest influences the diagnostic process or the placement of an individual in special treatment programs, independent of the individual's cognitive, emotional, and behavioral status. Several well-designed studies have investigated the influences of race and SES on diagnosis and the placement recommendations of school psychologists (i.e., bias in test interpretation). One of the studies investigated teacher bias as well.

Frame (1979) investigated the accuracy of school psychologists' diagnoses and consistency of treatment plans within the USA, with regard to bias effects associated specifically with race and SES. In Frame's study, 24 school psychologists from a number of school districts diagnostically rated and provided treatment plans for hypothetical cases in which all information except race, SES, and the achievement level of the child's school was held constant. No differences in the accuracy of diagnosis (as defined by interrater reliability) occurred as a function of race or SES. Differences did occur with regard to treatment recommendations, however. With all other data held constant, lower SES Black children were less likely to be recommended for special education placement than their White counterparts or higher SES Black children. A more general trend was for higher SES children to be recommended for special class placement more often than children of lower SES.

In a similar vein, Matuszek and Oakland (1979) asked whether SES and race influenced teacher or psychologist placement recommendations, independent of other characteristics such as adaptive behavior, IQ, and classroom achievement levels. Matuszek and Oakland concluded that "The data from this study clearly indicate that they [psychologists] did not make different recomendations on the basis of race." Consistent with the results of Frame (1979), psychologists were more likely to recommend special class placement for high SES status children than for low SES children when other varibles were held constant. Teachers showed no bias in regard to special education placement recommendations on the basis of race or SES. Upon investigating special education placement recommendations as a function of minority group status (Black, native American, or Oriental), Tomlinson, Acker, Canter, and Lindborg (1977) reported that psychologists recommended special education resource services more frequently for minority than for White children. Placement in a special education class, however, was recommended more frequently for White than minority children. A rather extensive study of placement in classes for the educable mentally retarded (EMR) in California also failed to find any racist intent in the placement of minority children in special classes (Meyers, MacMillan, & Yoshida, 1978). In fact, the tendency was not to place Black children in special education classes, even though they might be failing in the regular classroom. An even earlier study by Mercer (1971), one of the major critics of IQ testing with minorities, reached the same conclusion.

The general tendency not to label Black children also extends to community mental health settings. Lewis, Balla, and Shanok (1979) reported that when Black adolescents were seen in mental health settings, behaviors symptomatic of schizophrenia, paranoia, and a variety of psychoneurotic disorders were frequently dismissed as only "cultural aberrations" appropriate to coping with the frustrations created by the antagonistic White culture. Lewis et al. (1979) further noted that White adolescents exhibiting similar behaviours were given psychiatric diagnoses and referred for therapy and/or residential placement. Lewis et al. contended that this failure to diagnose mental illness in the Black population acts as bias in the denial of appropriate services. A tendency for psychologists to reward depressed performance on cognitive tasks by Blacks and low SES groups as a "cultural aberration" has also been shown. An early empirical study by Nalven, Hofmann, and Bierbryer (1969) demonstrated that psychologists generally rated the "true intelligence" of Black and lower SES children higher than that of White and middle-class children with the same Wechsler Intelligence Scale for Children (WISC) IQ. This tendency to "overrate" the intellectual potential of Black and low SES children probably accounts, at least in part, for psychologists' reluctance to recommend special education placement for these children; it could also be viewed as a discriminatory denial of services, depending on whether the provision of services is considered beneficial or harmful to the individual. Despite the outcome of these and other studies, it is common to read that psychologists overdiagnose psychopathology in cultural groups outside the mainstream culture (e.g. Dana, 1993).

Bias by ethnicity in diagnosis of specific forms of affective disturbance has been the subject of fewer examinations in the literature. However, there is little evidence to suggest that ethnicity or SES independently influence clinical diagnoses such as autistic disorders or attention-deficit hyperactivity disorder (e.g., Cuccaro, Wright, Rhownd, & Abramson, 1996).

These studies clearly indicate that the demographic variables of race and SES do not, independent of other pupil characteristics, influence or bias psychologists' diagnostic or placement behavior in a manner that would cause Blacks or lower SES children to be labeled inaccurately or placed inappropriately or in disproportionate numbers in special education programs. The empirical evidence, rather, argues in the opposite direction: in the USA, Black and low SES children are less likely to be diagnosed as having a form of psychopathology than their White or higher SES peers with similar cognitive, behavioral, and emotional characteristics. The data simply do not support William's (1970) and others (e.g., Dana, 1993; Guilford Press, 1997; Padilla, 1988) charges that ethnic minorities are more likely to be overly diagnosed with a variety of psychopathological disorders.

10.03.6 THE PROBLEM OF DEFINITION

The definition of test bias has produced considerable continuing debate among measurement and assessment experts (Angoff, 1976; Bass, 1976; Bernal, 1975; Bond, 1981; Cleary et al., 1975; Cole & Moss, 1989; Cronbach, 1976; Dana, 1993; Darlington, 1978; Einhorn & Bass, 1970; Flaugher, 1978; Gordon, 1984; Gross & Su, 1975; Helms, 1992; Humphreys, 1973; Hunter & Schmidt, 1976, 1978; Jackson, 1980; Linn, 1976; McNemar, 1975; Moreland, 1996; Novick & Petersen, 1976; Padilla, 1988; Petersen & Novick, 1976; Reschly, 1980; Reynolds, 1978; 1982b, 1995; Reynolds & Brown, 1984; Sawyer, Cole, & Cole, 1976; Schmidt & Hunter, 1974; Thorndike, 1971). Although the resulting debate has generated a number of selection models with which to examine bias, selection models focus on the decision-making system and not on the test itself. The various selection models are discussed at some length in Hunter and Schmidt (1974), Hunter, Schmidt, and Rauschenberger (1984), Jensen (1980), Peterson and Novick (1976), and Ramsay (1979). The choice of a decision-making system (especially a system for educational decision-making) must ultimately be a societal one; as such, it will depend to a large extent on the value system and goals of the society. Thus, before a model for test use in selection (whether ultimately selection is for a treatment program, a job, a college, etc.) can be chosen, it must be decided whether the ultimate goal of selection is equality of opportunity, equality of outcome, or representative equality (these concepts are discussed in more detail in Nichols, 1978).

"Equality of opportunity" is a competitive model wherein selection is based on ability. As more eloquently stated by Lewontin (1970), under equality of opportunity, "true merit ... will be the criterion of men's earthly reward" (p. 92). "Equality of outcome" is a selection model based on ability deficits. Schooling provides a good model to illustrate these concepts that are also applicable to mental health. Compensatory and remedial programs are typically constructed on the basis of the equality-of-outcome model. Children of low ability or children believed to be a high risk for academic failure are selected for remedial, compensatory, or other special educational programs. Adults vying for jobs may be placed in specialized job training programs. In a strictly predictive sense, tests are used in a similar manner under both of these models. However, under equality of opportunity, selection is based on the prediction of a high level of criterion performance; under equality of outcome, selection is determined by the prediction of "failure" or a preselected low level of criterion performance. Interestingly, it is the failure of compensatory and remedial education programs to bring the disadvantaged learner to "average" levels of performance that resulted in the charges of test bias now in vogue.

The model of "representative equality" also relies on selection, but selection that is proportionate to numerical representation of subgroups in the population under consideration. Representative equality is typically thought to be independent of the level of ability within each group; however, models can be constructed that select from each subgroup the desired proportion of individuals (i) according to relative ability level of the group, (ii) independent of group ability, or (iii) according to some decision rule between these two positions. Even under the conditions of representative equality, it is imperative to employ a selection device (test) that will rank order individuals within groups in a reliable and valid manner. The best way to ensure fair selection under any of these models is to employ tests whose scores are equally reliable and equally valid for all groups concerned. The tests employed should also yield the most reliable and most valid scores for all groups under consideration. The question of test bias *per se* then becomes a question of test validity. Test use (i.e., fairness) may be defined as biased or nonbiased only by the societal value system; at present, this value system within the USA is leaning strongly toward some variant of the representative-equality selection model. In other sociopolitical structures, other models may be more appropriate. As noted above, all models are facilitated by the use of a nonbiased test. That is, the use of a test with equivalent cross-group validities makes for the most parsimonious selection model, greatly simplifying the creation and application of the selection model that has been chosen.

This leads to the essential definitional component of test bias. "Test bias" refers in a global sense to systematic error in the estimation of some "true" value for a group of individuals. The key word here is "systematic"; all measures contain error and in all cultural settings, but this error is assumed to be random unless shown to be otherwise. Bias investigation is a statistical inquiry that does not concern itself with culture loading, labeling effects, or test use/test fairness. Concerning the last of these, Jensen (1980) comments,

> [U]nbiased tests can be used unfairly and biased tests can be used fairly. Therefore, the concepts of bias and unfairness should be kept distinct ... [A] number of different, and often mutually contradictory, criteria for fairness have been proposed, and no amount of statistical or psychometric reasoning per se can possible settle any arguments as to which is best. (pp. 375–376)

There are three types of validity as traditionally conceived: content, construct, and predictive (or criterion-related). Test bias may exist under any or all of these categories of validity. Though no category of validity is completely independent of any other category, each is discussed separately here for the purposes of clarity and convenience. (All true evidence of validity is as likely as not to be construct validity, and other, more detailed divisions including this one are for convenience of discussion.) Frequently encountered in bias research are the terms "single-group validity" and "differential validity." Single-group validity refers to the phenomenon of a score interpretation being valid for one group but not another. Differential validity refers to a condition where an interpretation is valid for all groups concerned, but the degree of validity varies as a function of group membership. Although these terms have been most often applied to predictive or criterion-related validity (validity coefficients are then examined for significance and compared across groups), the concepts of single-group and differential validity are equally applicable to content and construct validity.

10.03.7 RESEARCH STRATEGIES AND RESULTS

The methodologies available for research into bias in mental tests have grown rapidly in number and sophistication since the 1970s. Extensive reviews of the questions to be addressed in such research and their corresponding methodologies are available in Berk (1982), Camilli and Shepard (1994), Jensen (1980), Reynolds (1982b, 1995), and Reynolds and Brown (1984). The most popular methods are reviewed below, along with a summary of findings from each area of inquiry (these summaries are based almost entirely on research with ethnic subcultures within the USA). The sections are organized primarily by methodology within each content area of research (i.e., research into content, construct, and predictive validity).

10.03.7.1 Bias in Content Validity

Bias in the item content of intelligence tests is one of the favorite topics of those who decry the use of standardized tests with minorities (e.g., Hilliard, 1979; Jackson, 1975; Williams, 1972; Wright & Isenstein, 1977). The earliest work in cultural test bias centered around content. Typically, critics review the items of a test and select specific items as being biased because: (i) the items ask for information that ethnic minority or disadvantaged persons have not had equal opportunity to learn; and/or (ii) the scoring of the items is improper, since the test author has arbitrarily decided on the only correct answer and ethnic minorities are inappropriately penalized for giving answers that would be correct in their own culture but not that of the test maker; and/or (iii) the wording of the questions is unfamiliar, and an ethnic minority person who may "know" the correct answer may not be able to respond because he or she does not understand the question. Each of these and related criticisms, when accurate, has the same basic empirical result: the item becomes relatively more difficult for ethnic minority group members than for the majority population, for example, an ethnic minority and a member of the majority culture with the same standing on the construct in question will respond differently to such biased items. This leads directly to a definition of content bias for aptitude tests that allows empirical assessment of the phenomenon. An item or subscale of a test is considered to be biased in content when it is demonstrated to be relatively more difficult for members of one group than for members of another when the general ability level of the groups being compared is held constant and no reasonable theoretical rationale exists to explain group differences on the item (or subscale) in question.

With regard to achievement tests, the issue of content bias is considerably more complex. Exposure to instruction, general ability level of the group, and the accuracy and specificity of the sampling of the domain of items are all important variables in determining whether the content of an achievement test is biased (see Schmidt, 1983). Research into item (or content) bias with achievement tests has typically, and perhaps mistakenly, relied on methodology appropriate for determining item bias in aptitude tests. Nevertheless, research examining both types of instruments for content bias has yielded quite comparable results. Items on personality tests may be perceived differently across cultures as well or appropriate responses may vary dramatically and quite properly deserve different interpretations cross-culturally. If so, the items will behave differently across groups for individuals with the same relative standing. This too is detectable through analyses of item response data across groups.

One method of locating "suspicious" test items requires that item difficulties be determined separately for each group under consideration. If any individual item or series of items appears to be exceptionally difficult for the members of any group, relative to other items in the test, the item is considered potentially biased and removed from the test. An early, widespread approach to identifying biased items involved analysis of variance (ANOVA) and several closely related procedures wherein the group X item interaction term is of interest (e.g., Angoff & Ford, 1973; Cardall & Coffman, 1964; Cleary & Hilton, 1968; Plake & Hoover, 1979; Potthoff, 1966; Stanley, 1969).

The definition of content bias set forth above actually requires that the differences between groups be the same for every item on the test. Thus, in the ANOVA procedure, the group X item interaction should not yield a significant result. Whenever the differences in items are not uniform (a significant group X item interaction does exist), one may contend that biased items exist. Earlier in this area of research, it was hoped that the empirical analysis of tests at the item level would result in the identification of a category of items having similar biased, and that such items could then be avoided in future test development (Flaugher, 1978). Very little similarity among items determined to be biased has been found. No one has been able to identify those characteristics of an item that cause the item to be biased. It does seem that poorly written, sloppy, and ambiguous items tend to be identified as biased with greater frequency than those items typically encountered in a well-constructed standardized instrument. The variable at issue then may be the item reliability. Item reliabilities are typically not large, and poorly written or ambiguous test items can easily have reliabilities approaching zero. Decreases in reliability are known to increase the probability of the occurrence of bias (Linn & Werts, 1971). Informal inventories and locally derived tests are much more likely to be biased than professionally written standardized tests that have been scrutinized for bias in the items and whose item characteristics are known.

Once items have been identified as biased under the procedures described above, attempts have been made to eliminate "test bias" by eliminating the offending items and rescoring the tests. As pointed out by Flaugher (1978) and Flaugher and Schrader (1978), however, little is gained by this tactic. Mean differences in performance between groups are affected only slightly, and aptitude and achievement tests become more difficult for everyone involved, since the eliminated items typically have moderate to low difficulty. When race X item interactions have been found, the interaction typically accounts for a very small proportion of variance. For example, in analyzing items on the WISC-R, Jensen (1976), Sandoval (1979), and Mille (1979) found the group X item interaction to account for only 2–5% of the variance in performance. Using a similar technique with the Wonderlic Personnel Test, Jensen (1977) found the race X item interaction to account for only about 5% of the test score variance. Thus, elimination of the offending items can be expected to have little, if any, significant effect. These analyses have been of a *post hoc* nature (i.e., after the tests have been standardized), however, and use of empirical methods for determining item bias during the test development phase (as with tests like the K-ABC and the TOMAL) is to be encouraged.

The ANOVA methodology is appealing conceptually but has some significant problems, even though it was the dominant methodological approach to the issue of item bias through the

1980s. Camilli and Shepard (1987) have provided convincing examples, albeit using contrived data, that ANOVA methods often miss biased items, in both directions, and identify some items as biased which are not. An algebraic demonstration of the reasons for this is provided in Camilli and Shepard (1994) who conclude that ANOVA should no longer be used.

Based upon their thorough and compelling analysis of methods for detecting biased items, Camilli and Shepard (1994) recommend methods derived from item response theory (IRT) to detect what has come to be known as differential item functioning (DIF). IRT models are conceptually similar to what other models such as ANOVA attempt. IRT is concerned principally with the probability of a particular response to a test item as a function of the examinee's relative position on the latent trait assessed by the scale to which the item belongs. IRT models to detect DIF are primarily superior to prior methods because they are less sample dependent and they allow one to estimate multiple item statistics more precisely than a technique such as ANOVA. Using item characteristic curves, DIF is more accurately and readily detected when the probability of a particular response changes as a function of some nominal variable (e.g., ethnicity or gender) for individuals with the same relative standing on the latent trait being assessed.

Early studies using other approaches for the detection of DIF using a partial correlation procedure developed independently by Stricker (1982) and Reynolds, Willson, and Chatman (1984) have found no systematic bias against American Blacks or against women on measures of English vocabulary. Willson, Nolan, Reynolds, and Kamphaus (1989), using the same partialling methodology, examined DIF of the mental processing scales of the Kaufman Assessment Battery for Children, concluding " ... there appears to be little evidence of systematic race or gender bias ... " (p. 289).

With multiple-choice tests, another level of complexity is added to the examination of content bias. With a multiple-choice question, three or four distractors are typically given in addition to the correct response. Distractors may be examined for their attractiveness (the relative frequency with which they are chosen) across groups. When distractors are found to be disproportionately attractive for members of any particular group, the item may be defined as biased. When items are constructed to have an equal distribution of responses to each distractor for the total test population, then chi-square can be used to examine the distribution of choices for each distractor for each group (e.g., Burrill, 1975).

Jensen (1976) investigated the distribution of wrong responses for two multiple-choice intelligence tests, the Peabody Picture Vocabulary Test (PPVT) and Raven's Progressive Matrices (the Raven). Each of these tests was individually administered to 600 White and 400 Black children between the ages of six and 12. The analysis of incorrect responses for the PPVT indicated that the errors were distributed in a nonrandom fashion over the distractors for a large number of items. However, no racial bias in response patterns occurred, since the disproportionate choice of distractors followed the same pattern for Blacks and Whites. On the Raven, Blacks make different types of errors than Whites, but only on a small number of items. Jensen followed up these items and compared the Black response pattern to the response pattern of White children at a variety of age levels. For every item showing differences in Black–White response patterns, the Black response could be duplicated by the response patterns of Whites approximately two years younger than Blacks.

Veale and Foreman (1983) have advocated inspecting multiple-choice tests for bias in distractor or "foil" response distributions as a means of refining tests *before* they are finalized for the marketplace. They note that there are many instances whereby unbiased external criteria (such as achievement or ability) or culturally valid tests are not readily accessible for detecting bias in the measure under study. Veale and Foreman add that inspection of incorrect responses to distractor items can often lead to greater insight concerning cultural bias in any given question than would inspection of percentage of correct responses across groups. Veale and Foreman (1983) provide the statistical analyses for their "overpull probability model" along with the procedures for measuring cultural variation and diagraming the source of bias within any given item.

Investigation of item potential sources of bias during test development is certainly not restricted to multiple-choice items and methods such as those outlined by Veale and Foreman (1983). The possibilities are numerous (see Camilli & Shepard, 1994; Jensen, 1980, chap. 9). For example, Scheuneman (1987) has used the results of linear methods on Graduate Record Examination (GRE) item data to show interesting influences on Black–White performance when specific item characteristics (e.g., vocabulary content, one true or one false answer to be selected, diagrams to be used or not used, use of antonym items, etc.) are uniformly investigated. Although Scheuneman indicates that future research of this type should reduce the number of variables to address (there are 16 hypotheses therein), the results nonetheless suggest that bias methodology is a viable way in which to determine whether differential effects can "be demonstrated through the manipulation of relatively stable characteristics of test items" (p. 116). Scheuneman presented pairs of items, with the designated characteristic of a question format under study present in one item and absent or modified in the other. Paired experimental items were administered in the experimental section of the GRE General Test, given in December 1982. Results indicated that certain "item elements'—common in general form to a variety of questions—appeared to have a differential impact on Black and White performance. For example, significant group version interactions were seen for one correct true vs. one correct false response and for adding/modifying prefixes/suffixes to the stimulus word in antonym items. The question is thus raised as to whether the items showing differential impact are measuring the content domain (e.g., veral, quantitative, or analytial thinking) as opposed to an aspect of "element" within the presentation to some degree.

Another approach to the identification of biased items has been pursued by Jensen (1976). According to Jensen, if a test contains items that are disproportionately difficult for one group of examinees as compared to another, the correlation of *P* decrements between adjacent items will be low for the two groups. ("*P* decrement" refers to the difference in the difficulty index, *P*, from one item of a test to the next least or most item. Typically, ability test items are arranged in ascending order of difficulty.) Jensen (1974, 1976) also contends that if a test contains biased items, the correlation between the rank order of item difficulties for one race with another will also be low. Jensen (1974, 1976, 1977) calculated cross-racial correlations of item difficulties for large samples of Black and White children on five major intelligence tests: the PPVT, the Raven, the Revised Stanford–Binet Intelligence Scale Form L-M, the WISC-R, and the Wonderlic Personnel Test. Cross-racial correlations of *P* decrements were reported for several of the scales. Jensen's results are summarized in Table 1, along with the results of several other investigators also employing Jensen's methodology.

As is readily apparent in Table 1, little evidence to support any consistent content bias within any of the scales investigated was found. The consistently large magnitude of the cross-racial correlations of *P* decrements is impressive and indicates a general lack of content bias in the instuments as a whole. As previously noted, however, some individual items were identified as biased, yet they collectively accounted for only 2–5% of the variance in performance differences and showed no detectable pattern in item content.

This method has proved popular with some test publishers who desire to look at the items on a test as a group, despite the fact this approach may be overly sensitive due to the instability of estimates of *P* values (which would cause the correlation to be spuriously low). Using the most recent version of the Detroit Tests of Learning Aptitude (DTLA-3; Hammill, 1991), Hammill reported correlations of *P* decrements exceeding 0.90 for all subtests with most exceeding 0.95. Similar results have been reported for other aptitude measures. On the 14 subtests of the Test of Memory and Learning (TOMAL; Reynolds & Bigler, 1994), Reynolds and Bigler report correlations across *P* decrements by gender and ethnicity that all exceed 0.90 with most again above 0.95.

Another approach to this question is to use the partial correlation between a demographic or other nominal variable and item score, where the correlation between total test score and the variable of interest has been removed from the relationship. If a significant partial correlation exists, say, between race and an item score after the race–total test score relationship has been partialed, then the item is performing differentially across race within ability level. Bias has been demonstrated at this point under the definition offered above. Use of the partial correlation (typically a partial point-biserial *r*) is a simple yet powerful item bias detection approach, but its development is relatively recent and its use not yet common. The partial correlation approach also does not have the problems of ANOVA methods. An example of its application may be found in Reynolds, Willson, and Chatman (1984).

A common practice has been a return to including expert judgment by professionals and members of minority groups in the item selection for new psychological and educational tests. This approach was used in development of the K-ABC, the revision of the Wechsler Preschool and Primary Scale of Intelligence (WPPSI-R), the PPVT-R, PPVT-III, and a number of other contemporary tests. The practice typically asks for an "armchair" inspection of individual items as a means of locating and purging biased items in the measure under development. Since, as previously noted, no detectable pattern or common characteristic of content of individual items statistically shown to be biased has been observed (given reasonable care in the item-writing stage), it seems reasonable to question the "armchair" approach to determining biased

Table 1 Cross-racial analysis of content bias for five major intelligence scales.

Scale	Cross-racial correlation of rank order of item difficulties[a]	
	Black–White correlations[b]	White–Mexican–American correlations[b]
Peabody Picture Vocabulary Test (Jensen, 1974)	0.99 (0.79), 0.98 (0.65)	0.98 (0.78), 0.98 (0.66)
Raven's Progressive Matrices (Jensen, 1974)	0.99 (0.98), 0.99 (0.96)	0.99 (0.99), 0.99 (0.97)
Stanford-Binet Intelligence Scale (Jensen, 1976)	0.96	
Wechsler Intelligence Scale for Children-Revised		
(Jensen, 1976)	0.95	
(Sandoval, 1979)[c]	0.98 (0.87)	0.99 (0.91)
(Mille, 1979) (1949 WISC)	0.96, 0.95	
Wonderlic Personnel Test (Jensen, 1977)	0.94 (0.81)	

[a] Correlation of *P* decrements across race is included in parentheses if reported. [b] Where two sets of correlations are presented, data were reported separately for males and females and are listed males first. The presence of a single correlation indicates that data were pooled across gender. [c] Median values for the 10 WISC-R subtests excluding Digit Span and Coding.

items. The bulk of scientific data since the pioneering work of McGurk (1951) has not supported the position that anyone can—upon surface inspection—detect the degree to which any given item will function differentially across groups (Shepard, 1982). Several researchers since McGurk's time have identified items as being disproportionately more difficult for minority group members than for members of the majority culture and have subsequently compared their results with a panel of expert judges. The data have provided some interesting results.

Although examples of the failure of judges to identify biased items now abound (Camilli & Shepard, 1994) and show that judges are right about an item about as often as they are wrong, two studies demonstrate this failure most clearly. After identifying the eight least racially discriminating items on the Wonderlic Personnel Test, Jensen (1976) asked panels of five Black psychologists and five White psychologists to sort out the eight most and eight least discriminating items when only these 16 items were presented to them. The judges sorted the items at a level no better than chance. Sandoval and Mille (1980) conducted a somewhat more extensive analysis, using items from the WISC-R. These two researchers had 38 Black, 22 Mexican-American, and 40 White university students from Spanish, history, and education classes identify items from the WISC-R that would be more difficult for a minority child than a White child and items that would be equally difficult for each group. A total of 45 WISC-R items were presented to each judge; these items included the 15 most difficult items for Blacks as compared to Whites, the 15 most difficult items for Mexican-Americans as compared to Whites, and the 15 items showing the most nearly identical difficulty indices for minority and White children. The judges were asked to read each question and determine whether they thought the item was: (i) easier for minority than for White children, (ii) easier for White than for minority children, or (iii) of equal difficulty for White and minority children. Sandoval and Mille's (1980) results indicated that the judges were not able to differentiate accurately between items that were more difficult for minorities and items that were of equal difficulty across groups. The effects of the judges' ethnic background on the accuracy of item bias judgments were also considered. Minority and nonminority judges did not differ in their ability to identify accurately biased items, nor did they differ with regard to the type of incorrect identification they tended to make. Sandoval and Mille's (1980) two major conclusions were that "(1) judges are not able to detect items which are more difficult for a minority child than an Anglo child, and (2) the ethnic background of the judge makes no difference in accuracy of item selection for minority children" (p. 6). In each of these studies, the most extreme items were used, which should have given the judges an advantage.

Anecdotal evidence is also available to refute the assumption that armchair analyses of test bias in item content are accurate. The most widely cited example of a biased intelligence test item is item 6 of the WISC-R Comprehension subtest: "What is the thing to do if a boy (girl) much smaller than yourself starts to fight with you?" This item is generally considered to be biased against US Black children in particular, because of the scoring criteria. According to the item's critics, the most logical response for a Black child is to "fight back," yet this is a 0-point response. The correct (2-point) response is to walk away and avoid fighting with the child—a response that critics claim invites disaster in the Black culture, where children are taught to fight back and would not "know" the "correct White response." Black responses to this item have been investigated empirically in several studies, with the same basic results: the item is relatively easier for Black children than for White children. When all items on the WISC-R are ranked separately according to difficulty level for Blacks and Whites, this item is the 42nd least difficult item (where 1 represents the easiest item) for Black children and the 47th least difficult for White children (Jensen, 1976). Mille (1979), in a large *N* study of bias, reached a similar conclusion, stating that this item "is relatively easier for Blacks than it is for Whites" (p. 163). The results of these empirical studies with large samples of Black and White children in the USA are unequivocal: when matched for overall general intellectual skill, more Black than White children will get this item correct—the very item most often singled out as a blatant example of the inherent bias of intelligence test against Blacks, but so selected using anecdotal impressions and sterotypical views of Black cultural even by Black judges (see also Reynolds & Brown, 1984).

Even without empirical support for its accuracy, a number of prestigious writers support the continued use of the "face validity" approach of using a panel of minority judges to identify "biased" test items (Anastasi, 1986; Kaufman, 1979; Sandoval & Mille, 1979). Those who support the continued use of this technique see it as a method of gaining greater rapport with the public. As pointed out by Sandoval and Mille (1979), "Public opinion, whether it is supported by empirical findings, or based on emotion, can serve as an obstacle to the use of a measurement instrument" (p. 7). The elimination of items that are offensive or otherwise objectionable to any substantive segment of the population for whom the test is intended seems an appropriate action that may aid in the public's acceptance of new and better psychological asessment tools. However, the subjective-judgment approach should not be allowed to supplant the use of more sophisticated analyses in the determination of biased items. The subjective approach should serve as a supplemental procedure, and items identified through this method (provided that some interrater agreement can be obtained—an aspect of the subjective method yet to be demonstrated) as objectionable can be eliminated when a psychometrically equivalent (or better) item can be obtained as a replacement and the intent of the item is kept intact (e.g., with a criterion-referenced measure, the new item must be designed to measure the same objective).

Researchers such as Tittle (1982) have stressed that the possibility of and need for cooperation between those advocating statistical validity and those advocating face validity in nonbiased test construction is greater than one might think, given the above-cited research. Judgmental analysis allows for the perception of fairness in items, tests, and evaluations, and this perception should not be taken lightly. Tittle (1982) argues that "judgmental methods arise from a different, nonstatistical ground. In examining fairness or bias primarily on statistical grounds, we may again be witnessing a technical solution to a problem that is broader than the technical issues" (p. 34). Cronbach (1980) does not find the issue of fairness as determined by subjective judgment to be outside the realm of test validation. Cronbach states, "The politicization of testing ought not [to] be surprising. Test data influence the fortunes of individuals and the support given to human service programs" (p. 100). Tittle (1975, 1982) argues that the general field of test development requires greater consensus regarding specific, multidimensional steps taken in formulating "fair" measures, because "fairness" in testing will never be realistically viewed by the public from a unidimensional statistical standpoint.

Considerably less work has been conducted in all areas of bias relative to personality testing, where there would appear to be greater opportunity for cultural, social, and ethnic factors to act to produce bias. Research on item bias of personality measures, though less extensive than with aptitude measures, has produced results similar to those with aptitude measures (see especially Moran, 1990; Reynolds, in press; Reynolds & Harding, 1983).

Research evaluating behavior rating scales is also meager but at present supports the use of parent ratings in the diagnosis of childhood psychopathology independent of the child's ethnic background (e.g., see Mayfield & Reynolds, in press). A common set of items seems to measure consistently a variety of personality and behavioral traits for Whites, Blacks, and various Hispanic and Latin population residing in the USA (James, 1995; Mayfield & Reynolds, in press; Reynolds & Kamphaus, 1992).

Thus far, this section has focused on the identification of biased items. Several studies evaluating other hypotheses have provided data that are relevant to the issue of content bias of psychological tests, specifically the WISC-R (although now largely superseded in practice by WISC-III, little data regarding bias are available specifically on this new scale).

Jensen and Figueroa (1975) investigated Black–White differences in mental test scores as a function of differences in Level I (rote learning and memory) and Level II (complex cognitive processing) abilities. These researchers tested a large number of Blacks and Whites on the WISC-R Digit Span subtest and then analyzed the data separately for digits forward and digits backward. The content of the digits forward and digits backward procedures is the same. Thus, if score differences are due only to bias in content of the item validity, score differences across race should remain constant for the two tasks. On the other hand, since the information-processing demands of the two tasks are quite different (Reynolds, 1997b), the relative level of performance on the two tasks should not be the same, as Blacks and Whites differ in their ability to process information according to the demands of the two tasks. Jensen and Figueroa (1975) found the latter to be the case. The Black–White score difference on digits backward was more than twice the magnitude of the difference for digits forward. Granted, this methodology can provide only indirect evidence regarding the content validity of an instrument; however, its importance is in providing a different view of the issues and an alternative research strategy. Since the Jensen and Figueroa results do not indicate any content bias in the Digit Span subtest, they add to a growing body of literature that strongly suggests the lack of cultural bias in well-constructed, standardized tests, and their generalization within a common language and with some cultural diversity, at least for Black and for White US cultures.

Another study (Reynolds & Jensen, 1983) examined each of the 12 WISC-R subtests for cultural bias against Blacks using a variation of the group X item ANOVA methodology discussed earlier. Reynolds and Jensen matched 270 Black children with 270 White children from the WISC-R standardization sample on the basis of gender and WISC-R Full Scale IQ. Matching the two groups of children on the bases of the Full Scale IQ essentially equated the two groups for *g*. Therefore, examining Black–White differences in performance on each subtest of the WISC-R made it possible to determine which, if any, of the subtests were disproportionately difficult for Blacks or Whites. A summary of the Reynolds and Jensen (1983) results is presented in Table 2. Blacks exceeded Whites in performance on two subtests: Digit Span and Coding. Whites exceeded Blacks in performance on three subtests: Comprehension, Object Assembly, and Mazes. A trend was apparent for Blacks to perform at a higher level on the Arithmetic subtest, while Whites tended to exceed Blacks on the Picture Arrangement subtest. Although these results can be interpreted to indicate bias in several of the WISC-R subtests, the actual differences were very small (typically of the order of 0.10–0.15 standard deviation), and the amount of variance in performance associated with ethnic group membership was less than 5% in each case. The results are also reasonably consistent with Jensen's theory on mental test score differences and their relationship to Level I and Level II abilities. The Digit Span and Coding subtests are clearly the best measures of Level I abilities on the WISC-R, while Comprehension, Object Assembly, and Mazes are more closely associated with Level II abilities. Digit Span and Coding are also tasks adversely affected by increases in an examinee's anxiety level. The relatively higher level of performance by the Black children on these tasks is also inconsistent with arguments that the testing circumstance is more unfamiliar and more anxiety provoking to minority children relative to their White counterparts.

From a large number of studies employing a wide range of methodologies, a relatively clear picture emerges: content bias in well-prepared standardized tests is irregular in its occurrence, and no common characteristics of items that are found to be biased can be ascertained by expert judges (minority or nonminority). The variance in group score differences on mental tests associated with ethnic group membership when content bias has been found is relatively small (typically ranging from 2% to 5%). Even this small amount of bias has been seriously questioned, as Hunter (1975) describes such findings basically as methodological artifacts.

Harrington (1975, 1976) argued that traditional statistical methods would not detect DIF and that tests are designed in a psychometrically flawed manner so as to always favor the numerically superior group in a population. Although Harrington's research and logic are impressive, his results have not held and the Harrington Effect is not seen in a variety of works (e.g., Bayley, 1969; Beauchamp, Sammuels, & Griffore, 1974; Hickman & Reynolds, 1986; James, 1995).

Although the search for common "biased" item characteristics will continue, and psychologists must pursue the public relations issues of face validity, "armchair" claims of cultural bias in aptitude tests have found no empirical support in a large number of actuarial studies contrasting the performance of a variety of racial groups on items and subscales of the most

Table 2 Means, standard deviations, and univariate *F*s for comparison of performance on specific WISC-R subtests by groups of Blacks and Whites matched for WISC-R full scale IQ.

	Blacks		*Whites*				
WISC-R variable	$\bar{X}$	*SD*	$\bar{X}$	*SD*	D^a	F^b	*p*
Information	8.40	2.53	8.24	2.62	−0.16	0.54	NS
Similarities	8.24	2.78	8.13	2.78	−0.11	0.22	NS
Arithmetic	8.98	2.62	8.62	2.58	−0.36	2.52	0.10
Vocabulary	8.21	2.61	8.27	2.58	+0.06	0.06	NS
Comprehension	8.14	2.40	8.58	2.47	+0.44	4.27	0.05
Digit Span	9.51	3.09	8.89	2.83	+0.62	6.03	0.01
Picture Completion	8.49	2.88	8.60	2.58	+0.11	0.18	NS
Picture Arrangement	8.45	2.92	8.79	2.89	+0.34	1.78	0.01
Block Design	8.06	2.54	8.33	2.76	+0.27	1.36	NS
Object Assembly	8.17	2.90	8.68	2.70	+0.51	4.41	0.05
Coding	9.14	2.81	8.65	2.80	−0.49	4.30	0.05
Mazes	8.69	3.14	9.19	2.98	+0.50	3.60	0.05
Verbal IQ	89.63	12.13	89.61	12.07	−0.02	0.04	NS
Performance IQ	89.29	12.22	90.16	11.67	+0.87	0.72	NS
Full Scale IQ	88.61	11.48	88.96	11.35	+0.35	0.13	NS

NS, not significant.
[a] White $\bar{X}$–Black $\bar{X}$ difference. [b] Degrees of freedom = 1538.

widely employed intelligence and achievement scales in the USA; neither differential for single-group validity has been demonstrated. However, these results apply only to groups where a common language exists among examinees. Personality and interest measures fare likewise but there is less good research available for such tests. Test translations are a different issue and required a different line of study altogether.

10.03.7.2 Bias in Construct Validity

There is no single method for the accurate determination of the construct validity of educational and psychological tests. Defining bias in construct validity thus requires a general statement that can be researched from a variety of viewpoints with a broad range of methodologies. The following rather parsimonious definition is proffered: bias exists in regard to construct validity when a test is shown to measure different hypothetical traits (psychological constructs) for one group than for another; that is differing interpretations of a common performance are shown to be appropriate as a function of ethnicity, gender, or another variable of interest, one typically but not necessarily nominal.

As befits the concept of construct validity, many different methods have been employed to examine existing tests for potential bias in construct validity. One of the most popular and necessary empirical approaches to investigating construct validity is factor analysis (Anastasi, 1982; Cronbach, 1970). Factor analysis as a procedure identifies clusters of test items or clusters of subtests of psychological or educational tests that correlate highly with one another, and less so or not at all with other subtests or items. It thus allows one to determine patterns of interrelationships of performance among groups of individuals. For example, if several subtests of an intelligence scale load highly on (are members of) the same factor, then if a group of individuals score high on one of these subtests, they would be expected to score at a high level on other subtests that load highly on that factor. Psychologists attempt to determine, through a review of the test content and correlates of performance on the factor in question, what psychological trait underlies performance; or, in a more hypothesis-testing approach, they will make predictions concerning the pattern of factor loadings. Dana (1993) notes that factor analysis across various cultural groups can be a useful means of examining the cross-cultural validity of tests of personality, behavior, or cognitive skill. Dana argues that when "... the factor dimensions resulting from different factor analytic methods are stable, and therefore present an invariant structure across cultures, then cross-cultural validity may be inferred" (1993, p. 101). Reynolds (1982a, 1982b) has made similar albeit more detailed arguments as have others in specific domains such as intelligence. Hilliard (1979), one of the more vocal critics of IQ tests on the basis of cultural bias, has pointed out one of the potential areas of bias in comparisons of the factor-analytic results of tests across races:

> If the IQ test is a valid and reliable test of "innate" ability or abilities, then the factors which emerge on a given test should be the same from one population to another, since "intelligence" is asserted to be a set of mental processes. Therefore, while the configuration of scores of a particular group on the factor profile would be expected to differ, logic would dictate that the factors themselves would remain the same. (p. 53)

Although researchers do not necessarily agree that identical factor analytic results across groups speak to the innateness of the traits being measured, consistent factor-analytic results across populations do provide strong evidence that whatever is being measured by the instrument is being measured in the same manner and is, in fact, the same latent construct within each group. The information derived from comparative factor analysis across populations is directly relevant to the use of educational and psychological tests in diagnosis and other decision-making functions. Psychologists, in order to make consistent interpretations of test score data, must be certain that a test measures the same variable across populations.

Two basic approaches, each with a number of variations have been employed to compare factor-analytic results across populations. The first and more popular approach asks how similar the results are for each group; the second and less popular approach asks whether the results show a statistically significant difference between groups. The most sophisticated approach to the latter question has been the foundational work of Jöreskog (1969, 1971) in simultaneous factor analysis in several populations and now basically represented in the LISREL series of computer programs. However, little has been done with the latter approach within the context of test bias research. Mille (1979) has demonstrated the use of a simpler method (actually developed by Jensen and presented in detail in Jensen, 1980) for testing the significance of the difference between factors for two populations.

A number of techniques have been developed to measure the similarity of factors across groups. The two most common methods of determining factorial similarity or factorial invariance involve the direct comparison of factor loadings across groups. The two primary techniques for this comparison are (i) the calculation of a coefficient of congruence (Harman, 1976) between the loadings of corresponding factors for two groups, and (ii) the simple calculation of a Pearson product-moment coefficient of correlation between the factor loadings of the corresponding factors. The latter technique, though used with some frequency, is less satisfactory than the use of the coefficient of congruence, since in the comparison of factor loadings certain of the assumptions underlying the Pearson *r* may be violated. When one is determining the degree of similarity of factors, a value of 0.90 or greater is typically, though arbitrarily, taken to indicate equivalent factors (factorial invariance). However, the most popular methods of calculating factorial similarity produce quite similar results (Reynolds & Harding, 1983), at least in large *n* studies.

In contrast to Hilliard's (1979) strong statement that studies of factorial similarity across race have not been reported in the technical literature on IQ, a number of such studies have appeared dealing with a number of different tests. The focus here is primarily on studies comparing factor-analytic results across ethnic groups in the USA for aptitude tests, since these are the most controversial of tests.

Because the WISC (Wechsler, 1949) and its successor, the WISC-R (Wechsler, 1974; now superseded by the WISC-III, but as yet no such bias research is available on the latter scale), have been the most widely employed individual intelligence tests with school-age children in much of the world, it is appropriate that the cross-race structure of these two instruments has received extensive investigation for both normal and referral populations of children. Using a large, random sample, Reschly (1978) compared the factor structure of the WISC-R across four racially identifiable groups: Whites, Blacks, Mexican-Americans, and native American Papagos, all from the southwestern USA. Consistent with the findings of previous researchers with the 1949 WISC (Lindsey, 1967; Silverstein, 1973), Reschly (1978) reported substantial congruency of factors across races when the two-factor solutions were compared (the two-factor solution typically reiterated Wechsler's *a priori* grouping of the subtests on to a Verbal and a Performance, or nonverbal, scale). The 12 coefficients of congruence for comparisons of the two-factor solution across all combinations of racial groupings ranged only from 0.97 to 0.99, denoting factorial equivalence of this solution across groups. Reschly also compared three-factor solutions (three-factor solutions typically include Verbal Comprehension, Perceptual Organization, and Freedom from Distractibility factors), finding congruence only between Whites and Mexican-Americans. These findings are also consistent with previous research with the WISC (Mille, 1979; Semler & Iscoe, 1966), an intelligence scale originally developed and normed on an all-White sample.

The *g* factor present in the WISC-R was shown to be congruent across race, as was also demonstrated by Mille (1979) for the WISC. Reschly (1978) concluded that the usual interpretation of the WISC-R Full Scale IQ as a measure of overall intellectual ability appears to be equally appropriate for Whites, Blacks, Mexican-Americans, and Native American Papagos. Jensen (1985) has presented compelling data indicating that the Black-White discrepancy seen in major tests of aptitude reflects primarily the g factor. Reschly also concluded that the Verbal-Performance scale distinction on the WISC-R is equally appropriate across race and that there is strong evidence for the integrity of the WISC-R's construct validity as a measure of intelligence for a variety of populations.

Support for Reschly's (1978) conclusions is available from a variety of other studies of the WISC and WISC-R. Applying a hierarchical factor-analytic method developed by Wherry and Wherry (1969), Vance and Wallbrown (1978) factor analyzed the intercorrelation matrix of the WISC-R subtests for 150 referred Blacks from the Appalachian region of the USA. The two-factor hierarchical solution determined for Vance and Wallbrown's (1978) Blacks was highly similar to hierarchical factor solutions determined for the standardization samples of the Wechsler scales generally (Blaha, Wallbrown, & Wherry, 1975; Wallbrown, Blaha, & Wherry, 1973). Vance and Wallbrown's (1978) results with the WISC-R are also consistent with a previous hierarchical factor analysis with the 1949 WISC for a group of disadvantaged Blacks and Whites (Vance, Huelsman, & Wherry, 1976).

Several studies comparing the WISC-R factor structure across races for normal and referral populations of children have also provided increased support for the generality of Reschly's (1978) conclusions and the results of the other investigators cited above. Oakland and Feigenbaum (1979) factor analyzed the 12 WISC-R subtests' intercorrelations separately for stratified (race, age, sex, SES) random samples of normal White, Black, and Mexican-American children from an urban school district of the northwestern USA. Pearson *r*'s were calculated between corresponding factors for each group. For the *g* factor, the Black–White correlation between factor loadings was 0.95, the Mexican-American White correlation was 0.97, and the Black Mexican-American correlation was 0.96. Similar comparisons across all WISC-R variables produced correlations ranging only from 0.94 to 0.99. Oakland and Feigenbaum concluded that the results of their factor analyses "do not reflect bias with respect to construct validity for these three racial-ethnic ... groups" (1979, p.973).

Gutkin and Reynolds (1981) determined the factorial similarity of the WISC-R for groups of Black and White children from the WISC-R standardization sample. This study is particularly important to examine in determining the construct validity of the WISC-R across races, because of the sample employed in the investigation. The sample included 1868 White and 305 Black children obtained in a stratified random sampling procedure designed to mimic the 1970 US census data on the basis of age, sex, race, SES, geographic region of residence, and community size. Similarity of the WISC-R factor structure across race was investigated by comparing the Black and White groups for the two- and three-factor solutions on (i) the magnitude of unique variances, (ii) the pattern of subtest loadings on each factor, (iii) the portion of total variance accounted for by common factor variance, and (iv) the percentage of common factor variance accounted for by each factor. Coefficients of congruence comparing the unique variances, the *g* factor, the two-factor solutions, and the three-factor solutions across races all achieved a value of 0.99. The portion of total variance accounted for by each factor was the same in both the two- and three-factor racial groups. Gutkin and Reynolds (1981) concluded that for White and Black children the WISC-R factor structure was essentially invariant, and that no evidence of single-group or differential construct validity could be found. Subsequent studies comparing the WISC-R factor structure for referral populations of White and Mexican-American children have also strongly supported the construct validity of the WISC-R across races (e.g., Dean, 1979b; Gutkin & Reynolds, 1980).

DeFries et al. (1974) administered 15 mental tests to large samples of Americans of Japanese and Chinese ancestry. After examining the pattern of intercorrelations among the 15 tests for each of these two ethnic groups, DeFries et al. concluded that the cognitive organization of the two groups was virtually identical. In reviewing this study, Willerman (1979) concluded that "The similarity in factorial structure [between the two groups] suggests that the manner in which the tests are constructed by the subjects is similar regardless of ethnicity and that the tests are measuring the same mental abilities in the two groups" (p. 468). At the adult level, Kaiser (1986) and Scholwinski (1985) have analyzed the Wechsler Adult Intelligence Scale-Revised (WAIS-R; Wechsler, 1981) and reported substantial similarity between factor structures for Black and White samples obtained from the WAIS-R standardization data.

At the preschool level, factor-analytic results also tend to show consistency of construct validity across races, though the results are less clear-cut. In a comparison of separate factor analyses of the McCarthy Scales of Children's Abilities (McCarthy, 1972) for groups of Black and White children, Kaufman and DiCuio (1975) concluded that the McCarthy Scales showed a high degree of factorial similarity between the two races. The conclusion was not straightforward, however. Four factors were found for the Blacks and three for the Whites. Kaufman and DiCuio based their conclusion on factorial similarity on the finding that each "White" factor had a coefficient of congruence of 0.85–0.93 with one "Black" factor. One Black factor on the McCarthy Scales had no White counterpart with a coefficient of congruence beyond 0.74 (the Memory factor), and the Black and White Motor factors showed a coefficient of congruence of only 0.85.

When investigating the factor structure of the WPPSI across race, Kaufman and Hollenbeck (1974) found much "cleaner" factors for Blacks and Whites than with the McCarthy Scales. The two factors, essentially mirroring Wechsler's Verbal and Performance scales, were virtually identical between the races. Both factors also appear closely related to the hierarchical factor solution presented by Wallbrown at al. (1973) for Blacks and Whites on the WPPSI. When comparing factor analyses of the Goodenough–Harris Human Figure Drawing Test scoring item, Merz (1970) found highly similar factor structures for Blacks, Whites, Mexican-Americans, and native Americans.

Other investigators have found differences across races in the factor structures of several tests designed for preschool and primary-grade children. Goolsby and Frary (1970) factor-analyzed the Metropolitan Readiness Test (MRT) together for separate groups of Blacks and Whites, finding differences in the factor structure of this grouping of tests across races. When evaluating the experimental edition of the Illinois Test of Psycholinguistic Abilities, Leventhal and Stedman (1970) noted differences in the factor structure of this battery for Blacks and Whites. Two more studies have clarified somewhat the issue of differential construct validity of preschool tests across race.

The MRT (Hildreth, Griffith, & McGauvran, 1969) is one of the most widely employed of all preschool screening measures in the USA, and its 1969 version is composed of six subtests: Word Meaning, Listening, Matching, Letter Naming, Numbers, and Copying. Reynolds (1979b) had previously shown this to be essentially a one-factor (general Readiness) instrument. In a subsequent study, Reynolds (1979c) compared the general factor making up the MRT across races (Blacks and Whites) and genders. Substantial congruence was noted: coefficients of congruence across each pair of race–sex groupings ranged only from 0.92 to 0.99, with the lowest coefficient derived from the intraracial comparison for White females and White males. Eigenvalues, and subsequently the proportion of variance accounted for by the factor, were also highly similar for the race–sex groupings. The lack of differential or single-group construct validity across sex has also been demonstrated with aptitude tests for school-age children (Reynolds & Gutkin, 1980c).

In a more comprehensive study employing seven major preschool tests (the McCarthy Draw-a-Design and Draw-a-Child subtests, the Lee-Clark Reading Readiness tests, The Tests of Basic Experiences Language and Mathematics subtests, the Preschool Inventory-Revised Edition, and the MRT), Reynolds (1980a) reached a similar conclusion. A two-factor solution was determined with this battery for each of the four race–sex groups as above. Coefficients of congruence ranged only from 0.95 to 0.99 for the two factors, and the average degree of intercorrelation was essentially the same for all groups, as were eigenvalues and the percentage of variance accounted for by the factors. Reynolds (1980a) again concluded that the abilities being measured were invariant across race and that there was no evidence of differential or single-group construct validity of preschool tests across races or genders. The clear trend in studies of preschool tests' construct validity across race (and sex) is to uphold validity across groups. Such findings add support to the use of existing preschool screening measures with Black and White children of both sexes in the very necessary process of early identification (Reynolds, 1979a) of potential learning and behavior problems.

Taken individually but especially as a whole, these various cross-group factor analytic studies contradict sharply Helms' (1992) assertion that Black and White groups within the USA have significantly different latent cognitive structures. These results argue in favor of a common human organization of abilities and neuropsychological processes among the many ethnic groups studied thus far. Although majority–minority culturally related differences in level of performance differ in various ways across many ethnic groups, a common organization of latent ability structures seems clearly evident at this time.

As is appropriate for studies of construct validity, comparative factor analysis has not been the only method of determining whether single-group or differential validity exists. Another method of investigation involves comparing internal-consistency reliability estimates across groups. Internal-consistency reliability is determined by the degree to which the items are all measuring a similar construct. To be unbiased with regard to construct validity, internal-consistency estimates should be approximately equal across races. This characteristic of tests has been investigated with Blacks, Whites, and Mexican-Americans for a number of popular aptitude tests within the US population.

With groups of Black and White adults, Jensen (1977) calculated internal-consistency estimates (using the Kuder–Richardson 21 formula) for the Wonderlic Personnel Test (a frequently used employment/aptitude test). Kuder–Richardson 21 values of 0.86 and 0.88 were found, respectively, for Blacks and Whites. Using Hoyt's formula, Jensen (1974) determined internal-consistency estimates of 0.96 on the PPVT for each of three groups of children: Blacks, Whites, and Mexican-Americans. When children were categorized by gender within each racial grouping, the values ranged only from 0.95 to 0.97. On Raven's Progressive Matrices (colored), internal-consistency estimates were also quite similar across race and sex, ranging only from 0.86 to 0.91 for the six race–sex groupings. Thus, Jensen's (1974, 1977) research with three popular aptitude tests shows no signs of differential or single-group validity with regard to homogeneity of test content or consistency of measurement across groups.

Sandoval (1979) and Oakland and Feigenbaum (1979) have extensively investigated internal consistency of the various WISC-R subtests (excluding Digit Span and Coding, for which internal-consistency analysis is inappropriate) for Whites, Blacks, and Mexican-Americans. Both of these studies included large samples of children, with Sandoval's (1979) including over 1000. Sandoval found internal-consistency estimates to be within 0.04 of one another for all subtests except Object Assembly. This subtest was most reliable for Blacks (0.95), while being about equally reliable for Whites (0.79) and Mexican-Americans (0.75). Oakland and Feigenbaum (1979) reported internal-consistency estimates that never differed by more than 0.06 among the three groups, again with the exception of Object Assembly. In this instance, Object Assembly was most reliable for Whites (0.76), with about equal reliabilities for Blacks (0.64) and Mexican-Americans (0.67). Oakland and Feigenbaum also compared reliabilities across sex, finding highly similar values for males and females. Dean (1977) examined the internal consistency of the WISC-R for Mexican-American children tested by White examiners. He reported internal-consistency reliability estimates consistent with, although slightly exceeding, values reported by Wechsler (1974) for the predominantly White standardization sample. The Bender–Gestalt Test has also been reported to have similar internal-consistency estimates for Whites (0.84), Blacks (0.81), and Mexican-Americans (0.72), and for males (0.81) and females (0.80) (Oakland & Feigenbaum, 1979).

Several other methods have also been used to determine the construct validity of popular psychometric instruments across races. Since intelligence is considered a developmental phenomenon, the correlation of raw scores with age has been viewed as one measure of constrict validity for intelligence tests. Jensen (1976) reported that the correlations between raw scores on the PPVT and age were 0.79 for Whites, 0.73 for Blacks, and 0.67 for Mexican-Americans. For Raven's Progressive Matrices (colored), correlations for raw scores with age were 0.72 for Whites, 0.66 for Blacks, and 0.70 for Mexican-Americans. Similar results are apparent for the K-ABC (Kamphaus & Reynolds, 1987) and the Test of Memory and Learning (Reynolds & Bigler, 1994). Thus, in regard to increase in scores with age, the tests behave in a highly similar manner for Whites, Blacks, and Mexican-Americans. Similar findings occur in male–female comparisons.

In the review work of Moran (1990) and in a search for more recent work, it is apparent that only a few studies of the differential construct validity of personality tests have been undertaken, despite large mean differences across ethnicity and gender on such popular measures as the stalwart MMPI. Dana (1993) sharply criticizes even the meager work to date on the MMPI, stating that "[C]omparative MMPI research studies of Anglo-American and other cultural groups have typically not only used inappropriate statistics but also failed to equate groups adequately on socioeconomic criteria or even to define ethnicity" (p. 98). The lack of extensive research using method designed to detect test bias for such widely used scales as the MMPI is nothing short of appalling. A look at the newer MMPI-2 Manual suggests gender differs in construct validity but provides no real evidence either way. A few studies of factorial similarity of instruments such as the Revised Children's Manifest Anxiety Scale show little bias and high degrees of similarity by ethnicity and gender (Moran, 1990; Reynolds & Paget, 1981).

Constuct validity of a large number of popular psychometric assessment instruments has been investigated across races and genders with a variety of populations of minority and White children and with a divergent set of methodologies (see Reynolds, 1982b, for a review of methodologies). All roads have led to Rome: no consistent evidence of bias in construct validity has been found with any of the many tests investigated. This leads to the conclusion that psychological tests (especially aptitude tests) function in essentially the same manner, that test materials are perceived and reacted to in a similar manner, and that tests measure the same construct with equivalent accuracy for Blacks, Whites, Mexican-Americans, and other American minorities of both sexes and at all levels of SES. Single-group validity and differential validity have not been found and probably do not exist with regard to well-constructed and well-standardized psychological and educational tests of intellect, personality, or behavior although data are not as thorough for the latter two categories and much work is needed here.

10.03.7.3 Bias in Predictive or Criterion-related Validity

Evaluating bias in predictive validity of educational and psychological tests is less closely related to the evaluation of group mental test score differences than to the evaluation of individual test scores in a more absolute sense. This is especially true for aptitude (as opposed to personality or diagnostic) tests, where the primary purpose of administration is the prediction of some specific future outcome or behavior. Internal analyses of bias (such as in content and construct validity) are less confounded than analyses of bias in predictive validity, however, because of the potential problems of bias in the criterion measure. Predictive validity is strongly influenced by the reliability of criterion measures, which frequently is poor. The degree of relationship between a predictor and a criterion is restricted as a function of the square root of the product of the reliabilities of the two variables.

Arriving at a consensual definition of bias in predictive validity is also a difficult task, as previously discussed. Yet, from the standpoint of the practical applications of aptitude and intelligence tests, predictive validity is the most crucial form of validity in relation to test bias. Much of the discussion in professional journals concerning bias in predictive validity has centered around models of selection. These issues have been discussed in Section 10.03.6. Since this section is concerned with bias in respect to the test itself and not the social or political justification of any one particular selection model, the Cleary at al. (1975) definition, slightly rephrased here, provides a clear and direct statement of test bias with regard to predictive validity: a test is considered biased with respect to predictive validity if the inference drawn from the test score is not made with the smallest feasible random error or if there is constant error in an inference or prediction as a function of membership in a particular group. This definition is a restatement of previous definitions by Cardall and Coffman (1964), Cleary (1968), and Potthoff (1966), and has been widely accepted (though certainly not without criticism; e.g., Bernal, 1975; Linn & Werts, 1971; Schmidt & Hunter, 1974; Thorndike, 1971).

Oakland and Matuszek (1977) examined procedures for placement in special education classes under a variety of models of bias in prediction, and demonstrated that the smallest number of children are misplaced when the Cleary et al (1975) conditions of fairness are met. (However, under "quota" system requirements, Oakland and Matuszek favor the Thorndike, 1971 conditions of selection.) The Cleary et al. definition is also apparently the definition espoused in US government guidelines on testing and has been held in at least one court decision (Cortez v. Rosen, 1975) to be the only historically, legally, and logically required condition of test fairness (Ramsay, 1979), although apparently the judge in the Larry P. v. Riles (1979) decision (but overturned on appeal) in the US Federal court system adopted the "mean score differences as bias" approach. A variety of educational and psychological personnel long have adopted the Cleary et al. regression approach to bias, including: (i) noted psychological authorities on testing (Anastasi, 1986; Cronbach, 1970; Humphreys, 1973); (ii) educational and psychological researchers (Brossard, Reynolds, & Gutkin, 1980; Kallingal, 1971; Pfeifer & Sedlacek, 1971; Reynolds & Hartlage, 1978, 1979; Stanley & Porter, 1967; Wilson, 1969); (iii) industrial/organizational psychologists (Barlett & O'Leary, 1969; Einhorn & Bass, 1970; Gael & Grant, 1972; Grant & Bray, 1970; Ramsay, 1979; Tenopyr, 1967); and (iv) even critics of educational and psychological testing (Goldman & Hartig, 1976; Kirkpatrick, 1970; Kirkpatrick, Ewen, Barrett, & Katzell, 1968).

The evaluation of bias in prediction under the Cleary et al. (1975) definition (the regression definition) is quite straightforward. With simple regression, predictions take the form of $\hat{Y}_i = aX_i + b$, where a is the regression coefficient and b is a constant. When this equation is graphed (forming a regression line), a represents the slope of the regression line and b the Y intercept. Since our definition of fairness in predictive validity requires errors in prediction to be independent of group membership, the regression line formed for any pair of variables must be the same for each group for whom predictions are made. Whenever the slope or the intercept differs significantly across groups, there is bias in prediction if one attempts to use a common equation for all groups. However, if the regression equations for two (or more) groups are equivalent, prediction is the same for all groups. This condition is referred to variously as "homogeneity of regression across groups," "simultaneous regression," or "fairness in prediction." Homogeneity of regression across groups is illustrated in Figure 1. In this case, the single regression equation is appropriate with all groups, any errors in prediction being random with respect to group membership (i.e., residuals uncorrelated with group membership). When homogeneity of regression does not occur, for "fairness in prediction" to occur, separate regression equations must be used for each group.

In actual clinical practice, regression equations are seldom generated for the prediction of future performance. Instead, some arbitrary or perhaps statistically derived cutoff score is determined, below which "failure" is predicted. For school performance, IQs two or more standard deviations below the test mean are used to infer a high probability of failure in the regular classroom if special assistance is not provided for the student in question. Essentially, then, clinicians are establishing mental prediction equations that are assumed to be equivalent across ethnicity, gender, and so on. Although these mental equations cannot be tested readily across groups, the actual form of criterion prediction can be compared across groups in several ways. Errors in prediction must be independent of group membership. If regression equations are equal, this condition is met. To test the hypothesis of simultaneous regression, slopes and intercepts must both be compared. An alternative method is the direct examination of residuals through ANOVA or a similar design (Reynolds, 1980b).

In the evaluation of slope and intercept values, two basic techniques most often have been employed in the research literature. Gulliksen and Wilks (1965) and Kerlinger (1973) describe methods for separately testing regression coefficients and intercepts for significant differences across groups. Using separate, independent tests for these two values considerably increases the probability of a decision error and unnecessarily complicates the decision-making process. Potthoff (1966) has described a useful technique that allows one to test simultaneously the equivalence of regression coefficients and intercepts across K independent groups with a single F ratio (the Potthoff equations may be found also in Reynolds, 1982b). If a significant F results, the researcher may then test the slopes and intercepts separately if information concerning which value differs is desired. When homogeneity of regression does not occur, there are three basic conditions that can result: (i) intercept constants differ, (ii) regression coefficients (slopes) differ, or (iii) slopes and intercepts differ. These conditions are depicted pictorially in Figures 2, 3, and 4, respectively.

The regression coefficient is related to the correlation coefficient between the two variables and is one measure of the strength of the relationship between two variables. When intercepts differ and regression coefficients do not, a situation such as that shown in Figure 2 results. Relative accuracy of prediction is the same for the two groups (*a* and *b*), the use of a regression equation derived by combining the two groups results in bias that works against the group with the higher mean criterion score. Since the slope of the regression line is the same for all groups, the degree of error in prediction remains constant and does not fluctuate as a function of an individual's score on the independent variable. That is, regardless of group member *b*s score on the predictor, the degree of underprediction in performance on the criterion is the same. As illustrated in Figure 2, the use of the common score of Y_c for a score of X overestimates how well members of group *a* will perform and underestimates the criterion performance of members of group *b*.

In Figure 3, nonparallel regression lines illustrate the case where intercepts are constant across groups but the slope of the line is different for each group. Here, too, the performance of the group with the higher mean criterion score is typically underpredicted when a common regression equation is applied. The amount of bias in prediction that results from using the common regression line is the distance of the score from the mean. The most difficult, complex case of bias is represented in Figure 4 where the result of significant differences in slopes and intercepts is shown. Not only does the amount of bias vary but even the direction can reverse, depending on the location of the individual's score in the distribution of the independent variable. Only in the case of Figure 4 do members of the group with the lower mean criterion score run the risk of having their performance on the criterion variable underpredicted by the application of a common regression equation.

A considerable body of literature has developed regarding the differential predictive

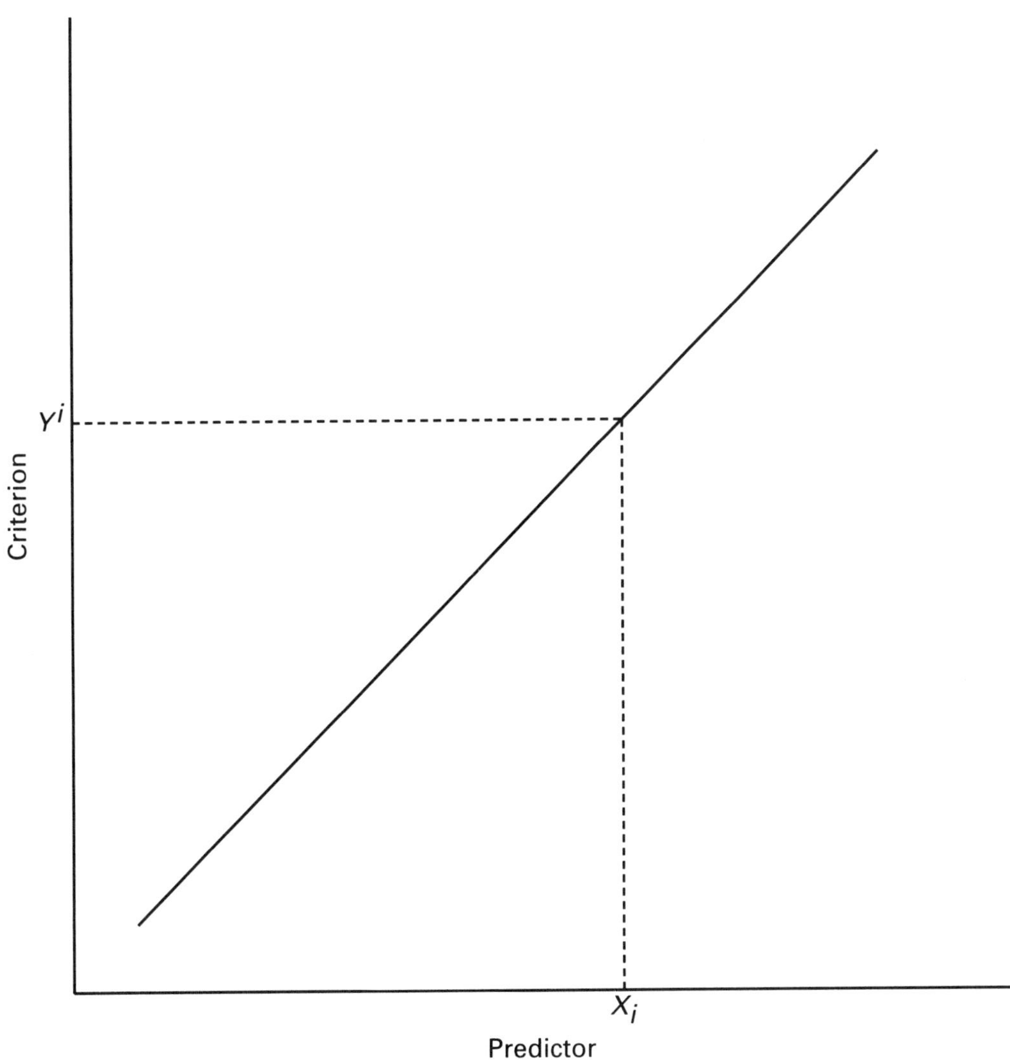

Figure 1 Equal slopes and intercepts result in homogeneity of regression that causes the regression lines for group *a*, group *b*, and the combined group *c* to be identical.

validity of IQ tests and for tests for employment selection and college admissions. However, virtually nothing appears in this regard with reference to personality tests (Dana, 1993; Moran, 1990) and this is a major weakness in the literature.

In a review of 866 Black–White test validity comparisons from 39 studies of test bias in personnel selection, Hunter, Schmidt, and Hunter (1979) concluded that there was no evidence to substantiate hypotheses of differential or single-group validity with regard to the prediction of job performance across races for Blacks and Whites. A similar conclusion was reached by Jensen (1980), O'Conner, Wexley, and Alexander (1975), and Reynolds (1982a, 1995) among others. A number of studies have also focused on differential validity of the Scholastic Aptitude Test (SAT) in the prediction of college performance (typically measured by grade point average, GPA). In general, these studies have found either no differences in the prediction of criterion performance for Blacks and Whites or a bias (underprediction of the criterion) against Whites (Cleary, 1968; Cleary et al., 1975; Goldman & Hewitt, 1976; Kallingal, 1971; Pfeifer & Sedlacek, 1971; Stanley, 1971; Stanley & Porter, 1967; Temp, 1971). When bias against Whites has been found, the differences between actual and predicted criterion scores, although statistically significant, have been quite small.

Reschly and Sabers (1979) evaluated the validity of WISC-R IQs in the prediction of Metropolitan Achievement Tests (MAT) performance (Reading and Math subtests) for Whites, Blacks, Mexican-Americans, and native American Papagos. The choice of the MAT as a criterion measure in studies of predictive bias is particularly appropriate, since item analysis

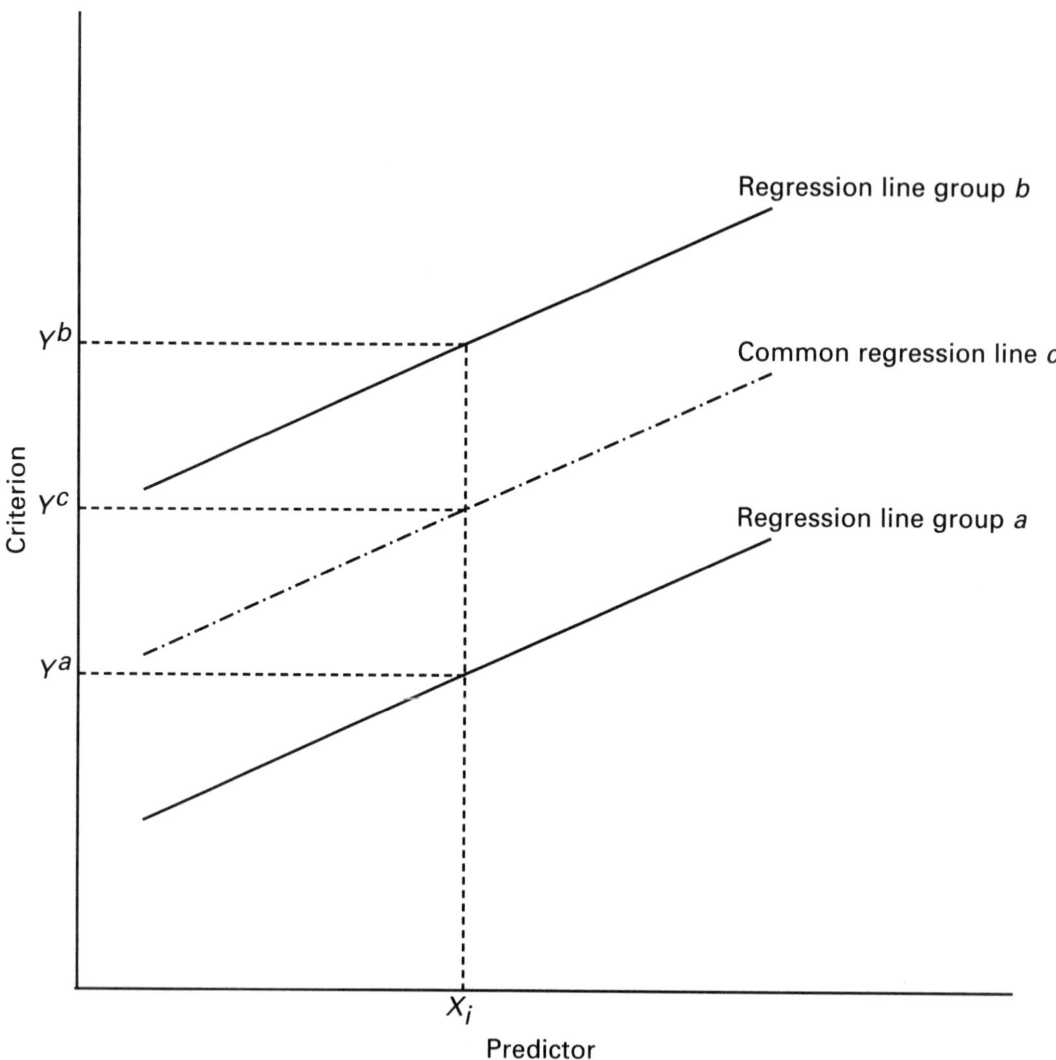

Figure 2 Equal slopes with differing intercepts result in parallel regression lines and a constant bias in prediction.

procedures were employed (as described earlier) to eliminate racial bias in item content during the test construction phase. Anastasi (1986) has described the MAT as an excellent model of an achievement test designed to reduce or eliminate cultural bias. Reschly and Saber's (1979) comparison of regression systems indicated bias in the prediction of the various achievement scores. Again, however, the bias produced generally significant underprediction of White performance when a common regression equation was applied. Achievement test performance of the native American Papago group showed the greatest amount of overprediction of all non-White groups. Using similar techniques, but including teacher ratings, Reschly and Reschly (1979) also investigated the predictive validity of WISC-R factor scores with the samples of White, Black, Mexican-American, and native American Papago children. A significant relationship occurred between the three WISC-R factors first delineated by Kaufman (1975) and measures of achievement for the White and non-White groups, with the exception of the Papagos. Significant correlations occurred between the WISC-R Freedom from Distractibility factor (Kaufman, 1975) and teacher ratings of attention for all four groups. Reschly and Reschly concluded that "These data also again confirm the relatively strong relationship of WISC-R scores to achievement for most non-Anglo as well as Anglo groups" (1979, p. 239). Reynolds and Hartlage (1979) investigated the differential validity of Full Scale IQs from the WISC-R and its 1949 predecessor, the WISC, in predicting reading and arithmetic achievement for Black and White children who had been referred by their

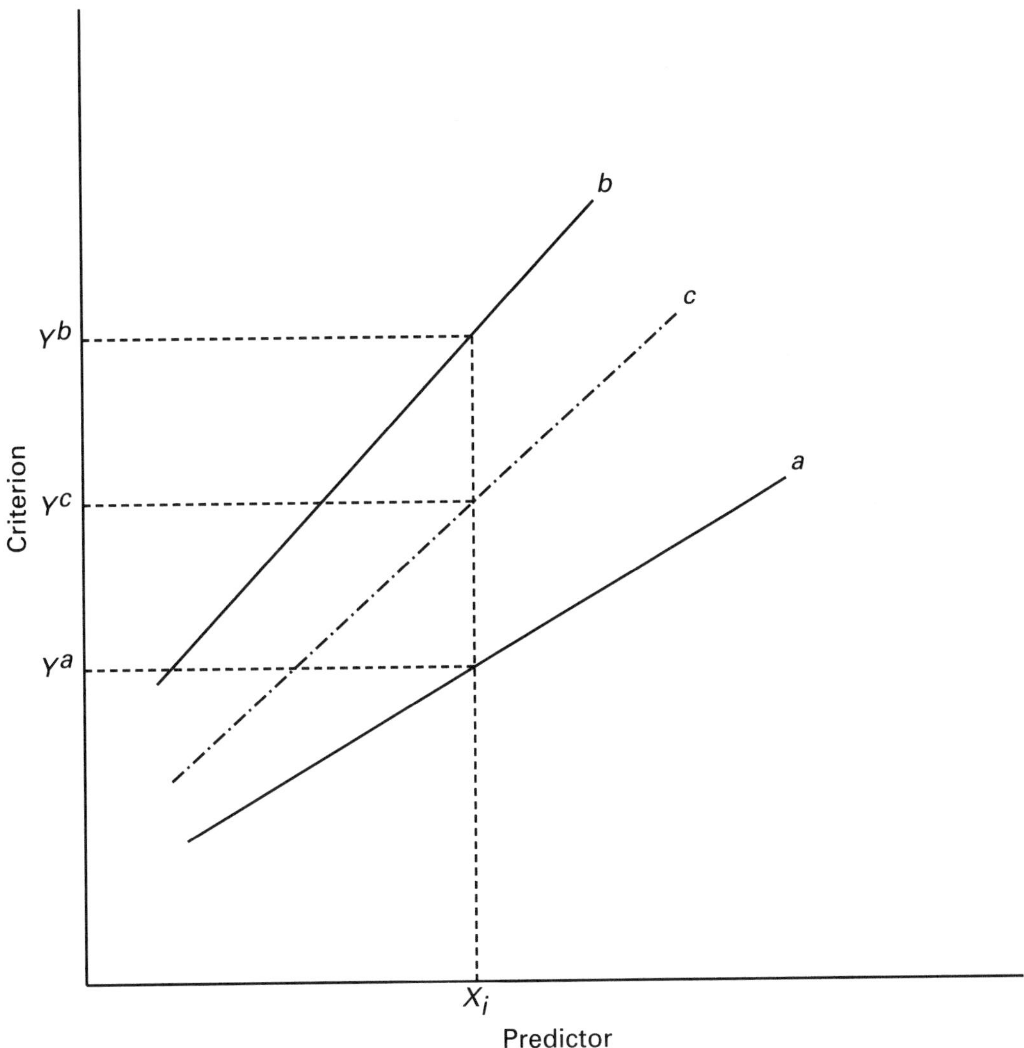

Figure 3 Equal intercepts and differing slopes result in nonparallel regression lines with the degree of bias dependent on the distance of the individual's score (x_i) from the origin.

teachers for psychological services in a rural Southern school district. Comparisons of correlations and a Potthoff (1966) analysis to test for identity of regression lines revealed no significant differences in the ability or function of the WISC and WISC-R to predict achievement for these two groups. Reynolds and Gutkin (1980b) replicated this study for the WISC-R with large groups of White and Mexican-American children from the Southwest. Reynolds and Gutkin contrasted regression systems between WISC-R Verbal, Performance, and Full Scale IQs and the "academic basics" of reading, spelling, and arithmetic. Only the regression equation between the WISC-R Performance IQ and arithmetic achievement differed for the two groups. The difference in the two equations was due to an intercept bias that resulted in the overprediction of achievement for the Mexican-American children. Reynolds, Gutkin, Dappen, and Wright (1979) also failed to find differential validity in the prediction of achievement for males and females with the WISC-R.

In a related study, Hartlage, Lucas, and Godwin (1976) compared the predictive validity of what they considered to be a relatively culture-free test (Raven's Progressive Matrices) with a more culture-loaded test (the 1949 WISC, a test developed and standardized on all White sample) for a group of low-SES, disadvantaged rural children. Hartlage et al. (1976) found that the WISC had consistently larger correlations with measures of reading, spelling, and arithmetic than Raven's Matrices. Although it did not make the comparison with other groups that is necessary for the drawing of firm conclusions, the study does support the validity of the WISC,

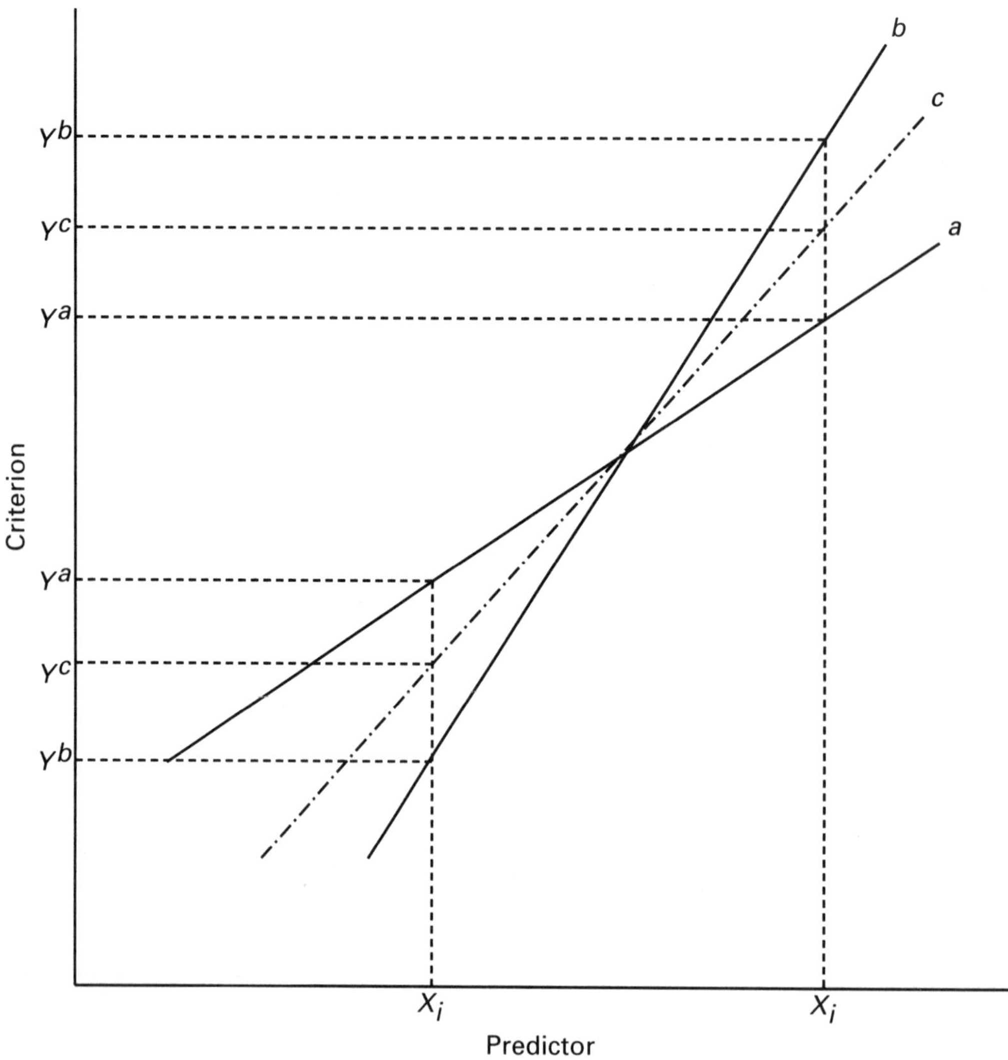

Figure 4 Differing slopes and intercepts result in the complex condition where the amount and the direction of the bias are a function of the distance of an individual's score from the origin.

which has been the target of many of the claims of bias in the prediction of achievement for low-SES, disadvantaged rural children. Henderson, Butler, and Goffeney (1969) also reported that the WISC and the Bender–Gestalt Test were equally effective in the prediction of reading and arithmetic achievement for White and non-White groups, though their study had a number of methodological difficulties, including heterogeneity of the non-White comparison group. Reynolds, Willson, and Chatman (1985) evaluated the predictive validity of the K-ABC for Blacks and Whites. Occasional evidence of bias was found in each direction, but mostly in the direction of overprediction of the academic attainment levels of Blacks.

Bossard et al. (1980) published a regression analysis of test bias on the 1972 Stanford–Binet Intelligence Scale for separate groups of Black and White children. Neither regression systems nor correlations differed at $p < 0.05$ for the prediction of the basic academic skills of reading, spelling, and arithmetic achievement for these two groups of referred children. An earlier study by Sewell (1979), a Black opponent of testing, did not compare regression systems, but also found no significant differences in validity coefficients for Stanford–Binet IQs predicting California Achievement Test (CAT) scores for Black and White first-grade children.

A series of studies comparing the predictive validity of group IQ measures across races has been reviewed by Jensen (1980) and Sattler (1974). Typically, regression systems have not been compared in these studies: instead, researchers have compared only the validity coefficients across races—a practice that tells only whether the test is potentially nonbiased. The comparison of validity coefficients is nevertheless relevant, since equivalence in predictive validities is a first step in evaluating differential validity. That is, if predictive validities differ, then regression systems must differ; the reverse is not necessarily true, however, since the correlation between two variables is a measure of the strength or magnitude of a relationship and does not dictate the form of a relationship. Although the number of studies evaluating group IQ tests across ethnicity is small, they have typically employed extremely large samples. The Lorge–Thorndike verbal and nonverbal IQs have been most often investigated. Jensen (1980) and Sattler (1974) concluded that the few available studies suggest that standard IQ tests in current use have comparable validities for Black and White children at the elementary school level.

Guterman (1979) reported on an extensive analysis of the predictive validity of the Ammons and Ammons Quick Test (QT; a measure of verbal IQ) for adolescents of different social classes. Social class was determined by a weighted combination of Duncan's SES index and the number of years of education of each parent. Three basic measures: (i) the Vocabulary subtest of the General Aptitude Test Battery (GATB); (ii) the test of Reading Comprehension from the Gates Reading Survey; and (iii) the Arithmetic subtest of the GATB were used. School grades in academic subjects for 9th, 10th, and 12th grades were also used to examine for bias in prediction. Guterman reached similar conclusions with regard to all criterion measures across all social classes: slopes and intercepts of regression lines did not differ across social class for the prediction of any of the criterion measures by the IQ derived from the QT. Several other social knowledge criterion measures were also examined. Again, slopes were constant across social class, and, with the exception of sexual knowledge, intercepts were also constant. Guterman concluded that his data provided strong support for equivalent validity of IQ measures across social class. In reanalyzing the Guterman (1979) study, Gordon and Rudert (1979) reached even stronger conclusions. Certainly with school-age children and adults, there is compelling evidence that differential and single-group predictive validity hypotheses must be rejected.

As with constrict validity, at the preschool level the evidence is less clear and convincing but points toward a lack of bias against minorities. Because of doubts expressed about the usefulness of customary readiness tests with students of certain racial and ethnic backgrounds and with low-SES children, Mitchell (1967) investigated the predictive validity of two preschool readiness tests used in the US Office of Education (Cooperative First-Grade Reading Study, 1964–1965 revision) and the Murphy–Durell Reading Readiness Analysis (1964 revision). Mitchell concluded that the two readiness tests performed their functions as well with Black as with White children and that the general level of predictive validity was similar. This overstates the case somewhat, since only validity coefficients and not regression systems were compared, but Mitchell's (1967) study does support the predictive validity of these readiness tests across race.

Oakland (1978) assessed the differential predictive validity of four readiness tests (the MRT, the Tests of Basic Experiences battery, the Slosson Intelligence Test, and the Slosson Oral Reading Test) across races (Black, White, and Mexican-American) for middle- and lower-SES children. The MAT, the CAT, and the California Test of Mental Maturity (CTMM) served as criterion variables. Since the CTMM is an IQ test, prediction of CTMM scores by the various readiness tests is excluded from the following discussion. Although Oakland (1978) did not use any test of statistical significance to compare the correlations between the independent and dependent variable pairs across ethnicity and SES, a clear pattern was found, showing higher levels of prediction for White as opposed to non-White groups. Oakland also did not compare regression systems, limiting his study to the report of the various validity coefficients for each race–SES grouping. Oakland's (1978) results clearly indicate potential bias in the prediction of early school achievement by individual readiness or screening tests. The lower correlations for non-White groups, however, given their lower mean criterion scores, led to anticipation of bias favoring non-Whites in the prediction of early school achievement.

To investigate this possibility, Reynolds (1978) conducted an extensive analysis of predictive bias for seven major preschool tests (the Draw-a-Design and Draw-a-Child subtests of the McCarthy Scales; the Mathematics and Language subtests of the Tests of Basic Experiences; the Preschool Inventory-Revised Edition; and the Lee–Clark Reading Readiness Test) across race and gender for large groups of Blacks and Whites. For each preschool test, validity coefficients, slopes, and intercepts were compared, with prediction of performance on four subtests of the MAT (Word Knowledge, Word Discrimination, Reading, and Arithmetic) as the criterion measures. The general advantage of the MAT as a criterion in external studies of bias has previously been pointed out.

In the Reynolds (1978) study, the MAT had the added advantage of being chosen by the teachers in the district: data were gathered on a large number of early achievement tests, and the teachers selected the MAT as the battery most closely measuring what was taught in their classrooms. Regression systems and validity coefficients were compared for each independent–dependent variable pair for White females (WF) vs. White males (WM), Black females (BF) vs. Black males (BM), WF vs. BF, and WM vs. BM, resulting in 112 comparisons of validity coefficients and 112 comparisons of regression systems. Although the mean correlations were slightly lower for Blacks, the 112 comparisons of pairs of correlations revealed only three significant differences, a less-than-chance occurrence with this number of comparisons. Using the Potthoff (1966) technique for comparing regression lines produced quite different results. Of the 112 comparisons of regression lines, 43 (38.4%) showed differences. For comparisons with race as the major variable (and gender controlled), 31 (55.2%) of the 56 comparisons showed significantly different regression lives. Clearly, racial bias was significantly more prevalent than gender bias ($p < 0.01$) in prediction. In comparing the various pretests, bias occurred most often with the Preschool Inventory and the Lee–Clark, whereas none of the comparisons involving the MRT showed bias. Though race clearly influenced homogeneity of regression across groups, the bias in each case acted to overpredict performance of lower-scoring groups; thus the bias acted against Whites and females and in favor of Blacks and males. A follow-up study (Reynolds, 1980b) has indicated one potential method for avoiding bias in the prediction of early school achievement with readiness or screening measures.

Brief screening measures, especially at the preschool level, typically do not have the high level of reliability obtained by such instruments as the WISC-R or the Stanford–Binet. Linn and Werts (1971) have demonstrated convincingly that poor reliability can lead to bias in prediction. Early screening measures, as a rule, also assess a very limited area of functioning, rather than allowing the child to demonstrate its skills in a variety of areas of cognitive functioning. The one well-researched, reliable, broad-based readiness test, the MRT, has failed to show bias with regard to internal or external criteria. Comprehensive and reliable individual preschool instruments such as the WPPSI and the McCarthy Scales, while showing no internal evidence of test bias, have not been researched with regard to predictive bias across race. Reynolds (1980b) examined the predictive validity of the seven preschool measures described previously when these were combined into a larger battery, thus increasing the scope and reliability of the assessment.

Since the definition of predictive bias noted earlier requires that errors in prediction be independent of group membership, Reynolds (1980b) directly examined residuals (a "residual term" is the remainder when the predicted score for an individual is subtracted from the individual's obtained score) across race and gender when the seven-test battery was used to predict MAT scores in a multiple-regression formula. Subtests of the seven-test battery were also examined. Results of a race X sex ANOVA of residuals for each of the MAT subtests when the seven-test battery was employed revealed no significant differences in residuals across races and genders, and no significant interactions occurred. When a subset of the larger battery was submitted to the same analysis, racial bias in prediction did not occur; however, a significant F resulted for gender effects in the prediction of two of the four MAT subscores (Word Discrimination and Word Knowledge). Examination of the residuals for each group showed that the bias in prediction was again against the group with the higher mean criterion scores: there was a consistent underprediction of performance for females. The magnitude of the effect was small, however, being of the order of 0.13–0.16 standard deviations. Thus, at the preschool level, the only convincing evidence of bias in predictive validity is a gender effect, not a race effect.

Kamphaus and Reynolds (1987) reviewed the available literature on predictive bias with the K-ABC and concluded that overprediction of Black children's performance in school is more common with the K-ABC, particularly the K-ABC Sequential Processing scale, than with other tests. The effects are small, however, and are mitigated in large part by using the K-ABC Mental Processing Composite. Some bias also occurs against Blacks, but when the extensive nature of the bias research with the K-ABC is considered, results with the K-ABC are not substantially different from the results with the WISC-R (with the exception of overprediction of Black academic performance by the K-ABC Sequential Processing scale).

Keith and Reynolds (1990) have suggested the use of path analysis as an alternative model for assessing bias is predictive validity. In such a path model, ability would be proposed to predict achievement, and group membership would be assessed as a moderator variable. A diagrammatic representation of a biased and an unbiased model is shown in Keith and Reynolds (1990). Bias in prediction would exist in such a model when group membership affects measured ability independent of true ability, that is, errors of measurement in testing of ability would be correlated with group membership. With regard to bias in predictive validity, the empirical evidence suggests conclusions similar to those regarding bias in content and construct validity. There is no strong evidence to support contentions of differential single-group validity. Bias occurs infrequently and with no apparently observable pattern, except when instruments of poor reliability and high specificity of test content are examined. When bias occurs, it is most often in the direction of favoring low-SES, disadvantaged ethnic minority children, or other low-scoring groups.

10.03.8 CROSS-CULTURAL TESTING WHEN TRANSLATION IS REQUIRED

When a test is translated from one language to another, the research findings discussed thus far do not hold. It is inappropriate simply to translate a test and apply it in a different linguistic culture. A test must be redeveloped from scratch (although constructs may be retained) basically before any such application would be appropriate. New items, new normative data, and new scaling would all be required. This has been known since the early days of psychological assessment and testing. In the early 1900s, when the Binet–Simon tests were brought to the USA from France, approximately 30 different versions of the test were developed in the USA by various researchers. However, most of these were mere translations or contained minor modifications to adapt to American culture. The Stanford–Binet Intelligence Scale, in its various incarnations, however, became the standard bearer for measurement of intelligence for nearly 60 years and was even more popular in France at one time than the original French Binet–Simon scales. The reason for the domination of the Stanford–Binet series was Lewis Terman's insight and tenacity in redeveloping the test in the USA. After determining that Binet's theory of intelligence applied, new items were written, tried out, and a new scale devised for norming that was conceptually consistent with the Binet–Simon scales but in its practical application was a new and different test.

The problems in translating verbal and nonverbal concepts across linguistic cultures are difficult but in any event the redevelopment of tests in such circumstances seems required. Cronbach and Drenth (1972) provide a book length treatment of these problems and various experiences with proposed solutions to cross-cultural adaptation of psychological tests stemming from some 30 nations from throughout the world. The various contributors describe both the strengths and limitations of adapting tests cross-culturally from one country to another, providing perspectives from such diverse discipline psychometrics, cognitive development, psychology, and anthropology. More recent guidelines and reviews of the issues involved in cross-cultural adaptation of psychological and educational tests can be found in Hambleton (1994), Hambleton and Kanjee (1995), and Van de Vijver and Hambleton (1996).

10.03.9 SUMMARY AND FUTURE DIRECTIONS

There is little question that the issue of bias in mental testing is an important one with strong historical precedence in the social sciences and, ultimately, formidable social consequences. Because the history of mental measurement has been closely wed from the outset to societal needs and expectations, testing in all forms has remained in the limelight, subjected to the crucible of social inspection, review, and (at times) condemnation in various cultures throughout the world. However, the fact that tests and measures of human aptitude and achievement continue to be employed in most modern cultures indicates strongly that the practice has value, despite the recurring storms of criticism over the years. The ongoing controversy related to test bias and the "fair" use of measures will undoubtedly remain with the social sciences for at least as long as we intertwine the nature–nuture question with these issues and affirm differences between–among groups in mean performance on standardized tests. Numerous scholars in the field of psychometrics have been attempting to separate the nature–nurture issue and data on mean score differences from the more orderly, empirically-driven specialty of bias investigation, but the separation will undoubtedly not be a clean one. A sharp distinction has developed between the popular press and scientific literature with regard to the interpretation of mental measurement research. The former all too often engenders beliefs that biased measures are put into use for socially pernicious purposes and psychology and education are often accused of courting political, social, and professional ideologies. The former appears to have created confusion in public opinion concerning the possibility of "fair" testing, to say the least. The latter—reported in this chapter—has been demonstrating through a rather sizable body of data that the hypothesis of cultural bias in tests is not a particularly strong one at present, at least in cultures with a common language and some degree (the extent or qualitative features of which are as yet indeterminant) of common experience. In any event, societal scrutiny and ongoing sentiment about testing have without question served to force the psychometric community to refine its definitions of bias further, to inspect practices in the construction of nonbiased measures, and to develop statistical procedures to detect bias when it is occurring. We can argue whether the social sciences have from the outset overstepped their bounds in implementing testing for social purposes before adequate data and methods were developed, but the resulting advancements made in bias technology in response to ongoing public inspection are undeniable.

Data from the empirical end of bias investigation do suggest several guidelines to follow in order to ensure equitable assessment. Points to consider include: (i) investigation of possible referral source bias, as there is evidence that persons are not always referred for mental health or special eductional services on the basis of impartial, objective rationales; (ii) inspection of test developers' data for evidence that sound statistical analyses for bias across groups to be evaluated with the measure have been completed; (iii) assessment with the most reliable measures available; and (iv) assessment of multiple abilities with multiple methods. In other words, psychologists need to view multiple sources of accurately derived data prior to making decisions concerning individuals. We may hope that this is not too far afield from what has actually been occurring in the practice on psychological assessment, though one continues to hear isolated stories of grossly incompetent diagnostic decisions being made (e.g., Mason, 1979). This does not mean that psychologists should be blind to a person's environmental background. Information concerning the home, community, and other environmental circumstances must all be evaluated in the individualized decision-making process. Exactly how this may be done is addressed in all other chapters and volumes of this work. Neither, however, can the psychologist ignore the fact that ethnic minority group members who score at levels indicative of psychopathology are just as likely to have problems and need intervention as are majority-class individuals. Indeed, it is the purpose of the assessment process to beat the prediction—to provide insight into hypotheses for environmental and biological interventions that will prevent the identified pathology from continuity to exert a negative influence on the person's life.

A philosophical perspective is emerging in the bias literature that is requiring test developers not only to demonstrate whether their measures demonstrate differential content, construct, and predictive validity across groups *prior* to publication, but also to incorporate in some form content analyses by interested groups to ensure that offensive materials are omitted. Although there are no sound empirical data to suggest that persons can determine bias upon surface inspection, the synergistic relationship between test use and pure psychometrics must be acknowledged and accommodated in an orderly fashion before tests gain greater acceptance within society. Ideally, a clear consensus on "fairness" (and steps taken to reach this end) is needed between those persons with more subjective concerns and those interested in gathering objective bias data during and after test construction. Accommodation along this line will ultimately ensure that all parties interested in any given test believe that the measure in question is nonbiased and that the steps taken to achieve "fairness" can be held up to public scrutiny without reservation. Given the significant and reliable methods developed over the last several decades in bias research, it is untenable at this point to abandon statistical analyses in favor of "armchair" determinations of bias. Test authors and publishers need to demonstrate factorial invariance across all groups for whom the test is designed in order to make the instrument more readily interpretable. Comparisons of predictive validity across races and genders during the test development phase are also needed. With the exception of some recent achievement tests, this has not been common practice, yet it is at this stage that tests can be altered through a variety of item analysis procedures to eliminate any apparent racial and sexual bias. As scientists, we must also inform the media of our results, whatever they may be.

Bias research in the area of personality testing must be expanded. Little has been done and this represents a major weakness in the literature. Only recently (e.g., Reynolds & Kamphaus, 1992) have publishers begun to give appropriate attention to this problem. Researchers in personality and psychodiagnostics must move ahead in this area of concern. Similar problems exist in the growing area of neuropsychological testing (e.g., Reynolds, 1997a).

10.03.10 REFERENCES

Abebimpe, V. R., Gigandet, J., & Harris, E. (1979). MMPI diagnosis of Black psychiatric patients. *American Journal of Psychiatry, 136,* 85–87.

Alley, G., & Foster, C. (1978). Nondiscriminatory testing

of minority and exceptional children. *Focus on Exceptional Children, 9,* 1–14.

American Psychological Association (1970). Psychological assessment and public policy. *American Psychologist, 25,* 264–266.

Anastasi, A. (1982). *Psychological testing* (5th ed.). New York: Macmillan.

Anastasi, A. (1986). *Psychological testing* (4th ed.). New York: Macmillan.

Angoff, W. H. (1976). Group membership as a predictor variable: A comment on McNemar. *American Psychologist, 31,* 612.

Angoff, W. H., & Ford, S. R. (1973). Item-race interaction on a test of scholastic aptitude. *Journal of Educational Measurement, 10,* 95–106.

Auerbach, A. G. (1971). The social control of learning disabilities. *Journal of Learning Disabilities, 4,* 369–378.

Bartlett, C. J., & O'Leary, B. S. (1969). A differential prediction model to moderate the effect of heterogeneous groups on personnel selection and classification. *Personnel Psychology, 22,* 1–19.

Bass, A. R. (1976). The "equal risk" model: A comment on McNemar. *American Psychologist, 31,* 611–612.

Bayley, N. (1969). *Bayley Scales of Infant Development.* New York: Psychological Corporation.

Beauchamp, D. P., Samuels, D. D., & Griffore, R. J. (1979). WISC-R Information and Digit Span scores of American and Canadian children. *Applied Psychological Measurement, 3,* 231–236.

Berk, R. A. (Ed.) (1982). *Handbook of methods for detecting test bias.* Baltimore: Johns Hopkins University Press.

Bernal, E. M. (1975). A response to "Educational uses of tests with disadvantaged students." *American Psychologist, 30,* 93–95.

Binet, A., & Simon, T. (1905). Methods nouvelles pour le diagnositic du nivea intellectual des anormaux. *L'AnnCe Psychologique, 11,* 191–244.

Binet, A., & Simon, T. (1916). *The development of intelligence in children.* New York: Arno (English translation reprinted, 1973).

Birch, H. G., & Gussow, J. D. (1970). *Disadvantaged children: Health, nutrition, and school failure.* New York: Saunders.

Blaha, J., Wallbrown, F., & Wherry, R. J. (1975). The hierarchical factor structure of the Wechsler Intelligence Scale for Children. *Psychological Reports, 35,* 771–778.

Bogen, J. E., DeZure, R., Tenhouten, N., & March, J. (1972). The other side of the brain: IV. The A/P ratio. *Bulletin of the Los Angeles Neurological Society, 37,* 49–61.

Bolles, R. C. (1975). *Theory of motivation* (2nd ed.). New York: Harper Collins.

Bond, L. (1981). Bias in mental tests. In B. F. Green (Ed.), *Issues in testing: Coaching, disclosure, and ethnic bias.* San Francisco: Jossey-Bass.

Bossard, M., Reynolds, C. R., & Gutkin, T. B. (1980). A regression analysis of test bias on the Stanford-Binet Intelligence Scale. *Journal of Clinical Child Psychology, 9,* 52–54.

Bouchard, T. J., & Segal, N. L. (1985). Environment and IQ. In B. Wolman (Ed.), *Handbook of intelligence: Theories, measurement, and applications* (pp. 391–464). New York: Wiley.

Bower, E. M. (1974). The three-pipe problem: Promotion of competent human beings through a preschool, kindergarten program and other sundry elementary matters. In G. J. Williams & S. Gordon (Eds.), *Clinical child psychology: Current practices and future perspectives.* New York: Behavioral Sciences Press.

Buros, O. K. (Ed.) (1978). *Eighth mental measurements yearbook.* Highland Park, NJ: Gryphon Press.

Burrill, L. (1975). *Statistical evidence of potential bias in items and tests assessing current educational status.* Paper presented at the annual meeting of the Southeastern Conference on Measurement in Education, New Orleans.

Burt, C. (1921). *Mental and scholastic tests.* London: King.

Camilli, G., & Shepard, L. A. (1987). The inadequacy of ANOVA for detecting test bias. *Journal of Educational Statistics, 12,* 87–99.

Camilli, G., & Shepard, L. A. (1994). *Methods for identifying biased test items.* Thousand Oaks, CA: Sage.

Cardall, C., & Coffman, W. E. (1964). *A method of comparing the performance of different groups on the items in a test* (RB-64-61). Princeton, NJ: Educational Testing Service.

Cattell, R. B. (1979). Are culture fair intelligence tests possible and necessary? *Journal of Research and Development in Education, 12,* 3–13.

Chambers, J. S., Barron, F., & Sprecher, J. W. (1980). Identifying gifted Mexican-American students. *Gifted Child Quarterly, 24,* 123–128.

Chinn, P. C. (1979). The exceptional minority child: Issues and some answers. *Exceptional Children. 46,* 532–536.

Cleary, T. A., (1968). Test bias: Prediction of grades of negro and White students in integrated universities. *Journal of Educational Measurement, 5,* 118–124.

Cleary, T. A., & Hilton, T. L. (1968). An investigation of item bias. *Educational and Psychological Measurement, 28,* 6–75.

Cleary, T. A., Humphreys, L. G., Kendrick, S. A., & Wesman, A. (1975). Educational uses of tests with disadvantaged students. *American Psychologist, 30,* 15–41.

Cole, N. S., & Moss, P. (1989). Bias in test use. In R. Linn (Ed.), *Educational measurement* (3rd ed., pp. 201–219). New York: Macmillan.

Council for Exceptional Children (1978). Minorities position policy statements. *Exceptional Children, 45,* 57–64.

Critchley, D. L. (1979). The adverse influence of psychiatric diagnostic labels on the observation of child behavior. *American Journal of Orthopsychiatry, 49,* 157–160.

Cronbach, L. J. (1970). *Essentials of psychological testing.* New York: Harper & Row.

Cronbach, L. J. (1976). Equity in selection—where psychometrics and political philosophy meet. *Journal of Educational Measurement, 13,* 31–41.

Cronbach, L. J. (1980). Validity on parole: How can we go straight? In W. B. Schraeder (Ed.), *New directions for testing and measurement: Vol 5. Measuring achievement: Progress over a decade.* San Francisco: Jossey-Bass.

Cronbach, L. J., & Drenth, P. J. D. (Eds.) (1972). *Mental tests and cultural adaption.* The Hague, Netherlands: Mouton.

Cuccaro, M. L., Wright, H. H., Rownd, C. V., & Abramson, R. (1996). Professional perceptions of children with developmental difficulties: The influence of race and socieconomic status. *Journal of Autism and Developmental Disorders, 26,* 461–469.

Dana, R. H. (1993). *Multicultural assessment perspectives for professional psychology.* Needham Heights, MA: Allyn & Bacon.

Dana, R. H. (1996). Culturally competent assessment practices in the United States. *Journal of Personality Assessment, 66,* 472–487.

Darlington, R. B. (1978). Cultural test bias: Comments on Hunter and Schmidt. *Psychological Bulletin, 85,* 673–674.

Dean, R. S. (1977). Reliability of the WISC-R with Mexican-American children. *Journal of School Psychology, 15,* 267–268.

Dean, R. S. (1979). *WISC-R factor structure for Anglo and Hispanic children.* Paper presented at the Annual Meeting of the American Psychological Association, New York.

DeFries, J. C., Vandenberg, S. G., McClearn, G. E., Kuse,

A. R., Wilson, J. R., Ashton, G. C., & Johnson, R. C. (1974). Near identity of cognitive structure in two ethnic groups. *Science, 183,* 338–339.

Dworkin, N., & Dworkin, Y. (1979). The legacy of Pygmalion in the classroom. *Phi Delta Kappan, 61,* 712–715.

Ebel, R. L. (1979). Intelligence: A skeptical view. *Journal of Research and Development in Education, 12,* 14–21.

Eells, K., Davis, A., Havighurst, R. J., Herrick, V. E., & Tyler, R. W. (1951). *Intelligence and cultural differences: A study of cultural learning and problem-solving.* Chicago: University of Chicago Press.

Einhorn, H. J., & Bass, A. R. (1970). Methodological considerations relevant to discrimination in employment testing. *Psychological Bulletin, 75,* 261–269.

Fine, B. (1975). *The stranglehold of the IQ.* Garden City, NY: Doubleday.

Flaugher, R. L. (1978). The many definitions of test bias. *American Psychologist, 33,* 671–679.

Flaugher, R. L., & Schrader, W. B. (1978). *Eliminating differentially difficult items as an approach to test bias* (RB-78-4). Princeton, NJ: Educational Testing Service.

Flynn, J. R. (1991). *Asian-Americans: Achievement Beyond IQ.* Hillsdale, NJ: Erlbaum.

Foster, G., & Ysseldyke, J. (1976). Expectancy and halo effects as a result of artificially induced teacher bias. *Contemporary Educational Psychology, 1,* 37–45.

Frame, R. (1979, September). *Diagnoses related to school achievement, chlient's race, and socioeconomic status.* Paper presented at the Annual Meeting of the American Psychological Association, New York.

Freeman, F. N. (1923). A referendum of psychologists. *Century Illustrated Magazine, 107,* 237–245.

Gael S., & Grant, D. L. (1972). Employment test validation for minority and non-minority telephone company service representatives. *Journal of Applied Psychology, 56,* 135–139.

Goldman, R. D., & Hartig, (1976). The WISC may not be a valid predictor of school performance for primary-grade minority children. *American Journal of Mental Deficiency, 80,* 583–587.

Goldman, R. D., & Hewitt, B. N. (1976). Predicting the success of black, Chicano, Oriental, and white college students. *Journal of Educational Measurement, 13,* 107–117.

Goldstein, H., Krantz, D. L., & Rains, J. D. (Eds.) (1965). *Controversial issues in learning.* New York: Appleton-Century-Crofts.

Goolsby, T. M., & Frary, R. B. (1970). Validity of the Metropolitan Readiness Test for white and Negro students in a Southern city. *Educational and Psychological Measurement, 30,* 443–450.

Gordon, R. A. (1984). Digits backward and the Mercer–Kamin law: An empirical response to Mercer's treatment of internal validy of IQ tests. In C. R. Reynolds & R. T. Brown (Eds.), *Perspectives on bias in mental testing* (pp. 357–506). New York: Plenum.

Gordon, R. A. & Rudert, E. E. (1979). Bad news concerning IQ tests. *Sociology of Education, 52,* 174–190.

Gould, S. J. (1981). *The mismeasure of man.* New York: Norton.

Grant, D. L., & Bray, D. W. (1970). Validation of employment tests for telephone company installation and repair occupations. *Journal of Applied Psychology, 54,* 7–14.

Gross, A. L., & Su, W. (1975). Defining a "fair" or "unbiased" selection model: A question of utilities *Journal of Applied Psychology, 60,* 345–351.

Guilford Press (1997). Culturally sensitive assessment: Paying attention to cultural orientation. *Child Assessment News, 6,* 8–12.

Gulliksen, H., & Wilks, S. S. (1965). Regression tests for several samples. *Psychometrika, 15,* 91–114.

Guterman, S. S. (1979). IQ tests in research on social stratification: The cross-class validity of the test as measures on scolastic aptitude. *Sociology of Education, 52,* 163–173.

Gutkin, T. B., & Reynolds, C. R. (1980). Factorial similarity of the WISC-R for Anglos and Chicanos referred for psychological services. *Journal of School Psychology, 18,* 34–39.

Gutkin, T. B., & Reynolds, C. R. (1981). Factorial similarity of the WISC-R for White and Black children from the standardized sample. *Journal of Educational Psychology, 73,* 227–231.

Gutkin, T. B., & Tieger, A. G. (1979). Funding patterns for exceptional children: Current approaches and suggested alternatives. *Professional Psychology, 10,* 670–680.

Hambleton, R. K. (1994). Guidelines for adapting educational and psychological test: A progress report. *European Journal of Psychological Assessment, 10*(3), 229–244.

Hambleton, R. K., & Kanjee, A. (1995). Increasing the validity of cross-cultural assessments: Use of improved methods for test adaptations. *European Journal of Psychological Assessment, 11,* 147–157.

Hammill, D. (1991). *Detroit tests of learning aptitude* (3rd ed.). Austin, TX: PRO-ED.

Harman, H. (1976). *Modern factor analysis* (2nd ed.). Chicago: University of Chicago Press.

Harrington, G. M. (1975). Intelligence tests may favour the majority groups in a population. *Nature, 258,* 708–709.

Harrington, G. M. (1976, September). *Minority test bias as a psychometric artifact: The experimental evidence.* Paper presented at the Annual Meeting of the American Psychological Association, Washington, DC.

Hartlage, L. C., Lucas, T., & Godwin, A. (1976). Culturally biased and culturally—fair tests correlated with school performance in culturally disadvantaged children. *Journal of Consulting and Clinical Psychology, 32,* 325–327.

Helms, J. E. (1992). Why is there no study of cultural equivalence in standardized cognitive ability testing? *American Psychologist, 47,* 1083–1101.

Helms, J. E. (1994). The conceptualization of racial identity and other "racial" constructs. In E. Trickett, R. Watts, & D. Birman (Eds.), *Human diversity* (pp. 285–311). San Francisco: Jossey-Bass.

Henderson, N. B., Butler, B. B., & Goffeney, B. (1969). Effectiveness of the WISC and Bender–Gestalt test in predicting arithmetic and reading achievement for white and non-white children. *Journal of Clinical Psychology, 25,* 268–271.

Herrnstein, R. J., & Murray, C. (1994). *The bell curve.* New York: Free Press.

Hickman, J. A., & Reynolds, C. R. (1986). Are race differences on mental tests an artifact of psychometric methods: A test of Harrington's experimental model. *Journal of Special Education, 20,* 409–430.

Hildreth, G. H., Griffiths, N. L., & McGauvran, M. E. (1969). *Metropolitan Readiness Tests.* New York: Harcourt-Brace Jovanovich.

Hilgard, E. R., & Bower, G. H. (1975). *Theories of learning* (4th ed.). Englewood Cliffs, NJ: Prentice-Hall.

Hilliard, A. G. (1979). Standardization and cultural bias as impediments to the scientific study and validation of "intelligence." *Journal of Research and Development in Education, 12,* 47–58.

Hobbs, N. R. (1975). *The futures of children.* San Francisco: Jossey-Bass.

Humphreys, L. G. (1973). Statistical definitions of test validity for minority groups. *Journal of Applied Psychology, 58,* 1–4.

Hunter, J. E. (1975, December). *A critical analysis of the use of item means and item-test correlations to determine the presence or absence of content bias in achievement test items.* Paper presented at the National Institute of

Education Conference on Test Bias, Annapolis, MD.

Hunter, J. E., & Schmidt, F. L. (1976). Critical analysis of the statistical and ethnical implications of various definitions of test bias. *Psychological Bulletin, 83*, 1053–1071.

Hunter, J. E., & Schmidt, F. L. (1978). Bias in defining test bias: Reply to Darlington. *Psychological Bulletin, 85*, 675–676.

Hunter, J. E., Schmidt, F. L., & Hunter, R. (1979). Differential validity of employment tests by race: A comprehensive review and analysis. *Psychological Bulletin, 86*, 721–735.

Hunter, J. E., Schmidt, F. L., & Rauschenberger, J. (1984). Methodological, statistical, and ethical issues in the study of bias in psychological tests. In C. R. Reynolds & R. T. Brown (Eds.), *Perspectives on bias in mental testing* (pp. 41–100). New York: Plenum.

Jackson, G. D. (1975). Another psychological view from the Association of Black Psychologists. *American Psychologist, 30*, 88–93.

Jackson, R. (1980). The scholastic aptitude test: A response to Slack and Porter's "Critical appraisal." *Harvard Educational Review, 50*, 382–391.

Jacobs, W. R. (1978). The effect of the learning disability label on classroom teachers' ability objectively to observe and interpret child behaviors. *Learning Disability Quarterly, 1*, 50–55.

James, B. J. (1995). *A test of Harrington's experimental model of ethnic bias in testing applied to a measure of emotional functioning in adolescents.* Unpublished doctoral dissertation. Texas A&M Univeristy, College Station, TX.

Jensen, A. R. (1974). How biased are culture loaded test? *Genetic Psychology Monographs, 90*, 185–224.

Jensen, A. R. (1976). Test bias and construct validity. *Phi Delta Kappan, 58*, 340–346.

Jensen, A. R. (1977). An examination of culture bias in the Wonderlic Personnel test. *Intelligence, 1*, 51–64.

Jensen, A. R. (1980). *Bias in mental testing.* New York: Free Press.

Jensen, A. R. (1985). The nature of the Black–White differences on various tests: Spearman's hypothesis. *Behavioral and Brain Sciences, 8*, 193–263.

Jensen, A. R., & Figueroa, R. (1975). Forward and backward digit span interaction with race and IQ: Predictions from Jensen's theory *Journal of Education Psychology, 67*, 882–893.

Jöreskog, K. G. (1969). A general approach to confirmatory maximum likelihood factor analysis. *Psychometrika, 34*, 183.

Jöreskog, K. (1971). Simultaneous factor analysis in several populations. *Psychometrika, 30*, 409–426.

Kaiser, S. (1986). *Ability patterns of Black and White adults on the WAIS-R independent of general intelligence and as a function of socioeconomic status.* Unpublished doctoral dissertation, Texas A&M University, College Station, TX.

Kallingal, A. (1971). The prediction of grades for black and white students at Michigan State University. *Journal of Educational Measurement, 8*, 263–265.

Kamphaus, R. W., & Reynolds, C. R. (1987). *Clinical and research applications of the K-ABC.* Circle Pines, MN: American Guidance Service.

Kaufman, A. S. (1973). Comparison of the performance of matched groups of Black children and White children on the Wechsler Preschool and Primary Scale of Intelligence. *Journal of Consulting and Clinical Psychology, 4*, 186–191.

Kaufman, A. S. (1975). Factor analysis of the WISC-R at 11 age levels between 6½ and 16½ years. *Journal of Consulting and Clinical Psychology, 43*, 135–147.

Kaufman, A. S. (1979). *Intelligent testing with the WISC-R.* New York: Wiley-Interscience.

Kaufman, A. S., & DiCiuo, R. (1975). Separate factor analyses of the McCarthy Scales for groups of Black and White children. *Journal of School Psychology, 13*, 10–18.

Kaufman, A. S., & Hollenbeck, G. P. (1974). Comparative structure of the WPPSI for Black and Whites. *Journal of Clinical Psychology, 30*, 316–319.

Kaufman, A. S., & Kaufman, N. L. (1973). Black–White differences at age 21/2–81/2 on the McCarthy Scales of Children's Abilities. *Journal of School Psychology, 11*, 196–206.

Kaufman, A. S., & Kaufman, N. L. (1983). *Kaufman assessment battery for children.* Circle Pines, MN: American Guidance Service.

Keith, T. Z., & Reynolds, C. R. (1990). Measurement and design issues in child assessment research,. In C R. Reynolds & R. W. Kamphaus (Eds.). *Handbook of psychological and educational assessment of children* (Vol. 1, pp. 29–61). New York: Guilford Press.

Kerlinger, F. N. (1973). *Foundations of behavioral research.* New York: Holt, Rinehart & Winston.

Kimble, G. A. (1961). *Hilgard and Marquis' conditioning and learning* (2nd ed.). New York: Appleton-Century-Crofts.

Kirkpatrick, J. J. (1970, September). *The psychological testing establishment: Vested interest versus responsibility.* Paper presented at the annual meeting of the American Psychological Association, Miami Beach, FL.

Kirkpatrick, J. J., Ewen, R. G., Barrett, R. S., & Katzell, R. A. (1968). *Testing and fair employment.* New York: New York University Press.

Lambert, N. M. (1979). *Adaptive behavior assessment and its implications for educational programming.* Paper presented to the Fourth Annual Midwestern Conference on Psychology in the Schools, Boys Town, NE, October 1979.

Larry, P. et al. v. Wilson Riles et al., C 71 2270 (United States District Court for the Northern District of California, October, 1979, slip opinion).

Leventhal, D. S., & Stedman, D. J. (1970). A factor analytic study of the Illinois Test of Psycholinguistic Abilities. *Journal of Clinical Psychology, 26*, 473–477.

Lewis, D. O., Balla, D. A., & Shanok, S. S. (1979). Some evidence of race bias in the diagnosis and treatment of the juvenile offender. *American Journal of Orthopsychiatry, 49*, 53–61.

Lewontin, R. C. (1970). Race and intelligence. *Bulletin of the Atomic Scientists, 26*, 2–8.

Lindsey, J. (1967). *The factorial organization of intelligence in children as related to the variables of age, sex, and subculture.* Unpublished doctoral dissertation, University of Georgia.

Linn, R. L. (1976). In search of fair selection precedures. *Journal of Educational Measurement, 13*, 53–58.

Linn, R. L. (Ed.) (1989). *Educational Measurement* (3rd ed.). New York: Macmillan.

Linn, R. L., & Werts, C. E. (1971). Considerations for studies of test bias. *Journal of Educational Measurement, 8*, 1–4.

Lippmann, W. (1923a). A judgment of the tests. *New Public, 34*, 322–323.

Lippmann, W. (1923b). Mr. Burt and the intelligence tests. *New Republic, 34*, 263–264.

Loehlin, J. C., Lindzey, G., & Spuhler, J. N. (1975). *Race differences in intelligence.* San Francisco: W. H. Freeman.

Lonner, W. J. (1985). Issues in testing and assessment in cross-cultural counseling. *The Counseling Psychologist, 13*, 599–614.

MacCorquodale, K., & Meehl, P. E. (1948). On a distinction between hypothetical constructs and intervening variables. *Psychological Review, 55*, 95–107.

MacMillan, D. L., Jones, R. L., & Aloia, G. F. (1974). The mentally retarded label: A theoretical analysis and

review of research. *American Journal of Mental Deficiency, 79,* 241–261.
Mandler, G. (1975). *Mind and emotion.* New York: Wiley.
Mason, E. J. (1979). A blessing dressed up like the plague? *The School Psychologist, 35,* 6.
Matuszek, P., & Oakland, T. (1979). Factors influencing teachers' and psychologists' recommendations regarding special class placement. *Journal of School Psychology, 17,* 116–125.
Mayfield, J. W., & Reynolds, C. R. (in press). Are ethnic differences in diagnosis of childhood psychopathology an artifact of psychometric methods? An experimental evaluation of Harrington's hypothesis using parent reported symptomotology. *Journal of School Psychology.*
McCarthy, D. (1972). *McCarthy Scales of Children's Abilities.* San Antonio, TX: The Psychological Corporation.
McCoy, S. A. (1976). Clinical judgments of normal childhood behaviors. *Journal of Consulting and Clinical Psychology, 44,* 710–714.
McGurk, F. C. (1951). *Comparison of the performance of negro and White high school seniors on cultural and noncultural psychological test questions.* Washington, DC: Catholic University of America Press.
McNemar, Q. (1975). On so-called test bias. *American Psychologist, 30,* 848–851.
Mercer, J. R. (1971). The meaning of mental retardation. In R. Koch & J. Dobson (Eds.), *The mentally retarded child and his family: A multidisciplinary handbook.* New York: Brunner/Mazel.
Mercer, J. R. (1976). *Cultural diversity, mental retardation, and assessment: The case for nonlabeling.* Paper presented to the Fourth International Congress of the International Association for the Scientific Study of Mental Retardation, Washington, DC, August, 1976.
Mercer, J. R. (1979). *System of multicultural pluralistic assessment: Conceptual and technical manual.* San Antonio, TX: The Psychologcial Corporation.
Merz, W. R. (1970). *A factor analysis of the Goodenough–Harris drawing test across four ethnic groups.* Unpublished doctoral dissertation, University of New Mexico.
Meyers, C. E., MacMillan, D. L., & Yoshida, R. K. (1978). Validity of psychologists' identification of EMR students in the perspective of the California decertification experience. *Journal of School Psychology, 16,* 3–15.
Mille, F. (1979). Cultural bias in the WISC. *Intelligence, 3,* 149–164.
Mitchell, B. C. (1967). Predictive validity of the Metropolitan Readiness Tests and the Murphy-Durrell Reading Analysis for white and for Negro pupils. *Educational and Psychological Measurement, 27,* 1047–1054.
Moran, M. P. (1990). The problem of cultural bias in personality assessment. In C. R. Reynolds & R. W. Kamphaus (Eds.), *Handbook of psychological and educational assessment of children. Vol. 2. Personality, behavior and context* (pp. 524–545). New York: Guilford Press.
Moreland, K. L. (1996). Persistent issues in multicultural assessment of social and emotional functioning. In L. A. Suzuki, P. J. Meller, & J. G. Ponterrotto (Eds.), *Handbook of multicultural assessement: Clinical, psychological, and educational applications.* San Francisco: Jossey-Bass.
Nalven, F. B., Hoffman, L. J., & Bierbryer, B. (1969). The effects of subject's age, sex, race, and socioeconomic status on psychologists' estimates of "True IQ" from WISC scores. *Journal of Clinical Psychology, 25,* 271–274.
Nichols, R. C. (1978). Policy implications of the IQ controversy. In L. S. Schulman (Ed.), *Review of research in education* (Vol. 6). Itasca, IL: F. E. Peacock.
Novick, M. R., & Petersen, N. S. (1976). Towards equalizing educational and employment opportunity. *Journal of Educational Measurement, 13,* 77–88.
Oakland, T. (1978). Predictive validity of readiness tests for middle and lower socioeconomic status Anglo, black and Mexican American children. *Journal of Educational Psychology, 70, 574–582.*
Oakland, T., & Feigenbaum, D. (1979). Multiple sources of test bias on the WISC-R and Bender–Gestalt Test. *Journal of Consulting and Clinical Psychology, 47,* 968–974.
Oakland, T., & Matuszek, P. (1977). Using tests of nondiscriminatory assessment. In T. Oakland (Ed.), *Psychological and educational assessment of minority group children.* New York: Brunner/Mazel.
O'Conner, E. J., Wexley, K. N., & Alexander, R. A. (1975). Single group validity: Fact or fallacy. *Journal of Applied Psychology, 60,* 352–355.
Padilla, A. M. (1988). Early psychological assessment of Mexican-American children. *Journal of the History of the Behavioral Sciences, 24,* 113–115.
Padilla, A. M., & Medina, A. (1996). Cross-cultural sensitivity in assessment: Using tests in culturally appropriate ways. In L. A. Suzuki, P. J. Miller, & J. G. Ponterotto (Eds.), *Handbook of multicultural assessment: Clinical psychological, and educational applications* (pp. 3–28). San Francisco: Jossey-Bass.
PASE: Parents in action on special education et al. v. Hannon et al. No. 74 C 3586 (United States District Court for the Northern District of Illinois, Eastern Division, July, 1980, slip opinion).
Petersen, N. S., & Novick, M. R. (1976). An evaluation of some models for culture—fair selection. *Journal of Educational Measurement, 13,* 3–29.
Pfeifer, C. M., & Sedlacek, W. E. (1971). The validity of academic predictors for black and white students at a predominately white university. *Journal of Educational Measurement, 8,* 253–261.
Pintner, R. (1931). *Intelligence testing.* New York: Holt, Rinehart & Winston.
Plake, B., & Hoover, H. (1979, September). *A methodology for identifying biased achievement test items that removes the confounding in a items by groups interaction due to possible group differences in instructional level.* Paper presented at the annual meeting of the American Educational Research Association, Toronto.
Potthoff, R. F. (1966). *Statistical aspects of the problem of biases in psychological tests.* (Institute of Statistics Mimeo Series No. 479). Chapel Hill: University of North Carolina, Department of Statistics.
Ramsey, R. T. (1979). *The testing manual: A guide to test administration and use.* Pittsburgh: Author.
Reschly, D. J. (1978). WISC-R factor stuctures among Anglos, blacks, Chicanos, and Native American Papagos. *Journal of Consulting and Clinical Psychology, 46,* 417–422.
Reschly, D. J., & Reschly, J. E. (1979). Validity of the WISC-R factor scores in predicting achievement and attention for four sociocultural groups. *Journal of School Psychology, 17,* 355–361.
Reschly, D. J., & Sabers, D. (1979). Analysis of test bias in four groups with the regression definition. *Journal of Educational Measurement, 16,* 1–9.
Reynolds, C. R. (1978). *Differential validity of several preschool assessment instruments for Blacks, Whites, males, and females.* Unpublished doctoral dissertation, University of Georgia.
Reynolds, C. R. (1979a). Should we screen preschoolers? *Contemporary Educational Psychology, 4,* 175–181.
Reynolds, C. R. (1979b). A factor analytic study of the Metropolitan Readiness Test. *Contemporary Educational Psychology, 4,* 315–317.
Reynolds, C. R. (1979c). The invariance of the factorial validity of the Metropolitan Readiness Tests for blacks,

whites, males and females. *Educational and Psychological Measurement, 39,* 1047–1052.
Reynolds, C. R. (1980a). Differential construct validity of intelligence as popularly measured: Correlations of age with raw scores on the WISC-R for Blacks, White, males and females. *Intelligence, 4,* 371–379.
Reynolds, C. R. (1980b). An examination for test bias in a preschool battery across race and sex. *Journal of Educational Measurement, 17,* 137–146.
Reynolds, C. R. (1980c). In support of "Bias in Mental Testing" and scientific inquiry. *The Behavioral and Brain Sciences, 3,* 352.
Reynolds, C. R. (1982a). The problem of bias in psychological assessment. In C. R. Reynolds & T. B. Gutkin (Eds.), *The handbook of school psychology.* New York: Wiley.
Reynolds, C. R. (1982b). Construct and predictive bias. In R. A. Berk (Ed.), *Handbook of methods for detecting test bias* (pp. 199–227). Baltimore: Johns Hopkins University Press.
Reynolds, C. R. (1990). Conceptual and technical problems in learning disability diagnosis. In C. R. Reynolds & R. W. Kamphaus (Eds.), *Handbook of psychological and educational assessment of children* (Vol. 1, pp. 571–592). New York: Guilford Press.
Reynolds, C. R. (1995). Test bias and the assessment of intelligence and personality. In D. Saklofske & M. Zeidner (Eds.), *International handbook of personality and intelligence* (pp. 545–573). New York: Plenum.
Reynolds, C. R. (1997a). Measurement and statistical problems in neuropsychological assessment of children. In C. R. Reynolds & E. Fletcher-Janzen (Eds.), *Handbook of clinical child neuropsychology* (2nd ed., pp. 180–203). New York: Plenum.
Reynolds, C. R. (1997b). Forward and backward memory span should not be combined for clinical analysis. *Archives of Clinical Neuropsychology, 12,* 29–40.
Reynolds, C. R. (in press). Need we measure anxiety differently for males and females. *Journal of Personality Assessment.*
Reynolds, C. R., & Bigler, E. D. (1994). *Test of memory and learning.* Austin, TX: PRO-ED.
Reynolds, C. R., & Brown, R. T. (1984). Bias in mental testing: An introduction to the issues. In C. R. Reynolds & R. T. Brown (Eds.), *Perspectives on bias in mental testing* (pp. 1–39). New York: Plenum.
Reynolds, C. R., & Gutkin, T. B. (1980a). A regression analysis of test bias on the WISC-R for Anglos and Chicanos referred for psychological services. *Journal of Abnormal Child Psychology, 8,* 237–243.
Reynolds, C. R., & Gutkin, T. B. (1980b, September). *WISC-R performance of Blacks and Whites matched on four demographic variables.* Paper presented at the Annual Meeting of the American Psychological Association, Montreal.
Reynolds, C. R., & Gutkin, T. B. (1980c). Stabillity of the WISC-R factor structure across sex at two age levels. *Journal of Clinical Psychology, 36,* 775–777.
Reynolds, C. R., & Gutkin, T. B. (1981). A multivariate comparison of the intellectual performance of Black and White children matched on four demographic variables. *Personality and Individual Differences, 2,* 175–180.
Reynolds, C. R., Gutkin, T. B., Dappen, L., & Wright, D. (1979). Differential validity of the WISC-R for boys and girls referred for psychological services. *Perceptual and Motor Skills, 48,* 868–870.
Reynolds, C. R., & Harding, R. E. (1983). Outcome in two large sample studies of factorial similarity under six methods of comparison. *Educational and Psychological Measurement, 43,* 723–728.
Reynolds, C. R., & Hartlage, L. C. (1978, March). *Comparison of WISC and WISC-R racial regression lines.* Paper presented at the annual meeting of the Southeastern Psychological Association, Atlanta.
Reynolds, C. R., & Hartlage, L. C. (1979). Comparison of WISC and WISC-R regression lines for academic prediction with Black and with White referred children. *Journal of Consulting and Clinical Psychology, 47,* 589–591.
Reynolds, C. R., & Jensen, A. R. (1983). *Patterns of intellectual performance among Blacks an Whites matched on "g."* Paper presented to the Annual Meeting of the American Psychological Association, Montreal, September, 1983.
Reynolds, C. R., & Kaiser, S. (1990). Test bias in psychological assessment. In T. B. Gutkin & C. R. Reynolds (Eds.), *The handbook of school psychology* (2nd ed., pp. 487–525) New York: Wiley.
Reynolds, C. R., & Kamphaus, R. W. (1992). *Behavior assessment system for children: Manual.* Circle Pines, MN: American Guidance Service.
Reynolds, C. R., & Paget, K. (1981). Factor analysis of the Revised Children's Manifest Anxiety Scale for Blacks, Whites, males, and females with a national normative sample. *Journal of Consulting and Clinical Psychology, 49,* 352–359.
Reynolds, C. R., Willson, V. L., & Chatman, S. P. (1984). Item bias on the 1981 revisions of the Peabody Picture Vocabulary Test using a new method of detecting bias. *Journal of Psychoeducational Assessment, 2,* 219–224.
Reynolds, C. R., Willson, V. L., & Chatman, S. P. (1985). Regression analyses of bias on the K-ABC. *Journal of School Psychology, 23,* 195–204.
Ross, A. O. (1974). A clinical child psychologist "examines" retarded children. In G. J. Williams & S. Gordon (Eds.), *Clinical child psychology: Current trends and future perspectives.* New York: Behavioral Publications.
Ross, A. O. (1976). *Psychological aspects of learning disorders of children.* New York: McGraw-Hill.
Samuda, A. J. (1975). *Psychological testing of American minorities: Issues and consequences.* New York: Dodd, Mead.
Sandoval, J. (1979). The WISC-R and internal evidence of test bias with minority groups. *Journal of Consulting and Clinical Psychology, 47,* 919–927.
Sandoval, J., & Mille, M. (1980). Accuracy judgments of WISC-R item difficulty for minority groups. *Journal of Consulting and Clinical Psychology, 48,* 249–253.
Sawyer, R. L., Cole, N. S., & Cole, J. W. (1976). Utilities and the issue of fairness in a decision theoretic model for selection. *Journal of Educational Measurement, 13,* 59–76.
Scheuneman, J. D. (1987). An experimental, exploratory study of causes of bias in test items. *Journal of Educational Measurement, 24,* 97–118.
Schmidt, W. H. (1983). Content biases in achievement tests. *Journal of Educational Measurement, 20, 165–178.*
Schmidt, F. L., & Hunter, J. E. (1974). Racial and ethnic bias in psychological tests: Divergent implications of two definitions of test bias. *American Psychologist, 29,* 1–8.
Schoenfeld, W. N. (1974). Notes on a bit of psychological nonsense: "Race differences in intelligence." *Psychological Record, 24,* 17–32.
Scholwinski, E. (1985). *Ability patterns of White and Black adults as determined by the subscales of the WAIS-R.* Unpublished doctoral dissertation, Texas A&M University, College Station, TX.
Semler, I., & Iscoe, I. (1966). Structure of intelligence in Negro and White children. *Journal of Educational Psychology, 57,* 326–336.
Sewell, T. E. (1979). Intelligence and learning tasks as predictors of Scholastic achievement in Black and White first-grade children. *Journal of School Psychology, 17,* 325–332.
Shepard, L. S. (1982). Definitions of bias. In R. A. Berk (Ed.), *Handbook of methods for detecting test bias.*

Baltimore: Johns Hopkins University Press.

Shuey, A. M. (1966). *The Testing of Negro intelligence* (2nd ed.). New York: Social Science Press.

Silverstein, A. R. (1973). Factor structure of the Wechsler Intelligence Scale for Children for three ethnic groups. *Journal of Educational Psychology, 65,* 408–410.

Stanley, J. C. (1971). Predicting college success of the educationally disadvantaged. *Science, 171,* 640–647.

Stanley, J. C., & Porter, A. C. (1967). Correlation of scholastic aptitude test scores with college grades for Negroes vs. whites. *Journal of Educational Measurement, 4,* 199–218.

Stern, W. (1914). *The psychological methods of testing intelligence.* Baltimore: Warwick & York.

Sternberg, R. J. (1980). Intelligence and test bias: Art and science. *Behavioral and Brain Sciences, 3,* 353–354.

Stricker, L. J. (1982). Identifying test items that perform differentially in population subgroups: A partial correlation index. *Applied Psychological Measurement, 6,* 261–273.

Temp, G. (1971). Validity of the SAT for blacks and whites in thirteen integrated institutions. *Journal of Educational Measurements, 8,* 245–251.

Tenopyr, M. L. (1967, September). *Race and socioeconomic status as moderators in predicting machine-shop training success.* Paper presented at the annual meeting of the American Psychological Association, Washington, DC.

Thorndike, R. L. (1971). Concepts of culture-fairness. *Journal of Educational Measurement, 8,* 63–70.

Tittle, C. K. (1975). Fairness in educational achievement testing. *Education and Urban Society, 8,* 86–103.

Tittle, C. K. (1982). Use of judgemental methods in item bias studies. In R. A. Berk (Ed.), *Handbook of methods for detecting test bias.* Baltimore: Johns Hopkins University Press.

Tomlinson, J. R., Acker, N., Canter, A., & Lindborg, S. (1977). Minority status, sex, and school psychological services. *Psychology in the Schools, 14,* 456–460.

Torrance, E. P. (1980). Psychology of gifted children and youth. In W. M. Cruickshank (Ed.), *Psychology of exceptional children and youth.* Englewood Cliffs, NJ: Prentice-Hall.

Tyler, L. E. (1965). *Psychology of human differences.* New York: Appleton-Century-Crofts.

Van de Vijver, F., & Hambleton, R. K. (1996). Translating tests: Some practical guidelines. *European Psychologist, 1,* 89–99.

Vance, H. B., & Wallbrown, F. H. (1978). The structure of intelligence for Black children: A hierarchical approach. *Psychological Record, 28,* 31–39.

Vance, H. B., Huelsman, C. B., & Wherry, R. J. (1976). The hierarchical factor structure of the Wechsler Intelligence Scale for Children as it relates to disadvantaged White and Black children. *Journal of General Psychology, 95,* 287–293.

Veale, J. R., & Foreman, D. I. (1983). Assessing cultural bias using foil response data: Cultural variation. *Journal of Educational Measurement, 20,* 249–258.

Wallbrown, F. H., Blaha, J., & Wherry, R. J. (1973). The hierarchical factor structure of the Wechsler Adult Intelligence Scale. *British Journal of Educational Psychology, 44,* 47–56.

Wechsler, D. (1949). *Wechsler Intelligence Scale for Children.* New York: Psychological Corporation.

Wechsler, D. (1974). *Wechsler Intelligence Scale for Children-Revised.* New York: The Psychological Corporation.

Wechsler, D. (1975). Intellegence defined and undefined: A relativistic appraisal. *American Psychologist, 30,* 135–139.

Wechsler, D. (1981). *Wechsler Adult Intelligence Scale-Revised.* San Antonio, TX: The Psychological Corporation.

Wherry, R. J., & Wherry, R. J., Jr. (1969). WNEWH program. In R. J. Wherry (Ed.), *Psychology department computer program.* Columbus, OH: Ohio State University.

Willerman, L. (1979). *The psychology of individual and group differences.* San Francisco: W. H. Freeman.

Williams, R. L. (1970). Danger: Testing and dehumanizing Black children. *Clinical Child Psychology Newsletter, 9,* 5–6.

Williams, R. L. (1972, September). *The BITCH-100: A culture specific test.* Paper presented at the annual meeting of the American Psychological Association, Honolulu.

Williams, R. L. (1974). From dehumanization to black intellectual genocide: A rejoinder. In G. J. Williams & S. Gordon (Eds.), *Clinical child psychology: Current practices and future perspectives.* New York: Behavioral Publications.

Williams, R. L., Dotson, W., Dow, P., & Williams, W. S. (1980). The war against testing: A current status report. *Journal of Negro Education, 49,* 263–273.

Willson, V. L., Nolan, R. F., Reynolds, C. R., & Kamphaus, R. W. (1989). Race and gender effects on item functioning on the Kaufman Assessment Battery for Children. *Journal of School Psychology, 27,* 289–296.

Wilson, K. M. (1969). *Black students entering CRC colleges: Their characteristics and their first year academic performance* (Research memo No. 69-1). Poughkeepsie, NY: College Research Center.

Wright, B. J., & Isenstein, V. R. (1977). Psychological tests and minorities. Rockville, MD: NIMH, DHEW Publication No. (ADM) 78–482 (reprinted 1978).

Zigler, E., & Butterfield, E. C. (1967). Motivational aspects of changes in IQ test performance of culturally deprived nursery school children. *Child Development, 39,* 1–14.

10.04
Cross-cultural Clinical Interventions

JOHN E. LEWIS
Nova Southeastern University, Fort Lauderdale, FL, USA

10.04.1 INTRODUCTION 94

10.04.2 PROXIMAL VS. DISTAL VARIABLES 95

10.04.2.1 Proximal Variables 95
10.04.2.2 Distal Variables 96

10.04.3 CLINICAL INTERVENTION PROCESSES 97

10.04.3.1 Cross-cultural Competence and Sensitivity 97
10.04.3.2 Intercultural Communication Style 98
10.04.3.3 Cross-cultural Verbal Communication 100
10.04.3.4 Nonverbal Communication 100
10.04.3.4.1 Proxemics 100
10.04.3.4.2 Kinesics 101
10.04.3.4.3 Paralinguistics 103
10.04.3.5 Use of Translators 103

10.04.4 THERAPIST–CLIENT MATCH 104

10.04.5 TREATMENT OUTCOME 107

10.04.5.1 Definition 107
10.04.5.2 Cross-cultural Outcome Research 107

10.04.6 METHODOLOGICAL CONSIDERATIONS 109

10.04.6.1 Reliability and Validity in Cross-cultural Research 109
10.04.6.2 Recommendations 110

10.04.7 FUTURE DIRECTIONS 111

10.04.7.1 Terminology 111
10.04.7.2 Ethical and Professional Issues 112
10.04.7.3 Future Research 112
10.04.7.3.1 Research agenda 113
10.04.7.3.2 Assessment techniques 114
10.04.7.3.3 Theory of multicultural counseling and therapy 114
10.04.7.3.4 Specific research topics 114
10.04.7.4 Global Psychology 115

10.04.8 SUMMARY 116

10.04.9 REFERENCES 116

10.04.1 INTRODUCTION

While attempts have been made to trace the evolution of multicultural counseling from ancient civilizations to the present day (Thompson, 1989), current thinking supports the notion that multicultural counseling is only several decades old. This is evidenced by the increased intercultural focus in publications from 1960 to 1995 (Jackson, 1995).

Early in the 1990s multicultural counseling and therapy (MCT) was hailed as the fourth force in psychology (Pedersen, 1990, 1991b, 1994; Pedersen & Ivey, 1993). As a result, the movement has been to formulate a framework for MCT in an attempt to describe and explain the impact of cultural diversity on psychotherapeutic interventions. This movement spawned a definitive explication of MCT theory in a conceptual treatise (Sue, Ivey, & Pedersen, 1996). The work provides a metatheory for cross-cultural interventions that espouses six basic propositions, encompassing 47 corollary suppositions.

The propositions and corollaries were originally proposed by Sue (1995), but were refined by Sue et al. (1996) to help psychologists move from a culture-bound theory of intervention to a theory that could encompass a variety of existing world views. The propositions and corollaries acknowledge that (i) both therapist and client identities are formed and embedded within a complex set of experiences that have a fluid dimension and a contextual salience, (ii) the development of one's cultural identity encompasses attitudes to one's own culture and other cultures; (iii) psychotherapeutic outcomes are more successful when goals and therapy modalities are consistent with a client's values, goals, and cultural experiences; and (iv) individual counseling may need to be balanced with models that incorporate family and societal units.

This new framework spawned critical debate (Casas & Mann, 1996; Corey, 1996) centered on the lack of adequate definitions within the field of MCT. The terms "race," "ethnicity," "minority," and "culture" have not been clarified and, thus, are constantly confused by professionals (Atkinson, Morten, & Sue, 1993). In 1994, Pedersen defined these terms. He stated that race is a classification based on genetic or biological differences and includes a shared genetic history and/or physical characteristics such as skin color; ethnicity refers to a common sociocultural history that can include political history, similar genealogy, and religion; minority is used to identify a group that has been treated unfairly or has suffered from collective discriminating practices due to the minorities' lack of power in the dominant culture; finally, culture has taken on broader implications in the literature of the 1990s to include demographic variables (e.g., age, gender, and region), status variables, affiliation variables, and the traditional variables of race and ethnicity. This view of culture focuses on its nonstatic nature, as culture also denotes patterns of behavior, family life, and beliefs (Fernando, 1995). Poortinga (1992) has argued that culture constitutes a set of shared constraints that limit individual members of groups in terms of their behavioral responses.

Goodchilds (1991) described race and ethnicity as dimensions not categories. Phinney (1996) argued that one needs to explore three dimensions that differ between and within ethnic groups: "First, cultural norms and attitudes that may be influential in psychological processes. ... Second, the strength, salience, and meaning of individuals' ethnic identities. ... Third, individuals' experiences as a member of a minority group with lower status and power" (p. 925). Readers are diverted to more complete explanations of the terminology concerning culture, race, and ethnicity (Gaw, 1993; Jackson, 1995; Marsella & Pedersen, 1981; Marsella & White, 1982; Pedersen, 1991b; Phinney, 1996).

This new emphasis has spawned concern about the terminology and definitions used by researchers and practitioners alike. In particular, current terms such as "multicultural counseling," "culture-centered counseling," cross-cultural intervention," "cross-cultural communication," "minority counseling," and "pluralism" have tended to obfuscate an already complex area of interest.

Pedersen (1991b) has suggested that psychologists use a broad definition of culture that includes demographic variables such as economics and education as well as informal and formal affiliation variables to supplement the traditional cultural variables of ethnicity, race, nationality, religion, and linguistic group. This wide view of culture seeks to balance culture-specific with universal perspectives that underlie a client's behavior, cognition, and affect. Pedersen (1991a) has also called for the term "multicultural counseling and therapy" to be used since it "implies a wide range of multiple groups without grading, comparing, or ranking them as better or worse than one another and without denying the very distinct and complementary perspective that each group brings with it" (p. 4).

Keeping in the forefront the concepts and definitions integral to MCT, this chapter will focus on issues pertaining to cross-cultural interventions. First, proximal and distal factors will be described. Second, interviewing and clinical interventions will be examined, by summarizing the research on effective intercultural communication, and verbal/nonverbal language factors in counseling and psychotherapy. Third, the issue of client and therapist match will be explored. This discussion will evaluate the notion that therapists and clients from similar backgrounds have more accurate communication and greater potential for successful therapeutic outcomes. Fourth, the treatment outcome literature will be examined with a view to evaluating the efficacy of particular intervention strategies with culturally different clients. Fifth, present and future methodological issues that relate to the clinical interventions with a culturally diverse clientele will be examined. Finally, future issues in this area will be discussed.

10.04.2 PROXIMAL VS. DISTAL VARIABLES

Two prerequisites of culturally responsive behavior are attitudes and beliefs (Ridley, Mendoza, Kanitz, Angermeier, & Zenk, 1994). These two constructs can be discussed by using Poortinga's (1992) notion that behavioral responses are dependent upon internal and external constraints which are governed by a person's sociocultural history. These constraints have been delineated into two variables: internal–proximal and external–distal. Proximal variables, also called proximal levels, include aspects of the immediate setting and behavior of the client, and the "related flux of affect and cognition during a particular interaction" (Fletcher & Fitness, 1990, p. 464). Distal variables, or levels, are generally "stable dispositional variables that predate the immediate proximal context" (Fletcher & Fitness, 1990, p. 464). Distal variables include personality characteristics, levels of effect, and client expectations. They also include ethnicity and race (Sue, Zane, & Young, 1994).

10.04.2.1 Proximal Variables

The effect of proximal variables on relationships and communication processes has emerged in studies originating in the field of social cognition (Bradbury & Fincham, 1988; Fletcher & Fitness, 1990; Kelly et al., 1983). The social cognition notion of proximal level can be expanded into cross-cultural interactions. The therapist must identify the thoughts and feelings experienced by the client immediately preceding a therapy session, especially values and beliefs (Bond & Smith, 1996).

The study of values within a cross-cultural framework is best exemplified in the work of Kluckhohn and Strodtbeck (1961). This model recognized that cultures differ in their perception of time, attitudes towards activity, their lineal versus collateral relationships, and their notion of the nature of people. These value orientations have been modified and expanded by Ibrahim, (1985) and Kohls (1979) to provide social/cultural interpretations and examples. Carter (1991) reviewed the research on the Kluckhohn–Strodtbeck model and concluded that a counselor needed to understand a culture's value structure if he or she hoped to understand both the unique and universal attributes of that culture.

Schwartz (1992, 1994) has examined the universal content and structure of values. He identified, through the results of a self-report values instrument, 10 universal value domains at the individual level and seven at the global cultural level. Scores were obtained for 38 different cultural groups (Schwartz, 1994). These culture-level scores have been compared to the results obtained in Hofstede's studies. Hofstede (1980, 1991) described a pattern of universal and culture-specific variables in 55 countries. He identified measures that related to thinking, feeling, and behaving and claimed that these patterns, or mental programs, were constructed differently by different cultures at different times. In addition, he described four dimensions that varied among the countries: small/large power distance, collectivism vs. individualism, femininity vs. masculinity, and weak/strong uncertainty avoidances. More recently, researchers (Kim, Triandis, Kagitcibasi, Choi, & Yoon, 1994; Smith, Peterson, Akande, Callan, & Cho, 1995) have examined specific value orientations in different countries and have illustrated clear patterns of cultural difference with respect to external–internal control and collectivism, respectively.

Whereas values exemplify what a culture or individual holds as important, beliefs encompass an individual's or culture's sense of how the world is construed. The most often studied variable in this area is locus of control. This concept was formulated by Rotter (1966) and incorporated the notion that people have differential beliefs about how outcomes are obtained in relation to personal power. Rotter described two dimensions, internal control and external control. Internal control referred to the idea that people can control their own outcomes. External control referred to the notion that outcomes are more determined by chance environmental circumstances rather than personal power. Through the socialization process, people learn one of these two views. These locus-of-control beliefs of clients are related to how a client experiences "control harmony, and submission with respect to the environment" (Bond & Smith, 1996, p. 211).

Locus of responsibility is closely related to locus of control. This belief, which has emerged largely from attribution theories in social cognition (Fiske & Taylor, 1991), is concerned with how much blame is placed on individuals or systems. Sue and Sue (1990) have described these emphases as important for a client's life orientation development. They believe that a person-oriented, person-blame individual tends to focus on individual responsibility attributes. He or she tends to focus on a person's motivations, values, feelings, and goals and tends to attribute successful or unsuccessful outcomes to a person's strengths and weaknesses. These individuals see a strong relationship between individual effort and success. This stance allows some members of the dominant culture to view minorities as totally responsible for their behavior and ignore contextually relevant information that may contribute to or cause a person's behavior. Some clients, on the other hand, tend to be situation-blaming. They tend to attribute successful and unsuccessful outcomes to variables outside of themselves, in the sociocultural environment. Sue and Sue believe that therapists need to view the individual–system blame continuum in an effort to understand their clients and to see the culturally relevant factors that may impact on a person's situation.

Other beliefs that are not universal, but culturally specific, have been suggested. They include the notion of justice (Furnham, 1993), global cooperation (Der-Kerabetian, 1992), and beliefs and attitudes about the work ethic (Furnham, Bond, Heaven, Hilton, & Lobel, 1993). Further research is needed to clarify and verify these variables.

10.04.2.2 Distal Variables

There has been a notable lack of empirical studies that have focused on external–distal factors. Bond and Smith (1996) have concluded that "almost all current models of cultural difference are thus proximal rather than distal" (p. 211). Sue and Zane (1987) discussed the proximal–distal issue by evaluating whether cultural knowledge or culture-specific techniques were linked to psychotherapeutic success. They formulated a proximal–distal model that suggested cultural knowledge and technique-oriented methods in therapy are of a distal nature and, therefore, may not contribute significantly to effective counseling and psychotherapy. Rather, they believe that "it may be wiser to focus on the proximal process of therapist credibility" (p. 39). This credibility involves a therapist's ability to conceptualize the client's problem, sensitivity to culturally appropriate means of problem resolution, and client–therapist goal compatibility. In other words, high achieved and ascribed credibility is likely to produce an effective therapeutic process, whereas low ascribed and achieved credibility will result in early termination of therapy.

Akutsu, Lin, and Zane (1990) stated that the proximal–distal model predicts that counselor credibility is related to continued involvement in treatment, whereas the distal variables, cultural knowledge, and techniques are mediated through the credibility that exists in the therapeutic relationship. They tested the proximal–distal model with Chinese students and concluded that counselor credibility was related to the client's intention to utilize therapy and that relationship variables and therapist style were mediated through the subject's evaluation of the counselor's credibility. Proximal factors, therefore, were seen as essential for continued intentions for therapy by culturally diverse clients.

Berry (1990) has studied distal factors with respect to ethnic group relationships. He identified a map of relationships that included three sociocultural factors: collective stereotypes, history–economics–politics, and collective behaviors. These categories influenced various psychological variables, including perception, attribution, attitudes, and behavior. Fiske (1992) has described sociocultural factors by proposing a four-component model, stating that social relationships in cultures include communal sharing, authority, ranking, equality matching, and market pricing. Berry (1990) and Triandis (1994) have called for more studies that are sensitive to external, distal ethnic variables.

The preceding discussion has encompassed the notion that universal and culture-specific thoughts, feelings, and behaviors affect client–therapist interaction. It was Frank (1961) that stated a "psychotherapist in any culture works to assist in the definition of subtle gradations of implicit rules governing behavior which derive from a vast array of norms, value systems, and ideologies present in the shared assumptive worlds of the patient and therapist" (p. 28). Therapists with culturally diverse clients are required to decode implicit rules that are culturally determined and to make them more situationally appropriate in therapy. It necessitates a therapist's close attention to what individual and sociocultural variables are salient at any given moment during the cross-cultural interaction. Failure to do so will result in cultural encapsulation, ineffective client–therapist relationships, and possible ineffective treatment outcomes.

The issues involved with distal and proximal variables are at the core of interviewing skills and clinical interventions. The act of interviewing and therapy involves the formation of a close relationship between client and therapist. This relationship, inevitably, exposes the proximal and distal factors present in the lives of both participants. Sensitivity to proximal and distal factors, as well as culture-specific and universal expressions of behavior from a client, are fundamental concerns in clinical interventions.

10.04.3 CLINICAL INTERVENTION PROCESSES

The area of clinical intervention process encompasses topics as diverse as cross-cultural sensitivity and competence, intercultural communication style, cross-cultural verbal communication, nonverbal communication, and the role of translators during therapy.

10.04.3.1 Cross-cultural Competence and Sensitivity

Cross-cultural counseling has been defined as "any counseling relationship in which two or more participants differ in cultural background, values, and lifestyle" (Sue et al., 1982, p. 47). This definition has led many counselors and therapists to the conclusion that *all* counseling could be considered to have a multicultural dimension (Pedersen, 1994; Speight, Myers, Cox, & Highlen, 1991; Sue, Ivey, & Pedersen, 1996). In fact, it is argued that within-group differences have at least equal impact as between-group differences on the clarification of cultural issues (Speight et al., 1991).

These definitions and statements have demanded the attention of organizations and policy makers concerned with the provision of psychological services. In 1992, the Association for Multicultural Counseling and Development (AMCD), a branch of the American Counseling Association (ACA), published a document that outlined multicultural counseling competencies and standards for inclusion in psychological service provider programs. This document espoused a three-by-three matrix for organizing and developing cross-cultural competencies. This matrix identified three areas of concern: (i) beliefs and attitudes, (ii) knowledge, and (iii) skills in relation to counselor self-awareness, counselor understanding of client's world view, and the development of culturally appropriate intervention strategies and techniques. Of particular relevance were the recommendations for interventions, which included the need for more accurate verbal communication, increased understanding of nonverbal communication, greater proficiency in dealing with clients' diverse behavioral and affective response styles, and increased understanding of the role of societal and familial issues in therapy.

In 1993, the American Psychological Association (APA) established guidelines for the provision of services to ethnic, linguistic, and culturally diverse populations. These guidelines stated: "Psychologists need a sociocultural framework to consider diversity of values, interactional styles, and cultural expectations in a systematic fashion" (p. 45). In response to this need for frameworks for effective cross-cultural interactions, psychologists have examined cultural differences and universal expressions of client behavior (Sue & Sue, 1990).

Culture tends to have a limiting or restructuring effect on universal expression. These cultural differences create stress on the therapeutic relationship. Problems can occur when the therapist becomes too enamored of his or her own cultural values. Wrenn (1962, 1985) created the term "cultural encapsulation" to describe the notion that some therapists: (i) substitute stereotypes for the real world, (ii) ignore cultural variations across cultures, and (iii) adhere to a technique-oriented, static notion of the therapeutic process. The result of cultural encapsulation is that the therapist's role becomes rigidly defined with an ensuing universal notion of health, normality, and pathology.

This notion of cultural encapsulation led Sue and Sue (1990) to outline the characteristics of the culturally skilled counselor and therapist. These characteristics involve the development of attitudes and beliefs that have understanding of the self and the client's world view at their core. The culturally skilled counselor (pp. 167–169):

(i) has moved from being culturally unaware to being aware and sensitive to his or her own cultural heritage and to valuing and respecting differences;

(ii) is aware of his or her own values and biases and how they might affect minority clients;

(iii) is comfortable with differences that exist between themselves and their clients in terms of race and beliefs;

(iv) is sensitive to circumstances (personal biases, stage of ethnic identity, sociopolitical influences, etc.) that may dictate referral of a minority client to a member of his or her own race or culture or to another counselor in general;

(v) is aware of his or her own racial attitudes, beliefs, and feelings;

(vi) must possess specific knowledge and information about the particular group he or she is working with;

(vii) must have a good understanding of the sociopolitical systems' operation with respect to its treatment of minorities;

(viii) has clear and explicit knowledge of the generic characteristics of counseling and therapy;

(ix) is aware of the institutional barriers that prevent minorities from using mental health services.

These attributes of the skilled multicultural therapist have been discussed more elaborately in the cross-cultural competencies and standards outlined by Sue, Arredondo, and McDavis (1992). Attempts to measure these competencies have been made with two rating scales: the Cross-cultural Competence Inventory (Hernandez & LaFromboise, 1985) and the Cross-cultural Competence Inventory–Revised (LaFromboise, Coleman, & Hernandez, 1991) and three self-report measures: the Multicultural Awareness–Knowledge–Skills Survey (D'Andrea, Daniels, & Heck, 1991), the Multicultural Counseling Awareness Scale (Ponterotto, Sanchez, & Magids, 1991), and the Multicultural Counseling Inventory (Sodowski, Taffe, Gutkin, & Wise, 1994).

Cultural sensitivity has been defined in various ways: cross-cultural competence, cross-cultural expertise, cross-cultural effectiveness, culture responsiveness, cultural awareness, and cultural skill. This has led to confusion in the vast literature surrounding cultural sensitivity (Ridley, 1984; Ridley et al., 1994) as authors have tended to use the terms interchangeably. Speigal and Papajohn (1986) have accordingly questioned how one can operationalize the terminology in order to construct treatment models.

Ridley et al. (1994) have called for cultural sensitivity that is linked to culturally responsive interventions. They formulated a model that proposed that cultural sensitivity can be viewed as being measured on a continuum which has underlying prerequisite behaviors, culturally responsive behavior, and the effects of this culturally responsive behavior. The assumptions that underlie this model are fivefold. First, the authors believe that cultural sensitivity depends on the personal meaning that a client has about events that depend on the broad spectrum of cultural attitudes available to the client (Pedersen, 1994). Second, therapists need to adopt a "naive" posture in processing information (p. 129). Third, cultural sensitivity is a prerequisite for interventions that are culturally responsive.

Fourth, cultural differences that exist between client and therapist may interfere with a therapist's information processing. Fifth, cultural sensitivity is grounded in the information processing theory of perceptual schemata; mental schemata develop likely as a natural process during client and therapist interactions. The authors have called for empirical studies that can verify or expand this model.

Culturally sensitive counselors, therefore, are seen as implicitly facilitating therapy that has more effective outcomes for diverse clients, while culturally insensitive counselors are seen as ineffective change agents. Culturally insensitive counselors have been viewed as a main contributor to problems of ethnocentrism, lack of empathy, misdiagnosis, and treatment selection errors (Gim, Atkinson, & Kim, 1991). In addition, the underutilization of mental health services and early termination by minorities have been attributed to the lack of sensitive therapy services (Romeo, 1985; Sue & Sue, 1990).

Pedersen and Lefley (1986), Sue and Sue (1990), and Sue et al. (1992) state that, for effective counseling to occur, the counselor and the client must also be able to appropriately and accurately send and receive both verbal and nonverbal messages. The next section of this chapter looks at the various factors that lead to effective interviewing and counseling. In order to understand effective interviewing and counseling strategies, however, one must first examine the elements of effective intercultural communication and the barriers present in non-effective communication. This necessitates a discussion of how communication styles differ between client and therapist.

10.04.3.2 Intercultural Communication Style

Communication style refers to those aspects that go beyond the literal content presented in verbal interactions. It includes the cadence of speech, inflection, tone, syntactical structure, fluidity, and depth. Communication styles are strongly correlated with race, ethnicity, and culture (Sue & Sue, 1990). For example, Yum (1991) has suggested that Confucianism has strongly impacted on communication styles with Asians; the main function of communication is to initiate, foster, and maintain social relationships. Communication, therefore, encourages these relationships and sets the framework for an infinite interpretation (Cheng, 1987).

In a multicultural setting the therapist usually conducts therapy without the familiar cultural guidelines that are normally present in counseling sessions with mainstream clients (Pedersen, 1994). Garza, (1981) focused on issues that emerge during initial diagnostic interviews with minorities. He discussed the notion that therapists, when confronted with a culturally different client, depart from their usual ways of interviewing. These departures include the use of cultural stereotypes as a distancing device. The therapist also tends to use generalizations which produce dehumanizing consequences. Furthermore, therapists are guilty of simplifying the task of diagnosis by overinterpreting, Garza stated:

> Overdiagnosing issues around cultural difference, precise and accurate as it may be, can at times serve the purpose not so much of enhancing the diagnostic process through the lens of a bicultural perspective, but of avoiding the task of really getting into the complexities of another's individual life. (p. 15)

Sue and Sue (1990) have delineated generic characteristics in Western counseling and psychotherapy. These characteristics incorporate culture, class, and language issues. Specifically, these generic characteristic include standard English, verbal communication, individual-centered therapy, verbal/behavioral/emotional expressiveness, openness, cause and effect attributions, and clear mental–physical dimensions. In addition, counseling models and techniques have traditional middle-class use of language, verbal communication, rigid time frames, long-range goals, and ambiguity. Sue and Sue (1990) describe these variables as being largely used in Western models of counseling and therapy. Non-Western cultures, on the other hand, have different modes of expressing affect, using silence, different language usage, differing time perspectives, nonstandard English, and a focus on individualism versus collectivism.

Sue (1977, 1981) has outlined in detail the barriers to effective cross-cultural counseling that have evolved as a natural consequence of utilizing generic modes of counseling with culturally diverse clients. Culture-bound values encompass several areas of concern. First, most forms of therapy are individually focused, emphasizing the importance of the client–counselor relationship. Some Western cultures, such as are found in the USA, have been identified as cultures that are based on individualism and competition between members. Individualism and competitiveness are seen as virtues within the culture. Not all cultures are based on this notion of individualism. Many cultures are socialized in a system of communality and codependence. The values in non-Western cultures differ markedly in that some might view individualism as an impediment to true mental health. Thus, counselors who do not deal with individualism versus group orientation will potentially create problems in the interview. An extensive review of cooperation and individualism in various cultures has provided support for this viewpoint (McGoldrick, Pearce, & Giordano, 1982).

Second, many therapists create an atmosphere within an interview that promotes verbal, emotional, and behavioral expressiveness. It is felt that such openness will allow a more accurate exploration of the problem and concomitant issues. Also, that it will provide a more focused emphasis on intrapsychic issues. This belief is especially important since it can lead to misperceptions and labeling of the client's reactions during the interview. Clients are in danger of being labeled as apathetic, repressed, or resistant if they do not exhibit expressiveness and openness. An open, expressive communication style is not predominant in Hispanic, Asian, or Aboriginal cultures (Sue & Sue, 1990). Studies have shown, for instance, that Chinese and Japanese cultures value restraint of feeling and circumspectual approaches when communicating (Samovar & Porter, 1991). Additionally, openness and expressiveness are antithetical to Native American communication styles (Dignes, Trimble, Manson, & Pasquale, 1981; Thomason, 1991).

Many interviews and psychotherapeutic interventions encourage and foster self-disclosure from the client. The problem with this approach is that self-disclosure has been determined to be a negative value trait among many cultures (Sue & Sue, 1990). Self-disclosure is a Western psychotherapeutic value. It has been called the *sine qua non* of most approaches to therapy (Poston, Craine, & Atkinson, 1991). Therapists may misinterpret a client's nondisclosure, as different cultures teach and validate different levels of self-disclosure (Pedersen, 1994).

Another culture-bound barrier involves the notion of "insight" in psychotherapy. Client insight is generally assumed to have positive or beneficial consequences, but clients from different cultures may place lower value on insight (Sue & Sue, 1990). This dichotomy can impede accurate communication. In addition, Sue and Sue described counseling and therapy within a Western context as linear and analytic with an emphasis on cause-and-effect explanations of healthy psychological functioning and psychological maladjustment. This reliance on scientific method and rationalism has contributed to

client–counselor barriers in therapy, since different attributions about the etiology of psychological problems may exist between client and therapist.

Finally, the culture-bound barrier of ambiguity is concerned with the level of structure that is present in an interview or counseling session. Sue and Sue (1990) state that lack of definitive structure may be confusing to clients from Hispanic backgrounds and may impede the communication process. They go on to state that the patterns of communication among culturally diverse clients are dependent upon one's cultural upbringing.

The focus on differing communication styles has led to an ever-increasing list of models, prescriptives, and resources for effective interviewing and counseling with specific populations (ACA, 1990; APA, 1994; Eisenbruch, 1990; Fiksdal, 1990; Gonzalez-Lee & Simon, 1990; Hollingsworth, 1987; Pedersen & Ivey, 1993; Song & Parker, 1995; University of Wisconsin, 1991). In particular, these differences in communication styles have led to a detailed examination of language issues that encompass verbal and nonverbal aspects of communication.

10.04.3.3 Cross-cultural Verbal Communication

Language issues constitute one of the most important differences and one of the greatest barriers to effective communication between cultures (Argyle, 1991). Labov and Fanshel (1977) state that the most important data during the counseling session are the words spoken by the client and counselor and, thus, whatever is construed from these words. Further, Ivey (1981) has stated that any person-to-person encounter must consider the language of helping. This is especially crucial in multicultural counseling since different cultures use different words, syntax, and constructs to convey meaning.

Ivey called for an examination of language patterns as central to effective cross-cultural interviewing and therapy. Language in therapy can be idiosyncratic and misunderstood by therapists who are not familiar with a particular culture (Draguns, 1981). Meaning is lost in therapy when the counselor is not attuned to the subtleties of specific cultural uses of affect, diagnosis, and treatment (Vontress, 1981; Yamamoto, Silva, Justice, Chang, & Leong, 1993).

Yum (1991) has indicated that east Asian communication patterns differ from those in North America. East Asian languages are very complex and there are honorific linguistic systems present in Asia which differentiate the use of words based on formality or informality of context (Ogino, Misono, & Fukushima, 1985). Dillard (1983) and McWhirter and Ryan (1991) have described the enormous number of dialects and language systems in North American native clients. Cross (1995), Dillard (1983), Pennington (1979), and Sue and Sue (1990) have described the language characteristics of African-Americans and their impact on therapy.

Language plays a critical role in psychotherapy, especially when the therapist and client do not share a common language. Westermeyer (1993) has stated that most cultures have a *lingua franca* or single major language. Comas-Diaz and Griffith (1988) have described the differential impact of a client using nonstandard English. They claimed that clients are diagnosed and assessed primarily on the basis of their ability to use standard English. They stressed the importance of accurate and meaningful client–therapist communication.

10.04.3.4 Nonverbal Communication

Effective intercultural counselors need to be aware of the total process of communication. They must be sensitive to the fact that communication is both verbal and nonverbal (Wolfgang, 1985). The study of nonverbal behavior has been divided into three areas: proxemics, kinesics, and paralinguistics. Overviews of the early work done in nonverbal communication can be found in Harper, Wiens, & Matarazzo (1978), Henley (1977), and LaFrance and Mayo (1978), and a comprehensive bibliography of the nonverbal literature from 1859 to 1983 has been compiled by Wolfgang and Bhardwaj (1984).

10.04.3.4.1 Proxemics

Hall (1959) initiated the study of proxemics. He demonstrated the impact of ethnicity and culture on various nonverbal behaviors such as eye contact, gestures, and personal space. The term "personal space" was introduced by Sommer (1959) to denote the area that separates ourself from others. The size of this area varies with situations and contexts. Hall (1969) delineated four zones of interpersonal distance that characterize Western culture: intimate (up to 18 inches), personal (18–48 inches), social (48 inches to 12 feet), and public (greater than 12 feet). Extensive research into proxemics has revealed that conversational distances vary cross-culturally and that these differences have an impact on formal and informal counseling interactions (Wolfgang, 1985).

Ramsay (1979) examined the studies that evolved from the proxemic inventory described by Hall (1959). These studies examined Arabs, Latin Americans, southern Europeans, northern Europeans, Indians, Pakistanis, east Asians, and Puerto Ricans. This body of literature served to illustrate that different cultures have different culturally determined ideas of appropriate social distance. Hanna (1984) studied the interactional distances between blacks and whites in the USA and discovered substantial variation in conversational distance. Jensen (1985) discovered smaller acceptable conversational distances for Latin-Americans, Africans, African-Americans, Indonesians, Arabs, and South Americans than Anglos.

Some studies have extended the investigation to include cultural attitudes toward crowding and its resultant effect on intimacy (Altman, 1975; Altman & Chemers, 1980; Pandey, 1978, 1990, 1996; Worchel & Teddlie, 1976). These studies illustrate that attitudes towards crowding differ around the world with respect to individual comfort level, as every culture has different tolerance levels for personal space. Further research is needed to clarify the relationship of these findings to the dynamics of interviewing.

10.04.3.4.2 Kinesics

The study of kinesics was originally described by Birdwhistell (1970) and focused on body movements. Kinesics include facial expressions, gestures, eye behavior, and posture. Kinesics are influenced strongly by the norms of one's culture (Smith, 1984). Rosenthal, Hall, Archer, Dimatteo, and Rogers (1979) discovered that subjects from outside of the USA, in countries that were culturally and/or linguistically similar (e.g., Canada, New Zealand, and the UK), scored higher than other nations on tests measuring the nonverbal accuracy of meaning. In other words, the subjects were able to interpret the body movements and gestures accurately. American subjects received the highest accuracy scores, indicating that culturally specific cues are present in a person's body language. Key (1975) described nonverbal acts within an overall structure that related kinesic qualities to communication channel, time, distance relationship, cultural affiliation, environmental considerations, and individual differences. She believed the preceding determinants of nonverbal language should be considered as interactional in nature.

Sue and Sue (1990) state that eye contact is "perhaps the non-verbal behavior most likely to be addressed by mental health providers ... counselors attribute negative traits to the avoidance of eye contact: shy, unassertive, sneaky, or depressed" (p. 55). Studies have illustrated that higher levels of gaze and eye contact invite more positive reciprocal nonverbal behavior (Smith, 1984). Studies on gaze behavior in Europe have been analyzed and summarized by Ellgring (1984); these studies showed cross-national differences among subjects.

Ramsey (1984) discovered differences between Eastern and Western cultures in eye gazing behavior largely through an analysis of studies conducted in Japan. Graham (1985) discovered differences in gazing behavior among Brazilian, Japanese, and American negotiators. Researchers have investigated the role of gaze-directed behavior and reciprocal interactions (Argyle & Cook, 1976; Argyle & Dean, 1965; Exline, Gray, & Schuette, 1985). Johnson (1972) discovered differences between black and white clients with respect to eye movements and discovered eye-rolling behavior in black American speakers. These eye movements were used to convey disapproval, impudence, and hostility.

Ivey (1994) identified the dimensions of attending. The first dimension concerned the use of the eyes. He stated that eye contact is desirable in some cultures, while in others it has negative connotations. He claimed that eye behavior had the universal characteristic of being used to convey meaning. Ivey concluded that eye contact should be modeled by the counselor as early in the relationship as possible. Pedersen and Ivey (1993) offer practical suggestions on improving one's eye contact and other attending skills for use in cross-cultural counseling and therapy.

Gestures refer to the types of hand movements that people make. Although there has been a great deal of disagreement as to what constitutes a gesture (Krauss, Chen, & Chawla, 1996), a typology of gestures has been proposed by Kendon (1983). This classification system describes symbolic, conversational, and adaptational gestures. The differentiation of gestures grew largely out of early anthropological studies with Darwin and included the work of Kleinberg and LaBarre (Efron, 1972; Ramsey, 1979). Morris, Collette, Marsh, and O'Shaughnessy (1979) studied the meaning given to various hand movements in British, Greek, Spanish, Turkish, and Italian subjects. They studied 20 forms of gestures and discovered that only two had universal use, and five had widespread use. The occurrences of the remaining gestures were found to be culturally specific. They concluded that people from various regions in Europe use substantively different gestures when communicating.

The most often studied area in cross-cultural interaction is conversational gestures, which are hand movements that accompany speech and seem to be related to the meaning of that speech. LaBarre (1985) documented the different gestures of politeness in south Asian, African, European, Pacific islander, east Asian, and American cultures. He also identified cross-cultural differences in gestures of contempt, beckoning behavior, kissing, and sticking out of one's tongue. These culturally determined nonverbals have been analyzed extensively by Krauss, Chen, and Chawla (1996). They have indicated that gestures contribute to comprehension and communicative intent in conversations and interviews. Touching another person has been studied from a cross-cultural perspective. It has been claimed that touching holds special significance in Anglo cultures because of its infrequency of occurrence (Henley & LaFrance, 1984). Touching behavior studies, even though generally focused on gender issues, have been reviewed by Knapp (1984).

Eakins and Eakins (1985) have gone beyond looking at hand movements to an examination of head movements. Jensen (1985) has illustrated that cultural differences exist in the meaning attached to head movements. A most detailed focus on head movements can be found in Erickson and Schultz (1982). The authors used a microethnographic approach to study social interactions. Head-nodding behavior was analyzed within a cultural context. It was discovered that head nodding was part of a conversational rhythm that contained culturally specific patterns. They described the impact of cultural organization or shared standards and communication traditions on nonverbal social interactions. They stated that "both the ends and means of communication are culturally defined as appropriate, effective, and intelligible. When persons meet who have learned different communicative traditions regarding intelligibility, effectiveness, and appropriateness, troubles can result in the social organization of their interaction" (p. 100).

Pearson (1985) believed counseling interpretations can be based on the facial expressions of a client. Early studies of facial expression focused on the universality of expressions and the culturally specific interpretations of facial movement (Ekman & Friesen, 1975; Izard, 1971). Ekman (1993) claimed that such psychological luminaries as Allport, Brunswik, Hull, Maslow, and Titchner all studied facial expressions early in their careers, each focusing on the dilemma of whether or not facial expressions are universal or culture-specific. Ekman concluded after considering the history of kinesics, "I found more than one answer. Different aspects of expression are both universal and culture-specific" (p. 391). In particular he studied facially active vs. facially inactive subjects.

The first issue of concern was specificity. This refers to any differences that exist in the manifestation of emotions. Are clients facially active with some emotions, yet facially inactive with others? Ekman (1993) concluded that individual differences are present with respect to specificity and that future research on these differences may shed light on the issue of universality. Yamamoto and Kubota (1983) described the differences in facial expressions between Asian and European clients. In particular, restraint of facial expressions was valued in Asian culture.

The second issue is threshold. Do individuals have a lower threshold for emotional experience than facial expression? Are clients able to experience psychological distress without showing physical signs? Izard and Izard (1980) theorized there was a cultural universality of emotion that was strongest in the area of primary emotions such as fear, sadness, and happiness. He argued the further one was removed from these basic primary emotions, the more cultural specificity occurred in the expression of emotion. Ekman (1993) has suggested further research is needed in this area.

Choosing one postural stance from the many options that are available appears to be culturally determined (Hewes, 1955; Ramsey, 1979). Mehrabian (1972) described posture as having two dimensions. These dimensions, immediacy and relaxation, were found to be related to how one communicates one's attitudes. Leaning forward increases immediacy of contact and communicates acceptance and liking. Leaning backwards tends to indicate relaxation and sometimes disinterest. These dimensions have been studied by Bond and Shirashi (1974) with Japanese subjects. They discovered preferences for counselors to lean forward, since flexibility and politeness were attributed to this postural movement. Scheflen (1964) linked the notion of posture congruence to successful psychotherapy. He claimed that if a therapist wished to communicate congruent feelings, he or she needed to have a relaxed posture that was reflective of his or her state of mind.

From the field of neurolinguistic programming there have begun to emerge studies on posture that are cross-cultural in scope. Sandhu (1984) found that therapists' mirroring of Choctaw adolescents in the USA increased adolescents' perceptions of empathy present in the therapists. Sandhu, Reeves, and Portes (1993) further studied the effects of mirroring on empathy with Native Americans. They concluded that postural mirroring may significantly aid in the building of rapport with culturally different clients.

10.04.3.4.3 Paralinguistics

Paralinguistics is the study of vocal cues that clients use to communicate meaning. Poyatos (1984) defined paralanguage as "the ever present co-occurrent voice modifications or alternating independent sounds of perfectly lexical value" (p. 433). These aspects of language include the higher volume used in conversation with Latins and Arabs, high-pitched or breathy intonations of some clients, tongue clicking as seen in South Africa, and sighing. It includes the use of silence, hesitations or pauses, rate of speech, inflections, and expressiveness (Sue & Sue, 1990).

Lass, Mertz, and Kimmel (1978), Mehrabian and Ferris (1976), and Poyatos (1976, 1984) concluded that paralanguage is culture specific. Wolfgang (1985) has described the use of extraverbal elements associated with speech, from a cross-culture perspective. He has described these elements as operating at the unconscious level in clients. Weitz (1972) outlined the effects of paralanguage in black American and white American communications. Crystal (1975) has looked at the various cultural uses of paralanguage. Apple, Streeter, and Krauss (1979) indicated that pitch and speech rate can significantly affect a person's attributions. Erickson and Shultz (1982) provided a detailed exploration of interactional rhythmic styles in social interactions. They explored cultural differences with regard to pauses, hesitation, and silences. The authors concluded "behavioral regularity, especially rhythmic regularity, may be *prima facie* evidence of shared interpretative frameworks among those engaged in interaction" (p. 143).

Nonmembers of the culture may display interactional arrhythmia and fail to engage a client in a smooth conversation or verbal interaction. Erickson and Shultz (1982) have claimed that when counseling occurs with ethnically and racially diverse clients, interactional arrhythmia occurs which causes discomfort in the one-on-one interview. These interactional differences may cause counselors who are unaccustomed to the interactional rhythm to be "out of sync in communicating" (Kim, 1988, p. 91) with different language proficient clients. In addition, Kim (1988) indicated that stuttering, accents, and other paralinguistic patterns which differ from the language used in therapy could also stifle the communication process.

Thomas (1995) has stated that, in Great Britain, English is the predominant language used in intercultural counseling. He believes that therapists experience difficulty in attending to the message delivered by the client because of differential usages of the English language. These paralinguistic patterns also include the notion of monochronic and polychronic time systems (Hall, 1976). Hall stated that monchronic time patterns are prevalent in the USA, where punctuality is valued, and the pace of the conversation differs from the polychronic time orientation found in Mexico and other Latin American countries. Kim (1988) stated that these vocal patterns help to establish the emotional and attitudinal foundations of social interaction and clarify the relationship between client and therapist.

10.04.3.5 Use of Translators

Translation has been described as "the exchange of the demonstrative meaning of a word, phrase, or sentence in one language for the same meaning in another language" (Westermeyer, 1993, p. 129). Some therapists call for literal translations when working with linguistically different clients; however, many therapists move beyond literalism to the interpretation of a client's words through the discovery of connotative meanings. The latter is attempted in order to achieve accuracy of meaning. De Figueiredo (1976) and de Figueiredo and Lemkau (1980) stressed the need for accurate translation when interviewing in Portuguese and Knokani in Goa, India. Kline, Acosta, Austin, and Johnson (1980) interviewed Spanish-speaking patients with the aid of an interpreter. They discovered increased patient satisfaction and greater client understanding.

Therapy with the use of translators has been shown to be time-consuming, inaccurate, and difficult (Carillo, 1982). Marcos (1976) has studied bilingual therapists and patients and discovered that language switching can be used by the patient to distance themselves from emotional issues in therapy. This process, labeled "code switching" (Pitta, Marcos, & Alpert, 1978), has been shown to occur in Hispanic clients (Price & Cuellar, 1981; Rivas-Vazquez, 1989). Russell (1988) determined that code switching during an interview or therapy session is a clear signal from the client that clinicians should ignore; it will have impact on the credibility of the therapist. In cultures where bilingualism is present, code switching can occur. The result is that communication accuracy is minimized (Berkanovic, 1980; Kline et al., 1980). Moreover, when bilingual clients switch to their mother tongue, an increase in emotional response has been observed (Marcos, Urcuyo, Kesselman, & Alpert, 1973). Santiago-Rivera (1995) has concluded that therapists need to assess a client's language dominance and preference prior to assessing their psychological and physical health.

Difficulties in translating mental health concepts into different languages occur when attempting to apply Western methods of therapy in other parts of the world. Westermeyer (1993) illustrated these issues with Thai-Lao language translators. Nichter (1981) discovered similar issues when working in south India where undesirable connotations occurred with translated terminology. Edgerton and Karno (1971) discovered differences between Mexican-American English speakers and Mexican-American Spanish speakers with respect to describing symptomatology. Jackson and Moto (1996) translated various forms of psychopathology and therapy terms from English into Chichewa, one of the main languages in Malawi, Africa. They discovered that some words lacked accurate English equivalents.

Acosta, Yamamoto, and Evans (1982) have called for non-Spanish-speaking therapists to use trained interpreters when conducting interviews with Spanish-speaking clients to ensure accuracy of communication. Trained bilingual interpreters have been used with success in community clinics in the USA (Acosta & Cristo, 1981). Baker (1981) advocated the use of interpreters with culturally diverse clients. He worked with south Asian refugees and recommended the creation of a group of interpreters who understood psychological and social processes. Additionally, Owan (1985) extensively discussed the successful use of interpreters when interviewing south east Asian clients.

Freed (1988) found that interpreters who had backgrounds in social work and psychology were effective largely due to the fact they could facilitate a therapeutic alliance with the therapist. She listed a series of translator considerations deemed important for the establishment of accurate and meaningful communication. These factors included role definition, assurance of confidentiality, cultural differences, and the individual characteristics of the translator.

While skillful translators appear to be desirable, evidence suggests that low socioeconomic clients use nonstandardized English which can create difficulties for middle-class formal language users. Forrest, Ryan, and Lazar (1978) showed that foreign medical graduates were more deficient in slang than in standard English. This factor caused them difficulty when communicating with clients. This prompted the creation of a course "American for Foreign Medical Graduate Psychiatric Residents" designed to equip therapists with slang, colloquial language, and subtleties of humor. Follow-up indicated that greater communication skills were present in the trained experimental group than in those in a nontrained control group.

The use of bilingual or bicultural counseling has received attention in the literature. Ruiz and Casas (1981) indicated that bicultural counseling can be considered as a blending of majority and minority approaches to communication. There is evidence that bicultural/bilingual therapists have increased flexibility, greater tolerance for ambiguity, and serve well as cultural mediators (Szapocznik, Rio, Perez-Vidal, Kurtines, & Sanisteban, 1986).

Song and Parker (1995) focused on bicultural Chinese-English and Korean-American young adults. They discovered their interviews were filled with shifting multiple positions as well as identifications rather than a single unitary focus on identification. This introduction of complexity into the interview has been deemed to have a positive impact on meaningful communication (Pedersen, 1991c, 1994). Rogler (1993) has examined the impact of bilingualism on the development of diagnostic errors with culturally diverse clients. He proposed a research framework designed to facilitate a culturally sensitive diagnostic interview that encompasses the assessment of symptoms from a culturally appropriate viewpoint.

Salzma (1995) discovered that cross-cultural interactions were replete with attributional discrepancies, partially based on linguistic factors. He studied Navajo and Athabascan Native Americans and discovered many assessment errors occurred during diagnostic interviews. These errors were due to linguistically based attribution biases which occurred because of differences between client and therapist. These differences included social distance, taciturnity, length of pause, and initiation of speech.

Ho (1987, 1992) calls for care in the assessment of a client's fluency in English and their dominant language when choosing a treatment modality. He delineated guidelines in this area for working with Asian-American families. Similarly, Nguyen (1992) examined Asian-American communication patterns and called for therapists to consider the metaphoric nature of Japanese, Chinese, and Vietnamese languages.

10.04.4 THERAPIST–CLIENT MATCH

There has been a long-standing debate over the issue of whether a client should be given therapy by a culturally similar therapist or one who is not of the same cultural background. Atkinson 1983, 1985) provided comprehensive reviews of the studies that occurred in the 1970s and early 1980s. Atkinson and Lowe (1995) updated the earlier reviews with a more contemporary discussion of preference for counselor ethnicity. They stated that early research on client–therapist match focused on the preferences of African-American clients. Most studies (e.g., Bernstein, Wade, & Hofmann, 1987; Greene, 1982; Harrison, 1975; Sattler, 1977) revealed that African-American clients preferred African-American counselors and that Asian-Americans preferred Asian-American therapists over white therapists. These studies were predicated on the work of Carkhuff and Pierce (1967), LeVine and Campbell (1972), Mitchell (1970), and Stanges and Riccio (1970) which indicated that clients prefer counselors who are culturally similar to them.

Higginbotham (1977) and Higginbotham, West, and Forsyth (1988) provided an alternative point of view by concluding that race or ethnicity may not be the most important variable in cross-cultural counseling. They believed that situational, rather than cultural, variables could evoke client outcome expectancies. In addition, Atkinson (1983) concluded that, even though African-American clients showed a preference for racially similar counselors, other ethnic groups showed no such preference. Instead, these studies have stressed that other variables of counselor effectiveness have a greater impact with ethnically diverse clients. Parloff, Waskow, and Wolfe (1978) have pointed out the need to include the sex, socioeconomic status, and attitude of the counselor in client preference studies. Some studies have concluded that clients actually prefer ethnically dissimilar counselors (Gamboa, Tosi, & Riccio, 1976). In addition, Flaskerud (1990) reviewed the literature on client match from 1970 to 1990 and concluded that there was no strong support for the notion that client–therapist match in ethnicity, language, and gender had positive effects on the process or outcome of therapy.

Many studies in the 1980s focused on the impact of racial identification on preference for counselors (Parham & Helms, 1981, 1985; Sanchez & Atkinson, 1983). These studies concluded that the more one identified with one's own cultural group, the greater likelihood of preference for an ethnically/racially similar therapist. In addition, some researchers have focused on the issue of clinical judgment as it is related to the ethnicity of the therapist (Lopez & Hernandez, 1987; Malgady, Rogler & Constantino, 1987; Pakov, Lewis & Lyons, 1989). They discovered that clients perceive ethnically/racially similar counselors as possessing greater clinical judgment skills than nonsimilar counselors.

In the 1990s, the majority of studies have tended to support the notion that ethnically/ racially diverse clients prefer ethnically/racially similar therapists (Coleman, Wampold, & Casali, 1995). The following three studies, however, have failed to support this notion. Steward, Gimenez, and Jackson (1995) studied the preferences of academically successful, culturally diverse students and concluded that ethnic match was not a well-defined preference among this group. Sue, Fujino, Hu, Takeuchi, and Zane (1991) failed to show any treatment effects when counselors were matched for ethnicity. Gottheil, Sterling, Weinstein, and Kurtz (1994) matched therapists and patients with respect to gender and race. The matching did not increase the proportion of cocaine-dependent patients that returned for a second session.

The following studies, however, have examined client preferences, and results support the notion that clients prefer same-race/ethnic counselors. These studies focus on Asian-American, Hispanic-American, African-American, and Native American subjects.

Yeh, Eastman, and Cheung (1994) investigated the effects of language and ethnic match with Asian-American clients and therapists. Ethnic match was a significant predictor of the dropout rate after the first session, while language match failed to predict early termination of counseling. Takeuchi, Mokuau, and Chun (1992) investigated the counselor matching among Asian-American and Pacific islander clients. They discovered that ethnic matching significantly reduced premature termination of therapy. In fact, when clients were matched with ethnically similar therapists they were five times less likely to prematurely leave therapy than clients matched with an ethnically similar therapist. They found, however, no subject differences in global functioning, an outcome measure of psychological, social, and occupational functioning as determined by the Global Assessment Scale.

Yeh, Takeuchi, and Sue (1994) discovered that Asian-American children and adolescents who received treatment at facilities with ethnically similar therapists were more likely to remain in therapy and achieve higher functioning upon termination than those at facilities with mainstream professionals. Flaskerud and Liu (1991) discovered that ethnicity match with Asian clients and therapists significantly reduced the early termination rate but did not affect global functioning scores. The researchers also examined the effect of counselor language and ethnicity on the outcome of therapy with southeast Asian clients (Flaskerud & Liu, 1990). Ethnicity match and language match significantly increased the number of client sessions but not the overall global functioning upon discharge. Flaskerud and Hu (1994) further studied the process of therapy for Asian-Americans suffering from major depression. They concluded that treatment by an ethnically similar therapist within an ethnically matched facility was related to the duration of treatment, not to the clients's global functioning upon termination of therapy. Fujino, Okazaki, and Young (1994) examined therapist–client match with Asian-American female clients. They concluded that ethnic match was significantly related to lowered premature termination, increased treatment duration, and higher functioning upon termination.

Tedeschi and Willis (1993) examined the attitudes of Asian international students toward counseling. Asian subjects were found to prefer an older counselor of similar ethnicity. Gim et al. (1991) examined the effects of counselor ethnicity on clients' perceptions of counselors credibility and efficacy. Asian-Americans were shown to attribute greater effectiveness and credibility to Asian counselors.

Atkinson and Matsushita (1991) discovered that Japanese-Americans were most apt to seek counseling from a directive Japanese-American counselor. Ngugen (1992) discovered that Asian-American patients extended therapy with Asian-American therapists. Several disadvantages were noted in the study with therapist matching. Some Vietnamese-American and Chinese-American clients preferred Western therapists, because of a fear of encountering breaches of confidentiality with Asian-American therapists, a concept apparently not totally adhered to in Asian-to-Asian encounters.

Lopez, Lopez, and Fong (1991) reviewed client preference among Mexican-Americans. They discovered that all studies supported the notion that Mexican-American clients prefer ethnically similar counselors. The authors stated they had conducted two studies of their own confirming this preference. A third study showed that medium and highly acculturated Mexican-Americans indicated greater preference for same-ethnicity counselors than Mexican-Americans with low acculturation.

Atkinson and Wampold (1993) critiqued the methodology used to obtain these conclusions. They called for the avoidance of simple choice methods to assess preference for counselors with Mexican-Americans. Further, Atkinson, Casas, and Abreu (1992) examined low-, medium-, and high-acculturated Mexican-Americans in relation to perceived counselor competence. They concluded that cultural competence was related to perceived cultural responsiveness, regardless of counselor ethnicity or client acculturation. Hess and Street (1991) studied Mexican-American high school students with respect to the effects of counselor ethnicity. No significant differences were found in the ratings of effectiveness in relation to ethnicity. Yeh et al. (1994) reported a lower therapy dropout rate when Mexican-American clients were matched with ethnically similar therapists. Sue et al. (1991) showed that ethnic match between Mexican clients and therapists increased the length of treatment and improved the effectiveness of therapy.

While most research indicates problems with matching of black clients with white therapists (Krause & Miller, 1995), problems associated with black therapists working with black clients have been observed (Montalvo & Gutierrez, 1988; Thomas, 1995). These matching studies have focused on the attractiveness and credibility of the therapist.

Tomlinson-Clarke and Cheatham (1993) matched ethnically/racially similar counselors with black and white clients. They discovered no significant differences in counselor judgments (i.e., clinical disposition, severity of diagnostic rating, need for psychological treatment, and predicted number of sessions) upon intake when clients were matched with similar counselors. Goldberg and Tidwell (1990) investigated perceived counselor–client similarity and its relationship to the clients' perceptions of attractiveness and the satisfaction derived from therapy. They investigated both gender and race with black and white counselors and students. They concluded that racial and gender differences appeared not to function as barriers to effective communication. They suggested instead that other counselor variables such as attitudes and personality were more important characteristics for perceived competence.

Redfern, Dancey, and Dryde (1993) examined the role of counselor ethnicity with English black and white undergraduate students. Black counselors were rated higher than white counselors on scales of attractiveness, competency, and trustworthiness. Tomlinson and Cheatham (1989) examined the effects of ethnicity match on intake interviews with black clients. They concluded that the race of the therapist affected the clinical judgments at the time of client intake.

Race and ethnicity have been studied within the psychoanalytic relationship (Leary, 1995). Three patients were paired with an African-American therapist. Qualitative descriptions showed the importance of client–therapist negotiation when racial characteristics differ. In addition, White (1994) investigated the impact of race and ethnicity on transference and countertransference in interracial group psychotherapy and discovered differential transference issues related to the race or ethnicity of the therapist.

Bennett and Bigfoot-Sipes (1991) examined Native American and white college student preferences for counselor ethnicity. They concluded that both American Indian and white students preferred counselors to have similar values, but Native Americans showed greater preferences for ethnically similar counselors, while white students showed no such preference. In addition, Johnson and Lashley (1989) examined the counselor preferences of Native American undergraduate students. They discovered that clients with a strong cultural commitment to Native American values placed great importance on the ethnicity of the counselor by preferring counselors with similar ethnic backgrounds.

Comas-Diaz and Jacobsen (1987) proposed that a client's ethnocultural identity be assessed as an auxiliary therapeutic tool. One aspect of their identity assessment focuses on the background of the therapist relative to that of the client. This assessment then aids in matching client and counselor. Hall and Maloney (1983) suggested that highly ethnoculturally dominant therapists should be matched with same-ethnicity clients while less ethnoculturally dominant therapists be matched with culturally different clients. Coleman et al. (1995) conducted a meta-analysis of studies that investigated perceptions and preferences of ethnically diverse clients. They concluded that ethnic minorities tended to prefer ethnically similar therapists and rated these therapists as more competent than European-American therapists.

The client–therapist match literature in the 1990s, therefore, has focused on the preferences for counselors of Asian-Americans, Hispanic-Americans, African-Americans, and Native Americans. Various topics in relation to client preference have been investigated, most notably: racial/ethnic identification, acculturation, counselor credibility, early termination from therapy, and outcome measures of global functioning. Investigation of these and other variables will continue into the next decade.

10.04.5 TREATMENT OUTCOME

10.04.5.1 Definition

Treatment outcome research was defined by Mowrer (1953) as a situation whereby the "emphasis is upon measuring significant aspects of personality before and after treatment and noting the nature and extent of the resulting changes" (p. 4). Sue and Zane (1987) have stated that therapeutic outcome is "the cumulative product of many discrete dynamics between client and therapist" (p. 44). Orlinski, Grawe, and Parks (1994) have asserted that the term "treatment outcome" has had a history of divergent meanings that have ranged from observational perspective to analysis levels. The authors pointed out that the definition and criteria for outcomes differ depending on who is completing the assessments before and after treatment is received. That is, differences are present if the assessment is completed by therapists, clients, nonparticipant observers, or nonprofessionals. They indicated that level of analysis also had critical issues in need of clarification. These issues included the outcomes occurring within, and external to, the therapy sessions and the use of evaluative or descriptive assessment instruments. The authors concluded that "treatment outcome should refer to changes in condition (psychological, somatic, physical, social, and cultural) reflecting favorable or adverse effects on the patients well being" (p. 284).

10.04.5.2 Cross-cultural Outcome Research

VandenBos (1996) presented a succinct history of outcome research beginning in the 1950s. He pointed out that most contemporary treatment outcome research has focused on the effectiveness of comparative treatment interventions and/or has focused on specific treatment methods targeting specific clinical problems. Goldfried and Wolfe (1996) examined the difficult relationship between psychotherapy practice and research. They called for a new outcome research paradigm that seeks to increase clinician and researcher collaboration. Other recent studies have examined many issues surrounding the outcome assessment of psychotherapy, pointing to methodological and conceptual problems (Barlow 1996; Hollon, 1996; Howard, Moras, Brill, Martinovich, & Lutz 1996; Jacobson & Christensen, 1996; Newman & Tejeda, 1996; Sechrest, McKnight, & McKnight 1996; Seligman 1996; Strupp, 1996).

While these studies examined many of the contemporary issues surrounding treatment outcome research, they conspicuously omitted any mention of ethnic or racial factors that contribute to the efficacy of treatment. Sue et al. (1994) have comprehensively analyzed the research on American minority clients. Specifically, they reviewed the outcome research using African-American, Asian-American, Native American, and Latino clients. The authors addressed the question: Is there any research evidence that reveals the efficacy of treatment with minority clients? Specifically, their paper addressed whether minority clients demonstrated differences in pre- and post-therapy assessment. It also investigated whether ethnic minority treatment outcomes differed from outcomes seen in majority clients, and whether various ethnic groups had differential treatment outcomes. They pointed out that research in these areas has historically been lacking and has not specifically addressed the outcome of psychotherapy. Sue et al. asserted that the relationship between ethnic/cultural/racial variables and psychotherapy outcome has not been determined with empirical evidence.

Zane and Sue (1991) stated that ethnic differences involve group membership, while cultural differences "constitute a host of cognitive variables which are limited to different cultural lifestyles and perspectives" (p. 32). They stated that these cognitive variables, rather than ethnic membership, have been responsible for the lack of conclusive psychotherapy outcome studies.

Sue et al. (1994) identified the reasons why outcome studies in cross-cultural psychology have been problematic. They pointed to four areas of concern: (i) the use of analogue studies, (ii) the heterogeneity of the sample, (iii) the insensitive or inappropriate use of dependent measures, and (iv) the lack of within-group design strategies. These methodological deficiencies have caused both researchers and clinicians to dismiss outcome research as being of limited practical value. With these limitations in mind, researchers have most often focused on treatment outcomes of African-Americans, Asian-Americans, Latino-Americans, and Native Americans. Research studies with these four groups will now be examined.

With regard to studies conducted with African-American subjects, Sue et al. (1994) state that, generally, "in no studies have African-Americans been found to exceed white Americans in terms of favorable treatment outcomes. Some investigators have revealed no ethnic differences and some studies have supported the notion that outcomes are less beneficial for African Americans" (p. 788). These conclusions were based on studies conducted in the 1970s and 1980s (Brown, Joe, & Thompson, 1985; Griffith & Jones, 1978; Jones, 1978, 1982; Lerner, 1972; Parloff et al., 1978; Sattler; 1977).

Latino/Hispanic-American studies have often been evaluated in terms of the utilization and retention rate of patients in therapy. Studies using more direct measures have been scarce in the literature. However, discussion on culturally appropriate modes of therapy and the effectiveness of therapies tailored for Latino/Hispanic clients have been studied (Sue et al., 1994; Szapocznik et al., 1989). Cuento therapy, utilizing Puerto Rican folktales, was examined by Constantino, Malgady, and Rogler (1986), and results from this study confirmed that culturally sensitive forms of therapy can reduce trait anxiety scores. Malgady, Rogler, & Constantino (1990) discovered that using culturally appropriate modeling therapy in conjunction with Cuento (folktales) therapy reduced anxiety symptoms and aggression in Puerto Rican children. Rey-Perez (1996), using a qualitative approach with five Hispanic families, constructed a comprehensive, culturally sensitive treatment program for Hispanic children and their families. Therapeutic gains were noted in each child; the subjects were Cuban, Puerto Rican, Nicaraguan, and Peruvian.

There have been a limited number of outcome studies using Asian-American subjects. Many studies have not studied specific groups of Asian-Americans (e.g., Vietnamese, Chinese, Japanese); rather they have viewed Asians as monolithic. Kinzie and Leung (1989), Mollica, Wyshak, Lavelle, Truong, Tor, and Yang (1990), and Snodgrass et al. (1993) found outcome gains in Vietnamese, Laotian, and Cambodian patients. Comparative studies with Asian and non-Asian clients have revealed few differences (Sue et al. 1994).

The authors stated that:

> any conclusions about the effectiveness of treatment for Asians would be premature given the limited data (four outcome studies), but that several empirical trends should be noted. First, some evidence suggests that certain Asian groups improve with psychotherapy and/or adjunct treatments. Second, with respect to differential outcome, divergent trends are found and these are associated with the type of outcome measure used....In summary, Asian clients appear to be deriving less positive experiences from therapy than whites but it is unclear if this difference in client satisfaction actually reflects ethnic differences in actual treatment outcomes (i.e., symptom reduction). (p. 798)

Native American populations, while culturally heterogenous, have been generally studied as an aggregate population. The number of outcome studies is limited in this area, and Manson, Shore, and Bloom (1985) and Neligh (1988) have reported that no research has been conducted to compare the efficacy of various treatment modalities with this population. Most outcome studies have focused on alcohol and drug use reduction and prevention (Bobo, Gilchrist, Cvetkovich, Trimble, & Schinke, 1988; Manson, 1982; Query, 1985; Schinke et al., 1988). Sue et al. (1994) have concluded that "it is apparent that research on intervention (i.e., treatment and prevention) has proceded very slowly, and it would be premature to try to address the question of the efficacy of mental health interventions with American Indians at this time" (p. 795).

The paucity of outcome studies in the literature suggest that more ethnically/racially specific studies on the efficacy of treatment are needed. In addition, methodological weaknesses need to be examined and corrected by future researchers. These methodological issues are explored in the next section.

10.04.6 METHODOLOGICAL CONSIDERATIONS

10.04.6.1 Reliability and Validity in Cross-cultural Research

The last decade has seen a focus on racial/ethnic research issues as they relate to shedding light on effective clinical interventions. Much of the literature has centered on the validity and usefulness of research studies that investigate racial and ethnic variables. The APA (1993) has outlined six areas that have been the focus of mental health research:

> (a) the impact of ethnic/racial similarity in the counseling process, (b) minority underutilization of mental health services, (c) relative effectiveness of directed versus nondirected styles of therapy, (d) the role of cultural values in therapy, (e) appropriate counseling and therapy models, and (e) competency in skills for working with specific ethnic populations. (p. 45).

Research designs using cross-cultural variables, as with all research designs, are expected to have adequate reliability and validity.

Ponterotto and Casas (1991) have carefully delineated the major criticisms leveled at racial/ethnic minority research. They have listed (pp. 78–79) the top 10 criticisms as:

(i) lack of conceptual/theoretical frameworks to guide research;

(ii) overemphasis on simplistic counselor/client process variables and a disregard for important psychosocial variables, within and outside the culture, that might impact counseling;

(iii) overreliance on experimental analog research;

(iv) disregard for within-group or intracultural differences;

(v) the use of easily accessible college student populations;

(vi) reliance on culturally encapsulated psychometric instrumentation;

(vii) failure adequately to describe one's sample in terms of socioeconomic status;

(viii) failure to delineate the study's limitations;

(ix) lack of adequate sample sizes; and

(x) overreliance on paper and pencil outcome measures.

In addition to the identification of the methodological weaknesses in ethnic/social research, the authors reviewed articles from the five journals that most often publish research in this area. They discovered that only about one-third of the studies had an adequate conceptual foundation. With regard to the second criticism, the authors discovered that, although many variables were investigated, key areas lacked systematic attention. Those areas included communication styles, socializing practices, learning styles, effects of poverty and discrimination, and acculturation. With respect to the third criticism, it was discovered that survey research was used in 72.5% of the studies, while analog research accounted for 12.5%, true experimental designs 8.8%, and archival designs 6.3% (p. 89). The authors concluded that researchers, rather than relying on analog studies, have overutilized a survey methodology.

The authors found overwhelming evidence to justify the veracity of their claim in the fourth criticism. They discovered that two-thirds of the literature did not include within-group designs or intracultural comparisons. The fifth criticism was justified, as it was discovered that over one-half of the studies used college and high-school student samples. The sixth criticism was also supported, as the authors discovered that only one-third of the studies used instruments that were designed for minority populations. The authors concluded this to be one of the most justified criticisms in ethnic/racial research studies.

Criticism (vii) was justified, as two-thirds of the studies failed to report social economic variables. The eighth criticism was not wholly justified, as 60% of the studies listed their limitations. Criticism (ix) was not justified, as sample size depends on many factors, including type of design and sampling characteristics. Finally, the tenth criticism was fully justified, as 90% of the studies utilized outcome measures that were paper-and-pencil instruments.

The authors concluded, therefore, that criticisms (i), (iv), (v), (vi), (vii) and (x) are justified; criticisms (ii) and (ix) partially justified; and criticisms (iii) and (viii) unjustified.

Stanfield (1993) has criticized cross-cultural research methods from an epistomological perspective. He examined the fallacies of homogeneity and monolithic identity, and the presumptions that underlie research ethics. He believed that the failure of researchers adequately to clarify these issues has led to exploitative research with ethnically and racially diverse subjects.

10.04.6.2 Recommendations

The comprehensiveness of Ponterotto and Casas's (1991) work can be seen in the methodological recommendations that they offer. These suggestions cover five areas of concern. First, because culture is complex (Pedersen 1991c), a variety of research methods need to be used. In particular, the authors called for researchers to "embrace qualitative methods that have been effectively employed in the related disciplines of ethnology, cultural anthropology, and sociology" (p. 96). Second, the authors suggest that studies focus on within-group differences rather than between-group differences. In so doing, research could avoid comparing racially and ethnically different clients to white or mainstream clients, a situation that usually implies majority behavior to be normal and minority behavior to be abnormal. Third, the authors suggest research that focuses on variables that "transcend culture" (p. 99). Those variables could include some of the universals of human experience such as economic deprivation, family loss, serious medical and psychological illness, and change in environmental conditions. Fourth, culture-specific instrumentation is recommended, especially for such psychological constructs as depression, self-concept, and assertiveness. Finally, the authors believe that more studies need to focus on the strengths of ethnically/racially different clients, rather than on their weaknesses. This suggestion also includes a focus on the positive aspects of biraciality and biculturality.

Mio and Iwamasa (1993) vociferously attacked the methodologies used in conducting ethnic minority research. They posed the question of whether or not researchers from a majority culture could and should conduct research with minority clients. Reactions to this position can be found in Atkinson (1993), Ponterotto (1993), Casas and San Miguel (1993), Helms (1993), Ivey (1993), Parham (1993), Pedersen (1993), and Sue (1993). These reactions suggested ways to improve the quality of ethnic/racial minority research.

Berry, Poortinga, Segall, and Dasen (1992) also explored methodological issues in cross-cultural psychology. They indicated that the two major methodological concerns in any empirical research study are the design and the analysis of results. The authors indicated that results from studies which focus on racially diverse subjects are more difficult to interpret validly than studies in which race and ethnicity are not considered as variables. They delineated four measures for accepting alternative hypotheses indicated by the data.

One method for increasing confidence is by selecting subjects on the basis of the variables race, ethnicity, and culture. Groups need to be included in a study based on their ethnic group inclusion. The authors point out that many studies involving ethnically/culturally diverse subjects have problems during the selection phase of the study. Differences between the groups can be due to factors that are present in the majority culture, the minority culture, or an interaction of factors between the two cultures.

Second, Berry et al. (1992) recommend the dependent variable be "expressed as a function of two or more separate scores. An example is the score that can be obtained by taking the difference betwween scores on two measurements" (p. 223); this strategy can help to eliminate rival hypotheses.

Third, they advocate the minimization of the effect of extraneous variables through statistical methods such as analyses of covariance and multiple regression analysis. Finally, they advocate that more than one dependent measure be used, through methods that include self-report measures, interviews, and archival information. This method increases the amount of data one has to use in the formulation of conclusions and interpretations.

Like Ponterotto and Casas (1991), Berry et al. (1992) show concern about the instrumentation utilized in cross-cultural studies. "Emic" approaches study behaviors of one culture from within the subjects' cultural system and use criteria that are related to the internal characteristics of that culture. "Etic" approaches study behaviors from outside of the culture, by comparing one or more cultures, using dependent measures that are considered universally applicable. The authors indicate that one must consider the emic–etic distinction when designing and interpreting research studies. Berry (1969), based on the work of Pike (1967), argued that researchers need to distinguish between culturally specific variables (emic variables) and culture-general, universal variables (etic variables). The authors advocate emic approaches to research. These recommendations reflect Ponterotto and Casas's suggestions that culturally relevant instruments be used for measuring variables in a study.

Berry et al. (1992), Hui and Triandis (1985), and Triandis (1978) have advocated a combined emic and etic approach to research. This approach identifies an etic construct to study, then operationalizes that construct through the development of emic instrumentation which evolves out of the culture studied. Bond and Smith (1996) have concluded that if future research is to proceed in a useful manner the "methodological problems stemming from the etic–emic dilemma must be more clearly addressed" (p. 226). Berry (1989) has suggested that research should proceed by investigating indigenously two or more cultures in order to arrive at a universally derived etic. This approach is in stark contrast to the more typical approach in cross-cultural psychology that uses etic measures from Western countries.

Mrinal, Mrinal, and Takooshian (1994) have outlined the various research methods that have historically been utilized by cross-cultural researchers. They discuss the use of experimentation, observation, sampling, and assessment. In particular they analyze the use of dependent measures by comparing various assessment methods and instruments. They call for flexibility and adaptation to be used when conducting research cross-culturally.

Stanfield (1993) has questioned the epistomological and methodological perspectives in contemporary cross-cultural studies. He believes that researchers have been pursuing the wrong question, or have answered incomplete questions concerning ethnically and racially diverse topics. He advocates a reorientation among researchers to re-evaluate and improve qualitative, quantitative, and comparative/historical research methods.

Qualitative researchers have advocated the improvement of cross-cultural research by focusing on class, race, or gender relations from within the culture (Andersen, 1993), participant observation (Dennis, 1993), ethnographic methods (Facio, 1993; Spradley, 1979; Williams, 1993), discourse analysis (Van Dijk, 1993), and personal narrative approaches (Jordan, 1995; Madrid, 1995; Moraga 1995). Quantitative suggestions range from re-evaluating demographic statistics (Marks 1993), to new ways of measuring and detecting discrimination (Myers 1993), to the assessment of outcomes (Patton 1993; Sue et al., 1994), and to survey research (Smith 1993). Comparative/historical methods have been suggested and outlined by Champagne (1993), Ragin and Hein (1993), and Stanfield (1993).

10.04.7 FUTURE DIRECTIONS

In 1989 three trends were predicted by Kagitcibasi and Berry. They predicted there would be an increasing focus on individualism and collectivism, on indigenous psychotherapies, and on the search for behaviors and values common to every culture (cultural universals). In 1996, Bond and Smith concluded that three trends have emerged during the 1990s in cross-cultural psychology. They suggested individualism and collectivism have been studied extensively but the other two areas have been plagued by methodological problems. They state that the emic–etic (i.e., culture-specific–universal) dilemma must be more clearly delineated. This clarification could provide new frameworks for research with culturally diverse subjects.

In addition, psychologists will have to focus on resolving issues of terminology and definition, clarifying professional and ethical concerns, addressing methodological weaknesses in research, and generating new topics for study. These areas of concern will be examined in this section of the chapter.

10.04.7.1 Terminology

The terms "ethnicity," "race," and "culture" have had a long history of clarification (Jackson, 1995; Jones, 1991). This history has been fraught with confusion and misunderstanding (Phinney, 1996). Ridley et al. (1994) and Westbrook and Sedlacek (1991) have criticized the inconsistent usage of terminology and pointed to the negative effects of labeling and stereotyping. LaFromboise, Foster, and James (1996) have suggested that the term "race" may be eliminated from future research studies, based on the conclusions of Yee, Fairchild, Weizmann, and Wyatt (1993), who indicated the lack of uniform use of the terms "race" and "ethnicity."

Alvidrez, Azocar, and Miranda (1996) have suggested methods to conceptualize, measure, and interpret ethnic or racial variables in studies of clinical interventions. The recommendations were that researchers should identify their definitions of race and ethnicity, provide more comprehensive information about subjects other than ethnicity or race (e.g., demographic information and language), identify social class variables, and indicate occupation level. The recognition that ethnicity is multifaceted has led to a re-examination of the terminology. Ragin and Hein (1993) have described the term "ethnicity" as interactive and contextual. Ethnicity and race have recently been viewed as dimensions rather than categories (Goodchilds, 1991). Phinney (1996) has suggested these dimensions "clearly cluster together in ways that make ethnicity a highly salient and meaningful construct" (p. 925).

Additionally, Phinney (1996) has also suggested that if psychologists wish to generate adequate explanations about treatment outcomes when ethnicity is a factor, they need to investigate three dimensions within and across ethnic groups. These are: significant cultural norms and attitudes, factors involved with a client's ethnic identification, and individual minority client experiences of decreased status and power.

Pedersen (1995) advocates the future use of the term "culture" as formulated by Betancourt and Lopez (1993). These authors have described culture as a learned, socially shared set of variables, incorporating individual, family, and societal variables. Fernando (1995) has examined the issue from the perspective of ethnic groups in Great Britain and has argued for a more dynamic conception of culture to be formulated in cross-cultural psychology. Pedersen and Ivey (1993) have outlined the complexity and dynamic nature of culture and have focused on the need to identify salient ethnic, racial, and cultural variables. The importance of these variables varies from moment to moment, and they include "ethnographic, demographic, status, and affiliation characteristics... particularly gender, ethnicity, life-style or other affiliations" (p. 188).

The consideration of these variables will allow researchers and practitioners to dissolve stereotypes of client behaviors based only on ethnic, cultural, and racial group membership. Pedersen and Ivey (1993) concluded that one needs to address the dynamics of culture by focusing on the salience and complexity of culture. This new focus will have greater relevance in future individual counseling discussions and is a foundation for an examination of ethical considerations in cross-cultural counseling (LaFromboise et al., 1996; Pedersen, 1995).

10.04.7.2 Ethical and Professional Issues

A 20 year historical analysis of cross-cultural counseling ethics, beginning with the 1973 Vail Conference, has been completed by Pedersen (1994). He traced the formulation of ethical principles in the professional associations of psychology. Ethical principles for conducting cross-cultural research were adopted in the 1970s by the International Association of Cross-Cultural Psychology (Tapp, Kelman, Triandis, Wrightsman, & Coelho, 1974). Ethical principles have also been formulated by the APA (1992) and the ACA (1988). The APA principles address the issues of race, ethnicity, and culture in an effort to minimize and dispel bias in therapeutic interventions, arising from stereotyping or discrimination. The ACA ethical principles indicate the need to respect the client's individuality and dignity with regard to cultural difference. In addition, guidelines have been provided for clinical interventions with ethnically, culturally, and linguistically different clients (APA, 1993).

Several future trends seem imminent in the area of ethics. Ethical principles are being revised and more specifically delineated. The ethics of caring and responsibility are beginning to receive more attention in the cross-cultural literature (Pedersen, 1995). Ethics in the area of multiculturalism will be expanded to delineate more fully the impact of psychotherapeutic training models on a counselor's multicultural competence (Sue et al., 1996). In addition, ethical issues concerning the types of, and approaches to, research with diverse populations will be elaborated in greater detail (Pedersen, 1995).

The issue of white American researchers conducting the majority of the research with minority clients is an area that will be examined with greater focus (Mio & Iwamasa, 1993). This issue will be expanded to incorporate the recruitment and retention of minorities in psychotherapy research, as there has been an under-representation of minorities in clinical research (Miranda, 1996). This under-representation has led to the formation of guidelines from the National Institutes of Health (NIH) in the USA concerning the inclusion of minorities and women in psychology research (NIH, 1994). These new NIH guidelines for the inclusion of minorities in clinical research will be evaluated and studied in greater depth (Hohmann, & Parron, 1996). The focus on recruitment and retention has centered on Native Americans (Norton & Manson, 1996), African-Americans (Thompson, Neighbors, Munday, & Jackson, 1996), Latinos (Miranda, Azocar, Organista, Munoz, & Lieberman, 1996), and elderly ethnic clients (Arean & Gallagher-Thompson, 1996). It is believed that the NIH guidelines will help encourage collaborative efforts between practitioners and researchers (Miranda, 1996). Specific recommendations will need to be formulated for recruiting and retaining other specific, racially, ethnically, and culturally diverse research subjects.

10.04.7.3 Future Research

Future cross-cultural research will address methodological, theoretical, and content issues. In particular, an examination of research agendas, assessment methods, multicultural counseling and therapy theory, and specific research topics, appear to be areas of future concern.

10.04.7.3.1 Research agenda

Sue and Sundberg (1996) have proposed 15 specific hypotheses to be tested in future research on individual counseling. These hypotheses are based on questions that range from client–counselor similarity, to worldview differences, to emic–etic issues. They are as follows (pp. 329–343).

(i) Entry into the counseling system will be affected by cultural conceptualization of mental disorders and socialization towards seeking help.

(ii) The more similar the expectations of the intercultural client to the goals and process of counseling the more effective the counseling will be.

(iii) Of special importance in intercultural effectiveness is the degree of congruence between the counselor and client in their orientations in philosophical values and views towards dependency, authority, power, openness of communication, and other special relationships inherent in counseling.

(iv) The more the aims and desires of the client can be appropriately simplified and formulated as objective behavior or information (such as university course requirements or specific tasks), the more effective the intercultural counseling will be.

(v) Cross-cultural empathy and rapport are important in establishing a working alliance between the counselor and the culturally different client.

(vi) Effectiveness will be enhanced by the counselor's general sensitivity to communications, both verbal and nonverbal. The more personal and emotionally laden the counseling becomes, the more the client will rely on words and concepts learned early in life, and the more helpful it will be for the counselor to be knowledgeable about socialization and communication styles in the client's culture.

(vii) The less familiar the client is with the counseling process, the more the counselor or the counseling program will need to instruct the client in what counseling is and in the role of the client.

(viii) Culture-specific modes of counseling will be found that will work more effectively with certain cultural ethnic groups than others.

(ix) Ethnic similarity between counselor and client increases the probability of a positive outcome.

(x) Within-group differences on variables such as acculturation and stage of racial identity may influence receptivity to counseling.

(xi) Credibility can be enhanced through acknowledgment of cross-cultural factors in cross-cultural encounters.

(xii) In general, women respond more positively than men to Western-style counseling.

(xiii) "The person who acts with intentionality has a sense of capability. She or he can generate alternative behaviors in a given situation and approach a problem from different vantage points. The intentional, functioning individual is not bound to one course of action but can respond in the moment to changing life situations" (cited from Ivey, Ivey, & Simek-Morgan, 1993, p. 8).

(xiv) Identity-related characteristics of white counselors can influence their reaction to ethnic minority clients.

(xv) Despite great differences in cultural contexts, in language, and in the implicit theory of the counseling process, a majority of the important elements of intercultural counseling are common across cultures and clients.

The authors have labeled their 15 hypotheses as protohypotheses because they acknowledge that the constructs and propositions need to be more fully sharpened, focused, and developed before effective research can be started. Their hope is to stimulate further thinking in this area. The testing of their hypotheses is proposed by the authors as an agenda for future research in the area of cross-cultural counseling and psychotherapy. Sue and Sundberg (1996) also have suggested that future research should broaden the criteria for inclusion into a study by using marginal and at-risk clients. They also advocate a detailed examination of the emic–etic controversy.

Ponterotto and Casas (1991) have identified areas of research that should constitute the agenda for the 1990s and beyond. The areas include: accurate epidemiological studies of psychological problems with various ethnic and racial identities, impact of Eurocentric political and social systems on clients, systemic racism, a focus on the strengths present in low socioeconomic groups, biracial identity development, ethnic minority youth research, primary prevention, assessment, and combination emic–etic studies.

Berry et al. (1992) predict a future focus on examining emic–etic issues. They envisage cross-cultural research that examines psychopathology from various perspectives. These perspectives are: invariate or present in all cultures (absolute); present in all cultures, but culturally determined (universal); and unique to specific cultures and emically definable (culturally relative). Helms (1994) has argued that the new focus on multiculturalism and pluralism has resulted in a neglect of racial factors that contribute to psychotherapy interventions. She has called for a greater focus on racial factors for the future.

10.04.7.3.2 Assessment techniques

Future research will inevitably include the development and validation of assessment techniques that are culturally appropriate. The use of traditional assessment techniques has been criticized extensively in the literature (APA, 1993; Dana, 1993; Lonner, 1990; Paniagua, 1994; Ponterotto & Casas, 1990; Samuda, 1975; Samuda, Kong, Cummins, Pascual-Leone, & Lewis, 1991; Sodowski & Impara, 1996). The issues of cross-cultural assessment and appraisal have most recently been examined by Lonner and Ibrahim (1996). The authors present a general overview of the issues involved when assessing culturally diverse clients by focusing on the impact of response sets and emic–etic issues. They have examined the use of cognitive ability tests and personality measures. In addition, they have provided a historical analysis of the assessment of the therapeutic process and the assessment of refugees. Subsequent to their extensive review they concluded that these areas need to have a greater focus in the future.

In addition to the investigation of traditional standardized cognitive and personality measures, researchers will need to develop future instruments, in various areas of concern, from an emic perspective (e.g., biracial identity and worldview). These instruments will need to be validated and thoroughly researched. Process-oriented techniques of assessment, such as those in the dynamic assessment movement (Feuerstein, 1979), will need to be considered for cross-cultural utility and feasibility (Samuda & Lewis, 1992). The area of assessment constitutes one of the most significant methodologic weaknesses (Ponterotto & Casas, 1991) and will, therefore, continue to occupy psychologists in the next decade.

10.04.7.3.3 Theory of multicultural counseling and therapy

Future research will focus on the theory of multicultural counseling and therapy (MCT). This new framework for delivery of psychotherapeutic services to culturally diverse clients, proposed by Sue et al. (1996), has six major propositions and 47 corollary suppositions. Research will undoubtedly focus on the specifics proposed by these authors.

The authors have advocated a future agenda that has researchers: (i) conduct a metareview of historical and current studies from a MCT perspective, (ii) examine the shift from a focus on the individual to a study of the individual within a context or in relation to others, and (iii) examine the positive attributes of individuals and cultures, rather than focusing on stereotyped behaviors and pathologies. Additionally, they have advocated the investigation of traditional research methods that generate epistemological assumptions that may not be universal. This future focus could incorporate a detailed examination of differing worldviews and how these differences impact on cross-cultural interventions. Finally, the authors recommend the use of qualitative research methodologies when working with a culturally diverse population. This approach, as well as quantitative methods, will need to be used effectively to "explore new methods that are culture centered rather than consider culture as peripheral" (p. 36).

The reactions to MCT theory (Arredondo, 1996; Ballou, 1996; Casas & Mann, 1996; Corey, 1996; Daniels, & D'Andrea, 1996; Highlen, 1996; LaFromboise & Jackson, 1996; Lee, 1996; Leong, 1996; Parham, 1996; Pope-Davis & Constantine, 1996; Vasquez-Nuttal, Webber, & Sanchez, 1996) and the counter-reactions (Sue et al., 1996) indicate that the dialogue will continue into the twenty-first century, with a refinement of the theory and an empirical validation of the underlying constructs.

10.04.7.3.4 Specific research topics

The methodological issues previously outlined and the research suggestions offered (APA, 1992; Berry et al., 1992; Ponterotto & Casas, 1990; Sue et al., 1996; Sue & Sundberg, 1996) provide a foundation for specific topic areas that appear to be receiving attention in the literature. Topics such as underserved populations, biraciality, the vocational behavior of diverse clients, and indigenous therapy, need more examination in the future. These four potential topics are now examined in greater detail.

In the 1990s, there has been a move to focus on specific ethnic/cultural/racial groups, rather than the more commonly studied four groups, in the USA: African-American, Asian-Americans, Latino-Americans, and Native Americans (Sue et al., 1994). This new focus on specific underserved populations and within-group populations could be a major focus in the next decade. In particular, the treatment of specific populations has begun to appear in the literature: traditional Arabic clients (Dwairy & Van Sickle,

1996), Puerto Ricans (Malgady, Rogler, & Rogler, & Constantino, 1990), Haitians (Gies, 1990), Guatemalan Mayans (Alger, 1996), Vietnamese (Snodgrass et al., 1993), Cambodians (Bemak & Greenberg, 1994), and Venezuelans (Villegas-Reimers, 1996). These authors have concluded that researchers need to go beyond the traditional ethnic/racial group categories to focus on the heterogeneity that exists within each ethnic/racial group. Future studies that examine these and other minority groups need to focus on both between- and within-group comparisons. Such a focus will provide an evaluation of the impact of the culture-specific versus universal variables on counseling and psychotherapy.

The focus on heterogeneity has revealed the presence of biracial/biethnic and multiracial/multiethnic variables. As the demographics change in countries, so do the number of intercultural and interracial marriages. Interracial, interethnic, and biracial families have become a reality in the 1990s and have received increasing attention in the psychological literature (Root, 1992). The term "biraciality" has been used to describe the children of racially different parents and is akin to biculturality and bilingualism (Kerwin & Ponterotto, 1995).

This area has evolved from early research on the biracial identity models as outlined by Kerwin and Ponterotto. The authors have suggested five research areas for future study: (i) effects of peer pressure on adolescent identity development, (ii) impact of cultural focus on identity development, (iii) dichotomous choices of identifying as multiracial/multicultural rather than choosing one racial/ethnic categorization, (iv) development of bicultural competence for biracial adolescents and adults, and (v) role of parents and educators in developing an adequate sense of identity in biracial children. This complex area of concern will receive greater study in the future.

During the 1980s and 1990s there has been an increasing focus on the vocational concerns of racial and ethnic minorities (Leong, 1995). This focus on career development of the culturally diverse has led to an exploration of the issues with African-Americans (Bowman, 1995; Brown, 1995), Hispanic-Americans (Arbona, 1995; Fouad, 1995), Asian-Americans (Leong & Gim-Chung, 1995; Leong & Serafica, 1995), and Native Americans (Johnson, Swartz, & Martin, 1995). This examination of career behavior has promulgated a multicultural theory of career development (Osipow & Littlejohn, 1995) and recommendations for vocational assessment and career counseling (Betz & Fitzgerald, 1995). Future literature on cross-cultural vocational counseling interventions will elucidate and attempt to validate this theory.

Another area of concern is the role of indigenous therapies. In many countries there is an acceptance of both standard, formal psychotherapeutic intervention methods and traditional healing methods. The role of traditional, or indigenous, healing practices has been examined by Lefley (1994) and Hiegel (1994). A comprehensive treatment of the subject is available in Kim & Berry (1993). This area of psychotherapy will inevitably continue to grow as emic approaches become more acceptable in both Western and non-Western cultures. Indigenous methods for investigation could include Morita, Naikan, Voodoo, Santoria, and Espiritismo therapy. Bemak, Chung, and Bornemann (1996) have proposed a multilevel model for counseling refugees that integrates Western therapies and indigenous methods of intervention. This integration of approaches has resulted in more effective psychotherapy outcomes (World Health Organization, 1992) and is a harbinger of future work in cross-cultural psychology.

10.04.7.4 Global Psychology

It has been suggested by Moghaddam (1987), that three worlds of psychology exist: the body of research derived from American research studies in the USA, research generated in other industrialized countries, and a third body of knowledge that has emerged from developing countries. Mays, Rubin, Sabourin, and Walker (1996) have stated: "Within this triumvirate, US psychology has been imported and serves as an important source of influence for a number of developed nations—the European communities, in particular—as well as the developing nations" (p. 485). Pawlik and d'Ydewalle (1996) have predicted the rise of international cooperation and exchange in psychology, occurring through international organizations, conferences, and publications. Gergen, Gulerce, Lock, and Misra (1996) have examined the global context of psychological practice. They delineated various indigenous issues present in India, New Zealand, and Turkey. They argue for a multicultural psychology that down plays the dominant influence of Western psychological models of theory and practice. Lunt and Poortinga (1996) have advocated the increase in European psychology studies that are based on the multicultural diversity present in European countries. The trend towards internationalizing psychology, therefore, appears to be one which will receive greater attention in the future and may have an impact on the area of cross-cultural intervention research.

10.04.8 SUMMARY

Multicultural counseling has been hailed as the fourth force in psychology (Pedersen, 1990). The area of cross-cultural interventions has evolved into a multidimensional field that encompasses several specific interest areas. First, the impact of proximal and distal variables upon behavior has been examined. This area has provided evidence that a therapist needs to understand both universal and culture-specific aspects of a client's functioning. Second, research on cross-cultural intervention processes has been reviewed. These processes include topics as diverse as counselor competence and sensitivity, communication style, and verbal and nonverbal communication. The research suggests that cross-cultural interventions can be facilitated and improved by a therapist having an understanding of the racial/ethnic/cultural differences that exist between the client and therapist. Third, the research on therapist–client match was examined. The majority of studies suggest that clients prefer ethnically/racially/culturally similar therapists and judge these therapists as more competent than dissimilar therapists. Other research, however, repudiates these notions, pointing to other therapist variables (e.g., sensitivity) as important. Fourth, the treatment outcome research has been examined. It was discovered that few methodologically sound studies exist in the literature and, also, that most studies have focused on minority groups in the USA. Fifth, methodological research concerns were explored. The weaknesses of cross-cultural studies were examined, and recommendations for future research were reviewed. Finally, this chapter has looked to future trends in cross-cultural intervention research. It predicted that terminology and ethical considerations will be more clearly delineated. In addition, future trends include the elucidation and validation of the theory of multicultural counseling and therapy, refinement and construction of culturally appropriate assessment and outcome measures, and a focus on specific within-group research topics. It is suggested that greater emphasis on global issues in psychology, and an increase in international research, will further the study of cross-cultural clinical interventions.

10.04.9 REFERENCES

Acosta, K., & Cristo, M. (1981). Development of a bilingual interpreter: An alternative model for Spanish-speaking services. *Professional Psychology, 12,* 474–482.

Acosta, K., Yamamoto, J., & Evans, L. (1982). *Effective psychotherapy for low-income and minority patients.* New York: Plenum.

Akutsu, P., Lin, C., & Zane, N. (1990). Predictors of utilization intent of counseling among Chinese and White students: A test of the proximal–distal model. *Journal of Counseling Psychology, 37*(4), 445–452.

Alger, M. (1996). *Counseling Guatemalan Mayans in South Florida.* Unpublished manuscript, Boca Raton, FL: Florida Atlantic University.

Altman, I. (1975). *The environment and social behavior.* Monterey, CA: Brooks/Cole.

Altman, A., & Chemers, M. M. (1980). *Culture and environment.* Monterey, CA: Brooks/Cole.

Alvidrez, J., Azocar, F., & Miranda, J. (1996). Demystifying the concept of ethnicity for psychotherapy researchers. *Journal of Consulting and Clinical Psychology, 64*(5), 903–908.

American Counseling Association (1988). *Ethical standards.* Alexandria, VA: Author.

American Counseling Association (1990). *Counseling the Black/African American client; Counseling the Mexican client; Counseling the Native American client; Counseling the Vietnamese client* [videocassettes]. (Available from the American Counseling Association, Alexandria, VA).

American Psychological Association (1992). Ethical principles of psychologists and code of conduct. *American Psychologist, 47*(12), 1597–1611.

American Psychological Association (1993). Guidelines for providers of psychological services to ethnic, and culturally diverse populations. *American Psychologist, 48,* 45–48.

American Psychological Association (1994). *Ethnocultural psychotherapy: Comas-Diaz* [videocassette]. (Available from the American Psychological Association, Washington, DC)

Andersen, M. (1993). Studying across difference: Race, class, and gender in qualitative research. In J. Stanfield II & R. Dennis (Eds.), *Race and ethnicity in research methods* (pp. 39–52). Newbury Park, CA: Sage.

Apple, W., Streeter, L., & Krauss, R. (1979). Effects of pitch and speech rate on personal attribution. *Journal of Personality and Social Psychology, 37,* 715–727.

Arbona, C. (1995). Theory and research on racial and ethnic minorities: Hispanic Americans. In F. Leong (Ed.), *Career development and vocational behavior of racial and ethnic minorities* (pp. 37–66). Mahwah, NJ: Erlbaum.

Arean, P., & Gallagher-Thompson, D. (1996). Issues and recommendations for the recruitment and retention of older ethnic minority adults into clinical research. *Journal of Consulting and Clinical Psychology, 64*(5), 875–880.

Argyle, M. (1991). Understanding intercultural communication. In L. Samovar & R. Porter, *Intercultural communication: A reader* (6th ed., pp. 33–45). Belmont, CA: Wadsworth.

Argyle, M., & Cook, M. (1976). *Gaze and mutual gaze.* Cambridge, UK: Cambridge University Press.

Argyle, M., & Dean, J. (1965). Eye-contact, distance, and affiliation. *Sociometry, 28,* 289–304.

Arredondo, P. (1996). MCT theory and Latina(o)-American populations. In D. W. Sue, A. Ivey, P. Pedersen (Eds.), *A theory of multicultural counseling and therapy* (pp. 217–235). Pacific Grove, CA: Brooks/Cole.

Atkinson, D. R. (1983). Ethnic similarity in counseling psychology: A review of research. *The Counseling Psychologist, 11*(3), 79–92.

Atkinson, D. R. (1985). A meta-review of research on cross-cultural counseling and psychotherapy. *Journal of Multicultural Counseling and Development, 13,* 138–153.

Atkinson, D. R. (1993). Who speaks for cross-cultural counseling research? *The Counseling Psychologist, 21*(2), 218–224.

Atkinson, D., Casas, A., & Abreu, J. (1992). Mexican-American acculturation, counselor ethnicity, and cultural sensitivity and perceived counselor competence.

Journal of Counseling Psychology, 39(4), 515–520.

Atkinson, D., & Lowe, S. (1995). The role of ethnicity, cultural knowledge, and conventional techniques in counseling and psychotherapy. In J. Ponterotto, J. M. Casas, L. A. Suzuki, & C. M. Alexander (Eds.), *Handbook of multicultural counseling* (pp. 387–414).

Atkinson, D., & Matsushita, Y. (1991). Japanese-American acculturation, counseling style, counselor ethnicity, and perceived counselor credibility. *Journal of Counseling Psychology, 38*(4), 473–478.

Atkinson, D., Morten, G., & Sue, D. (1993). *Counseling American minorities: A cross-cultural perspective* (4th ed.). Dubuque, IA: Brown and Benchmark.

Atkinson, D., & Wampold, B. (1993). Mexican Americans' initial preferences for counselors: Simple choice can be misleading: Comment on Lopez, Lopez, and Fong (1991). *Journal of Counseling Psychology, 40*(2), 245–248.

Baker, N. (1981). Social work through an interpreter. *Social Work, 26*, 391–397.

Barlow, D. (1996). The health care policy, psychotherapy research and the future of psychotherapy. *American Psychologist, 51* (10), 1050–1058.

Ballou, M. (1996). MCT theory in women. In D. W. Sue, A. Ivey, & P. Pedersen (Eds.), *A theory of multicultural counseling and therapy* (pp. 236–246). Pacific Grove, CA: Brooks/Cole.

Bemak, F., Chung, R. C., & Bornemann, T. (1996). Counseling and psychotherapy with refugees. In P. Pedersen, J. Draguns, W. Lonner, & J. Trimble (Eds.), *Counseling across cultures* (4th ed., pp. 243–265). Thousand Oaks, CA: Sage.

Bemak, F., & Greenberg, B. (1994). Southeast Asian refugee adolescents: Implications for counseling. *Journal of Multicultural Counseling and Development, 22*(4), 115–124.

Bennett, S., & Bigfoot-Sipes, D. (1991). American Indian and White college student preferences for counselor characteristics. *Journal of Counseling Psychology, 38*(4), 440–445.

Berkanovic, E. (1980). The effect of inadequate language translation on Hispanics' responses to health surveys. *American Journal of Public Health, 70*, 1273–1276.

Bernstein, B. L., Wade, P., & Hofmann, B. (1987). Students' race and preferences for counselor's race, sex, age, and experience. *Journal of Multicultural Counseling and Development, 15*, 60–70.

Berry, J. (1969). On cross-cultural comparability. *International Journal of Psychology, 4*, 119–128.

Berry, J. (1989). Imposed etics–emics–derived etics: The operationalization of a compelling idea. *International Journal of Psychology, 24*, 721–735.

Berry, J. (1990). The role of psychology in ethnic studies. *Canadian Ethnic Studies, XXII*(1), 8–21.

Berry, J., Poortinga, Y., Segall, M., Dasen, P. (1992). *Cross-cultural psychology: Research applications.* New York: Cambridge University Press.

Betancourt, H., & Lopez, S. (1993). The study of culture, ethnicity, and race in American psychology. *American Psychologist, 48*, 629–637.

Betz, N., & Fitzgerald, L. (1995). Career assessment and intervention with racial and ethnic minorities. In F. Leong (Ed.), *Career development and vocational behavior of racial and ethnic minorities* (pp. 263–279). Mahwah, NJ: Erlbaum.

Birdwhistell, R. (1970). *Kinesics and contexts.* Philadelphia, PA: University of Pennsylvania Press.

Bobo, J. K., Gilchrist, L. D., Cvetkovich, G. T., Trimble, J. E., & Schinke, S. P. (1988). Cross-cultural service delivery to minority communities. *Journal of Community Psychology, 16*, 263–272.

Bond, M. H., & Shirashi, D. (1974). The effect of body lean and status of an interviewer on the non-verbal behavior of Japanese interviewees. *International Journal of Psychology, 9*, 117–128.

Bond, M. H., & Smith, P. (1996). Cross-cultural social and organizational psychology. In J. Spence, J. Darley, & G. Foss (Eds.), *Annual review of psychology* (pp. 205–235). Palo Alto, CA: Annual Reviews.

Bowman, S. (1995). Career intervention strategies and assessment issues for African Americans. In F. Leong (Ed.), *Career development and vocational behavior of racial and ethnic minorities* (pp. 137–164). Mahwah, NJ: Erlbaum.

Bradbury, T., & Fincham, F. (1988). Individual difference variables in close relationships: A contextual model of marriage as an integrative framework. *Journal of Personality and Social Psychology, 54*(4), 713–721.

Brown, B. S., Joe, G. W., & Thompson, P. (1985). Minority group status and treatment retention. *International Journal of the Addictions, 20*, 319–335.

Brown, M. T. (1995). The career development of African Americans: Theoretical and empirical issues. In F. Leong (Ed.), *Career development and vocational behavior of racial and ethnic minorities* (pp. 7–36). Mahwah, NJ: Erlbaum.

Carillo, C. (1982). Changing norms of Hispanic families. In E. E. Jones & S. J. Korchin (Eds.), *Minority mental health* (pp. 250–256). New York: Praeger.

Carkhuff, R., & Pierce, R. (1967). Differential effects of therapist race and social class upon patient depth of self-exploration in the initial clinical interview. *Journal of Consulting Psychology, 31*, 632–634.

Carter, R. (1991). Cultural values: A review of empirical research and implications for counseling. *Journal of Counseling and Development, 70*(1), 164–173.

Casas, J., & Mann, D. (1996). MCT theory and implications for research. In D. Sue, A. Ivey, & P. Pedersen (Eds.), *A theory of multicultural counseling and therapy* (pp. 99–111). Pacific Grove, CA: Brooks/Cole.

Casas, J., & SanMiguel, S. (1993). Beyond questions and discussions, there is a need for action: A response to Mio and Iwamasa. *The Counseling Psychologist, 21*(2), 233–239.

Champagne, D. (1993). Toward a multidimensional historical comparative methodology: Context, process, and causality. In J. Stanfield II & R. Dennis (Eds.), *Race and ethnicity in research methods* (pp. 233–253). Newbury Park, CA: Sage.

Cheng, C. Y. (1987). Chinese philosophy and contemporary communication theory. In D. L. Kincaid (Ed.), *Communication theory: Eastern and western perspectives.* (pp. 39–58). New York: Academic Press.

Coleman, H. L., Wampold, B. E., & Casali, S. L. (1995). Ethnic minorities' ratings of ethnically similar and European American counselors: A meta-analysis. *Journal of Counseling Psychology, 42*(1), 55–64.

Comas-Diaz, L., & Griffith, E. (Eds.) (1988). *Clinical guidelines in cross-cultural mental health.* New York: Wiley.

Comas-Diaz, L., & Jacobsen, F. (1987). Ethnocultural identification in psychotherapy. *Psychiatry, 50*, 232–241.

Constantino, G., Malgady, R., & Rogler, L. (1986). Cuento therapy: A culturally sensitive modality for Puerto Rican children. *Journal of Counseling and Clinical Psychology, 54*, 639–645.

Corey, G. (1996). Theoretical implications of MCT theory. In D. W. Sue, A. Ivey, & P. Pedersen (Eds.), *A theory of multicultural counseling and therapy* (pp. 99–111). Pacific Grove, CA: Brooks/Cole.

Cross, W. Jr. (1995). The psychology of nigrescence: Revising the Cross model. In J. Ponterotto, J. Casas, L. Suzuki, & C. Alexander (Eds.), *Handbook of multicultural counseling* (pp. 93–122). Thousand Oaks, CA: Sage.

Crystal, D. (1975). Paralinguistics. In J. Benthall & T.

Polhemus (Eds.), *The body as a medium of expression* (pp. 49–74). New York: Dutton.

Dana, R. (1993). *Multicultural assessment perspectives for professional psychology*. Boston: Allyn & Bacon.

D'Andrea, M., Daniels, J., & Heck, R. (1991). Evaluating the impact of multicultural training. *Journal of Counseling and Development, 70*, 143–150.

Daniels, J. & D'Andrea, M. (1996). MCT theory and ethnocentrism in counseling. In D. W. Sue, A. Ivey, & P. Pedersen (Eds.), *A theory of multicultural counseling and therapy* (pp. 155–173). Pacific Grove, CA: Brooks/Cole.

de Figueiredo, J. (1976). Interviewing in Goa: Methodological issues in the study of a bilingual culture. *Journal of Social Science and Medicine, 10*, 503–508.

de Figueiredo, J., & Lemkau, P. (1980). Psychiatric interviewing across cultures: Some problems and prospects. *Social Psychiatry, 15*, 117–121.

Dennis, R. (1993). Participant observations. In J. Stanfield II & R. Dennis (Eds.), *Race and ethnicity in research methods* (pp. 53–74). Newbury Park, CA: Sage.

Der-Kerabetian, A. (1992). World-mindedness and the nuclear threat: Multinational study. *Journal of Social and Behavioral Personality, 7*, 293–303.

Dignes, N., Trimble, J., Manson, S., & Pasquale, F. (1981). Counseling and psychotherapy with American Indians and Alaska Natives. In A. Marsella & P. Pedersen (Eds.), *Cross-cultural counseling and psychotherapy: Foundations, evaluation and cultural considerations* (pp. 243–276). Elmsford, NY: Pergamon.

Dillard, J. M. (1983). *Multicultural counseling*. Chicago: Nelson.

Draguns, J. G. (1981). Cross-cultural counseling and psychotherapy: History, issues, current status. In A. J. Marsella & P. B. Pedersen (Eds.), *Cross-cultural counseling and psychotherapy* (pp. 3–27). New York: Pergamon.

Dwairy, M., & Van Sickle, T. (1996). Western psychotherapy in traditional Arabic societies. *Clinical Psychology Review, 16*(3), 231–249.

Eakins, B., & Eakins, R. (1985). Sex differences in nonverbal communication. In L. Samovar & R. Porter (Eds.), *Intercultural communication: A reader* (pp. 192–217). Belmont, CA: Wadsworth.

Edgerton, R. B., & Karno, M. (1971). Mexican-American biligualism and the perception of mental illness. *Archives of General Psychiatry, 24*, 286–290.

Efron, D. (1972). Gesture, race and culture. In T. A. Sebeok (Ed.), *Approaches to semibiotics* (pp. 44–59). The Hague, The Netherlands: Mouton.

Eisenbruch, M. (1990). The Cultural Bereavement Interview: A new clinical research approach for refugees. *Psychiatric Clinics of North America, 13*(4), 715–735.

Ekman, P. (1993). Facial expression and emotion. *American Psychologist, 48*(4), 384–392.

Ekman, P., & Friesen, W. V. (1975). *Unmasking the face: A guide to recognizing emotions from facial expressions.* Englewood Cliffs, NJ: Prentice-Hall.

Ellgring, H. (1984). The study of nonverbal behavior and its applications: State of the art in Europe. In A. Wolfgang (Ed.), *Nonverbal behavior* (pp. 115–138). Lewiston, NY: Hogrefe.

Erickson, F., & Shultz, J. (1982). *The counselor gatekeeper: Social interaction in interviews.* New York: Academic Press.

Exline, R. A., Gray, D., & Schuette, D. (1985). Visual behavior in a dyad as affected by interview content and sex of the respondent. *Journal of Personality and Social Psychology, 1*, 201–209.

Facio, E. (1993). Ethnography as personal experience. In J. Stanfield II & R. Dennis (Eds.), *Race and ethnicity in research methods* (pp. 75–93). Newbury Park, CA: Sage.

Fernando, S. (Ed.) (1995). *Mental health in a multi-ethnic society.* London: Routledge.

Feuerstein, R. (1979). *The dynamic assessment of retarded performers.* Baltimore, MD: University Park Press.

Fiksdal, S. (1990). *The right time and pace: A microanalysis of cross-cultural gatekeeping interviews.* Norwood, NJ: Ablex.

Fiske, A. (1992). The four elementary forms of sociality: Framework for a unified theory of social relations. *Psychological Review, 99*, 689–723.

Fiske, S., & Taylor, S. (1991). *Social cognition* (2nd ed.). New York: McGraw-Hill.

Flaskerud, J. (1990). Matching client and therapist ethnicity, language, and gender: A review of research. *Issues in Mental Health Nursing, 11*(4), 321–336.

Flaskerud, J., & Hu, L. (1994). Participation in and outcome of treatment for major depression among low income Asian-Americans. *Psychiatry Research, 53*(3), 289–300.

Flaskerud, J., & Liu, P. (1990). Influence of therapist ethnicity and language on therapy outcomes of Southeast Asian clients. *International Journal of Social Psychiatry, 36*(1), 18–29.

Flaskerud, J., & Liu, P. (1991). Effects of an Asian client–therapist language, ethnicity, and gender match on utilization and outcome of therapy. *Community Mental Health Journal, 27*(1), 31–42.

Fletcher, G., & Fitness, J. (1990). Occurrent social cognition in close relationship interaction: The role of proximal and distal variables. *Journal of Personality and Social Psychology, 59*(3), 464–474.

Forrest, D., Ryan, J., & Lazar, V. (1978). American familiar language and the FMG psychiatric resident. *The Journal of Psychiatric Education, 2*(1), 68–81.

Fouad, N. A. (1995). Career behavior of Hispanics: Assessment and career intervention. In F. Leong (Ed.), *Career development and vocational behavior of racial and ethnic minorities* (pp. 165–191). Mahwah, NJ: Erlbaum.

Frank, J. D. (1961). *Persuasion and healing: A comparative study of psychotherapy.* Baltimore, MD: Johns Hopkins University Press.

Freed, A. O. (1988). Interviewing through an interpreter. *Social Work, 46*, 315–319.

Fujino, D., Okazaki, S., & Young, K. (1994). Asian-American women in the mental health system: An examination of ethnic and gender match between therapist and client. *Journal of Community Psychology, 22*(2), 164–176.

Furnham, A. (1993). Just world beliefs in twelve societies. *Journal of Social Psychology, 133*, 317–329.

Furnham, A., Bond, M., Heaven, P., Hilton, D., & Lobel, T. (1993). A comparison of Protestant work ethic beliefs in thirteen nations. *Journal of Social Psychology, 133*, 185–197.

Gamboa, A., Tosi, D., & Riccio, A. (1976). Race and counselor climate in the counselor preference of delinquent girls. *Journal of Counseling Psychology, 23*, 160–162.

Garza, A. C. (1981). Potential pitfalls in the diagnosis and treatment of minority groups. *The Journal of Social Psychology, 114*, 9–22.

Gaw, A. C. (Ed.) (1993). *Culture, ethnicity, and mental illness.* Washington, DC: American Psychiatric Press.

Gergen, K. J., Gulerce, A., Lock, A., & Misra, G. (1996). Psychological science in cultural context. *American Psychologist, 51*(5), 496–503.

Giles, H. C. (1990). Counseling Haitian students and their families: Issues and interventions. *Journal of Counseling and Development, 68*, 317–320.

Gim, R. H., Atkinson, D., & Kim, S. (1991). Asian American acculturation, counselor ethnicity, and cultural sensitivity and ratings of counselors. *Journal of Counseling Psychology, 38*, 57–62.

Goldberg, B., & Tidwell, R. (1990). Ethnicity and gender similarity: The effectiveness of counseling for adolescents. *Journal of Youth and Adolescents, 19*(6), 598–603.

Goldfried, M., & Wolfe, B. (1996). Psychotherapy practice and research: Repairing a strained alliance. *American Psychologist, 51*(10), 1007–1016.

Gonzalez-Lee, T., & Simon, H. J. (1990). *Medical Spanish: Interviewing the Latino patient: A cross-cultural perspective.* Englewood Cliffs, NJ: Prentice-Hall.

Goodchilds, J. (Ed.) (1991). *Psychological perspectives on human diversity in America.* Washington, DC: American Psychological Association.

Gottheil, E., Sterling, R., & Weinstein, S. (1995). Generalizing from controlled treatment outcome studies: Sample data from a cocaine treatment program. *American Journal on Addictions, 4*(4), 331–338.

Gottheil, E., Sterling, R., Weinstein, S., & Kurtz, J. (1994). Patient/therapist matching and early treatment dropout. *Journal of Addictive Diseases, 13*(4), 169–176.

Graham, J. L. (1985). The influence of culture on business negotiations. *Journal of International Business Studies, 16,* 81–96.

Greene, C. J. (1982). *A study of community-college students' initial counselor preferences based on the nature of the personal problem and on the age, ethnicity, and sex of the counselor and student.* Unpublished doctoral dissertation, University of San Francisco.

Griffith. M. S., & Jones, E. E. (1978). Race and psychotherapy: Changing perspectives. In J. H. Masserman (Ed.), *Current psychiatric therapies* (Vol. 4, pp. 225–235). New York: Grune & Stratton.

Hall, E. T. (1959). *The silent language.* Garden City, NJ: Doubleday.

Hall, E. T. (1969). *The hidden dimension.* Garden City, NJ: Doubleday.

Hall, E. T. (1976). *Beyond culture.* Garden City, NJ: Anchor Press.

Hall, G., & Maloney, H. (1983). Cultural control in psychotherapy with minority clients. *Psychotherapy: Theory, Research, & Practice, 20*(2), 131–142.

Hanna, J. (1984). Black/white nonverbal differences, dance, and dissonance: Implications for desegregation. In A. Wolfgang (Ed.), *Nonverbal behavior: Perspectives, applications, intercultural insights* (pp. 373–410). Lewiston, NY: Hogrefe.

Harper, R. G., Wiens, A. N., & Matarazzo, J. D. (1978). *Nonverbal communication: The state of the art.* New York: Wiley.

Harrison, D. K. (1975). Race as a counselor–client variable in counseling and psychotherapy: A review of the research. *The Counseling Psychologist, 5,* 124–133.

Helms, J. E. (1993). I also said, "White racial identity influences White researchers". *The Counseling Psychologist, 21*(2), 240–243.

Helms, J. E. (1994). How multiculturalism obscures racial factors in the therapy process: Comment on Ridley et al. (1994), Sodowsky et al. (1994), Ottavi et al. (1994), and Thompson et al. (1994). *Journal of Counseling Psychology, 41*(2), 162–165.

Henley, N. (1977). *Body politics: Power, sex, and nonverbal communication.* Englewood Cliffs, NJ: Prentice-Hall.

Henley, N., & LaFrance, M. (1984). Gender as culture: Difference and dominance in nonverbal behavior. In A. Wolfgang (Ed.), *Nonverbal behavior:* (pp. 351–372). Lewiston, NY: Hogrefe.

Hernandez, A., & LaFromboise, T. (1985, August). *The development of the Cross-Cultural Counseling Inventory.* Paper presented at the 93rd Annual Convention of the American Psychological Association, Los Angeles, CA.

Hess, R., & Street, E. (1991). The effect of acculturation on the relationship of counselor ethnicity and client ratings. *Journal of Counseling Psychology, 38*(1), 71–75.

Hewes, G. (1955). World distribution of certain postural habits. *American Anthropologist, 52*(2) 231–244.

Hiegel, J. P. (1994). Use of indigenous concepts and healers in the care of refugees: Some experiences from the Thai border camps. In A. J. Marsella, T. Bornemann, S. Ekblad, & J. Orley (Eds.), *Amidst peril and pain: The mental health and well-being of the world's refugees* (pp. 293–310). Washington, DC: American Psychological Association.

Higginbotham, H. N. (1977). Culture and the role of client expectancy in psychotherapy. *Topics in Culture Learning, 5,* 107–124.

Higginbotham, H. N., West, S., & Forsyth, D. (1988). *Psychotherapy and behavior change: Social, cultural and methodological perspectives.* New York: Pergamon.

Highlen, P. (1996). MCT theory and implications for organizations/systems. In D. W. Sue, A. Ivey, & P. Pedersen (Eds.), *A theory of multicultural counseling and therapy* (pp. 65–85). Pacific Grove, CA: Brooks/Cole.

Ho, M. (1987). *Family therapy with ethnic minorities.* Newbury Park, CA: Sage.

Ho, M. (1992). *Minority children and adolescents in therapy.* Newbury Park, CA: Sage

Hofstede, G. (1980). *Culture's consequences: International differences in work related values.* Beverly Hills, CA: Sage.

Hofstede, G. (1991). *Cultures and organizations: Software of the mind.* London: McGraw-Hill.

Hohmann, A., & Parron, D. (1996). How the new NIH guidelines on inclusion of women and minorities apply: Efficacy trials, effectiveness trials and validity. *Journal of Consulting and Clinical Psychology, 64*(5), 851–855.

Hollingsworth, D. M. (1987). *The interview: A cross-cultural model, strategies and evaluative measures.* Unpublished doctoral dissertation, University of Arizona.

Hollon, S. (1996). The efficacy and effectiveness of psychotherapy relative to medications. *American Psychologist, 51*(10), A1020–1025.

Howard, K., Moras, K., Brill, P., Martinovich, Z., & Lutz, W. (1996). Evaluation of psychotherapy: Efficacy, effectiveness, and patient progress. *American Psychologist, 51*(10), 1059–1064.

Hui, C., & Triandis, H. (1985). Measurement in cross-cultural psychology: A review and comparison of strategies. *Journal of Cross-Cultural Psychology, 16(2),* 131–152.

Ibrahim, F. A. (1985). Effective cross-cultural counseling and psychotherapy. *The Counseling Psychologist, 13,* 625–638.

Ivey, A. E. (1981). Counseling and psychotherapy: Toward a new perspective. In A. Marsella & P. Pedersen (Eds.), *Cross-cultural counseling and psychotherapy* (pp. 279–311). New York: Pergamon.

Ivey, A. E. (1993). On the need for reconstruction of our present practice of counseling and psychotherapy. *The Counseling psychologist, 21*(2), 225–228.

Ivey, A. E. (1994). *Intentional interviewing in counseling: Facilitating client development.* Pacific Grove, CA: Brooks/Cole.

Ivey, A. E., Ivey, N. B., & Simek-Morgan, L. (1993). *Counseling and psychotherapy* (3rd ed.). Boston: Allyn & Bacon.

Izard, C. (1971). *The face of emotion.* New York: Appleton-Century-Crofts.

Izard, C., & Izard, B. (1980). Expressions of emotions as transcultural language in social interaction and theatrical performances. In W. von Raffer-Engel (Ed.), *Aspects of nonverbal communication* (pp. 78–102). Lisse, the Netherlands: Swets & Zeitlinger.

Jackson, K., & Moto, F. (1996, August). *Mental health concepts in Chichewa and English.* Poster session presented at the XIIIth Congress of the International Association of Cross-Cultural Psychology, Montreal, PQ, Canada.

Jackson, M. (1995). Multicultural counseling: Historical perspectives. In J. Ponterotto, J. Casas, L. Suzuki, & C. Alexander (Eds.), *Handbook of multicultural counsel-*

ing (pp. 3–16). Thousand Oaks, CA: Sage.

Jacobson, N., & Christensen, A. (1996). Studying the effectiveness of psychotherapy: How well can clinical trials do the job? *American Psychologist, 51*(10), 1031–1039.

Jensen, J. V. (1985). Perspective on non-verbal communication. In L. A. Samovar & R. E. Porter (Eds.), Intercultural communication: A reader (pp. 165–189). Belmont, CA: Wadsworth.

Johnson, D. R. (1972). Black kinesics: Some nonverbal communication patterns in the black culture. In L. A. Samovar & R. E. Porter (Eds.), *Intercultural communication: A reader* (pp. 231–254). Belmont, CA: Wadsworth.

Johnson, M., & Lashley, K. (1989). Influence of Native-Americans' cultural commitment on preferences for counselor ethnicity and expectations about counseling. *Journal of Multicultural Counseling and Development, 17*(3), 115–122.

Johnson, M. J., Swartz, J., & Martin, W. Jr. (1995). Applications of psychological theories for career development with Native Americans. In F. Leong (Ed.), *Career development and vocational behavior of racial and ethnic minorities* (pp. 103–133). Hillsdale, NJ: Erlbaum.

Jones, E. E. (1978). Effects of race on psychotherapy process and outcome: An exploratory investigation. *Psychotherapy: Theory, Research, and Practice, 15*(3), 226–236.

Jones, E. E. (1982). Psychotherapists' impressions of treatment outcome as a function of race. *Journal of Clinical Psychology, 38*(4), 722–731.

Jones, J. (1991). Psychological models of race: What have they been and what should they be? In J. Goodchilds (Ed.), *Psychological perspectives on human diversity in America* (pp. 7–46). Washington, DC: American Psychological Association.

Jordan, J. (1995). Report from the Bahamas. In N. R. Goldberger & J. B. Veroff (Eds.), *The culture and psychology reader* (pp. 605–617). New York: New York University Press.

Kagitcibasi, C., & Berry, J. W. (1989). Cross-cultural psychology: Current research and trends. *Annual Review of Psychology, 40*, 493–451.

Kelly, H. H., Berscheid, E., Christensen, A., Harvey, J. H., Huston, T. L., Levinger, G., McClintock, E., Peplau, L. A., & Peterson, D. (1983). *Close relationships.* San Francisco: Freeman.

Kendon, A. (1983). Gesture and speech: How they interact. In J. M. Weimann, & R. P. Harrison (Eds.), *Nonverbal interaction.* Beverly Hills, CA: Sage.

Kerwin, C., & Ponterotto, J. (1995). Biracial identity development: Theory and research. In J. Ponterotto, J. Casas, L. Suzuki, & C. Alexander (Eds.), *Handbook of multicultural counseling* (pp. 199–217). Thousand Oaks, CA: Sage.

Key, M. L. (1975). *Paralanguage and kinesics.* Metuchen, NJ: Scarecrow Press.

Kim, U., & Berry, J. (Eds.) (1993). *Indigenous psychologies: Research and experience in context.* Newbury Park, CA: Sage.

Kim, U., Triandis, H., Kagitcibasi, C., Choi, S., & Yoon, G. (Eds.) (1994). *Individualism and collectivism: Theory, method and applications.* Newbury Park, CA: Sage.

Kim, Y. Y. (1988). *Communication and cross-cultural adaptation.* Clevedon, UK: Multilingual Matters.

Kinzie, J. D, & Leung, P. (1989). Clonidine in Cambodian patients with post-traumatic stress disorder. *Journal of Nervous and Mental Disease, 177*, 546–550.

Kline, F., Acosta, F., & Austin, V., & Johnson, R. (1980). The misunderstood Spanish-speaking patient. *American Journal of Psychiatry, 137*(12), 1530–1533.

Kluckhohn, F. R., & Strodtbeck, F. L. (1961). *Variations in value orientation.* New York: Harper & Row.

Knapp, M. (1984). The study of nonverbal behavior vis-à-vis human communication theory. In A. Wolfgang (Ed.), *Nonverbal behavior* (pp. 15–40). Lewiston, NY: Hogrefe.

Kohls, L. R. (1979). *Survival kit for overseas living.* Chicago: Intercultural Press.

Krause, I., & Miller, M. C. (1995). Culture and family therapy. In S. Fernando (Ed.), *Mental health in a multi-ethnic society* (pp. 148–171). New York: Routledge.

Krauss, R. M., Chen, Y., & Chawla, P. (1996). Nonverbal behavior and nonverbal communication: What do conversational hand gestures tell us. In M. P. Zanna (Ed.), *Advances in experimental social psychology* (Vol. 28, pp. 389–450). San Diego, CA: Academic Press.

LaBarre, W. (1985). Paralinguistics, kinesics and cultural anthropology. In L. Samovar & R. Porter (Eds.), *Intercultural communication: A reader* (pp. 172–189). Belmont, CA: Wadsworth.

Labov W., & Fanshel, D. (1977). *Therapeutic discourse.* New York: Academic Press.

LaFrance, M., & Mayo, C. (1978). Cultural aspects on nonverbal communication: A review essay. *International Journal of Intercultural Relations, 2*, 71–89.

LaFromboise, T., Coleman, H., & Hernandez, A. (1991). Development and factor structure of the Cross-Cultural Counseling Inventory–Revised. *Professional Research and Practice, 22*, 380–388.

LaFromboise, T., Foster, S., & James, A. (1996). Ethics in multicultural counseling. In P. B. Pedersen, J. G. Draguns, W. J. Lonner, & J. E. Trimble (Eds.), *Counseling across cultures* (4th ed., pp. 47–72). Thousand Oaks, CA: Sage.

LaFromboise, T., & Jackson, M. (1996). MCT theory and Native-American populations. In D. W. Sue, A. Ivey, & P. Pedersen (Eds.), *A theory of multicultural counseling and therapy* (pp. 192–203). Pacific Grove, CA: Brooks/Cole.

Lass, N. J., Mertz P. J., & Kimmel, K. (1978). The effect of temporal speech alterations on speaker race and sex identification. *Language and Speech, 21*(3), 279–290.

Leary, K. (1995). "Interpreting in the dark": Race and ethnicity in psychoanalytic psychotherapy. *Journal of Psychoanalytic Psychology, 12*(1), 127–140.

Lee, C. C. (1996). MCT theory and implications for indigenous healing. In D. W. Sue, A. Ivey, & P. Pedersen (Eds.), *A theory of multicultural counseling and therapy* (pp. 86–98). Pacific Grove, CA: Brooks/Cole.

Lefley, H. (1994). Mental health treatment and service delivery in cross-cultural perspective. In L. Adler & U. Gielen (Eds.), *Cross-cultural topics in psychology* (pp. 179–199). Westport, CT: Praeger.

Leong, F. T. (Ed.) (1995). *Career development and vocational behavior of racial and ethnic minorities.* Mahwah, NJ: Erlbaum.

Leong, F. T. (1996). MCT theory and Asian-American populations. In D. W. Sue, A. Ivey, & P. Pedersen (Eds.), *A theory of multicultural counseling and therapy* (pp. 204–216). Pacific Grove, CA: Brooks/Cole.

Leong, F. T., & Gim-Chung, R. (1995). Career assessment and intervention with Asian Americans. In F. Leong (Ed.), *Career development and vocational behavior of racial and ethnic minorities* (pp. 193–226). Mahwah, NJ: Erlbaum.

Leong, F. T., & Serafica, F. (1995). Career development of Asian Americans: A research area in need of a good theory. In F. Leong (Ed.), *Career development and vocational behavior of racial and ethnic minorities* (pp. 67–102). Mahwah, NJ: Erlbaum.

Lerner, B. (1972). *Therapy in the ghetto: Political impotence and personal disintegration.* Baltimore, MD: Johns Hopkins University Press.

LeVine, R., & Campbell, D. (1972). *Ethnocentrism: Theories of conflict, ethnic attitudes and group behavior.* New York: Wiley.

Lonner, W. (1990). An overview of cross-cultural testing and assessment. In R. W. Brislin (Ed.), *Applied cross-cultural psychology* (pp. 56–76). Newbury Park, CA: Sage.

Lonner, W., & Ibrahim, F. (1996). Appraisal and assessment in cross-cultural counseling. In P. Pedersen, J. Draguns, W. Lonner, & J. Trimble (Eds.), *Counseling across cultures* (4th ed., pp. 223–267). Thousand Oaks, CA: Sage.

Lopez, S., & Hernandez, P. (1987). When culture is considered in the evaluation and treatment of Hispanic patients. *Psychotherapy, 24*, 120–126.

Lopez, S., Lopez, A., & Fong, K. (1991). Mexican Americans' initial preferences for counselors: The role of ethnic factors. *Journal of Counseling Psychology, 38*(4), 487–496.

Lunt, I., & Poortinga, Y. H. (1996). Internationalizing psychology: The case of Europe. *American Psychologist, 51*(5), 504–508.

Madrid, A. (1995). Diversity and its discontents. In N. R. Goldberger & J. B. Veroff (Eds.), *The culture and psychology reader* (pp. 617–626). New York: New York University Press.

Malgady, R., Rogler, L., & Constantino, G. (1987). Ethnocultural and linguistic bias in mental health evaluation of Hispanics. *American Psychologist, 42*, 228–234.

Malgady, R., Rogler, L., & Constantino, G. (1990). Culturally sensitive psychotherapy for Puerto Rican children and adolescents: A program of treatment outcome research. *Journal of Counseling and Clinical Psychology, 58*, 704–712.

Manson, S. M. (1982). *New directions in prevention among American Indian and Alaskan Native communities*. Portland, OR: Oregon Health Sciences University.

Manson, S. M., Shore, J. H., & Bloom, J. D. (1985). The depressive experience in American Indian communities: A challenge for psychiatric theory and diagnoses. In A. Kleinman & B. Good (Eds.), *Culture and depression* (pp. 331–368). Berkeley, CA: University of California Press.

Marcos, L. (1976). Bilinguals in psychotherapy: Language as an emotional barrier. *American Journal of Psychotherapy, 30*, 552–560.

Marcos, L., Urcuyo, L., Kesselman, M., & Alpert, M. (1973). The language barrier in evaluating Spanish-American patients. *Archives of General Psychiatry, 29*(5) 655–659.

Marks, C. (1993). Demography and race. In J. Stanfield II & R. Dennis (Eds.), *Race and ethnicity in research methods* (pp. 159–171). Newbury Park, CA: Sage.

Marsella, A. J., & Pedersen, P. B. (Eds.) (1981). *Cross-cultural counseling and psychotherapy*. New York: Pergamon.

Marsella, A. J., & White, G. M. (Eds.) (1982). *Cultural conceptions of mental health and therapy*. Dordrecht, The Netherlands: Reidel.

Mays, V. M., Rubin, J., Sabourin, M., & Walker, L. (1996). Moving toward a global psychology: Changing theories and practice to meet the needs of a changing world. *American Psychologist, 51*(5), 485–487.

McGoldrick, M., Pearce J., & Giordano, J. (Eds) (1982). *Ethnicity and family therapy*. New York: Guilford.

McWhirter, J. J., & Ryan, C. (1991). Counseling the Navajo: Cultural understanding. *Journal of Multicultural Counseling and Development, 19*, 74–82.

Mehrabian, A. (1972). *Nonverbal communication*. Chicago, IL: Aldine-Atherton.

Mehrabian, A., & Ferris, S. R. (1976). Influence of attitudes from nonverbal communication in two channels. *Journal of Consulting Psychology, 31*, 248–252.

Mio, J. S., & Iwamasa, G. (1993). To do, or not to do: That is the question for White cross-cultural researchers. *The Counseling Psychologist, 21*(2), 197–212.

Miranda, J. (1996). Introduction to the special section on recruiting and retaining minorities in psychotherapy research. *Journal of Consulting and Clinical Psychology, 64*(5), 848–850.

Miranda, J., Azocar, F., Organista, K., Munoz, R., & Lieberman, A. (1996). Recruiting and retaining low-income Latinos in psychotherapy research. *Journal of Consulting and Clinical Psychology, 64*(5), 868–874.

Mitchell, H. (1970). The Black experience in higher education. *The Counseling Psychologist, 2*, 30–36.

Moghaddam, F. (1987). Psychology in the three worlds: as reflected by the crisis in social psychology and the move towards indigenous Third World psychology. *American Psychologist, 42*(10), 912–920.

Mollica, R. F., Wyshak, G., Lavelle, J., Truong, T., Tor, S., & Yang, T. (1990). Assessment symptom change in Southeast Asian refugee survivors of mass violence and torture. *American Journal of Psychiatry, 147*(1), 83–88.

Montalvo, G., & Gutierrez, M. (1989). Nine assumptions for work with ethnic minority families. *Journal of Psychotherapy and the Family, 6*(1–2), 35–52.

Moraga, C. (1995). La guera. In N. R. Goldberger & J. B. Veroff (Eds.), *The culture and psychology reader* (pp. 596–604). New York: New York University Press.

Morris, D., Collette, P., Marsh, P., & O'Shaughnessy, M. (1979). *Gestures: Their origins and distributions*. London: Cape.

Mowrer, O. (Ed.) (1953). *Psychotherapy: Research and practice*. New York: Ronald Press.

Mrinal, N., Mrinal, U., & Takooshian, H. (1994). Research methods for studies in the field. In L. Adler & U. Gielen (Eds.), *Cross-cultural topics in psychology* (pp. 25–40). Westport, CT: Praeger/Greenwood.

Myers, S. (1993). Measuring and detecting discrimination in the post-civil rights era. In J. Stanfield II & R. Dennis (Eds.), *Race and ethnicity in research methods* (pp. 172–197). Newbury Park, CA: Sage.

Neligh, G. (1988). Major mental disorders and behavior among American Indians and Alaska Natives [Monograph]. In *Behavioral health issues among American Indians and Alaska Natives: Explorations on the frontiers of the biobehavioral sciences. American Indian and Alaska Mental Health Research, 1*, 116–159.

Newman, F., & Tejeda, M. (1996). The need for research that is designed to support decisions in the delivery of mental health services, *American Psychologist, 51*(10), 1040–1049.

Nguyen, N. (1992). Living between two cultures: Treating first-generation Asian Americans. In L. Vargas & J. Koss-Chioino (Eds.), *Working with culture* (pp. 204–224). San Francisco: Jossey-Bass.

Nichter, M. (1981). Idioms of distress, alternatives in the expression of psychosocial distress: A case study from South India. *Culture and Medical Psychiatry, 5*, 379–408.

National Institutes of Health (1994). NIH guidelines on the inclusion of women and minorities as subjects in clinical research. 59, Fed. Reg. 14, 508 (Document no. 94-5435).

Norton, I., & Manson, S. (1996). Research in American Indian and Alaska Native communities: Navigating the cultural universe of values and process. *Journal of Consulting and Clinical Psychology, 64*(5), 856–860.

Ogino, T., Misono, Y., & Fukushima, C. (1985). Diversity of honorific usage in Tokyo: a sociolinguistic approach based on a field survey. *International Journal of Sociology of Language, 55*, 23–39.

Orlinski, D., Grawe, K., & Parks, P. (1994). Process and outcome in psychotherapy–noch einmal. In A. Bergin & S. Garfield (Eds.), *Handbook of psychotherapy and behavior change* (4th ed., pp. 270–376). New York: Wiley.

Osipow, S., & Littlejohn, E. (1995). Toward a multicultural theory of career development: Prospects and dilemmas.

In F. Leong (Ed.), *Career development and vocational behavior of racial and ethnic minorities* (pp. 251–261). Mahwah, NJ: Erlbaum.

Owan, T. C. (Ed.) (1985). *Southeast Asian mental health: Treatment, prevention, services, training, and research.* Rockville, MD: National Institute for Mental Health.

Pakov, T., Lewis, D., & Lyons, J. (1989). Psychiatric diagnosis and racial bias: An empirical investigation. *Professional Psychology: Research and Practice, 20,* 364–368.

Pandey, J. (1978). Effects of crowding on human social behavior. *Journal of Social and Economic Studies, 6,* 85–95.

Pandey, J. (1990). The environment, culture, and behavior. In R. Brislin (Ed.), *Applied cross-cultural psychology* (Vol. 14, pp. 254–277). Newbury Park, CA: Sage.

Pandey, J. (1996, August). *Perceptions of crowding in India.* Paper presented at the XIII Congress of the International Association for Cross-Cultural Psychology, Montreal, PQ.

Paniagua, F. A. (1994). *Assessing and treating culturally diverse groups: A practical guide.* Thousand Oaks, CA: Sage.

Parham, T. (1993). White researchers conducting multicultural counseling research: Can their efforts be "mo betta"? *The Counseling Psychologist, 21*(2), 250–256.

Parham, T. (1996). MCT theory and African-American populations. In D. W. Sue, A. Ivey, P. Pedersen (Eds.), *A theory of multicultural counseling and therapy* (pp. 177–191). Pacific Grove, CA: Brooks/Cole.

Parham, T., & Helms, J. (1981). The influence of Black student's racial identity attitudes on preference for counselor's race. *Journal of Counseling Psychology, 28*(3) 250–257.

Parham, T., & Helms, J. (1985). Relation of racial identity attitudes to self-actualization and affective states of Black students. *Journal of Counseling Psychology, 32*(3), 431–440.

Parloff, M., Waskow, E., & Wolfe, B. (1978). Research on therapist variables in relation to process and outcome. In S. Garfield & A. Bergin (Eds.), *Handbook of psychotherapy and behavior change: An empirical analysis* (pp. 233–282). New York: Wiley.

Patton, J. (1993). Psychoeducational assessment of gifted and talented African Americans. In J. Stanfield II & R. Dennis (Eds.), *Race and ethnicity in research methods* (pp. 198–216). Newbury Park, CA: Sage.

Pawlik, K., & d'Ydewalle, G. (1996). Psychology and the global commons: Perspectives of international psychology. *American Psychologist, 51*(5), 488–495.

Pearson, J. C. (1985). *Gender and communication.* Dubuque, IA: Brown.

Pedersen, P. B. (1990). The multicultural perspective as a fourth force in counseling. *Journal of Mental Health Counseling: 12*(1), 93–95.

Pedersen, P. B. (1991a). Multiculturalism as a generic approach to counseling. *Journal of Counseling and Development: 70*(1), 6–12.

Pedersen, P. B. (Ed.) (1991b). Multiculturalism as a fourth force in counseling (Special issue). *Journal of Counseling and Development 70*(1).

Pedersen, P. B. (1991c). Complexity and balance as criteria of effective multicultural counseling. *Journal of Counseling and Development 68,* 550–554.

Pedersen, P. B. (1993). The multicultural dilemma of White cross-cultural researchers. *The Counseling Psychologist, 21*(2), 229–232.

Pedersen, P. B. (1994). *A handbook for developing multicultural awareness* (2nd ed.). Alexandria, VA: American Psychological Association.

Pedersen, P. B. (1995). Culture-centered ethical guidelines for counselors. In J. Ponterotto, J. Casas, L. Suzuki, & C. Alexander (Eds.), *Handbook of multicultural counseling* (pp. 34–49). Thousand Oaks, CA: Sage.

Pedersen, P. B., & Ivey, A. (1993). *Culture-centered counseling and interviewing skills.* Westport, CT: Greenwood/Praeger.

Pedersen, P. B., & Lefley, H. P. (Eds.) (1986). *Cross-cultural training for mental health professionals.* Springfield, IL: Thomas.

Pennington, D. L. (1979). Black–White communication: An assessment of research. In M. Asante, E. Newmark, & C. Balke (Eds.), *The handbook of intercultural communication* (pp. 383–401). Beverly Hills, CA: Sage.

Phinney, J. (1996). When we talk about American ethnic groups, what do we mean? *American Psychologist, 51*(9), 918–927.

Pike, K. (1967). *Language in relation to a unified theory of the structure of human behavior.* The Hague, The Netherlands: Mouton.

Pitta, P., Marcos, L., & Alpert, M. (1978). Language switching as a treatment strategy with bilingual patients. *American Journal of Psychoanalysis, 38*(3), 255–258.

Ponterotto, J. (1993). White racial identity and the counseling professional. *The Counseling Psychologist, 21*(2), 213–217.

Ponterotto, J., & Casas, M. (1991). *Handbook of racial/ethnic minority counseling research.* Springfield, IL: Thomas.

Ponterotto, J., Sanchez, C., & Magids, D. (1991, August). *Initial development and validation of the Multicultural Awareness Scale.* Paper presented at the 99th Annual Convention of the American Psychological Association, San Francisco, CA.

Poortinga, Y. (1992). Towards a conceptualization of culture for psychology. In S. Iawaki, Y. Kashima, & K. Leung (Eds.), *Innovations in cross cultural psychology* (pp. 3–17). Amsterdam: Swets and Zeitlinger.

Pope-Davis, D., & Constantine, M. (1996). MCT theory and implications for practice. In D. W. Sue, A. Ivey, & P. Pedersen (Eds.), *A theory of multicultural counseling and therapy* (pp. 112–122). Pacific Grove, CA: Brooks/Cole.

Poston, W. S., Craine, M., & Atkinson, D. L. (1991). Counselor dismilarity confrontation, client cultural mistrust, and willingness to self-disclose. *Journal of Multicultural Counseling and Development, 19*(2), 65–73.

Poyatos, F. (1976). *Man beyond words: Theory and methodology of nonverbal communication.* Oswego, NY: New York State English Council.

Poyatos, F. (1984). Linguistic fluency and verbal–nonverbal cultural fluency. In A. Wolfgang (Ed.), *Nonverbal behavior: Perspectives, applications, and cultural insights* (pp. 431–460). Lewiston, NY: Hogrefe.

Price, C., & Cuellar, I. (1981). Effects of language and related variables on the expression of psychopathology in Mexican psychiatric patients. *Hispanic Journal of Behavioral Science, 32*(2), 145–160.

Query, J. M. (1985). Comparative admission and follow-up study of American Indians and Whites in a youth chemical dependency unit on the North Central Plains. *The International Journal of the Addictions, 20,* 489–502.

Ragin, C., & Hein, J. (1993). The comparative study of ethnicity: Methodological and conceptual issues. In J. Stanfield II & R. Dennis (Eds.), *Race and ethnicity in research methods* (pp. 254–272). Newbury Park, CA: Sage.

Ramsey. S. (1979). Nonverbal behavior: An intercultural perspective. In M. Asante, E. Newmark, & C. Balke (Eds.), *The handbook of intercultural communication* (pp. 105–143). Beverly Hills, CA: Sage.

Ramsey, S. (1984). Double vision: Nonverbal behavior: Perspectives, applications, cultural insights. In A. Wolfgang (Ed.), *Nonverbal behavior* (pp. 139–167). Lewiston, NY: Hogrefe.

Redfern, S., Dancey, C., & Dryden, W. (1993). Empathy: Its effects on how counsellors are perceived. *British*

Journal of Guidance and Counselling, 21(3), 300–309.

Rey-Perez, A. (1996). *A culturally sensitive psychotherapeutic program for Hispanic children and families.* Unpublished doctoral directed study project, Nova Southeastern University, Fort Lauderdale, FL.

Ridley, C. (1984). Clinical treatment of the nondisclosing Black client: A therapeutic paradox. *American Psychologist, 39,* 1234–1244.

Ridley, C., Mendoza, D., Kanitz, B., Angermeier, L., & Zenk, R. (1994). Cultural sensitivity in multicultural counseling: A perceptual schema model. *Journal of Counseling Psychology, 41*(2), 125–136.

Rivas-Vazquez, R. (1989). *Assessing differential levels of affecting expression in bilingual subjects using the Thematic Apperception Test.* Unpublished doctoral dissertation, Nova Southeastern University, Fort Lauderdale, FL.

Rogler, L. (1993). Culturally sensitizing psychiatric diagnosis: A framework for research. *The Journal of Nervous and Mental Disease, 181*(7), 401–408.

Romeo, D. (1985). Cross-cultural counseling: Brief reactions for the practitioner. *The Counseling Psychologist, 13*(4), 665–671.

Root, M. (1992). Within, between, and beyond race. In M. Root (Ed.), *Racially mixed people in America* (pp. 3–11). Newbury Park, CA: Sage.

Rosenthal, R., Hall, J., Archer, D., Dimatteo, R., & Rogers, P. (1979). Measuring sensitivity to nonverbal communication: The PONS Test. In A. Wolfgang (Ed.), *Nonverbal behavior: Applications and cultural implications* (pp. 222–241). New York: Academic Press.

Rotter, J. (1966). Generalised expectancies for internal versus external control of reinforcement. *Psychological Monographs, 80,* 1–28.

Ruiz, R., & Casas, M. (1981). Culturally relevant and behavioristic counseling for Chicano college students. In P. Pedersen, J. Draguns, W. Lonner, & J. Trimble (Eds.), *Counseling across cultures: Revised and expanded edition* (pp. 203–226). Honolulu, HI: University of Hawaii Press.

Russell, D. (1988). Language in psychotherapy: The influence of nonstandard English in clinical practice. In L. Comas-Diaz & E. Griffith (Eds.), *Clinical guidelines in cross-cultural mental health* (pp. 33–68). New York: Wiley.

Salzma, M. (1995). Attributional discrepancies and bias in cross-cultural interactions. *Journal of Multicultural Counseling and Development, 23*(3), 181–193.

Samovar, L., & Porter, R. (Eds.) (1991). *Intercultural communication: A reader* (6th ed.). Belmont, CA: Wadsworth.

Samuda, R. J. (1975). *Psychological testing of American minorities: Issues and consequences.* New York: Harper & Row.

Samuda, R. J., Kong, S., Cummins, J., Pascual-Leone, J., & Lewis, J. E. (1991). Assessment and placement of minority students. Kingston, ON: Hogrefe/ISSP.

Samuda, R. J., & Lewis, J. E. (1992). Evaluation practices for the multicultural classroom. In C. Diaz (Ed.), *Multicultural education in the 21st century* (pp. 97–111). Washington, DC: National Education Association.

Sanchez, A., & Atkinson, D. (1983). Mexican American cultural commitment preference for counselor ethnicity and willingness to use counseling. *Journal of Counseling Psychology, 30*(2), 215–220.

Sandhu, D. (1984). *The effects of mirroring versus non-mirroring of clients' nonverbal behaviors on empathy, trustworthiness, and positive interaction in cross-cultural counseling dyads (NLP, neurolinguistic programming).* Unpublished doctoral dissertation, Mississippi State University, MS.

Sandhu, D., Reeves, T., & Portes, P. (1993). Cross-cultural counseling and neurolinguistic mirroring with Native American adolescents. *Journal of Multicultural Counseling and Development, 21*(2), 106–118.

Santiago-Rivera, A. L. (1995). Developing a culturally sensitive treatment modality for bilingual Spanish-speaking clients: Incorporating language and culture in counseling. *Journal of counseling and development,* 74, 12–17.

Sattler, J. (1977). The effects of therapist–client racial similarity. In A. Gurman & A. Razin (Eds.), *Effective psychotherapy: A handbook of research* (pp. 252–290). New York: Pergamon.

Scheflen, A. (1964). The significance of posture in communication systems. *Psychiatry, 27,* 316–331.

Schinke, S. P., Orlandi, M. A., Botvin, G. J., Gilchrist, L. D., Trimble, J. E., & Locklear, V. B. (1988). Preventing substance abuse among American-Indian adolescents: A bicultural competence skills approach. *Journal of Counseling Psychology, 35,* 87–90.

Schwartz, S. (1992). The universal content and structure of values: Theoretical advances and empirical tests in 20 countries. In M. Zanna (Ed.), *Advanced experimental social psychology* (pp. 1–65). New York: Academic Press.

Schwartz, S. (1994). Beyond individualism-collectivism: New cultural dimensions of values. In U. Kim, H. Triandis, C. Kagitcibasi, S. Choi, & G. Yoon (Eds.), *Individualism and collectivism: Theory, method, and applications* (pp. 85–119). Newbury Park, CA: Sage.

Sechrest, L., McKnight, P., & McKnight, K. (1996). Calibration of measures for psychotherapy outcome studies. *American Psychologist, 51*(10), 1065–1071.

Seligman, M. (1996). Science as an ally of practice. *American Psychologist, 51*(10), 1072–1079.

Smith, A. W. (1993). Survey research on African Americans: Methodological innovations. In J. Stanfield II & R. Dennis (Eds.), *Race and ethnicity in research methods* (pp. 217–232). Newbury Park, CA: Sage.

Smith, H. (1984). State of the art of nonverbal behavior in teaching. In A. Wolfgang (Ed.), *Nonverbal behavior: Perspectives, applications, and cultural insights* (pp. 171–202). Lewiston, NY: Hogrefe.

Smith, P., Peterson, M., Akande, D., Callan, V., & Cho, N. (1994). Organizational event management in 14 countries: A comparison with Hofstede's dimensions. In A. Bouvy, F. van de Vijver, P. Boski, & P. Schmitz (Eds.), *Journeys into cross-cultural psychology* (pp. 212–229). Amsterdam: Swets & Zeitlinger.

Snodgrass, L. L., Yamamoto, J., Frederick, C., Ton-That, N., Foy, D., Chan, L., Wu, J., Hahn, P. H., Shinh, D., Nguyen, N. H., de Jonge, J., & Fairbanks, L. (1993). Vietnamese refugees with PTSD symptomatology: Intervention via a coping skill model. *Journal of Traumatic Stress, 6*(4), 569–575.

Sodowski, G., & Impara, J. (Eds.) (1996). *Multicultural assessment in counseling and clinical psychology.* Lincoln, NE: Buros Institute of Mental Measurements.

Sodowski, G., Taffe, R., Gutkin, T., & Wise, S. (1994). Development of Multicultural Counseling Inventory: Self-report measure of multicultural competencies. *Journal of Counseling Psychology, 41,* 137–148.

Sommer, R. (1959). Studies in personal space. *Sociometry, 22,* 247–260.

Song, M., & Parker, D. (1995). Commonality, difference and the dynamics of disclosure in in-depth interviewing. *Journal of Sociology, 29*(2), 241–256.

Speigal, J., & Papajohn, J. (1986). Training program in ethnicity and mental health. In H. Lefley & P. Pedersen (Eds.), *Cross-cultural counseling for mental health professionals* (pp. 49–71). Springfield, IL: Thomas.

Speight, S. L., Myers, L. J., Cox, C., & Highlen, P. S. (1991). A redefinition of multicultural counseling. *Journal of Counseling and Development, 70*(1), 29–36.

Spradley, J. P. (1979). *The ethnographic interview.* New York: Holt, Rinehart, & Winston.

Stanfield, J. II (1993). Methodological reflections: An introduction. In J. Stanfield II & R. Dennis (Eds.), *Race and ethnicity in research methods* (pp. 3–15). Newbury Park, CA: Sage.

Stanges, B., & Riccio, A. (1970). A counselee preference for counselors: Some implications for counselor education. *Counselor Education and Supervision, 10*, 39–46.

Steward, R., Gimenez, M., & Jackson, C. (1995). A study of personal preferences of successful university students as related to race/ethnicity and sex: Implications and recommendations for training, practice, and future research. *Journal of College Student Development, 36*(2), 123–131.

Strupp, H. (1996). The tripartite model and the Consumer Reports study. *American Psychologist, 51*(10), 1017–1024.

Sue, D., & Sundberg, N. D. (1996). Research and research hypotheses about effectiveness in intercultural counseling. In P. B. Pedersen, J. G. Draguns, W. J. Lonner, & J. E. Trimble (Eds.), *Counseling across cultures* (4th ed., pp. 323–352). Thousand Oaks, CA: Sage.

Sue, D. W. (1977). Barriers to effective cross-cultural counseling. *Journal of Counseling Psychology, 24*, 420–429.

Sue, D. W. (Ed.) (1981). *Counseling the culturally different.* New York: Wiley.

Sue, D. W. (1990). Culture specific techniques in counseling: A conceptual framework. *Professional Psychology, 21*(6), 424–433.

Sue, D. W. (1991). A model for cultural diversity training. *Journal of Counseling and Development, 70*, 99–105.

Sue, D. W. (1993). Confronting ourselves: The White and racial/ethnic-minority researcher. *The Counseling Psychologist, 21*(2), 244–249.

Sue, D. W. (1995). Toward a theory of multicultural counseling and therapy. In J. A. Banks & C. A. McGee Banks (Eds.), *Handbook of research on multicultural education* (pp. 647–659). New York: Macmillan.

Sue, D. W., Arredondo, P., & McDavis, R. J. (1992). Multicultural competencies and standards: A call to the profession. *Journal of Counseling and Development, 70*, 477–486.

Sue, D. W., Bernier, J. E., Durran, A., Feinberg, L., Pedersen, P., Smith, E. J., & Vasquez-Nuttal, E. (1982). Position paper: Cross-cultural competencies. *The Counseling Psychologist, 1*, 45–52.

Sue, D. W., Ivey, A., & Pedersen, P. (Eds.) (1996). *A theory of multicultural counseling and therapy.* Pacific Grove, CA: Brooks/Cole.

Sue, D. W., & Sue, D. (1990). *Counseling the culturally different: Theory and practice* (2nd ed.). New York: Wiley.

Sue, S., Fujino, D. C., Hu, L. T., Takeuchi, D. T., & Zane, N. W. (1991). Community mental health services for ethnic minority groups: A test of the cultural responsiveness hypothesis. *Journal of Counseling Psychology, 59*, 533–540.

Sue, S., & Zane, N., (1987). The role of culture and cultural techniques in psychotherapy: A critique and reformulation. *American Psychologist, 42*(1), 37–45.

Sue, S., Zane, N., & Young, K. (1994). Research on psychotherapy with culturally diverse populations. In A. Bergin & S. Garfield (Eds.), *Handbook of psychotherapy and behavior change* (4th ed., pp. 783–820). New York: Wiley.

Szapocznik, J., Rio, A., Perez-Vidal, A., Kurtines, W., & Sanisteban, D. (1986). Family effectiveness training for Hispanic families. In H. Lefley & P. Pedersen (Eds.), *Cross-cultural training for mental health professionals* (pp. 245–261). Springfield, IL: Thomas.

Takeuchi, D., Mokuau, N., & Chun, C. (1992). Mental health services for Asian Americans and Pacific Islanders. *The Journal of Mental Health Administration, 19*(3), 237–244.

Tapp, J. L., Kelman, H., Triandis, H., Wrightsman, L., & Coelho, J. (1974). Advisory principles for ethical considerations in the conduct of cross-cultural research: Fall 1973 revision. *International Journal of Psychology, 9*(3), 240–249.

Tedeschi, G., & Willis, F. (1993). Attitudes toward counseling among Asian international and native caucasian students. *Journal of College Student Psychotherapy, 7*(4), 43–54.

Thomas, L. (1995). Psychotherapy in the context of race and culture: An inter-cultural therapeutic approach. In S. Fernando (Ed.), *Mental health in a multi-ethnic society* (pp. 172–190). London: Routledge.

Thomason, T. (1991). Counseling Native Americans: An introduction for non-Native American counselors. *Journal of Counseling and Development, 69*(4), 321–327.

Thompson, E., Neighbors, H., Munday, C., & Jackson, J. (1996). Recruitment and retention of African American patients for clinical research: An exploration of response rates in an urban psychiatric hospital. *Journal of Consulting Psychology, 64*(5), 861–867.

Thompson, L. (1989). *Romans and Blacks.* Norman, OK: University of Oklahoma Press.

Tomlinson, S., & Cheatham, H. (1989). Effects of counselor intake judgements on service to Black students using a university counseling center. *Counselling Psychology Quarterly, 2*(2), 105–111.

Tomlinson-Clarke, S., & Cheatham, H. (1993). Counselor and client ethnicity and counselor intake judgements. *Journal of Counseling Psychology, 40*(3), 267–270.

Triandis, H. (1978). Some universals of social behavior. *Personality in Social Psychology Bulletin, 4*, 1–16.

Triandis, H. (1994). *Culture and social behavior.* New York: McGraw-Hill.

University of Wisconsin (1991). *Cross-cultural interviewing in social work practice: The case of the Hmong* [videocassette]. (Available from the Social Work Department of the University of Wisconsin, Eau-Claire, WI)

VandenBos, G. (1996). Outcome assessment of psychotherapy. *American Psychologist, 51*(10), 1005–1006.

Van Dijk, T. (1993). Analyzing racism through discourse analysis: Some methodological reflections. In J. Stanfield II & R. Dennis (Eds.), *Race and ethnicity in research methods* (pp. 92–134). Newbury Park, CA: Sage.

Vazquez-Nuttall, E., Webber, J., & Sanchez, W. (1996). MCT theory and implications for training. In D. W. Sue, A. Ivey, & P. Pedersen (Eds.), *A theory of multicultural counseling and therapy* (pp. 123–138). Pacific Grove, CA: Brooks/Cole.

Villegas-Reimers, E. (1996). Self-development of Venezuelan adolescents. *Journal of Cross-Cultural Psychology, 27*(1), 25–36.

Vontress, C. (1981). Racial and ethnic barriers in counseling. In P. Pedersen, J. Draguns, W. Lonner, & J. Trimble (Eds.), *Counseling across cultures: Revised and expanded edition* (pp. 87–107). Honolulu, HI: University of Hawaii Press.

Weitz, S. (1972). Attitude, voice, and behavior: A repressed affect model of interracial interaction. *Journal of Personality and Social Psychology, 24*, 14–21.

Westbrook, F. D., & Sedlacek, W. E. (1991). Forty years of using labels to communicate about nontraditional students: Does it help or hurt? *Journal of Counseling and Development, 70*(1), 20–28.

Westermeyer, J. J. (1993). Cross-cultural psychiatric assessment. In A. C. Gaw (Ed.), *Culture, ethnicity and mental illness* (pp. 125–144). Washington, DC: American Psychiatric Press.

White, J. (1994). The impact of race and ethnicity on transference and countertransference in combined individual–group therapy. *Group, 18*(2), 89–99.

Williams, M. (1993). Urban ethnography: Anther look. In

J. Stanfield II & R. Dennis (Eds.), *Race and ethnicity in research methods* (pp. 135–158). Newbury Park, CA: Sage.

Wolfgang, A. (1985). Intercultural counselling and non-verbal behavior: An overview. In R. Samuda & A. Wolfgang (Eds.), *Intercultural counselling and assessment* (pp. 33–48). Lewiston, NY: Hogrefe.

Wolfgang, A., & Bhardwaj, A. (1984). Bibliography of 100 years of nonverbal study. In A. Wolfgang (Ed.), *Nonverbal behavior* (pp. 461–469). Lewiston, NY: Hogrefe.

Worchel, S., & Teddlie, C. (1976). The experience of crowding: A two factor theory. *Journal of Personality and Social Psychology, 34*, 30–40.

World Health Organization (1983). *Depressive disorders in different cultures*. Geneva, Switzerland: Author.

World Health Organization (1992). *Refugee mental health: Draft manual for field testing*. Geneva: Author.

Wrenn, C. (1962). The culturally encapsulated counselor. *Harvard Educational Review, 32*, 444–449.

Wrenn, C. (1985). Afterward: The culturally encapsulated counselor revisited. In P. Pedersen (Ed.), *Handbook of cross-cultural counseling and therapy* (pp. 323–329). Westport, CT: Greenwood.

Yamamoto, J., & Kubota, M. (1983). The Japanese American family. In J. Yamamoto, A. Romero, & A. Morales (Eds.), *The psychosocial development of minority group children* (pp. 65–84). New York: Brunner/Mazel.

Yamamoto, J., Silva, J., Justice, L., Chang, C., & Leong, G. (1993). Cross-cultural psychotherapy. In A. Gaw (Ed.), *Culture, ethnicity, and mental illness* (pp. 101–124). Washington, DC: American Psychiatric Press.

Yee, A. H., Fairchild, H. H., Weizmann, F., & Wyatt, G. (1993). Addressing psychology's problems with race. *American Psychologist, 48*, 1132–1140.

Yeh, M., Eastman, K., & Cheung, M. (1994). Children and adolescents in community mental health centers: Does the ethnicity or the language of the therapist matter? *Journal of Community Psychology, 22*, 153–163.

Yeh, M., Takeuchi, D., & Sue, S. (1994). Asian-American children treated in the mental health system: A comparison of parallel and mainstream outpatient service centers. *Journal of Clinical Child Psychology, 23*(1), 5–12.

Yum, O. (1991). The impact of Confucianism on interpersonal relationships and communication patterns in East Asia. In L. A. Samovar & R. E. Porter (Eds.), *Intercultural communication: A reader* (6th ed., pp. 71–78). Belmont, CA: Wadsworth.

Zane N., & Sue, S. (1991). Culturally-respective mental health services for Asian Americans: Treatment and training issues. In H. Myers, P. Wohlford, P. Guzman., & R. Echemendia (Eds.), *Ethnic minority perspectives on clinical training and services in psychology* (pp. 49–58). Washington, DC: American Psychological Association.

10.05
Cultural Competence Training in Clinical Psychology: Assessment, Clinical Intervention, and Research

FELIPE G. CASTRO
Arizona State University, Tempe, AZ, USA

10.05.1 INTRODUCTION 127

10.05.2 DEFINITIONS AND KEY CONCEPTS 128

10.05.2.1 Why the Need for Cultural Competence Training? 128
10.05.2.2 Cultural Competence as Good Science and Practice 128
10.05.2.3 Key Aspects of Cultural Competence 129
10.05.2.4 The Concept of Culture 130
10.05.2.5 Levels of Cultural Capacity 131

10.05.3 EVALUATING LEVELS OF CULTURAL CAPACITY 133

10.05.3.1 Evaluation Relevant to a Reference Group 133
10.05.3.2 Cultural Capacity in Assessment 135
10.05.3.3 Cultural Capacity in Clinical Intervention 136
10.05.3.4 Cultural Capacity in Research 137
10.05.3.5 A Life-long Professional Odyssey 138

10.05.4 FUTURE DIRECTIONS 139

10.05.5 SUMMARY 139

10.05.6 REFERENCES 139

10.05.1 INTRODUCTION

This chapter presents a three-factor model for describing and rating the capacity of a clinical psychologist or other health professional to conduct culturally effective assessments, clinical interventions, and research with members of ethnic minority populations. The overall aim of this model is to provide a specific and clinically useful system that guides skills training towards the development of cultural competence. Developing cultural competence in a new cohort of health professionals aims to enhance quality in the health services and research that is delivered to members of various ethnic minority groups, including African-Americans, Latinos/Hispanics, Asian-Americans and Pacific Islanders, and Native Americans.

This training model introduces a distinct minority perspective based on at least five assumptions. First, the model assumes that "culture" cannot be ignored, and that it must be well understood in order for a clinical psychologist or for a health program to work effectively with members of ethnic/racial populations. Second, this model assumes that the clinical psychologist must examine sociocultural factors in order to conduct effective assessments, treatments, and research with ethnic minority clients and communities. Third, it assumes that attaining the highest level of cultural capacity, which is cultural proficiency, requires the clinical psychologist to decenter himself or herself culturally, meaning that he or she must learn empathically to adopt the client's *emic* (cultural insider's) world view. A fourth assumption is that cultural proficiency in research and in community-based health service programs requires a social action research approach, an approach which invites the participation of ethnic minority community folks in the development and implementation of any intervention that is conducted within that ethnic minority community (Flores, Castro, & Fernandez-Esquer, 1995). Finally, within this perspective, a fifth assumption is that the culturally proficient clinical psychologist should exercise leadership by way of mentorship and an active involvement in advancing minority issues.

10.05.2 DEFINITIONS AND KEY CONCEPTS

10.05.2.1 Why the Need for Cultural Competence Training?

Today, the concept of cultural competence has emerged as the result of several converging social trends. First, the demographic face of the USA has changed since the early 1970s as several ethnic/racial populations have grown in size and significance. Several of the major ethnic/racial populations in the USA have shown growth rates that surpass the growth rate of the mainstream USA population. As these trends continue, for the year 2000, the projected sizes of the major ethnic racial populations of the USA in terms of size and percentage are: African-Americans, about 33.7 million (about 12.2%); Latinos/Hispanics, about 31.1 million (about 11.3%); Asian-Americans and Pacific Islanders, about 11.4 million (about 4.1%); and Native Americans/American-Indians, about 2.2 million (about 0.7%) (Department of Commerce, 1994).

As a second factor, the 1985 *Secretary's Task Force Report on Black and Minority Health* highlighted in greater detail what was known previously, which is that within the USA there exists a major gap in health status between the white mainstream (primarily middle class) population and the ethnic/racial minority and mostly lower class populations (Department of Health and Human Services, 1985). Moreover, a social process involving several interrelated behavioral, sociocultural, environmental, and economic factors has contributed to this disparity (Anderson, 1995). Thus, clinical psychologists and other providers of health services must comprehend the manner in which these various sociocultural factors have operated to influence the health status of these minority populations. Clearly then, clinical psychologists must acknowledge and understand the detrimental effects of certain sociocultural factors when conducting assessments, when developing clinical interventions, and when designing and conducting research that involves ethnic minority individuals, families, or communities. Within this context and at the level of the individual client, it is clear that ethnic minority clients have complex, and at times unique, needs that must be well understood within a cultural context in order to engage them successfully in treatment and/or research. This emerging recognition of the effects of sociocultural factors on physical and mental health underscores the need for cultural competence training, in order to improve the clinical psychologist's capacity to work effectively with members of these minority populations.

Third, the current need to develop cultural competence in clinical psychologists has also emerged as a result of the "pipeline issue." Trends regarding the educational progress of students of ethnic/racial backgrounds reveal low numbers of ethnic minority graduates who will be able to provide culturally relevant health services to members of their ethnic/racial group. Only a limited number of these minority graduates will enter the professional arena in order to address the large and growing need for services offered by minority professionals who understand the needs of ethnic/racial minority clients. Given this trend, and the growing need for culturally relevant health services, a more viable solution is to train and educate mainstream service providers, administrators, and researchers on essential aspects of the culture and health needs of clients from various ethnic/racial populations.

10.05.2.2 Cultural Competence as Good Science and Practice

Developing cultural competence in clinical psychologists of all backgrounds should not be seen as a "politically correct" gesture to demonstrate token responsiveness to a contemporary social concern. On the contrary, developing the cultural competence of clinical psychologists should be seen as an important training goal that offers them a broader range of capabilities for working more effectively clinically and in research with a broader and more diverse group of clients and research participants. Moreover, the American Psychological Association's Ethical Principles of Psychologists and Code of Conduct indicates that psychologists should "provide services, teach, and conduct research only within the boundaries of their competence, based on their education, training, supervised experience, or appropriate professional experience" (American Psychological Association, 1992, p. 1600; Standard 1.04—Boundaries of Competence).

In addition, these guidelines indicate that,

> in those emerging areas in which generally recognized standards for preparatory training do not yet exist, psychologists [should] nevertheless take reasonable steps to ensure the competence of their work and to protect patients/clients, students, research participants, and others from harm.

Clearly, in the late 1990s and in the early years of the twenty-first century, the guidelines that define cultural competence in clinical interventions with ethnic/racial populations are still evolving. Thus, in response to the American Psychological Association's Ethical Principles, all psychologists who work with clients from ethnic/racial backgrounds or who anticipate working with these clients should continually seek ways to enhance their cultural competence in order to conduct effective assessments, interventions, and/or research with these minority clients.

Moreover, from an organizational perspective, it can be noted that practically all organizations have a "culture," which consists of organizational operating characteristics. Based on these operating characteristics, some organizations can be described as having a healthy, accepting, collegial, supportive, comfortable, consumer-friendly, and culturally competent culture. By contrast, other organizations can be described as having a paranoid, judgmental, patriarchal, controlling, stressful, consumer-unfriendly, and culturally incompetent culture. The operating characteristics that govern a particular organization's culture affect the way that consumers will react to the services that the organization delivers, and this is especially true for the ethnic minority consumers who seek services within that organization. Human service organizations that have institutional policies, procedures, and structures that discount or devalue the importance of cultural competence are not likely to deliver culturally competent services to their minority clients, and they are likely to induce tension and demoralization among members of their staff who see the need for cultural competence in services that would be delivered to minority clients.

Finally, cultural competence training is also relevant to the conduct of good research and good science. In March 1994, the National Institutes of Health (NIH) published new guidelines for the inclusion of women and minorities in clinical research, guidelines which reflected the requirements of the NIH Revitalization Act 1993 (Public Law 103-43) (National Institutes of Health, 1994). The release of these guidelines gave formal recognition to the importance of gender and ethnic cultural factors in scientific clinical research (Hohmann & Parron, 1996). These guidelines indicate that studies of outstanding scientific merit cannot be conducted if such studies systematically or arbitrarily exclude a large and diverse sector of the population from their operating plans. Such studies are flawed if, without a sound rationale, they exclude women and/or minorities from their theoretical framework, their sampling design, their methodology, and thus from their findings and their conclusions. Here, cultural competence in research is demonstrated by an investigator who understands and can conceptualize the hypothesized effects of specific sociocultural factors on health outcomes, and who can design and implement studies that effectively recruit and retain women and minority participants (Areán & Gallagher-Thompson, 1996; Miranda, Azocar, Organista, Muñoz, & Lieberman, 1996; Thompson, Neighbors, Munday, & Jackson, 1996).

10.05.2.3 Key Aspects of Cultural Competence

Generally, cultural competence may be conceptualized as a capacity to work effectively with individuals from special populations, including clients from ethnic/racial communities. Cultural competence is expressed by communicating acceptance, deep understanding, and responsiveness to the needs and concerns of members of special populations. Cultural competence may also be conceptualized as a capacity level that supersedes cultural sensitivity, given that cultural competence involves a level of understanding and skills that moves beyond a basic awareness of the needs and concerns of members from a special population.

Cultural competence has been defined in various ways, although several definitions reveal certain common themes. For example, the Arizona Department of Health Services has defined cultural competence at the institutional level as

> knowledge, attitudes, and policies within an agency which allows individuals to work effectively in cross cultural situations. This requires the willingness and ability to utilize community-based values, traditions, and practices in developing and evaluating interventions, communication, and other activities. (Arizona Department of Health Services, 1995)

A definition that applies at the individual and institutional levels was developed by a behavioral health workgroup. This definition indicates that cultural competence

> includes the attainment of knowledge, skills, and attitudes to enable practitioners and systems of care to provide care for diverse populations, i.e., to work within the person's reality conditions, in particular minority populations, acknowledges and incorporates variance in normative acceptable behaviors, beliefs, and values in determining an individual's mental wellness/illness and incorporates those variables into assessment and treatment. (The National Latino Behavioral Health Workshop, 1996)

A few common themes have been stated or implied in these and other definitions of cultural competence as defined at both the macro institutional level, and the micro individual levels. These themes include the notions that cultural competence:

(i) consists of a complex set of knowledge, attitudes, and skills;

(ii) is characterized by an empathic and culturally relevant understanding of the client, using an insider's view of the client's presenting problem;

(iii) requires that the clinical psychologist or program exhibit cultural responsiveness, that is, a commitment towards understanding the client within the context of the client's own culture;

(iv) requires the use of culture-based insights in planning an intervention (individual/family therapy, or a program) that is culturally relevant and effective in alleviating the client's problem; and

(v) requires careful attention to the process of intervention, which is as important as the outcome, because in minority cultures expressions of respect and acceptance are indispensable aspects of the client–therapist relationship and will greatly influence client participation and treatment outcomes.

In addition, there are other aspects of cultural competence, primarily at the micro clinical level, that are less salient in the literature, but that are important in cultural competence training for clinical psychologists. These are:

(i) that cultural competence is a value-added capability where, under the current managed care environment, the culturally competent clinical psychologist is capable of delivering culturally responsive interventions that surpass the effectiveness of conventional interventions (The National Latino Behavioral Health Workshop, 1996);

(ii) that level of cultural competence is specific to a given cultural reference group, where, based on training and experience, a given clinical psychologist may exhibit cultural competence in working with one cultural group, for example with inner city African-American adolescents, but may only exhibit cultural sensitivity in addressing the needs of a different cultural group, such as elderly rural Mexican Americans;

(iii) that the concepts of culture and subculture are not synonymous with demographic ethnic labels (e.g., Hispanic), where cultural competence in program planning requires a segmentation of the targeted ethnic population into subcultural groups (Balcazar, Castro, & Krull, 1995), the members of which have distinct lifestyles, needs, and problems (e.g., Chicano gang adolescents from East Los Angeles vs. Navajo elderly who live on the reservation);

(iv) that culturally responsive interventions should be guided by culturally relevant intervention models and defining criteria, and by a management information system that gathers local data and that uses culturally relevant variables; and

(v) that truly effective training to develop cultural competence requires continuing education that systematically upgrades skills across levels of the cultural capacity continuum towards the ultimate goal of cultural proficiency (Bernal & Castro, 1994).

10.05.2.4 The Concept of Culture

The concept of "culture" is often difficult to grasp operationally, because, as a concept, culture is a rich, complex, and multidimensional concept. Indeed, one metaphor of culture as it relates to the heart and soul of ethnic minority peoples is the concept of "humidity" as it relates to the weather. You cannot see humidity, but you can definitely feel it when it is there. The same is true for culture. Given its rich complexity, well over 100 definitions of "culture" have been proposed (Murphy, 1986, cited in Baldwin & Lindsley, 1994). Indeed, culture has been defined broadly as

> the total body of tradition borne by a society and transmitted from generation to generation. It thus refers to norms, values, and standards by which people act, and it includes the ways distinctive in

each society of ordering the world and rendering it intelligible. (Baldwin & Lindsley, 1994; Murphy, 1986).

Across various definitions of culture, certain common themes have emerged. These are:

(i) that culture consists of the totality of learned behaviors of a people;

(ii) that it is transmitted from generation to generation, that is, from elders to children;

(iii) that people construct their own culture in order to give meaning to life by creating a world view that helps to explain their own reality;

(iv) that it consists of a people's shared beliefs, values, ways of making things, customs, behaviors, traditions, and lifestyles;

(v) that it offers a community of people with a set of social norms and moral values on how life should be lived;

(vi) that, via a culture's art, music, folklore, and other forms of creative expression, culture captures the soul, character, and essence of a people; and

(vii) that culture is important to a group of people because it promotes a sense of kinship, belonging, and group identity.

Given the breadth and richness of the concept of culture, for cultural competence training a more narrow concept and definition is needed as a reference point for the operationalization of levels of cultural capacity (cultural sensitivity, cultural competence, and cultural proficiency). The approach that we will use is to begin by identifying a specific targeted reference group, which is the group of clients that is targeted for a given intervention or program. This targeted group may be defined either broadly (e.g., African-Americans, Asian-Americans) or more narrowly (e.g., African-American elderly aged 65 years and older, low-acculturated Chinese adolescents). The more broadly defined groups are typically populations that share a common culture. By contrast, the more narrowly defined groups are typically subpopulations and subcultures that share a culture with the parent group, but that are also governed by additional and perhaps unique norms, values, and other local sociocultural conditions. Thus, a clinical psychologist's cultural capacity level can be defined more accurately, by describing specific capacity levels in the areas of assessment, clinical intervention, or research that are defined in relation to the culture of a specific targeted reference group.

10.05.2.5 Levels of Cultural Capacity

Figure 1 shows that the capacity for cultural competence varies along a graded continuum. This concept of a cultural capacity continuum has been proposed previously by various scholars (Cross, Bazron, Dennis, & Isaacs, 1989; Kim, McLeod, & Shantis, 1992; Orlandi, 1992). In our current model, we are taking this concept of a cultural capacity continuum and are modifying and expanding it.

On this cultural capacity continuum, the lowest level is "cultural destructiveness" (− 3), which consists of an ethnocentric orientation that harbors openly negative destructive attitudes that emphasize the superiority of one's own culture and the inferiority of other cultures. Attitude has been previously defined as a "readiness to respond," a learned "predisposition to respond in a particular way to a specific attitude object" (Oskamp, 1991). Within a health service organization, a given staff member's condescending attitude can serve as an expression of cultural destructiveness, and this attitude will destroy the client–provider relationship. Similarly, at the institutional level, an agency's policies or practices that promote stereotypes and a discrimination of lower class clients is an expression of institutional cultural destructiveness. Here a stereotype refers to a mental image or a set of beliefs about a group of people, beliefs that are highly simplistic (and often inaccurate), highly evaluative (often derogatory), and rigidly resistant to change (and thus not modified by corrective information) (Oskamp, 1991). Ironically, in contemporary American society, culturally destructive attitudes in individuals and culturally destructive policies within institutions still exist.

"Cultural incapacity"(−2) refers to a professional's or an organization's orientation that emphasizes separate but equal treatment. While this may seem to be a viable and fair approach, in reality it often results in an institutional incapacity to provide equal and effective treatment of those clients who are culturally different. Similarly, at the next level, an orientation describable as "cultural blindness" (− 1) emphasizes that all cultures and people are alike and equal. While this orientation appears unbiased and accepting, its subtle yet injurious effect on members of special populations is that this approach discounts the importance of culture and the need to consider multicultural perspectives. Indeed, in a well-meaning but culturally insensitive effort to be fair and to treat everyone the same, an administrator may use this orientation to discount or discredit programmatic efforts that aim to respond affirmatively and in a culturally sensitive manner to the unique needs of clients from special populations.

The first level of a positive cultural capacity is "cultural sensitivity" (+ 1). Cultural sensitivity is characterized by the presence of a basic

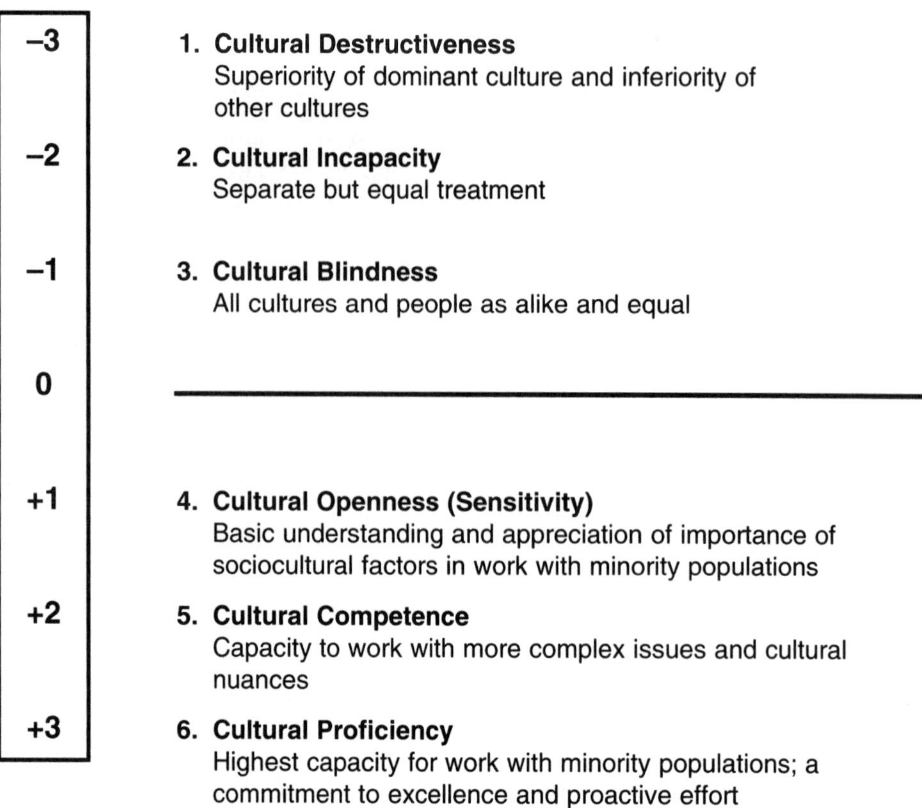

Figure 1 Levels of cultural capacity. Adapted from Kim et al. (1992).

understanding and appreciation of the importance of sociocultural factors as these affect the client and the most viable treatment that may be offered. For example, in a health promotion program for Latinos, cultural sensitivity is reflected by the program's attention to the role of linguistic factors, interpersonal factors (*personalismo*, *respeto*, *confianza*), and of familal factors (traditionalism, familism), as these affect the health-related behaviors of various Latinos.

Cultural sensitivity is also characterized by the presence of an elementary, but nonetheless critical, appreciation of the within-group variability, that is, of the diversity that exists within a given ethnic minority population. For example, among Latinos, scholars have regularly asserted that Hispanics/Latinos are a heterogeneous population characterized by large variability among its members in terms of racial background, educational attainment, household income, family size and composition, and even in the level of ethnic pride evident among its members (Montgomery, 1994).

"Cultural competence" (+2) represents a higher level of capacity to work with members of a special population. Relative to cultural sensitivity, cultural competence is characterized by a greater depth of skills and experience that allows the clinical psychologist to understand and work effectively with cultural nuances. By understanding cultural nuances, the clinical psychologist is able to detect the ethnic client's subtle communications, to interpret their meanings, and to do so within the client's specific cultural context. Based on this deeper level of understanding, the clinical psychologist is thus more capable of planning culturally potent interventions. Such interventions would appeal to the ethnic client, elicit the client's participation, and motivate sustained participation.

Similarly, in a community-based health promotion program, the cultural competence of the program's staff is characterized by their capacity to work actively with members of a community. This capacity includes an understanding of the cultural and political nuances that helps these staff members to develop trust and credibility with members of the local community, and to elicit their support and participation in the design and implementation of a health promotion program. Here also, cultural competence is characterized by the clinical psychologist's knowledge of the motivational dynamics that prevail within subgroups of a given population, as these motivational dynamics may be mediated by age, gender, cultural orientation, and other aspects of the group's subculture.

"Cultural proficiency" (+3) is the highest expression of cultural capacity. It serves as an ideal, rather than necessarily as a state that is attainable by all clinical psychologists. Cultural proficiency consists of a state of high mastery, a commitment to excellence, and a proactive attitude that facilitates the design and delivery of therapeutic services for members of a specific population. Here it is recognized that a given clinical psychologist or health program may exhibit cultural proficiency in service delivery to members of one targeted population (e.g., Latinos), but may only exhibit cultural sensitivity in service delivery to members of a different population. Thus, complete cultural proficiency with all special populations would be a rare accomplishment for many clinical psychologists, health programs, or human service agencies. Nonetheless, constantly striving to develop cultural proficiency in work with one or more special population is a laudable goal for any clinical psychologist, health program, or agency, although this calls for a commitment to life-long learning with the ultimate aim of developing depth and breadth in skills for working with members of one or more special population.

10.05.3 EVALUATING LEVELS OF CULTURAL CAPACITY

This section presents a more detailed discussion of key aspects of cultural capacity relevant to the training of clinical psychologists. Table 1 lists the specific knowledge, attitudes, and skills that serve as indicators of varying levels of cultural capacity in the areas of assessment, clinical intervention, and research. The table presents a progressive increase in the knowledge, attitude, and skills that serve as specific operational criteria to help gauge a clinical psychologist's progression across levels of cultural capacity from cultural sensitivity, to cultural competence, to cultural proficiency.

The criteria in Table 1 that describe levels of cultural capacity are presented as illustrative descriptors. They have not been validated empirically, although they are derived from the contemporary literature on cultural competence and from clinical and research experience (Allison, Crawford, Echemendia, Robinson, & Knepp, 1994; American Psychiatric Association, 1994; Dillard et al., 1992; La Fromboise & Foster, 1992; Szapocznik & Kurtines, 1993). Accordingly, these statements offer a viable system to evaluate levels of cultural capacity where these descriptive statements serve as guideposts for conceptualization and evaluation when conducting cultural capacity training in the areas of assessment, clinical intervention, and research. When using Table 1, cultural capacity should be evaluated in relation to a specific reference group, that is a specific and targeted cultural group or subgroup.

10.05.3.1 Evaluation Relevant to a Reference Group

One major problem in prior conceptualizations of cultural competence is that previous approaches have defined it in global and nonspecific terms. As a result, for the purpose of clinical training, cultural competence has remained a vague, unintelligible concept that is disassociated from critical clinical and organizational referents. Thus, as used previously, the concept of cultural competence has had limited practical usefulness to clinicians and to program planners. Missing is a conceptualization that defines cultural competence more accurately, as it is linked to a specific reference group. The present model aims to add greater precision and specificity to the conceptualization and measurement of cultural competence.

To operate as a construct that has practical applicability in the clinical, organizational, and community settings, cultural competence must therefore be defined in terms of skills for service delivery to members of a specific reference group. For example, through training and experience, a clinical psychologist may acquire the knowledge, attitudes, and skills that afford him or her the capacity to conduct effective therapeutic work with various African-American clients. Thus, this clinical psychologist could be rated as being culturally competent in the area of clinical interventions with African-American clients. By contrast, this same clinical psychologist may have never worked with a Asian-American client, and thus would not be culturally competent in service delivery with Asian-American clients. However, that clinical psychologist's knowledge about aspects of Asian-American cultural norms and values, his or her accepting attitude towards Asian-Americans and their culture, and his or her assessment skills for differential interpretation of tests conducted with various Asian

American subgroups, including a familiarity with scales of acculturation, could garner for this clinical psychologist a rating of cultural sensitivity for work with Asian-American clients in the area of assessment.

Based on these considerations, cultural capacity can be defined more accurately by

Table 1 General guidelines for evaluating levels of cultural capacity in assessment, clinical intervention, and research.

Assessment

Sensitivity (+1)

Is familiar with major cultural characteristics found among members of one or more cultural group, and understands basic aspects of the within-group variability that exists for a given cultural group

Is accepting of the concept of diversity, and is aware of the need to decenter oneself culturally in order to understand the world view of people from other cultures

Is capable of administering and interpreting tests and assessment instruments with a consideration of sources of bias or adjustment needed in order to interpret test results in a fair manner. Can formulate culturally relevant treatment recommendations

Competence (+2)

Is knowledgeable of and can understand apparent paradoxes and cultural nuances in the thoughts and behaviors of members of the cultural group

Has an affective attachment to the culture and a deeper understanding of issues within that culture. Has the capacity for empathic decentering

Is capable of understanding and working with nuances and apparent paradoxes in assessing, diagnosing, and interpreting more complex cultural aspects of thought and behavior. Can design a comprehensive treatment plan

Proficiency (+3)

Has developed a deep, integrated knowledge of a culture based on years of experience

Feels a deep attachment and appreciation for that culture

Is capable of understanding nuances and apparent paradoxes. Can distil deeper cultural meaning to obtain a deep understanding of cultural thoughts and behaviors in assessing or diagnosing a problem. Can plan an optimally effective treatment plan

Clinical intervention

Sensitivity (+1)

Is familiar with basic aspects of a culture and with the within-group variability in social norms that govern interpersonal relationships and the accepted manner in which various people communicate with one another

Is accepting of these social norms

Has developed ease and comfort in engaging persons from that culture in a culturally appropriate manner. Is able to decenter empathically and thus to gain an awareness of the world view of persons from the cultural reference group

Competence (+2)

Has greater knowledge of complex aspects of social norms and patterns of communication within the culture, and is able to understand nuances present in that communication

Has an affective bond with the culture and has a finer appreciation and acceptance of nuances and of apparent paradoxes. Is able to engage in advanced empathic decentering by understanding his or her own prejudices, as well as by being able to understand the reference culture from the "world view" perspective of members of that culture

Is able to conceptualize the client's problem using the most relevant therapeutic mode

Proficiency (+3)

Has deep, rich, culturally relevant knowledge of the culture and about the rich complexity that governs that culture

Feels a strong affective bond with the culture and expresses this in appreciation and respect for that culture and its people

Has the capacity to detect and to work with clinical nuances and to implement one of various therapeutic approaches as is most relevant to a client's central problem. In doing so, knows clearly where the case is going and can intervene efficiently and effectively. Is able to conduct potent culturally relevant interventions and/or design potent culturally relevant programs

Research

Sensitivity (+1)

Is familiar with variables such as race and ethnicity as important sociocultural factors in research design and methodology. Attends to issues involved in approaching and informing individuals and communities in a manner that protects their rights and fosters trust, respect, and mutual collaboration

Has an attitude of respect for the rights and sovereignty of individuals or communities from the culture who may participate in a proposed study

Is able to engage individuals or communities in an ongoing dialogue that promotes a partnership in research

Table 1 (continued).

Competence (+2)

Has a knowledge of the complexities of race, ethnicity, acculturation, and other sociocultural factors as these must be conceptualized and at times reconceptualized, in order to understand the more complex aspects of a culture. Can engage in theoretical decentering by evaluating the fit or lack of fit of Eurocentric models as applied to a cultural reference group

Has a commitment to establishing a partnership with individuals or communities from a culture in a manner that offers them a voice and active ownership of the research that is to be conducted

Is capable of working actively with individuals or communities from the culture in order to ensure their participation and active ownership of the study. Develops social action research

Proficiency (+3)

Has a deep and rich knowledge of the complexities and apparent paradoxes that exist and may emerge within a culture

Has a strong affection for the core values and traditions of a culture and has a strong commitment to ensuring that these values and traditions are acknowledged and respected in the design of proposed research. This respect includes ensuring that members of the culture have a voice and active ownership of the study

Is capable of establishing a strong and enduring collaboration with individuals or communities from the culture based on earned respect and trust. This strong research bond is also used to design research that has social action value, social action research, such that its findings or discoveries can be used to benefit the individuals or communities that have participated in that research. Also, takes a leadership role in offering scholarly critique on various minority issues and in serving as a role model and mentor for junior faculty and graduate students

conceptualizing it according to three dimensions: (i) capacity level (none, sensitivity, competence, proficiency; (ii) in a specialty area (assessment, clinical intervention, research); and (iii) in relation to a specific cultural reference group (African-Americans, Latinos, Asian-Americans, Native Americans). Thus, in assessing training-related cultural capacity, a clinical psychologist may be described as having *attained* cultural competence (capacity level) *in the area of* clinical intervention (specialty area) *for work with* African-Americans (reference group). This three-factor descriptive model provides a specific and meaningful approach to guide clinical training and professional communications about the relevant cultural capacity of a given clinical psychologist as he or she proceeds through a training program.

Regarding the dimension of reference group, a targeted reference group can be defined more generally, as a primary reference group, such as for example an entire ethnic/racial population that has a definable culture such as African-Americans or Latinos. Alternatively, this reference group may be defined more specifically as a secondary reference group, that is a smaller more specific subgroup—a subpopulation, such as African-American adolescents or Latino elderly. Referring to a more specific reference group may influence the level of cultural capacity that can be rated. As indicated earlier, a clinical psychologist may have attained cultural proficiency in conducting clinical interventions with African-American adolescents, but may only be rated as having attained cultural sensitivity in conducting clinical interventions with African-American elderly.

Similarly, this three-factor model can be applied at the organizational level, where an intervention program can be rated for its capacity to deliver culturally relevant services. Based on the service components of an intervention program, the skills of its providers, its institutional policies, and its clinical environment, a program may be rated in terms of cultural capacity (none, sensitivity, competence, proficiency), in a specialty area (assessment, clinical intervention, research, or other), with a given reference group (e.g., Native American elderly).

10.05.3.2 Cultural Capacity in Assessment

Assessment refers to the use of standardized tests, interview approaches, and other diagnostic methods for systematically learning about the client (Dana, 1993). A clinical psychologist's progressive increase in knowledge, attitudes, and skills characterizes his or her increased levels of cultural capacity in the area of assessment.

At the lowest capacity level, cultural sensitivity in assessment, the clinical psychologist should demonstrate an elementary knowledge of major cultural issues that affect the life experiences of members of a special population, such as members of one of the major ethnic/racial groups (African-Americans, Latinos,

Asian-Americans, Native Americans). The clinical psychologist should also be familiar with the need to decenter himself or herself from a solely Eurocentric world view in order to adopt an insider's *emic* view (i.e., one that takes the perspective of the indigenous client). This decentering allows the exploration of culturally specific concepts; these are concepts that may be unique to the indigenous culture, or concepts that are defined differently in the indigenous culture relative to how they are defined within the mainstream culture.

At the level of cultural sensitivity in assessment, the clinical psychologist should have an elementary knowledge of the within-group variability that exists within a given reference group, and should know about the moderator variables, such as the level of acculturation, that describe this within-group variability (Dana, 1993). This basic knowledge ideally facilitates an accepting attitude towards variability in culture, where variability is conceptualized as consisting of differences and not as deficits. Furthermore, this orientation should aid in reducing biased and stereotypical thinking (Oskamp, 1991), thus facilitating a more accurate assessment of clinical issues which are examined within the context of the client's cultural background.

In addition, this sensitivity in orientation should contribute to overall skills for conducting a basic assessment of the client's needs and clinical problems. This assessment should take into account the influence of cultural and social factors in drawing valid conclusions about the client's strengths and weaknesses, while also observing conflicts, relative skills deficits, and psychopathology if these are present. Attaining cultural sensitivity in assessment should enhance the clinical psychologist's capabilities for developing preliminary treatment recommendations that take into account the client's social, familial, and personal resources and barriers, as these may facilitate or impede participation in a treatment or intervention program.

As compared with cultural sensitivity, cultural competence in assessment constitutes a higher level of skills development. As contrasted with cultural sensitivity, attaining cultural competence in assessment requires a higher knowledge level, wherein the clinical psychologist understands more complex interactions and nuances as observed within the context of the client's culture. Apparent paradoxes when observed from a Eurocentric perspective may not necessarily appear as paradoxical or as psychopathology when observed from an indigenous cultural perspective. This capacity for empathic decentering when interpreting complex cultural meanings characterizes cultural competence in the area of assessment. The clinical psychologist's affective attachment to the reference group's culture would enhance his or her skills for working with cultural conflicts and with more subtle issues. Having advanced skills for interpreting manifest and more latent content, for organizing content, and for processing information would help the clinical psychologist to design an insightful and comprehensive treatment plan or intervention program.

As compared with cultural competence, at the level of cultural proficiency in assessment, the clinical psychologist would exhibit a deep and integrative knowledge of the client's culture. This knowledge would be coupled by a deep appreciation and bonding with that culture, based on having a deep personal involvement and years of experience. The culturally proficient clinical psychologist would have masterful skills for detecting and understanding subtle and complex cultural communications and for interpreting these accurately and in culturally appropriate ways. Such deep insight would allow the clinical psychologist to plan an optimally effective treatment plan or intervention program.

10.05.3.3 Cultural Capacity in Clinical Intervention

In a manner parallel with assessment, a level of cultural sensitivity in clinical intervention is characterized by a clinical psychologist's demonstrated knowledge about the prevailing social norms and patterns of interpersonal communication for a given cultural reference group. This includes having a basic understanding of the within-group variability that exists in that group. This knowledge would be supplemented by the clinical psychologist's accepting attitude towards the group's culture and values. This positive orientation towards that cultural group would also facilitate the clinical psychologist's ease and comfort in conducting therapeutic work with persons from that cultural reference group. The clinical psychologist's basic capacity for empathic decentering would also help in understanding the ethnic experience of members of that cultural reference group.

Cultural competence in clinical intervention would be characterized by the clinical psychologist's greater depth of knowledge about complex aspects of a culture's social norms, forms of communication, and types of interpersonal behavior, thus fostering the capacity to understand nuances and apparent cultural contradictions. Moreover, developing an affective bond and an appreciation for the reference culture and its people would foster the caring attitude that characterizes cultural competence in the clinical setting. This advanced level of knowledge and a caring attitude would enhance the clinical psychologist's understanding of the life conditions and the major ways of coping found among members of the reference group, and would aid in relating effectively to the client. Moreover, the clinician's ability to understand his or her own prejudices as one aspect of advanced empathic decentering would further enhance his or her cultural competence for conducting clinical interventions. This enhanced capacity to understand self and client as a dyad would also facilitate the clinical psychologist's capacity to conceptualize the client's problem using the most relevant therapeutic model, as it may apply within the client's life context. In addition, the culturally competent clinical psychologist would be able to plan and implement insightful and effective interventions or programs that address the ethnic client's most pressing needs.

As an even more advanced stage of clinical capability, cultural proficiency in clinical intervention would be characterized by a clinical psychologist's deep and rich knowledge of the reference group's culture and of the complex norms, values, and other factors that govern behavior within that culture. At this stage, the clinical psychologist would develop a strong affective bond with the reference group and its culture and would have a deep respect for its people. This combination of rich knowledge and a strong positive attitude would facilitate the clinical psychologist's capacity to comprehend the life situation of various clients from that reference group, to conceptualize a given client's problem from various theoretical perspectives, and to visualize clearly where the case is going. Thus, the culturally proficient clinician would also have the capacity to plan and implement potent clinical interventions and/or to design and implement culturally effective treatment programs.

10.05.3.4 Cultural Capacity in Research

In parallel with the knowledge, attitudes, and skills that serve as indicators of cultural capacity in a given specialty area, a clinical psychologist's cultural sensitivity in research would be characterized by his or her basic familiarity with sociocultural variables, including moderator variables, that must be incorporated into the research design and methodology of studies conducted with participants from a given cultural group. This knowledge-based sensitivity would include an awareness of procedures for the protection of potential research participants that would be recruited from that reference group. An attitude of respect for members of that culture and an awareness of their special linguistic and other needs would enhance the clinical psychologist's ability to safeguard the rights of these potential participants. In addition, cultural sensitivity would be reflected in the clinical psychologist's basic capacity to engage individuals or communities from the reference group with respect, and in his or her ability to develop a research partnership with members of that reference group.

As a more advanced stage of research capacity, cultural competence in research would be characterized by the clinical psychologist's greater knowledge of cultural interactions and of complex sociocultural processes, such as the process of acculturation, as these affect various members of the cultural reference group. This includes the clinical psychologist's capacity for theoretical decentering, which involves taking a critical examination of current Eurocentric models and their fit, or lack of fit, when applied with members of the cultural reference group. In cases in which model fit is poor, the culturally competent clinical psychologist is able to consider alternate constructivist models that feature an emic, insider's view of the ethnic person's life experiences and of the experience of being a minority person.

Moreover, the clinical psychologist's commitment to establishing a research partnership with individuals and communities in a manner that offers them a voice in the design and conduct of the proposed research would also characterize cultural competence in research (Flores et al., 1995; Norton & Manson, 1996). This in-depth knowledge and a proactive attitude that favors research partnerships and social action research would facilitate the clinical psychologist's capacity to work actively with individuals and communities from the cultural reference group in the design and implementation of social action research.

Beyond cultural competence, the more advanced level defined as cultural proficiency in research would involve advanced knowledge about the cultural reference group. This proficiency would be demonstrated by the clinical psychologist's deep and rich knowledge about the complexities and apparent paradoxes observed within the cultural reference group. This depth of knowledge would yield insights that facilitate the clinical psychologist's capacity to design significant new research. In principle, such research would be insightful and integrative, and would propose new culturally relevant models that could be adequately defined and tested. These models would include sociocultural variables, including moderator and culturally specific variables that capture, describe, and explain various sociocultural processes that affect the health of clients from the given cultural reference group.

In addition, cultural proficiency in research would be characterized by the clinical psychologist's strong appreciation for the core values and traditions of the cultural reference group and by a deep and abiding respect for these values and traditions. These proactive attitudes would be reflected in the clinical psychologist's strong commitment to safeguard the rights of prospective participants that are recruited from the cultural reference group.

The culturally proficient researcher would also exhibit research leadership in conceptualizing, designing, and implementing innovative research that examines critical issues of concern to members of the reference community. In conducting social action research, the culturally proficient researcher would pursue active solutions to contemporary social problems that affect the reference community. In such research, the investigator would exert leadership in building community partnerships and in building a research team that includes members of the targeted community in positions that contribute to the planning, design, and implementation of that social action research project.

Finally, the culturally proficient researcher would serve as a role model and as a mentor to junior faculty and graduate students, thus contributing to the training of future culturally competent investigators and teachers. The culturally proficient researcher would also adopt a leadership role in conducting critical yet helpful reviews of publication manuscripts and research proposals. This criticism would not only address issues of scientific merit, but would also address ethnic/racial issues, as well as issues of social inequality and scientific inaccuracy in manuscripts that examine ethnic minority communities and members of other special populations. In short, the culturally proficient researcher would take a proactive and leadership role in advancing a variety of minority research and training issues in the fields of clinical psychology, minority mental health, minority health, health promotion, and other related fields.

10.05.3.5 A Life-long Professional Odyssey

The road to cultural proficiency begins not with knowledge or skills, but with attitude. Given that "attitude" is defined as a predisposition to respond in a particular manner to a particular social situation (Oskamp, 1991), it is the clinical psychologist's positive attitude, an open-mindedness and willingness to learn about new cultures and people which characterizes that clinical psychologist's preparedness to embark on the journey towards cultural proficiency. Thus, instilling an attitude of openness in those who do not already have it is the first task in cultural competence training.

In addition, ethical practice in work with diverse populations requires a commitment on the part of the clinical psychologist continually to upgrade his or her cultural capabilities. To meet this need, clinical training programs should be proactive in developing curricula and resources that help clinical psychology trainees to develop their cultural competence. Here, Standard 6.01 of the Ethical Principles of Psychologists and Code of Conduct asserts that

> psychologists who are responsible for education and training [should] seek to ensure that the programs are competently designed to provide the proper experiences, and meet the requirements for licensure, certification, or other goals for which claims are made by the program. (American Psychological Association, 1992, Standard 6.01, Design of Education and Training Programs)

Relevant to this point, a study of 104 clinical training programs that examined changes in service and research with ethnic/racial populations across a 10-year period found some improvements among many of the 104 clinical training programs surveyed (Bernal & Castro, 1994). However, these improvements consisted primarily of introductory-level capabilities training, and did not offer the depth in training needed to develop cultural competence among program trainees. Bernal and Castro noted that, despite the tangible improvements in minority training in clinical psychology that have occurred since the mid-1980s relevant structural shifts have not taken place. These structural shifts refer to institutionalized programmatic changes that involve concerted plans to integrate key aspects of minority training across the clinical training curriculum, coupled with a commitment of resources to implement these plans. Indeed, only four of the 104 programs surveyed, all at professional schools, exhibited training program profiles for an integrated curriculum that would foster cultural proficiency among its trainees. Whereas many programs may express an in-principle endorsement of the importance of multicultural training, few have developed the infrastructure (coursework, minority faculty recruitment and retention, community links) for promoting cultural competence in clinical training. Given that departments and clinical training programs can also be rated on levels of cultural capacity, most programs nationally would fare no higher than being culturally sensitive. Clearly, based on the findings of the Bernal and Castro study, it can be concluded that most clinical psychology training programs in the USA can and should do more in order to develop their future capacity to promote cultural competence within their own clinical training program.

Within the context of our previous statements, we also recognize that not all clinical psychologists or students are necessarily interested in or prepared to participate in cultural competence training. Similarly, not all clinical training programs give sufficient value to cultural competence training, or do not seek to offer their students training in cultural competence as compared with other important clinical training needs. Unfortunately, those who could benefit most from cultural competence training are often those who are least interested in it. However, for those who do value learning about other cultures, and for those who can be convinced to try it, developing the cultural capacity to work with persons from various cultures is an odyssey of a professional lifetime that offers intellectual, affective, social, and spiritual rewards. The invitation to undertake this journey is there for those who are willing to take it.

10.05.4 FUTURE DIRECTIONS

The overview of the levels of cultural capacity that has been presented offers specific guidelines to help define cultural sensitivity, culture competence, and culture proficiency in the areas of assessment, clinical intervention, and research. However, in many ways, the present model only constitutes an early step towards a more detailed articulation of levels of cultural capacity. Additional work can and should be conducted to relate the guidelines presented here to a variety of specific cases with the aim of enhancing quality in assessment, treatment, and research with a diverse group of ethnic/racial clients.

Moreover, clinical training programs can and must do more to add depth of content and diversity in their clinical training activities, as these additions facilitate greater competence in assessment, clinical intervention, and research with members of ethnic/racial populations. One potential outcome of presenting the current three-factor model and its guidelines is that it may serve as a template from which to rate the level of cultural capacity of given clinical training program; that is, to rate the current capacity of the program to train culturally proficient clinical psychologists.

10.05.5 SUMMARY

In this chapter a three-factor model has been presented that aims to define operationally the various levels of cultural capacity (sensitivity, competence, proficiency) as related to three specialty areas (assessment, clinical intervention, research), and as related to a specific cultural reference group. It is recognized that attaining true cultural competence in the areas of assessment, intervention, and research for each of several ethnic/racial populations is a high ideal that will be achieved by only a few clinical psychologists in a lifetime of professional practice. However, this chapter has also identified and defined graded steps towards this ideal, and encourages the clinical psychologist to commit a sustained effort towards enhancing his or her level of cultural capacity. Here also, clinical training programs have a professional obligation to upgrade their training program by adding depth of content and activities in order to enhance their programmatic capacity to offer true depth in cultural competence training. It is recognized that the present three-factor model constitutes only an early step in the task of further articulating the characteristics of various levels of cultural capacity, as this articulation aids in clarifying further what it means to become culturally competent.

10.05.6 REFERENCES

Allison, K. W., Crawford, I., Echemendia, R., Robinson, L. V., & Knepp, D. (1994). Human diversity and professional competence: Training in clinical and counseling psychology revisited. *American Psychologist*, *49*, 792–796.

American Psychiatric Association (1994). *Diagnostic and statistical manual of mental disorders* (4th ed.). Washington, DC: Author.

American Psychological Association. (1992). Ethical principles of psychologists and code of conduct. *American Psychologist*, *47*, 1597–1611.

Anderson, N. B. (1995). Behavioral and sociocultural perspectives on ethnicity and health: Introduction to the special issue. *Health Psychology*, *14*, 589–591.

Areán, P. A. & Gallagher-Thompson, D. (1996). Issues and recommendations for the recruitment and retention of older ethnic minority adults into clinical research. *Journal of Consulting and Clinical Psychology*, *64*, 875–880.

Arizona Department of Health Services (1995). *Cultural competency in the administration and delivery of behavioral health services*. Phoenix, AZ: Author.

Balcazar, H., Castro, F. G., & Krull, J. L. (1995). Cancer risk reduction in Mexican American women: The role of acculturation, education, and health risk factors. *Health Education Quarterly*, *22*, 61–84.

Baldwin, J. R., & Lindsley, S. L. (1994). *Conceptualizations of culture*. Tempe, AZ: Urban Studies Center.

Bernal, M., & Castro, F. G. (1994). Are health professionals prepared for service and research with ethnic minorities? Report of a decade of progress. *American Psychologist*, *49*, 797–805.

Cross, T. L., Bazron, B. J., Dennis, K. W., & Isaacs, M. R. (1989). *Toward a culturally competent system of care*. Washington, DC: Georgetown University Child Development Center.

Dana, R. H. (1993). *Multicultural assessment perspectives for professional psychology*. Boston: Allyn and Bacon.

Department of Commerce (1994). *Statistical abstract of the United States: 1994* (114th ed.). Washington, DC: US Government Printing Office.

Department of Health and Human Services (1985). *Report of the Secretary's Task Force on Black and Minority Health*. Washington, DC: US Government Printing Office.

Dillard, M., Andonian, L., Flores, O., Lai, L., MacRae, A., & Shakir, M. (1992). Culturally competent occupational therapy in a diversely populated mental health setting. *The American Journal of Occupational Therapy*, *46*, 721–726.

Flores, E. T., Castro, F. G., & Fernandez-Esquer, M. (1995). Social theory, social action, and intervention research: Implications for cancer prevention among Latinos. *Journal of the National Cancer Institute Monographs*, *18*, 101–108.

Hohmann, A. A., & Parron, D. L. (1996). How the new NIH guidelines on inclusion of women and minorities apply: Efficacy trials, effectiveness trials, and validity. *Journal of Consulting and Clinical Psychology*, *64*, 851–855.

Kim, S., McLeod, J. H., & Shantis, C. (1992). Cultural competence for evaluators working with Asian American communities: Some practical considerations. In M. A. Orlandi, R. Weston, & L. G. Epstein (Eds.), *Cultural competence for evaluators* (pp. 203–260). Rockville, MD: Office of Substance Abuse Prevention.

La Fromboise, T. D. & Foster, S. L. (1992). Cross-cultural training: scientist–practitioner model and methods. *The Counseling Psychologist*, *20*, 472–489.

Miranda, J., Azocar, F., Organista, K. C., Muñoz, R. F., & Lieberman, A. (1996). Recruiting and retaining low-income Latinos in psychotherapy research. *Journal of Consulting and Clinical Psychology*, *64*, 868–874.

Montgomery, P. A. (1994). The Hispanic population in the United States: March 1993. *Current Population Reports—Population Characteristics* (Series P20-475). Washington, DC: US Government Printing Office.

Murphy, R. F. (1986). *Cultural and social anthropology: An overture*. Englewood Cliffs, NJ: Prentice-Hall.

National Institutes of Health. (1994). *Outreach notebook for the NIH guidelines on inclusion of women and minorities as subjects in clinical research*. Bethesda, MD: Author.

Norton, I. M., & Manson, S. M. (1996). Research in American Indian and Alaska Native communities: Navigating the cultural universe of value process. *Journal of Consulting and Clinical Psychology*, *64*, 856–860.

Orlandi, M. A. (1992). Defining cultural competence: an organizing framework. In M. A. Orlandi, R. Weston, & L. G. Epstein (Eds.), *Cultural competence for evaluators* (pp. 293–299). Rockville, MD: Center for Substance Abuse Prevention.

Oskamp, S. (1991). *Attitudes and opinions* (2nd ed.). Englewood Cliffs, NJ: Prentice-Hall.

Szapocznik, J., & Kurtines, M. (1993). Family psychology and cultural diversity: opportunities for theory, research and application. *American Psychologist*, *48*, 400–407.

The National Latino Behavioral Health Workshop (1996). *Cultural competence standards in managed care mental health services for Latino populations*. Phoenix, AZ: Author.

Thompson, E. E., Neighbors, H. W., Munday, C., & Jackson, J. S. (1996). Recruitment and retention of African American patients for clinical research: An exploration of response rates in the urban psychiatric hospital. *Journal of Consulting and Clinical Psychology*, *64*, 861–867.

10.06
Reconstructing Race, Rethinking Ethnicity

MARIA P. P. ROOT
University of Washington, Seattle, WA, USA

10.06.1 INTRODUCTION 141
10.06.1.1 Race and Ethnicity 143
10.06.1.2 Racial Identity Development as Racial Healing 144
10.06.2 PROCESS OF IDENTITY CONSTRUCTION 145
10.06.2.1 Process of Differentiation 145
10.06.3 RACIAL IDENTITY THEORIES 147
10.06.3.1 Nigrescence and Minority Racial Identity Stage Model Theories 147
10.06.3.2 White Racial Identity 148
10.06.4 ETHNIC IDENTITY MODELS 149
10.06.4.1 Comparison and Critique of Racial and Ethnic Identity Models 150
10.06.5 RETHINKING RACE AND ETHNICITY 151
10.06.6 CONTEMPORARY MODELS FOR RETHINKING THE RELATIONSHIP BETWEEN RACE AND ETHNICITY 152
10.06.6.1 Ecological Model of Race and Ethnicity 152
10.06.7 CLINICAL IMPLICATIONS 155
10.06.8 FUTURE DIRECTIONS: RETHINKING RACE AND ETHNICITY 157
10.06.9 SUMMARY 157
10.06.10 REFERENCES 158

10.06.1 INTRODUCTION

Ethnicity and race in the USA have become synonymous concepts in everyday language although they signify different experience. This chapter, which considers identity development in persons of mixed racial heritage, necessitates we differentiate these concepts. Increasingly, ambiguous phenotypes, proliferating since the biracial baby boom post-1967, defy instantaneous recognition or accurate assignment of ethnic group belonging (1967 marked the repeal of the last antimiscegenation laws in the USA forbidding and penalizing interracial marriage. Since this period of time the percentage of interracial marriages has approximately doubled with each subsequent decade. Correlated with this increase in legalized interracial unions has been a significant increase in the number of biracial and multiracial children and young adults, particularly in large cities of the USA (Root, 1992, 1996b)). These constructs seemingly collide when we consider the identities of people who claim multiple group memberships. This chapter uses the presence and experience of a growing presence of racially mixed people in the USA whose simultaneous, dynamic, and multiple identies require reexamination of assumptions about race and ethnicity.

How are racial and ethnic identity different? This has become an increasingly difficult differentiation as racial logic is somewhat circular and the distinctions between their historical constructions are suppressed (Gordon, 1995). Both exist because diversity in race and ethnicity have a social significance used to stratify society (Phinney, 1990). Much of the work on ethnic and racial identity stems from notions of the effects of marginality (Oetting & Beauvais, 1990–1991) and the observations and hypothesizing about the hybrids of race and culture (Park, 1931; Stonequist, 1964; Young, 1995).

Race and ethnicity become significant statuses relevant to experience of self and others when they are differentiated within a society. In his classic work on the roots of discrimination, Allport (1994, p. 221) lists 10 conditions which when present are accompanied by an increase in prejudiced personalities:

> Where the social structure is marked by heterogeneity
> Where vertical mobility is permitted
> Where rapid social change is in progress
> Where there are ignorance and barriers to communication
> Where the size of a minority group is large or increasing
> Where direct competition and realistic threats exist
> Where exploitation sustains important interests in the community
> Where customs regulating aggression are favorable to bigotry
> Where traditional justifications for ethnocentrism are available
> Where neither assimilation nor cultural pluralism is favored.

If one carries a visible status such as race, its socially constructed meaning results in a labeling process. Visible identities, whether they connote positive meaning or stigmatized status, effect the opportunities we encounter (Goffman, 1963). The process of incorporating a stigmatic status requires a personal understanding of human competition, oppression, and resilience. When these identities carry stigmatic statuses, the process by which they are incorporated into a positive aspect of self requires ego strength, resilience, and a repertoire of coping. Thus, identity is a very central concept for clinical, developmental, and social psychology.

The construction of race in the USA is not unique. Several scholars have elucidated the construction of racial and ethnic others as a colonial strategy (whether it be the Spanish, Dutch, Japanese, British, American, etc.) for justifying maltreatment of people (Foucault, 1978; Young, 1995). The construction of the racial or ethnic other sets the stage for justifying genocide whether it be in Bosnia, World War II Germany, the USA, or Africa at various points in history.

Because the mechanics of oppression have universal methods, the example of US history of race relations to examine current theories of racial identity development is used. In doing so, it becomes clear that our psychology exists within a political tangle of propaganda and oppression—past and present. The effects of our history of racial and ethnic oppression becomes evident in the critical examination of current racial identity theories from the experience of a growing minority in this country, persons of multiracial origin, who declare a biracial or multiracial heritage.

DuBois (1903) noted that the affirmation of a devalued self can create a depth of conscious awareness that possibly expands one's humanity. Almost three-quarters of a century later, the development of ethnic and racial identity theories elucidate the phenomenological process largely affected by a political history (Ramirez, 1983, 1997; Root, in press). Allport's (1954) conditions of almost a half century ago work well in understanding how sociology, politics, and psyche are interdependent. The 10 conditions he outlines shape the social intercourse of identity. Identity development will be necessarily a conscious and more complex status for racial and ethnic others. In this chapter, the biracial or multiracial person who chooses not to adhere to centuries-old rules of racial classification and insists upon simultaneous or blended identities is chosen as the example with which to explore race and ethnicity.

Differentiating between race and ethnicity becomes more important at this moment in history because of the trend in increasing miscegenation and the subsequent, significant biracial baby boom. This young, visible cohort, contests the virulent antimiscegenistic foundation upon which racial rules for belonging and identification derived and even Stonequist's hypothesized marginality (1964). Furthermore, recent research using multiracially identified individuals suggests that race is neither a necessary nor sufficient condition for establishing ethnic identity (Hall 1980, 1992; Stephan, 1992). The psychological models guiding and capturing racial identity are now dated and limited. Current and future directions must be plotted against the backdrop of a post-civil rights era that has spawned a biracial baby boom.

10.06.1.1 Race and Ethnicity

Some scholars suggest that the racially mixed person embodies one of the most tangible threats to the current racial order. In order to understand this threat, an historical understanding of the derivation of race is necessary. Without this examination, culture and ethnicity are misleading euphemisms for a construct laden with centuries of harm.

Colonists striving for an economic and political stronghold in new lands needed to create a system with which to distinguish themselves from the indigenous people. The construction of race was intrically aligned with economic systems of expansion. This system racialized gender and engendered race (Foucault, 1978; Stoler, 1995; Zack, 1997b). Whether this be through Dutch, Spanish, British, Japanese, or US colonization, the mechanisms have manufactured similar oppressions. Ethnocentric interpretations of differences in cultural practices are coded through the colonized group's bodies (Fanon, 1967; Foucault, 1978; Stoler, 1995; Young, 1995; Zack, 1997a). Subsequently, notions of group distinctions on moral and behavioral bases are attributed to lineage which eventually becomes accepted scientific folklore as biological heritability. A mythology and rationale for oppressive treatment of the colonized completes an irrational circle of logic to ensure that the physical demarcations provide clear markers of insider and outsider (Spickard, 1992). Utilizing paternalistic attitudes coupled with the belief in biological heritability of morality, intelligence, and civility (Young, 1995), the colonized group is considered helpless to change its outlook or status, which justifies paternalistic and missionary interventions introduced with imperial expansion.

Whereas racial classification systems are determined by those in power, those subjects disenfranchised by this system often unwittingly internalize it; subsequently, groups agree upon assignments between the colonizer and the colonized. For example, in the USA, hypodescent, a system by which a mixed race person is assigned to the group with the lowest social value, is now an agreed upon system. Using an extreme example, many black people will insist a person is black even if they grow up with a single white parent in a predominantly white neighborhood with little African-American ethnic group knowledge or shared customs, behaviors, or attitudes.

Weinreich (1986) suggests that ethnicity requires internal recognition and affiliation with the ethnic reference group. Mutual agreement between participant and group regarding group membership is based upon behavioral practices, rituals, customs, and values. However, because we are such an ethnically diverse society, and ethnicity is centrally defined by the previous variables and not defined phenotypically, ethnic ambiguity is reduced through using racialized bodies as signifiers of ethnic group membership. Whereas the enactment of ethnicity is dynamic over time and generation, race is repeatedly enacted within the constricture of laws of hypodescent and, until recently, laws against miscegenation. Among other purposes, these latter laws kept phenotypical signifiers of group belonging more visible. Given our country's history of racial tragedy, dialogue about race is avoided through the use of terms as ethnicity and culture that have come to be used interchangeably for race despite their essential difference.

Both ethnicity (Tajfel, 1981) and race (Cross, 1971; Helms, 1990) are salient identities of the self that provide a basis for interpreting the actions of others and one's internal experiences. Their similarities are perhaps bound both by the sense of reference group or belonging that one psychologically internalizes. One might construct their difference by viewing race as constructed by negative forces which subsequently require connectivity between members of a disenfranchised group for survival. In contrast, the connectivity between people derived from ethnicity includes positive experiences of sharing rituals and customs and language on daily basis. When negative forces drive definitions of ethnicity from outside the group, such as in anti-semitism, Jewishness is also constructed in racial rather than only ethnic terms, and the negative connectivity resulting from race also binds this ethnic group for survival.

Ironically, colonization and physical proximity between different populations inevitably leads to miscegenation of populations (Spickard, 1989; Stoler, 1995; Young, 1995). Initially the offspring may have the privileges, but when a critical mass starts to develop, these bodies may become viewed as the enemy within (Stoler, 1995), and this new group is relegated to another position. This system is challenged and breaks down when a critical mass of people refuse to collude with the system. This is the case with a portion of the contemporary generation of mixed racial heritage. The numbers of people born out of a biracial baby boom who do not wish to participate in conventional societal racial antagonisms has reached a critical mass.

In summary, race is based upon a delusional system of hierarchical difference marked by phenotypical differences. Systemically, race is not initially an agreed upon system. Assigned by those in power, group acceptance and belonging is based upon recognition and acceptance by the disenfranchised group. Whereas white society and groups of color are congruent in their assignments and acceptance of racial group membership, this system breaks down contemporarily with the refusal of many people of mixed heritage to agree to participate according to the rules of the system.

We must reexamine the assumptions upon which racial identity has been based as we reach the centennial anniversary of DuBois' observation that the color line would be one of the most significant issues of the twentieth century. We must shift our concern at the end of this millennium to the microcosm of this American dilemma—the individual who embodies multiple heritages and affirms multiple allegiances. What are the psychological implications of this for us as a nation and for individual identity development (Root, 1996b)? Current data suggest that the biracial baby boom is accelerating an unraveling of race as it has been practiced in the USA for centuries. These changes have implications for psychological constructions of race and racial identity through the dilemas posed by demographic changes.

10.06.1.2 Racial Identity Development as Racial Healing

Racial identity is necessarily defined in terms of a psychological process of healing from the insidious wounds of racism. In the broadest sense, the damage caused by justifying racial inferiority of nonwhite people has similar dynamics to hostage-taking during war. Interestingly, Banks' (1988) ethnic identity development theory posits the first stage as "ethnic psychological captivity." The tactics of isolation of the individual or group, deprivation, monopolizing of perceptions, and brainwashing result in a dependence on the captor, a belief in one's inferiority, and an aspiration to be more like the captor in hopes of survival, or even better treatment.

Furthermore, contemporary literature makes the case that race and gender are co-constructed (Zack, 1997a). Lerner (1986) suggest that men of color are constructed in the female gender. Historically, she makes the case for observing that desirable women have been constructed in the image of children. Paternalistic models of racism also construct people of color and indigenous people in images and caricatures of children.

Similarly, the dynamics of race relations have shared similar aspects to the chronic abuse of children or women in domestic households. In these positions women and children are often held hostage economically, materially, and psychologically. Their survival and welfare depends on developing a keen sensitivity to the whims and wishes of the captor or head of household. Feelings of inferiority, wishes to be other than female, and devaluing other women may follow (Griffin, 1992).

With the metaphors of war and the insidious psychological violence wreaked by the abuse of dominance, a healing process is required to establish a constructive sense of self which affirms the possibility of a positive racial and ethnic identity. In the meantime, however, what is the cost to individuals?

Rates of depression, schizophrenia, and stress reactions have been associated with race and social class which are confounded in this society (Dowrenhend & Dowrenhend, 1974). Although depression and schizophrenia exist across cultures, their rates vary across countries suggesting mediation by environmental influences. The US literature points to the stress caused by self-devaluation by racial system in terms of obstacles to economic advancement through glass ceilings and limited employment opportunities, and stress caused by living in unsafe neighborhoods that are also associated with impoverished levels of income, joblessness, and disillusionment by young people (Wilson, 1987). Recent literature investigates the relationship of stress caused by racial position and impact on mental health such that seeming personality disorders must be viewed in cultural contexts (Alarcon & Foulks, 1995). Unfortunately, the standard reference group unchallenged until more recent times has been similar to the researchers: white, male, and middle to upper middle class. Clients or students whose behaviors or psychological profile differed significantly tended to be pathologized or problematized. For example, a significant body of literature exists on the personality problems of the person of African-American heritage, particularly in the use of the Minnesota Multiphasic Personality Inventory. A debate over the intelligence of minority group children, particularly those of African heritage or of bilingual backgrounds, resurfaces every 15–20 years (Hilliard, 1996).

The civil rights movement, and legislation that accompanied it to extend equal rights guaranteed by the US constitution to all people, beginning in the 1950s and extending two more decades, might best mark the beginning of public awareness of the healing oppressed persons continued despite prevailing conditions in which prejudices thrived. Legislation attempted to correct previous misapplications of the US constitution and the Bill of Rights through formal desegregation of schools, workplaces, and neighborhoods. In time, a new body of literature emerged on ethnic and racial identity, produced primarily by people of color who were now part of a small and growing cohort of scholars. It was no coincidence that the primary originators of racial identity theories were people who were deeply influenced by the racial pride movements of the 1960s and 1970s, which occurred during their young adult years.

During this period in history, ethnicity and race essentially became the same; ethnic solidarity meant racial solidarity (Omi & Winant, 1986). Ironically, notions of ethnic/racial solidarity invoked an inside–outsider politic akin to the process outlined for individuals in racial identity theories; the oppressed person, in an attempt to selvage their racial self-esteem, separates themselves from the majority to seek refuge and absorb the positive aspects of identifying as a person of color. This period of refuge may also reflect a hatred of what is white and dominant, accompanied by an uncritical acceptance of racial group signifiers that one idealistically reveres. Phenotypic identification by styles of dress and physical appearance take on significant meaning as ethnic markers and symbols of racial pride and solidarity. Thus, a literature emerged on racial identity that was virtually synonymous with African heritage and ethnicity (Cross, 1971). Simultaneously, within the ethnic pride movements of the American Indian Movement (AIM), the Chicano Movement (La Raza), and the Asian American Movement, other theorists emerged who focused on the meaning and importance of biculturality (Ramirez, 1983).

10.06.2 PROCESS OF IDENTITY CONSTRUCTION

Human nature observes difference and leads us to differentiate ourselves at a basic level from "the other," someone different from us on a dimension that has meaning. Thus, part of building self-definition is through contrasting ourselves with the other (Sartre, 1976). This process of differentiation is initially primitive rather than complex, casting difference in binary, oppositional terms establishing poles of privilege and disenfranchisement (Zack, 1993): male, female; white, not-white; able bodied, disabled; same sex orientation, different sex orientation. Gordon (1995) outlines the logic of this transformation as it has been applied to race. A superior group is boundless from constraints and derives its justification from the proof of the inferior. In turn, the inferior is treated and constructed in less than human form. This oppressive process is the process of colonization of a people and colonization of the mind.

The body of the individual, through assigned social meaning, is stigmatized (Goffman, 1963; Young, 1995). In more recent work, Gordon (1997) uses a philosophical perspective to suggest that to have a race, in an antiblack world, is to be assigned the pole of raced, that is, black. To be white is raceless. A similar physical marker is assigned to gender. To have a gender is to be female; male is genderless. In contrast, Zack (1993) suggests that the polar opposites on race are to have a race (black, white, etc.) and its opposite is hybridity. Thus, racial mixing derived from either system of logic has the negative valence and has the most significant meaning attached to its embodiment. Racial mixing also brings in the topic of control of sexuality through privileged positions of bodies, both raced, and gendered.

In patriarchal societies the ideal self is referenced as male, white, able-bodied, and heterosexual. Sociological theories of anomy (Durkheim, 1966) and marginality (Stonequist, 1964) conclude that to possess other than the ideal and privileged position is to be inherently less powerful and more likely to be marginal. Activists and scholars concerned with the impact of colonialism make similar conclusions (Fanon, 1967; Friere, 1970). To function in the other position is to have more obstacles to overcome and to have to fight harder to derive a positive self-identity. Erikson's (1968) theory on the importance of identity and conscious identity process suggests that to be defined as other will predict at the least a more arduous task of positive self-identification. (Whereas he tackles the topic of race he does it also as a representative of the times in which he was produced; gender identity development receives relatively little attention (Burman, 1994).) The ethnic and racial identity theories that developed in the 1970s and 1980s are very much a consequence of this arduous task.

10.06.2.1 Process of Differentiation

Deriving a sense of self from contrast with the other begins a process of differentiation (Allport, 1954). Much contemporary literature has focused on the social construction of race and virtually little on the process of differentiation that gives rise to meanings assigned to differences. This process has different paths it can take. Root (in press) notes that the process of differentiation can be constructive or destructive, which promotes very different cognitive schemas around differences.

Tolerance for ambiguity of meaning and ability to operate fearlessly in the face of difference allows one to engage in the process of constructive differentiation. Tolerance for ambiguity allows the individual to suspend stereotyping and to refrain from applying conceptual frameworks that do not fit the situation. Differences may be observed, but neither a binary schema nor a valence is assigned. Thus, the other is observed side by side with the self rather than in competition or opposition. The other does not have to be inferior. Constructive differentiation observes difference outside of a hierarchical schema and allows one to expand one's world view, and even possibly find oneself in this difference. The ability to do this, particularly in light of observable physical differences, such as by color, by gender, or by height, is stifled early on by external inputs that impart hierarchical, competitive schemas and schemas of opposition. Categorization seems to be an important part of the cognitive process that allows the world to be made simpler. However, categorization is not necessarily synonymous with hierarchical stratification. It is the step from categorization to hierarchicalization which may shift the process of understanding difference into destructive differentiation.

Unfortunately, by the age of seven or eight, the process of destructive differentiation around race is well assimilated. Remember the song in the 1950s musical, *South Pacific* set during World War II: "you've got to be taught/before it's too late/before you are six, or seven, or eight/ to hate all the people your relatives hate." Underlying such a process is a tendency to interpret the other as threatening and to subsequently counter anxiety or threat with negative evaluation. Through a process of negative stereotyping, threatening differences are stratified (Berger, Cohen, & Zelditch, 1966) and stigmatized (Goffman, 1963).

Negative differentiation employs parsimonious, reductionistic strategies too early. Subsequently, this process yields primitive rather than complex understanding, though, complex and convoluted rationalization may develop to sustain these reductionistic schemas, as has been the case in using race as a reductionistic scheme. Racial epithets are an extreme example of destructive differentiation. With a few words, an overtly hostile act of differentiation relegates the target person to a less desirable position. In this act, the instigator defines themselves as superior in contrast to their target.

Ultimately, negative differentiation results in self-definition by what one is not—a distancing from feared association with the other. For example, a person may have ideas that they are not like Filipinos, not like Africans, but still not have a constructively defined notion of a racial self as a white person, that is, whiteness as the privileged position is inherently defined as raceless or without stigma. (In the USA, many white persons no longer have an ethnic affiliation, so that the primary identity is through white racial status rather than through an ethnic identity). Many researchers note that, unlike the identity process that persons who have been defined as other experience in this country, white persons do not have to think about themselves on a daily basis in terms of their race or ethnic belonging (Frankenburg, 1993; Helms & Carter, 1990). Destructive differentiation leaves little room for exploration on the very dimension one might use to expand one's world view. The mixed heritage person, socially located as other, and invisible, but feared and mistrusted, must struggle to create positive self-definition in the face of few positively valued reference groups or role models.

Destructive differentiation produces an identity that is inherently fragile, dependent upon maintaining distance from the other, and believing in the inferiority of the other in order to maintain a sense of self. Its unresolved conflicts regenerate itself; the oppressed may become the oppressor (identifying with the captor) as a survival strategy, yielding again, a fragile sense of identity. For example, given that this country's racial system is predicated on pure race, mixed-race people experience gatekeeping around racial belonging. Acceptance requires a singular belonging. Thus, persons who declare a biracial identity are often put to racial authenticity tests by other people of color. If they are also of white European origin, centuries-old rules of hypodescent automatically fail them in white authenticity. Multiple allegiances and affiliations of multiracial or multiethnic people may be vilified through the process of negative differentiation. On another level, women may be more oppressed than dictated by cultural rules as a means for men who feel oppressed to achieve a position of superiority. Unfortunately, this yields a fragile self construction. This juxtaposition of the inferiorizing of racial and gendered identity can provide the basis for some racial antagonisms between parents and mixed heritage children in some families (Kich, 1992).

Ironically, political consciousness pertaining to racial and ethnic identity is a response to negative differentiation in which being the other has simultaneous negative meaning and invisibility (Freire, 1970). Hurtado and Gurin (1995) discuss three interrelated aspects of racial and ethnic identity that originate out of a process of negative differentiation for individuals of

Mexican heritage. These issues are also relevant to other groups of people who may locate themselves in a multiracial and/or multiethnic context. First, the group is indignant over the lack of power; for example they might protest over lower wages than other ethnic groups in the same work environment performing the same work. Second, the group demonstrates that this social location and lack of power results in suffering healthwise, economically, and/or educationally. Third, collective action is necessary to improve the social standing of the group, such as strike action by groups of persons who occupy niches of wage work that capitalize on their lower status, but are necessary for the profit of a capitalist society. All three aspects of this increased political consciousness are directly implicated in the process of racial awareness and the personal meaning of racial identification.

Diminishing denigrating defensive strategies is difficult in a society that has colluded and condoned negative stereotyping such as that based on colorism, race, body size, gender, and so on. Bennett (1995, p. 36) suggests that confrontation of negative stereotyping or denigrating tactics may result in more overt protests that are denial defenses. In contrast to Bennett's suggestion that superiority or grandiosity is a defense that does not require overt denigration of the group constructed as other, it is a stratification defense against fragility. This defense, too, is a form of destructive differentiation through stratification driven by anxiety and primitive threat.

10.06.3 RACIAL IDENTITY THEORIES

10.06.3.1 Nigrescence and Minority Racial Identity Stage Model Theories

Numerous theories blend racial and ethnic identity. The most numerous models are found in the nigrescence models of racial identity offered by African-American researchers (Banks, 1988; Cross, 1971; Gay, 1984; Jackson, 1975; Milliones, 1980; Parham, 1989; Thomas, 1971; Vontress, 1971). Most of these models emerged in the context of working with clients of African-American heritage in counseling or educational settings. In both settings, the standard for behavior and mental health used a middle-class, white, male reference group similar to the majority of researchers. African-American researchers started depathologizing and renorming behavior in the social and historical context of healing from the wounds of racism. Significant reviews of this literature have been provided over the course of its development (Carter, 1995; Cross, 1978; Helms, 1990).

Although all these models imply some process that responds to racial traumatization, some might best be described as typology models and others as stage models. Helms (1990) summarizes the stages or categories proposed by each model in the early body of identity models. The models that have had most impact on contemporary thinking about racial identity are the stage models.

These models, particularly the early ones, were developed with little influence from each other. Thus, it is all the more remarkable how similar they are in process, varying in the number of stages from four to six. The assumption is that an individual proceeds linearly through the stages with the final stage synonymous with optimum mental health. Crises, which may be personally defined, are the catalysts to rethink one's experience and assumptions about race and how they fit into that schema.

First stages of these models typically suggest that the individual is hostage to the prevailing racial system. Both a racial and ethnic identity model, Banks' (1988) first stage is labeled "ethnic psychological captivity," connotating the culmination of destructive differentiation. In the first stage of these models, the individual holds the prevailing stereotypes which denigrate the group to which one is assigned. As a result, one may blame the self for plights and difficulties, ignoring systemic obstacles and barriers to success. They may insist that history has changed so that opportunities for equitable treatment exist. Thus, they are able to hold a just world hypotheses view of the world regarding race: People basically get what they deserve and that right behavior is rewarded and the individual is valued (Janoff-Bulman, 1992). When one encounters a significant challenge to this perception of the world, their assumptions are shattered and they must recreate a new understanding of how the world works.

A typical second stage in these models suggests that the individual withdraws into the black culture to reconstruct their world; simultaneously, they may employ negative differentiation by relabeling the binary poles of opposition. That which is associated with the dominant culture is worthless and reprehensible. The default racial label for dominance is white and engendered as male. Labels such as "encounter," "immersion," "separation," and "confrontation" characterize the process at work in this stage. Typical of the process of quick change which swings to an opposite pole, this stage might be characterized by over-idealization of the new world view, at times exaggeration of the evils of the dominant world view, and exaggeration of the flawlessness of one's racial/ethnic group. The racial pride movements of the 1960s and 1970s typified this stage of ethnic identity. Everything black, Chicano, Indian, or Asian was idealized by the respective groups. Those aspects of the culture that may not be positive may be ignored. Theorists reflected what they observed in the process of clients and peers. In order to counter the abundant negative messages one must denigrate the practices and identities associated with dominance. Out of this stage emerges a new basis for an identity that rebuffs the negative images of self. What has received little attention is that the default gender is black male, or male of color. Female gender and the co-constructed process of identity is not addressed.

With labels such as "internalization," "post-encounter," and "affirmation mode," the next stage suggests that one works to be able to internalize positive images of blackness that are not necessarily at the expense of denigrating whiteness or any other group. Thus, negative differentiation is less prevalent as an organizing strategy. One continues to build pride in one's self associated with ethnic and racial heritage.

Some models originally offered a stage that suggested it was possible to move towards a multicultural position and appreciation of diversity (Banks, 1988; Cross, 1971, 1991; Milliones, 1980; Thomas, 1971). Labeled as "integration," "internalization–commitment," or "global competency," individuals in this stage attempt to use experience and knowledge to fight oppression around them. Solidarity is defined less stereotypically as behaviors; symbols are not used for quick judgments or categorizations of other people. Constructive differentiation is an organizing schema. This stage implies a level of healing of rage and anger that requires life experience and some luck of positive encounters.

In more recent work and reworking of these models, a last stage seems to be informed by the life stage of the researchers. This stage is one in which there seems to be a transcendence of the constrictions of race, while maintaining an awareness that race does make a difference (Atkinson, Morten, & Sue, 1979; Carter, 1995; Cross, 1985, 1991).

Most of these models exist within a dichotomous racial framework of white and not white, thus, capturing the prevalent racial paradigm and the prevailing racial politics of the time in which they emerged. They assume that the two major operating rules of race (pure race and hypodescent) abound so that there is a racial hierarchy and the races are separate. Atkinson et al. (1979) developed a minority identity model to reflect similar process in ethnic identity and racial identity development across groups. However, this model as the other racial identity models, does not explain the process of identity development when a multiracial paradigm exists and other aspects of identity coconstruct identity.

10.06.3.2 White Racial Identity

Starting in the late 1970s through the 1980s researchers conceptualized white identity stage models (Carney & Kahn, 1984; Ganter, 1977; Helms, 1984). Again, Helms (1990) provides a summary of these models. An identifiable process of white racial identity formation has been offered, that is, moving from assuming a raceless position to acknowledging that whiteness comes with inherent privileges and power.

These models suggests that a white person's linear movement through the stages progresses towards establishing egalitarian relationships with persons different from oneself. Such an accomplishment would again require an active use of constructive differentiation to interpret differences. These models vary between offering three to six stages. These descriptions of the process through which an individual moves are not as uniform as the black identity models. The labels are less descriptive in these models, some preferring to refer to stages as phase or stage 1, 2, 3, and so on.

Although it is hard to typify the stages across models, the first and last stages bear similarities across models. The first stage typically captures the acceptance of the white dominant position in society with an obliviousness to this being a racial identity. Without acknowledgment of white racial identity at work, an individual can protest the notion that the status quo associated with white domination economically and politically promotes racism—or that these white individuals serve as pawns in the racial machinery governing the social structure of this country.

In the last stage of the models, the individual acknowledges the significance of white racial identity and accepts responsibility for the losses associated with white superiority and domination. The individual moves to broaden their standards and values of reference beyond their own. Unlike the nigrescence or minority models, none of the models reviewed by Helms (1990) suggest that fighting oppression is inherent to transcending the constrictures of race as constructed in this country.

The racial identity models, that developed out of the counseling and educational contexts, have been conceptually linked to mental health: well-being, beliefs, and behaviors. However, the empirical testing is just beginning. No conclusive data is available.

10.06.4 ETHNIC IDENTITY MODELS

Outside the bipolar black–white racial framework, multiracial populations exist which are primarily defined by ethnicity (e.g., Mexican, Latino, Puerto Rican, Native Hawaiian, Native American, and Filipino) rather than race (e.g., black, white). Although the embodiment of this ethnicity may be physically blended with non-European features, these groups fall outside of the most contrasted borders of black–white. Examination of the process of identity that occurs for these groups of people is important when considering the question of how race and ethnicity might be different despite phenotypic variation within a population (Ramirez, 1983, 1997). The ethnic identity models do not contend with race directly as much as they do with cultural difference and shared cultural elements that define an ethnic community.

Sociological theories suggest that several interactional factors affect ethnic identity: the individual, the society, and the group to which an immigrant is assigned reactions, positive or negative, and the interaction of these three social locations (Mittelberg & Waters, 1992). The symbolic interactionist theories highlight the interaction between the individual or collective and the environment from the actor's point of view (Lal, 1995). These models become precursors for multidimensional psychological models which emphasize the ecology of the environment within which the individual acts. Furthermore, many sociological concepts of ethnicity explore which factors influence the boundaries of ethnic identity. Within this framework, certain visible characteristics of an individual restrict options for ethnic identification, such as race and language facility (Mittelberg & Waters, 1992; Waters, 1990).

Psychological models of ethnic identification introduce concepts of acculturation and assimilation as source of stress, directing the outcome of attempts to integrate a bicultural world view (Olmedo, 1979; Padilla, 1980; Ramirez, 1983, 1997). Much of this work emerges from research with youth (Oetting & Beauvais, 1990–1991; Padilla, 1980; Phinney, 1989; Ramirez, 1983; Trimble, 1996, in press). Gurin, Hurtado, and Peng (1994) concluded the macrosocial conditions, such as language dominance, length of residence, geographic dispersal, and the diversity of work settings, that influenced the opportunities for group contact which in turn influence the formation of social ethnic identities in Chicanos and Mexicanos in the Southwest and Chicago. Ramirez (1983, 1997) uses the term mestizo(a) as a world view perspective rather than a racial term for bicultural individuals who are capable of blending distinct cultural influences. More recently, Huang (1994) provides a model for identity formation for Asian Americans. Acknowledging the interplay between internal and external identities, she notes that an important aspect of ethnic identity is the degree to which the individual perceives it to have salience in life and the degree to which the person's external identity is mediated by the congruence or conflict between their acceptance and belonging to an in group and out group. The centrality of a salience hierarchy, and the flexibility posed by separating internal from external identities, provides for a host of profiles of identity which can accommodate the range of ethnic identity outcomes discussed in the literature. Thus, her model moves towards a newer wave of multidimensional models.

Oetting and Beauvais (1990–1991) suggest that the precursors to ethnic or cultural identification models stem from Park's (1931) and his student's, Stonequist's (1964), seminal work on hybridity and marginality, respectively. Similar to the racial identity models, these ethnic or cultural identification models emerge out of attempts to explain problematic behavior in persons who are culturally different to the dominant reference group, deemed American. They provide a summary of models that have prevailed from the linear continuum models to more complex multidimensional models. Finally, they propose the orthogonal cultural identification theory. The dominant majority models suggest movement away from the culture of origin to the new. Furthermore, Anglo culture is good and to be emulated. Simple transitional models suggest that, in the process of movement there is inherent stress that is always difficult and may result in problematic behaviors such as drinking. Another form of transitional model, the alienation model, suggests that in the transition there may be a good or a bad outcome, depending on coping. Good coping results in movement towards the adoption of Anglo ways, whereas failed coping results in alienation. To some degree these models are invoked at various times in the research literature or in everyday life explanations for the success and failure of people who are originally culturally different from the dominant, European-derived culture.

Three multidimensional models are also summarized, including their own. Multidimensional models allow multiple values to co-exist at different points along the continuum from culture of origin to European derived culture. Bicultural models are the first models to suggest that an individual can be simultaneously identified with two cultures. Although they explain and predict that people who are adept and involved in both cultures become more flexible, these models do not generally have explanatory power for the individual who is marginal to both cultures, who demonstrates low involvement or identification with both cultures. Lastly, the orthogonal identification model suggests that identification with one culture is independent of another. Thus, unlike other models, this one allows for any and all combinations of identifications.

It is important with the multidimensional models not to believe that the bicultural models are inferior to the orthogonal models, but to examine which model fits which contexts best. Ramirez (1983) offers a bicultural model born out by research which strongly suggests that biculturality does seem to increase some cognitive flexibility. In educational settings, this model may be advantageous (Banks, 1988). With increasing trends for some populations to live in two countries, the notions of biculturality will continue to be reinforced and be a reality for many populations of Latino and Asian origin.

On a process level, Bennett (1995) suggests that the defenses of denial, minimization, acceptance, adaptation, and integration are employed as people move through a process of interethnic and intercultural valuation related to identity. This model is unique in that process is discussed in terms of developmental strategies with an emphasis on the role of intrapsychic defenses against inferior status.

10.06.4.1 Comparison and Critique of Racial and Ethnic Identity Models

The ethnic identity models have grappled with reference group orientation multiple alliances, and more recently with the transnational identities. Often referred to as a process of ethnogenesis, immigrants reformulate their identity after entering the USA. This reformulation often requires accomodating a new definition of race and being relegated to a minority status. This process is impacted by the way in which bodies are racially assigned meaning. The destructive differentiation based on race in the process of ethnogenesis is illustrated succinctly in a recent study by Mittelberg and Waters (1992) of identity formation in two immigrant groups: middle-class Haitians and secular kibbutz-born Israelis. The authors observe, unsurprisingly, that the Israelis have fewer constraints in reformulating their identities than do Haitians, because of the primacy of the meaning of blackness as a race in this country.

The racial identity models seem the more limited in contemporary context because they are still embedded in an undimensional model of racial belonging, as centuries-old rules remain unquestioned. The linear nature of the models of nigrescence and minority racial identity development assume that an individual will retreat from white society's denigration and refuge in the community of color. However, biracial people, particularly of European heritage, do not have a guaranteed refuge because of their marginalized status by multiple groups. With other people in this stage of development, such as high school and college age peers, they may not be viewed as authentic members due to their biracial status, particularly if they are not willing to denigrate and denounce in an exaggerated way that which is white. To do this is to potentially denounce part of one's heritage and people one loves (Root, 1990). Thus, the biracial person may be subjected to racial or ethnic authenticity tests which are charicatures of socially constructed race and ethnicity. Many biracial persons find this neither a natural nor only process for achieving a positive racial and ethnic identity (Root, 1992a, 1996b). Many young adults enact multidimensional models of race which are more similar to models of ethnicity. Identities can be dynamic fluctuating in salience contextually and be orthogonal (Duffy, 1978; Hall, 1980, 1992; Stephan, 1992; Williams, 1992). Contextually, the salient identity of someone of black and Asian heritage may sometimes be black, at other times Asian. An orthogonal experience of identity would be manifested in the declaration of being both black and Asian.

However, despite some of the strengths of applicability of multidimensional models of ethnicity to mixed heritage individuals, neither the racial nor ethnic identity development models consider other simultaneous influences of other salient statuses integral to identity, such as gender or sexual orientation. Huang's (1994) model can acccomodate this through the identity salience hierarchy and the consideration that other identities interact and inform personal internal identity. Even the diversity of social economic class orientation, often erroneously assumed homogeneous within ethnic and racial groups, may be critical to the construction of identity. For example, Singelis, Triandis, Bhawuk, and Gelfand (1995) observe that individualism and collectivism vary cross-culturally within a culture according to class: wealthy and impoverished classes are much more individualistic than middle classes. Thus, class location may affect value systems as much or more man race; class and race are often confounded.

Stage models of racial identity do not explain the fluidity of exchange of different aspects of identity between background and foreground, such as gender and race, race and class and gender, sexual orientation and race. These models assume to some degree that either gender has negligible effect or—consistent with much research of the time—did not critically assess how gender informs and shapes life experience and worldview. Notably, most of these researchers being male did not have access to the gendered experience of femaleness and its secondary status within their ethnic and racial groups. Also with a more privileged gendered status, they were not as compelled to consider simultaneously the role of female experience as a female researcher might be.

It is also very likely that the models which prevail have been implicity generation specific; it was no coincidence that early racial and ethnic identity models emerged out of the movements of the 1960s and 1970s. However, the contemporary generation of teenagers and adults have inherited many of the benefits of the civil rights movement of the third quarter of this century. Subsequently, they have not experienced the extremes of racial injustice experienced by persons a generation or more before them. There is also a large segment of the Asian American community who is adjusting to the social construction of race in the USA, having moved from racially homogenous cultures to a racially diverse society that stratifies according to race. Many of these immigrants are learning to identify the racism that blocks their opportunities or explains the differential treatment they receive.

When primary identities are without significant ties and markers specific to ethnicity, more fragile identities are constructed through race For example, consider the genre of US movies and trade books that describe someone who is white discovering they have a black ancestor and consider the deep emotional reaction someone has to this revelation. Why should this be such an unravelling experience if one already knows who one is? Such reactions suggest that the primary identity occurs through race and whiteness rather than through ethnicity.

10.06.5 RETHINKING RACE AND ETHNICITY

Both race and ethnicity are socially constructed. Thus, they are dynamic and influenced by many factors including history, gender, and other aspects of identity that are socially salient and specific to the macro- and microsocial compositions of regions or neighborhoods and ethnic group histories. With the legacy of civil rights legislation in the third quarter of this century, many young people grow up with more latitude to cross racial boundaries in friendship and intimacy. Technological advances in transportation and communication have increased the numbers of persons involved in international and cross-cultural marriages. Again, we can expect that the products of these unions will have the options to be multiethnically, multiracially, and even multinationally identified. This forecast necessitates that we rethink the meaning of race and ethnicity and their relationship.

Consider these demographic trends (Root, 1996b). Since the repeal of antimiscegenation laws in 1967, the rates of racial intermarriage have almost doubled with each subsequent decade. The number of babies of mixed racial heritage has boomed since the late 1980s. Also, the number of persons writing in racial identifiers to elaborate on the other choice has caused the US Bureau of the Census enough concern to entertain a multiracial way of identifying for the year 2000 census. In July 1997, the Office of Management and Budget which oversees the Bureau of the Census decided after much research that the year 2000 decennial census will allow people to mark more than one box in response to the race question. This is an historical change in the accounting of population in the USA.

Whereas the folklore sustaining racial boundaries has purported that racially mixed people will be marginally located and accepted in society, this marginality is being explored and challenged in the academic literature (Anzaldua, 1987; Root, 1992, 1996a; Zack, 1993; 1995), literary essays (Funderburg, 1994; Jones, 1994), novels, and mainstream cinema. The social location of an increasing number of multiracially and multiethnically identified people is often positively constructed, in contemporary time and particular on the west coast of the USA.

More than ever, current research on ethnicity and race suggests that we must attempt to disengage these constructs so that, although at times they admittedly remain confounded, they are not synonymous. For example, Stephan's (1992) research in Hawaii and New Mexico points out geographic differences in how race and parents' ethnicity effects the identification of multiracial Asians and multiracial Mexican American young adults. Her conclusion is that race is neither a necessary nor sufficient condition for making an assumption about ethnic identification. She found that when offered an open ended response option to ethnicity in different situations, few respondents identified themselves consistently across all situations. The conclusion was that identity has contextually constructed Hall (1980) found that neither self-assessed phenotypical resemblance to either black or Japanese reference groups or language facility predicted ethnic identity in her black Japanese sample.

The person of mixed heritage experiences many of the psychological assaults and injuries that their generation cohort of people of color experience. Furthermore, many assaults and insults stem from and are specifically directed to their racial ambiguity. These assaults come from groups of people with whom the biracial person shares heritage and identifies. Table 1 provides a summary of 40 racial experiences commonly experienced by many persons whose racial classification is ambiguous or interpreted by others as mixed. Experienced repeatedly throughout a lifetime, these items potentially influence one's understanding of race relations, race rules, and racial identity. Inherent to this inventory is the negative stereotyping of mixed race, boundary policing of authentic racial behavior, physical objectification of phenotype, and denigration of whiteness. Therapists, teachers, and school counselors might use such a list to provoke discussion. Therapists might further use such an inventory to generate discussion about coping, identity formation, and psychological defenses against exclusion, authenticity testing, denigration, and idealizing that the person of mixed heritage may experience.

10.06.6 CONTEMPORARY MODELS FOR RETHINKING THE RELATIONSHIP BETWEEN RACE AND ETHNICITY

Current trends to reformulate racial formation or ethnogenesis should not ignore the conceptual and empirical information gleaned from earlier research. However, current trends necessitate that we move beyond bipolar conceptualizations of race, reexamine assumptions about racial identity formation, and differentiate race and ethnicity. Contextual spheres of influence from large macrodimensions of geographic region to microdimensions of family interaction and personality must be considered in identity formation.

10.06.6.1 Ecological Model of Race and Ethnicity

Figure 1 represents an ecological identity model of influences on identity development. It evolved out of observing the identity process and differential outcomes for persons of multiracial ancestry, often of multiethnic background, in both clinical and nonclinical settings. The model can accommodate several different outcomes of identity for both monoracially and multiracially identified people from very fragile identities to well-grounded and stable identities. It also accomodates some previous work which states that identity is indeed dynamic and can change over a lifetime due to changing contexts and developmental issues over the lifespan (Root, 1990, in press). However, unlike the stage models which may reflect an underlying linear process, this change of identity does not necessarily invoke a linear movement. Social identities are informed by the interaction of micro and macro influences on identity. This model breaks away from the longstanding constraints of bipolar racial frameworks and assumed rules of hypodescent. In line with the symbolic interactionist theories and models, this one proposes reflexive interaction between variables.

In the proposed model, all boxes are lenses and are present to some degree. The drawing serves as a conceptual organizing tool with which to consider influences in identity. The lenses recognize individual factors, familial factors, community influences—both imagined and factual such as historical influence and experience that transcends generations. Through these lenses, the inherited influences, traits, and social interactions with community determine identity development. The inherited influences include biological and environmental inheritance. Biological inheritance, such as sexual orientation and phenotype, significantly influence life. The other inherited influential lenses are environmental: languages spoken at home; parent's identification ethnically, racially, and nationally; nativity; presence and socialization influence of extended family; given names and nicknames; and home values. All of these variables have been documented in different literatures as having influence on identity. All the environmental influences provide cultural markers to a lesser or greater degree of distinctiveness. The lenses with inherited influences interact with one another.

These inherited influences interact with traits: temperament, social skills, talents, and coping skills. These influences may have both elements of nature and nurture. The traits are some of those aspects of the individual that together are often summarized as personality. The traits are differentiated from inherited influences through what the individual has control over. This model assumes the individual has little control over their inherited influences, whether they be biological or environmental. In contrast, the traits, are deemed to be majorly subject to social influence and learning, even when there may be different degrees of natural talents, coping, sociability and its skills, and even temperament.

Table 1 Items from the racial experiences questionnaire.

1. Told, "You have to choose; you can't be both"
2. Your ethnicity misidentified
3. People assume your race to be different by phone and in person
4. Accused of not acting or wanting to be ... (Latino, black, Asian, etc.)
5. Told, "Mixed race people are so beautiful/handsome"
6. Strangers look between you and your parent(s) to figure out if you are related
7. Told, "You don't look ... (Asian, black, native, etc.)"
8. Asked, "What are you?"
9. People might not say certain things in front of you if they knew how you think about race
10. Asked, "Where are you from?"
11. Stared or looked at by strangers
12. Told, "You look exotic"
13. Your choice of friends is interpreted as your selling out or not being authentic
14. Accused of acting or wanting to be white
15. Judgments of your racial authenticity are based upon your partner's race
16. Comments are made about your physical attributes (hair/hairstyle, skin color, eyes, shape, etc.)
17. You are subjected to jokes about people of mixed heritage
18. Told, "You think you're too good for your own kind"
19. Grandparent(s) or relatives don't accept you because of your parents' interracial relationship
20. Your parents/relatives compete to claim you for their own racial or ethnic group
21. Told, "You have the best of both worlds"
22. Asked about your racial heritage
23. Upon meeting you, people seem confused by your name(s)
24. People assume you are confused about your racial identity
25. People speak to you in foreign languages because of how they intepret your physical appearance
26. Told, "Society doesn't recognize mixed race"
27. Told, "you aren't really ... (Asian, black, Hispanic/Latino, native, etc.)"
28. Mistaken for another person of mixed heritage who does not resemble you
29. Told you must be full of self-loathing or hatred because of how you racially identify yourself
30. Told, "You are a mistake"
31. People's racial identification of you varies and is colored by the race of the people you are with
32. The race people assume you are varies in different parts of the USA
33. You have difficulty filling out forms requiring you to check one race only
34. You identify your race differently to how others identify your race
35. Told, "You aren't like other ... (blacks, Latinos, native Americans, Asians, etc.)"
36. Your siblings identify their race differently than you identify yours
37. Called racial slurs of groups who aren't part of your heritage
38. When friends suggest dating partners for you, they stick within a single racial or ethnic group
39. Your parents identify your race differently than you identify yourself
40. Told, "You aren't ... (native, Asian, black, Latino, etc.) enough"

These interactions takes place in contexts. Such interpersonal contexts allow for the communications about rules of belonging whether it be to the outgroup or ingroup. Reflections of who we are outside of our families serves as frame for further reconciling the private and public experience of identity. For most of us, five social contexts encapsulate most of our social interactions: home; school and/or work; community groups; friendships, and communities in which we are strangers. This last social context is important because it may challenge an individual's construction of self when community environments differ from one another or a person's identity is in some way ambiguous. In the case of phenotypically ambiguous people, whether or not they are multiracially or multiethnically identified, a community to which they are a stranger may provide them with feedback that affects how they experience themselves in relationship to others—and it may be different to what they are used to. The most dramatic stories emerge from recent biographical stories of persons raised white who change living situation or state and then, though phenotypically white, must assume the life of a black person (Williams, 1995).

Lastly, the summation of this interactive life experience filtered through the interaction of the different lenses posed by inherited influences, traits, and social contexts helps us understand identity—both ethnic and racial identity in the context of history and gender. These identities, in turn, provide a lens through

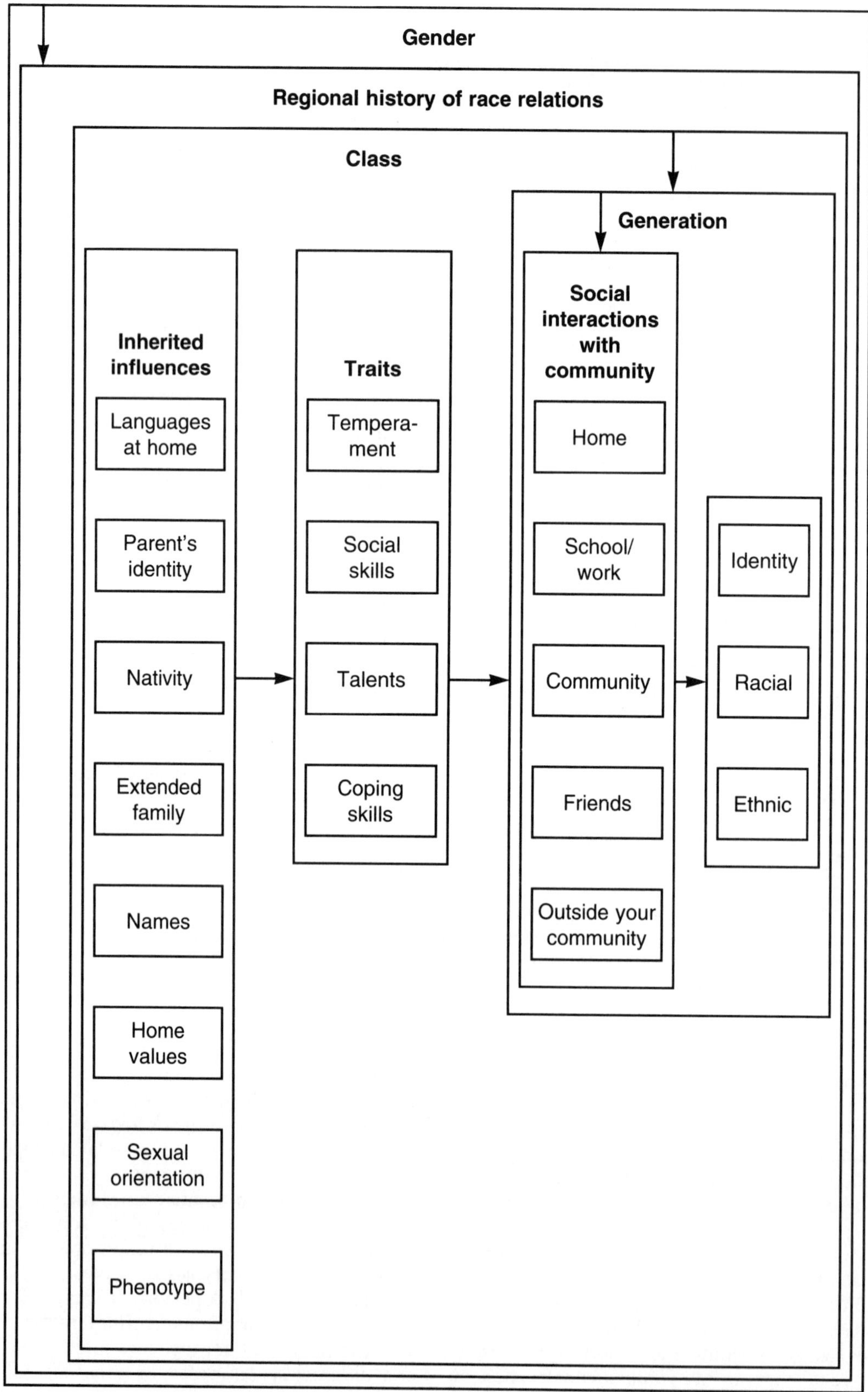

Figure 1 Ecological identity model; all boxes are interactive.

which life is experienced. As one moves through milestones in one's life course, racial and ethnic identity can influence what is passed on as inherited influences to the next generation.

This model suggests that the sociohistorical construction of gender and race are lenses through which most of our life experiences are filtered. However, the construction and connotations of race and gender are also informed by geographical regional context and the historical generational cohort. These additional filters allow us to understand how race and gender have been constructed through paradigms of domination and submission (Lerner, 1986; Stoler, 1995; Zack, 1997b). Patriarchal and imperialistically driven cultures construct racial and ethnic hierarchies with imperialist or the colonial schemes (Freire, 1970; Stoler, 1995; Young, 1995). Therefore, in this model gender and ultimately racial identity are viewed as lenses that are layered upon one another. These two lenses interact dynamically, exchanging salience in relationship to one another as foreground or background filters. This conceptual relationship also explains why some persons assert that gender is the primary organizing factor in life experience, whereas others assert that race is the primary organizing factor in life. However, at all times there is an interaction as described above that makes it certain that the social address of men and women differ when we filter their location through the lenses of gender and race.

Other secondary statuses are significant dimensions or lenses through which life is experienced, for example, class and sexual orientation. Both of these locations may be accompanied by denigrating and oppressive or affirming reflections of self. Again, psychological defenses and coping skills are necessary to be able to incorporate these aspects of experience, and ultimately identity into the larger concept of self.

Likewise, racial and ethnic experience in this country, by region, yield different experiences between two individuals despite the similarity of a host of other life variables. For example, the rates of intermarriage between whites and blacks is very different in the south compared to the west. The histories of these regions are also very different. The prominence of lynchings of black men who dared to interact or even look at white women is well documented in the south, particularly prior to this century. Through the lens of race, the socially constructed groups in the USA are Asian and Pacific Islander American, American Indian, African-American, and white. Whereas persons of Hispanic origin may be any race, this country's history of race relations has constituted this category as a race based on attitudes (Root, 1996b). There will be points at which the experiences of each of these groups will overlap. However, if the gender lens is more prominent, an African-American woman may share more in common in a given context with a Chicana than with an African-American man. For example, the threat to one's body through sexual violence is an experience shared by women and much less so by men. The lense of historical race relations suggest that women of color have been less protected by the legal system in matters of violations of their body, whether it be child abuse, domestic violence, or rape.

This model can accommodate the process described in racial identity development models described earlier in this chapter. However, it does not predict or require that an individual will go through the first stage of negative feelings about their minority racial or ethnic group; it can accomodate such a process, though. This is important because in contemporary times, perhaps due to some of the benefits of the civil right movement, many young people do not feel badly about their ethnic or racial reference group which society ascribes to them.

The ecological identity model also accommodates typology models. It evolved from an earlier work (Root, 1990) in which types of identity were proposed for multiracial people. The process by which people might get to those identities is subsumed in this model. Thus, it is possible to change identity over time, and sometimes this move is simply precipitated by a geographic move, such as from mainland USA to Hawaii where a multiracial and multiethnic identity is the norm. It also provides an increased number of variables with explanatory power for differences in identity absent in other racial identity models.

10.06.7 CLINICAL IMPLICATIONS

The ecological identity model may be useful in clinical settings. It acknowledges trauma which in fact determines some of the salient lenses through which one experiences life (Root, 1992). If a patient has been sexually violated because she is female, and links her suffering to this status, the lens of gender will be prominent. If life chances have been compromised by skin color, and this link has been made, the lens of race will operate prominently. But both lenses will interact. Therapists and counselors can understand the possibility and impact of transgenerational trauma as part of inherited influence: stories of genocide, slavery, incarceration, colonization, and domination imparted from an early age are part of a parent's or relative's identity. The stories may be passed on in the inherited influences of names and family interactions within the community. Parenting is extremely important in the passing on of both coping with a secondary status and the formation and interpretation of both racial and ethnic identity.

Kich (1992) provides one of the best clinical explanations of the processes and outcomes that the biracial person may experience through his three stages. One of his most significant contributions is that his model provides for an understanding of how internal family dynamics may interact with lessons around race and ethnicity. Given that society stratifies race, this hierarchy may be replicated in family dynamics. A child may develop a distance and ambivalent relationship with the parent of color if emotional denigration or the process of destructive differentiation occurs around cultural differences.

The model has implications for different developmental periods that can be further elucidated by the ecological framework suggested in this chapter. For example, if the parent with higher racial or ethnic status denigrates the other parent, a child may feel simultaneously victimized or denigrated. Simultaneously, if this child feels helpless to help, she or he may develop an acute awareness of self which is akin to the vigilance typical of post-traumatic responding. Several aspects of his or her existence may serve as subsequent environmental cues which trigger vigilance in certain settings. For those children who have been raised in psychologically or emotionally denigrating households, the statements, questions, and experiences in Table 1 may all serve as cues leading to experiences of marginalization and rejection.

Therapists and clinicians may want to explore how these experiences have had impact on a person at different stages in their life, and how their coping deflects or defends against society's unresolved anger stemming from the consequences of the racial system. In this system anger and anxiety is projected onto the body of the mixed-race person and subsequently creates a gestalt of experience unique to the mixed-race individual's experience. Major themes are rejection, marginalization, societal anxiety, and objectification as represented by the items of Table 1. These experiences may be specific to certain social environments which feed into definition of self through acceptance and rejection experiences which also seem critical to ethnic identity of racially mixed people (Hall, 1992; Root, 1990; Stephan, 1992). Each of these themes is explained below.

Rejection is captured by items such as, "You are a mistake," "Grandparents or relatives don't accept you because of your parents' interracial relationship," and "Told society doesn't recognize mixed race." It also encompasses the accusations of passing into a dominant desired group with statements such as "You think you're to good for your own kind," "Ethnicity misidentified," or "Accused of acting white." Ironically, because of the past history of racially mixed people passing into a desired group group because their phenotype allowed this, many racially mixed persons are struggling for acceptance from an ethnic group or racial group of their heritage because their phenotype creates suspicion about their intent to belong and their trustworthiness.

Marginalization relates to rejection through authenticity tests and applications of rigid boundaries. Cues for this experience may occur with statements such as, "You have to choose, you can't be both" or "Told you must be full of self-loathing or hatred because of how you racially identify" or "Your racial authenticity is based upon your partner's race."

Much societal anxiety about race is projected onto the mixed race person who refuses to comply with the implicit rules of race which guide daily interactions. This anxiety manifests in questions and statements such as, "Asked about your racial heritage," "Asked what are you?" and "Accused of not wanting to be Latino/black/Asian, etc."

Objectification encompasses the deindividualization and sexualization projected onto race and gender and their interaction. Such a process sets the stage for cruel treatment and relegating persons of mixed heritage to otherwise invisibility. Experiences such as being "told you look exotic" and "stared or looked at by strangers" signal this process.

In increasing attempts at individuation, particularly during adolescence in western cultures, anger at the parent with perceived lower status may be a dysfunctional attempt to attempt to avoid taking on the denigrated status. Also of this racial group, the adolescent is caught in a cycle of anger or even hate that precludes them from realistic affirmation of their whole self. Whereas adolescence in the USA is replete with anger, racial dynamics and gender dynamics may become entwined in a way that makes it very difficult for a child to cope and determine psychologically adaptive ways of responding that may serve them into adulthood. For example, if a white father repeatedly denigrates an Asian mother, not only does this set up the possible dynamics above, it may perpetuate misogyny and denigration of female status, particularly women of color, and set up an idealization of white women.

The status of parents' relationship to one another and society may also be formative in identity. Stephan (1992) discusses the possible influence of the gender of parents in patriarchally organized societies as it may differentially influence identity formation in Hawaii versus New Mexico. Results from her study suggest that for persons of mixed heritage, having an Hispanic father in New Mexico may be more of a determining factor in New Mexico, where such status is lower than having a Japanese American father in Hawaii, where Japanese Americans have relatively high social status. Kich (1982, 1992) further suggests that the absence of a parent and how that absence occurs and is explained may be very critical to how race is interpreted in the family. More recently, with high rates of divorce, increasing attention is paid to white single parenting of mixed heritage children so that they can defend themselves in a society that has been antimiscegenistic and anxious about their existence. Similarly, children of single parents of color must also be aware of the intense discrimination towards racially mixed people that may occur in some closed communities of color. McRoy and Hall's (1996) clinical work on transracial adoption is applicable here. They essentially point out that basic needs of a child must be met even before the tasks of racial defense are relevant, that is, a child must feel loved and secure.

Root (1994) identifies the issues in therapy for mixed race women, although most of the issues are applicable to men. Whereas few people enter therapy to work on their mixed racial heritage, the experiences society has dealt around this status can manifest in issues around self-definition, acceptance and belonging, interpretations of power, sources of self-esteem, and independence.

Gibbs and Hines (1992) suggest that adolescent biracial identity resolution revolves around several developmental questions: Who am I? Where do I fit? What is my social role? Who is in charge of my life? Where am I going? These questions are windows into several areas of developmental conflicts including, racial/ethnic identity, social marginality, sexuality, autonomy and independence, and education and career aspirations. Bradshaw (1992) cautions therapists to take the time to understand the contemporary multiracial experience to contextualize the acute and at times everpresent self-consciousness present in people's lives. Lastly, Root (1994) cautions therapists not to assume that being of mixed heritage is an unresolved issue for persons coming into therapy.

10.06.8 FUTURE DIRECTIONS: RETHINKING RACE AND ETHNICITY

There are several factors driving the need for a reexamination of how we think about race and ethnicity. Unless we rethink race, the process of differentiation between ourselves and those who look different from us will often times be a destructive process of differentiation driven by unresolved conflicts and fraught with stigmatizing of bodies we have inherited from this country's history of race relations. Unless we reopen the dialogue—and a new one that considers a contemporary meaning for mixed race—we may not be able to understand contemporary ethnicity in America. Without separating the concepts of ethnicity and race, dialogues will remain confused as discomfort with the construct of race, can be evaded by changing the dialogue to one that shifts emphasis to the other construct of ethnicity, despite the negative differentiating driving the construct.

Likely the racial identity models of the 1970s and 1980s were necessary to understand and be able to educate people oppressed by the racial system in a way that promoted healing. We are now challenged to see if we can undertake a next step in healing. Can we develop models that allows us to explore the fluidity of identity in the social contexts of current and past historical moments?

10.06.9 SUMMARY

A biracial baby boom became possible with the repeal of the last antimiscegenation laws in the USA in 1967, changes in immigration laws, and global mobility of people and populations. Changes in the psychology of race and ethnicity in this last part of the century are integrally linked to these demographic changes. Nevertheless, the 10 conditions Allport (1954) hypothesized correlate with prejudicial attitudes still exist. A more critical understanding of how racial politics derive from a process of negative rather than constructive differentiation is highlighted by examining the current experience, identity process, and social location of the person of mixed racial heritage. An ecological framework for thinking about the different outcomes of racial identity is presented. Gender, geographical history, class, and generation are significant, dynamic lenses which filter many life experiences which have not been put forth in previous racial identity models. The ecological identity model can accomodate the processes proposed by past identity models. However, it accomodates increasingly more common identity development processes that do not involve traumagenic experiences despite prevailing conditions towards prejudicial attitudes. Psychological processes in resolution and integration of a multiracial location and identity are discussed in this chapter with cautions that therapists should not assume that a multiracial identity is inherently problematic. For many young people, the work of the generation before has allowed them to open a different dialogue on race. This is a challenge to society and to therapists trying to understand the process by which these people negotiate their daily lives.

10.06.10 REFERENCES

Alarcon, R. D., & Foulks, E. (1995). Personality disorders and culture: Contemporary clinical views. *Cultural Diversity and Mental Health, 1,* 3–17.

Allport, G. W. (1954). *The nature of prejudice.* Reading, MA: Addison-Wesley.

Anzaldua, G. (1987). *Borderlands/La Frontera: The New Mestiza.* San Francisco: Spinsters/Aunt Lute.

Atkinson, D. R., Morten, G., & Sue, D. W. (Eds.) (1979). *Counseling American minorities: A cross-cultural perspective.* Dubuque, IA: William C. Brown.

Banks, J. A. (1988). The stages of ethnicity: Implications for curriculum reform: In J. A. Banks (Ed.), *Multi-ethnic education: Theory and practice* (pp. 129–139). Boston: Allyn & Bacon.

Bennett, M. J. (1995). A developmental model of intercultural sensitivity. In R. M. Paige (Ed.), *Education for the intercultural experience* (pp. 29–71). Washington, DC: Intercultural Press.

Berger, J., Cohen, B. P., & Zelditch, M. J. (1966). Status characteristics and expectation states. In J. Berger, M. Zelditch, & B. Anderson (Eds.), *Sociological theories in progress 1.* Boston: Houghton Mifflin.

Bradshaw, C. K. (1992). Beauty and the beast: On racial ambiguity. In. M. P. P. Root (Ed.), *Racially mixed people in America* (pp. 77–90). Thousand Oaks, CA: Sage.

Burman, E. (1994). *Deconstructing developmental psychology.* New York: Routledge.

Carney, C. G., & Kahn, K. B. (1984). Building competencies for effective cross-cultural counseling: A developmental view. *The Counseling Psychologist, 12*(1), 111–119.

Carter, R. T. (1995). *The influence of race and racial identity in psychotherapy: Toward a racially inclusive model.* New York: Wiley.

Cross, W. E., Jr. (1971). The Negro-to-Black conversion experience: Toward a psychology of Black liberation. *Black World, 20* (9), 13–27.

Cross, W. E., Jr. (1978). Models of psychological nigrescence: A literature review. *Journal of Black Psychology, 5*(1), 13–31.

Cross, W. E., Jr. (1985). Black identity: Rediscovering the distinction between personal identity and reference group orientation. In M. Spencer, G. Brookins, & W. Allen (Eds.), *Beginnings: The social and affective development of Black children* (pp. 155–171). Hillsdale, NJ: Erlbaum.

Cross, W. E., Jr. (1991). *Shades of black: Diversity in African–American identity.* Philadelphia: Temple University Press.

Dohrenwend, B. P., & Dohrenwend, B. S. (1974). Social and cultural influences on psychopathology. *Annual Review of Psychology, 25,* 417–452.

DuBois, W. E. B. (1903, 1989). *The souls of Black folks.* New York: Bantam.

Duffy, L. K. (1978). *The interracial individuals: Self-concept, parental interaction, and ethnic identity.* Unpublished master's thesis, University of Hawaii, Honolulu.

Durkheim, E. (1966, c1951). *Suicide: A study in sociology.* (Translated by John A. Spaulding and George Simpson.) New York: Free Press.

Erikson, E. (1968). Race and the wider identity. In E. H. Erikson, *Identity, youth and crisis.* New York: Norton.

Fanon, F. (1967). *Black skin: White masks.* New York: Grove Press.

Foucault, M. (1978). *The history of sexuality: An introduction.* New York: Random House.

Frankenberg, R. (1993). *The social construction of whiteness: White women, race matters.* Minneapolis, MN: University of Minnesota Press.

Friere, P. (1970). *Pedagogy of the oppressed.* New York: Seabury.

Funderburg, L. (1994). *Black, white, and other: Biracial Americans talk about race and identity.* New York: William Morrow.

Ganter, G. (1977). The socio-conditions of the White practitioner: New perspectives. *Journal of Contemporary Psychotherapy, 9*(1), 26–32.

Gay, G. (1984). Implications of selected models of ethnic identity development for educators. *The Journal of Negro Education, 54*(1), 43–52.

Gibbs, J. T., & Hines, A. M. (1992). Negotiating ethnic identity: Issues for black–white biracial adolescents. In M. P. P. Root (Ed.), *Racially mixed people in America* (pp. 223–238). Thousand Oaks, CA: Sage.

Goffman, E. (1963). *Stigma: Notes on the management of spoiled identity.* Englewood Cliffs, NJ: Prentice-Hall.

Gordon, L. R. (1995). Critical "Mixed Race"? *Social Identities, 1*(2), 381–395.

Gordon. L. R. (1997). Race, sex, and matrices of desire in an antiblack world: An essay in phenomenology and social role. In N. Zack (Ed.), *Race/sex: Their sameness, difference and interplay* (pp. 117–132). New York: Routledge.

Griffin, S. (1992). *A chorus of stones: The private life of war.* New York: Doubleday.

Gurin, P., Hurtado, A., & Peng, T. (1994). Group contacts and ethnicity in the social identities of Mexicanos and Chicanos. *Personality and Social Psychology Bulletin, 20*(5), 521–532.

Hall, C. C. I. (1980). *The ethnic of racially mixed people: A study of Black-Japanese.* Unpublished doctoral dissertation, University of California, Los Angeles.

Hall, C. C. I. (1992). Please choose one: Ethnic identity choices for biracial individuals. In M. P. P. Root (Ed.), *Racially mixed people in America* (pp. 250–264). Thousand Oaks, CA: Sage.

Helms, J. E. (1984). Toward a theoretical explanation of the effects of race on counseling: A black and white model. *The Counseling Psychologist, 12*(4), 153–165.

Helms, J. E. (1990). An overview of Black racial identity theory. In J. E. Helms (Ed.), *Black and White racial identity: Theory, research, and practice* (pp. 9–32). New York: Greenwood Press.

Helms, J. E., & Carter, R. T. (1990). Development of the White Racial Identity Inventory. In J. E. Helms (Ed.), *Black and White racial identity: Theory, research, and practice* (pp. 67–80). New York: Greenwood Press.

Hilliard, A. G., III (1996). Either a paradigm shift or no mental measurement: The nonscience and the nonsense of the Bell curve. *Cultural Diversity and Mental Health, 2,* 1–20.

Huang, L. N. (1994). An integrative view of identity

formation: A model for Asian Americans. In E. P. Salett & D. R. Koslow (Eds.), *Race, ethnicity and self* (pp. 42–59). Washington, DC: National Multicultural Institute.

Hurtado, A., & Gurin, P. (1995). Ethnic identity and bilingualism attitudes. In A. M. Padilla (Ed.), *Hispanic psychology: Critical issues in theory and research* (pp. 89–103). Thousand Oaks, CA: Sage.

Jackson, B. (1975) Black identity development. In L. Golubchick & B. Persky (Eds.), *Urban social and educational issues* (pp. 158–164). Dubuque, IA: Kendall-Hall.

Janoff-Bulman, R. (1992). *Shattered assumptions: towards a new psychology of trauma.* New York: The Free Press.

Jones L. (1994). *Bulletproof diva: Tales of race, sex and hair.* New York: Praeger.

Kich, G. K. (1982). *Eurasians: Ethnic/racial identity development of biracial Japanese/white adults.* Unpublished doctoral dissertation, Wright Institute Graduate School of Psychology, Berkeley, CA.

Kich, G. K. (1992). The developmental process of asserting a biracial, bicultural identity. In M. P. P. Root (Ed.), *Racially mixed people in America* (pp. 304–320). Thousand Oaks, CA: Sage.

Lal, B. B. (1995). Symbolic Interaction Theories. *American Behavioral Scientist, 38*(3), 421–441.

Lerner, G. (1986). *The creation of patriarchy.* New York: Oxford University Press.

McRoy, R. G., & Hall, C. C. I. (1996). Transracial adoptions: In whose best interest? In M. P. P. Root (Ed.), *The multiracial experience: Racial borders as the new frontier* (pp. 63–78). Thousand Oaks, CA: Sage.

Milliones, J. (1980). Construction of a Black consciousness measure: Psychotherapeutic implications. *Psychotherapy: Theory, Research, and Practice, 17*(2), 175–182.

Mittelberg, D., & Waters, M. C. (1992). The process of ethnogenesis among Haitian and Israeli immigrants in the United States. *Ethnic and Racial Studies, 15*(3), 412–435.

Oetting, E. R., & Beauvais, F. (1990–91). Orthogonal cultural identification theory: The cultural identification of minority adolescents. *The International Journal of Addictions, 25* (5A & 6A), 655–685.

Olmedo, E. L. (1979). Acculturation: A psychometric perspective. *American Psychologist, 34,* 1061–1070.

Omi, M., & Winant, H. (1986). *Racial formation in the United States from the 1960s to the 1980s.* New York: Routledge & Kegan Paul.

Padilla, A. M. (Ed.) (1980). *Acculturation: Theory, models and some new findings.* Boulder, CO: Westview.

Parham, T. (1989). Cycles of nigrescence. *The Counseling Psychologist, 17,* 187–226.

Park, R. E. (1931). Mentality of racial hybrids. *American Journal of Sociology, 36,* 534–551.

Phinney, J. (1989). Stages of ethnic identity development in minority group adolescents. *Journal of Early Adolescence, 9,* 34–39.

Phinney, J. (1990). Ethnic identity in adolescents and adults: A review of research. *Psychological Bulletin, 108,* 499–514.

Ramirez, M., III (1983). *Psychology of the Americas: Mestizo perspectives on personality and mental health.* New York: Pergamon.

Ramirez, M., III (1997). *Multicultural/multiracial psychology: Mestizo perspectives in personality and mental health.* Northvale, NJ: Jason Aronson.

Root, M. P. P. (1990). Resolving "Other" status: Identity development of biracial individuals. In L. S. Brown & M. P. P. Root (Eds.), *Diversity and complexity in feminist therapy.* New York: Harrington Park Press.

Root, M. P. P. (Ed.) (1992). *Racially mixed people in America.* Thousand Oaks, CA: Sage.

Root, M. P. P. (1994). Mixed race women. In L. Comas Diaz & B. Greene (Eds.), *Women of color and mental health: The healing tapestry.* New York: Guilford Press.

Root, M. P. P. (Ed.) (1996a). *The multiracial experience: Racial borders as the new frontier.* Thousand Oaks, CA: Sage.

Root, M. P. P. (1996b). The multiracial experience: Racial borders as a significant frontier in race relations. In M. P. P. Root (Ed.), *The multiracial experience: Racial borders as the new frontier.* Thousand Oaks, CA: Sage.

Root, M. P. P. (in press). The biracial baby boom: Understanding ecological constructions of racial identity in the twenty-first century. In E. Hollins & R. H. Sheets (Eds.), *Racial, ethnic, cultural human development: Implications for education.* New York: Erlbaum.

Sartre, J.-P. (1976) translation by A. Sheridan-Smith). *Critique of dialectical reasoning: Theory of practical ensembles.* London: New Left Books.

Singelis, T. M., Triandis, H. C., Bhawuk, D. P. S., & Gelfand, M. J. (1995). Horizontal and vertical dimensions of individualism and collectivism: A theoretical and measurement refinement. *Cross-cultural Research, 29*(3), 240–275.

Spickard, P. R. (1989) *Mixed blood: Intermarriage and ethnic identity in twentieth-century America.* Madison, WI: University of Wisconsin Press.

Spickard, P. R. (1992). The illogic of American racial categories. In M. P. P. Root (Ed.), *Ratially mixed people in America* (pp. 12–23). Thousand Oaks, CA: Sage.

Stephan, C. W. (1992) Mixed-heritage individuals: Ethnic identity and trait characteristics. In M. P. P. Root (Ed.), *Racially mixed people in America* (pp. 50–63). Thousand Oaks, CA: Sage.

Stoler, A. (1995). *Race and the education of desire: Foucault's history of sexuality and the colonial order of things.* Durham, NC: Duke University Press.

Stonequist, E. V. (1964). The marginal man: A study in personality and culture conflict. In E. Burgess & D. J. Bogue (Eds.), *Contributions to urban sociology.* Chicago: University of Chicago Press.

Tajfel, H. (1981). *Human groups and social categories.* Cambridge, UK: Cambridge University Press.

Thomas, C. (1971). *Boys no more.* Beverly Hills, CA: Glencoe Press.

Trimble, J. E. (1996). Accumulturation, ethnic identification, and the evaluation proces. In A. H. Buyer, F. L. Brisbane, & A. Romirez (Eds.), *Advanced methodological issues in culturally competent evaluation for substance abuse prevention.* Center for Substance Abuse Prevention, Cultural Competence Series 6, Department of Human and Health Services, Publication (SMA) 96-3110

Trimble, J. E. (in press). Social psychological perspectives on changing self-identification among American Indian and Alaska natives. In R. H. Dana (Ed.), *Handbook of cross-cultural/multi-cultural personality assessment.* Mahweh, NJ: Erlbaum.

Vontress, C. E. (1970). Counseling Blacks. *Personnel and Guidance Journal, 48,* 713–719.

Waters, M. S. (1990). *Ethnic options: Choosing identities in America.* Berkeley, CA: University of California Press.

Weinreich, P. (1986). The operationalisation of identity theory in racial and ethnic relations. In J. Rex & D. Mason (Eds.), *Theories of race and ethnic relations* (pp. 299–320). Cambridge, UK: Cambridge University Press.

Williams, G. H. (1995). *Life on the color line: The true story of white boy who discovered he was black.* New York: Dutton.

Williams, T. K. (1992). Prism Lives: Identity of Binational Amerasians. In M. P. P. Root (Ed.), *Racially mixed people in America* (pp. 280–303). Thousand Oaks, CA: Sage.

Wilson, W. J. (1987). *The truly disadvantaged: The inner city, the underclass, and public policy*. Chicago: University of Chicago Press.
Young, R. (1995). *Colonial desire: Hybridity in theory, culture and race*. New York: Routledge.
Zack, N. (1993). *Race and mixed race*. Philadelphia: Temple University Press.
Zack, N. (Ed.) (1995). *American mixed race: The culture of microdiversity*. Lanham, MD: Rowman & Littlefield.
Zack, N. (Ed.) (1997a). *Race/Sex: Their sameness, their difference*. New York: Routledge.
Zack, N. (1997b). The American sexualization of race. In N. Zack (Ed.), *Race/Sex: Their sameness, difference, and interplay* (pp. 145–156). New York: Routledge.

10.07
The Psychology of Gender and Health

RICHARD M. EISLER
Virginia Polytechnic Institute and State University, Blacksburg, VA, USA

10.07.1 INTRODUCTION 161
10.07.2 GENDER AND EPIDEMIOLOGY OF HEALTH PROBLEMS 162
10.07.3 HISTORICAL PERSPECTIVE ON GENDER DIFFERENCES 163
10.07.4 THEORETICAL OVERVIEW OF GENDER DIFFERENCES 164
10.07.4.1 Biological Perspective 164
10.07.4.2 Social Psychological Perspective 165
10.07.4.3 Cross-cultural Perspective 165
10.07.4.4 Summary of Gender and Health Perspectives 166
10.07.5 THE ROLE OF PSYCHOLOGICAL STRESS IN WOMENS' AND MENS' HEALTH 166
10.07.5.1 Gender and Biological Vulnerability to Stress 166
10.07.5.2 Gender and Cognitive Vulnerability to Stress 167
10.07.5.3 Gender Role Stress 167
10.07.5.4 Gender Roles and Coping with Stress 168
10.07.6 GENDER DIFFERENCES IN SELF-DISCLOSURE AND HELP SEEKING 168
10.07.6.1 Gender and Emotional Expression 169
10.07.6.2 Gender and Social Support 169
10.07.6.3 Gender and Help Seeking 170
10.07.7 FUTURE DIRECTIONS 170
10.07.8 SUMMARY 171
10.07.9 REFERENCES 171

10.07.1 INTRODUCTION

Why is it important for a discourse on the psychology of health to focus on gender issues? Most importantly, there has been a shift in the conception of healthcare practices over the past few decades from the biomedical model to the biopsychosocial model. The biomedical model had limited the assessment and treatment of disease to the biological components of organs, biochemicals, and infectious agents. In this model biochemical problems caused by faulty organs or infectious agents resulted in illness. The biomedical model served us well 100 years ago, when the leading causes of death were tuberculosis, pneumonia, and influenza. The leading causes of death today, however, such as cardiovascular disease and lung cancer, have psychosocial etiologies that may be more comprehensively evaluated and treated by understanding cultural risk factors, including gender determinants.

In the current biopsychosocial model of health, biological disease processes are acknowledged, but psychosocial factors that predispose one to illness are strongly emphasized. The psychosocial components encompass engaging in high-risk behaviors, appraising and coping with stress, utilizing social support systems, and the seeking of appropriate help from the healthcare system. In all the aforementioned psychosocial areas, recent research has shown that there are important sex or gender distinctions, the evaluation of which is crucial for the prevention of illness and the maintenance of health. These psychosocial issues are the focus of this chapter.

It has been evident that many health problems occur with different frequencies among men and women. Paradoxically, while women are more likely than men to have most of the nonfatal chronic illnesses and acute medical conditions, more men than women die of each of the 12 leading causes of death (Wingard, 1984). There are also important differences in the types of stress to which each gender is subjected. For example, research has shown that working women have greater gender role stresses than working men, in that they have to manage both family and work roles (Frankenhaeuser, Lundberg, & Chesney, 1991). Further, it appears that marriage itself contributes differentially to the health of women as contrasted to men. Married men report lower rates of mental and physical health problems than single men. Married women, on the other hand, report higher rates of mental health problems than single women. Finally, women are far more vulnerable to sexual and physical abuse than men in their intimate relationships (Koss et al., 1994).

Another gender-related health issue is the frequency and quality of each sex's interaction with the professional healthcare system. Across most age categories men have a lower frequency of physician office visits than women, and less than a third as many visits to a mental health professional. Pennebaker (1982) theorized that underutilization of the healthcare system by men compared to women may be the result of men's tendency to disregard the importance of their symptoms. Another possibility could be that men are reluctant to visit caregivers because it conflicts with masculine gender role imperatives to appear strong and tolerate pain (Eisler & Blalock, 1991). Not only do women and men utilize healthcare systems differently, but healthcare systems may also respond differently to each gender. If similar kinds of symptoms are reported by each sex, women are more likely than men to be diagnosed with a mental or nervous condition (Travis, 1988). In addition, physicians may be less likely to diagnose women with diseases that they consider to be most prevalent in men, such as heart disease.

Thus, we may conclude that there are very significant reasons for including gender in studying the psychology of health. More than half of the mortality from the 10 leading causes of death may be traced to lifestyle risk factors on which women and men differ significantly (Verbrugge, 1989). Divergent gender roles produce large variations in exposure to and coping with stress, which result in different vulnerabilities to various disorders. Also, men and women have different values regarding the importance of social support and preventive healthcare practices. Finally, existing research protocols have primarily been designed to assess the causes of health problems in white males. It is clear that this is inadequate for understanding treatment issues for women and other cultural groups.

It is instructive to note here that the current convention is to use the term "sex" when referring to reliable biological distinctions between males and females. Sex refers to biological characteristics including chromosome pattern, and genital structure. However, "gender" is the term preferred by psychologists to denote the idea that men and women are socialized to display "masculine" and "feminine" characteristics and behavior patterns. The term sex will be used henceforth to denote the biological aspects of individuals, and gender will be used to refer to the socially constructed roles deemed socially appropriate for either men or women.

10.07.2 GENDER AND EPIDEMIOLOGY OF HEALTH PROBLEMS

Recent epidemiological data on the association between gender and health have documented gender differences in "premature mortality" based on more hazardous lifestyles and behavior patterns engaged in by men compared to women (Harrison, Chin, & Ficarrotto, 1989). In the USA, women live, on average, about seven years longer than men. The death rate for men is higher than for women at all ages and for all leading causes of death (Verbrugge, 1985). Men have twice the rate of premature death from coronary artery disease, and they are three times more likely to die in motor vehicle accidents than are women. In addition, Waldron and Johnson (1976) have noted that mens' death rates from lung cancer have been nearly six times that of women, and twice as high from cirrhosis of the liver.

In terms of psychological dysfunction, men are much more prone to a higher incidence of personality and behavior disorders. In a review of epidemiological studies, Cleary (1987) noted that men have been three times more likely to be problem drinkers and four times as likely to be diagnosed with alcoholism than are women. It was also evident in this review that men were more likely than women to abuse drugs and to be diagnosed with antisocial personality disorder. In addition, a review by Widom (1984) cited evidence that men, far more than women, are involved in violent crime, including armed robbery and homicide. Widom also noted that men are much more likely than women to be involved in sexual deviance and more frequently are perpetrators of child and spouse abuse. Taken together, these statistics suggest that men more than women tend to employ antisocial and aggressive means in dealing with conflicts and personal problems. This is consistent with the evidence reported by Huselid and Cooper (1994) that men are more inclined than women to "externalize" their distress through aggressive and hazardous coping strategies.

On the other hand, there is convincing evidence that women may suffer from more "internalized" psychological distress than men (Huselid & Cooper, 1994). Women's stereotypic gender roles associated with passivity and self-blame may be responsible for their greater vulnerability to internalizing disorders such as anxiety and depression. In an early study, Weissman and Klerman (1977) reviewed 40 studies in over 30 countries before concluding that women were two to three times more likely than men to suffer from depression. The greater incidence of depression in women has been confirmed in a large-scale community study of the mental health of over 20 000 residents in different US cities (Robins et al., 1984). With respect to the anxiety disorders, Robins et al. showed that women had higher prevalence rates of agoraphobia, panic disorder, and obsessive-compulsive disorders than men. In an extensive review, Attie and Brooks-Gunn (1987) described weight concerns and chronic dieting as the focus of constant stress in women as being directly responsible for the extraordinarily high ratio of eating disorders (anorexia and bulimia) in women compared to men.

From the above discussion, we may conclude that there have been significant gender differences in incidence of different disorders, including psychological dysfunction. It is also apparent that gender roles mediate male vs. female differences in expressions of psychopathology in response to stress. In the remaining sections of this chapter, we will be concerned with the historical and theoretical studies of gender differences, gender roles and one's vulnerability to stress, and how each gender handles and expresses emotional distress. In addition, we discuss how each gender seeks help for their psychological problems through informal support systems and professional counseling. Finally, we explore how these perspectives may influence the future directions of the investigations concerned with gender and health.

10.07.3 HISTORICAL PERSPECTIVE ON GENDER DIFFERENCES

While philosophers and social scientists have deliberated for ages about the essential qualities of women compared to men, the first systematic attempt by psychologists to synthesize a large body of research data about the psychological differences between the sexes may be traced to Maccoby and Jacklin's classic work *The Psychology of sex differences* published in 1974. Maccoby and Jacklin's volume reviewed over 1400 of the available psychological studies which conducted statistical comparisons of the sexes on their intellectual abilities and social behavior. Their purpose, as stated in the introduction, was to "sift the evidence" to determine which of the many (stereotypic) beliefs about presumed differences between the sexes had a solid basis in fact and which did not. Overall, they concluded from the data that the sexes differed much less than commonly held cultural stereotypes had indicated. Based on the evidence, the authors found sex differences in a few intellectual abilities: verbal, quantitative, and spatial skills. However, Maccoby and Jacklin argued that the evidence was negative or inconclusive with regard to differences in social behavior, with the notable exception that boys tended to display more aggression than girls. Finally, they drew attention to the fact that differences among individuals within each gender were often as great as the average differences between genders. Once again, the point was made that the ability of the individual, not the individual's gender, was most important.

With respect to the potential sources of verified sex differences, such as aggression, Maccoby and Jacklin acknowledged that biological predispositions based on sex could interact with psychosocial experiences to determine the psychological and social characteristics of the person. However, the authors indicated that the biological bases for these psychological characteristics of women and men could not be specified with any degree of certainty.

Interestingly, and probably not coincidently, the publication of Maccoby and Jacklin's (1974) volume coincided with the early phases of the feminist movement in the USA. At that time feminist theory had a political as well as a scientific stake in gender research (Eagly, 1995). Two of the major feminist political agendas were to discover scientific data to show that: (i) women were intellectually just as capable as men, and (ii) gender stereotypes that depicted women socially or emotionally at a disadvantage compared to men were false. This agenda required an interpretation of the data that showed there were no meaningful differences between the basic abilities of men and women, which would then give women equal opportunity with men to succeed in society. While feminist ideology may have biased gender research of the 1970s toward the conclusion that there was little evidence of sex differences, research in the mid-1980s and 1990s returned to more refined theoretical questions about the origin and health implications of gender similarities and differences.

A thorough critique of Maccoby and Jacklin's (1974) synthesis regarding the evidence of significant gender differences in intellectual and social abilities is beyond the scope of this chapter. Suffice it to say that subsequent to their review, more sophisticated quantitative analyses comparing gender differences in a variety of skills and social behavior have followed. These have included meta-analytic studies of gender differences in decoding nonverbal cues (Hall, 1978), conformity and influenceability (Becker, 1986), and helping and aggressive behaviors (Eagly & Crowley, 1986), to name just a few. While the significance of these newer findings is hotly debated, the conclusions reached by more recent work have been that there are in fact functional gender distinctions in such areas as empathy (Eisenberg & Lennon, 1983), leadership (Eagly & Karau, 1992), and the incidence of psychological disorders such as depression (Nolen-Hocksema, 1987). In addition, nontrivial gender differences in important social behaviors have been reviewed and discussed by gender researchers (Daly & Wilson, 1988; Deaux & Major, 1987; Eagly & Wood, 1991).

10.07.4 THEORETICAL OVERVIEW OF GENDER DIFFERENCES

Having established that gender differences exist in certain psychological and behavioral domains, we can turn to questions more pertinent to the present chapter on the relationship between gender and health psychology. For instance, why do males and females sometimes differ considerably, moderately, or not at all in their vulnerability to physical and psychological disorders? To what extent are the sources of these distinctions biological, environmental, or an interaction between both?,Furthermore, how does the health of the individual depend on her or his social roles and abilities? Shifting from the question of whether gender differences exist to explaining why males and females are predisposed to different health problems requires testable theories about how gender differences come about and what biopsychosocial forces maintain them.

Most modern theories about the origin of gender difference adopt an "interactional" perspective, whereby the biological features of each sex interact with the social environment to produce the observed gendered behavior of men and women. On the one hand, however, it is fair to say that theories that give prominence to "biological" features treat gendered behavior as arising primarily from characteristics that are built into the person prior to social experience. On the other hand, social psychological theories regard gendered behavior as primarily arising out of the interaction between the person and his or her social environment.

10.07.4.1 Biological Perspective

Few modern theories attempt to explain the differences in the behavior of men and women solely in terms of biological forces. Recently, Buss and Schmitt (1993) and Kenrick (1994) have advocated what has been termed "evolutionary psychological theory" to account for some different features in the behavior of the sexes. Evolutionary psychology, which was first applied to nonhuman species, is based on the premise that biologically based sex differences have evolved over time, employing the Darwinian notion of sexual selection (Buss, 1995). These biologically oriented psychologists have postulated that there are sex differences in genetic make-up or differences in the structural features of females' and males' brains. Presumably, these biological distinctions have evolved over time to produce functionally useful aspects of masculine behavior for men, and feminine behavior for women. Evolutionary psychology predicts that males and females will be similar in those domains in which the sexes have faced similar adaptive problems. For example, both sexes have similar preferences for fats, sugars, and salt because both sexes have faced similar food consumption problems. However, in some domains the sexes will have faced different problems. For instance, men have evolved to have greater skills in spatial visualization than women, because men have had a greater need to develop these skills for hunting. Women, on the other hand, have faced the adaptive challenge of securing sufficient food to carry them through pregnancy and lactation; therefore, evolution might have favored selection of women who developed the ability and features to attract mates to help them through this period. Thus, evolutionary psychology predicts distinctive male and female behavior in areas where sexual selection has favored the development of the physically and psychologically different adaptive characteristics for men and women. Presently, the evolutionary account of sex differences is regarded by many gender researchers as highly speculative. However, this perspective has presumably generated testable hypotheses (Eagly, 1995).

10.07.4.2 Social Psychological Perspective

Over the past several decades, a diverse group of scientists has contributed to the social psychology of gender, which in its simplest description investigates how gendered behavior is defined, created, and maintained for each sex through social norms and social interaction. Social psychological theories that feature discussions about the acquisition of disparate gender roles and how "sex-typed" gender roles create stress-related problems for men compared to women have generated much of the recent data on gender and behavior for clinical health psychologists. For example, the masculine gender imperative for men always to appear invulnerable may be related to their reluctance to seek medical or psychological care. Similarly, the feminine gender imperative for women to be ever youthful and attractive may contribute to excessive dieting among women, which may in turn render women especially vulnerable to eating disorders.

The following are a few examples of the contributions of social psychologists that view gender distinctions more as a social construction than a biological reality. Bem (1981, 1982) contributed to gender role theory by supposing that children develop cognitive schema to organize information about the world and themselves in terms of socially desirable masculine or feminine traits. That is, at an early age, boys and girls learn to judge their adequacy as people based on whether their thoughts and behavior are in conformity with social norms for their gender. For example, women may be reluctant to be assertive about their needs because it conflicts with their gender schema about appearing appropriately conciliatory. A man's gender schema might direct him not to express his true worries and concerns because it is inconsistent with masculine values to show one's emotional vulnerability. "Never let them see you sweat" was an often quoted line from a men's deodorant commercial. Indeed, an individual's own behavior is constantly being scrutinized by his or her own cognitive commitments to being in conformity with masculine or feminine ideology.

In addition to what we as women or men consider is acceptable behavior for our gender, social psychological research has shown that a great deal of our behavior is based on what others expect from us solely on the basis of our being male or female. Geiss (1993) and Maccoby (1990) have reviewed research which showed that our sex-typed expectations of each sex tends to generate "self-fulfilling prophecies" in producing the behavior expected of our gender. For example, if we expect a woman to be submissive in the presence of a dominant male colleague, she may well conform to this "feminine" expectation in his presence. However, she might not act submissively with her husband who does not expect her to act in a stereotypically feminine way. Because we expect males not to show their pain, we might see a little leaguer get up smiling defiantly after being knocked down by a fast ball at the plate. Moreover, it is evident that our own beliefs about how each gender should think and act, as well as others' expectations about how we as women or men should think and act are major determinants of our behavior. The notion that gendered behavior is socially constructed and enforced by society to provide distinctive roles and behaviors for men and women has important implications for people who live in diverse cultures. If the behavior of women is largely the result of cultural imperatives, we would expect the behavior of women to differ depending on the culture in which they live.

10.07.4.3 Cross-cultural Perspective

Cross-cultural research on gender has been concerned with the degree to which each gender's attitudes and behaviors are either invariant across cultures or may be different depending on the distinctive features of one's cultural environment. Let us frame the question in another way. Are men less expressive of tender emotions than women in all cultures? If the answer to this question is yes, it would mean that inexpressiveness is intrinsic to all individuals who are biologically male, no matter what their social environment. On the other hand, if a man's emotional expressiveness depends on the particular culture in which he is found, then we would have evidence that expressiveness in men is largely determined by cultural forces.

While the study of cultural differences in gendered behavior is still in its infancy, Williams and Best (1990) have collected some interesting data on sex role ideology, sexual stereotypes, and work values in 14 different countries. Their results showed a high degree of agreement between men and women living within a given country about expected gender roles. However, there were important differences in social expectations about distinctive gender roles across different cultures. For example, within developed Protestant countries, both genders emphasized the importance of men behaving assertively and having power and possessions to a greater extent than women and men in the less economically developed countries. Also, men and women were seen as necessarily more distinctive in their gender roles by people in developed countries, while people from less developed countries tended to see the gender roles of males and females as more similar. Williams and Best (1990) concluded that the effect of culture was greater than the effect of biological sex in determining the expected behavior of women compared with men.

10.07.4.4 Summary of Gender and Health Perspectives

Taken as a whole, research examining the basis for gendered behavior seems to demonstrate that biological differences between the sexes may establish predispositions for certain kinds of health problems. Female hormones have been found to offer protection from heart disease prior to women's menopause. Greater cardiovascular reactivity in men may predispose males to coronary artery disease. However, most researchers would agree that sociocultural forces appear to have the most profound effect on predisposing each gender to different health risks. In the following sections we hope to show that the mechanisms linking gender to health involves, to a great extent, gender differences in beliefs about health, exposure to certain health risks, gender determined roles, and gender relevant stresses and coping styles.

10.07.5 THE ROLE OF PSYCHOLOGICAL STRESS IN WOMENS' AND MENS' HEALTH

At this point we have some theoretical perspectives about the acquisition and maintenance of socially constructed gender roles related to socially accepted behavior for women as distinct from acceptable behavior for men. We now move to a discussion about how each gender evaluates and copes with the stressors to which each may be exposed. This is crucial in our understanding of the nature of the relationship between gender and vulnerability to specific health problems. We begin with an orientation to the biological and psychological features of stress and coping as they relate to health.

10.07.5.1 Gender and Biological Vulnerability to Stress

Modern theories of how stressful situations produce health problems for each sex are based on the notion that psychological responses to stress produce aberrant physiological or cognitive responses that may be different for women and men. For example, it has been demonstrated that men produce larger increases in blood pressure in response to some forms of stress than women (Stoney, Davis, & Matthews, 1987). The question of how differences in the sex hormones estrogen, progesterone, and testosterone affect gender differences in health has also been a novel area of study. There has been some evidence that the female hormone estrogen is protective against atherosclerosis for women, whereas testosterone may enhance the risk of this disease for men (Polefrone & Manuck, 1987). In addition, there appear to be consistent differences between women and men in healthy immune function, which is suppressed by gender related stresses (Kiecolt-Glaser & Glaser, 1987). Women, for example, exhibit higher immunoglobulin levels than men, and produce larger antibody response to infection than do men (Michaels & Rogers, 1971).

Psychologists and other scientists who have accumulated large quantities of data over the years about stress have concluded that stress is prominently involved in the production of a myriad of physical and psychological disorders (see Goldberger & Breznitz, 1982; Neufield, 1989). During the latter part of the twentieth century, conceptions of stress have evolved and have repeatedly shown that biological responses and the psychological make-up of a person interact with environmental pressures to produce deleterious somatic and mental health problems. Psychological stress has been acknowledged to pose health risks for both medical and psychological types of disorders (Goldberger & Breznitz, 1982; Neufield, 1989). The fact that psychological stressors may be the origin of either mental or somatic health problems, and the fact that biological and psychological systems have been shown to interact have tended to blur earlier distinctions between the two categories of health problems.

Currently, sophisticated views about stress describe an interaction between biological and psychosocial factors. First, there are gender differences in the probability that each gender will be exposed to a particular stressful situation. For example, women are more likely to be exposed to the stress of sexual harassment and rape than men. Divorced women compared to divorced men are more likely to be exposed to the dual stresses of having to earn a living and manage a family. However, men may be more stressed than women at some work sites because men have been expected to deal with physically hazardous situations (e.g., working in a coal mine) to a greater extent than women. In addition to the nature of the environmental events, modern views about stress focus on the individual's cognitive appraisal of the threat and her or his psychological coping strategies.

10.07.5.2 Gender and Cognitive Vulnerability to Stress

Mediating the relationship between traumatic events and physiological stress arousal are cognitive processes that assess the nature of the threat (Lazarus & Folkman, 1984; Neufield, 1989). According to Lazarus and Folkman (1984), psychological stress involves the relationship between the person and the environment that is appraised by the person as taxing or exceeding his or her coping resources and endangering his or her well-being. Thus, the interaction between our cognitive evaluations of particular situations and our assessment of our abilities to manage those problems physically and psychologically defines the stress process for us as individuals.

Furthermore, according to Lazarus and Folkman, the strength of one's commitment to a particular outcome increases vulnerability to stress. Therefore, should a woman become extremely committed to losing weight, her vulnerability to stress will be proportional to the strength of her commitment to weight loss. These concepts about stress have been adopted by most clinical health psychologists, whether they work with psychological disorders such as anxiety and depression, or with the effects of stress on biological systems, such as in the cases of gastric ulcers and coronary heart disease.

10.07.5.3 Gender Role Stress

A fair amount of evidence has linked sex differences in the incidence of various health problems to gender differences in appraisal of stress and utilization of coping responses (see Barnett, Biener, & Baruch, 1987; Baum & Grunberg, 1991; Collins & Frankenhaeuser, 1978). Building on the previous cognitive conceptualizations of stress, the present author and his colleagues have developed a paradigm describing gender role stress to explain how one's commitment to gender role ideology produces stress that may lead to gender-related health problems.

Incorporating Pleck's (1981) initial notions about the stress imposed by gender roles, we have developed a model that independently evaluates masculine gender role stress (MGRS) for men and feminine gender role stress (FGRS) for women. This gender role stress model reflects our attempt to account for some of the vulnerability of women and men to contrasting health problems (Eisler, 1995; Eisler & Blalock, 1991; Eisler & Skidmore, 1987; Eisler, Skidmore, & Ward, 1988; Gillespie & Eisler, 1992; Lash, Eisler, & Schulman, 1990; Lash, Gillespie, Eisler, & Southard, 1991; Martz, Handley, & Eisler, 1995; Watkins, Eisler, Carpenter, Schectman, & Fisher, 1991).

The gender role stress paradigm includes several major components. The first of these is the development of gender schema through social learning environments, which tend to reward the development of masculine conceptions of self for boys and feminine conceptions of self for girls. Opposite gender conceptions of self tend to be strongly discouraged. For example, boys are rewarded for acting tough and girls for being nice. Boys are punished for acting feminine (sissy) and girls for acting aggressively (bitchy). These gender schema are then utilized to evaluate whether or not a particular situation may be threatening. Expressing feelings of vulnerability tends to be far more stressful for men than women. On the other hand, many women are much more concerned about their looks than men so that a substantial weight gain is more stressful to women. Finally, one's gender schema guide each person's choice of coping responses. A man whose masculine gender schema promotes highly vigorous means of coping with stress may rely extensively on aggression to cope with stress, whereas a woman might feel that aggressive displays were inconsistent with her feminine gender schema of how women should act.

According to this paradigm, gender role stress may result from faulty gender determined appraisals of the situation, in that a man's expression of fear (feminine) need not lead to environmental stress for him, whereas acting in a forceful (masculine) manner might reduce the environmental pressures felt by a woman. Alternatively, gender role stress may result from excessive reliance on socially approved masculine or feminine coping styles. For example, a man's reliance on a hostile or combative style of coping with stress may be dysfunctional in that it produces chronic physiological arousal leading to a heart attack. A woman who copes with stresses by the continual expression of dysphoric emotions and rumination about her difficulties could end up feeling helpless and depressed. Consequently, gender role norms have helped create gender role coping strategies for an individual based purely on his or her gender. Living up to these culturally defined masculine or feminine expectations may, in itself, be difficult for each gender, and produce stress or dysfunctional appraisal and coping behavior.

10.07.5.4 Gender Roles and Coping with Stress

A major issue linking gender role stress and health has involved gender differences in coping with stress. As we alluded to earlier, consistent with their gender roles, men are more likely to externalize and women internalize their stress (Huselid & Cooper, 1994). Therefore, masculine ideology specifies different kinds of coping behavior for men than feminine ideology does for women. Because of social norms, men are more likely to utilize instrumental aggressive behaviors and displays of dominance to cope with their problems than women. However, women may be more likely to ruminate and engage in self-blame in response to crises in their lives because this behavior is more consistent with feminine gender role expectations.

When we look at gender-related coping styles, we can see that some health problems may result from dysfunctional coping styles associated with one's gender role. For example, most psychological disorders involving antisocial and abusive behavior reflect exaggerated aggressive coping styles typically used by men. This might explain why there is a strikingly high incidence of men compared to women who commit crimes of violence (Widom, 1984). Also, women make more suicide attempts than men, yet men are more likely to succeed in killing themselves. Psychological disorders utilizing passive, stereotypical feminine coping styles are disorders that show higher prevalence rates for women, such as anxiety disorders and obsessive-compulsive disorders. Learned helplessness (Seligman, 1975), a major cognitive theory of depression, is more consistent with enacting the feminine rather than the masculine role. Admittedly, much research remains to be done to demonstrate that there are direct relationships between masculine or feminine gender roles and gender role coping strategies responsible for particular disorders. However, the possibilities are intriguing, and we have conducted a number of preliminary studies to evaluate the possible association between gender role stress and coping and potentially adverse health effects.

Utilizing the MGRS scale (Eisler and Skidmore, 1987), we found that there were significant associations between the MGRS scale measure and self-reported anger, anxiety, anger, and poor health habits in men (Eisler & Skidmore, 1987; Eisler, Skidmore, & Ward, 1988). In addition, Lash, Eisler, and Schulman (1990) showed that men with a high score on the MGRS scale, compared to men with a low score, were subject to greater increases in blood pressure when the stressor dealt with masculine relevant tasks in which men were expected to perform well. No differences between men with high and low MGRS scale scores were noted when the task was concerned with feminine behaviors or tasks not particularly relevant to expected male gender roles. Additional studies by Lash et al. (1991) showed that women had greater increases in their blood pressure responses than men if the stress threatened areas that were inherent in the female gender role, including nurturance and child rearing. Watkins et al. (1991) showed that high gender role stress was associated with coronary-prone type A behavior and elevated blood pressure in both men and women. Martz et al. (1995) found that FGRS scores could distinguish women who had eating disorders from women who had other psychiatric conditions. Gillespie and Eisler (1992) showed that women who had high scores on the FGRS scale reported more depression than did women low in feminine role stress.

As a whole, these studies have demonstrated that responses to stress have gender components in that women are more likely than men to be stressed by events that the culture has specified as especially important to women's gender roles. Similarly, men are more subject to stress when the situation requires expected masculine behaviors. These studies have also tended to indicate that gender differences in favored coping styles may be predictive of the types of disorder that men compared with women are prone to develop.

10.07.6 GENDER DIFFERENCES IN SELF-DISCLOSURE AND HELP SEEKING

In this section we consider gender issues in the expression of emotion, the ability to elicit or utilize social support, and the inclination to seek help for personal problems. These are gender differences that may have profound implications for the health of women compared to men. The majority of verbal psychological therapies used in Western countries rely on the assumption that expressing one's feelings about past traumatic or painful events has a healing effect. Pennebaker (1995) has been foremost among researchers attempting to understand the beneficial effects of emotional disclosure on psychological and physical health. In the introductory chapter of his book *Emotion, disclosure, and health*, Pennebaker (1995) has reviewed the evidence that full expression of emotion reduces rumination and worry and promotes cognitive resolution of disturbing events. He also cites laboratory studies which show that disclosure of upsetting events has produced reductions in sympathetic nervous system arousal, including blood pressure and muscle tension. Other studies have shown that improvement in immune function is another benefit of self-disclosure (Petrie, Booth, & Davison, 1995). In reviewing the research detailed in chapters in Pennebaker's book by experts on psychopathology, psychophysiology, and counseling, one is struck by the evidence that the tendency to share emotional experiences has great power in increasing interpersonal intimacy, which in turn tends to buffer stress for the individual.

How do the genders compare on the tendency to express emotion and create social support networks to buffer stress? Is the ability to express innermost feelings related to an individual's tendency to seek help for emotional turmoil? These questions about emotional expression, social support, and the willingness to seek help for psychological and other health problems are very much interrelated issues. Hence we now turn to a discussion of gender differences in emotional expression, gender distinctions in the ability to develop social support networks, and the tendency for women as contrasted to men to seek professional help for health problems.

10.07.6.1 Gender and Emotional Expression

In a review of literature on gender differences in emotional expression Sauer and Eisler (1990) found that, almost without exception, women were more self-disclosing than men. However, it did appear that men self-disclosed more to women than to other men. Eagly and Wood (1991) explained these gender differences in terms of the widespread belief in our culture that women are more emotionally sensitive, more socially skilled, and more concerned with maintaining personal relationships than are men. Eisler and Blalock (1991) proposed an alternative possibility: that expressing feelings other than anger is perceived by men as "feminine" behavior, which is contrary to their masculine role. Finally, while developing a measure of MGRS, Eisler and Skidmore (1987) found that men found it significantly more stressful than women to express feelings of affection or fear. However, this might not be true for men in other cultures.

10.07.6.2 Gender and Social Support

The evaluation of social support in psychology has been hampered by a lack of agreement on a single definition of support and a broad range of measures. However, most researchers agree that the functions of social support include providing assistance in obtaining resources, problem solving, and bolstering self-worth (Belle, 1987). Research has shown that other mechanisms by which social support is associated with health are: (i) decreasing the supported persons's feelings of isolation and loss of self-esteem; (ii) attenuating the perception of certain events as highly threatening; and (iii) reducing physiological reactivity to stress (Shumaker & Hill, 1991).

Throughout the lifespan, evidence indicates that females are more likely to have supportive confidants than men. While the relative size of womens' and mens' support networks varies, womens' investment in supportive disclosing relationships consistently tends to exceed those of men (Belle, 1987). While mens' supportive relationships center around shared activities and experiences, womens' relationships emphasize shared emotional intimacy. Females are more likely both to seek and to receive social support in times of stress than men (Wolchik, Sandler, & Braver, 1984). Women are also more likely than men to be supportive as friends. Finally, the evidence indicates that men have much more restricted social networks than women. In fact, married men tend to rely almost exclusively on their spouses for support, whereas married women utilize other relatives and friends for support (Belle, 1987). The potential downside of this for women is that large social networks may be emotionally stressful as well as being supportive.

The impact of social support on the overall health of women compared to men is far from clear. We do know from the above data that women are more likely than men to participate in stress-buffering social networks and are more able to mobilize social support in times of stress. Women also provide more frequent and more effective support to others of both sexes.

Schumaker and Hill (1991) have concluded that the role of social support in womens' and mens' health awaits greater numbers of women to add power to the comparative health studies and more sophisticated measures of social support. We now turn to some data from the counseling literature on the relationship between gender and the tendency to seek help for health problems.

10.07.6.3 Gender and Help Seeking

A crucial determinant of preventing disorder and maintaining health involves the desire and ability to seek help for problems at an early stage of difficulty. Nearly 70% of all clients seeking psychological help are female. Furthermore, one in three women, as compared to one in seven men, has sought help from a mental health professional at some point during her life (Collier, 1982). Psychologists concerned with gender issues have written extensively about a strong association between the masculine gender role and the comparative reluctance of men to seek help for psychological problems (Eisler, 1990; Good, Dell, & Mintz, 1990; Scher, 1990). Until recently, most forms of psychotherapy were developed by men to be practiced on women by male psychotherapists. This unfortunate evolution of the provider–client relationship has created problems in the delivery of health services to both women and men.

In order to understand why men seek psychological and other health services as a last resort, we need to appreciate the demands of the masculine gender role and the fact that most forms of counseling have required behavior that may be regarded as feminine. Writers on mens' issues have theorized that client characteristics required by most forms of counseling and psychotherapy are completely antithetical to the masculine gender role (Eisler, 1990; Eisler & Blalock, 1991; Scher, 1990). Conventional wisdom is that, for counseling to be successful, the client must acknowledge personal problems, be willing to self-disclose, tolerate feelings of interpersonal vulnerability, and be willing to submit control of the central issues in one's life to an outsider. All these therapeutic expectations are completely contrary to what males have been taught is essential to perform adequately as a man.

Men are raised to see their world as an adversarial place where a man must attain mastery of the world by being independent and cope with stress by wielding power and not by revealing his vulnerabilities. Men perceive a basic incongruity between what is expected from them as men in society and what is expected of them as consumers of health services. The result of this is that men typically perceive going for help with personal problems as an intolerable loss of personal control and power. Psychotherapists perceive the behavior of most of their male clients as defensive, emotionally constricted, and insensitive because the male role of "invincibility" appears inconsistent with seeking help. We must conclude that, for many men, entrenched masculine values continue to be an important obstacle to seeking and receiving help for health problems.

10.07.7 FUTURE DIRECTIONS

Expanding our understanding of health from a biomedical enterprise to a biopsychosocial paradigm requires a greater understanding of health beyond assessment and treatment of disease processes and infectious agents. More comprehensive views of health require an understanding of psychological and sociocultural factors. An individual's beliefs and attitudes, and his or her perception of and exposure to stress that differentially affect the risk of illness have been shown to have important gender and cultural components. How these psychosocial components interact with biological systems continues to be a fascinating area for further theory and research. Research on health should endeavor to employ a more equal distribution of women and men, as well as to sample more individuals from different ethnic groups.

Many of the health problems of the twenty-first century that are reflected in premature mortality and morbidity will be preventable by attention to changes in lifestyle risk factors and creation of lower stress environments for people of different gender and cultural backgrounds. For example, preliminary research has shown that cultural and gender differences in dietary patterns, smoking, alcohol consumption, and high-risk sexual and aggressive behaviors are significantly related to differential risks of mortality and morbidity in different cultural groups (Anderson, 1995).

More research is needed to understand the different kinds of stress factors to which women and men and people from different cultural groups are exposed. Clearly, racism, sexism, and economic hardship variously constitute major stress and health risks for different groups. Presently, health research has focused on specific health problems such as heart disease, the effectiveness of smoking cessation programs, cancer screening tests, and blood pressure monitoring programs. Perhaps this should be supplemented by comprehensive studies examining the health risks to which diverse populations are exposed. For example, how are the dietary patterns and smoking habits of diverse populations including Asian, Black, White, and Latino women and men related to different rates of acute and chronic illness?

Based on these analyses, it appears that preventive health interventions are inadequately guided if they do not consider individuals as inseparable from their gender and cultural beliefs and roles. Men experience, appraise, and cope with stress differently than women, and these cognitions and behaviors undoubtedly vary for women and men belonging to different cultural groups as well. Therefore, to be successful in providing health interventions to diverse populations, we will need to address the social and cultural differences among these diverse groups of women and men.

10.07.8 SUMMARY

As stated in the introduction, research and practice in healthcare delivery has recently focused our attention on psychosocial risk factors in addition to the traditional emphasis on biology. A major aspect of this shift has been to study gender and cultural variables that affect group differences in prevention practices, health maintenance, activities, and differences in outcome. Many of our conclusions have been based on differences in cultural responses to stress and studying lifestyle risk factors for different groups.

It was apparent from our review that women and men experience different rates of both somatic and mental health problems, including anxiety disorders, excessive anger problems, certain types of cancer, and premature heart disease to cite just a few examples. Taken as a whole, the bases for differences in womens' and mens' health were found to be related to an interaction of biological differences with psychosocial risk factors or lifestyles. More specifically, gender differences in appraisal and coping with stress was discussed as a major factor accounting for a significant amount of variance in mens' and womens' health problems.

For example, gender differences in expressing emotion and tendency to seek help from the healthcare system were shown to have major implications for gender variations in health outcome. Gender differences in social support were difficult to evaluate because of problems of definition for empirical research. We concluded that the improved health care of the twenty-first century will be more attuned to research on the psychosocial characteristics of individuals who have different risk profiles for different medical and psychological disorders throughout their lifespan.

10.07.9 REFERENCES

Anderson, N. B. (1995). Behavioral sociocultural perspectives on ethnicity and health: Introduction to the special issue. *Health Psychology, 14,* 589–591.

Attie, I., & Brooks-Gunn, J. (1987). Weight concerns as chronic stressors in women. In R. C. Barnett, L. Biener, & G. K. Baruch (Eds.), *Gender and stress* (pp. 219–254). New York: Free Press.

Barnett, R. C., Biener, L., & Baruch, G. K. (Eds.) (1991). *Gender and stress.* New York: Free Press.

Baum, A., & Grunberg, N. E. (1991). Gender, stress, and health. *Health Psychology, 10*(2), 80–85.

Becker, B. J. (1986). Influence again: An examination of reviews and studies of gender differences in social influence. In J. S. Hyde & M. C. Linn (Eds.), *The psychology of gender: Advances through meta-analysis* (pp. 178–209). Baltimore: Johns Hopkins University Press.

Belle, D. (1987). Gender differences in the social moderators of stress. In R. C. Barnett, L. Biener, & G. K. Baruch (Eds.), *Gender and stress* (pp. 257–277). New York: Free Press.

Bem, S. (1981). Gender schema theory: A cognitive account of sex typing. *Psychological Review, 88,* 354–364.

Bem, S. (1982). Gender schema theory and self-schema theory compared: A comment on Markus, Crane, Bernstein, and Siladi's "Self-schemas and gender." *Journal of Personality and Social Psychology, 43,* 1192–1194.

Buss, D. M. (1995). Psychological sex differences: Origins through sexual selection. *American Psychologist, 50,* 164–168.

Buss, D. M., & Schmitt (1993). Sexual strategies theory: An evolutionary theory on human mating. *Psychological Review, 100,* 204–232.

Cleary, P. D. (1987). Gender differences in stress related disorders. In R. C. Barnett, L. Biener, & G. K. Baruch (Eds.), *Gender and stress* (pp. 39–72). New York: Free Press.

Collier, H. V. (1982). *Counseling women: A guide for therapists.* New York: Macmillan.

Collins, A., & Frankenhaeuser, M. (1978). Stress responses in male and female engineering students. *Journal of Human Stress, 4,* 43–48.

Daly, M., & Wilson, M. (1988). *Homicide.* New York: Aldine de Gruyter.

Deaux, K., & Major, B. (1987). Putting gender into context: An interactive model of gender-related behavior. *Psychological Review, 94,* 369–389.

Eagly, A. H. (1995). The science and politics of comparing women and men. *American Psychologist, 50,* 145–158.

Eagly, A. H., & Crowley, M. (1986). Gender and helping behavior: A meta-analytic view of the social psychological literature. *Psychological Bulletin, 100,* 283–308.

Eagly, A. H., & Karau, S. S. (1991). Gender and the emergence of leaders: A meta-analysis. *Journal of Personality and Social Psychology, 60,* 685–710.

Eagly, A. H., & Wood, W. (1991). Explaining sex differences in social behavior: A meta-analytic perspective. *Personality and Social Psychology Bulletin, 17,* 306–315.

Eisenberg, N., & Lennon, R. (1983). Sex differences in empathy and related capacities. *Psychological Bulletin, 94,* 100–131.

Eisler, R. M. (1990). Gender role issues in the treatment of men. *Behavior Therapist, 13,* 57–60.

Eisler, R. M. (1995). The relationship between masculine gender role stress and men's health risk: The validation of a construct. In R. F. Levant & W. S. Pollack (Eds.), *A new psychology of men.* New York: Basic Books.

Eisler, R. M., & Blalock, J. (1991). Masculine gender role stress: Implications for the assessment of men. *Clinical*

Psychology Review, 11, 45–60.
Eisler, R. M., & Skidmore, J. R. (1987). Masculine gender role stress: Scale development and component factors in the appraisal of stressful situations. *Behavior Modification, 11,* 123–136.
Eisler, R. M., Skidmore, J. R., & Ward, C. H. (1988). Masculine gender role stress: Predictor of anger, anxiety, and health risk behaviors. *Journal of Personality Assessment, 52,* 133–141.
Frankenhaeuser, M., Lundberg, U., & Chesney, M. (1991). *Women, work, and health: Stress and opportunities.* New York: Plenum.
Geiss, F. L. (1993). Self-fulfilling prophecies: A social psychological view of gender. In A. E. Beall & R. S. Sternberg (Eds.), *The psychology of gender* (pp. 9–55). New York: Guilford Press.
Gillespie, B. L., & Eisler, R. M. (1992). Development of the feminine gender role stress scale. *Behavior Modification, 16,* 426–438.
Goldberger, L., & Breznitz, S. (Eds.) (1982). *Handbook of stress: Theoretical and clinical aspects.* New York: Free Press.
Good, G. E., Dell, D. M., & Mintz, L. B. (1989). Male role and gender role conflict: Relations to help seeking in men. *Journal of Counseling Psychology, 36,* 295–300.
Hall, J. A. (1978). Gender effects in decoding non-verbal cues. *Psychological Bulletin, 85,* 845–857.
Harrison, J., Chin, J., & Ficarrotto, T. (1989). Warning: Masculinity may be dangerous to your health. In M. S. Kimmel & M. A. Messner (Eds.), *Men's lives* (pp. 296–309). New York: Macmillan.
Huselid, R. F., & Cooper, M. L. (1994). Gender roles as mediators of sex differences in expressions of pathology. *Journal of Abnormal Psychology, 103,* 595–603.
Kenrick, D. T. (1994). Evolutionary social psychology: From sexual selection to social cognition. In M. P. Zanna (Ed.), *Advances in experimental social psychology* (Vol. 26, pp. 75–121). San Diego, CA: Academic Press.
Kiecolt-Glaser, J., & Glaser, R. (1987). Psychosocial moderators of immune function. *Annals of Behavioral Medicine, 9*(2), 16–40.
Koss, M. P., Goodman, L. A., Browne, A., Fitzgerald, L. F., Keita, G. P., & Russo, N. F. (1994). *No safe haven: Male violence against women at home, at work, and in the community.* Washington, DC: American Psychological Association.
Lash, S. J., Eisler, R. M., & Schulman, R. S. (1990). Cardiovascular reactivity to stress in men. *Behavior Modification, 14,* 3–20.
Lash, S. J., Gillespie, B. L., Eisler, R. M., & Southard, D. R. (1991). Sex differences in cardiovascular reactivity: Effects of the gender relevance of the stressor. *Health Psychology, 6,* 392–398.
Lazarus, R. S., & Folkman, S. (1984). *Stress, appraisal and coping.* New York: Springer.
Maccoby, E. E. (1990). Gender and relationships: A developmental account. *American Psychologist, 45,* 513–520.
Maccoby, E. E., & Jacklin, C. N. (1974). *The psychology of sex differences.* Stanford, CA: Stanford University Press.
Martz, D. M., Handley, K. B., & Eisler, R. M. (1995). The relationship between feminine gender role stress, body image, and eating disorders. *Psychology of Women Quarterly, 19,* 493–508.
Michaels, R. H., & Rogers, K. D. (1971). A sex difference in immunologic responsiveness. *Pediatrics, 47,* 120–123.
Neufield, R. W. (Ed.) (1989). *Advances in the investigation of psychological stress.* New York: Wiley.
Nolen-Hocksema, S. (1987). Sex differences in unipolar depression: Evidence and theory. *Psychological Bulletin, 101,* 259–282.
Pennebaker, J. W. (1982). *The psychology of physical symptoms.* New York: Springer.
Pennebaker, J. W. (Ed.) (1995). *Emotion, disclosure, & health.* Washington, DC: American Psychological Association.
Petrie, K. J., Booth, R. J., & Davison, K. P. (1995). Repression, disclosure, and immune functioning: Recent findings and methodological issues. In J. W. Pennebaker (Ed.), *Emotion, disclosure, and health.* New York: Springer.
Pleck, J. (1981). *The myth of masculinity.* Cambridge, MA: MIT Press.
Polefrone, J. M., & Manuck, S. B. (1987). Gender differences in cardiovascular and neuroendocrine response to stressors. In R. C. Barnett, L. Biener, & G. K. Baruch (Eds.), *Gender and stress* (pp. 13–38). New York: Free Press.
Robins, L. N., Helzer, J. E., Weissman, M. M., Orvaschel, H., Gruenberg, E., Burke, J. D., & Regier, D. A. (1984). Lifetime prevalence of specific psychiatric disorders in three sites. *Archives of General Psychiatry, 41,* 949–958.
Sauer, M. H., & Eisler, R. M. (1990). The role of masculine gender role stress in expressivity and social support network factors. *Sex Roles, 23,* 261–271.
Seligman, M. E. (1975). *Helplessness: On depression, development, and death.* San Francisco: Freeman.
Scher, M. (1990). Effect of gender role incongruities on men's experience as clients in psychotherapy. *Psychotherapy, 27,* 322–326.
Shumaker, S. A., & Hill, D. R. (1991) Gender differences in social support and physical health. *Health Psychology, 10(2),* 102–111.
Stoney, C. M., Davis, M. C., & Matthews, K. A. (1987). Sex differences in physiological responses to stress and in coronary heart disease: A causal link? *Psychophysiology, 24,* 127–131.
Travis. C. (1988). *Women and health psychology.* Hillsdale, NJ: Erlbaum.
Verbrugge, L. M. (1985). Gender and health: An update on hypothesis and evidence. *Journal of Health and Social Behavior, 26,* 156–182.
Verbrugge, L. M. (1989). The twain meet: Empirical explanations of sex differences in health and mortality. *Journal of Health and Social Behavior, 30,* 282–304.
Waldron, I., & Johnson, S. (1976). Why do women live longer than men? *Journal of Human Stress, 2,* 19–29.
Watkins, P. L., Eisler, R. M., Carpenter, L., Schectman, K. B., & Fisher, E. B. (1991). Psychosocial and physiological correlates of male gender role stress among employed adults. *Behavioral Medicine, 17,* 86–90.
Weissman, M., & Klerman, G. L. (1977). Sex differences in the epidemiology of depression. *Archives of General Psychiatry, 34,* 98–111.
Widom, C. S. (Ed.) (1984). *Sex roles and psychopathology.* New York: Plenum.
Williams, J. E., & Best, D. L. (1990). *Measuring sex stereotypes: A thirty-nation study* (Rev. ed.). Beverley Hills, CA: Sage.
Wingard, D. (1984). The sex differential in morbidity, mortality, and lifestyle. *Annual Review of Public Health, 5,* 433–458.
Wolchik, S. A., Sandler, I. N., & Braver, S. L. (1984). *The social support networks of children of divorce.* Paper presented at the American Psychological Association meeting, Toronto.

10.08
A Cultural Perspective on Families Across the Life Cycle: Patterns, Assessment, and Intervention

Outline

NADINE J. KASLOW and KEITH A. WOOD
Emory University School of Medicine, Atlanta, GA, USA
and
MONICA R. LOUNDY
Georgia State University, Atlanta, GA, USA

10.08.1 INTRODUCTION 174

10.08.2 DEFINITION OF TERMS AND CONCEPTS 175

10.08.2.1 Culture 175
10.08.2.2 Family 175
10.08.2.2.1 Normal and dysfunctional family processes 176

10.08.3 CULTURE AND THE FAMILY LIFE CYCLE 177

10.08.3.1 Family Life Cycle 177
10.08.3.2 Significance of Family Life Transitions Across Cultures 177
10.08.3.3 Rituals Denoting Family Transitions Across Cultures 177
10.08.3.4 Migration: A Life Cycle Transition Unique to Immigrant Families 178

10.08.4 FAMILY LIFE CYCLE STAGES: A CULTURAL PERSPECTIVE 179

10.08.4.1 The Joining of Families Through Marriage: The New Couple 179
10.08.4.1.1 Marriage: a life cycle transition 179
10.08.4.1.2 Intermarriage 181
10.08.4.2 Becoming Parents: Families with Young Children 181
10.08.4.2.1 Childbirth 181
10.08.4.2.2 Childrearing 181
10.08.4.2.3 Attachment 182
10.08.4.2.4 Developing a personal identity 182
10.08.4.2.5 Developing an ethnic identity 183
10.08.4.2.6 Developing effective coping strategies 184
10.08.4.3 Families of Adolescents 184
10.08.4.3.1 Separation-individuation 185
10.08.4.3.2 Ethnic identity development 185
10.08.4.3.3 Achievement 186
10.08.4.3.4 Dating and sexuality 186
10.08.4.4 Launching Children, Single Young Adults Leaving Home, and the Middle Generation Moving On 187
10.08.4.4.1 Cultural values and norms on launching 188

10.08.4.4.2 Leaving home: single young adults 188
10.08.4.4.3 Conflicts experienced by the middle generation 189
10.08.4.4.4 Dealing with parental illness and death 189
10.08.4.5 Families in Later Life 189
10.08.4.5.1 Definition of the elderly 190
10.08.4.5.2 Issues confronting the elderly 190
10.08.4.5.3 Immigrant elderly 190
10.08.4.5.4 Ethnic identity 191
10.08.5 CULTURALLY SENSITIVE FAMILY ASSESSMENT AND INTERVENTION 191
10.08.5.1 Values 191
10.08.5.2 Help-seeking Patterns 192
10.08.5.3 Adherence 193
10.08.5.4 Culturally Sensitive Techniques 193
10.08.5.4.1 Stance of the therapist 193
10.08.5.4.2 Development of the working alliance 194
10.08.5.4.3 Assessment process 194
10.08.5.4.4 Intervention process 195
10.08.5.5 Culturally Sensitive Techniques Across the Life Cycle 197
10.08.5.5.1 The joining of families: culturally sensitive assessment and intervention 197
10.08.5.5.2 Families with young children: culturally sensitive assessment and intervention 198
10.08.5.5.3 Families with adolescents: culturally sensitive assessment and intervention 199
10.08.5.5.4 Launching children, single young adults leaving home, and the middle generation moving on: culturally sensitive assessment and intervention 200
10.08.5.5.5 Families in later life: culturally sensitive assessment and intervention 200
10.08.6 FUTURE DIRECTIONS 201
10.08.7 SUMMARY 202
10.08.8 REFERENCES 202

10.08.1 INTRODUCTION

Family theory and therapy and the multicultural perspective offer complementary views on assessment and intervention (Gushue & Sciarra, 1995). Both approaches share the assumption that the individuals must be understood within their larger familial and sociocultural context (Gushue & Sciarra, 1995). Thus, a comprehensive assessment and intervention should attend to the complex interactions among the individual, the family, and the culture across the family life cycle (Carter & McGoldrick, 1989; Szapocznik & Kurtines, 1993).

Family theorists and therapists increasingly have underscored the importance of the cultural context in which family therapy is conducted (e.g., Falicov, 1983; Ho, 1987; McGoldrick, Giordano, & Pearce, 1996; McGoldrick, Pearce, & Giordano, 1982). They have come to appreciate therapeutic models as reflecting the culture within which they are developed and practiced. Family theorists have become attuned to the role of culture and values in the conceptualization of interactive processes. Consistent with this, family therapists have become more cognizant of the impact of culture, values, and theoretical stance on the assessment and intervention process and outcome. These changes in perspective have led more family theorists and therapists to view each individual as a member of a family system that exists within a context of cultural diversity (Szapocznik & Kurtines, 1993).

After defining terms and concepts (e.g., culture, family) central to a discussion of a cultural perspective on families across the life cycle, a detailed presentation of cultural characteristics of families across the family life cycle is offered. Adapting the work of Carter and McGoldrick (1989), information is provided on cultural group differences across the major family life cycle stages. The aforementioned sections lay the groundwork for a discussion of culturally sensitive family assessment and intervention across the family life cycle. The theoretical underpinnings of family therapy from a culturally informed perspective are reviewed and culturally sensitive family assessment and intervention approaches in the United States are delineated. Hopefully, the information provided will inform psychologists about ways to adapt and modify current practices to enhance the cultural fit between the assessment and intervention approach and the family. Additionally, given the considerable intra- and intercultural variation in family patterns, it is our goal to present information that will help psychologists better treat families with whom they share a common cultural heritage and families from a different cultural background than their own.

We hope the reader will bear in mind the following caveats regarding our presentation. First, there is a lack of clarity in the literature regarding the distinction between culture and ethnicity. We use the term culture to refer broadly to values, attitudes, and behaviors that characterize groupings of people who are influenced by their culture of origin, religion, race, and socioeconomic status (SES). Second, the cultural characterizations presented are not meant as stereotypes of specific groups. Instead, the depictions reflect generalizations regarding common family patterns associated with a given cultural group (Falicov, 1983). These generalizations require validation at the level of the individual family. Third, and in a related vein, this chapter incorporates an intercultural perspective in which the definitions of what is appropriate or normal family structure, values, communication patterns, and interactional processes are seen as varying across different cultures. Although this chapter does not attend to individual differences between families within a given culture (intracultural perspective), we want to underscore the importance of attending to the unique characteristics of each family, which are often affected by such variables as the phase of acculturation, the stage of ethnic identity, and each members' choice of a primary language(s) both within the family system and in the larger community (Gushue & Sciarra, 1995). Fourth, due to space considerations, only a limited number of examples of some family cultures are provided. For in-depth reviews of families from specific cultures, and for coverage of a greater breadth of families, the reader is referred to McGoldrick, Pearce, and Giordano (1982) and McGoldrick, Giordano, and Pearce (1996). Fifth, it is not our intention to suggest that culture is the only or primary factor that impacts the family life cycle. Culture is one variable that interacts with multiple factors in influencing a family's presentation and effective assessment and intervention approaches. The salience of cultural issues differs across families, as does the significance of cultural factors in assessment and intervention. Thus, it behoves clinicians and researchers to incorporate culture as a key, albeit not sole, element in their work with families.

10.08.2 DEFINITION OF TERMS AND CONCEPTS

To set the stage for a discussion of culture and the family life cycle and culturally sensitive assessment and intervention, a number of terms warrant definition.

10.08.2.1 Culture

For this chapter, culture is defined as the totality of tacit behaviors, ideas and knowledge, attitudes, values, beliefs, customs, language, and technology shared by a group of people and transmitted by families from one generation to the next (Bullrich, 1989). Cultural patterns are influenced by multiple factors, including ethnicity, race, SES, education, gender roles, sexual orientation, country of origin, current residence, migration, religious and political affiliations, and family life cycle stage. Cultural norms and values inform family members' roles and rules regarding family membership and structure, rituals, help seeking behavior, problem definition and resolution, communication styles, expression of affect, and feelings about life, death, and illness (Carter & McGoldrick, 1996). In sum, culture is a dynamic and evolving process reflecting the interaction between a family's and a group's collective history and ongoing experiences in a particular context.

10.08.2.2 Family

Historically, the dominant American definition of family has focused on the intact, nuclear, heterosexual family unit, connected by blood or legal bonds, the members of which typically reside in one domicile. During the past few decades, the definition of the American family has expanded to include myriad constellations of emotional subsystems, such as step and remarried families, foster and adopted families, and cohabitating heterosexual, lesbian, gay, and bisexual couples.

With the multifaceted complexion of America, the definition of "family" varies among cultural groups (McGoldrick et al., 1996). For example, African-Americans' definition of family often refers to a wide network of kin and community and extended family members (e.g., grandparents, aunts, uncles, cousins) and non-family members (e.g., very close neighbors and friends, church leaders, boyfriends) who function as part of one's psychological family. It is understood that all members of this family will provide assistance and guidance in various aspects of family life including child rearing, caring for the elderly, providing material resources, and offering support during crises and transitions (Billingsley, 1992; Boyd-Franklin, 1989).

In the Latino community, the term family frequently connotes a close network of blood relatives that spans three or four generations. This network often includes nonblood members (e.g., godparents, legally adopted children whose adoptions have not been formalized). The traditional concept of the nuclear family has little meaning or applicability in the Latino subculture (Garcia-Preto, 1996).

Historically, the definition of family in certain Asian cultures (e.g., Chinese) included ancestors and descendants as well as living nuclear and extended family members. These families were patriarchal in structure. However, the Chinese-American family has evolved such that the contemporary family consists primarily of members of the nuclear family in which there is a more egalitarian sharing of roles across gender lines. This shift in family structure may reflect an accommodation to the dominant culture, the reality that only certain family subgroups immigrated to the US, and an increased emphasis on functional relationships (Lee, 1996).

In some Native American cultures, the primary parental functions are played by the grandparents and thus the key bond is between the children and the grandparents. The term grandparent in these families may refer to grandparents by blood, godparents, maternal or paternal great aunts, and so on. In many Native American families, no distinctions are made between one's family of origin and in-law family; these families are blended, rather than joined by marriage (Sutton & Nose, 1996).

10.08.2.2.1 Normal and dysfunctional family processes

Historically, family theories (for review, see N. J. Kaslow, Celano, & Dreelin, 1995) have portrayed the family as structured according to clearly defined, static, gender-based roles and family composition and have viewed the stability of the family household as the major family unit (Wamboldt & Reiss, 1991). These models also delineated the primary tasks to be accomplished by the typical family (Wamboldt & Reiss, 1991). For the most part, however, until recently, when detailing normal family structure and processes, these models failed to consider the effects of gender, social class, ethnicity, race, and sexual orientation (N. J. Kaslow et al.). This is unfortunate given that a Eurocentric model of normalcy is not applicable across cultures (e.g., Jamaican-Americans, Japanese-Americans, African-Americans) (e.g., Boyd-Franklin, 1989; Dechesnay, 1986; Hsu, Tseng, Ashton, McDermott, & Char, 1985).

For instance, while the role of the parental child is often viewed as indicative of dysfunction in the family structure, in many low-income African-American families, parentification of children may reflect a family's adaptive response to their economic conditions (Boyd-Franklin, 1989). In these families, the presence of a parentified child is dysfunctional only when these young people are inundated with abdicated, rather than delegated, responsibilities at the expense of their development (Boyd-Franklin, 1989). As another example, the extent to which triangulation (two opposing family members demand that a third person support him or her against the opposing party) within the family should be interpreted as reflecting maladaptive family patterns depends on the cultural context. In nuclear family structures common to EuroAmericans, triangulation reflects family pathology and thus may destabilize the family unit. In extended family structures common to many African-American, Asian, and Latino families, in which cross-generational executive subsystems (e.g., mother and grandmother) are normative, triangulating a child is less likely to affect the marital dyad negatively because authority lines are clear and the exclusion of one parent is not perceived as rejection (Falicov, 1983).

These examples highlight the fact that the cultural validity of various family theories and theoretical constructs (e.g., kinship, division of labor, proximity and hierarchy, triangulation, parentification) require empirical examination prior to making claims about universal v. culturally specific models of family normality and dysfunction (Boyd-Franklin, 1989; Fisek, 1991; Tseng, 1985). In addition, differences in family interactions between cultural groups (e.g., Japanese-American vs. Caucasian families in Hawaii) may be attributed to cultural factors, thus, it is essential that culture-specific profiles of healthy family functioning be devised (Hsu et al., 1985). If distinct, culture-specific portrayals of normal family functioning are not developed and validated empirically, normal interactions among family members that are disparate from those observed in the majority culture may be misconstrued as pathological (Hsu et al.).

Theories on normal and abnormal family functioning are socially constructed and shaped by the evolving cultural context (Walsh, 1993). Even the value placed on distinguishing between functional (i.e., normal) and dysfunctional family processes varies across cultures. While such a distinction has been of paramount importance in mainstream American culture, the conceptual dichotomy associated with the distinct categories of normal and abnormal is antithetical to the underlying assumptions of human behavior characteristic of many non-western societies (Foulks, 1991). Given that definitions of normal behavior vary across cultural groups, and the utility of the construct of normality differs between Western and non-Western societies, it behoves therapists to refrain from classifying certain family patterns as dysfunctional solely because they deviate from the norms of the dominant culture (Walsh, 1993). Rather, only families who manifest interactional processes discordant with the cultural context in which they are embedded and/or are associated with elevated levels of distress or problems establishing relationships with other cultural group members, require intervention (Foulks, 1991; Wamboldt & Reiss, 1991). For example, a person raised in a Southern African-American family affiliated with a Pentecostal Church who believes that their symptoms can be attributed to rootwork (a malevolent form of magic) may not be psychotic, particularly if these beliefs are shared by the family (Hillard, 1982). Although mental health services may be required, the patient and family may benefit from the assistance of a rootdoctor, who can remove a hex from the patient (Hillard, 1982). This example highlights that it is a challenge for therapists both to refrain from falsely ascribing dysfunction to a culturally normative pattern or exaggerating the significance of culture at the cost of failing to identify dysfunctional patterns (Falicov, 1983).

10.08.3 CULTURE AND THE FAMILY LIFE CYCLE

To present coherently the wealth of material on cultural characteristics of families across the life span, we organize our discussion using a family life cycle framework (Carter & McGoldrick, 1989), which provides a breadth and depth of insight into family functioning in all stages of development. This rubric is applicable to families from myriad cultures.

10.08.3.1 Family Life Cycle

The family life cycle, a circular model of normal family development, identifies key transitional stages of the family. First applied to intact, middle class, mainstream Euro-American families, this model divides the life span into six stages reflecting significant events in the lives of family members: unattached young adulthood, young couples, transition to parenthood, families with adolescents, launching, and families in later life (Carter & McGoldrick, 1989). As the composition of family units has evolved, the model has been revised to incorporate additional life cycle stages observed in families who experience divorce, single parenthood, and remarriage (Carter & McGoldrick, 1989). An additional life cycle transition pertinent to immigrant families, and thus relevant to this chapter, is that of migration.

Significant intra- and extrafamilial stress are evidenced by many families during family life cycle transitions. Elevated stress levels are associated with disruption in the emotional processes identified with each stage, as well as with the requisite second-order changes in family status that accompany each family life cycle stage. Thus, families often seek or require mental health services during key transition points.

10.08.3.2 Significance of Family Life Transitions Across Cultures

Cultural factors impact families' definitions of the nature, timing, tasks, and rituals of life cycle transitions, as well as the significance the family attaches to each transition (Carter & McGoldrick, 1989). For example, in Amish-American families, births are understood as gifts from God and associated with increased standing in the community; thus, births represent a transition of particular importance in the Amish community (Emery, 1996). Births are major events in many other groups, including most Latino cultures.

The shift from adolescence to adulthood, marked by the ritual of the Bar or Bar Mitzvah, is the most salient transition in Jewish-American tradition (Davis, 1988). The transition to adulthood is also one of importance in the Amish culture, denoted by the individual's decision to join the church and marriage (Emery, 1996). In many Latino cultures, *quinceaneras* (at 15, girls are given a party in honor of their coming of age) mark the adolescence to adulthood transition. Depending on the country of origin and the social class, the elaborateness of these festivities and the associated religious ceremonies vary.

Marriage is a highly valued family life cycle stage that carries considerable status in many cultural groups (e.g., Italian-American, Puerto Rican, West Indian). Finally, in some cultures, death is the most significant transition. This is the case for Irish-American families who emphasize rituals associated with mourning (e.g., wake).

10.08.3.3 Rituals Denoting Family Transitions Across Cultures

Cultures also differ in the rituals used to connote major life events (Carter & McGoldrick, 1989). For example, there are notable differences in the rituals associated with a child's birth. In the Jewish-American tradition, the birth of a son includes a celebration (*bris*) when the circumcision takes place. In response to the increased value placed upon females in the Jewish culture, baby naming ceremonies and parties have become more common for girls. In the Roman Catholic community, birth is marked by the baptism. In some Latino Catholic subcultures, baptism is accompanied by parties marking the beginning of a life long relationship among the child, parents, and godparents.

Marriage and wedding rituals are strikingly different across ethnic groups. An African tradition, adopted by many African-Americans, is jumping the broom, in which the couple jump together over a broom to mark their union. The broom signifies the beginning of homemaking for the couple. Consistent with ancient Chinese tradition, Chinese-American women may wear red wedding gowns. Red symbolizes prosperity, fertility, and good luck. In addition, before the wedding, the groom and bride give tea to elder family members as a token of appreciation for having been nurtured. Family members bless them with red packets of money that represent support for having a good life. In the Iranian community, the wedding is a spontaneous occasion, held at the bride's family's home in the presence of close relatives. Family members stand and clap during the ceremony, and the bride and groom are seated as they take their marriage vows.

Family and community behaviors that mark death differ significantly (McGoldrick, Hines, Lee, & Preto, 1986). For example, for Irish-American families, funerals are times of drinking and story and joke telling. In the African-American community, funerals are marked by a public expression of grief and moving spirituals. The funerals of Puerto Rican families are characterized by crying, screaming, and *ataques* (i.e., hysterical, convulsive reactions). In Chinese-American families, survivors are expected to cry without inhibition at the wake and funeral. To facilitate the deceased person's transition to the afterlife, and to insure that the next life is a good one, loved ones burn paper money and clothing and present elaborate spreads of food. Other dealth-related rituals that differ across cultural groups relate to the timing of the funeral (e.g., African-American Muslims and Jews bury the dead person quickly, whereas Hindus in America allow many days to elapse between one's death and burial) (McGoldrick et al., 1996) and the preparation of the deceased for the burial (e.g., in the African-American Muslim and Orthodox Jewish communities, often the deceased person's corpse is cleansed by individuals of the same sex as the deceased and given a ritual ablution) (McGoldrick et al., 1996).

Consistent with the evolving nature of the American family, rituals have been designed to mark transitions in a broader array of family constellations, such as welcoming adopted members, addressing remarriage, supporting lesbian and gay couples in making public their commitment to one another, and acknowledging divorce (Imber-Black, Roberts, & Whiting, 1988; F.W. Kaslow, 1993; Scrivner & Eldridge, 1995). Although historically, certain cultures (e.g., Orthodox Jews) have had divorce ceremonies for the purpose of freeing each partner to remarry and for acknowledging the legitimate birth of subsequent children, only recently has such a ritual been recommended for individuals across cultures. F. W. Kaslow (1993) presents a framework for conducting a divorce ceremony to help each partner heal from the pain of the termination of a failed union. In this ceremony, each partner affirms the positive aspects of the relationship and acknowledges that the children represent an important product of their union. The children are encouraged to process the impact of the divorce and to articulate expectations regarding future involvements with each parent.

10.08.3.4 Migration: A Life Cycle Transition Unique to Immigrant Families

Migration, a unique life cycle transition of immigrant families, reflects a developmental process of family adjustment with impact across multiple generations. The process of the immigrant family's transition to a new culture occurs on a continuum, and includes a number of specific stages: preparatory, active migration, overcompensation, decompensation, and transgenerational phenomena (Sluzki, 1979). Successful immigration is associated with both maintenance of the family's cultural identity and integration into the new culture; both tasks require reorganization of the family unit and the development of complex elaborations of family structure and processes (Bullrich, 1989). Although the migration process varies across cultures and is affected by the family's stage of development, cultural patterns, and the characteristics of the new culture, there are similarities in family patterns associated with the migratory process across cultures (Carter & McGoldrick, 1989; Sluzki, 1979).

Many refugee families seek mental health services in response to the stress associated with immigration and acculturation, in addition to the traumas experienced in their country of origin. Typical presenting complaints relate to intergenerational conflicts, marital discord, guilt and anxiety mixed with anger secondary to the tensions experienced between family members and relatives left behind, and conflicts with the sponsor/sponsor organization (McGoldrick et al., 1996). Often, a family assessment reveals that intergenerational difficulties are a screen for a more fundamental problem, namely a clash between the family's culture of origin and the host culture. In such cases, it is recommended that the therapist reframe the subsystem conflicts as culture conflicts, which ameliorates the fixed subsystem–culture alliances (Szapocznik, Santisteban, Kurtines, Perez-Vidal, & Hervi, 1984).

10.08.4 FAMILY LIFE CYCLE STAGES: A CULTURAL PERSPECTIVE

The following sections address cultural influences on each major family life cycle stage. Due to space considerations, only key stages are detailed. (i) The joining of families through marriage: The new couple. (ii) Families with young children. (iii) Families with adolescents. (iv) Launching children, single young adults leaving home and the middle generation moving on. (v) Families in later life. We deviate some from the family life cycle sequence provided by Carter and McGoldrick (1989), since the family life cycle is a circular process that can be conceptualized as begining at any stage. One of our modifications reflects our decision to initiate the family life cycle with the marriage of the young couple, which is the begining of a new family unit. Our second modification is our decision to combine two stages, launching children and moving on (Stage 5 in the Carter and McGoldrick model) with the leaving home: single young adult phase (Stage 1 in the Carter and McGoldrick model) because these processes often occur simultaneously in the younger and middle generations. Although cultural variations in patterns and belief systems across the family life cycle have been delineated, there is a dearth of empirical data on this topic (N. J. Kaslow et al., 1995). Relevant empirical data will be cited when available.

10.08.4.1 The Joining of Families Through Marriage: The New Couple

The decision to marry represents a commitment to a new family unit and a marital subsystem. This entails maintaining an intense attachment to someone outside of one's family of origin and renegotiating one's family of origin and peer group relationships. Such renegotiation includes redefining the structure and process of the relationships in order to incorporate a new member, and a change in the family member's identity. Forming a new family (family of creation, family of choice) also requires that the couple make decisions regarding routines and rituals, and customs and traditions.

Historically, in the majority of cultures, the ritual of marriage was the primary marker of the transition to adulthood. The significance and universality of this life cycle stage have shifted with changes in the onset of sexual involvements (earlier), increased incidence of cohabitation among nonmarried partners, increased reliance on nontraditional marital arrangements (e.g., same-sex couples, couples who cohabitate for long periods without having a legal ceremony marking their commitment), greater acceptance of people's choices to remain single or divorce or remarry, and later onset of marriages due to changes in educational and career paths. Also, although many groups prohibit intermarriages, there has been a significant rise in intermarriage rates since the mid-1970s.

10.08.4.1.1 Marriage: a life cycle transition

Virtually every cultural group has traditions and rituals associated with one's choice of a partner and the marital process. Between-group differences are noted on such factors as: process of mate selection, age at time of marriage, presence of a formal marital contract, meaning of marriage, marital roles and responsibilities, and expectations regarding monogamy and marital fidelity.

In the past, many cultures advocated arranged marriages. In some groups, arranged marriages are still common (Iranians, Greeks). In many Islamic Arab-American families, marriage is a family matter, in which partners are chosen by one's family and not on the basis of romantic love, as is the norm in most Western cultures (McGoldrick et al., 1996). In other communities (Chinese-American), arranged marriages of two young adults residing in their parents' homes used to be the norm. However, cultural shifts have resulted in many more marriages occurring after the adult children leave the family home and form a romantic attachment with a partner (McGoldrick et al., 1996).

In terms of age at time of marriage, in some cultures (e.g., Amish) it is expected that individuals marry young (late adolescence or young adulthood), whereas in other cultures (e.g., Jewish), people tend to marry at an older age. Further, sex differences exist within cultures regarding the expected age of marriage. For instance, among Iranian-Americans, females typically marry during adolescence or young adulthood, whereas males tend to be 10–15 years older than their partners (McGoldrick et al., 1982). In addition, the expectations regarding one's financial status often influence the typical age at the time of marriage. As an example, Jamaican males often marry 10 years after their Euro-American male counterparts, due to the expectation that they be financially secure prior to marriage (Comas-Diaz & Greene, 1994).

In the majority of cultural groups, heterosexual couples have a formal legal marital agreement. However, this is not true for couples of all socioeconomic levels in a given cultural group. As an example, formalized marriages are the norm among middle and upper class Haitians, but the equivalent of common-law marriages (i.e., *placage*) are common among low-income Haitian couples (McGoldrick et al., 1996). In the West Indian culture, although legal marriages are valued, many couples cohabit for lengthy periods of time to test their compatibility and they often procreate during this period (McGoldrick et al., 1982). Among some cultural groups, two types of formal marital contracts are obtained. Many Jews have a Jewish marriage certificate (*ketubah*) and a state-approved marriage certificate, with separate rituals associated with the receipt of each document.

There are myriad ways in which the meaning of the marital bond differs across cultural groups. For some groups, the formation of a marital unit indicates the creation of a new family designed to enable individuals to meet individual needs (e.g., Anglo-American); for others, it marks a continuation of the man's family line (e.g., Asian-American), and for still others it represents an alliance between two extended families (e.g., Nigerian, Puerto Rican) (McGoldrick et al., 1982, 1996). In some communities, getting married is a sign of status. Within the West Indian culture, a man only marries once he is capable of providing his spouse with economic security and material goods (e.g., house). In other cultures, getting married is an expectation and is not associated with status (Anglo-Americans). Finally, in some communities, marriage is conceived of as a symbolic rite of passage into adulthood (e.g., Amish), whereas other nodal events mark the transition from adolescence to adulthood in other communities.

With regard to marital roles and responsibilities, significant intercultural variations, often reflecting differences in gender roles, have been noted. In many cultural groups, the traditional marriage is one in which the male is the dominant member who has key roles outside the family system, whereas the women's major role is at home and with the family. Within many Mexican-American families, the ideal of machismo is expected from the husband; that is, the male member of the marital dyad is expected to have considerable sexual experience, and to be brave, pugnacious, and sheltering of his partner. Normative behavior of married women within Mexican-American homes is consistent with submission and humility. However, despite these gender role based social presentations, within the home, the domineering and patriarchal male member of the marital dyad often depends on his female partner for major family-related decisions (Falicov, 1996). In the Puerto Rican community and in many Dutch families, women have the primary responsibility for home and family, whereas men are responsible for protecting and providing for the family (Garcia-Preto, 1996). However, among Dutch partners, the husband often solicits his wife's input on business, career, and family financial matters. A reverse pattern of gender roles in marriage is observed among many Hungarian families (Smith, 1996). Hungarian women often are powerful in politics, business, and community affairs, yet have a clearly delineated role in the family typically confined to childrearing decisions and domestic tasks. In these families, the husband has ultimate power regarding domestic decisions. Among Amish-Americans, marriage is viewed as a practical matter and thus partners are expected to cooperate and be respectful of one another, but there is no expectation of romantic love or physical affection (Emery, 1996).

There are also within-culture variations regarding marital roles that often reflect the era of one's birth. As an example, Japanese-American couples in which both partners were born prior to 1935 tend to exhibit traditional, patriarchal, and hierarchical family structures in which the overt expression of affection and love is minimal, whereas couples with members born subsequent to 1935 more often assume an egalitarian relationship in which physical displays of affection are normative. Although these younger couples appear to have marriages more similar to that observed in many Euro-American families, they typically retain their cultural heritage by continuing to hold traditional Japanese attitudes, values, and beliefs (Matsui, 1996). Similar generational differences are exhibited among other cultural groups (e.g., Korean-Americans).

Fidelity is a value shared by members of virtually all cultural groups. However, the consequences of infidelity differ significantly. Among West Indians, adultery is an acceptable reason to divorce. In Vietnamese families, divorce is only an option if adultery is committed by the women. Although polygamy is illegal in America and thus is illegal for Vietnamese individuals residing in the US, the practice of men having female sexual partners in addition to their wives is somewhat acceptable and overlooked by the wife if her position in her extended family is secure and her children receive adequate provisions (McGoldrick et al., 1996). In the Jamaican community, although monogamy is supported, many Jamaican men maintain a mistress and their mutual children in a separate household (practice of "twin households") (Comas-Diaz & Greene, 1994).

10.08.4.1.2 Intermarriage

More than 50% of people in the US marry someone who is not a member of the same cultural group and 33 million adults reside in homes in which at least one other adult has a different religious background (Mayer & Kosmin, 1994). In 1990, 1.5 million children lived in families in which one caregiver was Caucasian American and another caregiver was of African, Asian, or Native American descent. The rates of African-American–Caucasian marriages have tripled since the mid-1960s, even though the actual numbers of such marriages remain relatively low (Wright, 1995). Within the Asian-American community, inter-racial marriages constitute 10–15% of marriages, with such marital unions being most common among Japanese-Americans and least evidenced by Korean-Americans (Karnow & Yoshihara, 1992). The increasing rates of intimate partnerships between individuals of different ethnic, religious, and racial backgrounds suggest that American society is becoming more tolerant of differences. However, couples from intercultural marriages often need therapy to address their cultural differences.

Inter-racial marriage complicates the successful negotiation of this family life cycle phase. Conflicts regarding values, religious beliefs and practices, communication styles, childrearing, and relations with in-laws are common (McGoldrick et al., 1996). The more salient the cultural differences between the partners, the more difficulty they are likely to experience in accommodating to married life (McGoldrick et al., 1996). It has been hypothesized that ethnic intermarriages reflect an effort on the part of each partner to redefine the most important ethnic characteristics and to abandon those ethnic traits that are valued least (McGoldrick et al., 1996).

10.08.4.2 Becoming Parents: Families with Young Children

Within the Euroamerican culture, the transition to this life cycle stage requires that the new parents develop a primary identity as caretakers for the next generation. Typical issues addressed are associated with childbearing, childrearing, and parenting (Carter & McGoldrick, 1989). Young children in families form attachments, develop increased competencies, and begin to develop a sense of self and an ethnic identity. This section reviews the major tasks for the adults associated with this family life cycle phase, including childbirth and childrearing. Then, attention is paid to issues focal in the child's development: attachment, developing a personal identity, developing an ethnic identity, and learning effective coping strategies.

10.08.4.2.1 Childbirth

Variations are noted in birth practices across cultures. In the US, the birth process has been considered a medical event, one that usually occurs in the hospital. With the influence of other cultures on American customs, more American families choose naturalistic approaches (e.g., home births, midwives, involvement of multiple family members) (McGoldrick et al., 1996).

10.08.4.2.2 Childrearing

Cultural differences in childrearing, parenting styles, and socialization practices are significant and often reflect the conditions (e.g., economics, work demands) and values (e.g., independence vs. dependence) of the culture in which they are formed (Matsumoto, 1994). For example, Mexican-American and Puerto Rican parents value family closeness and thus often socialize their children to be obedient and respectful and to prefer familial support over self-reliance (e.g., Zayas & Solari, 1994). As another example, Caucasian American mothers are more likely than African-American or Haitian mothers to use modeling and reassurance to help their children cope with fearful situations; Haitian mothers are more likely than either Caucasian American or African-American mothers to use force when their children confront anxiety-producing stimuli (Reyes, Routh, Jean-Gilles, Sanfilippo, & Fawcett, 1991). These differential parenting patterns could be construed as mothers using parenting styles that encourage adaptive survival in their home country.

The structure of the family affects childrearing and caregiving practices. In Euroamerican culture, the primary responsibility for childrearing has been the purview of the mother, and more recently the parental dyad, while in many non-Anglo-American cultures, children have been raised by extended family members (e.g., grandparents, aunts, and uncles) older siblings, nannies, wet nurses, or in group settings (e.g., kibbutz) (Matsumoto, 1994; McGoldrick et al., 1996). For example, African-

American children living in poverty are often raised in multigenerational families in which maternal grandmothers are the primary caregivers. Frequently, these grandmothers coreside with their daughter and her children, often with no adult male in the home (Harrison, Wilson, Pine, Chan, & Buriel, 1990). Although this family constellation differs from what has been considered the typical American family (i.e., heterosexual, married parents, who coreside with their biological children), it is often associated with healthy African-American child and family development (Canino & Spurlock, 1994; Wilson, 1989). In addition, a significant percentage of minority single-parent families are successful (Lindblad-Goldberg, 1989). As another example, in a number of cultures (e.g., Latino, Filipino), godparents serve as important models for young children and as sources of support for the young child's parents (Matsumoto, 1994). Although the composition of the extended family varies across groups, extended family networks are all characterized by a sharing of resources, emotional support, and caregiving responsibilities (Matsumoto, 1994).

In addition to cross-cultural differences in the identity of the primary caretaker(s), there are variations between cultures in terms of how caretaking occurs and the values communicated to young children within the family. These variations reflect differences in both beliefs regarding childrearing and in standards of living (e.g., family economic status, country of origin). In many Western European cultures, teaching some independence early is emphasized. Toddlers are raised in their own rooms, some crying is tolerated so the child learns not to cry manipulatively, strong verbal feedback during childhood is accepted, and the reward–punishment system emphasizes the gain or loss of possessions or privileges (Matsumoto, 1994). In many other cultures (e.g., Asian-American, African-American, Native-American) communicating a value on dependence and interdependence is emphasized (Matsumoto, 1994). For some, the young child may sleep in the parents' bed for several years and may be breast fed until age three or four. Often in cultures in which dependence and interdependence are emphasized, crying is not tolerated and thus may result in positive (e.g., picking up, cuddling) or negative (e.g., spanking) attention, disrespect in the form of talking back to elders (parental figures) is unacceptable, and the reward–punishment system frequently means the presence or absence of corporal consequences (e.g., Greek-American, Puerto Rican). These differential rearing and parenting practices prepare youth to live in the cultural context in which they are embedded.

10.08.4.2.3 Attachment

Cultural values in childrearing practices impact upon the nature and perception of the parent–child attachment bond. While many attachment behaviors are found across cultures, the selection, shaping, and interpretation of these attachment behaviors are culturally determined (IJzendoorn, 1990). Empirical investigations reveal frequency differences of the major forms of attachment (anxious avoidant, anxious resistant, securely attached, disorganized/disoriented) between and within cultures (across regional and socioeconomic groups) (Bretherton & Waters, 1985; IJzendoorn, 1990). These data underscore the importance of ascertaining the contextual meanings of attachment behavior, as well as whether or not attachment patterns are differentially adaptive across cultures (Harwood, Miller, & Irizarry, 1995).

Studies examining attachment behavior in Anglo vs. Puerto Rican mother–infant dyads indicate that Anglo-American mothers value child qualities associated with individualism (e.g., autonomy, self-control, activity), whereas Puerto Rican mothers prefer child factors consistent with interpersonal relatedness (e.g., affection, dignity, respectfulness, responsiveness to others, proximity seeking) (Harwood, 1992; Harwood & Miller, 1991). These preferences mirror the differences in values within the two cultures as individuation is promoted in Anglo-American culture, whereas relatedness is considered optimal in Puerto Rican culture. Despite these differences in valued child characteristics, both Anglo-American and Puerto Rican mothers rate the securely attached child as more positive than the insecurely attached child. However, the basis for this preference differs between the two groups of women. Anglo mothers note the confidence and independence of the securely attached child; Puerto Rican mothers find the child's demeanor, obedience, and relatedness most appealing (Harwood & Miller, 1991).

10.08.4.2.4 Developing a personal identity

The challenge for young children is learning, through interactions with key attachment figures, the adaptive patterns of their social group (Canino & Spurlock, 1994). Early in life, a child begins negotiating different affiliation styles, communication strategies, coping patterns, and family hierarchy and approaches to discipline. As the young children struggle with these issues and conflicts, they begin to form a personal identity.

The development of a personal identity is complicated when the child has to adapt to various, changing, and/or conflicting social rules and expectations. This is particularly true when the child must meet the demands of different cultures or adapt to a culture in rapid transition. Understandably, the child may have difficulty finding that adaptive skills in one culture may be a liability in another. For example, the openness valued in the Euro-American culture may be shamed in the Asian-American family context, and the gender-associated aggresiveness praised in the Latino culture may be punished in the Euroamerican culture. Many first-generation immigrant children become confused and overwhelmed by the need for their family to adapt to the dominant cultural demands. They may feel rejected by their peer group when their family engages in behaviors consistent with their culture of origin (e.g., afternoon siesta) and rejected by their family if they fail to conform with culturally normative rituals. In addition, these children often receive contradictory messages from their family as the family tries to meet the demands of the American culture (e.g., forego the afternoon siesta).

10.08.4.2.5 Developing an ethnic identity

As part of a personal identity, each child develops an ethnic identity, that is, a sense of belonging to an ethnic group with shared values, attitudes, language, behavior, perceptions, and social interaction patterns (Phinney, 1990a). The relevance of ethnic identity and awareness of this aspect of a person's identity are particularly important when children realize that their personal ethnic or cultural identity differs from the culture in power (Erikson, 1958). Therefore, being a "minority" or a member of a nondominant culture automatically predisposes a child to different identity development contingencies. For example, the dark, slanted eyes common in Asian-American children are not dark or slanted (they are normal) when everyone else's eyes are that way; but when a child realizes that beautiful and normal equals bluer and rounded eyes, that child has to deal with different identity-related issues than blue, round-eyed children. How this difference impacts identity is significant, and the family's role in helping the child develop a positive identity is crucial.

Accepting differences in personal characteristics is a developmental process. Children proceed from wanting to be something other than who they are (pre-encounter phase) to only wanting to be with and trusting others who are like themself (encounter and immersion–emersion stages), to accepting and appreciating variety (internalization stage) (Parham & Helms, 1981). This is a challenging task, especially when the socialization process (adult guided) is not clear on such issues. Older siblings and caretakers must model for younger children the internalization phase and help them negotiate earlier phases to facilitate their attainment of a more mature ethnic identity.

The best known empirical studies on ethnic identity in youth focus on minority children's preference for stimuli associated with Caucasian culture (e.g., white dolls) vs. their own culture (e.g., Banks, 1976; Clark & Clark, 1940). These findings initially were interpreted as indicating low self-esteem and a preference for the dominant culture vs. one's own culture. Many researchers criticized these early studies on methodological grounds (Banks, 1976). Also, the findings are dated and with the increased Afrocentric pride evidenced in most African-American families (Mahon, 1976) and the greater availability of black dolls in stores, African-American children are more likely to prefer black dolls. The other well-researched topic relates to children's self-identification, or self-definition, and capacity to correctly label their own ethnic identity (Aboud, 1987). Some suggest that incorrect self-definition vis-à-vis one's ethnicity indicates a negative self-concept, and thus may merit attention.

Much of ethnic identity is developed in the communication style in which the child is surrounded. For example, in many African-American social groups, the meaning of a message may be more in how (rhythm, tonal range) something is said than what is said. Part of the identity of the Italian language is the use of hand motions which are absent in Asian cultures. For certain African groups, much of the meaning of a message is in the nonword sounds that accompany the language, whereas for some Native Americans certain sounds are their words.

Cultures take possession of their unique ways of communication and generally are intolerant of deviations. In each culture, there are idiosyncratic words, phrases, grammar patterns, accents, and nonverbal behaviors that are understood by group members. For example, Jewish phrases help identify one's Jewishness. Children learn these language patterns and are reinforced for using these words in their family and with their Jewish peers, but may be teased if they incorporate these phrases into their communication with their non-Jewish peers. Black children sounding White to sound intellectual in the school environment may be perceived as rejecting their cultural communication identity, which could result in them having to deal with derogatory perceptions and comments from peers and family members. Cultural communication is also developed in musical types and unique sounds are associated with each culture. Learning these patterns of communication is a crucial aspect of children developing their ethnic identity.

Communication conflicts occur when one group defines the "right" way to speak and views certain cultural subtypes as "wrong" or inferior. Children struggle with their language identity when they learn different rules at school and at home. For some immigrant families, attempting to fit in with the major culture's language style has been critical and, as a result, their native language or dialects are not taught to their children. As an example, many Japanese families who were in internment camps during World War II discourage the use of Japanese by their children and grandchildren. This is in an effort to reduce their own pain and to be more "American," but may also function to hinder the development of a positive ethnic identity as a Japanese-American in their children or grandchildren (Vargas & Koss-Chiono, 1992).

Issues around appearance are another domain of ethnic socialization often associated with parent–child tensions. The young female whose family is from East India who wants to cut her hair in a stylish fashion (rather than never to cut it as is the cultural custom) like her friends poses issues for herself (identity formation), and is likely to meet with resistance from her parents who may feel distressed that their ability to control her ethnic identity is threatened. The Native American boy who only wants to perform the "in" (i.e., Macarena) is engaging in behavior that is likely to conflict with the traditional cultural patterns being enforced at home. What could be interpreted as "rebellious" may more appropriately be framed as the child's efforts to fit in.

Children must learn the subtleties of how to act appropriately within each unique cultural context. Much of this learning is acquired through parental modeling. Mothers and fathers struggling to negotiate their cultural practices in an environment intolerant of certain customs (corporal punishment is encouraged in some cultures, but is illegal in America) often send confusing messages to their children. This learning process is complicated further by possible cultural clashes at school, where appropriate behavior, modeled and reinforced by teachers and students, can be drastically different from the home environment (e.g., asking questions and challenging authority may be the norm in school, whereas deference to authority is expected in Asian-American families).

10.08.4.2.6 Developing effective coping strategies

A major challenge of childhood is developing a coping style for handling the obstacles further developmental stages present. If the child looks or sounds different from the majority of Americans, strategies must be formed for coping with being a minority and facing discrimination. Effective use of such tactics enables the child to establish a healthy self-view and a respect for others. While myriad coping strategies are potentially efficacious, it is the child's capacity to use a range of tactics flexibly that determines the overall coping ability. It is helpful to the child if these strategies are taught by elders. For example, African-American children can learn to cope with racism if their caretakers share African cultural values and practices and instil in them a sense of pride in their racial background (Vargas & Koss-Chioino, 1992).

When developing strategies for handling discrimination, it is often a challenge for children to find an approach that is respected in their own culture and the dominant culture. Withdrawing from or attacking the majority culture may be praised by one's own culture, but may result in rejection from the majority culture. Thus, this approach is inconsistent with developing bicultural competence.

The child must also form strategies for negotiating differences between the family's culture and the majority culture. Applying traditions associated with the environmental, social, or economic demands of a non-American country may have limited applicability to successful matriculation the US. One common coping strategy for maintaining important elements from one's culture of origin, while accommodating to one's culture of choice, is culture blending. This involves the Americanization of traditional practices, thoughts, and perceptions. Culture blending is noted throughout the US, including among the Creole population in New Orleans (French and American) and the Gullah population on the coast of South Carolina and Georgia (African and American). Culture blending is often manifested in the use of amalgamated language forms, such as Patwah (Caribbean dialect and English), Gullah (African dialect and English), and Spanglish (Spanish and English).

10.08.4.3 Families of Adolescents

The transition to this stage in the family life cycle often brings marked changes in the roles that adults and children take in the family. In Euroamerican culture, this stage is marked by the establishment of boundaries between adolescents and younger children, as well as parents relinquishing complete authority over the adolescent (Carter & McGoldrick, 1989). In addition, the married couple begin to address midlife marital and career issues and start to care for the older generation. This section focuses on cultural differences in negotiating the major issues of adolescence, separation-individuation, ethnic identity development, achievement, and dating and sexuality.

10.08.4.3.1 Separation-individuation

Families who experience problems in this stage often have difficulty negotiating flexible boundaries in which the adolescent is encouraged to be both independent and dependent. The shift in parenting patterns from childhood to adolescence is often problematic. As an example, some Irish-American families move from a structured, controlling parenting style in childhood to a permissive, laissez-faire style in adolescence, a shift often associated with increased behavior problems in the teenager (Carter & McGoldrick, 1989). Parents may be confused about how much autonomy is appropriate and norms on the balance between dependence and independence vary across cultural groups. In Arab-American families, adolescents are not expected to challenge parental authority, to engage in behaviors that conflict with parental expectations, or to place individual concerns over family interests (Timimi, 1995). Those Arab-American adolescents who rebel to attain increased autonomy are engaging in culturally unacceptable behavior and are likely to meet with intense parental resistance (Timimi, 1995). In a related vein, whereas Euroamerican families believe that healthy development in adolescence is associated with the young people's capacity to both love and leave their parents, in Japanese American families, the value is on family cohesion and support; leaving home is not viewed as an important aspect of adolescent development (McGoldrick et al., 1996).

In the most cultures, adolescent males are afforded more latitude to exert independence than their female counterparts, who often experience rigid and restricted rules. For example, an Italian-American family presents for help because their 16-year old daughter is "disrespectful, rejecting, and unappreciative." They report that she asserts her plan to stay out after midnight following her prom, intends to apply to and attend an out-of-state college, and prefers to buy her own clothes rather than wear clothes made by her mother. The 16-year-old claims her parents are old-fashioned and controlling. If the therapist holds the dominant value orientation, valuing autonomy more than responsibility to a collectivity (Papajohn & Spiegel, 1975), the cultural basis of the conflict, may not be acknowledged. As a result, the therapist will have problems supporting the family's negotiation of a mutually acceptable solution.

During this family life cycle stage, adolescents often fight to spend more time away from the family as peer relations become paramount. Similarly, as adolescents seek to fine tune their personal identity, they will often bring friends home who may expose the family to new values and ideas. While including nonblood relatives is welcomed in some cultures (e.g., Irish-Americans) it may be frowned upon as an intrusion in other cultures (e.g., Italian-Americans).

10.08.4.3.2 Ethnic identity development

Given the centrality of identity development concerns during adolescence, ethnic identity is of great importance during this developmental stage (Phinney, 1990a). Whereas the primary question for young children regarding ethnic identity relates to the accuracy of self-definition, during adolescence the major issues relate to the labels one chooses to use to define oneself, the degree to which one examines one's ethnic identity, and the degree and nature of group identification (Phinney, 1990a). In terms of labels, do adolescents whose parents migrated from Cuba refer to themselves as Cuban, Cuban-American, Hispanic, or Latino? Do adolescents whose parents grew up in Poland and moved to the US prior to their birth refer to themselves as Polish-American or simply American? Such decisions are complex for an adolescent, particularly if the parents are of different heritages, as parental heritage may not be consistent with the adolescent's ethnic self-identification (Phinney, 1990a). Further, each ethnic label has a different connotation regarding the adolescent's ethnic identity and group identification.

Research reveals that adolescents with a well-defined ethnic identity manifest more positive psychological adjustment than their counterparts with limited ethnic self-identification. In a group of African-American, Asian-American, and Mexican-American high school students, those who revealed more mature stages of ethnic identity during an interview had higher self-esteem, a greater sense of mastery, and more positive relationships than their peers who endorsed lower levels of ethnic identity (Phinney, 1989).

The degree and nature of group identification can often be inferred from the degree to which individual adolescents manifest positive vs. negative attitudes toward their ethnic group, and their involvement in the social activities and cultural practices of their ethnic group. The adolescent's involvement in such activities is evident via language choice, friends' ethnic background, religious practices, and participation in structured ethnic social groups (Phinney, 1990a). It is interesting to note that there are sex differences in adolescents' ethnic group identification; research suggests that females are more involved with their ethnic heritage and manifest more mature levels of ethnic identity than males (Phinney, 1990a; Plummer, 1995).

One important aspect of personal and ethnic identity is the expression of gender role, which is influenced by cultural factors. For Latino males, becoming a man often involves learning to physically fight, and taking a dominant role with females. These behaviors could be considered chauvinistic and threatening to those from a Euro-American culture that takes a more egalitarian view regarding gender differences. Traditional *Chicano* ways by a Mexican-American adolescent male toward a White girl could be interpreted as rude or discriminatory and result in a very negative social interaction, despite the fact that the behaviors reflect cultural differences in communication between the sexes.

10.08.4.3.3 Achievement

The arenas in which achievement is valued differ across cultural groups (Gibbs & Huang, 1989). Native American youth may become estranged from their community if they receive recognition for their academic successes, particularly if they choose education over tribal activities. For many Asian-American families, strong academic success is the focus of the family and the source of praise and attention. Excellence in sports, for example, is less valued among many Asian-American families compared to African-American families.

One aspect of achievement that has received considerable attention is academic achievement. A burgeoning body of research underscores ethnic differences in school performance among children and adolescents (Slaughter-Defoe, Nakagawa, Takanishi, & Johnson, 1990; Steinberg, Dornbusch, & Brown, 1992). Data indicate that African-American and Latino youth perform more poorly in academic settings than their Caucasian counterparts in terms of grades obtained and amount of education completed (e.g., Mickelson, 1990). Conversely, there is evidence that the academic performance of Asian-American students surpasses that of their Caucasian, African-American, and Latino peers (Sue & Okazaki, 1990). Environmental factors proposed to explain the impact of culture on adolescents' school performance focus on parenting practices, familial values regarding education, and beliefs communicated within the family regarding the benefits of education. The data on each of these variables are complex and do not provide a clear picture (Steinberg et al., 1992). Evidence suggests, however, that although the authoritarian parenting patterns often found in Asian-American families may not be optimal for superior academic performance, these parenting styles are typically counterbalanced by high levels of peer support for superior academic performance. Caucasian adolescents tend to have optimal academic performance when their parents use an authoritative parenting style and they receive support from their peer group regarding academic achievement. In addition, difficulties in academic success among both African-American and Latino youth may be attributed to low levels of peer support for academic excellence. This low level of peer support is often accompanied by authoritarian parenting practices in the homes of Latino youth, a combination of factors that often interferes with academic success. These data underscore the importance of focusing on cultural values and expectations, as well as family and peer relations, in assessing academic difficulties and devising intervention programs. The development and implementation of such preventive intervention programs must be sensitive to the child's economic conditions.

10.08.4.3.4 Dating and sexuality

Another important task of adolescence is managing dating and sexuality. The major issues that differ across cultures regarding dating relate to the presence of a chaperon and who chooses who the adolescent will date (and ultimately marry). The tradition in many Cuban-American families continues in which chaperons accompany the dating couple (McGoldrick et al., 1982). The chaperon's presence may be a major source of parent–adolescent conflict for adolescents who are more acculturated than their parents. The custom of parental mate selection persists in a number of cultures outside the US. Families from some of these cultures continue this practice upon immigrating to America (e.g., Arab-Americans, East Indians). Again, this practice may cause disagreement between acculturated adolescents and their families. A major issue among many cultural groups relates to parental and extended family concerns regarding the adolescent's decision to date someone outside the family's culture, race, or religion. Interethnic, interracial, and interfaith dating on the part of the adolescent is often a controversial family matter.

Many immigrant populations (e.g., Portuguese, Amish) have strong beliefs that sex is reserved for marriage. However, other cultural groups are permissive of sexual experiences prior to marriage. Italian-American families often encourage and expect their adolescent sons (not daughters) to become sexually proficient as a sign of masculinity and mastery of interpersonal relations. Given that premarital sex is the norm in present day American culture, it is common for a family whose heritage views premarital sex as unacceptable and deserving of punishment to seek mental health services for the adolescent engaged in sexual relations. With this presenting problem, a family intervention rather than individual therapy for the adolescent is warranted. The goal of the family intervention is to help all members address the conflicting norms and understand one another's behavior and attitudes within the larger sociocultural context. In families such as Chinese-American families in which sexuality is a taboo subject, the therapist must form a strong working alliance with the family prior to addressing issues of sexuality (Gibbs & Huang, 1989).

One possible consequence of sexual behavior is pregnancy. The rates of pregnancy and teenage parenthood differ significantly across cultural groups. For example, adolescent childbearing and parenthood are more likely to occur in low-income African-American samples than in demographically matched Caucasian samples or middle-income African-American groups (Franklin, 1987). Also, the rates of teenage pregnancy in the US are increasing, most notably among African-Americans and Latinas (Jacobs, 1994). Multiple psychosocial factors have been proposed to explain differential pregnancy rates among adolescents from different ethnic groups. It has been suggested that African-American teenagers from low-income or single-parent homes become more active sexually than their Caucasian peers and at a younger age. Their increased exposure to sexual behavior in the overcrowded environments in which they reside, the greater level of peer socialization associated with an enhanced awareness of sexuality at an early age, and the higher levels of involvement in adult responsibilities including sexual roles are hypothesized as factors to explain this discrepancy (Staples & Johnson, 1993). In addition to higher rates of sexual activity, low-income African-American adolescents are less likely than their demographically matched Caucasian peers to use contraception or to get abortions (Franklin, 1987). Further, there is increased tolerance of teenage pregnancy in many low-income African-American families and communities and such a pattern has a long history (Boyd-Franklin, 1989). In addition, extended family members are more likely to assist in raising children of teen mothers in the African-American community than in the Caucasian community (Boyd-Franklin, 1989).

10.08.4.4 Launching Children, Single Young Adults Leaving Home, and the Middle Generation Moving On

We have modified Carter and McGoldrick's (1989) family life cycle stages by combining the "Launching Children and Moving On" and the "Leaving Home: Single Young Adults" phases; these typically occur simultaneously in the family's life. This family life cycle stage for EuroAmericans refers to family functioning once children become of age and begin to leave the home.

For the middle generation, the major tasks of this transition are the negotiation and acceptance of adult children leaving the family unit and welcoming their partners and children into the extended family system (Carter & McGoldrick, 1989). The launching of adult children facilitates restructuring of the parent subsystem back to the marital dyad. In addition, it is likely that the couple will have to endure the disability and death of their parents. Families at this stage often present for therapy when parents, particularly mothers who worked as homemakers, experience depression and the "empty nest syndrome" at the loss of the family unit as defined since the mid-1970s. The couple's role as parents is no longer paramount and, as such, they may experience difficulties finding meaningful new life activities. This period may be the first time the couple has lived alone since their early marriage, and thus, they may need to become reacquainted as husband and wife. This may be a period of reinvestment in the relationship or a time when the couple move toward dissolving the marriage. For those who renew their marital commitment, this phase of the family life cycle often brings greater financial freedom, allowing the couple to engage in activities that may have been postponed earlier in the relationship (e.g., vacations, new careers, relocation).

For the younger generation of young adults from Euroamerican backgrounds, during the leaving home phase, the major emotional tasks are that of accepting responsibility (emotional, financial) for themselves, differentiating as an adult from their family of origin, developing intimate relationships, and gaining increased academic and/or occupational self-definition (Carter & McGoldrick, 1989). The individuation characteristic of this phase of development entails clear articulation of personal and ethnic identities (Phinney, 1990a).

10.08.4.4.1 Cultural values and norms on launching

There is a continuum of normative launching behavior across cultural groups, ranging from no expectation of launching to a high degree of expectation regarding launching at an early age and to a significant extent (Carter & McGoldrick, 1989). For example, in many Italian-American families, older adolescent and young adult children are not launched but are expected to remain in the family home or neighborhood, and the family integrates their partners and children into the family. In these families, interdependence is valued and autonomy strivings are experienced as disloyalty to the family unit. In some cultural groups (Iranian-American), the middle generation consider their adult children, even those who are married with offspring, to be children (McGoldrick et al., 1996). Further, in many refugee families, especially those who were traumatized in their homeland (e.g., Cambodian), the launching phase of the family cycle is threatening. The middle generation feels isolated and abandoned when the younger generation attempts to separate, particularly if their extended kin and social support network have remained in their homeland (McGoldrick et al., 1996).

Conversely, in many White Anglo Saxon Protestant families, value is placed on launching older adolescents and young adults and in their assuming significant independence. In such families, an 18-year-olds' inability or unwillingness to leave the family home and function with limited family support is perceived as pathological. Many cultural groups fall in the middle of this continuum, although the specific characteristics of this middle group vary. As an example, many Jewish-American families give mixed messages about separation during this family life cycle phase. Increased autonomy and success is valued highly on the one hand, but high levels of contact and intimate sharing continue to be expected on the other. These conflictual messages are often associated with guilty distancing or ambivalent closeness (Carter & McGoldrick, 1989).

10.08.4.4.2 Leaving home: single young adults

For single young adults, this stage of development includes continued separation–individuation, self-definition, and definition of ethnic identity, processes begun earlier in life. The recently "launched" young adults must grapple with the degree and nature of contact with their family of origin. Young adults from certain ethnic backgrounds (e.g., Jewish, Greek) maintain frequent contact (telephone, letters, email, visits) with their family of origin, yet attain a significant degree of autonomy to pursue success in their chosen endeavors. When they fail to attain such success, increased family involvement occurs (Carter & McGoldrick, 1989). Conversely, young adults from ethnic backgrounds that value independence beginning in older adolescence or young adulthood (White Anglo Saxon Protestants, Germans, Scandinavians) may be rejected by their family of origin if they cannot function autonomously due to personal limitations (e.g., disabilities) or need for continued financial support to pursue life goals (e.g., advanced training and education) (Carter & McGoldrick, 1989). Young adults often need to find a way to negotiate their personal desires for autonomy, their family's and culture's expectations about independent functioning, and the majority population's values on age-appropriate adult behavior. This negotiation is quite complex for young adults who leave their ethnic community and engage actively in mainstream culture.

Young adults' ethnic involvement during this phase is manifested in their choice of friends and partners, religious practices, structured ethnic social groups, political ideology and activity, area of residence, and career path (Phinney, 1990a). Studies examining ethnic identity among college students fail to yield consistent results regarding the association between positive or negative feelings about individual's ethnic identity, self-esteem, and psychological adjustment (Phinney, 1990a). However, research on the stage model of ethnic identity reveals an association between college students' achieved level of ethnic identity and self-esteem (Parham & Helms, 1985a, 1985b; Phinney & Alipuria, 1990). This relation is particularly evident in African-American, Asian-American, and Mexican-American young adults, and less obvious in Caucasian American college students (Phinney & Alipuria, 1990). Data also indicate that college students' stage of ethnic or racial identity is associated with their preferences regarding the race or ethnicity of their therapist (Parham & Helms, 1981). Specifically, older African-American adolescents and young adults who endorse early stages of racial identity (i.e., pre-encounter) often prefer Caucasian therapists and are nonaccepting of African-American counselors, whereas African-American adolescents and young adults who exhibit higher levels of racial identity (i.e., encounter, immersion–emersion, internalization) manifest varying degrees of both preference for same-race therapists and lack of interest in working with Caucasian counselors (Parham & Helms, 1981). These data suggest an association between identity formation and self-esteem; the more young adults accept their ethnicity, the more positive they feel about themselves. These data also underscore the need to consider the young adults' level of ethnic identity in making decisions regarding therapist assignments.

A major foci of the young adults' development relates to their choice of friends and intimate partners, and decisions about whether to be involved in a relationship or remain single. Once older adolescents and young adults leave the family home, they often feel an increased sense of personal choice regarding the ethnicity of their friends and partners and their sexual orientation. While this may be a relief for young adults, it often forces them to become more clear about their preferences and values regarding interpersonal relationships as distinct from those held by the family. Should young adults choose to engage in relationships not acceptable to their family's cultural norms and expectations (e.g., interracial, interfaith, or interethnic dating; same-sex relationships), the risk of being ostracized or criticized by the family of origin may be considerable and certainly depends to some extent on the family's ethnic heritage. For instance, since the African-American family often buffers its members from racism, these families are unlikely to reject a lesbian young adult family member, despite the fact that a lesbian life style may be considered unacceptable (Comas-Diaz & Greene, 1994). This stance does not imply acceptance of the young adult's sexual orientation but rather reflects tolerance and a desire to protect the young person from additional discrimination. This stance of tolerance, however, is often relinquished should the lesbian young adult openly define herself as a lesbian (Comas-Diaz & Greene, 1994). In the Native American community, young adult women who choose a lesbian life style are most often accepted in the lesbian community within the mainstream culture and rejected by their family and community on the reservation (Comas-Diaz & Greene, 1994). As a result, these young women often experience a loss of support if they explore a nontraditional sexual orientation.

10.08.4.4.3 Conflicts experienced by the middle generation

Realignment of the marital subsystem in response to the launching of young adult children and the manner in which marital dyads deal with the illness and death of their parents are influenced by the middle generation's culture of origin. Sex roles, an aspect of one's culture of origin, impact the negotiation of these family life cycle tasks (Carter & McGoldrick, 1989). For families whose cultural traditions emphasize the primacy of the woman's role as mother and wife (e.g., Italian-American, Puerto Rican), the launching phase may be associated with a crisis in the marriage if the woman becomes involved in activities outside the home. Conversely, in communities in which the woman's role outside the home is valued or accepted (e.g., Irish-American, African-American, White Anglo Saxon Protestant), the likelihood of this type of marital crisis at this stage is minimal. This is particularly true for those cultural groups in which limited emphasis is placed on intimacy within the marital dyad (e.g., Irish-American) or in which parent–child connectedness is valued more highly than the husband–wife bond (e.g., Mexican-Americans) (McGoldrick et al., 1996).

10.08.4.4.4 Dealing with parental illness and death

There are differences among ethnic groups about the responsibility the middle generation experiences regarding caring for their aging and dying parents (Carter & McGoldrick, 1989). In some ethnic groups (e.g., Greeks, Italians, Chinese, African-Americans), the middle generation expects to be the primary caretakers for their elderly parents and placing a loved one in a nursing home is rarely considered an option. Among certain groups (e.g., Germans, Scandinavians, Jews), the decision to place an elderly parent in a nursing home is commonly accepted. For some of these families, it is considered essential to provide aging parents with a familiar cultural environment (e.g., Jewish nursing home) in which familiar ethnic rituals and customs are practiced.

10.08.4.5 Families in Later Life

The elderly face many pressing challenges in the US, and as such the role of culture has often been overlooked by clinicians, researchers, and, at times, the elderly. As individuals get older, there is a greater emphasis on changing roles in the intergenerational family, the "culture of poverty," age discrimination, victimization, retirement, meaningfulness of life, health and vitality, loss of significant relationships and death of loved ones, and preparation for their own death. Such issues entail life review and integration. Families with elderly loved ones generally function best when they acknowledge and experience the wisdom of the elderly and support the older generation without overfunctioning for them (Carter & McGoldrick, 1989). The multitude of issues experienced by the elderly and their family often obscure the importance of culture in this period. This section begins by defining the term elderly. This is followed by a review of issues confronting the elderly, with specific attention paid to the immigrant elderly. Then, ethnic identity in the elderly is examined. It should be noted that cultural information regarding the elderly is minimal and the data are limited to a few subcultures (American Psychiatric Association, 1994a).

10.08.4.5.1 Definition of the elderly

In general, old is defined as 65–84, whereas old-old refers to age 85 and above. However, in some groups, being elderly starts at 55. In the US, some benefits associated with age begin at 55, others begin at 65 or 70. These numbers have changed over the years, partially due to the fact that the average life span has increased.

The onset of old age varies among cultures, in part because individuals of various cultures die at different ages (American Psychiatric Association, 1994a). The definition of old age is complicated further by the within-group variability in typical age of death. For instance, African-Americans tend to die younger than Euro-Americans. However, African-American individuals who survive past 75 have a longer life expectancy than Caucasian persons of the same age (Baker, 1994). Differences in life expectancies and health status raise questions about when a family and cultural group views an older loved one as elderly.

10.08.4.5.2 Issues confronting the elderly

The elderly confront myriad issues during the stage referred to as "Families in Later Life." First, non-Euro-American elderly individuals often experience discrimination, based on their age and cultural background. Latino elders often are the object of prejudice because of their Spanish surnames and inability to speak English (Jimenez & de Figueiredo, 1994). Due to their limited command of English, combined with the fact that interpreters often fail to capture accurately the perspective of the elderly, Latino elderly are often unable to defend themselves against discrimination and their behaviors and attitudes are often misinterpreted.

Appearance (e.g., clothing, accessories) and diet are variables associated with discrimination against minority elderly. For instance, because it is most common for the elderly to wear traditional dress, many elderly Asian-Indian women are ridiculed if they don a sari. Elderly people who retain their culture's traditions may feel particularly ostracized if their younger family members criticize their choices to retain their language and/or dress of origin.

The maintenance of beliefs from the homeland may also increase the elderly's vulnerability to oppression. The Chinese-American value placed on stoicism often conflicts with the American medical system, as well as the family system (Sakauye & Chacko, 1994). Medical personnel and younger family members often express frustration and confusion regarding the severity of an elderly Chinese-American's pain given their tendency to refrain from articulating the seriousness of their problems.

Many minority elderly face a sense of isolation and alienation due to their memories of traumatic experiences in the US and/or their country of origin. Elderly African-Americans who talk about slavery, elderly European Jews who reflect upon the Holocaust, and elderly Japanese-Americans who discuss the internment camp experiences of World War II may feel that their pain is discounted by younger family members who fail to appreciate the ongoing significance of such traumatic times. This sense of rejection by family members, who are unlikely to ever encounter such tragedies, further compounds the suspiciousness often associated with postslavery, the Holocaust, or internment camp experiences.

Some elderly people struggle to maintain a sense of autonomy and independence, despite increased family dependence due to economic limitations or physical or mental deterioration. This conflict is most pronounced in cultural groups in which caretaking of parents is not the norm (e.g., Germans, Scandinavians, Jews). Conversely, for those groups (e.g., African-Americans, Latinos, Native Americans, Asian-Americans) in which it is common for older family members to reside with, and be cared for by, younger members, independence–dependence struggles may be less central.

10.08.4.5.3 Immigrant elderly

From a cultural perspective, the immigrant elderly deserve specific attention. With the exception of African-Americans, Native Americans, Alaskan, and Hawaiian Natives, and those from cultures whose families immigrated to the US hundreds of years ago (e.g., White Anglo Saxon Protestants), many minority elders are relatively new immigrants to the country (e.g., Soviet Jews) (American Psychiatric

Association, 1994a). These elderly immigrants must adapt to a novel environment with new expectation while losing much of their accumulated experience from their culture of origin. As a consequence, they may lose much of their value within the family. Superimposed on this are the other issues surrounding getting older, resulting in the immigrant elderly feeling extremely challenged and overwhelmed. The intensity of these struggles appears correlated with the recency of immigration, with less recent immigrants manifesting fewer problems (American Psychiatric Association, 1994a). In spite of the aforementioned challenges, the elderly, particularly those who are immigrants, tend to be survivors who are resilient and exhibit a pleasure in life that is not quelled by age, suffering, or loss (Myerhoff, 1979).

10.08.4.5.4 Ethnic identity

Elders often assume the role of maintaining their own and their family's ethnic identity despite the family's assimilation into mainstream culture and associated loss of cultural knowledge, language, and traditional values and beliefs (American Psychiatric Association, 1994a). In the Native American community, this may be particularly problematic given that much of the tradition is maintained through oral history. A second aspect of ethnic identity of concern to many minority elderly is that they are no longer being as honored because of their strong ethnic identification (Thompson, 1994). Again, in some Native American families, as the younger generations become more Americanized, the elderly are less valued despite their wealth of experience. A similar process is evident in other groups (e.g., Asian-Americans).

10.08.5 CULTURALLY SENSITIVE FAMILY ASSESSMENT AND INTERVENTION

The conduct of culturally sensitive assessments and interventions is predicated on the incorporation of a conceptual model that emphasizes the behaviors, perceptions, beliefs, and values of different groupings of individuals. Clinicians and service delivery systems must be knowledgeable about, and attentive to, their own cultural backgrounds and those of the client and their family. Awareness of these cultural factors must inform the assessment and intervention process with families from all cultural groups (i.e., cultural competence) (Dana, 1993; Zayas, Torres, Malcolm, & DesRosiers, 1996).

According to Zayas et al. (1996) and Dana (1993), therapists transverse a number of stages in becoming culturally sensitive practitioners:

(i) unawareness and/or denial, defensiveness and minimization of the importance of cultural issues;

(ii) heightened awareness and acceptance of culture;

(iii) burden of considering culture and doing therapy and adapting behavior and thinking accordingly; and

(iv) integration and synthesis of culture into the assessment and intervention process.

Psychologists who engage in culturally informed assessments and interventions consider myriad variables, including the family's group identity, the family's identity as a subsystem, and the identity of each individual member. Also, the clinician focuses on the beliefs, values, and language of each family member and the family unit as a whole (Dana, 1993).

The following section reviews the conceptual issues and assumptions that guide family assessment and intervention in a culturally informed manner (Kaslow et al., 1995; Odell, Shelling, Young, Hewitt, & L'Abate, 1994). The topics covered include values, help-seeking behavior, and adherence issues. These issues are of paramount importance given the considerable variation in the presenting problem, nature and rate of help-seeking, views of mental health services, and the nature and rate of premature termination among diverse cultural groups (Kazdin, Stolar, & Marciano, 1995). Next, techniques for assessment and intervention appropriate across cultural groups and family life cycle stages are described. This information provides the background for the later section on culturally sensitive assessment and intervention across each specific phase of the family life cycle.

10.08.5.1 Values

To conduct culturally sensitive assessments and interventions, psychologists must be cognizant of their own biases and prejudicial reactions regarding various cultural groups, their personal and culturally based values, and the cultural values of the family with whom they are working. Since families often seek help when their norms are disparate from the cultural values represented by other family members and/or the community, values play a central role in family work.

If the clinician and family differ in their values about the presenting problem, but these differences do not reflect significant conflict or indicate pathological functioning in the family's cultural context, it is recommended that the therapist incorporates the family's cultural framework throughout the assessment and intervention. This recommendation assumes that the therapist's and family's values are equally valid. Another possible stance is for the therapist and family to acknowledge their differences of opinion and the acceptability of such differences.

If during evaluation or treatment the practitioner discovers that the family's value system leads them to engage in behaviors considered illegal or unethical in the relevant jurisdiction, the clinician must inform the family and take appropriate steps. Harsh physical punishment of children may be normative in certain cultural groups (e.g., Jamaican families), but such behavior is illegal in the US and thus requires that the therapist report the family to the appropriate authorities (e.g., Gibbs & Huang, 1989). In such instances, the therapist needs to work with the family to help them modify their disciplinary practices in accordance with the law. This needs to be done sensitively, without the therapist invalidating the family's cultural practices.

If the behaviors associated with the family's values are contrary to normative practices for the relevant cultural groups in the current ecological context, but the behaviors are not illegal or unethical, the therapy helps the family modify these values and associated behaviors in an effort to foster healthy development and enhance family functioning. To accomplish this goal, the psychologist must help the family examine the cultural origins of these values, ascertain the positive and negative consequences of engaging in behaviors associated with the values, and learn culturally sanctioned alternative practices. It is helpful if the therapist underscores that the family's cultural values may lead to problems in some contexts and be beneficial in others, and that values developed in one historical context may be maladaptive in a new sociocultural context.

When there are conflicts among family members regarding key values, and the therapist shares the values of only some family members, the therapeutic process becomes complicated. Often, the therapist will be most aligned with those family members who have the most similar acculturation status and/or cultural identity to the therapist. It is common for the therapist working with immigrant or refugee families to conflict with the grandparent generation regarding gender roles in the family system and to support the gender roles desired by the adult children who are likely to have acculturated more rapidly.

Classes among family members and/or generations regarding values are a necessary consideration in the assessment and treatment of minority families (Gibbs & Huang, 1989). Failure to attend to the processes of value orientation and value clashes may result in an overemphasis on intrapsychic or family dynamics, and may limit the treatment efficacy. Thus, an ecologically oriented approach, that attends to contextual issues as these influence the values of each family member, must be incorporated in all assessment and intervention endeavors with families from nondominant cultural groups.

10.08.5.2 Help-seeking Patterns

The family's cultural background often influences the type of help the family seeks for a loved one's problems. Many families from minority cultures prefer to receive help from both trained and not formally trained members of their own community. This preference often results in their being less likely to seek medical or mental health services from qualified professionals, given the relative dearth of well-trained minority providers and culturally sensitive service programs. For example, African-American and Latino families are less likely than Euroamerican families to seek support from agencies and professionals in the initial stages of responding to the a family members' difficulties. (McMiller & Weisz, 1996). Different help-seeking patterns appear to reflect more negative views toward professionals by majority families and the increased availability of alternative social networks (e.g., extended family, clergy) in many minority communities as compared to Euroamerican communities. In a related vein, in many minority communities there is considerable stigma associated with revealing personal and/or cultural values and beliefs to someone outside the family unit, particularly to someone outside the culture.

These differential help-seeking patterns must be considered when forming an alliance with minority group families, assessing the index person's and family's problems, and designing, implementing, and evaluating culturally based community outreach programs (McMiller & Weisz, 1996). Specifically, during the initial stages of the evaluation process with African-American and Latino families, the psychologist must address the family's concerns and reluctance about mental health services and educate the family about mental health services. Only by doing so will the clinician earn the family's trust sufficiently to conduct a thorough, accurate assessment (McMiller & Weisz, 1996).

10.08.5.3 Adherence

Given the data on minority families' reluctance to use professional mental health services and the high rates of attrition among culturally diverse groups, it behoves the therapist to become familiar with risk factors associated with dropping out of treatment. While several factors of premature termination (e.g., parental stress, antisocial behavior of the parent and/or child, adverse parenting styles, low SES) are common among most families, specific differences among ethnic groups in the rate and nature of intervention drop out have been found (Kazdin et al., 1995). As an example, African-American families leave treatment more frequently and earlier than their Caucasian counterparts (Kazdin et al.). Predictors of African-American drop out also differed, with compliance often predicated on child academic functioning.

There are a number of techniques that may reduce attrition rates, however, many of these strategies are ineffective with families from culturally diverse groups (Paniagua, 1994). To effectively prevent premature termination of family therapy, the psychologist's interventions must attend to the family's culture and the impact of the family's culture on attrition. Separate guidelines have been proposed to prevent attrition in African-American, Latino, Asian-American, and Native American families. For example, when working with African-American families, it is suggested that racial differences be addressed, mental health problems not be linked to parental behaviors, medication not be recommended as the initial treatment of choice, and the psychologist "not give the impression that he or she is the protector of the race when discussing racial issues" (Paniagua, 1994, p. 93). To minimize the likelihood of attrition when working with Native American families, the psychologist should emphasize listening and collaboration rather than talking and authority, de-emphasize the issue of time, discuss the administration rather than the control of the problem, and avoid personalism.

10.08.5.4 Culturally Sensitive Techniques

Cultural issues influence the therapeutic stance, the development of the working alliance, and the assessment and intervention process (Sue & Zane, 1987). In addition to attending to cultural factors as these influence family dynamics, the psychologist conducting the family assessment and intervention must consider the unique aspects of each family to distinguish culturally based and idiosyncratic family relational patterns (Goldenberg & Goldenberg, 1994).

10.08.5.4.1 Stance of the therapist

Nonspecific therapist characteristics associated with the conduct of competent assessments and interventions (e.g., empathy, warmth, genuineness, acceptance, respect) are necessary but not sufficient to assess adequately cultural issues (Sue & Sue, 1990). Culturally informed clinicians must also: (i) be knowledgeable about their own cultural background and its influence on clinical practice; (ii) comprehend the impact of culture on the lives of the families with whom they work; (iii) be cognizant of the variability of normative family structures and functioning across and within cultural groups to avoid stereotyping; (iv) be attuned to subtle cultural variations in language, nonverbal behavior, and expressions of distress; (v) adjust their style to be compatible with the family's culturally influenced patterns of relating to one another and to outsiders in authority; (vi) modify the therapeutic strategies used to facilitate behavior change in a manner consistent with the family's cultural values; (vii) recognize and use the family's natural support systems in the community; and (viii) be willing to incorporate other culturally acceptable clinicians from multiple disciplines into the assessment and intervention process (London & Devore, 1988; Odell et al., 1994; Sue & Sue, 1990).

The American Psychological Association's guidelines for ethical practice for the provision of psychological services to ethnic, linguistic, and culturally diverse populations (American Psychological Association, 1993) maintain that it is only ethical to assess and intervene with individuals and families from the nondominant culture if the professional is trained in multicultural assessment and intervention. According to these guidelines, the therapist's stance must reflect their recognition of cultural diversity, understanding of the role that culture, ethnicity, and race play in psychosocial development, awareness that economic and political factors influence psychosocial development, and knowledge of the impact of culture, gender, and sexual orientation on behavior. Psychologists working with culturally diverse families must communicate a value on helping families understand, maintain, and resolve their own sociocultural identification (American Psychological Association, 1993).

10.08.5.4.2 Development of the working alliance

Joining, a key component of forming a working alliance between the therapist, each family member, and the family system as a whole, is crucial to the conduct of effective assessment and intervention. This process is facilitated when the therapist's space (office, agency) includes culturally familiar objects and symbols to the family (Vasquez-Nuttall, Avila-Vivas, & Morales-Barreto, 1984). Through the joining process, a trusting relationship is forged between the therapist and the family.

Through the process of joining, the clinician becomes cognizant of the culturally influenced rules, roles, structure, communication and problem-solving patterns, and traditional sources of help that impact on family interactional processes. To enhance the working alliance with a family from a cultural group unfamiliar to the psychologist, or when the family engages in culturally driven family patterns to which the therapist is unaccustomed, it is suggested that the therapist assume a position of humility coupled with benign curiosity (Odell et al., 1994). Such a stance can be assumed most readily if the clinician requests the family's aid in learning relevant cultural norms and patterns. If the family is unable to provide adequate information to insure an empathic awareness of the family's interactions within their cultural context, the therapist must glean such data from others knowledgeable about the particular family's culture.

Credibility is associated with effective joining (Sue & Zane, 1987). Professionals' credibility, a reflection of their status, may be determined by the position assigned by the family (ascribed credibility) or by their competencies (achieved credibility). When therapists exhibit culturally consistent assessment and intervention strategies, they may be considered credible by a given family system. The lack of ascribed credibility of formalized mental health services may account for low utilization rates among certain cultural groups, and the lack of achieved credibility may contribute to explanations of nonadherence.

10.08.5.4.3 Assessment process

Once psychologists have begun to form a working alliance with the family, the assessment may begin. The psychologist who gathers family assessment data in a culturally sensitive manner communicates a respect of the cultural diversity of families (Hanson, Lynch, & Wayman, 1990). In conducting a family evaluation, the ways in which the family's culture impacts on their symptom presentation and interactional patterns must be considered (Zayas et al., 1996). Evaluators must be mindful of the ways in which their own culture may affect the assessment process. In addition to cultural biases influencing the assessment of intellectual, psychiatric, and behavioral functioning, these biases may impact upon the evaluator's perception and evaluation of family functioning (Canino & Spurlock, 1994; Dana, 1993). Given the growing literature on cultural considerations in assessing psychological symptoms and psychiatric conditions in people across the life span (e.g., Alarcon, 1995; American Psychiatric Association, 1994a; Canino & Spurlock, 1994; Gaw, 1993), and in diagnosing psychiatric disorders in the recent *Diagnostic and statistical manual of mental disorders* (*4th ed.; DSM-IV*) (American Psychiatric Association, 1994b), our comments on assessment only address considerations pertinent to families.

During the evaluation, the clinician must gather information about the ethnic, racial, and religious background of the family and data about the historical and current political, social, and economic conditions of the family's cultural group. The construct of a genogram may be useful (McGoldrick & Gerson, 1985). Genograms, which graphically provide personal data regarding individual members (e.g., ethnicity, religion, current residence), and information about family structure, relationships, and patterns, enable the psychologist and family to develop systemic hypotheses about family functioning and its connection to the larger family and sociocultural context.

Some therapists question the appropriate timing and nature of genogram construction with families from certain cultural groups. Boyd-Franklin (1989) asserted that with African-American families, genogram work may be most meaningful later in the treatment after trust has been established, rather than during the evaluation. Similarly, Odell et al. (1994) have noted that since constructing a genogram may elicit painful memories for many immigrant and refugee families, this technique may sabotage the development of the initial working alliance and thus may best be introduced during the intervention. For many families who have lost a loved one due to sociopolitical conditions (e.g., Holocaust survivors, Bosnian refugees), projective genogramming elicits effectively distressing) yet important information and feelings (F. W. Kaslow, 1995). Thus, while genograms may be an important assessment tool with families from most cultural groups, the family's cultural background should inform the timing of this task.

An assessment strategy related to the genogram, but devised for work with diverse family groups, is the culturagram (Congress, 1994). With the culturagram, psychologists glean information from the family regarding: reasons for immigration, length of time in the community, citizenship status, language spoken at home and in the community, health beliefs, major holidays, and values on family, education, work, gender roles, religion, and money. Constructing a culturagram enables clinicians to ascertain the effects of culture on the family system and to individualize ethnically similar families. As a result, clinicians are more culturally empathic and more able to empower the families with whom they work.

Enumerable tools and methodologies have been devised to assess multiple aspects of family functioning. These include self-report scales, micro- and macroanalytic coding schemas to code interactional patterns, and projective techniques (for review, see Fredman & Sherman, 1987; Jacob, 1987; L'Abate & Bagarozzi, 1993). Unfortunately, few of these measures or coding schemas have been developed, normed, or empirically tested for specific cultural groups, and thus their utility across groups remains questionable (Dana, 1993). In addition, generalizations about findings gleaned from using standard assessment protocols must be limited and made with caution. Given the scarcity of culture-free assessment strategies, the assessor must take the family's cultural context into account when interpreting findings from assessment protocols not standardized with the family's cultural group. This requires including an evaluation of culturally valid constructs (e.g., racial or ethnic identity, level of acculturation, belief systems, culture-specific syndromes) (Lasry & Sayegh, 1992; Phinney, 1990b). For example, the psychologist may use Gushue's (1993) recent adaptation of Parham and Helms (1985b) Black and White interaction model for assessing and working with families. This assessment strategy enables the clinician to incorporate cultural identity data in making an initial family assessment.

The final phase of the assessment process is problem definition and goal-setting. Cultural variables that may impact this phase include the role of authority, preferred decision-making strategies, the view of psychological problems and potential solutions, and culturally based values. Thus, with Latino families, the goals should address immediate and concrete concerns (Ho, 1987). These families prefer to focus on goals that affect family subsystems, particularly the parent–child subsystem, rather than individual family members or the marital dyad. When working with many Asian-American families, it is recommended that the goals be well-defined, objective, and address practical matters. Asian-American families prefer the therapist to be confident and active in the goal-setting process, while simultaneously communicating respect for the family (Ho, 1987). With Native American families, goal-setting should be collaborative. Given the value on interdependence in the Native American community, all relevant nuclear and extended family members should be included in setting intervention goals (Ho, 1987). When setting goals with low-income, African-American families, a mutual process should be assumed, with a focus on survival needs and the incorporation of an ecostructural framework (Ho, 1987).

In addition to setting goals specific to the given family, many culturally competent practitioners recommend that cultural intentionality and bicultural competence be defined as therapeutic goals for families across cultural groups who seek mental health services (Boyd-Franklin, 1989; Ivey, Ivey, & Simek-Morgah, 1993; Szapocznik et al., 1984). Cultural intentionality refers to the ability to communicate competently with others within the cultural group and with individuals from multiple cultural backgrounds. Bicultural competence connotes the simultaneous processes of accommodating to the host culture and retaining aspects of the culture of origin.

10.08.5.4.4 Intervention process

Throughout the intervention phase, the psychologist is a cultural interpreter or culture broker, helping the family recognize and resolve conflicts between the demands and values of the minority and majority cultures (Canino & Spurlock, 1994; Glordano & Giordano, 1995). Issues that may require interpretation include: kinship relations, respect for roles and family hierarchy, personalization in the therapeutic relationship, and the need to involve additional people from the family's community (e.g., clergy). To assume the role of cultural interpreter, the therapist may incorporate Boyntons (1987) ESCAPE model, according to which the therapist, as cultural interpreter, must: Engage the family within its context; be sensitive to the family's culture; communicate an awareness of the culture's potential and positives; and know the environment in which culture clashes are likely to occur.

When intervening with families from either the same or a different cultural background as themselves, therapists must be mindful that interpersonal behaviors may be interpreted differently. For example, whereas listening may be experienced by some as reflecting empathy and concern, families from certain cultural backgrounds are likely to perceive listening as not caring. Thus, it is crucial that the family and the therapist discuss their differing perceptions and experiences throughout the course of the family work. Awareness of these differences should inform subsequent interventions.

A major focus of family interventions is the introduction and utilization of adaptive problem-resolution tactics. Problem-resolution strategies are most effective when system and cultural variables are taken into account. Since culturally specific intervention approaches for problem resolution have been offered to families from multiple cultural groups (for detailed discussions, see Boyd-Franklin, 1989; Falicov, 1983; Ho, 1987; McGoldrick et al., 1982, 1996; Paniagua, 1994), this section reviews, briefly, techniques for problem resolution with families from the most often encountered cultural groups in the US.

The optimal family intervention approach for African-American families, regardless of SES, is time-limited, problem-focused, and present-oriented with all significant family members and members of the kinship and caregiving networks included (Boyd-Franklin, 1989; Ho, 1987; McGoldrick et al., 1996). The psychologist, who needs to assume an active stance, should inform the family about the goals, process, structure, and limits of family therapy, and serve as a role model, educator, and advocate. Effective family therapy underscores and utilizes family strengths and resources to empower the family to solve its own problems, exert more control over the environment, cope constructively with racism and oppression, and extricate itself from the victim system (Boyd-Franklin, 1989; Pinderhughes, 1989). Psychoeducation and skills training, role clarification, and boundary setting are useful strategies. The unique power and value conflicts of middle-class African-American families may require additional treatment modifications, such as the therapist relabeling behaviors that appear maladaptive as manifestations of the family's determination to negotiate effectively between cultures with competing demands (Corner-Edwards & Spurlock, 1988).

When intervening with Asian-American families, the psychologist must respect key values in the community (e.g., the central role of family solidarity, the emphasis on connectedness and integration rather than separation and individuation) and must be sensitive to the families' culturally sanctioned reluctance to expose conflict to outsiders because it reflects disloyalty (Gaw, 1993; Tamura & Lau, 1992). Although these family values and patterns of relating characterize Asian-American families from multiple countries of origin, effective interventions must take into account the family's specific ethnic background and level of acculturation (Gaw, 1993). When working with Asian-American families, it is suggested that the intervention approach be relatively formal and structured, and focus on pragmatic concerns rather than underlying affects. The therapist must balance showing respect for parental authority and the family's culture of origin with the assumption of an authoritative stance. Family members should be encouraged to communicate verbally and the value of democratic communication should be highlighted (Gaw, 1993). Since many Asian-American families prefer negotiation of differences rather than direct conflict, it may help to hold separate sessions with individual members prior to addressing family conflict directly (Berg & Jaya, 1993; Ho, 1987).

The mental health services literature on work with Latino populations has focused on improving the accessibility of mental health services, choosing interventions according to the cultural characteristics of Latinos, and modifying traditional intervention approaches based on a familiarity and evaluation of ethnic characteristics or creatively deriving the intervention program in response to the cultural milieu (Rogler, Malgady, Constantino, & Blumenthal, 1987). For example, home visits may be an essential component of family interventions with Latino families (Ho, 1987). In addition, or when home visits are not possible, the psychologist should become acquainted with extended family members and assimilated into the family's power hierarchy in order to exert the influence necessary to help the family change. The therapist must appreciate the positive aspects of roles within Latino families that may have negative connotations within middle class, Anglo American culture (e.g., machismo in the father figure). It is essential that the therapist function as cultural translator, mediator, and role model to facilitate the family's active engagement in the community.

It is often the case that Native American families' explanation of a family problem (e.g., marital discord, parent–child conflict) is that the problem is a response to the family's inability to provide for essential needs (e.g., food, shelter) (Ho, 1987). As such, the early stages of a family intervention must address these basic needs and the psychologist should provide advice and information to enhance the family's capacity to fulfill these basic needs. Such a stance communicates the therapist's sensitivity to the family's basic needs and willingness to provide immediate services (Panigua, 1994). Such a stance is likely to foster the development of a working alliance with the family. When undertaking the problem-resolution phase of family interventions with Native American families, the therapist should emphasize group decision-making by including nuclear and extended family members and key community members (medicine man or woman, tribal leaders) (Ho, 1987), and must be mindful of this culture's holistic, interdependent world view and the fact that relationships with kin are of prime significance (Ho, 1987). Suggestions must be delivered to the family in a thoughtful, pragmatic, and calm manner (Ho, 1987; Panigua, 1994). One of the major goals of family interventions with Native American families is the promotion of interdependence. This can be achieved most readily when the therapist functions as a role model, committed to engaging all relevant parties in problem assessment and resolution. Involving all family members in the intervention process typically entails allowing the family to determine the issues to be addressed (Ho, 1987; Panigua, 1994). The use of structural and strategic interventions such as reframing and relabeling are likely to be particularly effective. Strategies experienced by the family as indicating the family's causal role in the identified patient's symptoms are likely to meet with considerable opposition.

Given the consistency between Jewish family values (family membership and loyalty, egalitarianism with regard to roles, intellectual achievement, verbal expression of feelings) and those of psychotherapy, Jewish families often appear to engage readily in family therapy (Rosen & Weltman, 1996). However, the culture's pride in suffering and emphasis on insight over behavior change may complicate the family therapy process. Jewish families often seek services when there is a conflict within the system regarding the degree of closeness vs. separateness. When working with these families, the psychologist must communicate to the family a respect for their value on family cohesion, while simultaneously addressing the ways in which closeness in the family system may interfere with the development and maintenance of family members' personal boundaries and age-appropriate separation–individuation.

Irish-Americans tend to minimize problems, have difficulty articulating their feelings, and use humor and alcohol to manage stress (McGoldrick, 1996). These coping strategies are often associated with a reluctance to seek psychological services. When Irish-American families do enter therapy, the psychologist is likely to encounter guilt, resentment, and self-reproach. To intervene effectively with Irish-American families, family clinicians should ask specific questions to elicit all relevant information, maintain a friendly distance, and avoid exploration of painful effects and embarrassing topics (Jalali, 1988; McGoldrick, 1996). Thus, a structured approach, focusing on the presenting problem, is suggested (McGoldrick, 1996).

The family is of prime importance in Italian-American communities. Families in these communities are often reluctant to support members' differentiation. In addition, many Italian-American families attempt to resolve conflicts within the nuclear and extended family. The therapist, therefore, must respect the family as a cohesive unit. Attempts to decrease family closeness by strengthening internal and weakening external boundaries are likely to be resisted and met with the family's refusal to let the therapist enter the family system. This impedes the family work, which can only be effective when the therapist is treated as a member, albeit distant, of the family. Because these families often seek therapy during life cycle transitions associated with separation, it may be difficult for the therapist to refrain from challenging the family's strong emotional ties. Thus, family therapists can help most by coaching individuals to remain close to the family, without becoming engulfed (Giordano & McGoldrick, 1996). Given the Italians' penchant for "histrionics," the therapist must ascertain the actual severity of the problem (Jalali, 1988). Despite their emotionally expressive presentation, they frequently deny family conflicts and secrets until they trust the therapist. It is important, therefore, to provide timely advice regarding the chief complaint, while patiently waiting for the family to examine underlying patterns (Giordano & McGoldrick, 1996).

10.08.5.5 Culturally Sensitive Techniques Across the Life Cycle

10.08.5.5.1 The joining of families: culturally sensitive assessment and intervention

Given the significant cultural variations in the nature of marital relationships among diverse families, an assessment of a couple must include attention to those cultural variables most likely to impact upon the functioning of the dyad. In addition, when conducting an assessment, the psychologist must be mindful of accepted cultural practices, many of which may be unfamiliar to the clinician (e.g., arranged marriages, lack of emphasis placed on love). When assessing newly formed couples, whether or not they are married, the psychologist must examine each person's perspective on the meaning of an intimate partnership (values on intimacy, fidelity, divorce), appropriate gender roles within a couple, and the degree of autonomy vs. interdependence expected by each partner both within the dyad and between the dyad and the extended family. Attention must be paid to each person's notions regarding the degree to which each party has an equal role and value in the partnership and the responsibilities to be assumed by each person. It is also crucial that the psychologist investigates physical abuse in all couples, regardless of their ethnic heritage, as domestic violence is prevalent in all cultures (Levinson, 1989). Finally, given the increasing rates of intermarriage and the fact that intimate relationships between people of different ethnic, religious, and racial backgrounds compound the issues faced by couples from a single ethnic group, similarities and differences between partners based upon their cultural heritage must be examined.

The joining of two families through marriage requires that the two individuals choosing to marry renegotiate with one another about areas of concern. Difficulties in negotiating and compromising on such issues as core values, the role of the family, communication styles, roles and responsibilities, level of intimacy, religion, and politics often lead couples to seek couples' therapy (Carter & McGoldrick, 1989). When intervening with newly formed couples, the psychologist must first help each partner to feel comfortable in sharing their perceptions, opinions, and wishes regarding various areas of disagreement (e.g., Falicov, 1983). One way in which a nonjudgemental context can be created to facilitate this sharing is by the therapist encouraging both members of the dyad to examine how their views are influenced by their cultural background. During this process of disclosure, it behoves the therapist to validate for the couple the complexities of negotiating different life styles and different cultural stereotypes. The couple also needs help in realizing the importance of integrating their differences, rather than choosing between polar opposites. The process of working through similarities and differences enables the couple to form their own identification as a new family unit, both related to and separate from their respective families of origin.

10.08.5.5.2 Families with young children: culturally sensitive assessment and intervention

In working with culturally diverse families with young children, psychologists need to choose and administer assessment devices and interpret the results from a culturally informed perspective (Canino & Spurlock, 1994). This involves using and producing culturally and developmentally sensitive instruments, techniques, and explanations. Direct observation of children playing, drawing, and interacting with their family can provide metaphors for the child's thoughts and feelings (Grizenko, Sayeghm, & Migneault, 1991). Such metaphors are particularly helpful when language differences complicate the assessment process. The psychologist must guard against any personal biases and shed cultural stereotypes when conducting and interpreting a family assessment of a young child (Grizenko et al., 1991). When evaluating a child's presenting problem, the psychologist must ascertain the meaning of the symptoms in the child's culture and the degree to which the symptoms are viewed as pathological in the child's culture (Grizenko et al.). An assessment of a young child, individually as well as in the context of the family, must consider the cultural context of the child's socialization. For example, deferential behavior may raise questions about the Caucasian child's self-confidence and or a rigid family structure; such behavior is expected in many Latino cultures and thus is most appropriately understood as reflecting the child's efforts to conform to cultural expectations.

When intervening with families with young children, the therapist must consider the family's cultural values on various aspects of childrearing and socialization. For example, when working with many traditional Latino families, it may be inappropriate for the therapist to emphasize the need for the child to be behaviorally and verbally assertive, as such a recommendation may be perceived by the family as undermining of the parents' role (Zayas & Solari, 1994). The therapist must join such family systems by acknowledging, not challenging, the parents' authority. Gradually, this will enable the family to trust the therapist, which in turn will facilitate the family's increased comfort with the expression of a full range of emotions from the children (Zayas & Solari, 1994).

One complicated dilemma that may be encountered when working with families with young children occurs when the child is the only family member fluent in English (Vasquez-Nuttall et al., 1984). For example, for a Cuban-American family in which Spanish is the sole language of the adults, a Spanish speaking therapist may be optimal. If such a therapist is unavailable or if the family prefers an English speaking therapist who can introduce them to the majority culture, a translator may be an option. Unfortunately, however, translations often misrepresent the actual meaning and cultural significance of family expressions and fail to consider implications of nonverbal behaviors. While some families prefer using the young child as an interpreter, this is problematic in families from cultural groups in which respect for parental authority is of utmost importance. In such instances, the child as interpreter may be perceived as being insubordinate, disrespectful, and intruding on adult concerns.

One particular form of intervention that impacts significantly on the family of a young child is that of early interventions (Hanson et al., 1990). Because early interventions focus on the young child with a disability, these programs interact with cultural views and values. Early interventionists often work with the young child with a disability in the family's home. This experience offers an inside view of family rituals, communication, and caretaking patterns, and a perspective on children and child-rearing, and family and family roles. In addition, it typically is sanctioned for early interventionists to consult with the family regarding health and mental health care. Such involvements with the family heighten the early interventionist's awareness of different cultural perspectives and the need to respect the family's boundaries while simultaneously imparting the views of the larger culture so that they can receive optimal care for their young child (Hanson et al., 1990).

10.08.5.5.3 Families with adolescents: culturally sensitive assessment and intervention

Defining deviant adolescent behavior in the context of culturally diverse families is complicated. The degree to which rebellion, deviance, and separation–individuation strivings are tolerated varies with different ethnic and cultural groups. For example, the Latino family's awareness that their adolescent daughter is sexually active with her boyfriend may lead to their seeking services for their child. Once the psychologist is familiar with the family's cultural norm that premarital sex among adolescent females is unacceptable, the therapist must assess the adolescent's sexual activity (solely with significant other vs. with multiple partners, safe sex practices) and other potentially maladaptive or self-destructive behaviors. Based on these data, the psychologist can ascertain if the adolescent's behavior is inconsistent with her family's cultural norms but in keeping with the practices of the majority culture, or deviant from the expectations of both cultures. This information should be shared with the family during the assessment.

Among immigrant families from such diverse cultures as Mexico, Nigeria, and Kuwait, adolescents are expected to seek, respect, and obey their parents' guidance (Baptiste, 1993). After living in the US, adolescents from these families often begin to behave in a more individualistic fashion, place a greater value on autonomy than is accepted in their family and culture of origin, and seek advice from nonfamily members. Such actions are perceived by older family members as a reflection of the family's inability to cope effectively with immigration and are experienced as threatening and disrespectful. As a consequence, a rigidification of family rules is common. If such a response fails to reduce the adolescent's autonomy strivings, the family may seek a mental health evaluation. It is incumbent upon the psychologist evaluating such families to bear in mind the conflictual values regarding family hierarchy and dependence vs. independence manifested by members of different generations. Feedback from such an assessment must incorporate the therapist's evaluation of the extent to which the adolescent's behaviors and attitudes are consistent with, or discrepant from, the different cultures in which the adolescent embedded. If based on this feedback, the therapist recommends treatment and the family concurs, the therapist should serve as a family intermediary, whose primary function is to translate cultural behavior in a developmental perspective. In working with some families (e.g., Mexican-Americans), this may entail conducting separate sibling and parent sessions to discuss sexual matters, prior to holding sessions with all family members present (Falicov, 1996). Such an approach demonstrates the therapist's respect for the parents' view that discussion of intimate matters with their children is inappropriate and undermining of their authority (Garcia-Preto, 1996).

There is a burgeoning body of research on racial and ethnic similarities and differences in adolescent substance abuse patterns and risk factors (e.g., Gottfredson & Koper, 1996). Data from these studies have been used to guide the development and implementation of culturally informed preventive intervention programs, such as the State-wide Indian Drug Prevention Program (IDPP) (Bobo, Gilchrist, Cvetkovich, Trimble, & Schinke, 1988). In addition, these data have laid the foundation for treatment outcome studies. For example, an excellent example of culturally sensitive treatment outcome research has been conducted with the families of Cuban-American adolescents with substance abuse problems (e.g., Kurtines & Szapocznik, 1996; Szapocznik et al., 1984; 1986). Bicultural effectiveness training (BET), a brief family intervention model that incorporates culture as a key content area upon which to base family interventions, has been found to be equally effective in improving family functioning as structural family therapy, a standard family approach that is not necessarily culturally based. These findings support the use of a culturally informed family intervention for enhancing the functioning of adolescents with substance abuse problems from families that experience conflicts associated with cultural and generational differences (Szapocznik et al., 1986).

10.08.5.5.4 Launching children, single young adults leaving home, and the middle generation moving on: culturally sensitive assessment and intervention

Given cultural variations in what is considered normative behavior during the launching stage of the family life cycle, it is crucial that the psychologist takes cultural norms into account when ascertaining whether or not family conflicts during this time reflect significant individual or family dysfunction, differences in values across generations about independence v. interdependence, differences in perspectives on healthy behavior during this phase between the family's cultural group and the majority culture, or simply normal family processes. It is useful to learn if previous generations of the family migrated during this phase, as these family of origin experiences would intensify the significance of this period (Carter & McGoldrick, 1989). When assessing the single young adult leaving home, it is recommended that information be gleaned regarding how the person's parents managed this phase of their own development. Questions should be asked about the young adult's internal struggles and conflicts with cultural norms regarding separation and individuation. Also, data should be gathered regarding the individual's view of acceptable gender roles vs. those held by the family and cultural group (e.g., views on remaining single as a woman). Finally, given that this process requires a restructuring of the marital relationship, the parent's marital history and current marital status deserve attention.

It is often recommended that family work with single young adults or with young adults in the launching phase be conducted primarily with the young adult, using a family of origin approach (Bowen, 1978). It is useful for the psychologist to help young adults examine the relation between multigenerational patterns of relating and their own personal development. To facilitate this awareness, the psychologist can "coach" or guide young adults in both the emancipation process and in renegotiating family relationships in order to develop a healthier balance between autonomy and attachment that meets the needs of both the individual and the family, and that takes cultural considerations into account. The coaching process must address cultural norms when focusing on the reduction of extreme enmeshment, radical disengagement, and the active use of triangulation. Specific strategies that may facilitate this process include: detriangling, person-to-person contact, reversals, and reconnecting (Carter & McGoldrick, 1989). These strategies enable the family system to alter patterns of relating that are dysfunctional given the family's current cultural context and foster mature communication among family members.

When couples seek mental health services during this family life cycle stage, culturally sensitive interventions must take at least a three-generation perspective. A multigenerational view allows the psychologist to help the couple deal with their independence from their offspring and their increased commitment to the older generation. In addition, they may need help in dealing with the separation and loss associated with the death of older family members who often serve as culture bearers. The negotiation of new relationships with children and parents is often complicated by the need to renegotiate the marital dyad. Thus, family interventions must address all relevant relationships, with particular attention to the ways in which the cultural values of individuals across the generations impact on the interpersonal difficulties that emerge. Further, for individuals from many cultural groups, this may be the first family life cycle stage in which their own individual development is paramount. Thus, personal difficulties camouflaged by the demands of family life at other stages in the family life cycle may come to the fore, and may require individual attention.

10.08.5.5.5 Families in later life: culturally sensitive assessment and intervention

For psychologists to assess accurately the functioning among culturally diverse families with elderly members, they must first build a therapeutic relationship with all family members. This may be complicated when working with elderly family members, as these individuals from different cultural groups are often suspicious of professionals who they perceive as having little in common with them. They suspect that mental health and health care professionals may have biases against their age, race, sex, and culture.

Hays' (1996) framework for the conduct of culturally responsive assessments underscores the importance of attending to a number of influences that impact on the functioning of diverse older adults. She uses the acronym ADRESSING (albeit incorrectly spelled) to organize the key influences to be taken into account when assessing elderly family members: age, disability, religion, ethnicity, social status, sexual orientation, indigenous heritage, national origin, and gender. Attention to these variables facilitates the building of rapport, enhances the psychologist's understanding of the elderly family member's cultural identity and heritage, and improves the psychologist's awareness of elderly family members' cultural environment, needs, and strengths (Hays, 1996).

When assessing elderly clients in a family context, it behoves the psychologist to use strategies that enhance rapport and communication. Possible techniques that may facilitate positive interactions include sitting closer and speaking clearly, talking to "the good ear," using titles (Mr, Mrs, Dr, etc.) before names, using respectful and culturally sensitive interpreters when language differences exist, being equipped with conveniences for physical disabilities, and having culturally diverse artifacts in the office (Hays, 1996). When gathering a history from elderly family members, the psychologist should be cognizant of the importance of gathering extensive background information and encouraging the older family members to tell their life stories. During the assessment process, it is recommended that some time be spent with all family members present and some time should be devoted to separate meetings with the older people.

During the multigenerational meetings, the psychologist can communicate respect for the elderly by encouraging the eldest family member to speak first and by valuing the input offered by elderly family members (Kim, 1985). When conducting diagnostic interviews with the elderly or administering and interpreting test results, the psychologist must bear in mind the pernicious problem of misdiagnosis of psychiatric disorders in minority older adults (American Psychiatric Association, 1994a). Elderly clients are likely to view testing as humiliating, confusing, too time-consuming; and not relevant to them, and thus may respond with excessive anxiety and a lack of focus and effort to the process. Frequently, the instruments used and the process of assessing intelligence or personality have been created and indexed around younger, Euroamerican cultural values and constructs (Berry, Poortinga, Segall, & Dasen, 1992), and thus may not be valid or reliable for use with diverse older adults. When such instruments or processes are used with elderly ethnic minority individuals, misdiagnoses, confusion, and inappropriate interventions can occur (Hilliard, 1992). The likelihood of misdiagnosis can be minimized if the psychologist takes the time to use observations and interviews, and to look for "intrapersonal strengths related to specific cultural identities as well as interpersonal or social supports related to minority group membership" (Hays, 1996, p. 192).

There is a dearth of information on clinical interventions with the ethnic minority elderly and their families (American Psychiatric Association, 1994a). Little data exist regarding whether or not efficacious interventions for nonminority elderly will be effective for minority elderly. The extant literature underscores the importance of engaging as many extended family members as possible in the care of older family members. Unfortunately, however, for many immigrants, family support may be inadequate or absent and family relations are often marked by significant intergenerational conflicts (Goldstein, 1989). Thus, adequate mental health services must include outreach efforts and the availability of mental health resources in conjunction with medical care (Sakauye, 1989).

Family interventions with diverse older adults should be primarily directive (Paniagua, 1994) and include the provision of education to the patient and family. The psychologist should assume an active stance and incorporate a problem focus. All interventions should communicate respect for the elderly and an appreciation of the elderly's perspective on the role of the therapist. For example, Native American elderly typically view the therapist as akin to the medicine man, whereas Latino elderly often perceive the therapist as a folk healer (Paniagua, 1994). Further, family interventions should be geared toward the acceptance of intergenerational differences and the resolution of associated conflicts.

10.08.6 FUTURE DIRECTIONS

Given the relative dearth of empirical literature from a culturally sensitive perspective regarding family patterns, family-oriented assessment, and family interventions, it is incumbent upon psychologists to conduct research on all of these topics. One specific area that deserves immediate attention is the delineation, based on research findings, of family patterns among different ethnic groups across the various family life cycle stages. A second research topic that merits further investigation is the development and collection of normative data on culturally sensitive assessment tools (e.g., questionnaires, observational coding schemas, semistructured interviews) for various aspects of family functioning across a multitude of cultural settings. The need for assessment methodologies specific to each given culture requires special attention. A third avenue for research exploration relates to the development, implementation, and evaluation of family interventions designed to be culturally and developmentally sensitive. The conduct of assessment and intervention research must include a focus on the validity, reliability, and efficacy of various techniques based upon the culture of the therapist and the family.

Due to the rapidly changing nature of the family in America and throughout the world, as well as increased levels of multiculturalism, clinicians and researchers must devote efforts to understanding more about families embedded in cultures in transition. This will require more attention to such issues as cultures within cultures (e.g., a lesbian couple in which one member is Latino and her partner is Asian-American), and intergenerational conflicts within families associated with levels of acculturation and/or sense of connection to the culture of origin.

Fortunately, diversity training for clinicians and researchers has advanced significantly. However, it is incumbent upon us as psychologists to insure that cultural considerations be given paramount importance in coursework, supervision, and continuing education programs related to family assessment and intervention. This entails the utilization of a cultural formulation for family case conceptualization, increased and ongoing discussion of the family's cultural context as it impacts on family relationships, and enhanced sensitivity to cultural issues in all aspects of the family assessment and intervention process. Such a shift in our orientation as psychologists and family therapists will result in the delivery of more ethical and effective interventions.

10.08.7 SUMMARY

Since the 1970s, family theory and therapy has come to recognize the significant impact that a family's cultural context has on assessment and intervention across the family life cycle. Increasingly, family theorists and therapists view each individual as apart of a family system embedded in a larger culture, the structure and process of which depends on the family's stage of development. The current chapter focused on a cultural perspective on families across the life cycle and implications for the conduct of culturally sensitive assessment and intervention. While conceptualizations of culture often include ethnicity, race, SES, gender, sexual orientation, country of origin, and religious and political affiliations, we have chosen to concentrate on cultural issues relevant to ethnic groups living in the US. A thorough review of the literature suggests that effective family assessment and intervention is characterized by:

(i) the therapists' acknowledgement of their own cultural origins and the impact of this background on the assessment and intervention process;

(ii) a sensitivity to the family's cultural background;

(iii) an appreciation of the unique interactional patterns, attitudes, feelings, and behaviors of each family;

(iv) a recognition of the family's location in the family life cycle;

(v) validation and strengthening of the ethnic identity of each family member and the family unit as a whole; and

(vi) an incorporation of relevant support systems (Giordano & Giordano, 1995; N.J. Kaslow et al., 1995).

To provide culturally sensitive family assessments and interventions, the clinician must strive to overcome cultural barriers while demonstrating respect for the cultural identity and integrity of each family member, the family system, and the therapist (Tyler, Brome, & Williams, 1991). As the dramatic increase in cultural diversity in the US is expected to continue into the twenty-first century, there is a strong need for empirically validated multicultural and culture specific family theories and therapies. However, until such theories and therapies are available, psychologists are charged with helping families negotiate the reconnection with their cultural heritage in order to establish or preserve a sense of belonging and cultural identity, while concurrently adapting to an evolving cultural context (N.J. Kaslow et al., 1995).

10.08.8 REFERENCES

Aboud, F. (1987). The development of ethnic self-identification and attitudes. In J. Phinney & M. Rotheram (Eds.), *Children's ethnic socialization: Pluralism and development* (pp. 32–55). Newbury Park, CA: Sage.

Alarcon, R. D. (Ed.) (1995). Cultural psychiatry (special issue). *The Psychiatric Clinics of North America, 18*(3).

American Psychiatric Association (1994a). *Ethnic minority elderly: A task force report of the American Psychiatric Association*. Washington, DC: Author.

American Psychiatric Association (1994b). *Diagnostic and*

statistical manual of mental disorders (4th ed.). Washington, DC: Author.

American Psychological Association (1993). Guidelines for providers of psychological services to ethnic, linguistic, and culturally diverse populations. *American Psychologist, 48,* 45–48.

Baker, F. M. (1994). Issues in the psychiatric care of African American elders. In American Psychiatric Association (Ed.), *Ethnic minority elderly: A task force report of the American Psychiatric Association* (pp. 21–62). Washington, DC: American Psychiatric Association.

Banks, W. (1976). White preference in Blacks: A paradigm in search of a phenomenon. *Psychological Bulletin, 83,* 1179–1186.

Baptiste, D. A., Jr. (1993). Immigrant families, adolescents and acculturation: Insight for therapists. *Marriage and Family Review, 19,* 341–363.

Berg, I. K., & Jaya, A. (1993). Different and same: Family therapy with Asian American families. *Journal of Marital and Family Therapy, 19,* 31–38.

Berry, J. W., Poortinga, Y. H., Segall, M. H., & Dasen, P. R. (1992). *Cross-cultural psychology: Research and applications.* New York: Cambridge University Press.

Billingsley, A. (1992). *Climbing Jacob's ladder: The enduring legacy of African American families.* New York: Simon and Schuster.

Babo, J. K., Gilchrist, L. D., Cvetkovich, G. T., Trimble, J. E., & Schinke, S. P. (1988). Cross-cultural service delivery to minority communities. *Journal of Community Psychology, 16,* 263–272.

Bowen, M. (1978). *Family therapy in clinical practice.* New York: Jason Aronson.

Boyd-Franklin, N. (1989). *Black families in therapy: A multi-systems approach.* New York: Guilford Press.

Boynton, G. (1987). Cross-cultural family therapy: The ESCAPE model. *American Journal of Family Therapy, 15,* 123–130.

Bretherton, I., & Waters, E. (Eds.) (1985). Growing points of attachment theory and research. *Monographs of the Society for Research in Child Development, 50 (1–2, Serial No. 209).*

Bullrich, S. (1989). The process of immigration. In L. Combrinck-Graham (Ed.), *Children in family contexts: Perspectives on treatment* (pp. 482–501). New York: Guilford Press.

Canino, I., & Spurlock, J. (1994). *Culturally diverse children and adolescents: Assessment, diagnosis and treatment.* New York: Guilford Press.

Carter, E., & McGoldrick, M. (1989). *The changing family life cycle: A framework for family therapy* (2nd ed.). Boston: Allyn and Bacon.

Clark, K. B., & Clark, M. P. (1940). Skin color as a factor in racial identification of Negro preschool children. *Journal of Social Psychology, 11,* 156–169.

Comas-Diaz, L., & Greene, B. (Eds.) (1994). *Women of color: integrating ethnic and gender identities in psychotherapy.* New York: Guilford Press.

Coner-Edwards, A. F., & Spurlock, J. (Eds.) (1988). *Black families in crisis: The middle class.* New York: Brunner Mazel.

Congress, E. P. (1994). The use of culturagrams to assess and empower culturally diverse families. *Families in Society, 75,* 531–540.

Dana, R. H. (1993). *Multicultural assessment perspectives for professional psychology.* Boston: Allyn and Bacon.

Lavis, J. (1988). Mazel tov: The Bar Mitzvah as a multigenerational ritual of change and continuity. In E. Imber-Black, J. Roberts, & R. Whiting (Eds.), *Rituals in families and family therapy* (pp. 177–208). New York: Norton.

Dechesnay, M. (1986). Jamaican family structure: The paradox of normalcy. *Family Process, 25,* 293–300.

Emery, E. (1996). Amish families. In M. McGoldrick, J. Giordano, & J. Pearce (Eds.), *Ethnicity and family therapy* (2nd ed., pp. 442–450). New York: Guilford Press.

Erikson, E. H. (1958). *Identity: Youth and crisis.* New York: Norton.

Falicov, C. J. (Ed.) (1983). *Cultural perspectives in family therapy.* Rockville, MD: Aspen.

Falicov, C. J. (1996). Mexican families. In M. McGoldrick, J. Giordano, & J. Pearce (Eds.), *Ethnicity and family therapy* (2nd ed., pp. 169–182). New York: Guilford Press.

Fisek, G. O. (1991). A cross-cultural examination of proximity and hierarchy as dimensions of family structure. *Family Process, 30,* 121–133.

Foulks, E. F. (1991). Transcultural psychiatry and normal behavior. In D. Offer & M. Sabshin (Eds.), *The diversity of normal behavior* (pp. 207–238). New York: Basic Books.

Franklin, D. L. (1987). Black adolescent pregnancy: A literature review. *Child and Youth Services, 9,* 15–39.

Fredman, N., & Sherman, R. (1987). *Handbook of measurements for marriage and family therapy.* New York: Brunner Mazel.

Garcia-Preto, N. (1996). Latino families: An overview. In M. McGoldrick, J. Giordano, & J. Pearce (Eds.), *Ethnicity and family therapy* (2nd ed., pp. 141–154). New York: Guilford Press.

Gaw, A. C. (Ed.) (1993). *Culture, ethnicity, and mental illness.* Washington, DC: American Psychiatric Press.

Gibbs, J. T., & Huang, L. N. (1989). *Children of color: Psychological interventions with minority youth.* San Francisco: Jossey Bass.

Giordano, J., & Giordano, M. A. (1995). Ethnic dimensions in family therapy. In R. Mikesell, D. Lusterman, & S. McDaniel (Eds.), *Integrating family therapy: Handbook of family psychology and systems theory* (pp. 347–356). Washington, DC: American Psychological Association.

Giordano, J., & McGoldrick, M. (1996). Italian families. In M. McGoldrick, J. Giordani, & J. Pearce (Eds.), *Ethnicity and family therapy* (2nd ed., pp. 567–582). New York: Guilford Press.

Goldenberg, H., & Goldenberg, I. (1994). *Counseling today's families* (2nd ed.). Pacific Grove, CA: Brooks/Cole.

Goldstein, M. Z. (1989). *Family involvement in treatment of the frail elderly.* Washington, DC: American Psychiatric Press.

Gottfredson, D. C. & Koper, C. S. (1996). Race and sex differences in the prediction of drug use. *Journal of Consulting and Clinical Psychology, 64,* 305–313.

Grizenko, N., Sayegh, L., & Migneault, P. (Eds.) (1991). *Transcultural issues in child psychiatry.* Verdun, PQ: Editions Douglas.

Gushue, G. (1993). Cultural-identity development and family assessment: An interaction model. *Counseling Psychologist, 21,* 487–513.

Gushue, G. V., & Sciarra, D. T. (1995). Culture and families: A multidimensional approach. In J. G. Ponterotto, J. M. Casas, L. A. Suzuki, & C. M. Alexander (Eds.), *Handbook of multicultural counseling.* Thousand Oaks, CA: Sage.

Hanson, M. J., Lynch, E. W., & Wayman, K. I. (1990). Honoring the cultural diversity of families when gathering data. *Topics in Early Childhood Special Education, 10,* 112–131.

Harrison, A. O., Wilson, M. N., Pine, C. J., Chan, S. Q., & Buriel, R. (1990). Family ecologies of ethnic minority children. *Child Development, 61,* 347–362.

Harwood, R. L. (1992). The influence of culturally derived values on Anglo and Puerto Rican mothers' perceptions of attachment behavior. *Child Development, 63,* 822–839.

Harwood, R. L., & Miller, J. G. (1991). Perceptions of attachment behavior: A comparison of Anglo and Puerto Rican mothers. *Merrill-Palmer Quarterly, 37,* 583–599.

Harwood, R. L., Miller, J. G., & Irizarry, N. L. (1995). *Culture and attachment: Perceptions of the child in context.* New York: Guilford Press.

Hays, P. A. (1996). Culturally responsive assessment with diverse older clients. *Professional Psychology: Research and Practice, 27,* 188–193.

Hillard, J. R. (1982). Diagnosis and treatment of the rootwork victim. *Psychiatric Annals, 12,* 705–714.

Hilliard, A. S. (1992). IQ and the courts: Larry P. v. Wilson Riles and PASE v. Hannon. In A. K. H. Burlew, W. C. Banks, H. P. McAdoo, & D. A. Azibo (Eds.), *African American psychology* (pp. 199–217). Newbury Park, CA: Sage.

Ho, M. K. (1987). *Family therapy with ethnic minorities.* Newbury Park, CA: Sage.

Hsu, J., Tseng, W. S., Ashton, G., McDermott, J. F., & Char, W. (1985). Family interaction patterns among Japanese-American and Caucasian families in Hawaii. *American Journal of Psychiatry, 142,* 577–581.

IJzendoorn, M. H. Van (Ed.) (1990). Cross-cultural validity of attachment theory (special issue). *Human Development, 33.*

Imber-Black, E., Roberts, J., & Whiting, R. (Eds) (1988). *Rituals in families and family therapy.* New York: Norton.

Ivey, A. E., Ivey, M. B., & Simek-Morgan, L. (1993). *Counseling and psychotherapy: A multicultural perspective* (3rd ed.). Boston: Allyn and Bacon.

Jacob, T. (Ed.) (1987). *Family interaction and psychopathology: Theories, methods, and findings.* New York: Plenum Press.

Jacobs, J. L. (1994). Gender, race, class, and the trend toward early motherhood: A feminist analysis of teen mothers in contemporary society. *Journal of Contemporary Ethnography, 22,* 442–462.

Jalali, B. (1988). Ethnicity, cultural adjustment and behavior: Implications for family therapy. In L. Comas-Diaz & E. Griffith (Eds.), *Clinical guidelines in cross-cultural mental health* (pp. 9–32). New York: Wiley.

Jimenez, R. G., & Figueiredo, J. M. de (1994). Issues in the psychiatric care of Hispanic American elders. In American Psychiatric Association (Ed.), *Ethnic minority elderly: A task force report of the American Psychiatric Association* (pp. 63–90). Washington, DC: American Psychiatric Association.

Karnow, S., & Yoshihara, N. (1992). *Asian Americans in transition.* New York: The Asia Society.

Kaslow, F. W. (1993). The divorce ceremony: A healing strategy. In T. Nelson & T. Trepper (Eds.), *101 favorite family therapy interventions* (pp. 341–345). New York: Haworth Press.

Kaslow, F. W. (1995). *Projective genogramming.* Sarasota, FL: Professional Resource Press.

Kaslow, N. J., Celano, M., & Dreelin, E. D. (1995). A cultural perspective on family theory and therapy. *Psychiatric Clinics of North America, 18,* 621–633.

Kazdin, A. E., Stolar, M. J., & Marciano, P. L. (1995). Risk factors for dropping out of treatment among White and Black families. *Journal of Family Psychology, 9,* 402–417.

Kim, S. C. (1985). Family therapy for Asian Americans: A strategic structural framework. *Psychotherapy, 22,* 342–348.

Kurtines, W. M., & Szapocznik, J. (1996). Family interaction patterns: Structural family therapy in contexts of cultural diversity. In E. D. Hibbs & P. S. Jensen (Eds.), *Psychosocial treatments for child and adolescent disorders: Empirically based strategies for clinical practice* (pp. 671–697). Washington, DC: American Psychological Association.

L'Abate, L., & Bagarozzi, D. A. (1993). *Sourcebook of marriage and family evaluation.* New York: Brunner Mazel.

Lasry, J. C., & Sayegh, L. (1992). Developing an acculturation scale: A bidimensional model. In N. Grizenko, L. Sayegh, & P. Migneault (Eds.), *Transcultural issues in child psychiatry* (pp. 67–86). Verdun, PQ: Editions Douglas.

Lee, E. (1996). Chinese families. In M. McGoldrick, J. Giordano, & J. Pearce (Eds.), *Ethnicity and family therapy* (2nd ed., pp. 249–267). New York: Guilford Press.

Levinson, D. (1989). *Family violence in cross cultural perspective.* Newbury Park, CA: Sage.

Lindblad-Goldberg, M. (1989). Successful minority single-parent families. In L. Combrinck-Graham (Ed.), *Children in family contexts: Perspectives in treatment* (pp. 116–134). New York: Guilford Press.

London, H., & Devore, W. (1988). Layers of understanding: Counseling ethnic minority families. *Family Relations, 37,* 310–314.

Mahon, J. (1976). Black and White children's racial identification and preference. *Journal of Black Psychology, 3,* 47–58.

Matsui, W. T. (1996). Japanese families. In M. McGoldrick, J. Giordano, & J. Pearce (Eds.), *Ethnicity and family therapy* (2nd ed., pp. 268–280). New York: Guilford Press.

Matsumoto, D. (1994). *People: Psychology from a cultural perspective.* Pacific Grove, CA.: Brooks/Cole.

Mayer, E., & Kosmin, B. (1994). *National survey of religious identification.* New York: University of New York.

McGoldrick, M. (1996). Irish families. In M. McGoldrick, J. Giordano, & J. Pearce (Eds.), *Ethnicity and family therapy* (2nd ed., pp. 544–566). New York: Guilford Press.

McGoldrick, M., & Gerson, R. (1985). *Genograms in family assessment.* New York: Norton.

McGoldrick, M., Hines, P., Lee, E., & Preto, N. G. (1986). Mourning rituals: How culture shapes the experience of loss. *Family Therapy Networker, November/December,* 28–36.

McGoldrick, M., Pearce, J. K., & Giordano, J. (Eds.) (1982). *Ethnicity and family therapy.* New York: Guilford Press.

McGoldrick, M., Pearce, J. K., & Giordano, J (Eds.) (1996). *Ethnicity and family therapy* (2nd ed.). New York: Guilford Press.

McMiller, W. P., & Weisz, J. R. (1996). Help-seeking preceding mental health clinic intake among African-American, Latino, and Caucasian youths. *Journal of the American Academy of Child and Adolescent Psychiatry, 35,* 1086–1094.

Mickelson, R. (1990). The attitude-achievement paradox among Black adolescents. *Sociology of Education, 63,* 44–61.

Myerhoff, B. (1979). *Number our days: Culture and community among elderly Jews in an American ghetto.* New York: Meridian.

Odell, M., Shelling, G., Young, K. S., Hewitt, D. H., & L'Abate, L. (1994). The skills of the marriage and family therapist in straddling multicultural issues. *American Journal of Family Therapy, 22,* 145–155.

Panigua, F. A. (1994). *Assessing and treating culturally diverse clients.* Thousand Oaks, CA: Sage.

Papajohn, J., & Spiegel, J. P. (1975). *Transactions in families: A modern approach for resolving cultural and generational conflict.* San Francisco: Jossey-Bass.

Parham, T. A., & Helms, J. E. (1981). The influence of Black students' racial identity attitudes on preferences for counselor's race. *Journal of Counseling Psychology,*

28, 250–257.

Parham, T. A., & Helms, J. E. (1985a). Attitudes of racial identity and self-esteem of Black students: An exploratory investigation. *Journal of College Student Personnel, 26*, 143–147.

Parham, T. A., & Helms, J. E. (1985b). Relation of racial identity attitudes to self-actualization and affective states of Black students. *Journal of Counseling Psychology, 32*, 431–440.

Phinney, J. S. (1989). Stages of ethnic identity in minority group adolescents. *Journal of Early Adolescence, 9*, 34–49.

Phinney, J. S. (1990a). Ethnic identity in adolescents and adults: Review of research. *Psychological Bulletin, 108*, 499–514.

Phinney, J. S. (1990b). The multi-group ethnic identity measure. A new scale for use with diverse groups. *Journal of Adolescent Research, 7*, 156–176.

Phinney, J. S., & Alipuria, L. (1990). Ethnic identity in older adolescents from four ethnic groups. *Journal of Adolescence, 13*, 171–183.

Pinderhughes, E. (1989). *Understanding race, ethnicity, and power*. New York: Guilford Press.

Plummer, D. L. (1995). Patterns of racial identity development of African American adolescent males and females. *Journal of Black Psychology, 21*, 168–180.

Reyes, M. B., Routh, D. K., Jean-Gilles, M. M., Sanfilippo, M. D., & Fawcett, N. (1991). Ethnic differences in parenting children in fearful situations. *Journal of Pediatric Psychology, 16*, 717–726.

Rogler, L. H., Malgady, R. G., Constantino, G., & Blumenthal, R. (1987). What do culturally sensitive mental health services mean? The case of Hispanics. *American Psychologist, 42*, 565–570.

Rosen, E. J., & Weltman, S. F. (1996). Jewish families: An overview. In M. McGoldrick, J. Giordano, & J. Pearce (Eds.), *Ethnicity and family therapy* (2nd ed., pp. 611–645). New York: Guilford Press.

Sakauye, K. M. (1989). Ethnic variations in family support of the frail elderly. In M. Zucker-Goldstein (Ed.), *Family involvement in treatment of the frail elderly* (pp. 63–106). Washington, DC: American Psychiatric Press.

Sakauye, K. M., & Chacko, R. C. (1994). Issues in the psychiatric care of Asian/Pacific American elders. In American Psychiatric Association (Ed.), *Ethnic minority elderly: A task force report of the American Psychiatric Association* (pp. 115–148). Washington, DC: American Psychiatric Association.

Scrivner, R., & Eldridge, N. S. (1995). Lesbian and gay family psychology. In R. Mikesell, D. D. Lusterman, & S. H. McDaniel (Eds.), *Integrating family therapy: Handbook of family psychology and systems theory* (pp. 327–345). Washington, DC: American Psychological Association Press.

Slaughter-Defoe, D. T., Nakagawa, K., Takanishi, R., & Johnson, D. J. (1990). Toward cultural/ecological perspectives on schooling and achievement in African and Asian American children. *Child Development, 61*, 363–383.

Sluzki, C. E. (1979). Migration and family conflict. *Family Process, 18*, 379–390.

Smith, D. (1996). Hungarian families. In M. McGoldrick, J. Giordano, & J. Pearce (Eds.), *Ethnicity and family therapy* (2nd ed., pp. 530–543). New York: Guildford Press.

Staples, R., & Johnson, L. B. (1993). *Black families at the crossroads: Challenges and prospects*. San Francisco: Jossey-Bass.

Steinberg, L., Dornbusch, S. M., & Brown, B. B. (1992). Ethnic differences in adolescent achievement: An ecological perspective. *American Psychology, 45*, 913–920.

Sue, D. W., & Sue, D. (1990). *Counseling the culturally different: Theory and practice* (2nd ed.). New York: Wiley.

Sue, S., & Okazaki, S. (1990). Asian American educational achievements: A phenomenon in search of an explanation. *American Psychology, 45*, 913–920.

Sue, S., & Zane, N. (1987). The role of culture and cultural techniques in psychotherapy: A critique and reformulation. *American Psychologist, 42*, 37–45.

Sutton, C. T., & Nose, M. A. B. (1996). American Indian families: An overview. In M. McGoldrick, J. Giordano, & J. Pearce (Eds.), *Ethnicity and family therapy* (2nd ed., pp. 31–44). New York: Guilford Press.

Szapocznik, J., & Kurtines, W. M. (1993). Family psychology and cultural diversity. *American Psychologist, 48*, 400–407.

Szapocznik, J., Rio, A., Perez-Vidal, A., Kurtines, W., Hervis, O., & Santisteban, D. (1986). Bicultural effectiveness training (BET): An experimental test of an intervention modality for families experiencing intergenerational/intercultural conflict. *Hispanic Journal of Behavioral Sciences, 8*, 303–330.

Szapocznik, J., Santisteban, D., Kurtines, W., Perez-Vidal, A., & Hervis, O. (1984). Bicultural effectiveness training: A treatment intervention for enhancing intercultural adjustment in Cuban American families. *Hispanic Journal of Behavioral Sciences, 6*, 317–344.

Tamura, T., & Lau, A. (1992). Connectedness versus separateness: Applicability of family therapy to Japanese families. *Family Process, 31*, 319–340.

Thompson, J. W. (1994). Issues in the psychiatric care of American Indian and Alaska Native elders. In American Psychiatric Association (Ed.), *Ethnic minority elderly: A task force report of the American Psychiatric Association* (pp. 91–114). Washington, DC: American Psychiatric Association.

Timimi, S. B. (1995). Adolescence in immigrant Arab families. *Psychotherapy: Theory, Research, Practice, and Training, 32*, 141–149.

Tseng, W. (1985). Cultural aspects of family therapy. *International Journal of Family Psychiatry, 6*, 19–31.

Tyler, F. B., Brome, D. R., & Williams, J. E. (1991). *Ethnic validity, ecology, and psychotherapy: A psychological competence model*. New York: Plenum Press.

Vargas, L. A., & Koss-Chiono, J. D. (1992). *Working with culture: Psychotherapeutic interventions with ethnic minority children and adolescents*. San Francisco: Jossey-Bass.

Vazquez-Nuttall, E., Avila-Vivas, A., & Morales-Barreto, G. (1984). Working with Latin American families. *Family Therapy Collections, 9*, 74–90.

Walsh, F. (Ed.) (1993). *Normal family processes* (2nd ed.). New York: Guildford Press.

Wamboldt, F. S., & Reiss, D. (1991). Task performance and the social construction of meaning: Juxtaposing normality with contemporary family research. In D. Offer & M. Sabshin (Eds.), *The diversity of normal behavior* (pp. 164–206). New York: Basic Books.

Wilson, M. N. (1989). Child development in the context of the Black extended family. *American Psychologist, 44*, 380–385.

Wright, L. (1995, November 6). One drop of blood. *The New Yorker*.

Zayas, L. H., & Solari, F. (1994). Early childhood socialization in Hispanic families: Context, culture, and practice implications. *Professional Psychology: Research and Practice, 25*, 200–206.

Zayas, L. H., Torres, L. R., Malcolm, J., & DesRosiers, F. S. (1996). Clinicians' definitions of ethnically sensitive therapy. *Professional Psychology: Research and Practice, 27*, 78–82.

10.09
Sexual Orientation

BEVERLY GREENE
St. John's University, Jamaica, NY, USA

10.09.1 INTRODUCTION 207
10.09.2 DEFINING AND CONCEPTUALIZING SEXUAL ORIENTATION: CHALLENGES 209
10.09.3 DEMOGRAPHICS 210
10.09.3.1 Etiology Theories 213
10.09.4 UNIQUE PSYCHOLOGICAL AND DEVELOPMENTAL TASKS CHALLENGING LGB PERSONS 215
10.09.4.1 Identity Development 216
10.09.4.2 Resilience in LGB People 217
10.09.5 UTILIZATION OF PSYCHOLOGICAL SERVICES 218
10.09.5.1 Psychotherapy with LGB Persons 219
10.09.6 LGB PERSONS AND FAMILY ISSUES 222
10.09.6.1 Gay and Lesbian Couples 223
10.09.6.2 Gay and Lesbian Parents 224
10.09.6.3 Gay and Lesbian Youth 225
10.09.7 TRAINING 226
10.09.7.1 Hetrosexist Bias in the Delivery of Psychological Services 226
10.09.8 FUTURE DIRECTIONS 228
10.09.9 SUMMARY 229
10.09.10 REFERENCES 229

10.09.1 INTRODUCTION

Sexual orientation is generally defined by the sex of the person that an individual is sexually and emotionally attracted to (Bohan, 1996) and includes heterosexual, lesbian, gay, and bisexual orientations. The meaning of sexual orientation and what it represents, like other aspects of sexuality, is contextual. The context in which sexual orientation is defined and a brief history of its conceptualization is required to assess its meaning appropriately both in our society and as an aspect of human identity.

Despite the fact that sexual orientation conceptually encompasses all orientations, the study of sexual orientation in American psychology has focused generally on individuals with lesbian, gay, and bisexual (LGB) sexual orientations. Heterosexuality traditionally has been considered normative and because of this it has not been the object of study or the focus of the kinds of questions that LGB sexual orientations are subject to. The presumption of heterosexuality as the only form of sexual orientation that is psychologically normal and legitimate, and the subsequent depiction of other sexual orientations as deviant or pathological, is referred to as heterosexism (Bohan, 1996; Gonsiorek & Weinrich, 1991; McWhirter, 1990).

The failure of psychological research to ask relevant questions about the origins and determinants of all sexual orientations, rather than selective, nontraditional orientations, obscures information about all of them and leads to a range of erroneous assumptions about sexual orientation in general. Traditionally, nontraditional sexual orientations have been assumed to represent the presence or manifestation of a psychological disturbance or pathological developmental arrest.

Hooker (1957) was among the first empirical studies in psychology to broadly contradict the pathology model of homosexuality in mental health (McWhirter, 1990). Hooker administered batteries of projective tests to 30 homosexual male and 30 heterosexual male subjects. Results were reviewed by experts who could not distinguish homosexual and heterosexual subjects on the basis of their test results. Gonsiorek (1977, 1991), Meredith and Reister (1980), and Reiss (1980) provide detailed reviews of psychometric studies on homosexuality. These studies generally conclude that homosexuality *per se* is not pathological, nor is it related to psychological adjustment. The presence of such evidence, however, has not led to a complete abandonment of the pathology model in mental health practice.

An intense period of political activism and advocacy for social justice for lesbians and gay men, and the efforts of lesbian and gay mental health professionals, led to formal challenges to pathological views and subsequent changes in the diagnostic nomenclature. The details of that struggle are beyond the scope of this chapter, however, the reader is referred to Greene (1994b) and Giusti and Katz (1992) for a more detailed description of them.

In 1973, the American Psychiatric Association (APA) removed the diagnosis homosexuality from the *Diagnostic and statistical manual of mental disorders* (*DSM*), replacing it with the diagnosis of "ego dystonic homosexuality" (Haldeman, 1991, 1999). This diagnosis was used to describe individuals who were unhappy with their lesbian or gay sexual orientation and who wanted therapy to make them heterosexual. The absence of a diagnostic category for people who were dissatisfied with their heterosexuality was another manifestation of the presumed normative nature of heterosexuality. Opponents to the use of ego dystonic homosexuality as a diagnostic entity argued that it continued to pathologize homosexuality, albeit indirectly (Bohan, 1996; Gonsiorek, 1991; Haldeman, 1991, 1994, 1999). Diagnosing this predictable response to society's intolerance as if it were a condition that required repair fails to address the pathology of homophobia (Weinberg, 1972), heterosexism, and the unfair treatment of lesbians and gay men. Rather, it unfairly stigmatized the victims of unfair treatment. Furthermore, it is unlikely that individuals who face hostility and stigma as a result of an LGB sexual orientation would not at different stages of their sexual identity development manifest levels of ego dystonia or distress. In a climate that is hostile to LGB, persons, it would be likely that some would wish to be heterosexual or express distress about their sexual orientation. Bohan (1996) and Haldeman (1994, 1999) argue that a period of ego dystonia does not represent the individual's distress with their sexual orientation *per se*, but with the attitudes of a society that stigmatize that orientation and make its adoption painful. Acknowledging an LGB sexual orientation means not only the loss of heterosexual privilege but also carries the realistic danger of becoming the target of hostility, derision, potential rejection from loved ones, loss of employment, loss of child custody, and even violence (Herek, 1989). The ego dystonia observed should be regarded as a predictable and understandable part of the evolution of an LGB identity and a "normal aspect of the process of managing denigrating attitudes" associated with those identities rather than as a condition that warrants attempts at conversion to heterosexual sexual orientation (Bohan, 1996, p. 19). The diagnostic entity, ego dystonic homosexuality, was removed from the *DSM* in 1988.

In 1975, the American Psychological Association (APA) adopted an official policy statement that: homosexuality *per se* implies no impairment in judgment, stability, reliability, or general social and vocational capabilities (Committee on Lesbian and Gay Concerns [CLGC], 1986; Morin & Rothblum, 1991). At that time, APA urged all mental health professionals to take the lead in removing the stigma of mental illness that was associated historically with lesbian and gay sexual orientations in Western psychology. After years of lobbying efforts, in 1980 the CLGC was approved as a standing committee and an official part of APA's governance. The Committee, whose name has been recently changed to include Bisexual concerns, (CLGBC), was charged with establishing standards for eliminating heterosexist bias in psychological research and practice with LGB persons, as well as developing policy statements on lesbian and gay issues for the Association. Since its adoption, the committee has developed a range of guidelines for affirmative practice and research with LGB persons. Prior to the adoption of this policy, however, reproductive sexuality was legitimized as the only form of sexual orientation that was psychologically normal and morally correct. This assumption widely pervaded research, training, and practice in psychology. Some would argue that despite many changes, the association between pathology and LGB sexual orientations still lingers broadly in various corners of this discipline.

In the 23 years since the introduction of APA policy changes regarding LGB sexual orientations, LGB persons assume a higher level of visibility among those who seek professional psychological services (Liddle, 1997). However, despite major changes in the diagnostic nomenclature aimed at removing the stigma of psychopathology from gay and lesbian sexual orientations, negative bias and misinformation about lesbians and gay men continues and is still observed in clinical practice, research, and training efforts (Brown, 1996; CLGC, 1990; Garnets, Hancock, Cochran, Goodchilds, & Peplau, 1991; Garnets & Kimmel, 1991; Markowitz, 1991; Rothblum, 1993).

In 1986, the CLGC conducted a survey investigating bias in psychotherapy with lesbians and gay men. Two thousand five hundred and forty-four psychologists were surveyed to elicit themes suggestive of biased and sensitive practice. The results suggested the presence of a wide range of variance in the degree to which psychologists conform to unbiased practice standards with lesbian and gay clients (CLGC, 1990; Garnets et al., 1991). Data from this study and other research (DeCrescenzo, 1985; Rudolph, 1988) suggests that practice does not conform to APA policy standards. This suggests that despite major strides in depathologizing lesbian and gay sexual orientations *per se*, there is still much to be done with respect to educating psychologists about sexual orientation and that attitudes within organized psychology toward sexual orientation remain ambivalent (CLGC, 1990; Garnet et al., 1991; Rothblum, 1993).

10.09.2 DEFINING AND CONCEPTUALIZING SEXUAL ORIENTATION: CHALLENGES

"Homosexual" was the traditional, clinical term used to refer to people whose erotic, sexual, and affectional attractions were to individuals of the same sex. Many objections to the use of this term came from lesbians and gay men themselves as it was originally used to describe a form of psychiatric disorder or psychopathology. Other objections focused on the term's perceived emphasis on the sexual component of lesbian and gay men's experiences in isolation from other complex and integral aspects of their identities. Still other objections focused on the gender neutrality of the term and its masking of the differences between lesbians' and gay men's experiences and issues based on gender (Bohan, 1996; Gonsiorek, 1991). Since most early psychological and medical studies on sexual orientation focused on males, the continued use of the term homosexual was deemed methodologically imprecise in its application to both men and women. In the 1990s, LGB sexual orientations or lesbian, gay man, and bisexual man and woman are the terms preferred by APA reflected in their 1994 publication standards (APA, 1994).

Lesbian and gay sexual orientation is defined as an erotic and or affectional disposition to the same sex (Bohan, 1996; Gonsiorek & Weinrich, 1991). Bisexuality is defined as an affectional and/or erotic attraction to members of both sexes, serially or simultaneously (Bohan, 1996). While distinctions are made between members of these groups for the sake of descriptive clarity, human sexuality exists along a continuum in most persons, rather than as dichotomous and discrete categories. Any form of sexual orientation represents an interaction of biological, cultural, historical, and psychosocial influences (Bohan, 1996; Garnets & Kimmel, 1991; McWhirter, 1990).

The definition of sexual orientation in Western cultures is based explicitly on the biological sex of the person an individual is sexually and emotionally attracted to (Ames, 1996; Bohan, 1996). In this context, there is an inextricable link between the sociopolitical meanings of gender and sexual orientation in Western culture (Ames, 1996; Bohan, 1996; Greene, 1994a, 1996a, 1999; Kaschak, 1992; Kitzinger, 1987). Sexual attraction to members of the other gender is a central part of the way that being a normal man or woman has always been defined in American society (Ames, 1996; Bem, 1993; Bohan, 1996; Greene, 1994a, 1994b, 1994c, 1999). It is not surprising that in this context, lesbians and gay men are presumed to want to be members of the other sex or are viewed as defective examples of their own sex.

Bohan (1996) discusses the extent to which certain questionable assumptions about sexual orientation are embedded in psychological theories and paradigms that are also a function of societal gender and sex roles. Lesbian or gay sexual orientation is assumed to entail cross-gender behavior, with the assumption that gender roles are and should be inextricably linked to and defined by a person's biological sex. Bohan (1996) reviews a range of studies and scales in the psychological literature that serve as illustrations of these assumptions. The first psychological scale designed to measure masculinity and femininity assumed that lesbians and gay men would have M–F scores that differed from their biological sex. M–F scores measure the degree to which a person's behavior is consistent with that of male vs. female gender roles. The assumption is that a person's behavior and therefore their score should be consistent with their biological sex. Therefore, a basic assumption of the scale was that adherence to sex role stereotypes defined heterosexual sexual orientation. Departures from those stereotypes marked a person lesbian or gay. These kinds of assumptions are prevalent among lay persons as well as mental-health professionals. They are more of a reflection of what society values and wants people to be rather than an accurate reflection or measure of who they are. In other studies, when animal or human behavior was not consistent with traditional gender role stereotyped behavior, the presence of homosexuality or the potential for its development was presumed (Bohan, 1996; Haumann, 1995; Parker & DeCecco, 1995). The latter is reflected in the assumption that children who behave in gender atypical ways will become lesbian or gay. There is some evidence to suggest a link between extreme gender atypical behavior and later gay sexual orientation in boys. It does not, however, explain the development of lesbian sexual orientation in women, nor does it explain the presence of heterosexual sexual orientations in adults who were gender atypical children (Bohan, 1996). Another assumption related to the latter is expressed in the belief that if you are able to inhibit gender atypical behavior in children you will prevent them from becoming lesbian or gay. Of course there is no evidence to support this belief. All of these assumptions highlight the contextual nature of sexual orientation as a concept. Gender and sex role behaviors and expectations differ across cultures and differ over time within the same culture. Because of these variations, the concept of sexual orientation would vary as well. However, the ethnocentric nature of American psychological research has obscured important differences in gender and sex role expectations across cultures and in doing this has also obscured the effect of those differences on the psychological conceptualization of human sexual orientation.

Gonsiorek (1991) goes on to discuss the problems defining lesbian or gay sexual orientations that contribute to methodological challenges and flaws in empirical research. Problems establishing precise definitions of sexual orientation also affect the degree to which even our estimates of the number of LGB persons and heterosexual persons in the general population can be considered accurate. The concept of sexual orientation may be viewed from essentialist or social constructionist perspectives. Essentialist perspectives view sexual orientation as an intrinsic characteristic of a person, that endures over time, whether it can be observed by the individual possessing it, by others, or not. From this perspective, sexual orientation is an element of identity that has always existed in every person, in every culture, and in every point in time. For the most part, psychology has studied LGB sexual orientations as if they were enduring traits of people whose determinants could be discovered, quantified, and measured objectively and understood. The social constructionist perspective views sexual orientation as a construct that varies over time and place and has meaning only in the context of a particular culture, in a specific point in time. Sexual orientation from this perspective is viewed as contextual. It is a category that has meaning only because in Western culture we choose to imbue it with specific meaning. This meaning of sexual orientation is created out of the importance we give to the sex of a person that an individual is romantically attracted to. As previously discussed, that meaning is also a function of the meaning we give to gender and sex roles. In the absence of such "constructs," sexual orientation *per se* has no special meaning. In cultures where gender and sexuality have different meanings, sexual orientation may not even exist as an entity to be studied or deemed important enough to label (Tafoya, 1997).

10.09.3 DEMOGRAPHICS

Gonsiorek and Weinrich (1991) estimate that the number of lesbians and gay men in the USA ranges from 4 to 17% of the general population depending on the sampling methods and sources used. These estimates may be deceptive, however, given the imprecision of the definitions used and the hidden nature of this population. Both of these problems make obtaining representative samples a major challenge in conducting empirical research.

Kirk and Madsen (1996) observe that one of the seven myths that straight Americans believe is that all LGB persons can be easily identified by their outward appearance. This is based in part on gendered definitions of heterosexual and LGB orientations. Despite these beliefs, for the most part, LGB persons are invisible. They may not be identified solely on the basis of observation as they are a part of every social group in society. Unlike people with physical distinctions or challenges that readily identify them, LGB persons who are subjects in research are deemed to be LGB because they self-identify or say that they are. Just as we regard individuals in research studies to be LGB because they say they are, we do not assume that someone is LGB unless they actually tell us so. Therefore, we cannot be certain about the numbers of heterosexual or LGB participants in such studies. Unfortunately, for a variety of reasons this problem is not completely resolved by simply asking subjects to identify their sexual orientation.

Gonsiorek (1991), Bohan (1996), and McWhirter (1990) assert that problems defining LGB orientations make it difficult to derive accurate population estimates and to obtain appropriate samples. Attempts to define sexual orientation based on sexual behavior are less than reliable. Bohan (1996) observes that a person may experience themselves as or may be appropriately labeled lesbian or gay before they have ever had sexual relationships. Other individuals may have both male and female sexual partners and/or relationships. Some of these individuals would consider themselves LGB while others would not self-label in this way. Still other people may have sexual partners that are not consistent with the content of their fantasies. As observed in the previous example, some would self-label as LGB while others would not.

Gonsiorek (1991) observes that defining and obtaining a representative sample of LGB persons is the largest methodological problem in the scientific study of LGB sexual orientation. If subjects are considered LGB because they say that they are, it is important that the individual subjectively identifies themselves as having an LGB orientation if they are LGB. It is equally important that they do not identify themselves as such if they are not. This approach cannot account, however, for persons who do not yet acknowledge an LGB orientation, or those who are in an ego dystonic period. It also fails to account for individuals who maintain intimate relationships with members of the same sex but do not consider themselves or conceptualize their relationships (for cultural and other reasons) as lesbian or gay (Tafoya, 1997). There are other problems as well. Acknowledging an LGB sexual orientation is often associated with negative consequences. As such, many individuals who may be LGB may not openly acknowledge that they are. Class, ethnic, and other distinctions may also compound the consequences of disclosure and affect the degree to which many people will or will not take those risks. On the one hand, many people who are successful professionally but who are not out will not risk the embarrassment or loss of stature that may be associated with disclosure (Gonsiorek, 1991). On the other hand, many LGB persons who are economically marginal may be unable, for example, to risk the loss of their jobs, child custody, or visitation rights if their sexual orientation is discovered (Bradford, Ryan, & Rothblum, 1994; Fassinger, 1991; Greene 1994a, 1999). Many members of ethnic minority groups may conceal their LGB orientation from their families and ethnic communities to a greater degree than their white counterparts (Chan, 1992; Greene, 1990, 1994b, 1996a, 1997; Morales, 1992). In fact, in many families of people of color, a lover or life partner may be accepted as long as they are not labeled, as long as the family member does not label themselves lesbian or gay, and as long as they do not attempt to discuss their sexual orientation openly. The failure to make such statements about LGB sexual orientation to family members must be understood in the context of the ethnic group the person belongs to, the level of tolerance within that group, and traditional ways of managing members who deviate from family norms without causing family strife (Chan, 1990; Croom, in press; Fygetakis, 1997; Greene, 1994a, 1994b, 1999; Liu & Chan, 1996; Morales, 1992). Fygetakis (1997) observes that many white lesbians and gay men who belong to ethnic or religious groups that are intolerant of LGB sexual orientations may not be "out" to their families or in their ethnic/religious communities for reasons that are similar to those expressed by lesbians and gay men of color. She warns that it is inappropriate to use Western models of being out (particularly to family) as a measure of LGB self-acceptance or well-being for all LGB persons (Fygetakis, 1997). Accordingly, such individuals may not openly acknowledge their LGB orientation as research subjects, despite assurances of confidentiality.

Studies of LGB sexual orientations based on samples of psychiatric patients, prison inmates, psychoanalytic patients, and patients seeking aversion therapy, the primary subject pool for early studies, are not considered representative of LGB persons and therefore are not generalizable to them (Gonsiorek, 1991). Their continued use in making such generalizations is considered methodologically inappropriate. In early studies of sexual orientation, the use of psychiatric patients, patients in psychotherapy, and psychoanalysis was widespread. Many of these studies compared nonpatient heterosexual controls to homosexual patients. Individuals drawn from clinical populations by virtue of their status as patients are not representative of nonpatient LGB samples (Bohan, 1996; Gonsiorek, 1991). Even if this population were representative, comparisons to nonpatient heterosexual controls lack validity. Gonsiorek (1991) observes that samples drawn from individuals in psychoanalysis are atypical of the general population of LGB persons and may be atypical of psychotherapy patients as well. On average they are better educated and must be highly motivated to engage in a form of therapy that requires frequent visits over a protracted period of time and as such is expensive to maintain. Samples drawn from the armed forces, prison, or other law enforcement sources are also dubious. The presence of the same sex sexual behavior in prison or in places where heterosexual behavior is not available does not mean that its participants are LGB persons.

Gonsiorek (1991) also warns that individuals whose sexual behavior has come to the attention of law enforcement officials may include a higher proportion of individuals whose reality testing, impulse control, and capacity for good judgement are impaired. Often, such individuals may have been involved in sexual activity that was not conducted in private, was not consenting, was not with another adult, or was the specific result of entrapment (Gonsiorek, 1991).

Still, there are problems with other samples as well. Gonsiorek (1991) observes that studies whose samples are drawn from LGB bars and clubs are skewed toward people who drink alcohol, are young, able-bodied, extroverted, urban, lack a consistent sexual partner, and who can economically afford to socialize in those venues (Bradford et al., 1994; Croom, in press; Greene, 1999). Other samples drawn from LGB organizations will over-represent people who are out and who do not fear disclosure of their LGB orientation. Those samples obtained via social, friendship networks, experimenter contacts, and the like tend to be biased in their homogeneity (Gonsiorek, 1991).

Generally, samples of LGB persons are sought in venues that tend to be labeled as such, an approach that would seem to make sense. However, the diversity of LGB persons warrants understanding that many of them will not be found in such venues for a variety of reasons, some of which have been addressed here. Whether or not they would respond to requests for participation in such research is questionable. We know that there are many persons who would never be asked to participate by virtue of their absence in the kinds of venues targeted for obtaining samples. Hence, they are invisible to us. Largely, research is based on samples that are predominantly white, middle-class, able-bodied, North American, English speaking, and well educated (Bradford et al., 1994; Croom, in press; Gonsiorek, 1991; Greene, 1999). Because of these limitations, results of LGB research should be approached with caution as its generalizability is often limited to very specific subgroups. Similarly, suspicion is warranted when evaluating population estimates of LGB persons. It is likely that those estimates are an under-representation of the total population of LGB persons in the USA (Bohan, 1996). It is wise to ask how we know what we propose to know about the group in question, how that information was acquired, and who would have been omitted by virtue of the sampling methods chosen.

LGB persons are often presumed to be a part of a monolithic community. This obscures the wide range of diversity within them as a group that crosses all cultural, ethnic, racial, economic, social, age, geographic locale, and other lines. There is little research on or about LGB realities outside of the USA. Brown (1989) suggests that there is no unitary lesbian or gay reality; rather, there are multiple realities as diverse as lesbians and gay men themselves (Bell & Weinberg, 1978). While generalizations are made about a range of psychological realities for LGB persons, they are always embedded in other aspects of human experience and cannot be understood realistically when examined in isolation. LGB persons with multiple identities may experience their sexual orientation and heterosexism very differently than those who do not have multiple identities (Croom, in press; Greene, 1994b; 1999; Potgieter, 1997).

For the most part, American psychology as well as LGB psychology has understood human behavior from decidedly Western cultural perspectives. It is important to view LGB psychology from diverse perspectives within and outside of the USA. There is often a glaring absence of international perspectives on LGB persons' lives. Assumptions about what is helpful or healthy in one context may not have the same meaning or implications in another. For example, in American LGB psychology, the demise of pathology models of LGB sexual orientation is viewed as a major step toward affirming LGB sexual orientations as equal in status to heterosexual sexual orientations. It is difficult to consider that this would not be the case for LGB men and women around the world, however, this may not be as simple as it appears. Potgieter (1997) interviewed a sample of 30 Black South African lesbians from rural and urban settings and from a wide range of class and educational backgrounds in South Africa. Many of the women she interviewed had never even spoken to another lesbian. Potgieter's (1997) study documents, with the exception of dissertations, the absence of a single published article on homosexuality by any South African psychology journal, as well as the prominent role of South African psychologists in supporting the entrenchment of apartheid, and the view that homosexuality is both a sickness (that can be cured) and a sin (that the individual is responsible for) that warrants criminalization.

It would seem on the face of things that the eradication of the pathology model would benefit South African lesbians and gay men of all ethnicities. Potgieter (1997), however, points out that among Black South Africans, families are required to maintain contact with and provide family support for any member who is deemed ill. Despite the fact that lesbian or gay sexual orientation is viewed as both pathological and sinful and is disapproved of, the LGB family member is explicitly entitled to support and is not evicted to the degree that LGB persons in Western culture might be treated by disapproving family members. Potgieter (1997) asserts that we must consider what would happen, in Black South African culture, if the lesbian or gay family member were not viewed as sick, but simply sinful, particularly in a country where the gay and lesbian rights movement *per se* is fledgling at best. The entire basis of an entitlement to family support could be questioned. Hence, the impact of rejecting the pathology model poses different consequences for LGB persons in different cultures. This highlights the importance of viewing LGB psychologies and imperatives from a wide range of perspectives.

10.09.3.1 Etiology Theories

The "cause" of LGB sexual orientations has long been a focus of interest in psychological and medical research in the USA. However, the very question suggests that we know the origins of heterosexuality. The reality is that we presume to know because it is a preferred orientation and whatever is believed to be characteristic of it is deemed normative. When the question of causation of LGB sexual orientations arises, it prompts us to ask why its origins are important, particularly since similar questions are not raised about heterosexual sexual orientation. The latter is presumed to be an evolutionary and adaptive means of continuing the species. This assumption prevails despite what we know about the complexity of human sexuality and relationships that goes far beyond propagation.

The importance of determining a cause for LGB orientations assumes that if a cause is identified, interventions may be designed to prevent the development of LGB orientations. This is consistent with the prevalence of the disease and pathology models of homosexuality, although some proponents of conversion would say that their position does not rest on the presumption of pathology. This group of advocates of conversion would suggest that LGB sexual orientation is problematic for individuals because it is stigmatized and because it results in the LGB person being disadvantaged. The logic is that it is kinder to convert the individual to something that society will more readily accept. Despite the formal changes in the diagnostic nomenclature, inquiries about causation are embedded in the need to justify conversion. Altering LGB sexual orientations, in this context, is couched in what appears to be a benign assumption. If being a member of a stigmatized group is difficult, removing the stigma will make a child or adult's life easier. LGB sexual orientations, in this context, are still deemed the cause of the problem. Alter it and the problem goes away.

Bohan (1996) points out another way that the pathology model continues to inform the way that LGB persons are understood. She writes that when explanations for LGB orientations are sought, it is with the assumption that whatever markers are used or traits that are found will be, by definition, abnormal in LGB persons. Conversely, whatever is found in heterosexual persons will be considered normal. For example, she observes that the research sought to find hormonal imbalances in LGB samples to explain the presence of their orientation. This approach, however, presumed that whatever levels were measured in heterosexuals were normal. Bohan (1996) suggests that the presence of bisexuality in different societies in different historical times gives credence to the bisexual potential in all persons and suggests that legitimizing only one sexual orientation is arbitrary.

Explanations for LGB sexual orientations range from one extreme in which biological underpinnings are presumed to totally account for them, and at the other, that environmental determinants are deemed causative. There is also a range of approaches that postulate the presence of combinations of determinants that fall between the polarities of these extremes and contain elements from both of them. These theories fall roughly into three categories.

Explanations based on psychodynamic theory are well known and longstanding. Overall traditional psychoanalytic explanations of LGB sexual orientation view them as a symptom of a developmental conflict and early fixation (Isay, 1990). Isay (1990) observes that traditional analysts believe that homosexuality represents an unfavorable unconscious solution to a developmental conflict and that the entire personal life of the individual reflects the effects of the early fixation. While this view is based on Freud's (1922/1959) early models, Isay (1990) notes that post-Freudian analysts ignore the ambiguities in his theory of object choice. Freud suggested that all human beings were innately bisexual, and supported decriminalizing and depathologizing homosexuality (Bohan, 1996; Freud, 1922/1959; Isay, 1990; Jones, 1965). Despite this, American psychoanalysts viewed LGB sexual orientations as illnesses in need of a cure. A range of explanations developed that posit the presence of dysfunctional relationships between parents and children accounting for the development of LGB orientations. Their common themes are based on the assumption that a key task in psychosexual development is to identify with a parent of the same sex and transform oneself psychologically into that parent. Based primarily on studies with psychoanalytic patients as subjects, psychoanalytic research alleged that the fathers of gay men were aloof, distant, and uninvolved with them, while their mothers were smothering and overprotective (Isay, 1990). Lesbianism was deemed a manifestation of incest fears, an expression of a wish to adopt a masculine role, or "a girl's anger at her father for rejecting her causing her to hate men" (Bohan, 1996, p. 76). Critiques of these explanations cite their reliance on patient samples and the presence of other methodological problems. There is also too much variation in the families and family dynamics of lesbians and gay men to make such generalizations (Bohan, 1996; Isay, 1990). Furthermore, the same kinds of dynamics ascribed to the families of lesbians and gay men may be found among heterosexual men and women. There are no adequate explanations in these paradigms for why heterosexual men and women with like family dynamics do not become lesbian or gay.

Biological explanations enjoy great popularity in the 1990s and tend to look for genetic and/or hormonal markers of lesbian or gay sexual orientation. There is some evidence that there may be a genetic element in the development of LGB orientations for some individuals, but it is far from conclusive (Bohan, 1996; Diamond, 1993; McGuire, 1995). Bohan (1996) provides a detailed review of concordance studies that are summarized briefly. Concordance studies seek to determine the degree to which there is agreement between two individuals on a particular trait. In this case, the trait would be LGB sexual orientations. We would expect, if sexual orientation were 100% genetically determined, to find a near 100% concordance rate between monozygotic twins, and a 50% rate on measures between fraternal siblings. Studies in this area (Bailey & Pillard, 1991) produce results that show higher concordance rates for identical twin brothers than for fraternal siblings, however, not at the levels we would expect to find to demonstrate 100% genetic determination. Similar findings for women are not reported. Other biological theories analyze the role of hormones in prenatal development (Bailey, 1995; Hamer, Hu, Magnusson, Hu, & Pattatucci, 1993 Meyer-Bahlberg, 1995) and sex differences in brain organization. In the former theories, sex differences in behavior are attributed to hormonally related brain organization. Despite contradictory findings in studies attempting to replicate this work (Byne, 1995), these models seem to have some measure of validity (when sexual behavior is the variable measured) in research with lower animals. However, making the leap to encompass the complexity of an LGB orientation is questionable. Gendered assumptions about LGB orientations are evident in these approaches. It is presumed that brain development is influenced by the presence of prenatal hormones and that sex-typical behaviors are a reflection of brain organization rather than cultural influences. Lesbians are presumed to have brain organizations similar to those of heterosexual men, and gay men are presumed to have brain organizations similar to those of heterosexual women. A familiar problem in this schema is that gendered behaviors may have specific meaning in Western culture that they do not have in other cultures. The most recent study conducted by LeVay (1991) is based on autopsied brains of heterosexual and gay men. LeVay (1991) hypothesized that a forward region of the hypothalamus would be smaller in the brains of gay men (as it would in heterosexual women) than in heterosexual men. These findings were confirmed. Despite this, the meaning of these findings is unclear. LeVay's (1991) sample was small and involved the use of subjects who died as a result of complications from AIDS. Furthermore, there was no evidence that the differences in size of these brain structures were prenatal. Overall, the results of these studies are intriguing but far from definitive. Bohan (1996) and McWhirter (1990) observe that research in the biology of sexual orientation has failed to produce any conclusive findings.

Another group of explanations are based on social learning or learning theories. These theories suggest that sexual orientation is a constellation of complex, learned behavior based on prior experiences that have been reinforced. One example posits the existence of previous heterosexual encounters that are unpleasant or traumatic, or same-sex sexual encounters early in life that are seductive in nature. Still others suggest that "gender deviance," particularly in boys, goes unpunished and evolves into an LGB orientation. Bohan (1996) explains that it is possible that some children may cope with their gender atypical identity by internalizing the identity that the culture provides them with to explain their difference, therefore defining themselves as lesbian, gay, or bisexual. These are the labels they are given to choose from. There is little to support perspectives based solely on social learning models. This is particularly so given the degree to which LGB persons often identify themselves as such long before they have any same-sex or heterosexual contact. There is also evidence that individuals who engage in same-sex sexual behavior do not necessarily adopt an LGB orientation. Furthermore, same-sex sexual contact is more likely to be delayed because of the stigma associated with LGB orientations. The notion that there is reinforcement for them seems questionable. Clinicians observe clients who want nothing more than to avoid the societal rejection that accompanies the adoption of an LGB identity.

In a shift toward a more interactionist approach, Bem (1996) proposes that biological determinants predispose temperaments and that it is temperaments that predispose behavior which is sex-typical or atypical. Bem's theory asserts that a child who is sex-atypical will feel different from his or her same-sex peers and may be rejected by them. Children whose temperament predisposes them to be sex-typical experience themselves as different from peers of the other sex. The rejection from peers and a sense of difference from them is presumed to create anxiety and discomfort which then triggers physiological arousal. He proposes that this is the crucible in which an association between same-sex peers and physiological arousal leads to erotocizing those peers. Bohan (1996) suggests that this theory fails to explain why in this situation anxiety becomes eroticized rather than leading to avoidance of same-sex peers.

The question of causality in LGB sexual orientation research is intriguing but leaves us with no definitive conclusions. McWhirter (1990) observes that there does not seem to be a single cause or a simple developmental path that determines sexual orientation of any type. Bell and Weinberg (1978) suggest that our understanding of sexual orientation would be greatly enhanced by recognizing and considering that there is great diversity among LGB persons, just as there is among heterosexual men and women; that there may be many homosexualities as well as many multiple paths to any single form of sexual orientation (Garnets & Kimmel, 1991).

Sexual orientation is likely established by adolescence, usually before sexual activity begins, often preceded by a subjective awareness of same gender attraction (Bell, Weinberg, & Hammersmith, 1981; Garnets & Kimmel, 1991; Gonsiorek & Weinrich, 1991). Still other LGB persons may not be aware of same-sex attractions until later in life. It is difficult to determine how, at what stage of development, or chronological age LGB sexual orientation would emerge were it not for the pervasive societal messages condemning it. Many individuals who have same-sex attractions may suppress or repress an awareness of them because of the ways that LGB identity is stigmatizing. This is reflected in the tendency among many LGB persons to reject or experience confusion about their orientation initially. Sexual orientation appears to be a stable characteristic over the life span for some individuals; for others, one orientation may be adopted after lengthy experience with the other as an adult. Money (1988) refers to the latter as sequential bisexuality (Bohan, 1996; Garnets & Kimmel, 1991; Golden, 1996).

Because LGB individuals are not readily identifiable on the basis of physical characteristics, they are often presumed to be and treated as if they were heterosexual. Such treatment forces LGB persons to make conscious decisions about whether or not to reveal their sexual orientation routinely. This raises one of the core psychological tasks confronting LGB persons, "coming out."

10.09.4 UNIQUE PSYCHOLOGICAL AND DEVELOPMENTAL TASKS CHALLENGING LGB PERSONS

Coming out has been defined at its simplest as the realization or conscious acknowledgment of one's LGB sexual orientation and the subsequent disclosure of that orientation to others (Bohan, 1996; Dworkin & Gutierrez, 1992; Garnets & Kimmel, 1991; Isay, 1990). While this definition describes the salient features of coming out as a developmental event, it is a deceptively simplistic depiction of an extremely complex lifelong task. Because of the presumption of heterosexuality in our society, most LGB persons will be presumed to be heterosexual unless they say otherwise. For members of many ethnic minority groups, skin color and other features make their group membership visible and a given that is beyond their control. Unlike visible minority group members, LGB persons must consciously decide whether or not to disclose their sexual orientation to others. This also means that to some extent, they have some degree of control over who has information about their orientation and who does not, affording a measure of safety under certain circumstances. This control, however, has benefits as well as disadvantages. The need to make decisions about coming out surfaces whenever the individual is in a new situation such as a new job with new colleagues, and is usually stressful. Whether or not to disclose, to whom, at what point in time, and weighing the risks vs. benefits, is a lifelong task for most LGB persons.

Perhaps the most anxiety provoking stage of coming out is the initial stage of self-awareness. Bell, Weinberg, and Hammersmith (1981) report that 70% of lesbians and gay men in their sample reported having a vague sense of feeling different from same-sex peers as young as age four or five and that the vague feeling of difference had or developed a sexual component. Savin-Williams (1996) reports that LGB youth move from the stage of awareness to that of attempting to name or define the sense of difference that they experience. This period of self-definition, that for some but not all LGB people begins in early childhood, is usually resolved by early adolescence or young adulthood. The resolution of self-definition, however, may be postponed from several years to decades depending on the degree to which negative attitudes toward LGB people are internalized (Savin-Williams, 1996).

Following the period of self-awareness, another anxiety-provoking period may be marked by the desire to come out to family members, about not wanting to do so, or the uncertainty of which course to take. Many individuals, however, endure constant concern about being "outed" before they have chosen to personally disclose their sexual orientation to someone. Individuals who do not disclose their sexual orientation are considered closeted (Bohan, 1996). However, being closeted, like being out, is not a dichotomous, either/or state. Most LGB persons are out to some people in their lives and closeted to others.

Coming out is a major source of stress for LGB persons and is frequently cited as a major source of anxiety among LGB clients entering psychotherapy (Bell & Weinberg, 1978; Bradford & Ryan, 1988). Coming out is, in reality, a process that incorporates an important element of a person's identity, an element that the individual may not have always been aware of. The LGB individual is required to incorporate this perhaps newly discovered aspect of themselves, in affirmative ways, in the midst of a culture which is anything but affirming. This is reflected in its legitimized intense, negative reactions to LGB persons (Bohan, 1996; Garnets & Kimmel, 1991; Gonsiorek, 1991; Isay, 1990).

There is research that documents the benefits of coming out. Decreased feelings of loneliness and guilt, identity synthesis, integration, and commitment (Cass, 1979; Coleman, 1981/1982), healthy psychological adjustment and positive self-esteem (Savin-Williams, 1990), positive gay identity, a greater sense of freedom to be oneself, of not living a lie, and experiencing genuine acceptance were reported as benefits of disclosure (Savin-Williams, 1996). Despite the benefits of disclosure, for some LGB persons negative reprisals may outweigh benefits depending on the unique aspects of an individual's life, that may change over time and in different situations. For some LGB persons, reluctance to come out may be attributed to a reluctance to confront fears of the unknown, an avoidance of rejection, or harassment or abuse by society and/or loved and trusted figures in the individual's life (Savin-Williams, 1996). Some individuals structure their lives around two completely separate worlds, their LGB friends and acquaintances with whom they can be out, and their co-workers, families, friends, or other persons with whom they are closeted.

It is important to remember that coming out is a contextual process, and that it will be experienced, timed, and understood by the individual in concert with that person's gender, ethnicity, socioeconomic class, age, and other distinctions. For example, there may be differences in the process that are a function of gender that make it different for gay men and lesbians. Gonsiorek (1988) suggests that coming out may be more abrupt for males who come out during the adolescent period than for females, and that men may tend to act on their sexual feelings at an earlier stage than women. Women in Western cultures are permitted to display a broader range of emotions and behaviors with other women that do not violate their traditional gender role expectations. Physical contact and physical displays of affection between women are not necessarily presumed to mean that such contact is sexual or that they are lesbians. Their male counterparts do not enjoy the same latitude of behaviors and in the expression of emotions. Men engaging in physical displays of affection with other men would be deemed suspicious as such conduct is not in keeping with the Western male stereotype of masculinity. However, there are subcultural differences in the latitude men are allowed for such conduct. For example, African-American males who have close emotional or familial ties are very likely to hug one another or exchange unique handshakes or other displays on greeting one another. This can be understood as a means of displaying solidarity as well as affection (Boyd-Franklin, 1990). In the context of African-American and Latino communities, such behavior is not presumed to represent suspicious conduct, but rather may represent a more culturally syntonic value of touch. This underscores the importance of understanding the cultural reference point of the person as it will play a significant role in that person's response to their own as well as other's behaviors.

10.09.4.1 Identity Development

Theories of sequential stages in identity development in LGB persons are similar in structure to those for ethnic group members (Bohan, 1996; Cass, 1984; Coleman, 1981/1982; Fassinger, 1991; Weinberg, 1983). However, smooth transitions through the stages of any of these models will be complicated by the pervasive presence of negative attitudes toward and discrimination against group members. Members of ethnic minority groups, who come from healthy families and affirming communities, usually receive positive cultural mirroring during the course of their development that LGB people do not receive. That is, ethnic minority individuals are often socialized to actively challenge rather than accept the dominant culture's assertions about them from their families and community. LGB persons, however, learn a range of negative stereotypes and attitudes about LGB persons, not simply from the dominant culture but from loved and trusted figures (Greene, 1994a, 1994b; Greene & Boyd-Franklin, 1996). To complicate matters, they are likely exposed to such attitudes long before they are aware of their own sexual orientation. When LGB persons have uncritically accepted such values and attitudes, moreover, when they have internalized them, the process of self-acceptance becomes complicated and often fraught with ambivalence. It is not uncommon during this period to observe what has been previously described as ego dystonic feelings about one's LGB orientation. The internalization of hateful and denigrating attitudes toward LGB persons has been defined as internalized homophobia (Bohan, 1996; Gonsiorek, 1982; Shidlo, 1994; Weinberg, 1972). Internalized homophobia may be manifested in a hatred or contempt for any quality or characteristic attributed to LGB persons. It may also be manifested in depression, suicidal ideation or attempts, verbal or physical aggression toward other LGB persons, substance abuse, and other self-destructive behaviors. Addressing internalized homophobia and eliminating it is an important aspect of psychotherapy with LGB persons whenever it is present.

Successfully moving through the different stages of any model may take years or, for some individuals, a lifetime to accomplish. The precise length of time required, however, will also vary from person to person depending on other circumstances and other psychological tasks they must perform. There is frequently a delay in time between the discovery of an LGB sexual orientation and its acceptance as a healthy and acceptable part of an individual's identity (Bohan, 1996; Garnets & Kimmel, 1991; Gonsiorek, 1991).

10.09.4.2 Resilience in LGB People

D'Augelli (1994) suggests that development in LGB persons should be approached from the perspective of exceptionality given the superior coping strategies required for them to negotiate developmental tasks successfully in an antagonistic environment. Such an approach, he suggests, will be more likely to yield important information about adaptive and perhaps even exceptional strategies that might otherwise be overlooked. The concept of resilience in LGB persons is rarely explored. Jones (1997) attempts to analyze the components of resilience by examining the paradoxical life of jazz composer Billy Strayhorn. Strayhorn, an African-American gay man in a viciously racist and homophobic climate, was also the victim of childhood physical abuse and other troubled family dynamics. Despite those obstacles, he came to be known as a major figure in American jazz music idioms, and developed what appeared to be satisfying adult relationships of all types. His adult life was not entirely free of the residual psychological effects of his childhood struggles with adversity. In many ways the effects of those struggles were compounded by the double layers of societal discrimination that were routine features of American society at that time. Jones (1997) identifies a range of key ingredients in the psychological resilience found in members of many groups, including sexual minorities, who have been forced to endure "patterned injustice" (p. 13). Among those ingredients, Jones (1997) observes that carefully constructed, segregated communities can facilitate the development of self-constructed psychological realities and a form of psychological independence observable in members of disadvantaged groups. People who move within those communities can develop a high level of resilience in part because these communities provide them with the opportunity to engage in a process of independent self-construction. LGB subcultures have always existed. They have offered LGB persons the opportunity to have small corners of the world in which they may safely be themselves and experience other people who are like them directly. Despite their often secretive nature, these subcultures nevertheless provide members with the important opportunity to develop the alternative self-images needed to challenge the negative labels applied to them from members of the dominant group (Greene, 1999; Greene & Boyd-Franklin, 1996; Jones, 1997). The opportunity to engage in a process that allows group members to define themselves rather than accept negative definitions of them is a salient ingredient in their mental health.

The process of coming out is further complicated by the frequent absence of routinely available and explicit role models that socially affirm LGB identities. Media images of LGB persons, with rare exceptions, routinely depict them as seriously flawed, tragic, or comedic characters, when they are visible at all. Such depictions leave many persons struggling with their new found identity, reluctant to identify with a group which is perceived to have many negative features that are deemed to characterize them. As a result, many individuals must develop their own personal framework for identity and for maintaining self-esteem (Garnets & Kimmel, 1991; Peplau, 1991).

10.09.5 UTILIZATION OF PSYCHOLOGICAL SERVICES

Lesbians and gay men are more likely to see a therapist or seek psychological services than their heterosexual counterparts (Bell & Weinberg, 1978; Bradford et al., 1994; Morgan, 1992; Morgan & Eliason, 1992). This is not surprising as group members are vulnerable to oppression and discrimination, the denial of many basic legal rights, as well as exposure to the same life stressors that their counterparts must negotiate (Fassinger, 1991; Greene, 1999). Some seek therapy to have a place where they can safely discuss their feelings about their sexual orientation, where their "secret" cannot be divulged to anyone else without their permission. Over 50% of lesbians in a national sample reported being the target of verbal attacks, 13% reported losing their jobs, and others reported discrimination against or being stereotyped by mental health professionals because of their sexual orientation (Bradford et al., 1994). This kind of treatment often results in fears of disclosure even to mental health professionals. Such fears of disclosure may represent another factor that indirectly affects our estimates of the numbers of LGB persons receiving mental health services, as some remain invisible to us, even in the therapy hour. Bradford et al. report that three-quarters of their sample reported seeking mental health services at some time, the majority reported finding it helpful.

Most LGB persons seek psychological services for many of the same reasons that other people do, normal life transitions as well as unexpected trauma. However, they must manage those stressors in the context of an environment that is hostile to them. They also tend to see therapists for longer periods than their heterosexual counterparts (Liddle, 1997; Morgan, 1992). Many of their presenting problems, however, focus on or are related to the presence of societal and internalized homophobia, issues that heterosexual persons do not have to manage, often exposing them to chronic, high levels of stress (Morgan, 1992). These issues are compounded for LGB persons who are members of ethnic minority or other societally disadvantaged groups as they must manage multiple levels of discrimination (Chan, 1989; Greene, 1999; Greene & Boyd-Franklin, 1996). Liddle (1997) observes that LGB clients tend to choose LGB therapists 41% of the time; gay men tend to choose gay or bisexual male therapists; lesbians tend to choose lesbian or bisexual female therapists (Modrcin & Wyers, 1990). When the sexual orientation of the therapist is unknown, lesbians are more likely to see female therapists, with 89% of Liddle's (1997) lesbian sample choosing female therapists (Modrcin & Wyers, 1990). Morgan (1992) finds that lesbians hold unusually positive attitudes about seeking professional help. However, this is consistent with the demographics of lesbians that tend to be sampled. Members of groups sampled tended to be young, White, and better educated than their heterosexual counterparts (Morgan, 1992; Trippet, 1994). Higher levels of education are associated with positive attitudes toward seeking professional help.

Presenting mental health concerns in therapy include homophobia and stress (Niesen, 1990), depression (Rothblum, 1990), relationship issues (not being out or coming out to family members, limited support for or disparaging attitudes toward relationships), and conflicts about being closeted or out (e.g., being closeted at work and out socially; whether or not to come out and to whom). Bradford et al. (1994) found depression present in half of their sample, in fact depression was often the factor precipitating a referral. They also determined that the degree to which a subject was out affected their mental health. In a national survey of lesbian health care and mental health concerns, Bradford et al. found that relationships were a major focus of attention in therapy. Problems with lovers were reported as a major focus by 44% of participants, with family (34%), and with friends (10%), respectively. Loneliness was also a significant focus of attention (21%). In the Bradford et al. sample, 68% of respondents reported experiencing a range of mental health problems in the past. Those problems included long-term depression and sadness, constant anxiety and fear, as well as other mental health concerns. However, only 23% of that group reported being in therapy prior to the present time. 49% of that group, however, reported having been in therapy for one year or less. These patterns suggest the presence of coping and survival skills, reliance on friends, and the presence of social supports as alternatives to therapy (Bradford et al., 1994; Fassinger, 1991).

Concerns about money and financial well-being were reported by 57% of the Bradford et al. (1994) sample. The percentages of African-American lesbians and lesbians aged 54 and younger were somewhat higher in the group reporting financial concerns. While most respondents reported a preference for private therapy, the lack of third-party payments and insufficient personal resources impinged on those preferences. One-third of the sample reported seeking professional services for "personal growth," however, this was less frequently cited as a reason for referral among African-American and Latin, lesbians. Rates of eating disorders and sexual abuse among the respondents in this group were similar to those of their heterosexual counterparts. Higher percentages of suicidal ideation and attempts were reported, however, among the younger aged groups, suggesting that the potential for suicide among LGB adolescents warrants serious attention (Bradford & Ryan, 1989; Bradford et al., 1994). Researchers caution that the samples in the research studies cited tended to be young, White, better educated, and accessible to major cities. Older, non-White, financially less well off LGB persons in rural or isolated communities are not well represented. In isolated settings, people may be at even higher risk for distress and the development of mental disorders, however, they may be more likely to be cut off from a supportive and sympathetic community when they are in greatest need of one.

10.09.5.1 Psychotherapy with LGB Persons

Prior to changes in the diagnostic nomenclature, most psychotherapy with lesbian and gay clients focused on changing their sexual orientation. Despite changes in the nomenclature and organized mental health's rejection of pathology theories, efforts to change the sexual orientation of gay and lesbian clients have persisted and are referred to as conversion therapies (Haldeman, 1991, 1994; 1999; McWhirter, 1990). There is no credible empirical evidence to warrant the assumption that therapies aimed at altering sexual orientation are successful. Haldeman (1999) documents psychology's evolution from this position to its current policy and offers guidance to clinicians who deliver services to clients who may be distressed by their LGB sexual orientation.

Groups under the auspices of fundamentalist Christian denominations touting the sanctity of literal biblical interpretations as superior to scientific studies on LGB sexual orientations are the "main purveyors" of conversion therapies. In addition to these groups, the National Association for Research and Therapy of Homosexuality (NARTH), founded by Charles Socarides and Joseph Nicolosi, is committed to the pathology model of LGB sexual orientation. Its members believe that the removal of homosexuality as a diagnostic entity from the *DSM* was the result of the power of gay rights lobbyists and reject any scientific studies challenging the pathology model. Group members are committed to the pathology model and use of reparative therapies to change LGB sexual orientations to heterosexual orientations. Generally, the use of conversion therapies rests on the assumption that LGB sexual orientations are expressions of psychopathology. Gonsiorek (1991) and Haldeman (1994, 1999) provide comprehensive discussions of the weaknesses of the pathology models. Briefly summarized, these studies suffer from a range of methodological problems. Among them, it is not clear if the subjects who are labeled homosexual in fact are homosexual, as opposed to bisexual or even heterosexual. As previously discussed, they often compare lesbian or gay subjects drawn from patient populations to nonpatient heterosexual controls, and frequently use outcome measures of questionable validity. Furthermore, there is data to support the contention that there is no difference between LGB persons and their heterosexual counterparts on instruments measuring psychological adjustment. Haldeman (1999) further documents the methodological weaknesses in studies that purport to demonstrate that sexual orientation can be altered. Selection criteria, subject classification, and outcome measures are cited as major flaws (Haldeman, 1991, 1994, 1999).

As previously examined in the discussion of ego dystonic homosexuality, there are serious questions about the origins of requests from LGB clients to alter their sexual orientation. In this context, Haldeman (1999) raises an even more important question. Whether or not LGB sexual orientations can be changed, should they be? In a climate of hostility and derision, where acknowledging an LGB sexual orientation results in a loss of societal privilege, at the very least, the offer of "treatment" or "conversion" may serve to reinforce negative societal attitudes. It would be difficult to conduct such treatment without supporting the idea that something is wrong with the LGB person that warrants correction, and in doing so, reinforcing heterosexist bias. The LGB person becomes the focus of change, rather than the pathology of heterosexism and homophobia and its advocates. Furthermore, Haldeman (1994, 1999) argues that such treatments are not benign. In some studies, patients complain of significant discomfort following attempts to convert their sexual orientation. Such reactions include chronic depression, anxiety, intimacy avoidance, and sexual dysfunction.

APA, in an attempt to address ethical questions raised by the use of conversion therapies, approved (in a near unanimous vote) a resolution, "Appropriate Therapeutic Responses to Sexual Orientation" at its 105th Annual Convention in August 1997. The resolution holds clinicians responsible for rejecting depictions of LGB persons as mentally ill and acknowledges the role of societal prejudice in prompting many LGB persons to seek conversion therapies (Haldeman, 1999). Another aspect of the resolution requires clinicians to disclose the theoretical underpinnings and scientific basis for their interventions. As conversion therapies do not enjoy the support of empirical evidence, it would make it more difficult to ethically offer them as suitable responses to an LGB client's distress about their sexual orientation. APA commentary on conversion therapies states, "these findings suggest that efforts to repair homosexuals are nothing more than social prejudice garbed in psychological accoutrements" (Welch, 1990, in Haldeman, 1991, p. 160).

Different stages of the coming out process may be extremely anxiety provoking. The discovery or confirmation of a lesbian or gay sexual orientation may be experienced as frightening, ego alien, and/or a source of great subjective distress (Gonsiorek, 1982, 1988). It is also a frequently cited reason LGB persons give for seeking psychological services. As such, it may lead to the expression of behaviors or feelings which resemble symptoms of severe psychopathology. However, the presence of this behavior, particularly under these circumstances, does not warrant the immediate assumption that an underlying psychiatric disorder is present (Gonsiorek, 1982). For many clients, the clinician is observing the individual's difficult struggle confronting the real nature of their sexual orientation, perhaps for the first time. For other clients, however, the intense stress inherent in this process may, like any other stressor, precipitate the expression of serious underlying psychiatric disorders. In either case, a person is required to manage this realistically stressful life event. Clients who have underlying psychopathology must do this with fewer emotional resources. Another diagnostic variation is observed in the client who is consumed with great anxiety or fears of delusional proportions that they may be gay or lesbian despite the absence of any rational foundation for such beliefs. It is important to attend to diagnostic distinctions in these situations. A comprehensive discussion of differential diagnostic issues can be found in Gonsiorek (1982).

The relative invisibility of gay men and lesbians allows them to "pass" as heterosexual. Passing in the LGB community is also referred to as being closeted. Both "passing" and being "out" have their own distinct negative and positive consequences. Passing may conceal group members from other LGB persons. Both passing and being out are accompanied by varying types and degrees of psychological demands and the stress that is a result of those demands. Gay men and lesbians pass or are closeted when they do not challenge the assumption that they are heterosexual or when they actively conceal their sexual orientation.

Passing can be an adaptive coping strategy when used strategically. It has been used historically by ethnic minorities in threatening situations and can be an adaptive survival tool. It was often effective in helping its users avoid or escape imminent harm or to obtain goods, services, or jobs which would be otherwise inaccessible to them because of discrimination (Greene, 1994a, 1994b, 1994c). When used as a long-term survival tool, however, it deprives its user of the spontaneity required for authenticity in interpersonal relationships. Individuals live with a consistent pressure to conceal major aspects of their lives and may often live with the constant dread of being discovered (Bradford et al., 1994; Greene, 1992). When passing is accompanied by the belief that being gay or lesbian is a sign of inferiority or pathology, it represents an expression of internalized homophobia. Lesbians and gay men who pass or are forced to remain closeted, particularly when it is dangerous not to do so, are confronted with a chronic stressor which can leave them at risk for negative psychological outcomes (Bradford et al., 1994; Fassinger, 1991; Trippet, 1994).

Not only are lesbians and gay men unprotected by legislation which prohibits discrimination based on group membership, some legislation exists which actually requires discrimination against them, for example, military regulations.

Bisexual persons are frequently the objects of hostility from gay men, lesbians, and heterosexuals as well. Bohan (1996) uses the term biphobia to describe the discomfort people experience about bisexuality. The negative treatment bisexual men and women receive from the lesbian and gay community can include their exclusion from LGB social events, as well as a denial of the legitimacy of bisexual identity. They may be perceived by members of the gay and lesbian community as persons who are really gay or lesbian, but who conceal or deny their true identity to avoid the stigma of being gay, and to allow them to benefit from heterosexual privilege (Bohan, 1996; Garnets & Kimmel, 1991).

Their bisexuality may also be perceived as an expression of their internalized homophobia. Bohan (1996) argues that many lesbians and gay men consider the presence of a singular commitment to one's own sex as a statement of loyalty to lesbians and gay men, the absence of such a commitment as disloyal, and perhaps the fear that such a person will ultimately reject their lesbian or gay sexual orientation if it is opportune to do so. Conversely, they may be viewed by heterosexuals as less normal or inferior to persons who are exclusively heterosexual (Garnets & Kimmel, 1991).

Heterosexism and its concomitant negative stereotypes of gay men and lesbians has been so much a part of the definition of psychological normalcy that it predisposes practitioners to make a range of erroneous assumptions about LGB clients. Many of these assumptions represent ideas of questionable validity, which they have not been sensitized to recognize during their training (Brown, 1996; CLGC, 1990, 1991; Garnets et al., 1991; Glassgold, 1992; Gonsiorek, 1991; Liddle, 1997; Markowitz, 1991; Morin, 1977).

One example of such errors is the presumption that clients are heterosexual until proven otherwise. This can be particularly problematic for individuals who are in the early stages of coming out, who lack a sense of clarity about their sexual orientation, who are distressed by the possibility that they may have an LGB sexual orientation, or who have internalized the dominant culture's heterosexist bias. The client may not necessarily disclose their LGB orientation to the therapist at all or they may do so at any point in treatment (Bradford et al., 1994; Fassinger, 1991; Garnets & Kimmel, 1991; Greene, 1994b; Markowitz, 1991; Liddle, 1997; Youngstrom, 1991). Like other factors which vary from person to person, sexual orientation may be centrally or distantly related to the presenting problem. Many individuals, however, may depend on the therapy process and the therapist's acceptance to help them navigate this uncharted and frequently anxiety-ridden course to self-acceptance (Greene, 1994b).

A former therapy client recounted: "not one of them (therapists) was prepared or brave enough to ask me the one question that might have saved me and two ex-wives a lot of pain ... Do you think you might be gay?" (Woolley, 1991, p. 30).

Errors in treatment can occur at either of two extremes and, of course, at any point along the continuum between those extremes. On the one hand, the therapist may minimize the importance of the client's sexual orientation and the negative impact of heterosexism on the client's life (Garnets et al., 1991; Greene, 1994b; Youngstrom, 1991). On the other hand, the therapist may tend to focus on the client's lesbian or gay sexual orientation as pathological and the source of all of the client's problems, ignoring matters that are more troubling to the client (Garnets et al., Markowitz, 1991). Similarly, therapists may focus on the client's sexual orientation in a voyeuristic manner, wishing to hear unnecessary details about the client's sexual practices for the therapist's own titillation, neglecting other areas of inquiry important to the client's treatment (Dworkin & Gutierrez, 1992; Garnets & Kimmel, 1991; Gonsiorek & Weinrich, 1991; Markowitz, 1991).

Many clients report finding that when they raise questions or attempt to explore their confusion about their sexual orientation, they find themselves confronted with the therapist's anxiety about the topic. This anxiety may take the form of the therapist's failure to ask questions or assist the client in explorations of these issues. Other clients report the therapist's outright denial that the client could be gay. This may be accompanied by the therapist actively discouraging the client from having or adopting a gay or lesbian sexual orientation (Brown, 1996; Garnets et al., 1991; Youngstrom, 1991) or selectively encouraging heterosexual relationships. On these occasions, many clients simply drop the issue. Others move on to another therapist. Still others leave therapy, sometimes the worse for the experience.

Generally, therapists who work with LGB persons must appreciate the individual client's dilemma in the context of real and not fantasised prejudice and discrimination. Heterosexism often assumes the form of physical violence directed at LGB persons (Fassinger, 1991; Herek & Berrill, 1992). Data on bias crimes suggest that 92% of lesbians and gay men report being targets of antigay verbal abuse or threats, and that 24% report physical attacks, of which some result in death (Herek, 1989). Gay men and lesbians face the routine tasks of assessing realistic dangers associated with divulging the nature of their sexual orientation. Many endure painful isolation from families of origin who do not accept their identity, as well as the painful process of rejection which often precedes it. They are challenged by their own internalized homophobia, which can negatively affect their psychological adjustment (Fassinger, 1991; Trippet, 1994; Weinberg, 1972).

Those who are out face the formidable task of negotiating nontraditional relationships and family structures with few models and little support for doing so in a ubiquitously hostile environment. In such a climate, many people who would consider expressions of racism or ethnic bigotry wholly inappropriate are quite comfortable expressing heterosexist bigotry and find support for doing so. These issues are further complicated for gay men and lesbians who are members of ethnic minority or other marginalized groups (Chan, 1992; Greene, 1994a, 1994b, 1994c, 1996a, 1996b, 1999; Morales, 1992).

Therapists must begin to assess the impact of a legacy of negative stereotypes about LGB persons on their own thinking, and they must do so before a client ever appears before them. Markowitz (1991) warns that therapists must acknowledge and understand the extent to which they have internalized society's negative depictions of gay men and lesbians. It is not sufficient to simply not believe the stereotypes and to be unbiased without an inquiry into their personal effects on deeper levels (Brown, 1996; Liddle, 1997; Markowitz, 1991).

Unexamined fears in the therapist may be triggered by a range of interactions with LGB clients. The client may, if angry, accuse the therapist of being homophobic. Conversely, if the therapist is supportive and understanding, some LGB clients may assume that they share sexual orientations. The therapist may assume a defensive posture, rather than exploring the client's feelings in an uncritical manner. The therapist may respond to the client's accusation that the therapist is homophobic by failing to set or maintain appropriate limits, as if this disproves the client's assumptions. Such behavior on the therapist's part is not done with the client's interests in mind, rather it is often the therapist's response to their own feelings of guilt or discomfort (Greene, 1994a, 1994b, 1994c).

This does not mean that whenever a client perceives homophobia in the therapist, it must be a distortion on the client's part. It means that it is always the clinician's responsibility to be familiar with their own personal feelings and attitudes toward LGB persons and the ways they may be manifested in the therapy process. The therapist must then assess the client's complaint in this context, while simultaneously exploring the range of conscious and unconscious purposes which may be served by the client's beliefs about the therapist (Brown, 1996; Greene, 1994b, 1999; Liddle, 1997).

The issue of therapist neutrality, common in psychodynamic therapies, must be managed delicately. Because LGB persons are frequently the objects of intense disapproval from both loved ones and society, a client may read a therapist's neutrality as disapproval. The therapist in these situations must also be careful not to advance their own agenda for the client, no matter how well intentioned. It is inappropriate to push the client toward acknowledging a gay or lesbian sexual orientation before the client is psychologically prepared to manage it. Rather, the therapist must be affirming and supportive of the client, regardless of the client's choice about their sexual orientation or the management of challenges associated with adopting LGB orientations. Furthermore, therapy with members of oppressed groups must address the pathology of the oppressive behavior rather than exclusively focusing on victims' responses to oppressive behavior. In this context, helping the client understand negative responses to LGB persons (heterosexist bias) as an example of societal pathology, and not the client's flaw or defect, must be an explicit part of the therapeutic work (Brown, 1996; Dahlheimer & Feigal, 1991; Greene, 1994b).

Just as the authentic inclusion of any previously excluded minority group forces the larger group to transform itself into a realistic reflection of the diversity of its members, the visible presence of LGB persons who seek psychological services forces us to rethink our traditional notions about personality development, developmental tasks and stressors, and about what kinds of constellations of persons constitute a couple, a marriage, or a family (Greene, 1994b).

10.09.6 LGB PERSONS AND FAMILY ISSUES

LGB persons come from diverse family constellations as do their heterosexual counterparts. They also require the same tangible and emotional support that all people need, usually provided for by family members. It may be said that strong family ties are even more crucial to LGB persons given the hostility and rejection they routinely confront in the outside world. They may not, however, presume the support that heterosexual family members facing any challenge might take for granted. Therapists should be attuned to the possibility that the absence of such support has more negative consequences for LGB persons than for their heterosexual counterparts. Some research suggests that White lesbians report that they are as much as three times more likely to depend on friends for support over family members (Bradford et al., 1994; Kurdek & Schmidt, 1987; Morgan, 1992). Other research suggests that ethnicity may play a role in the extent to which family or friends are more salient sources of support. Mays and Cochran (1986; 1988) report that African-American lesbians tend to depend on family members for tangible and emotional support to a greater degree than their White counterparts. This may contribute to making African-American lesbians more reluctant to come out to family members than their White counterparts.

Many lesbian and gay clients struggle at some point in their lives with crises related to maintaining secrecy about their sexual orientation, the true nature of their relationships, and the ongoing problems that are a consequence of that decision. An expected developmental issue involves the decision to come out to family members, and the consequences of that decision. Many clients may feel very conflicted about what they want to do and will express great confusion in making this decision. Some may even feel guilty about their disclosure if it upsets family members. The therapist in these situations must be careful not to reinforce the client's guilt by discouraging disclosure when it is appropriate or by suggesting that the family's rejection is justified.

While it may be expected that a family member's disclosure may upset some family members or disrupt family functioning, there is no uniform way in which families respond. Each client's family is different and the range and intensity of their responses will vary from acceptance, or perhaps disappointment, to outrage and outright rejection. Ethnicity, socioeconomic class, religious belief, age at the time of coming out, and other variables will affect the responses of family members as well as the consequences of those responses to the LGB person. Previous family dynamics, rivalries, close ties, and strengths will also affect the process differentially. Over time, some families will come to accept the lesbian or gay member's sexual orientation to varying degrees and others will not. Responses of families will be as diverse as the racial, ethnic, and class groups they represent. Clients may need to be reminded of the often lengthy and difficult process of coming out that they have previously negotiated. This process required that they reevaluate their previously accepted attitudes about LGB persons and come to accept and embrace their identity over time. Just as they required time and understanding to do so, as painful or infuriating as the process may be for them personally, their family members will require time as well. Strommen (1989), Liu and Chan (1996), Greene and Boyd-Franklin (1996), and Brown (1988) provide a detailed discussion of the complexities inherent in the coming out processes for diverse LGB persons and their families of origin

10.09.6.1 Gay and Lesbian Couples

LGB persons seek, form, and sustain relationships in a context where there is little support for them. Most lesbians and gay men grew up in families where their parents were heterosexual and where they had few useful role models for understanding what normal transitions and developmental periods in gay and lesbian relationships would be like (Garnets & Kimmel, 1991). For some couples, there may be a tendency to idealize relationships with members of the same gender. This belief may have some of its origins in the assumption that their gender similarity makes them the same, and that sameness presumes an ease in relating. While this may be true for some couples, it is certainly not generalizable to all of them. Gender similarity does not preclude conflicts, disagreements, or dysfunction in relationships and in some cases may even intensify it. Hence, many gay and lesbian couples are surprised and disappointed when they encounter problems or conflicts within their relationships, even when they are representative of the normal range of challenges for all couples. They may harbor the notion that they are the exception to their idealized image of lesbian or gay relationships, or conversely that all lesbian or gay relationships are doomed to fail. For example, some women believe that battering does not occur in lesbian relationships. They believe that women, unlike men, are not physically abusive. Hence, lesbians in battering relationships may be confused and unable to appropriately label such behavior out of the belief that it does not occur between women, despite the fact that it is happening to them. Renzetti (1992) documents the problem of partner abuse in lesbian relationships and offers a helpful analysis. Kanuha (1990) offers special insights into this problem as it occurs in lesbian women of color.

If lesbian and gay couples are out, their relationship may be constantly minimized and challenged. If they are not out the invisibility of their relationship can be just as problematic. The invisible relationship goes unnoticed. While this is in part the idea, it means that the legitimate status accorded relationships and the social and economic privileges that accompany them are lost. The special pressures and stressors that accompany them remain unacknowledged as well. Family members who perceive a relative to be single, or without the responsibility of a family of their own, may be more demanding of a relative's time or resources. They may fail to understand the responsibility to a partner or relationship which they do not see or one which they choose not to recognize. On this informal level, when the couple has a relationship problem, loss or termination of the relationship, responses to such problems from heterosexual peers or family members may be inconsistent with the realistic magnitude and significance of the loss, or with the attentiveness that would be given to a marital partner in a heterosexual relationship. Thus, members of couples may not derive appropriate support during critical times from resources commonly available to heterosexual couples. Lack of legal status for gay and lesbian relationships in most cities in the USA has direct economic consequences reflected in part in the loss of employee benefits that would normally be extended to a marital partner.

Therapists who are unfamiliar with gay and lesbian couples, and some couples themselves, may attempt to impose male–female models on them, as there are no similar models for same-sex couples (Markowitz, 1991). The myth that in lesbian and gay couples gender roles are reversed is not supported, rather it is contradicted by empirical research on couples. Peplau (1991) and Peplau and Cochran (1990) find that in most lesbian and gay relationships surveyed participants actively reject traditional gender roles as models. Appropriate models would need to take into account differences between male and female socialization and its effects on relationships in which both persons received the same gender socialization (Markowitz, 1991; Schreurs, 1993).

Peplau (1991) discusses a range of commonly believed stereotypes about gay and lesbian couples. Among them, gay men and lesbians neither wish to have, nor are they capable of forming, enduring relationships, most lesbians and gay men grow old unhappy and alone, their relationships are inferior imitations of heterosexual relationships, or that traditional husband and wife and other traditional gender roles are reversed. Such stereotypes are still believed by many therapists despite the absence of any credible evidence to support them and in the presence of a growing body of evidence which disputes such contentions. Bell and Weinberg (1978) report that 40–60% of the participants in their research were in steady relationships. Peplau and Cochran (1990) suggest that the invisibility of long-term couples in research can be attributed in part to sampling bias. LGB research subjects are often recruited in venues that over-represent young, White, urban participants, often in bars. They suggest that couples, particularly long-term partners, do not frequent bars as often as their younger, single counterparts. If older LGB people are not sufficiently sampled, we would not expect to see longer relationships among young subjects. The fact that LGB persons cannot legally marry also means that there are no marriage records that would document the existence of long-term partnerships rendering them less visible (Peplau & Cochran, 1990). Clunis and Green (1988) provide a detailed review of issues facing lesbian couples which may be particularly helpful to the therapist with no experience or training in this area. Kurdek (1994), Kurdek and Schmidt (1987), Peplau (1991), Peplau and Cochran (1990), and Modrcin and Wyers (1990) report on extensive studies of cohabiting gay, lesbian, and heterosexual couples. Findings suggest that lesbian and gay couples are no more prone to relationship dissatisfaction or problems than their heterosexual counterparts. While they may have special problems and challenges, they are no more likely to have marital problems or impoverished social support networks than their heterosexual counterparts and generally report satisfaction in their relationships.

10.09.6.2 Gay and Lesbian Parents

It has been traditionally, albeit incorrectly, presumed that gay men and lesbians do not wish to have children and that they do not make appropriate parents (Greene, 1990, 1994b). Nonetheless, gay men and lesbians become parents in many different ways, as do heterosexual parents. However, they do so amidst the pervasive assumption that their sexual orientation makes them inappropriate parenting figures. This assumption is often based on the false belief that they will increase the likelihood that their child will be gay, lesbian, or psychologically defective. Research on children of LGB parents does not support these contentions (Bigner & Bozett, 1989; Patterson, 1994, 1996). Patterson (1994) provides a systematic study of the behavioral adjustment, self concepts, and sex role identity of children of the lesbian baby boom.

Many LGB persons choose to limit their social world to other LGB people whenever possible. Those who have children, however, are forced to both interact with and negotiate systems, for example, schools, that they might otherwise choose to avoid. They find themselves presented with the dilemma of how to present their unique family constellation in ways that maintain its integrity, protect its privacy, and are sensitive to the child's needs as well. Those who are involved in shared custody arrangements with a former heterosexual spouse often face the realistic danger of having the courts remove their children from their custody if the true nature of their relationship is exposed. The problem of maintaining secrecy in families where a gay or lesbian parent is not out is complex. Care must be taken to determine how to create the privacy or secrecy the family needs without leaving children feeling so fearful or burdened that it interferes with their own emotional needs and development (Greene, 1994b).

Disclosure of lesbian or gay sexual orientation to children is an anxiety-laden process for the parent and child. Many of the dynamics discussed in Strommen (1989) and Brown (1988) can be applied to an understanding of problems which may arise in such disclosures to children. Bigner and Bozett (1987), Crawford (1987), Falk (1989), and Green and Bozett (1991) provide detailed reviews of the issues faced by gay and lesbian parents relevant to disclosure, family dynamics, clinical strategies, and pertinent research.

10.09.6.3 Gay and Lesbian Youth

Gay and lesbian youth force us to take a second look at traditional assumptions about developmental tasks and tensions during the adolescent period. Despite the highly sexualized nature of popular culture in the USA, most adolescents have little accurate information about sexuality at a time when they may be in greatest need of it. They have even less knowledge about gay and lesbian sexual orientation which is not pejorative.

Gonsiorek (1988), Herdt (1989), Savin-Williams (1989, 1990, 1996) describe a range of intense social and personal pressures facing gay and lesbian adolescents. All are complicated by the normative rigidity and intolerance of differences adolescents maintain toward themselves and others. Adolescents who disclose their concerns about their sexual orientation are almost sure to find themselves in the midst of conflict with other family members and peers as well. The negative stereotypes associated with gay and lesbian sexual orientations and the dominant culture's denials of sexuality during this developmental period intensify this conflict. This denial is manifested in a conspicuous absence of institutional support for these youngsters. Coping strategies may also include withdrawal from social activities, denial, overcompensation, emotional constriction, and self-destructive behavior (Gonsiorek, 1988; Savin-Williams, 1989, 1990, 1996).

Savin-Williams (1990, 1996) and Golden (1996) caution that there are important gender differences in the process of self-awareness and disclosure of LGB orientation. Golden (1996) tells us that self-labeling is more fluid in women over the lifespan than men and that the concept of sexual orientation may not be as stable for women as it seems to be for their male counterparts. Women are more likely to initially disclose their awareness of a lesbian sexual orientation in the context of an emotional and affectionate relationship with another woman, and are less likely to disclose prior to coming to a more personal, internal resolution for themselves (Savin-Williams, 1996). Men, on the other hand, are more likely to disclose earlier and to use external social and sexual activity to develop a sense of self-acceptance, a more external process (Savin-Williams, 1990, 1996).

Many adolescents do not reveal their concerns about their sexual orientation to their families or other people who are close to them out of realistic fears of rejection as well as punishment (Hersch, 1991). When they do, Savin-Williams (1996) observes that they are likely to tell a close friend first rather than a family member. They may tell family members as much as decades later or for some LGB persons, never. Some may often withdraw at a time when they are in critical need of support. The high rate of suicide among adolescents believed to be gay and lesbian underscores the dire implications of this problem and warrants the serious attention of mental health practitioners. Support groups, accessible health and social services, the availability of healthy role models, advocacy and education, and education with respect to sexually transmitted diseases, particularly AIDS, are suggested as needed services for gay and lesbian adolescents, a vulnerable population (Gonsiorek, 1988; Hersch, 1991).

The visibility of LGB persons as consumers of psychological services requires practitioners to rethink traditional definitions of family constellations. Practitioners in the 1990s may find themselves confronted by the family in crisis after an adolescent member has disclosed that they are lesbian or gay, or by the adolescent who is in the throes of deciding whether or not, or who, to tell. Similarly, they may be consulted by the wife or husband who has chosen or struggles with the decision about whether or not to leave a heterosexual marriage to come out. They may also be consulted by the confused and angry heterosexual spouse.

Practitioners may also be confronted with family and couple constellations with which they are totally unfamiliar. Aside from issues of custody and marital conflict in parents, it is not uncommon to be asked to treat a child or children, in both the public and private sectors, who must in these arrangements acknowledge this previously feared or unknown aspect of their parent's life. This may occur in conjunction with the sudden upheaval and breakup of their family unit. As gay men and lesbians actively embrace their lifestyles and choose to form their own families, therapists are frequently consulted to assist them in addressing difficulties in their own relationships, as well as making decisions to have and raise children in nontraditional situations. It is incumbent on therapists in these scenarios to be aware of the unwarranted but realistic level of prejudice and discrimination, particularly in custody hearings and court proceedings, against gay and lesbian parents that persists.

10.09.7 TRAINING

10.09.7.1 Hetrosexist Bias in the Delivery of Psychological Services

Educational institutions are not exempt from pervasive heterosexist bias in Western culture. In fact, they have often communicated and legitimized that bias. Institutions responsible for the training of clinical psychologists are no exception. Practicing psychologists, therefore, are not immune to the effects of the pervasive themes of heterosexist bias in the dominant culture. Such bias has often served as an integral part of the underpinnings of theoretical and research paradigms. Hence, this bias insidiously pervades research and practice despite the intentions of many well-meaning research scientists and practitioners. For example, psychoanalytic theories evolved out of traditional culturally-bound views of gender roles. Its theory of etiology of sexual orientation has its origins in views which privilege reproductive sexuality as the only healthy outcome of psychosexual development. Simoni (1999) reports on the review of 24 college-level textbooks in social, abnormal, and developmental psychology. Overall her study reveals inadequate coverage and segregated treatment of the topic of lesbian and gay sexual orientation. Notably, there was little attention given to the systematic incorporation of lesbians and gay men in contexts other than sexual orientation or sexual behavior, such as commitment, parenting, and other routine aspects of human behavior and relationships.

The work of Hooker (1957), Kinsey, Pomeroy and Martin (1948), Kinsey, Pomeroy, Martin, and Gebhard (1953) and others established that lesbian and gay sexual orientations were not synonymous with poor psychological adjustment. Despite this, ignorance and heterosexist bias, which formal training rarely addresses directly, continues to significantly influence the delivery of psychological services to gay and lesbian clients, as well as research in areas relevant to developing a better understanding of this group (Greene, 1994b).

Buhrke's (1989a) findings suggest that students receive little exposure to information relevant to the delivery of services to gay and lesbian clients during the course of their formal training. Garnets et al. (1991), Graham, Rawlings, Halpern, and Hermes (1984), Liddle (1997), and Youngstrom (1991) recommend that current research and findings on lesbians and gay men should be discussed in graduate programs, continuing education and inservice training, as well as in undergraduate courses. Liddle (1997) asserts that being unbiased is not sufficient to demonstrate competence or expertise in clinical work with LGB persons.

Since the late 1980s we have witnessed the growth of a significant body of psychological literature which appropriately addresses the aforementioned concerns. It has not, however, found its way into the mainstream of clinical psychology training programs and curriculums. Browning and Kain (1999), Buhrke (1989b), Chan (1996), Greene and Croom (1999), King (1988), and Simoni (1999) review a range of resources and strategies (see also Dworkin & Gutierrez, 1989; Stone, 1991) which may be useful in the design, implementation, and supplementation of traditional graduate and undergraduate psychology courses, rendering them more sensitive and relevant to LGB persons.

LGB sexual orientations are topics which most persons socialized in the USA have intense feelings about. Hence, it is important that psychologists learn to explore and understand these issues appropriately in both their clients and themselves. Few topics, however, are more scrupulously avoided in the formal training of clinical psychologists. Just as members of ethnic minority groups have been harmed by a legacy of racially stigmatizing psychological folklore, gay and lesbian clients are also harmed by negative heterosexist bias and the misinformation which pervades psychotherapy practice and has similarly pervaded psychological research. Just as ethnic minority clients can be harmed by the unexamined racism in the therapist or inherent in a research design, gay and lesbian clients can be similarly harmed by unexamined and untransformed heterosexist bias in those areas.

As greater numbers of gay and lesbian individuals and families seek counseling and psychotherapy, many therapists find themselves ill-equipped to provide services sensitive to what may be seen as a distinct cultural group. It is important that therapists be aware of the ways in which routine life stressors may be intensified for individuals who are actively discriminated against by the dominant culture and who, unlike members of oppressed ethnic groups, may not find mentoring, support from, or identification with family members. Such identification and sense of shared struggle with family members has been an important coping mechanism in the adaptive "banding together against the outside oppressor" for many members of oppressed ethnic groups. While family members of ethnic minority group members often teach their children to actively challenge the dominant culture's views of them, they are more likely to embrace heterosexist attitudes and join in the dominant culture's rejection of LGB persons.

The ethnic minority LGB person depends on the protective armoring of their family and ethnic community more than their White counterparts but may find themselves on the outskirts of that protective buffer against racism. In addition to the dominant culture's racism, LGB people of color are challenged by the additional stress of coping with the LGB community's racism, the dominant culture's heterosexism, as well as the heterosexist bias of their own ethnic group. This results in a complex inter-relationship of loyalties and estrangements (Chan, 1992; Greene, 1994a, 1994b, 1994c, 1996; Greene & Boyd-Franklin, 1996; Morales, 1992).

Clinicians in these encounters are confronted with the difficult and challenging task of disentangling characterological issues from the personal distress that results from the pressures of societal inequities and their effects on mental health. This cannot be accomplished without a realistic portrayal of the institutional barriers which regularly confront LGB people. This includes an understanding of the role of heterosexist bias in many psychological treatment and research paradigms. Despite the extreme hostility and discrimination that LGB people routinely encounter, they are not inevitable psychological cripples. The resilience and unique skills which many out gay men and lesbians develop, despite the hostility and barriers they face, must be more fully explored as well as the negative outcomes (Greene 1994b, 1999). While the realistic need for secrecy, and often justifiable suspicion LGB persons hold for mental health practitioners and research scientists often complicates research endeavors, they are not impossible to negotiate.

Garnets et al. (1991) suggest the continued use of survey research as a means of reducing sampling bias found in many studies on lesbians and gay men. Caution must exercised when making generalizations from samples which are nonrepresentative and replication of results is important (Gonsiorek, 1991).

While APA has charged psychologists with the task of challenging heterosexist bias in both research and practice, it has provided little in their formal training to assist them in making the necessary shifts in practice as well as attitude. Just as clients are presumed to be heterosexual, faculty members and psychologists in training are similarly regarded. Heterosexist bias in training programs continue to make it unsafe for some faculty members and lesbian and gay students to divulge their sexual orientation. The locus and levels of danger assume different forms.

D'Augelli (1989) observes that LGB students and faculty members continue to suffer from discrimination in the workplace. Three-quarters of the lesbians and gay men in his sample in university environments reported experiences of verbal abuse, 26% reported being threatened with violence, and 17% reported having their personal property damaged. Kitzinger (1996) reports that British studies have similar findings. Tierney (1992), in a report from the University of Oregon, finds the university environment neither consistently safe, tolerant, nor academically inclusive of LGB persons or of research relevant to them. The study concurred with D'Augelli (1989) and Kitzinger (1996) who report higher incidences of verbal and physical attacks on LGB students than on their heterosexual counterparts. Kitzinger (1996) reports that the British Psychological Society has refused on three occasions to consider the establishment of a specific forum or unit devoted to the psychological study of LGB issues.

For many LGB students in graduate programs, disclosing their sexual orientation before their formal training is completed puts them at risk for discrimination that may be subtle but nonetheless can adversely affect their training status within their programs. The requirement to manage the heterosexism of faculty members, supervisors, and fellow students can leave LGB students with additional challenges that are neither appropriate nor shared by their heterosexual counterparts. It also deprives them of the opportunity to authentically explore their own feelings, ideas, and appropriate use of self as a clinical instrument in their work with clients. Hence, there is a failure to appropriately explore countertransference problems as well as issues which may arise when the therapist and client are both LGB persons (Greene, 1994b).

Dahlheimer and Feigal (1991) suggest that therapists may use a variety of techniques in conjunction with didactic training to develop greater sensitivities toward gay and lesbian clients. They suggest the use of role-playing and the review of case material for insensitive approaches. Case material may be used that requires students or supervisees to review data or client histories and determine how they might view the case if the heterosexual client were an LGB person (Greene, 1994b).

Another suggestion directs therapists as a part of their training to purchase a gay or lesbian magazine (which is clearly labeled as such), to carry it visibly throughout the course of their day, to monitor their feelings about doing so as well as their internal and overt responses to the inquiries and responses of others, and to discuss these experiences in supervision. It is suggested that these exercises be used to develop a subjective sense of the level of self-consciousness, shame, fear, vulnerability, or anger that many of their clients must manage routinely (Dahlheimer & Feigal, 1991). Participation in such exercises does not mean that doing so will give a heterosexual therapist a complete understanding of what life is like for their LGB client. Rather it is intended to provide the therapist with some realistic, albeit minimal, understanding of what their client must manage on an ongoing basis without the luxury of terminating the "exercise" when they are uncomfortable or in danger (Greene, 1994b). Browning and Kain (1999) present a range of exercises and other strategies that may be useful in training.

Practitioners who lack formal training in or experience working with LGB clients and their families are advised to use cogroup and cofamily therapist arrangements; others may use peer and/or other forms of supervision with practitioners who have this professional experience and training as an additional means of augmenting their skills (Liddle, 1997).

David Scasta, editor of the *Journal of Gay and Lesbian Psychotherapy* (Markowitz, 1991), observes that the treatment of gay men and lesbians is a specialized field that requires a heightened level of self-awareness in the clinician and a commitment to being educated about gay and lesbian issues. It is important that all current and prospective therapists examine their conscious and unconscious levels of heterosexist bias to assure that they do not intrude into their client's therapy (Brown, 1996; Liddle, 1997).

10.09.8 FUTURE DIRECTIONS

As we approach the twenty-first century, clinical psychology is confronted with the need to be more inclusive if it is to serve the needs of consumers of psychological services appropriately. It is also challenged with the need to create theoretical paradigms and develop research that is a reflection of a wider range of human behavior and realities.

Chan (1996) asserts that academic institutions play a major role in perpetuating heterosexist bias and can play a major role in eliminating it. Listing sexual orientation in the nondiscrimination policies of institutions and seriously implementing that policy is one step. The assumption of a proactive, rather than reactive, affirmative stance among the leadership of academic institutions is an important means of establishing and implementing such policies.

A new line of inquiry must include acknowledgment, exploration, and understanding of the role of heterosexist bias in psychological practice, research, and the development of theoretical paradigms. It must also include international perspectives on assessments of the role of negative attitudes toward LGB sexual orientations on the development of identities in lesbians, gay men, bisexual, and heterosexual persons. LGB research must develop the means of sampling a wider range of LGB persons if studies are to be more representative of the population of LGB persons. This information is critical to the establishment of a reliable database as well as to the development of culturally and contextually sensitive methods of understanding the complex issues that arise when treating a diverse range of LGB clients (Croom, in press).

It is essential that the treatment of LGB clients and research with this population be given formal and explicit attention in the training of clinical psychologists. Initially, the invisibility of LGB issues that should be integrated in and across disciplines must be addressed. This can assume many different forms including the incorporation of required course work and clinical supervision (Buhrke, 1989a; Greene, 1994b; Liddle, 1997). The active recruitment of psychologists with research, supervision, teaching, and other forms of expertise and interest in this area and the inclusion of openly gay or lesbian faculty and staff members in academic and training institutions must also be accomplished in order to meet the goals of competent practice.

This may also be accomplished by supporting the creation of LGB scholarship by rewarding (rather than punishing or failing to prioritize) course development, providing tangible resources, supporting the acquisition of state-of-the-art publications and collections in university libraries, and providing support for interdisciplinary LGB research and teaching that develops scholarship from diverse perspectives (Chan, 1996; Simoni, 1999). Simoni (1999) advocates the identification, definition, and confrontation of heterosexism in psychology as the explicit responsibility of an effective instructor in the academy.

Accreditation teams must be serious in their efforts to hold training institutions, practicum, externship, and internship sites accountable for upholding meaningful standards of competence. Establishing requirements for demonstrating proficiency as an integral requirement for graduate comprehensive examinations, licensing, and certification should be undertaken as well. This can be accomplished by including relevant items on LGB issues on licensing, certification, and advanced practice specialty examinations (i.e., American Board of Professional Psychology).

10.09.9 SUMMARY

Sexual orientation is an important and complex psychological variable that has long been an object of scientific scrutiny. Its study has undergone critical change since the late 1970s. However, there is still much to be done. Potgieter (1997) documents the long history of struggle against racism and heterosexism in South Africa. In the fall of 1995, the first gay and lesbian colloquium took place in South Africa. In its final constitution, South Africa became the first country to include sexual orientation in its nondiscrimination clause. Since the late 1980s, the South African National Gay and Lesbian Coalition has become a prominent and active lobby for lesbian and gay rights. Even in quarters where change is slow, change takes place nonetheless. To collectively promote more accurate understandings of LGB sexual orientations, dichotomous and categorical attempts to classify it must be abandoned. Our task is the development of broader, more inclusive questions that explore the complex origins and determinants of all affectional and erotic attractions as they interact with other salient aspects of human beings as collective reflections of a healthy range of human diversity.

10.09.10 REFERENCES

American Psychological Association (1994). *Publication Manual of the American Psychological Association* (4th ed). Washington, DC: Author.

Ames, L. J. (1996). Homo-phobia, homo-ignorance, homo-hate: Heterosexism and aids. In E. Rothblum & L. Bond (Eds.), *Preventing heterosexism and homophobia* (pp. 239–265). Thousand Oaks, CA: Sage.

Bailey, J. M., & Pillard, R. C. (1991). A genetic study of male sexual orientation. *Archives of General Psychiatry, 48,* 1089–1096.

Bell, A. P., & Weinberg, M. S. (1978). *Homosexuality: A study of diversity among men and women.* New York: Simon & Schuster.

Bell, A. P., Weinberg, M. S., & Hammersmith, S. K. (1981). *Sexual preference: Its development in men and women.* Bloomington, IN: Indiana University Press.

Bem, D. J. (1996). Exotic becomes erotic: A developmental theory of sexual orientation. *Psychological Review, 103,* 320–335.

Bem, S. J. (1993). *The lenses of gender: Transforming the debate on sexual inequality.* New Haven, CT: Yale.

Bigner, J. J., & Bozett, F. W. (1989). Parenting by gay fathers. *Marriage and Family Review, 14,* 155–175.

Bohan, J. (1996). *Psychology and sexual orientation: Coming to terms.* New York: Routledge.

Boyd-Franklin, N. (1989). *Black families in therapy: A multisystems approach.* New York: Guilford Press.

Bradford, J., & Ryan, C. (1988). *The National Lesbian Health Care Survey: Final Report.* National Lesbian and Gay Health Foundation.

Bradford, J., Ryan, C., & Rothblum, E. (1994). National lesbian health care survey: Implications for mental health care. *Journal of Consulting and Clinical Psychology, 62,* 228–242.

Brown, L. S. (1988). Lesbians, gay men and their families: Common clinical issues. *Journal of Gay and Lesbian Psychotherapy, 1,* 65–77.

Brown, L. (1989). New voices, new visions: Toward a lesbian and gay paradigm for psychology. *Psychology of Women, 13,* 445–458.

Brown, L. (1996). Preventing heterosexism and bias in psychotherapy and counseling. In E. Rothblum & L. Bond (Eds.), *Preventing heterosexism and homophobia* (pp. 36–58). Thousand Oaks, CA: Sage.

Browning, C., & Kain, C. (1999). Teaching lesbian, gay and bisexual psychology: Issues and resources. In B. Greene & G. L. Croom (Eds.), *Psychological perspectives on lesbian, gay and bisexual issues Vol 5—Education, research and practice in lesbian, gay, bisexual and transgendered psychology: A resource manual.* Thousand Oaks, CA: Sage.

Buhrke, R. A. (1989a). Female student perspectives on training in lesbian and gay issues. *The Counseling Psychologist, 17,* 629–636.

Buhrke, R. A. (1989b). Incorporating lesbian and gay issues into counselor training: A resource guide. *Journal of Counseling and Development, 68,* 77–80.

Byne, W. (1995). Science and belief: Psychobiological research and sexual orientation. *Journal of Homosexuality, 28,* 303–344.

Cass, V. C. (1984). Homosexual identity formation: A theoretical model. *Journal of Sex Research, 20,* 143–167.

Chan, C. S. (1989). Issues of identity development among Asian-American lesbians and gay men. *Journal of Counseling and Development, 68,* 16–20.

Chan, C. S. (1992). Cultural considerations in counseling Asian American lesbians and gay men. In S. Dworkin & F. Gutierrez (Eds.), *Counseling gay men and lesbians: Journey to the end of the rainbow* (pp. 115–124). Alexandra, VA: American Association for Counseling and Development.

Chan, C. S. (1996). Combating heterosexism in educational institutions: Structural changes and strategies. In E. Rothblum & L. Bond (Eds.), *Preventing heterosexism and homophobia* (pp. 20–35). Thousand Oaks, CA: Sage.

Clunis, D. M. & Green, G. D. (1988). *Lesbian couples.* Seattle, WA: Seal Press.

Coleman, E. (1981/1982). Developmental stages of the coming out process. *Journal of Homosexuality, 7,* 31–43.

Committee on Lesbian and Gay Concerns (1986). APA policy statement on lesbian and gay issues. Washington, DC: American Psychological Association.

Committee on Lesbian and Gay Concerns (1990). Final report of the Task Force on Bias in Psychotherapy with Lesbians and Gay Men. Washington, DC: American Psychological Association.

Crawford, S. (1987). Lesbian families: Psychosocial stress and the family building process. In Boston Lesbian Psychologies Collective (Ed.), *Lesbian psychologies* (pp. 195–214). Chicago: University of Illinois Press.

Croom, G. L. (in press). Lesbian, gay and bisexuals of color: A challenge to representative sampling in empirical research. In B. Greene & G. L. Croom (Eds.), *Psychological perspectives on lesbian, gay and bisexual issues, Vol 5—Education, research and practice in lesbian, gay, bisexual and transgendered psychology: A resource manual.* Thousand Oaks, CA: Sage.

Dahlheimer, D., & Feigal, J. (1991, Jan.–Feb.). Bridging the gap. *The Family Therapy Networker, 15,* 26–29; 31–35.

D'Augelli, A. (1989). Lesbian and gay men's experiences of discrimination and harassment in a university community. *American Journal of Community Psychology, 17,* 317–321.

D'Augelli, A. (1994). Lesbian and gay male development: Steps toward an analysis of lesbians' and gay men's lives. In B. Greene & G. Herek (Eds.), *Lesbian and gay psychology: Theory, research and clinical applications* (pp. 118–132). Thousand Oaks, CA: Sage.

DeCrescenzo, T. (1985). Homophobia: A study of attitudes of mental health professionals toward homosexuality. In R. Schoenberg, R. Goldberg, & D. Shore (Eds.), *With compassion toward some: Homosexuality and social work in America* (pp. 115–136). New York: Harrington Park Press.

Diamond, M. (1993). Some genetic considerations in the development of sexual orientation. In M. Huang, R. E. Whalen, C. Aron, & K. Olsen (Eds.), *The development of sex differences and similarities in behavior* (pp. 291–309). Dordrecht, The Netherlands: Kluwer.

Dworkin, S., & Gutierrez, F. (Eds.) (1989, Sept./Oct.). Special Issue: Gay, lesbian and bisexual issues in counseling. *Journal of Counseling and Development, 68,* 6–96.

Dworkin, S., & Gutierrez, F. (1992). Opening the closet door. In S. Dworkin & F. Gutierrez (Eds.), *Counseling gay men and lesbians: Journey to the end of the rainbow* (pp xvii–xxvii). Alexandria, VA: American Association of Counseling and Development.

Falk, P. J. (1989). Lesbian mothers: Psychosocial assumptions in family law. *American Psychologist, 44,* 941–947.

Fassinger, R. E. (1991, April). The hidden minority: Issues and challenges in working with lesbian women and gay men. *The Counseling Psychologist, 19,* 157–176.

Freud, S. (1922/1959). *Group psychology and the analysis of the ego* (James Strachey, Ed. and trans.). London: Hogarth Press. (Original work published in 1922).

Fygetakis, L. (1997). Greek American Lesbians: Identity odysseys of honorable good girls. In B. Greene (Ed.), *Ethnic and cultural diversity among lesbians and gay men* (pp. 152–190). Thousand Oaks, CA: Sage.

Garnets, L., Hancock, K. A., Cochran, S. D., Goodchilds, J., & Peplau, L. A. (1991). Issues in psychotherapy with lesbians and gay men: A survey of psychologists. *American Psychologist, 46,* 964–972.

Garnets, L., & Kimmel, D. (1991). Lesbian and gay male dimensions in the psychological study of human diversity. In J. Goodchilds (Ed.), *Psychological perspectives on human diversity in America: Master lectures* (pp. 143–192). Washington, DC: American Psychological Association.

Giusti, I., & Katz, R. (1992). *The history of the organization of gay and lesbian psychology: How it all began.* New York: Unpublished manuscript.

Glassgold, J. (1992). New directions in dynamic theories of lesbianism: From psychoanalysis to social constructionism. In J. Chrisler & D. Howard (Eds.), *New directions in feminist psychology: Practice, theory, and research* (pp. 154–164). New York: Springer.

Golden, C. (1996). Whats in a name? Sexual self-identification among women. In R. C. Williams & K. M. Cohen (Eds.), *The lives of lesbians, gays and bisexuals: Children to adults* (pp. 229–249). Fort Worth, TX: Harcourt Brace.

Gonsiorek, J. (1977). Psychological adjustment and homosexuality. *Social and Behavioral Sciences Documents, MS 1478.* San Raphael, CA: Select Press.

Gonsiorek, J. (1982). The use of diagnostic concepts in working with gay and lesbian populations. In J. Gonsiorek (Ed.), *Homosexuality and psychotherapy: A practitioners handbook of affirmative models* (pp. 9–20). Thousand Oaks, CA: Sage.

Gonsiorek, J. (1988). Mental health issues of gay and lesbian adolescents. *Journal of Adolescent Health Care, 9,* 114–122.

Gonsiorek, J. (1991). The empirical basis for the demise of the illness model of homosexuality. In J. Gonsiorek & J. Weinrich (Eds.), *Homosexuality: Research implications for public policy* (pp. 115–136). Thousand Oaks, CA: Sage.

Gonsiorek, J., & Weinrich, J. (1991). The definition and scope of sexual orientation. In J. Gonsiorek & J. Weinrich (Eds.), *Homosexuality: Research implications for public policy* (pp. 1–12). Thousand Oaks, CA: Sage.

Graham, D., Rawlings, E. I., Halpern, H. S., & Hermes, J. (1984). Therapists' needs for training in counseling lesbians and gay men. *Professional Psychology, 15,* 482–496.

Green, G. D., & Bozett, F. (1991). Lesbian mothers and gay fathers. In J. Gonsiorek & J. Weinrich (Eds.), *Homosexuality: Research implications for public policy* (pp. 197–214). Thousand Oaks, CA: Sage.

Greene, B. (1990, December). African American lesbians. *BG Magazine, 26,* 6.

Greene, B. (1992). Black feminist psychotherapy. In E. Wright (Ed.), *Feminism and psychoanalysis: A critical dictionary* (pp. 34–35). Oxford, UK: Basil Blackwell.

Greene, B. (1994a). Lesbian women of color. In L. Comas-Diaz & B. Greene (Eds.), *Women of color: Integrating ethnic and gender identities in psychotherapy* (pp. 389–427). New York: Guilford Press.

Greene, B. (1994b). Lesbian and gay sexual orientations: Implications for clinical training, practice and research. In B. Greene & G. Herek (Eds.), *Psychological Perspectives on lesbian and gay issues. Vol. 1—Lesbian and gay psychology: Theory, research & clinical applications* (pp. 1–24). Thousand Oaks, CA: Sage.

Greene, B. (1994c). Ethnic minority lesbians and gay men: Mental health and treatment issues. *Journal of Consulting and Clinical Psychology, 62*(2), 243–251.

Greene, B. (1996a). Lesbians and gay men of color: The legacy of ethnosexual mythologies in heterosexism. In E. Rothblum & L. Bond (Eds.), *Preventing heterosexism and homophobia* (pp. 59–70). Thousand Oaks, CA: Sage.

Greene, B. (1996b). Psychotherapy with African American women: Considering diverse identities and societal barriers. *Annals of the New York Academy of Sciences-Women & Mental Health, 789,* 191–210.

Greene, B. (1997, June). Psychotherapy with African-American women: Integrating feminist and psychodynamic models. *Journal of Smith College Studies in Social Work—Theoretical, Research, Practice and Educational Perspectives for Understanding and Working with African-American Clients, 67*(3), 299–322.

Greene, B. (1999). Beyond heterosexism and across the cultural divide: Privilege, invisibility and future lesbian, gay and bisexual psychology. In B. Greene & G. L. Croom (Eds.), *Psychological perspectives on lesbian, gay and bisexual issues. Vol. 5—Education, research & practice in lesbian, gay, bisexual and transgendered psychology: A resource manual.* Thousand Oaks, CA: Sage.

Greene, B., & Boyd-Franklin, N. (1996). African American lesbians: Issues in couples therapy. In J. Laird & R. J. Green (Eds.), *Lesbians and gay men in couples and families: A handbook for therapists* (pp. 251–271). San Francisco: Jossey-Bass.

Greene, B., & Croom, G. L. (Eds.) (1999). *Psychological Perspectives on Lesbian, Gay, and Bisexual and Issues, Vol. 5—Education, Research and Practice in Lesbian, Gay, Bisexual and Transgendered Psychology: A Resource Manual.* Thousand Oaks, CA: Sage.

Haldeman, D. (1991). Sexual orientation conversion therapy for gay men and lesbians: A scientific examination. In J. Gonsiorek & J. Weinrich (Eds.), *Homosexuality: Research implications for public policy* (pp. 149–160). Newbury Park, CA: Sage.

Haldeman, D. (1994). The practice and ethics of sexual orientation conversion therapy. *Journal of Consulting and Clinical Psychology, 62,* 221–227.

Haldeman, D. (1999). Therapeutic responses to sexual orientation: Psychology's evolution. In B. Greene & G. L. Croom (Eds.), *Psychological perspectives on lesbian, gay and bisexual issues, Vol. 5—Education, research and practice in lesbian, gay, bisexual and transgendered psychology: A resource manual*. Thousand Oaks, CA: Sage.

Hamer, D. H., Hu, S., Magnuson, V. L., Hu, N., & Pattatucci, A. (1993). A linkage between DNA markers on the X chromosome and male sexual orientation. *Science, 261*, 321–327.

Haumann, G. (1995). Homosexuality, biology and ideology. *Journal of Homosexuality, 28*, 57–77.

Herdt, G. (1989). Gay and lesbian youth. *Journal of Homosexuality, 17*, 1–4.

Herek, G. M. (1989). Hate crimes against lesbians and gay men. *American Psychologist, 44*, 948–955.

Herek, G. M., & Berrill, K. (Eds.) (1992). *Hate crimes: Confronting violence against lesbians and gay men*. Newbury Park, CA: Sage.

Hersch, P. (1991, Jan.–Feb.). Secret lives: Lesbians and gay teens in fear of discovery. *The Family Therapy Networker, 15*, 36–39; 41–43.

Hooker, E. (1957). The adjustment of the male overt homosexual. *Journal of Projective Techniques, 21*, 18–31.

Isay, R. A. (1990). Psychoanalytic theory and psychotherapy of gay men. In D. P. McWhirter, S. A. Sanders, & J. M. Reinisch (Eds.), *Homosexuality/heterosexuality* (pp. 283–301). New York: Oxford University Press.

Jones, E. (1965). *The life and work of Sigmund Freud*. New York: Basic Books.

Jones, F. (1997, March). *Eloquent anonymity*. [Review of the book *Lush Life: A Biography of Billy Strayhorn*]. *Readings: A Journal of Reviews and Commentary in Mental Health, 12*(1), 10–14.

Kanuha, V. (1990) Compounding the triple jeopardy: Battering in lesbian of color relationships. In L. S. Brown & M. P. P. Root (Eds.), *Diversity and complexity in feminist therapy* (pp. 169–184). New York: Haworth Press.

Kashak, E. (1992). *Engendered lives: A new psychology of women's experience*. New York: Basic Books.

King, N. (1988). Teaching about lesbians and gays in the psychology curriculum. In P. A. Bronstein & K. Quina (Eds.), *Teaching a psychology of people: Resources for gender and sociocultural awareness* (pp. 168–174). Washington, DC: American Psychological Association.

Kinsey, A., Pomeroy, W. B., & Martin, C. E. (1948). *Sexual behavior in the human male*. Philadelphia: Saunders.

Kinsey, A., Pomeroy, W. B., Martin, C. E., & Gebhard, P. H. (1953). *Sexual behavior in the human female*. Philadelphia: Saunders.

Kirk, M., & Madsen, H. (1996). A field trip to straight America. In K. Rosenblum & T.-M. C. Travis (Eds.), *The meaning of difference: American constructions of race, sex and gender, social class, and sexual orientation* (pp. 400–412). New York: McGraw-Hill.

Kitzinger, C. (1987). *The social construction of lesbianism*. London: Sage.

Kitzinger, C. (1996). Speaking of oppression: Psychology, politics and the language of power. In E. Rothblum & L. Bond (Eds.), *Preventing heterosexism and homophobia* (pp. 3–19). Thousand Oaks, CA: Sage.

Kurdek, L. A. (1994). The nature and correlates of relationship quality in gay, lesbian and heterosexual cohabiting couples. In B. Greene & G. Herek (Eds.), *Lesbian and gay psychology: Theory, research and clinical applications* (pp. 133–155). Thousand Oaks, CA: Sage.

Kurdek, L. A., & Schmidt, J. P. (1987). Perceived emotional support from family and friends in members of homosexual, married, and heterosexual cohabiting couples. *Journal of Homosexuality, 14*, 57–68.

LeVay, S. (1991). A difference in hypothalamic structure between heterosexual and homosexual men. *Science, 253*, 1034–1037.

Liddle, B. J. (1997). Gay and lesbian clients' selection of therapists and utilization of therapy. *Psychotherapy, 34*, 11–18.

Liu, P., & Chan, C. S. (1996). Lesbian, gay and bisexual Asian Americans and their families. In J. Laird & R. J. Green (Eds.), *Lesbians and gays in couples and families* (pp. 137–152). San Francisco: Jossey-Bass.

Markowitz, L. M. (1991, Jan.–Feb.). Homosexuality: Are we still in the dark? *The Family Therapy Networker, 15*, 26–29; 31–35.

Mays, V. M., & Cochran, S. D. (1986, August). Relationship experiences and the perception of discrimination by Black lesbians. Paper presented at the 94th Annual Convention of the American Psychological Association, Washington, DC.

Mays, V.M., & Cochran, S. D. (1988). The Black women's relationship project: A national survey of Black lesbians. In M. Shernoff & W. Scott (Eds.), *The sourcebook on lesbian/gay healthcare* (2nd ed., pp. 54–62). Washington, DC: National Lesbian and Gay Health Foundation, Inc.

McGuire, T. R. (1995). Is homosexuality genetic? A critical review. *Journal of Homosexuality, 28*, 115–145.

McWhirter, D. P. (1990). Homosexuality/Heterosexuality: An overview. In D. P. McWhirter, S. A. Sanders, & J. M. Reinisch (Eds.), *Homosexuality/heterosexuality* (pp. xiv–xxvii). New York: Oxford University Press.

Meredith, R. L., & Reister, R. W. (1980). Psychotherapy responsibility and homosexuality: Clinical examination of socially deviant behavior. *Professional Psychology, 11*, 174–193.

Meyer-Bahlberg, H. (1995). Psychoneuroendocrinology and sexual pleasure: The aspect of sexual orientation. In P. R. Abramson & S. D. Pinkerton (Eds.), *Sexual nature/sexual culture* (pp. 135–153). Chicago: University of Chicago Press.

Modrcin, M. J., & Wyers, N. L. (1990). Lesbian and gay couples: Where they turn when help is needed. *Journal of Gay and Lesbian Psychotherapy, 1*, 89–104.

Money, J. (1988). *Gay, straight and in between: The sexology of erotic orientation*. New York: Oxford University Press.

Morales, E. (1992). Counseling Latino gays and Latina lesbians. In S. Dworkin & F. Gutierriez (Eds.), *Counseling gay men and lesbians: Journey to the end of the rainbow* (pp. 125–139). Alexandria, VA: American Association for Counseling and Development.

Morgan, K. S. (1992). Caucasian lesbians use of psychotherapy: A matter of attitude? *Psychology of Women Quarterly, 16*, 127–130.

Morgan, K. S., & Eliason, M. J. (1992). The role of psychotherapy in Caucasian lesbians' lives. *Women & Therapy, 13*, 27–52.

Morin, S. (1977). Heterosexual bias in psychological research on lesbianism and male homosexuality. *American Psychologist, 32*, 629–637.

Morin, S., & Rothblum, E. (1991). Removing the stigma: Fifteen years of progress. *American Psychologist, 46*, 947–949.

Niesen, J. P. (1990). Heterosexism: Redefining homophobia for the 1990s. *Journal of Gay and Lesbian Psychotherapy, 1*, 21–23.

Parker, D. A., & DeCecco, J. P. (1995). Sexual expression: a global perspective. *Journal of Homosexuality, 28*, 427–430.

Patterson, C. (1994). Children of the lesbian baby boom. In B. Greene & G. Herek (Eds.), *Lesbian and gay psychology: Theory, research and clinical Applications* (pp. 156–175). Thousand Oaks, CA: Sage.

Patterson, C. (1996). Lesbian mothers and their children:

Findings from the Bay Area Study. In J. Laird & R. J. Green (Eds.), *Lesbians and gays in couples and families* (pp. 420–437). San Francisco: Jossey-Bass.

Peplau, L. A. (1991). Lesbian and gay relationships. In J. Gonsiorek & J. Weinrich (Eds.), *Homosexuality: Research implications for public policy* (pp. 177–196). Newbury Park, CA: Sage.

Peplau, L. A., & Cochran, S. (1990). A relationship perspective on homosexuality. In D. P. McWhirter, S. A. Sanders, & J. M. Reinisch (Eds.), *Homosexuality/heterosexuality* (pp. 321–349). New York: Oxford University Press.

Potgieter, C. (1997). From apartheid to Mandela's constitution: Black South African Lesbians in the Nineties. In B. Greene (Ed.), *Ethnic and cultural diversity among lesbians and gay men* (pp. 88–116). Thousand Oaks, CA: Sage.

Reiss, B. F. (1980). Psychological tests in homosexuality. In J. Marmor (Ed.), *Homosexual behavior: A modern reappraisal* (pp. 293–311). New York: Basic Books.

Renzetti, C. (1992). *Violent betrayal: Partner abuse in lesbian relationships*. Newbury Park, CA: Sage.

Rothblum, E. (1990). Depression among lesbians: An invisible and unresearched phenomenon. *Journal of Gay and Lesbian Psychotherapy, 1*, 67–87.

Rothblum, E. (1993). Gay and lesbian faculty face issues in academia. *APA Monitor, September*, 4.

Rudolph, J. (1988). Counselors attitudes toward homosexuality: A selective review of the literature. *Journal of Counseling and Development, 67*, 165–168.

Savin-Williams, R. (1989). Gay and lesbian adolescents. *Marriage and Family Review, 14*, 197–216.

Savin-Williams, R. (1990). *Gay and lesbian youth: Expressions of identity*. Washington, DC: Hemisphere.

Savin-Williams, R. C. (1994). Verbal and physical abuse as stressors in the lives of lesbian, gay male and bisexual youths: Associations with school problems, running away, substance abuse, prostitution and suicide. *Journal of Consulting and Clinical Psychology, 62*, 261–269.

Savin-Williams, R. (1996). Self labeling and disclosure among gay, lesbian and bisexual youths. In J. Laird & R. J. Green (Eds.), *Lesbians and gays in couples and families* (pp. 153–182). San Francisco: Jossey-Bass.

Schreurs, K. M. G. (1993). Sexuality in lesbian couples. *Annual Review of Sex Research, 4*, 49–66.

Shidlo, A. (1994). Internalized homophobia: Conceptual and empirical issues in measurement. In B. Greene & G. Herek (Eds.), *Lesbian and gay psychology: Theory, research and clinical applications* (pp. 176–205). Thousand Oaks, CA: Sage.

Simoni, J. (1999). Confronting heterosexist bias in the teaching of psychology. In B. Greene & G. L. Croom (Eds.), *Education, research and practice in lesbian, gay, bisexual and transgendered psychology: A resource manual*. Thousand Oaks, CA: Sage.

Stone, G. L. (Ed.) (1991, April). Counseling lesbian women and gay men—Special issue. *The Counseling Psychologist, 19*, 155–248.

Strommen, E. (1989). Hidden branches and growing pains: Stressful aspects of negotiating their lives. Homosexuality and the family tree. *Marriage and Family Review, 14*, 9–34.

Tafoya, T. (1997). Native gay and lesbian issues: The two spirited. In B. Greene (Ed.), *Ethnic and cultural diversity among lesbians and gay men* (pp. 1–10). Thousand Oaks, CA: Sage.

Tierney, W. G. (1992). Enhancing diversity: Toward a better campus climate. Report of the Committee on Lesbian and Gay Concerns. University Park: Pennsylvania State University.

Trippet, S. E. (1994). Lesbians' mental health concerns. *Health Care for Women International, 15*, 317–323.

Weinberg, G. (1972). *Society and the healthy homosexual*. New York: St. Martins.

Weinberg, T. S. (1983). *Gay men, gay selves: The social construction of homosexual identities*. New York: Irvington.

Welch, B. (1990, January 26). Statement on homosexuality [Available from American Psychological Association, 750 First St., NE, Washington, DC. 20002–4242].

Woolley, G. (1991, Jan.–Feb.). Beware the well intentioned therapist. *The Family Therapy Networker, 15*, 30.

Youngstrom, N. (1991, July). Lesbians and gay men still find bias in therapy. *APA Monitor, 22*, 24–25.

10.10
Diversity Matters: Religion and the Practice of Clinical Psychology

DONALD W. PREUSSLER, RICHARD E. BUTMAN, and STANTON L. JONES
Wheaton College, IL, USA

10.10.1 INTRODUCTION 233

10.10.2 THE DIVERSITY OF THE WORLD'S RELIGIONS 236

10.10.2.1 Cognitive Dimension 237
10.10.2.2 Ritualistic and Symbolic Dimension 237
10.10.2.3 Moral Dimension 237
10.10.2.4 Institutional Dimension 238
10.10.2.5 Community and Lifestyle Dimension 238
10.10.2.6 Experiential Dimension 238

10.10.3 RELIGION AND/OR VS. SPIRITUALITY 239

10.10.4 PHILOSOPHICAL BASIS FOR APPRECIATING RELIGIOUS DIVERSITY IN CLINICAL CARE 239

10.10.4.1 The Philosophical Conflict Between Clinical Care and Religious Belief 240
10.10.4.2 A Philosophy of Clinical Practice that Appreciates Religious Belief 240
10.10.4.3 A Paradigm for Dialog on Religious Beliefs in Clinical Care 241

10.10.5 CLINICAL ASSESSMENT AND DIAGNOSIS: APPRECIATING RELIGIOUS DIVERSITY IN THE PROCESS OF MEASUREMENT 243

10.10.6 THE EMPIRICAL BASIS FOR APPRECIATING RELIGIOUS DIVERSITY IN CLINICAL CARE 245

10.10.6.1 Religious Persons and Mental Health 245
10.10.6.2 Psychotherapy and Values 246
10.10.6.3 Religion in Psychotherapy 246
10.10.6.4 Religion and Clinical Judgment, Technique and Behavior 247
10.10.6.5 Religion and Clinical Research 248

10.10.7 THE RELIGIOUS COMMUNITY AS A RESOURCE FOR SUPPORT 248

10.10.8 TRAINING CLINICAL PSYCHOLOGISTS IN RELIGIOUS DIVERSITY 249

10.10.9 FUTURE DIRECTIONS 250

10.10.10 SUMMARY 252

10.10.11 REFERENCES 252

10.10.1 INTRODUCTION

In this chapter, the aim is to promote the inclusion of spirituality and religion as potentially important and salient factors in the assessment, diagnosis, and treatment of clients by mental health professionals, particularly clinical psychologists. To do this, an attempt will be made to lay the philosophical, empirical, and clinical bases for such a treatise. The chapter will conclude with thoughts about future directions for the inclusion of spirituality and religion in clinical care.

"Probably nothing in human history has sparked more controversy and debate than religion" (Paloutzian, 1996, p. 2). The etymology of the word religion is interesting. It comes from the Latin word *legare,* which means that which binds or connects. As Paloutzian (1996) suggests, religion is a process of rebinding or reconnection. In the psychology of religion, it is less clear whether that binding or connecting is to "God, Nature, a state of mind, a cosmic force, each other as individuals or their communities" (Paloutzian, 1996, p. 7).

Historically, religion has not been a prominent diversity issue for the field of clinical psychology. Most often the field of psychology has embraced tolerance of diversity in the world of ideas and experience, with the notable exception of religious ideas and spirituality (Kauffmann, 1991). It is remarkable that an issue of *The Clinical Psychologist* devoted to diversity (Comas-Díaz & Striker, 1993) did not focus on, and barely mentioned, religion as a diversity variable. Bergin (1991) has asserted that "Psychologists' understanding and support of cultural diversity has been exemplary with respect to race, gender, and ethnicity but the profession's tolerance and empathy has not adequately reached the religious client."

There is historical precedent for the inclusion of religion in the practice of clinical psychology. The pioneering psychologist William James wrote in 1910 on the pragmatics of religious diversity in his essays on the philosophical construct of pluralism (James, 1910/1963). In his classic text on the psychology of religion, *The varieties of religious experience*, James wrote that "Religion is an essential organ of our life, performing a function which no other portion of our nature can so successfully fulfill." Beyond James, there is a long and established tradition of studies in the psychology of religion that lends support to the notion of "interest" in the psychological study of religion. Unfortunately, the psychology of religion literature conceptualizes religion primarily as a psychosocial variable or examines the functional utility of religion and rarely speaks to the issue of religion as a clinically relevant diversity variable that may transcend a unidimensional psychological or functional analysis.

Clearly, religion and spirituality are important to most people served by health care providers. Gallup polls in 1990 indicated that 95% of Americans believe in God and 85% believe the Bible to be the word of God. Polls also suggest that approximately 75% of Americans view their religious faith to be the most important influence in their life and large numbers (approximately 42%) would embrace the label of being "born again" (as cited in Larson, Lu, & Swyers, 1996, p. 1). There is also evidence that there is no difference between the religious beliefs and practices of mental health patients and the general population (Larson et al., 1996).

These religious believers often see their faith as relevant to their health and lifestyle concerns. Studies (e.g., Matthews, 1997) have found that 77% of patients in hospitals wanted their physician to consider their spiritual needs and 64% wanted their physician to pray for them if they requested it. Larson et al. (1996) review studies suggesting that most patients view spiritual health as relevant and important to their general health. Further, studies cited by Larson et al. suggest that religious coping is a major asset to elderly patients with psychiatric and mental disorders, and that there is a significant relationship between church attendance and lower rates of mental illness, as well as a beneficial relationship between religious commitment and lower suicide rates.

Research documents the positive contribution of religion to mental health and quality of life. A study of over 1000 university students found that religious students had better overall health and fewer injuries as well as less frequent use of tobacco, drugs, and alcohol, leading the researchers to conclude that religion had a positive effect on healthy lifestyle and behavioral choices (Matthews, 1997, p. 13). Worthington, Kurusu, McCullough, and Sandage (1996) concluded, after an exhaustive review of the empirical literature, that religious clients cannot reliably be labeled as having poor mental health. Many draw on their religion to cope with stress and the challenges of everyday living, especially when crisis strikes and options are limited (Hood, Spilka, Hunsberger, & Gorsuch, 1996). Hood et al. (1996, p. 378) summarize the work of Pargament and others saying, "People do not face stressful situations without resources. They rely on a system of beliefs, practices, and relationships which affects how they deal with difficult situations. In the coping process, this orienting system is translated into concrete situation-specific appraisals, activities, and goals. Religion is part of this general orienting system. A person with a strong religious faith who suffers a disabling injury must find a way to move from the generalities of belief to the specifics of dealing with that injury." In particular, prayer and social support may be viewed as positive coping strategies (Kauffmann, 1991).

Worthington et al.'s (1996, p. 457) analysis of empirical findings in the field from the last 10 years suggests that there are seven positive effects religion may have on mental health: (i) religion may produce a sense of meaning; (ii) religion may stimulate hope; (iii) religion may give religious people a sense of control by a beneficent God, which compensates for reduced personal control; (iv) religion prescribes a healthier lifestyle that yields positive health and mental health outcomes; (v) religion may set positive social norms that elicit approval, nurturance, and acceptance from others; (vi) religion may provide a social support network; (vii) religion may give a person a sense of the supernatural that is certainly a psychological boost but may also be a spiritual boost that cannot be measured phenomenologically.

Further, Hood et al. (1996) suggest that religion has the potential to meet the needs for meaning, control, and self-esteem. No doubt there are some positive and proactive ways this can take place, while other efforts might best be understood as avoidant or self-defeating (Malony, 1991). But to view prayer and social support as only means to control emotions seems potentially reductionistic and even patronizing. Perhaps naturalistic assumptions limit full appreciation of more adaptive "problem-focused" or "emotion-focused" possibilities? Even speculations of sociobiologists would suggest that religion has the potential to be a species-wide coping mechanism that has aided humans to cope successfully with life, and has enhanced their chances for physical survival (Wright, 1994).

Hood et al. (1996) have also concluded that the research evidence would "appear to be quite strong that religion, through offering a sense of meaning, control and self-esteem, does support an optimistic outlook. This in turn helps people deal constructively with life, and seems to have long-range beneficial effects." Especially pronounced are the potential for coping with death and the stresses often associated with the natural aging process. This is not to say that religion, in and of itself, "guarantees" stress inoculation; however, religiously based coping strategies appear to be quite effective for large numbers of persons in our society. Beliefs, rituals, prayer, and social support are important resources in the coping and adjustment of many people; religion may actually change a person since new interpretations are offered that might make problems less distressing and threatening.

As Hood et al. (1996) suggest, for those individuals whose religious orientation is intrinsic-committed rather than extrinsic-consensual:

> Religion probably helps because it provides individuals with personally useful meanings for upsetting circumstances. Concurrently, it offers, through a variety of avenues, opportunities for an enhanced sense of power and control over what is taking place. The result of both these tendencies and of faith itself is buttressing of self-esteem. Things no longer seem as bad as they once were, and since the individuals now believe they are doing the best that is possible, they can feel good about themselves. For the overwhelming majority of North Americans, the message of the 46th Psalm thus holds: "God is our refuge and strength, a very present help in time of trouble. (p. 401)

Still, there can be no doubt that in certain expressions of psychopathology, there is overt religious content and symbolism. Whether the connection is causal or consequential is far less clear (Paloutzian, 1996). Considering the fact that the concept of mental health itself is hard to pin down precisely, it is exceedingly difficult to draw sweeping conclusions in this vast and rapidly growing literature. Hood et al. (1996) note that the research has not been organized along productive theoretical lines. Further, they assert that antireligious biases were especially evident in earlier studies, and that serious methodological flaws limit the generalizability of those tentative conclusions. They remark:

> Personal religious expression may still reflect underlying mental disturbance, and for some, institutional faith remains a danger to their mental health. In most instances, however, faith buttresses people's sense of control and self-esteem, offers meanings that oppose anxiety, provides hope, sanctions social facilitating behavior, enhances personal well-being, and promotes social integration. All of these possibilities work to the benefit of distressed persons; ideally, they will be increasingly employed by mental health professions, to the advantage of those who seek their help. (p. 436)

Friedman and Benson (1997) suggest, "Many spiritual and religious individuals believe that the positive relationship that may exist between spirituality, religion, and health involves more than psychology and behavior" (pp. 1–12). Unfortunatley, as a study by Bergin and Jensen (1990) points out, of all the providers of psychotherapy, clinical psychologists are the least religious of the group (as measured by formal institutional involvement and investment) and they may also therefore be the least informed about religious behavior, particularly as it is represented in its institutional forms. They also appear to be significantly less likely than the general population to view religion as having an important role in their lives. It could therefore be argued that there is not only a lack of religious diversity in the profession but there may also be a lack of personal understanding and investment in the important religious concerns of our clients.

The American Psychiatric Association (cited in Larson et al., 1996, pp. 5–6) issued "Guidelines Regarding Possible Conflict Between Psychiatrists' Religious Commitments and Psychiatric Practice" in which they stated explicitly that psychiatrists should not only "maintain respect for their patient's beliefs" but also "obtain information on the religious or ideological orientation and beliefs of their patients so that they may properly attend to them in the course of treatment." However, as Larson et al. point out in their psychiatric residency curriculum, "While well intended and vital as an important first step, these guidelines may prove difficult for mental health professionals to follow due to their lack of familiarity with religious issues in the clinical environment."

These important guidelines are germane to the practice of clinical psychology as well. The American Psychological Association's revision (1992) of its "Ethical Principles of Psychologists and Code of Conduct" includes religion in the list of other matters of diversity as an area that may require special competence (Standard 1.08). It is suggested that clinicians need to not only respect but also increase competency by being sensitive to this multicultural diversity issue through awareness, knowledge, and skills related to addressing religion as a diversity variable in treatment (cf. Brems, 1993, p. 74). A lack of understanding and appreciation for the role that religion plays in the lives of clients may reduce the clinician's effectiveness in assessing and aiding clients to change, and may significantly influence the ability to build rapport and trust. At a minimum, clinicians need to avail themselves of opportunities to learn more about religious traditions different from their own.

It is also important to acknowledge that religion has provided some unique challenges as clinicians have embraced diversity in all its important expressions. A commitment to diversity is associated in the minds of most with the presumed notion that diversity should be celebrated in a pluralistic spirit. By implication, if I recognize and respect your religion as on par with mine, you should reciprocate, a notion not necessarily endorsed by all religions (Kung, 1985). Some of the world's religions do embrace diversity which in turn may even lead to syncretism or universalism (respectively, the combination or reconciliation of two belief systems). However, some of the world's major religious systems are "intolerant" and "authoritarian," and are compelled to embrace their own notions *a priori* and reject, or at least devalue, those of other religions (exclusivism). Indeed, the study of world religions would suggest that it is easier to internalize exclusive claims to truth, a reality which can complicate any search for common ground. Therefore, religion, by its nature, at times precipitates a philosophical conflict between those who embrace exclusive religious systems and those who anticipate reciprocity in the celebration of diversity.

10.10.2 THE DIVERSITY OF THE WORLD'S RELIGIONS

A chapter on the proper appreciation of religion as a powerful diversity variable ought to contain a terse summary of the major religions and their major distinctives, but such a summary would fill an entire chapter itself and do an injustice to the exquisitely complex realities of the religious faiths. Instead an attempt will be made to mention some of the most important dimensions on which religions vary.

Several caveats are in order. First, it should be noted that there is the need for humility in attempting to understand different religions; few people are experts in the world religions and all their variants (for orienting surveys, see Nielsen; 1993; Noss & Noss, 1993; Smart, 1989), and even less can people truly be appreciative supporters of all religions equally. There should be a readiness to acknowledge the limits of knowledge, and of the limited attitudinal flexibility which can be mustered in confronting beliefs that are different. Of particular danger to psychologists is the temptation to confuse their personal synthesis of religions, often via some sort of psychological functional analysis, with a genuine appreciation of all religions. Such a synthesis is necessarily a variant on religious belief itself and hence in tension with other religious beliefs; for example, an analysis of all religions as "particularistic cognitive renderings of the universal human pursuit of transcendent purpose, the ethical good, and of community" is a competing definition of, rather than an apt summary of, any particular religion.

Second, often there is greater diversity within religious categorizations than across them. For example, conservative Catholics and conservative Protestants have, on many dimensions, more in common than liberal and conservative Protestants. Hence, some very diverse religious groups are able to build remarkable consensus on certain foundational issues.

There have been many attempts to do what amounts to a conceptual factor analysis of religion, with varying outcomes (there have been empirical attempts as well; see Gorsuch, 1984). This chapter draws on the work of Glock (1962), Smart (1989), and others and discusses the multidimensionality of the religions in terms of their cognitive dimension (religious beliefs), ritualistic and symbolic dimension (religious practice), moral dimension (religious action), institutional dimension (religious organization), community and lifestyle dimension (religious community), and experiential dimension (religious feelings).

10.10.2.1 Cognitive Dimension

Religions vary cognitively in a number of ways. Myths play a central role in most religions, where myth is understood not in the general use of the term as a fantastic fictional tale, but rather as a set of religious stories that "quiver with special or sacred meaning" (Smart, 1983, p. 7). The importance of these are made clear in the care and honor given to the sacred texts that record them: the Christian Bible, the Hebrew Torah, the Hindu Bhagavad-Gita, Islam's Koran. The abiding power (i.e., the value of the narrative whether oral or written) of such sacred stories vibrates in the communities which have been transformed and sustained by such stories as the Jewish Exodus from Egypt or the visions of Lao-tzu of the early Taoist movement. For some believers, the historicity of the founding myths is vital, while others regard them as symbols pointing to meanings not tied to specific events in history. Christians, for example, have traditionally insisted on the historical reality of the death and resurrection of Jesus Christ (literalism); some continue that tradition while others regard that story as a nonhistorical emblem of the ability to overcome evil and adversity through the transforming power of God's love (symbolism). Recognition of the literalism vs. symbolism hermeneutic typically reaches beyond just one dogma or belief of the group but often pervades into other areas of interpretation within the group's religious belief system.

Religions vary according to the content of their founding myths, and also according to the place of doctrine in the religious community, its sophistication, and degree of elaboration. Smart (1983, p. 8) defines religious doctrine as "an attempt to give system, clarity and intellectual power to what is revealed through the mythological and symbolic language of religious faith and ritual." In essence, doctrine is an attempt to systematize divine revelation and render it applicable to everyday life. Some religious traditions have given rise to extensive systematized literatures (e.g., Christianity, Judaism, Islam, and Hinduism), while others have not (e.g., Animism and Shintoism).

Myth and doctrine together can contribute to the formation of the world views of religious adherents. Some religions have limited general application; some animistic faiths prescribe rituals by which to appease or petition their gods, but have few broader implications. But a religion can give broad definition to the world which its faithful inhabit. In essence, a religious faith can constitute the lenses (i.e., cognitive-perceptual "style," world view, or control beliefs) through which believers see the world, and those lenses are clearly different from those through which the unfaithful peer. The central focus around which a religious world organizes is the sacred or divine. This understanding of the divine is so striking that it literally shapes how an individual, indeed, how a community, understands the greater order of existence. For a Christian this picture orients around a creative, redemptive, and present God. To Shinto believers, the kami, a spirit or divinity, completes their understanding of holiness in this world. The Muslim believer finds certainty in existence in Allah's Five Pillars of Faith.

10.10.2.2 Ritualistic and Symbolic Dimension

Most obvious to an outside observer are the differing roles played by ritual in the world religions. Common forms of religious ritual are worship, singing, fasting, and prayer. In general these are "some form of outer behavior coordinated to an inner intention to make contact with, or take part in, the invisible world" (Smart, 1968, p. 6). Rituals can be daily practices such as the yoga of Hindus, the prayers of the Shinto or the purity rituals of Orthodox Judaism, weekly participation in services such as Catholic mass or Jewish temple, or annual celebrations such as Islam's Ramadan or the Hindu Divali. Each is a unique attempt to connect with, through discipline and remembrance, the divine which provides an orientation to self, others, and moral good.

10.10.2.3 Moral Dimension

Religions vary in the degree of elaboration of their accompanying ethical systems, but such systems are connected vitally to religious faith and the consequences of belief. At its most basic level, ethics is the way in which religious systems answer the challenge of evil in the world and deal with the profane (Paden, 1988, p. 144). Inherent in religious ethics is a call to live in a manner which reflects one faith in an unbelieving world. Thus for a Muslim, love for Allah will be reflected in distributing wealth among those in need, while for a Sikh it involves, but is not exhausted by, wearing uncut hair, a dagger, breeches, a comb, and iron bangle (Smart, 1989, p. 98). Religious ethics systems vary according to their overt applicability to society; Islam and ancient Judaism have ethical systems seemingly designed for implementation on a societal basis, while New Testament Christianity articulated an ethical code for members of a disenfranchised and powerless subculture. Religious ethical systems typically have individual, interpersonal, and communal implications.

10.10.2.4 Institutional Dimension

The religions differ in terms of their formalization as enduring human institutions. At one end of the continuum, imagine an autonomous American who distills a set of idiosyncratic religious beliefs which can be embraced, and who then quietly, privately, and with dignity lives consistently with those beliefs without the formation of an organization at all. At the other extreme contemplate the Roman Catholic Church with its high degree of institutionalization. While some degree of institutionalization is probably inevitable with growing size of the adherent body, religions differ in terms of how readily they engender institutionalization.

10.10.2.5 Community and Lifestyle Dimension

World understandings formed and framed by religious belief serve social functions. They draw boundaries which allow believers to understand themselves (the insider) in contrast to others (the outsiders); thus, a Jew is able to clearly define themselves as distinct from a Muslim or a Buddhist, both in terms of differences and commonalties. A communal consensus on "who we are," common understandings of proper and improper behavior and values, the power of shared rituals, language and symbols, common engagement with religious institutions, and even an emphasis on the importance of community itself all contribute to a sense of belonging to a religious community and a cohesive sense of lifestyle. Some religious believers have a diffuse sense of engagement with their religious community, while others are deeply engaged with a highly visible and formalized community. Williams notes that it has been common in the sociology of religion to distinguish between church and sect according to the degree of rejection of the dominant social environment, with members of sects disengaged from majority culture. "Compared with members of churches, members of sects are poorer, less educated, contribute more money to their religious organizations, attend more services, hold stronger and more distinctive religious beliefs, belong to smaller congregations, and have more of their friends as members of their denomination" (Williams, 1993, p. 127). This is a helpful distinction as long as the term sect is understood in a nonpejorative sense. Such a distinction may also be an important indicator of potential individual differences in ego-strength or assertiveness between groups as well as relevant to understanding counterculture tendencies and conformity pressures for individuals within the sect.

10.10.2.6 Experiential Dimension

Religious experience is often regarded as the *sine qua non* of religious life and its goal. Historically, such experience has often occurred at the founding moments of a religious tradition: the Koran tells of Mohammed's overwhelming, painful experience of receiving revelation from Allah; Buddhists" honor the light that filled Buddha's mind under the Bodhi tree, allowing him to see the antidote for the suffering of this world; and Christians recall the blinding, life altering vision the apostle Paul received on the road to Damascus. Believers across the spectrum regularly celebrate and search after the same. Thus, many Christians refer to their entrance in the faith as being "born again," Taoists search for inner illumination that will lead to a "mystic union," and Hindu's practice yoga to catch a glimpse of Nirvana. Such desires recognize the unique and holy place of the divine in the world of a believer and may in fact be one dimension that drives clients in psychotherapy.

Psychology as a discipline has often attempted to understand religious experience, but in doing so has often imperialistically presumed that only certain types of experiences are properly religious. Lash (1988), for example, argued against the account of religious experience of William James (articulated in his classic *The varieties of religious experience*) on the basis that it is an exclusivist account of religious experience, one which looked for a particular and peculiar type of experience as qualifying as religious experience and which ruled out as "true" religious experience on *a priori* grounds any experience which was tightly connected to a particular religious tradition. Such an *a priori* definition misses the reality that there is no such thing as generic and pure religious experience, and that the forms of religious experience are intimately connected with and vary according to the faith systems in which they occur (Lash, 1988). A variety of religious experiences within Christianity—of shame and guilt for sin, of repentance, of gratitude for God's mercy—have no direct parallel in other faiths such as Buddhism, a reality which may produce some unique challenges for engagement of the two religious systems.

In attempting to understand the religion of a client and its impact upon their presenting concerns, understanding these dimensions of religion—cognitive, ritual and symbol, moral, institutional, community and lifestyle, and experiential—can serve as a guide for exploration of a client's particular religious faith. Awareness of these factors can assist psychologists to catch a general glimpse of how faith affects and is interwoven into the lives of clients, and the unique differences between the many faiths which will be encountered.

10.10.3 RELIGION AND/OR VS. SPIRITUALITY

Even a cursory reading of standard texts in the psychology of religion (Hood et al., 1996; Kauffmann, 1991; Malony, 1991; Meadow & Kahoe, 1984; Paloutzian, 1996; Wulff, 1991) would suggest that there is no consensus in the field about the definition of either religion or "spirituality." The use of the term "spirituality" is almost a "hot" topic in clinical psychology although the term is being historically redefined in the psychology of religion literature. As Worthington et al. (1996) have noted, the fascination has more to do with an interest in mysticism and very private spiritualities rather than with the more institutionalized, corporate, and communal expressions of institutional worship, fellowship, and service. This focus on spirituality, in deference to the more classical understandings of the psychology of religion, trivializes more well-defined constructs like intrinsic-committed or extrinsic-consensual religiosity or the quest orientation as well as the major religious orientations derived from decades of research. Many clinicians who focus strictly on the notion of spirituality lack significant familiarity with institutionalized religion. This has a tendency to make it difficult for the clinicians to fully appreciate the complex and subtle ways that persons of corporate and institutionalized faith interact within their communities.

Zinnbauer, Pargament, Cowell, and Scott (1996), in a paper entitled "Religion and Spirituality: Unfuzzying the Fuzzy," recognized the inherent definitional difficulty in attempting to study "spirituality" in contrast to "religion." They conducted a study to measure how individuals define religiousness and spirituality. They were interested in how the individual's definition might be associated with different demographic, religio/spiritual, and psychosocial variables. They concluded, first, that religiousness and spirituality are probably different concepts. They found that religiousness was associated with higher levels of such things as "authoritarianism, religious orthodoxy, intrinsic religiousness, parental religious attendance, self-righteousness, and frequency of prayer," while spirituality was more closely associated with "mystical experiences, new age beliefs and practices, higher SES, and frequency of prayer" (p. 9). Whereas spirituality seemed to be more closely aligned with both personal and experiential dimensions, religion seemed to connect specifically with organizational or institutional beliefs as well.

On the other hand, they also concluded that individuals tend to integrate both spirituality and religion into their lives. In particular, they found that for the majority of individuals, spirituality and religion were irrevocably tied together. Their third conclusion was that "most believers approach the sacred through the personal, subjective, and experiential path of spirituality, but they differ in whether they also include organizational or institutional beliefs and practices" (p. 10). The researchers described their study as having particular importance for mental health workers, who as a group tend not to integrate their spirituality into religiousness. Thus, mental health workers may have a potential bias toward spirituality but against religiousness when for the general population they are typically linked. In light of the fact that their study found most people to identify themselves as both spiritual and religious, mental health workers prone to defining themselves as spiritual but not religious may fail to be sensitive to this integration. They may fail to appreciate the religious side of the majority of their clients.

Finally, it should be noted that formal and informal attempts have been made throughout history to engage in acts of kindness and healing under the auspices of spiritual direction. In contrast, disciplines like clinical psychology have a relatively recent history of such work. Unfortunately, only a minority of the mental health providers are even remotely aware of the rich and centuries-old traditions of pastoral care and spiritual formation (Benner, 1988; Browning, 1987; Coles, 1990; Groeschel, 1992; Jones & Butman, 1991; Malony, 1991; Miller & Jackson, 1995; Shafranske, 1996; Worthington et al., 1996). In many ways, psychotherapy is an heir to a rich tradition of altruistic service and compassion performed by spiritual directors.

10.10.4 PHILOSOPHICAL BASIS FOR APPRECIATING RELIGIOUS DIVERSITY IN CLINICAL CARE

It could be argued that religion and mental health care have much in common metaphysically. This is particularly true in the broad philosophical areas of ultimate meaning and morality. In fact, there are those in the field of clinical psychology and mental health care who would argue that the constructs and application of psychological theory are "religious" in nature and form a pragmatic basis for the replacement of institutional and/or personal religion in the lives of "believers" (Gross, 1978; Szasz, 1977; Zilbergeld, 1983). Perhaps no one has made the case more clearly than London (1986) in regard to the moral and religious nature of psychology, particularly applied psychology, and the enterprise of psychotherapy. In many ways it would appear that religion and psychotherapy are both activities that involve the search for a coherent world view and attempt to link beliefs with behaviors.

10.10.4.1 The Philosophical Conflict Between Clinical Care and Religious Belief

There is a potential for philosophical conflict between clinical psychology, as a presuppositionally religious enterprise attempting to answer broad questions of ultimate reality and morality, and the control beliefs of other religious systems. Thinking about clinical work as controlled by a belief system that influences how humans view themselves and their world makes it particularly important to consider how the clinicians" view of religion impacts the practice of clinical psychology. The clinician's control belief system clearly impacts the lives of religious clients.

For example, for the client who presents with marital difficulties and comes with a religious background that contains strict teachings about gender roles within the family or community, the control beliefs of the client based on the teachings of their religion may come into conflict with the control beliefs of the clinician regarding gender roles. For the clinician, this difference may be based on the theoretical orientation which forms their frame of reference or world view. Hypothetically, the hierarchical view of gender roles embraced by the clinician may come into direct conflict with the client's own chosen response to the egalitarian control beliefs of their religion. In fact, for the clinician, the client's religious beliefs about gender roles may in fact suggest presence of psychopathology or at least unhealthy thinking. The client is left with the dilemma of either embracing the control beliefs of the clinician (and getting "well" or becoming "healthy" in the process) or maintaining their own beliefs and being "sick" or "unhealthy." Further, it is important to recognize the religious context from which the client comes and the role of their control beliefs in maintaining important psychosocial resources in their life. These resources are often a direct result of the corporate and/or communal dimensions of their religion. To fail to do so may force the client into a painful choice between accepting the control beliefs of the clinician and losing important psychosocial resources or rejecting the control beliefs of the clinician and being abandoned.

Another example might involve questions of ultimate reality. The religious client who comes to the clinician family a number of stresses as well as feelings of depression in the aftermath of the death of a spouse may find religious beliefs about an afterlife minimized or even pathologized. Confrontation might be faced over being in "denial," or a challenge made to express suppressed anger toward religious deity, or to abandon a fantasy about reincarnation or reunion with the spouse. Such interventions by the clinician fail to appreciate the positive role that religion may be playing in the life of the client. In the worst cases, the clinician may also assume that in some way the religious control beliefs of the client are inferior to the psychologized control beliefs of the clinician. In these cases, the clinician presupposes that the client's religious beliefs are totally ineffective in helping the client manage his life.

10.10.4.2 A Philosophy of Clinical Practice that Appreciates Religious Belief

A starting point for the dialog about clinical practice and religious belief may be to think about clinical psychology as a postpositivistic science that is not value free. Further, in the practice of clinical care, it should also be noted that the scientific enterprise involves metaphysical presuppositions that reflect the world view and belief system of the scientist. Obviously, the potential exists for the clinician's control beliefs about ultimate reality and morality to be different from the presuppositional control beliefs of a client's religious system. It is further suggested (cf. Jones, 1994) that the relationship between religion and clinical work is in part an issue of addressing the religious diversity that may exist between the clinician and the client. An explicit acknowledgment of control beliefs, is recommended, on the part of both the client and clinician, as an important point of dialogical contact.

Following the "Ethical Principles of Psychologists and Code of Conduct" (American Psychological Association, 1992) with respect to "Principle A: Competence" and "Principle D: Respect for People's Rights and Dignity" would, on a very practical level, seem to involve the clinician acknowledging awareness (or lack thereof) of the person's particular religion, articulating a level of knowledge in regard to the control beliefs of the religion, and finally describing any skills or previous experience in working with individuals with similar religious beliefs. It would also seem logical that such a discussion would involve an articulation of the contrasting or similar control beliefs of the clinician as well as the clinician's theoretical orientation. Obviously, the role of religion in clinical work may be very different depending on the clinician's theoretical orientation. Further, the extent of the discussion regarding religious diversity may ebb and flow with the importance of the issue in the presenting problem of the client as well.

10.10.4.3 A Paradigm for Dialog on Religious Beliefs in Clinical Care

Dialogical contact between clinical psychology and religion may be enhanced by an articulation of the nature of the dialog, particularly if it is understood and applied in terms of multicultural notions of religious diversity. In an article on religion and multiculturalism, Dell'Olio (1996) attempted to address three philosophical constructs related to religious diversity: exclusivism, pluralism, and inclusivism. If the control beliefs of the clinician, whether personal or based on her theoretical orientation, are considered as overlapping metaphysically (e.g., issues of ultimate meaning, morality, etc.) with the religious control beliefs of the client, Dell'Olio's (1996) proposal for the management of religious diversity may contain merit for understanding the relationship between the clinician's perspective on these overlapping metaphysical issues and the client's religious control beliefs.

Dell-Olio (1996) rejects the construct of religious exclusivism on moral grounds. He believes it is immoral to reject totally the beliefs of another simply because they are different or ancillary to one's own. In addition, he rejects the religious pluralism of John Hick, arguing that in his underlying assumptions Hick's "perspective presumes to know more about what the religions themselves know about what they know, and thus refuses to recognize the legitimacy of the other's perspective regarding religious truth." Dell'Olio (1996) argues for "inclusivism" which allows for limited reciprocity on the basis of what he refers to as the multicultural mandate of the "morality of recognition." Limited reciprocity refers to a process whereby individuals seek common ground in regard to their individual control beliefs and gain an understanding of the distinctives of each others control beliefs and, even when their control beliefs are irreconcilable respecting the control beliefs of the other without abandoning one's own control beliefs. To Dell'Olio, (1996), limited reciprocity or "inclusivism" is the moral "high ground" or what he refers to as the "morality of recognition." In other words, the individual is free to acknowledge the sincerity of another's perspective even when they would sincerely disagree with some, much, or all of it.

Dell'Olio's (1996) conceptualization (morality of recognition) applied to the relationship between religion and clinical psychology would suggest that clinicians need to recognize with sincerity the client's perspective regarding religious truth even if the clinician disagrees with some, much, or all of it. This is particularly important when clinical work addresses the broader questions of ultimate reality and morality. However, the religious perspective of the client may not only be very important to the client's understanding of ultimate reality and morality but also the client's sense of self.

Dell'Olio's (1996) notion of inclusivism holds promise as a paradigm for the dialogical relationship between religious beliefs and the practice of clinical psychology. Inclusivism allows the person to remain committed to their religious beliefs while recognizing that religion does not have exclusive claim to all "truth." In this way, the religious client can remain open to the truth-claims of the clinician. On the other hand, the clinician can remain committed to the religious dimensions of their truth-claims while recognizing that they do not have exclusive claim to all "truth." Inclusivism allows the religious person to appreciate the truth-claims of the clinician and also be free to note where and when the truth-claims of the clinician are inadequate in describing or appreciating their religious experience. Inclusivism allows the clinician to appreciate the truth-claims of the client's religion as well as to note where and when the client's religion is inadequate in describing or appreciating the nature of the client's problems or their clinical work.

The morality of recognition principle in the care of clients means that the clinician is not obligated to embrace all of the religious control beliefs of the client in order to work with the client, nor is the client obligated to embrace all of the control beliefs of the clinician in order to benefit from therapy. Rather, it is the open acknowledgment on the part of both the client and clinician of control belief similarities and differences that may impact their work together, particularly as it relates to the presenting problem and the experience of the clinician.

For example, a religiously liberal Christian client being treated with cognitive therapy for depression may have little difficulty with the morality of recognition principle when being cared for by a religiously liberal Jewish or Muslim clinician or visa versa. In contrast, a conservative Christian being treated for a generalized anxiety disorder who is prescribed an Eastern meditation technique will likely have difficulty embracing the acceptableness of that approach in light of their religious teachings, regardless of the clinician's beliefs or intent. The clinician's awareness of such a conflict based on knowledge of the religious beliefs of the client may cause the clinician to consider alternative treatments in light of the morality of recognition principle. However, in some cases, the client or clinician may feel that the clinician's awareness, knowledge, and skill related to the client's religious diversity issues are inadequate for their work to be as productive as it might be if the client was referred to another clinician more aware, knowledgeable, or skillful in the religious diversity issues of the client. In all three situations, there is an expression of the morality of recognition principle.

Paradigmatically, inclusivism avoids the imperialism of exclusivism but in contrast to the pluralism, inclusivism "realizes that judgments must be made from a particular perspective" and that neither the clinician nor the client needs to "give up their particular (religious) perspective" when engaged in the process of clinical care. Clinicians are not required to give up their control beliefs in appreciating their own and the client's experience of religion and spirituality.

It is necessary for those who practice clinical psychology to seek an understanding of religion and spirituality in the context of an inclusive diversity while appreciating the contribution of both psychology and religion to the welfare of the human family. While applied postpositivistic psychology (as relativistic "science") and religion (as absolutist "divine or natural" law) may share very similar subject matter, they come to the human family with very different epistemological and methodological notions. The morality of recognition principle goes beyond just the awareness and knowledge of different control beliefs and the skills to address those differences. The morality of recognition is also an awareness and knowledge of different epistemologies and methods for arriving at those control beliefs. For the clinician this involves the development of skills to navigate these different epistemological and methodological approaches.

For example, for the client who endorses the "absolute authority" of a sacred text, anything the "science" of psychology may conclude from empirical investigation or theoretical development that would oppose or contradict the sacred text would be discounted because of the primary authority given to the text. Conversely, teachings of a sacred text are often discounted by "scientific" findings. The lack of awareness and knowledge of both epistemologies will be a deficit to the clinician who requires skill to navigate these issues in therapy. The clinician needs to recognize how the client understands the authority of religious truth and the role the client ascribes to "scientific" truth and work with the tensions that may arise in both the client and clinician as a result.

Religion and clinical psychology share similarities in subject matter and are human enterprises (Jones, 1994), and in their pragmatic forms both attempt to understand and interpret the behavior and experience of human beings. They also share constructs such as cognition, consciousness, emotion, motivation, and relation to name just a few (Tisdale, 1980). As clinical psychology and religion attempt to share the same constructs, their contrasting differences are pronounced by the fact that they may come from different epistemological and methodological bases. The result may often lead to different conclusions about the same matters. This affects the practice of clinical psychology because it affects not only how the clinician and client view the nature of the client's problem but also the resources that should be accessed in treatment of the problem and the validity and reliability of the treatment outcome.

For example, many clinicians have wondered about the immediate positive effects of antidepressant medicine in clients who have been suffering from depression. This is particularly true when psychiatric colleagues explain the pharmacology of the drug. Many clinicians may have also wondered about the client who informed them that their depressed mood had lifted as a result of prayer or some other prescribed spiritual discipline. In the first case, there is no pharmacological basis to adequately explain the effect. However, in the second there is often a clearly defined religious control belief or teaching for the religious intervention effect. Both situations could be potentially explained psychologically as the classic "placebo" effect, but it may be a lack of epistemic humility that makes the latter is so hard to accept. In fact, even though there may be no pharmacological explanation for the immediate effect of the antidepressant in some clients, most clinicians still refer severely depressed clients for medical treatment. Is it any less appropriate to refer a religious client for a religious intervention that is consistent with the client's religious belief system?

Clinical psychology and religion share similar concerns about outcomes. It could be argued that both disciplines are attempting to interpret and manipulate human experience in meaningful ways that will produce "ultimate good." Again, the disagreement often comes in the epistemology and methodology used (e.g., divine revelation vs. materialistic determinism; Stevenson, 1987). In fact, what ultimately may matter to both is what or who gets the credit for any "good" outcome.

Clinicians have also witnessed the lack of efficacy of medical treatments for a number of mental disorders. Should the practice of referring clients for medical treatment for that reason be abandoned totally? Why should it be any different for religious interventions? In fact, many religious systems have developed systems for explaining the limited efficacy, or the conditions of efficacy, for their religious interventions. It is a lack of epistemic humility that keeps clinicians from taking full advantage of the religious interventions found in the religious beliefs of many clients.

Even in light of these commonalties and significant metaphysical differences, we have an obligation to do "good" psychology, while recognizing the important role that religious presuppositions play in all of our lives. The multicultural mandate of the morality of recognition principle is important as is the fact that religion is an important multicultural variable in the lives of both clinicians and their clients.

10.10.5 CLINICAL ASSESSMENT AND DIAGNOSIS: APPRECIATING RELIGIOUS DIVERSITY IN THE PROCESS OF MEASUREMENT

There is a rich tradition in psychology and sociology of measuring and assessing religion and religiosity in its many complexities. For an introduction to this vast literature, the interested reader is urged to turn to Gorsuch (1984) and Williams (1993), or to one of the excellent survey texts in the psychology of religion, such as Hood et al. (1996), Paloutzian (1996), or Wulff (1995). Additionally, MacDonald, LeClair, Holland, Alter, and Friedman (1995) provide an analysis of instruments which attempt to measure spiritual experience and spirituality disconnected from traditional forms of institutionalized Western religion; for example, "spiritual orientation," mysticism and mystical experience, peak experiences, self-transcendence, paranormal beliefs and experiences, altered states of consciousness, holistic living, and so forth.

Religious beliefs and behaviors are complex, multidimensional variables. Attempts to measure religious variables have two principle historical roots: Allport's intrinsic and extrinsic orientations and Batson's quest approach (Batson, Schoenrade, & Ventis, 1993). In the broadest sense, an intrinsic person appears to live the faith whereas an extrinsic person uses the faith (see any of the above noted overviews for more in-depth discussions). The assumption is that an extrinsic orientation is a less mature or developed orientation. The quest orientation is one in which an individual adopts a critical but open-ended approach to existential questions. Other formulations tend to combine elements of the quest and intrinsic orientations. These are hardly "pure" categorizations.

Researchers and theoreticians alike assert that the overwhelming majority of people in the Anglo-American context show elements of all three tendencies in the ebb and flow of everyday life. It has been noted that all three orientations stress "process" more than "content," as do measures of moral, cognitive, and psychosocial development. Perhaps the most helpful formulation is to use an attributional perspective that is respectful of the phenomena studied, appreciates the potential contributions of the intrinsic, extrinsic, and quest orientations, and strives to find connections between motivational and cognitive patterns that are at the heart of religious experience and behavior.

For decades, attempts have been made to measure aspects of the dimensions of religious commitment. Hundreds of decent measures are available. Gorsuch (1984) has argued that there is a need to refine existing measures rather than create new ones. Hill, Butman, and Hood (1997) have published a collection of such measures; this should help address the fact that few clinicians seem to be aware of the existence of such measures or where to find them. Familiarity with a range of assessment instruments can enrich an understanding of the range of religious experience. Further, not all of the assessment effort has been targeted at individual differences; Pargament and his colleagues have done innovative work in assessing the differing organizational climates of religious congregations (Pargament, Silverman, Johnson, Echemendia, & Snyder, 1983; Pargament, Tyler, & Steele, 1979), finding that they differ on such dimensions as order and clarity, sense of community, openness to change, social concern, autonomy, stability, activity, expressiveness, problem solving, and participation.

The utility of existing measures is, however, limited. There is little convincing data on their "relevance" beyond the majority culture in the Anglo-American context. They tend to stress behaviors (e.g., church attendance) more than religious beliefs, or often contain a mixture of questions about belief content, attitudes, values, morality, actions, and experiences which makes interpretation of the resulting scores difficult. Gorsuch (1984) criticizes their heavy reliance on self-report and tendency to self-distorting bias or impression management. They are usually confined to an objective format and, thus, do not allow for a more complete understanding of the motivational and cognitive patterns that undergird so many of our decisions to act, qualities that perhaps can only be fully explored in a more open-ended interview format. Many instruments tend only to measure broad dimensions of religious orientation; it would be helpful if these measures could evaluate the more specific and concrete aspects of religiosity for descriptive/prescriptive purposes. Finally, psychological measurement of religion appears to often be contaminated by the theoretical commitments of the researcher; Gartner (1996, pp. 187–203) has noted that "hard measures" of health and well-being (such as death rate) almost without exception show the positive health benefits of religion, while "soft measures" of personality traits and other theoretically-grounded psychological variables often show negative outcomes to be associated with religion, suggesting that the soft measures are biased or contaminated in some way.

Drawing from this vast assessment literature, it is suggested that intake questionnaires in clinical practice be used to increase the clinician's awareness of religious variables and issues in the life of the client. Profitably they could include a few initial items regarding religion to set the stage for further examination of these issues if merited. Brief items querying how frequently the person attends religious services and functions, and how frequently the person engages in personal religious practices and activities such as prayer, meditation, or bible reading, can both be answered on a five- or seven-point scale from daily to never. The vast assessment literature indicates that the action or behavioral dimension of religion is important to assess, as there is a direct tie between what people do and their degree of commitment to religion; participation in personal or institutionalized religious activities may be regarded as a proxy for religious commitment generally. Clients can be asked to rate how important or significant religious faith is to them, from extremely important and at the center of life to not important at all. Enquiries can be made about their current religious affiliation, and what other important religious affiliations have had a major impact upon them in the past. The degree to which they believe their religious faith is relevant to their presenting concerns can be rated.

As the assessment of religion and religious faith in considered for the sake of better understanding clients and the difficulties they present, however, the limitations of questionnaire assessment methods are confronted. In the area of sexuality, a variety of measures exist which are well suited for research but which have little clinical utility and which can never duplicate the richness of data which can be generated by competent clinical assessment; so also in this area.

As in all areas of clinical interview assessment, the clinician will only get useful information if religion is queried sensitively and with respect for whatever answer may result. Clinicians should be wary of the functional equivalent of the "You aren't still masturbating, are you?" question in the area of religion. Introductory questions can include: "People in our community hold to a wide variety of religious faiths and beliefs, and sometimes a person's religion is quite important to the issues and concerns being addressed in the counseling relationship. Where are you on the matter of religion? Do you see your religious faith as being related to this problem in any way?"

In responding to client output, clinicians must be prepared for religion to serve a complex array of roles, none of which are mutually exclusive: motivation for change ("God wants me to overcome this problem"), cause ("My fundamentalist upbringing is what made me sexually unresponsive"), effect ("This problem has brought my faith to life as I have realized how much I need God" or "I gave up believing as I have suffered through this problem for years and found no relief in my church"), potential obstacle to change ("But the people in my church would ostracize me if I were to be more assertive with them"), coping strategy ("When I get stressed out, it helps to meditate"), potential resource for change ("A number of men in the synagogue are very willing to serve to keep me on target in this change plan"), apparent locus of pathology (religious delusions and religious content to depressogenic cognitions), and others.

It is best to look at the client's religious faith developmentally and as a dynamic reality rather than as a static one. The various religious or faith development theories are not regarded as normative in this area, though they can be helpful. For example, Fowler's (1981) theory suggests that faith development parallels cognitive and moral development as understood from the work of Piaget and Kohlberg as the individual moves from highly concrete and literalistic faith to a religion of universal abstraction. Such an analysis, while engaging, may overestimate the role of rationality in religious growth and may impose an inappropriate normative model that psychologizes faith and obscures differences across religions. A more open-ended querying of religious change over the life span is suggested. If a client indicates or comes to understand that their religious faith is relevant to the clinical concerns, it may be fruitful to explore the major epochs in the religious life, asking for information about those periods when religious faith was most central to the person, the major factors producing change in religious belief and experience, and important formative persons and events in the life of faith. The clinician's ability to show respect and empathy for the client's journey will pay dividends in rich information which can inform intervention. The clinician's ability to empower the client to believe that it is acceptable to talk about religion/religious issues and even to probe the clinician's religious perspectives is a very helpful way to build rapport and facilitate the assessment process.

Religion serves a variety of functions in the lives of participants, and psychological interpretation of those functions can enrich clinical understanding. Interpretations, however, may be distorted by prejudices and theoretical systems, and such a functional analysis can be alien to the fundamental views and instincts of the client. The shape of a functional analysis is driven by the basic theoretical assumptions which the clinician brings to the case, and so functional analysis from a classic psychoanalytic perspective will come up with a fundamentally different portrait of the dynamics of religious faith than that from a behavioral or a cognitive perspective. Psychological analyses also usually presume that there is no supernatural dimension to religious experience, a presumption which goes well beyond what science can demonstrate. Religiously grounded guilt may mediate avoidance of and restraint of unacceptable sexual impulses, or may represent the internalization of interpersonal patterns of approval and disapproval in the social environment, but it may also be the natural outcome of doing something wrong and a sign of a supernatural presence quickening one's need for repentance. Collaborative exploration of the variety of meanings of religious phenomena with a client can facilitate growth in awareness and understanding in the client and the clinician.

It is important to remember that much of the research on the psychology and sociology of religion has been done on white middle-class populations, and may not tap dimensions of relevance to minority populations, whether racial/ethnic (the experience of African-Americans) or religious (the experience of Jehovah's Witnesses) minorities. This should highlight how important it is for the clinician to be sensitive to all minority issues, particularly when the individual's life is diverse in many ways from the life of the clinician. As in expressing empathy with affective responses of clients, so also in the area of religion should clinicians check their understandings of the client's experiences regularly and with a spirit of willingness to be instructed and corrected by our clients.

Diagnostically, the *Diagnostic and statistical manual of mental disorders,* 4th ed. (1994) devotes only a single paragraph to "religious or spiritual problem." This would hardly seem to demand the development or use of diagnostic assessment instruments measuring religious constructs. Even within the multiaxial system, there is little or no place to address religious or spiritual factors in formulation of the client's "clinical picture." Considering the importance of the religious diversity for the majority of persons, this relative neglect is striking.

10.10.6 THE EMPIRICAL BASIS FOR APPRECIATING RELIGIOUS DIVERSITY IN CLINICAL CARE

Our brief and selective overview of empirical research on religion and clinical care will be organized around the findings of the excellent review by Worthington et al. (1996) of empirical research since the late 1980s.

10.10.6.1 Religious Persons and Mental Health

Worthington et al. (1996, p. 451) recall that religion has been viewed by many (such as Albert Ellis) as associated with irrationality and psychopathology. A large number of studies have produced relatively consistent findings that religion *per se* does not negatively impact mental health in general, and that the mental health of religious persons is often positively effected by their religiosity in a variety of ways as discussed earlier.

A number of studies discussed in Worthington et al. (1996, p. 451) have found superior mental health outcomes for intrinsically religious individuals; extrinsically oriented persons may even experience some negative impact from their religiosity. Therefore, assessing the religious orientation (intrinsic vs. extrinsic) of the client may provide some important data for the clinician as to the potential impact of religion on the mental health of the client in the process of clinical care. Bergin (1991, cited in Worthington et al., p. 457) found that intrinsically oriented religious persons, while they may tend to frustrate the clinician with their religious explanations for their behavior and experiences, are more likely to be open to therapeutic change than the extrinsically oriented person. Pargament (1987, cited in Worthington et al.) found that religiously conservative people may be more open to therapeutic change than people who typically associate themselves with more mainline religious groups. As in other matters of diversity, stereotypes (in this case the stereotype that highly religious individuals are defensive and rigid) can be very dangerous.

Intrinsically and extrinsically oriented people differ on other life dimensions as well. Worthington et al. (1996, pp. 451, 457) cited the findings of Hood et al. (1996) that there are significant differences in how intrinsically religious students, extrinsically oriented students, and proreligious students (both intrinsically and extrinsically oriented) describe identical sensory experiences. Intrinsically oriented students give religious descriptions of their experience spontaneously, while extrinsically oriented students do not use religious descriptions of their experience even when prompted to do so, and proreligious students tend to only mention religion in their descriptions if prompted. Clinically understanding the different ways in which the religious orientation of the client may predispose the client's use of religious explanations in therapy could be of significant help in the clinical care of the client.

10.10.6.2 Psychotherapy and Values

It is widely recognized that successful psychotherapy often entails a certain degree of convergence in values, with the values of the client moving to be more like those of the clinician. It appears that psychotherapy does not typically result in movement in basic religious values of clients, but the close articulation of so many values with religious faith makes this an area of concern for many religious persons seeking counseling and psychotherapy (Worthington et al., 1996). Schwartz and Huismans (1995) report in their article on value priorities and religiosity that there is a negative correlation between religiosity and values such as universalism (understanding, appreciation, tolerance, and protection for the welfare of all people and for nature), stimulation (excitement, novelty, and challenge in life), and self-direction (independent thought and action; choosing, creating, exploring). Their research also suggested that "valuing openness to change and free self-expression inclines people to become less religious." Conversely, they found that "valuing certainty, self-restraint and submission to superior external verities inclines people to become more religious in general."

Given that psychotherapists are disproportionately nonreligious compared to their clientele, and that psychotherapy is a value-changing relationship, such findings can be seen as justifying concerns about value influence for religious clients; it becomes obvious that value differences based on religiosity may significantly impact the work of clinicians who are not sensitive to the values reflected in the religious beliefs of their clients. It may be for this very reason that the data suggests that the world views of religious people may lead them to prefer religious counselors (Worthington et al., 1996). Highly religious persons appear to prefer therapists of very similar religious beliefs. They may also have clear expectations of religious counseling. Highly religious individuals may tend to view the world with religious schema and may view psychotherapy differently as a result.

Shafranske and Malony (1990) discovered in their study of the nature of clinical psychologists" religiousness that, while their sample of clinical psychologists appeared to value the role of religion in human experience in general terms, they were also less likely to be involved with religious institutions. "Less than one in five declared organized religion to be their primary source of spirituality." Approximately 25% reported negative feelings regarding past religious experiences. They also found support for the findings of previous studies that personal attitudes appear to play a more important role than clinical training when it comes to therapeutic interventions related to religion. In fact, they suggest that "it may be that religious beliefs function as a meta-theory that significantly influences psychotherapy in both implicit and explicit ways." As Jones (1994) points out, "... it seems that the concerns presented by clients often push the practitioner beyond the limits of what consensually validated scientific research has established. 'Given that research supplies only a small fraction of the information needed to completely understand the psychotherapeutic process, we are often compelled to rely on our tacit, background metaphysical notions'" (p. 191).

10.10.6.3 Religion in Psychotherapy

Religion can be best viewed as a multidimensional variable that includes facets such as what people believe, feel, do, know, and how they respond to their beliefs. Thinking in terms of the many important dimensions of religious experience helps to avoid the possibility of reductionistic thinking (e.g., their religion is "nothing but . . . ") and encourages more holistic and integrated thinking, that is, the type of thinking that should characterize the psychotherapy process.

The "bias" among clinical psychologists appears to be overwhelmingly functional. In other words, when they speak about the religiosity of a client, they are most often referring to the intersection of psychodynamics and faith, that is, how it operates in an individual's life (Groeschel, 1992). It is suspected that it is exceedingly rare for most clinical psychologists to be able to speak directly to religion as both a process and as a set of particular beliefs (Shafranske, 1996). Clearly, institutional identification with a particular religious tradition is not generally seen as a top priority of the majority of clinical psychologists (Worthington et al., 1996). If the majority of clients are religious and if the majority of providers do not identify with institutional religion or are unable to think about religiosity beyond the functional, there is a clear possibility that clinical psychologists and their clients may find it difficult to connect on issues which give them focus and meaning in their lives (see for further discussion Hood et al., 1996, Kauffmann, 1991; Paloutzian, 1996).

Worthington et al. (1996) summarize their findings by saying, "highly religious people may prefer religious counselors and explicitly religious counseling .... Despite preferring religious counselors, people do not want their counseling to focus mainly on religion" (p. 460). While it may be a truism, it is difficult to appreciate the impact of the experience of another human being upon themselves or upon clinicians if they have no reference point with which to compare or have no particular knowledge with which to interpret that experience. Clearly, if clinical psychologists are going to do therapy with religious persons, it would seem logical that they should have some reference point or knowledge of religious experience. It is contended that the religious knowledge and experience of the clinician plays an important role in clinical work with religious persons even if the client is not in therapy to address religious or spiritual issues.

10.10.6.4 Religion and Clinical Judgment, Technique and Behavior

Worthington et al. (1996, p. 467) refer to previous studies more than 10 years old which found that the religious orientation of the clinician did not seem to influence the diagnosis given to either religious or nonreligious clients. They also found that religious orientation did not appear to influence the ability of clinicians to discriminate between religious experiences that were either real or fabricated as well as the pathological or responsible use of religion. However, more recent research does not appear to be as clear. According to Worthington et al. (1996), studies done since the mid-1980s have had more mixed results. In fact, they cite a particularly methodologically sound study by Gartner, Harmatz, Hohmann, and Larson (1990) which found that clinician ratings were affected by patient ideology. It seems that in light of the "Ethical Principles of Psychologists and Code of Conduct" (APA, 1992), it would be important for clinicians to be aware of this potential bias.

Religious variables can affect the formation of a therapeutic relationship. Worthington et al. (1996) summarize the research by noting that "When counselors disclose their religious beliefs or values, their disclosure will likely affect both the client's behavior and expectations about the counseling process and outcome. Disclosing a counselor's religious beliefs and values can facilitate counseling if the counselor and client are quite similar in beliefs and values and if the counseling does not focus mainly on religion" (p. 460). In the light of managed care and the concerns of the public about accountability in the practice of psychotherapy, it may be well for us to be concerned about the values clients bring to therapy and their dissonance with the clinician's.

Research studies cited by Worthington et al. (1996) have investigated the role religion plays in other clinical behaviors. It appears that there is a positive correlation between clergy exposure to mental health issues and training and the propensity of clergy to do counseling and to refer. There would also appear to be a relationship between the clinician's theoretical orientation and the referral behaviors of clergy. It appears that mainline Protestant clergy are more likely to refer to humanistic or behavioral therapists and that clergy from more conservative fundamentalist or orthodox faiths are more reluctant to refer to therapists of a psychodynamic orientation. Interestingly, they also state that "Secular professionals rarely refer to clergy, even when difficult spiritual issues arise in counseling" (p. 468). It would seem important for clinicians to give clergy the same referral treatment we do other helping professionals. Perhaps it is an imperialistic attitude or a lack of relationships that prevents such from happening.

Holden et al. (cited in Worthington et al., 1996, p. 468) found that both counselors and clergy demonstrated equally developed skills in assessing the interpretation accuracy of Judeo-Christian principles in the religious ideation of a depressed client. Further, counselors were more reluctant than clergy to challenge those religious beliefs. The question might be asked; if clinicians are reluctant to challenge religious beliefs that they accurately perceive as distorted, why don't they refer the client to someone who may help the client by doing just that?

Some explicitly or implicitly religious techniques are used regularly in psychotherapy. Worthington et al. (1996) state, "The use of religious techniques by explicitly religious therapists stands in some contrast to the general field of clinical psychology" (p. 469). They cite an important study by Shafranske and Malony (1990) in which they did a national survey of clinical psychologists. They reported that 59% of the clinicians surveyed supported the use of religious language in psychotherapy but 55% opposed the use of scriptures. Further, only 19% of the clinician found it acceptable to pray with a client while 68% believed it inappropriate. However, as previously noted, the public seems to feel prayer is important to their physical health and the majority would like their physician to pray for them. Clearly, the issue of prayer in mental health care needs to be investigated further. Worthington et al. (1996) state, "Prayer appears to be the most common form of religious coping by most religious people, and even nonreligious people often turn to prayer in the throes of suffering" (p. 474).

Another religious behavior that has found its way frequently into clinical work is forgiveness. Worthington et al. (1996, p. 475) note that forgiveness has been almost as popular in the psychological literature as the religious journals. Unfortunately, they make a similar assessment of research on forgiveness as other religious interventions. While forgiveness is used with self-reported efficacy in case studies, little empirical attention has been given to its potential efficacy in clinical populations. Also, while forgiving may have efficacy as an intervention, few studies have investigated the potential effect of seeking forgiveness in clinical populations. This may have particular interest for those investigating personality disorders such as antisocial personality disorder.

A particularly problematic clinical intervention for clients of the Western religious traditions has been the Eastern Hindu and Buddhist oriented meditation techniques. Because of their close connection with specific practices of a religious system, many highly religious persons have objected to their use or have been surprised, given their religious connections, at their acceptance by the clinical community. A study by Carlson, Bacaseta, and Simanton (1988, cited in Worthington et al., 1996) found progressive relaxation and Christian meditation equal in their efficacy. Worthington et al. (1996) state, "Most of what can be accomplished therapeutically with meditation can be accomplished with relaxation training which is generally easier and avoids religious associations of meditation" (p. 475). This is an example of an exclusive religious practice that has mental health benefits and can be used inclusively when modified to meet the religious diversity concerns of others.

10.10.6.5 Religion and Clinical Research

Worthington et al. (1996) note that religion has become an increasingly acceptable topic for research in counseling and psychotherapy in part due to the "fourth force" in psychology, i.e. multiculturalism. According to the authors, religion and spirituality has moved into the mainstream of clinical care in many ways. This has been demonstrated by the increase in religiously oriented professional organizations in the field, the development of doctoral level training programs that have a religious orientation, the number of conferences and workshops presented in mainstream marketplaces such as the APA preconvention workshops, and the publishing of a "plethora of theoretical, polemic, and conceptual works" (p. 448). They suggest that there has been an improvement in the scientific study of counseling for the religious and of religious counseling since the mid-1980s. They conclude that "religious counseling by religious counselors of religious clients has recently assumed an increased prominence" (p. 449), and note that the changes occurring in the mental health care marketplace will have a continuing effect on how religious clients and religious counselors experience mental health care (p. 480).

10.10.7 THE RELIGIOUS COMMUNITY AS A RESOURCE FOR SUPPORT

It seems clear that there are many signals in contemporary North American society that persons are looking for the kind of social support that can only be found in a community (Kauffmann, 1991). This phenomenon appears to be particularly relevant to the Christian church. When the church is at its best, there is concern for the total welfare of its members and friends: "By prayer and petition for the Spirit's leading, by identifying the resources it possesses, and by framing programs consistent with the best empirical findings, congregations can provide a much needed service to both believers and nonbelievers" (Kauffmann, 1991, pp. 134–135).

Particularly in the era of decreased resources due to managed care, it might be useful to think about a religious group as a potential therapeutic community. Indeed, the data (Miller & Jackson, 1995) would support the observation that religious professionals, rather than mental health or health care providers, are often the first persons contacted and sought out when individuals or families are in a crisis. A failure to recognize this pattern and to consider networking with local religious groups might be one way to guarantee that even the best effort in the consulting room will not generalize or maintain beyond the immediate professional involvement. Religious professionals and members of local religious communities should be viewed as resources and as potential collaborators. Indeed, professional isolation (Guy, 1987) may be hazardous to clinicians" well-being as well as that of clients.

10.10.8 TRAINING CLINICAL PSYCHOLOGISTS IN RELIGIOUS DIVERSITY

It is hard to find truly balanced and informed treatments of creative and even curative possibilities of the resources of faith and religious communities in theoretical and research literature, although there are some encouraging trends in the field (Browning, 1987; Hood et al., 1996; Jones & Butman, 1991; Malony, 1995; McLemore, 1982; Meyer & Deitsch, 1996; Miller & Jackson, 1995; Shafranske, 1996; Worthington et al., 1996; Wulff, 1991). The lack of epistemic humility when studying the traditions of others is a truly disturbing characteristics of training programs and clinical practice.

Shafranske and Malony (1990) concluded in their study of the religiousness of clinical psychologists that only one-third of their subjects "expressed personal competence" to intervene in the religious aspects of their clients" lives. This was contrasted with the finding that the majority felt they had the knowledge and ability to deal with religious issues. Further, 85% reported the frequency of discussion related to religious issues in their training experiences to be rare or never. Along with other past reviewers, they concluded that clinical psychologists should "receive limited training respective of religious and spiritual issues" and that:

> in light of the limited training opportunities, the profession may have failed to heed the admonition of Perry London that while modern psychotherapists have grown up in the tradition of medicine, the nature of the ailments they deal with and the way they treat them, make them function much like clergy.

The profession's concern about diversity in all its form is to be applauded. It can be argued that religious diversity is an important multicultural factor that has not been treated equally with others in addressing the need for training. Petersen (1988, cited in Brems, 1993, pp. 72–86) proposes a threefold approach to increase multicultural sensitivity: awareness, knowledge, and skills. Petersen's model is developmental in that each of the areas builds on the other and thereby assumes a process of growth.

Awareness would be the first step in becoming sensitive to the issue of religious diversity as a multicultural issue. Brems (1993, p. 74) describes seven characteristics of an aware clinician. First, an aware clinician would have an awareness of their own cultural heritage. The clinician could participate in this by self-reflection on their own religious or spiritual journey and seek to share that story with a colleague. Second, Brems proposes that the clinician be conscious and embracing of all the diversity memberships in their life. This may involve the clinician making an intentional connection between ethnic heritage, gender identification, and religious background and how these issues in concert may impact her clinical work with others, particularly in light of the fact that they may not share all of the same diversity issues with the client. Third, the clinician should "value and respect" the diversity of others. This may involve the intentional exposure to other religious groups, orientations, and variety of religious experiences through attending institutional functions or reading popular literature or even dialoging with a colleague or friend who has a religious experience very different from one's own. Fourth, the clinician should become aware of their own values and potential bias and the potential effect they may have on therapy. This could come as a result of dialoging with a colleague or being supervised by a colleague with more knowledge and expertise about the particular religious affiliation of a client. This would hopefully enable the clinician to become more aware of the salient differences and their potential impact on therapy.

Fifth, Brems (1993) would suggest that the aware clinician should be careful not to "overemphasize" or "underemphasize" the differences from the client. This might be observed by the clinician or the client. The clinician might consider seeking common religious ground with the client by comparing and contrasting religious ideas. They might ask about the client's concern with regard to religious symbols in their office, for example, or might seek clarification of the religious language used by the client. Sixth, the clinician should seek to be comfortable with and diversity that exists between themself and their client. This might be accomplished by the clinician asking to be "educated" by the client with regard to the client's religious background while expressing genuine interest in understanding the impact religion has for the client. The clinician might read about the client's religion independently and dialog about that with the client. Finally, the clinician should seek to be sensitive to the need for referral should that be in the best interest of the client and the diversity issues present.

Brems (1993) also describes the further development of knowledge in the process of becoming sensitive to multicultural issues in therapy. The development of knowledge involves gaining accurate information about the client's religion. It also involves being sensitive to the fact that, even within very structured religious groups, individuals within the group may think, feel, and act differently than their cohorts as it relates to their religious expression. Accurate information should not be limited to just the writing of psychologists but should also involve the writings of both supporters and critics of the religion. First-hand experience can also be a powerful source of imagery as it relates to understanding the client's experience. Finally, the clinician should become aware of the past injustices and inadequacies of the mental health system to adequately address the needs of the religious client. The clinician may need to rethink their conclusions about psychopathology when religious variables predominate.

Brems (1993) describes the skills necessary to successfully deal with multicultural issues in therapy. This includes the matching of communication and therapeutic orientation to meet the client's specific diversity needs, being careful not to stereotype or categorize, and remaining flexible in meeting the client's needs. This may involve being an agent for social change by using language that is appropriate and not prejudicial. Most importantly for the religious client, a therapist may need to have the contacts and relationships within the client's religious community to promote or participate in institutional interventions or referrals. This process is no different to that of the establishment of referral relationships with other mental health care providers who intervene in ways unique to their discipline.

10.10.9 FUTURE DIRECTIONS

According to *The encyclopedia of American religions* (1993), there are 1730 "primary religious bodies" in America alone (cited in Paloutzian, 1996, p. 7). Collectively, these groups are described in the psychology of religion as churches, denominations, sects, or cults. As Paloutzian (1996) has noted, if to this the full scope of world religions is added including varieties of Buddhism, Hinduism, New Age religions, Spiritualist, Wisdom religions, and others, the numbers are staggering. Even a full-time student of domestic or world religions would have to devote decades of serious study in order to fully appreciate the complexities and subtleties of the ideological, ritualistic, experiential, intellectual, and consequential dimensions of all these religious commitments. Certainly, this would be an unrealistic task for even the most interested and committed clinician or clinician-in-training.

It is not proposed that clinicians become experts in religion or spirituality any more than it is expected that clinicians be experts in law (although some are experts in forensic psychology) or medicine (although some are very knowledgeable about psychopharmacology). Even if limiting oneself to Anglo-American religions (assuming one is from an Anglo-American religious and cultural heritage), it would be an unnecessary and daunting task. What is being argued in this chapter is a need for sensitivity, awareness, and acknowledgment of the religious diversity (or lack thereof) of clinicians and of the religious diversity of clients. Further, it has been the intention to make the case for understanding the role of religion in the experience of clients not only from a psychosocial perspective but from a transcendent one as well.

It is suggested that religion be treated with the same respect and concern for competency as other areas of diversity and that clinicians recognize their abilities as well as lack of ability to deal with religious issues in the assessment, diagnosis, and treatment of their clients. A model is proposed for such clinical activity that is consistent with other models of competency including forensic psychology, or even more appropriately, psychopharmacology.

What is required is an Assess–Treat–Refer model of clinical care as it relates to clinicians" religious diversity and that of their clients. The "Assess" aspect of this model involves identifying control beliefs, religious beliefs, and commitments, and the impact they may have on the care of clients. The clinician should not keep this totally to themself, but rather in keeping with ethical guidelines be explicit with the client about differences that may impact clinical care.

The clinician might attempt to articulate spirituality/religiosity through a self-assessment by reflecting on the dimensions of religion noted (cognitive, ritualistic and symbolic, moral, institutional, community and lifestyle, and experiential). Further, the clinician may need to increase sensitivity to the limits of knowledge and the limits of attitudinal flexibility. They may also need to reflect on the implicit assumption that nobody can support all religions equally and assess the level of empathy with different traditions. Finally, in the assessment of their own control beliefs about religion and spirituality the clinician should be careful not to make personal synthesis of religion a "reality" but rather recognize it as a variant of religious belief itself.

Additionally, the assessment aspect of this model would involve exploring the client's religious background and control beliefs in an attempt to not only understand the psychosocial aspects of their religious experience but also the potential resource that religion might be in their clinical care. The clinician should be careful not to only make a functional analysis of the client's religious beliefs and behaviors (as helpful as that can be), but rather consider the implications that religion has for the client's interpretation of ultimate reality.

While there are many instruments available for measuring the religious aspects of a client's experience, the assessment of religion/spirituality as part of the regular clinical interview may be the most helpful place to start. As previously noted, the clinical interview should explore the various dimensions of religious experience and behavior as well as serve as a helpful understanding of the role of religion in the life of the client. The assessment process should be sensitive to bias that may be inherent in soliciting such information. Clinicians should pay careful attention to and encourage the continuing explosion of research on clinical processes and outcomes which includes careful study of religion and spirituality and how they interact with clinical variables.

The "treat" aspect of the model recognizes that some clinicians may identify readily with a particular religious tradition in ways that make them uniquely qualified to care for particular clients. These clients may present with religious issues that are very significant, in not only formalizing their case, but also in treating them.

It is important to note that the standard of care has changed and continues to evolve in mental health care. The focus on managed care and utilization review has produced a system of care that is multidisciplinary and interdisciplinary. This model of care is held out to be not only in the best interest of the client, but it also recognizes that the clinician cannot provide all of the beneficial care that a client deserves or that may be available. While some clinicians may be relative experts in a particular religious context or identify with particular religious systems, even then the benefits of accessing clergy or other religious professionals may be more appropriate in meeting the client's religious and/or spiritual needs as part of a multidisciplinary approach to mental health care.

Certainly, the competence to treat involves not just multicultural awareness, knowledge, and skills but will ultimately be decided on by effectiveness in dealing with a particular client with a particular problem and in a particular context. With the increasing call for accountability and responsibility for clinical care, it would appear to be important to focus on outcomes as a particular measure in the care of the religiously diverse client. Outcome measures should certainly have clinical utility (changes in symptoms, behaviors, mood, relationships, and so on), but also need to measure consumer satisfaction. Broadly understood, this could involve the client, significant others in the client's life, and, for the religiously diverse client, the religious community. A potentially important measure of the effectiveness in treating the religiously diverse client may be the evaluation by the religious community of the impact of work on the client in the context of their faith.

Finally, the "Refer" aspect of the model would suggest the obvious. There are times when competencies are clearly limited in cases that involve religious issues. We should seek to network with religious professionals similar to networks we may have with other healers. Clinicians should be open and clear with clients that deference in caring for them is not a function of inability to morally recognize their religious diversity but rather it is a matter of limited competence and the specialized ability of others to whom they can be referred.

A case example may illustrate the model. An 18-year-old male was referred for psychological evaluation by his public school because of "aggressive and violent behavior" towards peers and staff. The young man was a new immigrant from Bosnia. His primary language was Bosnian, and so there was a language barrier that would require the assistance of a translator. An initial hypothesis was that this "language barrier" in other relationships and the resulting isolation and frustration may have played a role in this young man's "aggressive and violent behavior."

While the examiner was aware of a "religious war" in the former Yugoslavia, the "religious" aspect of the war was not well understood by the clinician. In taking the clinical history of this young man it was discovered that he had immigrated to the US through the auspices of a "Christian" organization. Prior to that, he had been held in a refugee camp which he described as very undesirable. While at the camp, he was identified as one who could immigrate because of his "circumstances," those circumstances being the murder of his entire family, in his presence, by "Christians." They were killed, he stated, because they were "Muslims."

He was a Muslim. He stated that he would die for Islam. He also stated that his chief end in life was to revenge the death of his family and that this was dictated by his Muslim religion. Having only a rudimentary understanding of Islam and noting that revenge was not one of the five pillars of faith, the clinician was compelled to seek the assistance of a Muslim cleric who could clarify the issues and counsel this young man about this issue in particular. It seemed better to the client to discuss his religious beliefs with a Muslim cleric than with a Christian clinician.

It became clear in conceptualizing the nature of the "aggressive and violent behavior" that this young man was very angry over the loss of his family, had struggled to understand and be understood in a culture with a language very different from his own, and that the client was conflicted over his hatred for "Christians" and their apparent goodwill toward himself. Obviously, the assessment of this young man's presenting problem hinged upon an understanding of his religious and sociocultural background. The treatment of his problem required the special expertise of a Muslim cleric as well as a recognition of the therapist's identification as a "Christian" Ultimately, his care involved the multidisciplinary involvement of a foreign language teacher, a Muslim cleric, and a clinical psychologist.

10.10.10 SUMMARY

Clinical psychologists are nonrepresentative of the general population in terms of their lack of commitment to traditional religious faiths. Religious faith, like other vital diversity variables such as race, gender, ethnicity, age, sexual orientation, and others, shapes and contextualizes the clinical concerns of persons who present for psychological assessment and treatment. Clinical psychologists have an ethical obligation to become more knowledgeable, aware, and skilled in managing the impact which religious variables, broadly conceived, can have on the process and outcome of psychological service delivery. They must also become more aware of their own biases and limitations in dealing with such material, more aware of the degree to which their own religious assumptions color their theories and practices in clinical psychology, more tolerant of the wide array of religious beliefs and practices which characterize the people they serve, more respectful of the resource which religious beliefs, practices, communities, and institutions are to many clients, and more cognizant of the extensive and growing research base on the role of religion in human life generally and in psychological practice in particular. Contrary to the prevailing mindset in psychological circles, for most of the population, to be spiritual is to be religious, and psychologists must avoid the tendency to "reduce" the religious faith of those they serve to either a bland, generic spirituality or to a set of sociopsychological processes.

10.10.11 REFERENCES

American Psychiatric Association (1994). *Diagnostic and statistical manual of mental disorders* (4th ed.). Washington: American Psychiatric Association.

American Psychiatric Association Task Force on Religion and Psychiatry (1975). *Psychiatrists viewpoints on religion and their services to religious institutions and the ministry.* Washington, DC: American Psychiatric Association.

American Psychological Association (1992). Ethical principles of psychologists and code of conduct. *American Psychologist, 47,* 1597–1611.

Batson, C. D., Schoenrade, P., & Ventis, W. L. (1993). *Religion and the individual: A social-psychological perspective,* New York: Oxford University Press.

Benner, D. G. (Ed.) (1988). *Psychology and religion.* Grand Rapids, MI: Zondervan.

Bergin, A. E. (1991). Values and religious issues in psychotherapy and mental health. *American Psychologist, 46,* 394–403.

Bergin, A. E., & Jensen, J. (1990). Religiosity of psychotherapists: A national survey. *Psychotherapy, 27,* 3–7.

Brems, C. (1993). *A comprehensive guide to child psychotherapy.* Boston: Allyn & Bacon.

Browning, D. S. (1987). *Religious thought and the modern psychologies: A critical conversation in the theology of culture.* Philadelphia: Fortress Press.

Coles, R. (1990). *Harvard diary: Reflections on the sacred and the secular.* New York: Crossroad.

Comas-Díaz, L., & Striker, G. (1993). Special issue: Diversity in clinical psychology. *The Clinical Psychologist, 46*(2), 88–89.

Dell'Olio, A. (1996). Multiculturalism and religious diversity: A Christian perspective. *Christian Scholars Review, 25,* 459–477.

Fowler, J. (1981). *Stages of faith.* San Francisco: Harper & Row.

Friedman, R., & Benson, H. (1997). Spirituality and medicine. *Mind/Body Medicine, 2*(1), 1.

Gartner, J. (1996). Religious commitment, mental health, and prosocial behavior: A review of the empirical literature. In E. P. Shafranske (Ed.), *Religion and the clinical practice of psychology* (pp. 187–214). Washington, DC: American Psychological Association.

Gartner, J., Harmatz, M., Hohmann, A., & Larson, D. (1990). The effect of client and counselor values on clinical judgment. *Counseling and Values, 35*, 58–62.

Glock, C. (1962). On the study of religious commitment: Review of recent research bearing on religious and character formation. *Religious Education, 57*(4), S98–S110.

Gorsuch, R. L. (1984). Measurement: The boon and bane of investigating religion. *American Psychologist, 39*(3), 228–236.

Groeschel, B. J. (1992). *Spiritual passages: The psychology of religious development*. New York: Crossroad.

Gross, M. L. (1978). *The psychological society*. New York: Random House.

Guy, J. D. (1987). *The personal life of the psychotherapist*. New York: Wiley.

Hill, P. C., Butman, R. E., & Hood, R. W., Jr. (Eds.) (1997). *Measures of religious behavior*. Birmingham, AL: Religious Education Press..

Hood, R. W., Spilka, B., Hunsberger, B., & Gorsuch, R. (1996). *The psychology of religion* (2nd ed.). New York: Guilford Press.

James, W. (1910/1963). Pragmatism. In P. R. Reynolds (Ed.) *William James: Pragmatism and other essays* (pp. 119–132). New York: Simon & Schuster.

Jones, S. L. (1994). A constructive relationship for religion with the science and profession of psychology: perhaps the boldest model yet. *American Psychologist, 49*(3), 184–199.

Jones, S. L., & Butman, R. E. (1991). *Modern psychotherapies: A comprehensive Christian appraisal*. Downers Grove, IL: InterVarsity Press.

Kauffmann, D. (1991). *My faith's ok—your faith's not: Reflections on the psychology of religion*. Goshen, IN: Goshen College.

Kung, H. (1985). *Christianity and world religions*. Maryknoll, NY: Orbis Books.

Larson, D., Lu, F., & Swyers, J. (1996, May). *Model curriculum for psychiatric residency training programs: religion and spirituality in clinical practice* (available from first author and used by permission. Published by The National Institute for Healthcare Research, Rockville, MD).

Lash, N. (1988). *Easter in ordinary: Reflections on human experience and the knowledge of God*. Notre Dame, IN: University of Notre Dame Press.

London, P. (1986). *The modes and morals of psychotherapy* (2nd ed.). Washington, DC: Hemisphere.

MacDonald, D. A., LeClair, L., Holland, C. J., Alter, A., & Friedman, H. L. (1995). A survey of measures on transpersonal constructs. *Journal of Transpersonal Psychology, 27*(2), 171–235.

Malony, H. N. (1991). *The psychology of religion: Personalities, problems, possibilities*. Grand Rapids, MI: Baker.

Malony, H. N. (1995). *The psychology of religion for ministry*. Pasadena, CA: Integration Press.

Matthews, D. A. (1997). Religion and spirituality in primary care. *Mind/Body Medicine, 2*(1), 9–19.

McLemore, C. W. (1982). *The scandal of psychotherapy*. Wheaton, IL: Tyndale.

Meadow, M. J., & Kahoe, R. D. (1984). *Psychology of religion: Religion in individual lives*. New York: Harper and Row.

Meyer, R. G., & Deitsch, S. E. (1996). *The clinician's handbook: Integrated assessment in adult and adolescent psychopathology* (4th ed.). Boston: Allyn and Bacon.

Miller, W. R., & Jackson, K. A. (1995). *Practical psychology for pastors* (2nd ed.). Englewood Cliffs, NJ: Prentice-Hall.

Nielsen, N. C. (1993). *Religions of the world* (3rd ed.). New York: St. Martins Press.

Noss, J. B., & Noss, D. S. (1993). *A history of the world's religions* (9th ed.). New York: Macmillan.

Paden, W. E. (1988). *Religious worlds: The comparative study of religion*. Boston: Beacon Press.

Paloutzian, R. G. (1996). *Invitation to the psychology of religion* (2nd ed.). Boston: Allyn and Bacon.

Pargament, K., Silverman, W., Johnson, S., Echemendia, R., & Snyder, S. (1983). The psychosocial climate of religious congregations. *American Journal of Community Psychology, 11*, 351–381.

Pargament, K., Tyler, F. B., & Steele, R. E. (1979). The church/synagogue and the psychosocial competence of the member: An initial inquiry into a neglected dimension. *American Journal of Community Psychology, 7*, 649–664.

Schwartz, S. H., & Huismans, S. (1995). Value priorities and religiosity in four western religions. *Social Psychology Quarterly, 58*(2), 88–107.

Shafranske, E. P. (Ed.) (1996). *Religion and the clinical practice of psychology*. Washington, DC: American Psychological Association.

Shafranske, E. P., & Malony, H. N. (1990). Clinical psychologists" religious and spiritual orientations and their practice of psychotherapy. *Psychotherapy, 27*(1), 72–78.

Smart, N. (1968). *The religious experience of mankind*. New York: Charles Scribner.

Smart, N. (1983). *Worldviews: Cross-cultural explorations of human beliefs*. New York: Charles Scribner.

Smart, N. (1989). *The world's religions*. Cambridge, UK: Cambridge University Press.

Stevenson, L. (1987). *Seven theories of human nature* (2nd ed.). New York: Oxford University Press.

Szasz, T. (1977). *The theology of medicine*. Syracuse, NY: Syracuse University Press.

Tisdale, J. R. (1980). *Growing edges in the psychology of religion*. Chicago: Nelson-Hall.

Williams, D. R. (1993). The measurement of religion in epidemiologic studies: Problems and prospects. In J. S. Levin (Ed.), *Religion in aging and health: Theoretical formulations and methodological frontiers* (pp. 125–148). Thousand Oaks, CA: Sage.

Worthington, E. L., Kurusu, T. A., McCullough, M. E., & Sandage, S. J. (1996). Empirical research on religion and psychotherapeutic processes and outcomes: A 10-year review and research prospectus. *Psychological Bulletin, 119*(3), 448–487.

Wright, R. (1994). *The moral animal: The new science of evolutionary psychology*. New York: Pantheon.

Wulff, D. M. (1991). *Psychology of religion: Classic and contemporary views*. New York: Wiley.

Zilbergeld, B. (1983). *The shrinking of America: Myths of psychological change*. Boston: Little, Brown, and Company.

Zinnbauer, B. J., Pargament, K. I., Cowell, B., & Scott, A. B. (1996). *Religion and spirituality: unfuzzying the fuzzy*. Paper pressented at the American Psychological Association Annual conference. Toronto, Canada. August, 1996.

10.11
Mental Health in Rural Society

MICHAEL MURRAY
Memorial University of Newfoundland, St. John's, NF, Canada
DAVID S. HARGROVE
University of Mississippi, MS, USA
and
MICHAEL BLANK
University of Virginia, Charlottesville, VA, USA

10.11.1 INTRODUCTION 256
10.11.2 STRUCTURE OF RURAL SOCIETY 256
10.11.2.1 Changing Demographics 256
10.11.2.2 Definitions of Rural 256
10.11.2.3 Diversity 257
10.11.2.4 Age and Education 257
10.11.2.5 Work 257
10.11.2.6 Income 258
10.11.2.7 Living Conditions 258
10.11.3 LIFE IN RURAL SOCIETY 258
10.11.3.1 Social Life 258
10.11.3.2 Women and Family Life 259
10.11.3.3 Working Life 259
10.11.3.4 Change in Rural Society 260
10.11.4 HEALTH ISSUES 261
10.11.4.1 Stress in Rural Society 261
10.11.4.2 Impact of Crisis 261
10.11.4.3 Social Cohesion 261
10.11.4.4 Mental Illness 262
10.11.5 MENTAL HEALTH SERVICES 263
10.11.5.1 Healthcare Utilization 263
10.11.5.2 Specialty Mental Health Services 263
10.11.5.3 Public Policy 264
10.11.5.4 Empirical and Theoretical Basis for Planning Services 264
10.11.5.5 Healthcare Reform 265
10.11.5.6 Primary Care 265
10.11.5.7 Telemedicine 266
10.11.6 PSYCHOLOGY AND RURAL MENTAL HEALTH 267
10.11.6.1 Historical Background 267
10.11.6.2 Roles of Psychologists in Rural Communities 267
10.11.6.3 Training Psychologists for Rural Practice 268

10.11.7 TYPES OF INTERVENTION 269
10.11.7.1 Fitting the Intervention to the Context 269
10.11.7.2 The Rural Psychologist as a Generalist 270
10.11.7.3 The Concept of Community and Psychological Intervention 270
10.11.7.4 Ethical Dilemmas in Rural Practice 271
10.11.8 FUTURE DIRECTIONS 272
10.11.9 SUMMARY 272
10.11.10 REFERENCES 273

10.11.1 INTRODUCTION

The twentieth century has seen a dramatic shift in the distribution of the population over most parts of the globe, including North America. Whereas in the early part of this century the majority of the world's population lived in small communities relatively isolated from population centers, the world has now become a predominantly urban society. Large metropolitan centers have not only become the location for an increasing proportion of the world's population but also of service provison and, indeed, of human research interest.

This change has led to an orientation towards understanding and providing for the needs of urban society and a lesser interest in the nature of rural society and of the various problems it faces. The purpose of this chapter is to focus attention specifically on rural society in North America. It begins by outlining the demographic structure of rural society, proceeds to describe some of the problems rural society is currently experiencing, describes some of the main mental health problems, and then considers the character of health service provision, and the role of psychologists in rural mental health care.

10.11.2 STRUCTURE OF RURAL SOCIETY

10.11.2.1 Changing Demographics

According to the most generous estimates, approximately 25% of North Americans currently live in rural areas. This proportion has declined steadily throughout the twentieth century. However, the absolute number of people living in rural settings has actually increased. Between 1930 and 1990 the rural population in the USA increased by 7.9 million (15%) to 53 million (22%), whereas in Canada it increased from 4.4 million (51%) in 1921 to 6.4 million (23%) in 1991 (45% increase) (Statistics Canada, 1993). This increase in population confirms what Cordes (1990) describes as the myth of a shrinking rural America.

Admittedly, these overall figures conceal a decline in the population of certain rural areas. This decline in population is due to a steady increase in outmigration from those rural regions that are experiencing economic difficulties. Part of the reason for the absolute increase in the rural population is the movement of urban residents to rural or semirural areas from which they commute to urban centres for employment. These numbers are also supplemented by those former urban residents who retire to rural areas.

10.11.2.2 Definitions of Rural

In attempting to describe the character of rural society one endemic problem is the actual definition of rural. There has been ongoing debate about the term. The three most common dimensions used in definitions are (see Bealer, Willis, & Kuvlesky, 1965):

(i) *Ecological.* This concerns the spatial distribution of the population. According to this definition a rural area is one where the population is small, widely distributed, and remote from more urban settings.

(ii) *Occupational.* This suggests that rural refers to a limited number of occupations, specifically those that are involved with agriculture and, to a lesser extent, with fishing, forestry, and mining.

(iii) *Sociocultural.* This refers to the complex of values and behaviors that typify a particular group of people. Stereotypically, rural people are considered to be socially conservative, provincial, and resistant to change.

Admittedly, most studies do not make use of all three dimensions (see Bosack & Perlman, 1982). In compiling statistics it is important to have a common definition. In the USA the favored definition is that developed by the Bureau of Census. It defines urban areas as central cities of 50 000 or more and adjacent territory of more than 2500 residents living outside the geopolitical boundary. From this definition, rural is then defined as the residual category.

Statistics Canada (1993) uses a similar definition describing an urban area as having attained a population concentration of at least

1000 and a population density of at least 400 per square kilometer at the previous census. All territory lying outside urban areas is considered rural. Recently a more sophisticated definition has been developed which classifies US Census returns according to both the population of the locality and the proximity to urban centers. This scheme produces a 17 category continuum from core counties with a population greater than one million to nonmetropolitan nonadjacent counties with no community greater than 2500. This classification scheme has recently been used to clarify the demographics of the USA (Miller, Farmer, & Clarke, 1994). Admittedly, even when using a classification as sophisticated as this, there remains the problem of the substantial variations that exist between and within regions.

10.11.2.3 Diversity

An overall characteristic of rural society in North America is the broad sociocultural diversity of its population. From Southern Blacks, Hispanics in the Southwest, through American indians and Appalachian whites, to Canadian natives and Innuit in the Arctic north, the diversity of cultures, languages, and traditions is extensive.

It is estimated that about 8.3% of the rural population in the USA is Black as opposed to 11.8% in urban areas. Similarly, less than 2.5% of the rural population is Hispanic compared with over 7.5% in urban areas (Cordes, 1989). However, these minorities are concentrated in certain regions. Snipp (1996) argues that racial segregation is as much a feature of rural as of urban America. Besides the enduring poverty of rural society, these minorities also experience discrimination and the threat of physical harm.

While the overall level of poverty is higher in rural than in urban areas, it peaks among the ethnic minorities. According to Lichter (1989), rural blacks "remain among the most economically disadvantaged groups in the United States" (p. 444). Although there was an improvement in the economic position of these minorities during the 1960s and 1970s the evidence suggests that there has been a deterioration since the 1980s (Jensen & Tienda, 1989).

10.11.2.4 Age and Education

The ongoing economic difficulties facing rural America have led to an outflow of young adults and a consequent aging of the rural population. According to 1990 US figures, whereas 11.3% of the population of core urban areas was 65 years and older, 16.2% of those resident in the most rural counties were of a similar age (Miller et al., 1994). In certain pockets, the median age can be much higher. The exodus of many young people in search of employment has led in certain areas to a graying of rural America. Johnson and Beale (1992) note that in many rural communities more than one in four of the population is over 65 years.

These elderly people are a mixture of those who have lived all or most of their lives in rural areas and urban seniors who have retired to a rural setting. The latter tend to be wealthier and to have fewer immediate family connections. There is also evidence that elderly rural residents will migrate to small towns to retire (Li & MacLean, 1989).

The general pattern of education is one with rural residents having poorer educational qualifications than urban residents. For example, whereas only 6.2% of the population of the fringe suburban counties in the USA had less than nine years of schooling, the figure for the most rural counties was 17.7% (Miller et al., 1994). In Canada, while 26% of the general working population has a university education, only 13% of farm opeators have that level of education (Statistics Canada, 1996).

10.11.2.5 Work

While the traditional image of rural work is that of farming, in fact farmers represent only a small proportion of workers in rural areas. According to the 1990 US Census only 11% of the workforce in rural areas was involved in farming (Miller et al., 1994). Admittedly, agriculture may form a central component of the economy of certain rural regions as do the fishery, forestry, and mining industries in others. The central position of these industries in local communities can result in substantial dislocation of the whole community if that industry is threatened. This has occurred in many rural areas since the mid-1970s.

With the decline in the relative importance of these natural resource-based industries, increasingly the largest proportion of the rural workforce is now employed as private wage and salary workers in service and manufacturing industries. In addition, farmworkers will seek temporary nonfarm employment. For example, Bollman and Smith (1988) report that between 1951 and 1981 the number of off-farm work days reported annually by farm operators in Canada increased from 75 to 171. Also during the period 1941 to 1981 the proportion of farm operators reporting working full-time off the farm increased from 3% to 14%.

Increasingly, residents of rural areas have become more dependent upon other sources of income. According to Bender et al. (1985) only

29% of US nonmetropolitan counties are farming-dependent, 28% are manufacturing-dependent, 21% are retirement-dependent, and 8% are mining- and energy-dependent. Further, while the farming-dependent counties only account for 13% of the rural population, the manufacturing-dependent counties account for 40%. Indeed, as some large firms relocate to rural areas in search of cheaper rents and labor, the proportion of rural jobs now attributed to manufacture is similar to that in urban centers (Bluestone & Daberkow, 1986).

The job crisis affecting urban America has its counterpart in rural America. It has been estimated that approximately half the work-force in rural America either does not have a job or has an inadequate one (DeLeon, Wakefield, Schultz, Williams, & VandenBos, 1989). Young people without jobs will move to urban centers in search of employment, while older unemployed workers will tend to remain in the small communities.

10.11.2.6 Income

The average income of rural areas is generally lower than that in urban areas. Analysis across the 17 US census categories revealed that while the median income in core urban areas was \$32 000 and in the more suburban fringe counties it reached \$38 000, it was only \$20 000 in the most rural counties (Miller et al., 1994). In comparison with urban centers a greater proportion of rural dwellers are classified as poor—17% in rural areas compared with 12% in urban areas (Cordes, 1989).

Again, these figures conceal substantial variations even within a single area. For example, in Canada it was estimated that 30% of rural households had an income less than \$20 000 but 25% had an income greater than \$45 000 (Bolaria, Dickinson, & Wotherspoon, 1991). Similarly, a study of the Atlantic fishery (Task Force, 1993) found that while two-thirds of fishermen made less than \$20 000 per annum and nearly one-quarter made less than \$10 000, 11% had average incomes of over \$35 000. Thus while rural areas are generally poorer than urban areas, there also exist pockets of relative affluence and of substantial poverty within these areas.

Further, the evidence suggests that along with the rest of America, rural America is experiencing increasing inequalities in the distribution of wealth (Tolbert & Lyson, 1992). This increasing inequality has implications for the health of the community over and above that due to the adverse effects of the absolute level of poverty (Wilkinson, 1996).

10.11.2.7 Living Conditions

In general, housing in rural areas is of a lower standard than in urban areas. According to White House (1979) figures, rural people in the USA are three times more likely to live in substandard housing than those in urban areas. Similarly, the 1981 Canadian census found that while 1 in 15 homes overall required major repairs in order to meet basic accommodation standards, the comparable figure for rural areas was less than 1 in 10. Further, while 90% of urban homes had central heating, the comparable figure for rural homes was 80% (Bolaria et al., 1991).

Again, these figures conceal substantial variation within rural areas. The same 1981 Canadian Census found that 21% of native people in rural areas lived in housing that required major repairs, 46% lived in housing that lacked central heating, and 27% did not have a bathroom.

10.11.3 LIFE IN RURAL SOCIETY

10.11.3.1 Social Life

There has been much discussion in the rural sociology literature about the so-called duality between rural and urban life (see Labao, 1996). The popular image of rural life is that of pastoral tranquillity. Short (1991) summarized the features of this image as follows:

> a less-hurried lifestyle where people follow the seasons rather than the stock market, where they have more time for one another and exist in more organic community where people have a place and an authentic role. The countryside has become the refuge from modernity. (p. 34)

This bucolic image of rural life is often contrasted with the murder and mayhem that is supposed to typify urban America. Srole (1972) traced this distinction back to the Old Testament with the city life of Sodom and Gomorrah being portrayed as an example of evil. Herzlich (1974) in her study of contemporary social representations (popular beliefs) of health and illness found that lay people tend to characterize urban life as the major source of ill health.

To investigate this image further, Melton and Hargrove (1987) asked a sample of American university students to write a short paragraph describing an urban scene, an urban person, a rural scene, and a rural person. Content analysis of their replies revealed that their descriptions of a rural person were generally positive and frequently referred to warmth, friendliness, and simplicity of lifestyle. Less frequently mentioned were slowness of pace, family centeredness, and conformity. These findings led Melton and Hargrove to concur with the following comment of Coward and Jackson (1983):

> there is little empirical support for this folklore [of a family immersed in a strong and pervasive social support network of kin, friends, and church. To the extent that kin, friends, and neighbors can serve to support families during periods of stress, the conclusion to be drawn from the research literature is that rural families are not particularly advantaged. (p. 196)

In North America, the decline of the family farm, the rise of agribusiness, and the integration of rural areas into urban society has contributed to the undermining of the traditional communitarian culture (Cordes, 1990). Murray and Kupinsky (1982) found that now fewer rural Americans participate in community activities, such as granges, church functions, and civic groups, than in the past. They suggest that changes in communication patterns and the geographic dispersal of extended families have led to strains on traditional sources of social support.

One seemingly enduring attribute of rural societies is a high value placed on self-sufficiency and self-reliance (Dengerink & Cross, 1982). A consequence of this can be a reduced demand for health care. Bigbee (1990) found less evidence of health problems in a rural community and suggested that this was due to under-reporting by residents who wished to maintain a sense of self-reliance.

10.11.3.2 Women and Family Life

Women have traditionally played a central role in rural society. Although there are substantial variations, there is evidence that rural women are more likely than urban women to be married, have more children, and live in larger families (Mansfield, Preston, & Crawford, 1988). The greater frequency of larger extended families is due to a variety of social and economic factors. Many young rural couples initially establish their families in their original family homes and some single-parent mothers return to their home of origin. This living arrangement can be a source of social support at times of difficulty, but can also be a source of conflict (Bushy, 1990).

There is evidence that rural women more frequently adopt traditional gender roles in terms of family care and household responsibilities (see Bushy, 1993). In addition, those who are farmers' wives have the dual responsibilities of assisting with a wide range of farming tasks. Despite these increased demands, rural women have fewer sources of support. For example, Bushy (1993), in a study of the health needs of rural women found that they were less likely than urban women to identify a large network of social support that could be of benefit during times of difficulty. The rate of female participation in the labor force also tends to be lower in rural areas (Swanson & Butler, 1987).

10.11.3.3 Working Life

Rural occupations are not confined to farming and related activities. Indeed, increasingly there is a widespread range of occupations in rural areas, although admittedly there are fewer professionals and white-collar workers than in urban centres. Despite this change, an image persists that working life in rural areas is gentle and easygoing. Behind this image there exist quiet desperation and much hardship.

Farming would seem to be an inherently stressful occupation (Keating, 1987). There are a variety of reasons for this. An important factor is the very uncertainty of the job in terms of the market and the weather. This lack of control would be expected to lead to feelings of unease (see Belyea & Labao, 1990). Another factor is the multiple responsibilities a farmer has in terms of work on and off the farm and with respect to the family. Finally, there is the changing rural scene which threatens the whole farming way of life.

Keating (1987) considered the level of stress among farming couples on Canadian grain farms. She found that personal resources, which was a measure of perceived mastery, was the best predictor of stress. In a comparable study of Ohio farmers, Belyea and Labao (1990) found that relatively young farmers with a large number of children and a large proportion of acreage in grain crops were most vulnerable economically as measured by the debt-to-asset ratio and the net family income. Further, those who were most vulnerable reported more feelings of economic hardship and stress. In turn, perceived hardship and stress were related to depression.

One factor that deters many rural residents from leaving despite difficulties is the sense of family and community history. Many of the rural residents will come from families who have lived in a specific community for generations. Their whole lives are defined by the character of their work and their community and it is difficult for them to imagine another way of living. Often, they will have been working on the farm or in the family business before they left school and expect to do so until retirement as their parents did before them. Their work is not just a job but a way of life. It is integrated into their daily lives. It is for this reason that a threat to their jobs becomes a threat to their whole way of life (Schroeder, Fliegel, & VanEs, 1985).

Another feature of rural employment, at least that which is based upon the exploitation of natural resources, is its seasonal nature. This has given rise to large numbers of migrant workers in both the USA and Canada. These workers are largely drawn from ethnic and racial minorities (Burawoy, 1976). For example, most farmworkers in British Columbia are East Indians, Chinese, native Indians, Francophones, and migrant youth (Sharma, 1983). These workers often work in atrocious conditions and are clearly exploited by their employers. A 1973 Canadian Task Force study of migrant farmworkers found evidence of "child labor, sick, pregnant, and otherwise unfit adults working with only the head of the family being paid" (Sanderson, 1974, p. 405). Hopefully, conditions have improved since then.

Finally, a large proportion of rural workers are without regular employment. These individuals would be expected to experience the various deleterious effects of loss of employment (see Jahoda, 1972). Admittedly there is some evidence that this impact may be ameliorated in rural areas owing to the presence of social support (Harding & Sewel, 1992; Murray & Dolomount, 1995). However, the apparent decline of such support leaves these individuals at increased risk of psychological distress.

10.11.3.4 Change in Rural Society

Rural communities have been adversely affected by both economic and natural problems over the past decade or so. One major change has been the rapid decline of the medium-sized family farm. There are various economic and political explanations for this but the result has been that many small farmers have had their farms seized by the banks and large lending institutions. According to the US Department of Agriculture (1985) about one-third of American farmers with sales over \$100 000 are at risk of losing their operations. Between 1981 and 1986 650 000 farms in the USA were foreclosed. About half a million rural jobs were lost between 1981 and 1983 (Human & Wasem, 1991). According to the US Office of Technology over a million farmers will leave the land by the year 2000 (Rosemann & Delworth, 1990).

It would seem that the farmers who have been most vulnerable to this economic threat have been those with medium-sized farms and those who are younger and well educated. These are the farmers who took advantage of loans in the 1970s to expand their operations but found it difficult to maintain their payments when the market changed in the 1980s.

A survey of Canadian prairie provinces by the National Farmers' Union (1989) concluded that "over the past ten years ... thousands of farm families have been dispossessed" (p. 4). The report further adds that:

> the *corporate ownership* of land means that an increasing amount of the value of farm production leaves the community in the form of payment to corporate owners. This means less spending power will remain with rural communities which, in turn, will influence their future viability. (p. 8)

In view of these economic difficulties it is perhaps not surprising that farmers generally view financial problems as the principal source of stress (Olson & Schellenberg, 1986).

Throughout the twentieth century there has been a steady decline in the number of farms and what has been described as the rise of a dualistic system of agriculture (Albrecht & Murdock, 1988). On the one hand are the small family-run farms which are increasingly economically nonviable and where the farmer often seeks part-time employment off the farm in order to survive. On the other hand are the large industrial-type farms owned by corporations. These large farms are run as capitalist enterprises with more mechanized methods of cultivation and lesser requirement for human labor. In Canada the total number of farms has dropped from a peak of 732 832 in 1941 to 280 043 in 1990 (Statistics Canada, 1996). Currently 8% of Canadian farms account for 43% of Canadian farmland.

The crisis hitting small farmers and fishermen has an impact beyond the immediate worker and threatens the survival of the worker's family and of the local community. Hoyt, O'Donnell, and Mack (1995) note that the farm crisis had two major impacts on the immediate community. First, there is the direct economic impact which removes money from the local economy, threatens small businesses, reduces employment opportunites, and accelerates the exodus of young people in search of alternative employment. Davidson (1989) compared the effects of this rural upheaval to the more visible degradation of urban ghettos.

A second, more indirect, consequence of the farm crisis is the decline of support resources. The decline in the population base is followed by the loss or consolidation of formal support services such as hospitals, community organizations, and churches. Thus, the remaining elderly population has more difficulty gaining access to these services. Human and Wasem (1991) describe this process as a vicious cycle: "when times are bad, the need for health services—particularly mental health services—is greater, but because times are bad, the ability to purchase services is lower, as is the ability of the communities to provide services" (p. 234).

It is not just the natural resource-based industries that have been restructured but also the small rural-based service and manufacturing industries (Fitchen, 1991). Brooks, Stucker, and Bailey (1986) argue that as the small farms disappear so, too, do the small shops, to be relaced by fewer and larger firms with a total of fewer employees. Like the large farms, these large firms are often owned by nonrural corporations whose primary interest is extracting profit from their investment and not with the economic maintenance of rural society.

These changes have had a widespread impact on the character of traditional rural society. Naples (1994) found that rural residents frequently report increasing dissatisfaction with community life and fewer feelings of community cohesiveness. These feelings would be expected to contribute to feelings of social isolation and hopelessness and subsequent psychological distress.

10.11.4 HEALTH ISSUES

10.11.4.1 Stress in Rural Society

As already mentioned, farm life has a variety of associated stressors. Rosmann and Delworth (1990) distinguished between social stressors and more work-related stressors. The former are the range of social pressures from commercial and government agents that the farmer has to deal with on a regular basis. The work-related pressures derive directly from the uncertainty of farm life. These concern the variability of prices and production costs, the variability of the weather, and the variability of government and other regulations.

The psychological consequences of such economic uncertainty affects the whole farming family and not just the farmer. Rosenblatt and Keller (1983) studied a small sample of Minnesota farming couples. They found that economic vulnerability was related to perceptions of economic distress and also to evidence of interpersonal conflict.

Some research has explored gender differences in the character of psychological distress experienced by farmworkers. The results of this work would suggest that women farmworkers experience higher levels of stress (Walker & Walker, 1987). This may be because they are the ones who shoulder more of the problems that affect rural families, including those experienced by male farmworkers.

10.11.4.2 Impact of Crisis

Several studies have examined the impact of farm crises and foreclosure on the health of farming families. This research has shown that economic hardship is followed by a rise in psychological distress (e.g., Armstrong & Schulman, 1990; Belyea & Labao, 1990).

One important longitudinal study was conducted in Nebraska (see Ortega, Johnson, Beeson, & Craft, 1994). A sample of farm families was followed throughout the 1980s and it was found that the level of self-reported depression significantly increased following the economic downturn but improved when there was a recovery in the economy. This would suggest that the negative mental health effects were short term.

Hoyt et al. (1995) found greater evidence of psychological distress among residents living in small rural communities than among those living on farms or in larger towns. This distress was particularly pronounced among those with low levels of social support. This would suggest that the effect of place on distress may be due to the erosion of communal identity and decreasing sense of collective concern.

10.11.4.3 Social Cohesion

One of the most important factors in understanding mental health, and indeed physical health, in rural society is the degree of social cohesion. Traditionally this has been considered a defining aspect of rural societies. Brody (1973) argues that mutual aid is virtually a defining characteristic of small farming communities. He quotes the Russian anarchist Kropotkin (1939):

> the mutual-aid tendency in man has so remote an origin, and is so deeply interwoven with all the past evolution of the human race, that it has been maintained by mankind up to the present time, notwithstanding all vicissitudes of history. (p. 180)

It is the undermining of this social solidarity that is possibly the greatest threat to the mental health of rural society.

Social interdependence leads to substantial social interaction as a requirement both for work and also for entertainment. This was so in traditional rural communities. It was based upon the large degree of social equality that existed within these communities. This meant that people shared in times of need and celebrated together in times of plenty. The breakdown of the family farm and small rural businesses has meant the rise of a social hierarchy in rural communities that undermines this basis of social solidarity. A classic example of this change is the case of Roseto, the small Italian community in Pennsylvania. The reason for initial research interest in this community was the low death rates despite the presence of the standard behavioral risk factors. It was noticed that Roseto was a very egalitarian and close-knit community. Bruhn and Wolf (1979) summarized the impact as follows:

> The sense of common purpose and the camaraderie precluded ostentation or embarrassment to the less affluent, and the concern for neighbors ensured that no one was ever abandoned. This pattern of remarkable cohesion ... provided security and cohesion against any catastrophe [and] was associated with the striking absence of myocardial infarction and sudden death. (p. 136)

Sadly, the death rate in the community rose as the degree of social integration declined (Egolf, Lasker, Wolf, & Potvin, 1992; Wilkinson, 1996).

The decline of social solidarity is, perhaps, one of the most negative consequences of the social changes in rural America. It has also been argued that the change in the social composition of rural America away from an interdependent society towards one that in many ways is more comparable to mainstream America has introduced more individualistic attitudes and values to the detriment of rural mental health (Zahner, Jacobs, Freeman, & Trainor, 1993).

10.11.4.4 Mental Illness

The results of studies comparing mental illness in urban and rural communities are confusing. One problem with early work was that it was limited to rates of admission to mental institutions and did not control for differences in the regional provision of such facilities (see Cochrane, 1983, for commentary). For example, Srole (1972) refers to the early work which suggested that black slaves in the southern states had lower rates of admission to mental hospital than freed slaves in the north. These studies neglected to point out that there were no mental hospital beds for blacks in the south.

Another problem is that early studies neglected to consider sociodemographic differences between urban and rural areas. More recent work that attempted to control for such differences, for example, Neff (1983) and Scheidt (1985), concluded that there were few differences between urban and rural mental health. Zahner et al. (1993) found that urban–rural differences in emotional and behavioral problems among children largely disappeared after statistically adjusting for mobility and cultural and economic differences.

The Epidemiological Catchment Area study (ECA; Robins & Regier, 1991) and National Co-morbidity Study (NCS; Kessler et al., 1994) found only minor differences in prevalence rates among some diagnostic categories of mental illness among individuals living in rural and urban areas. Prevalence data for rural populations in general and particularly for rural African-American and poor populations are limited and have provoked some controversy. The NCS failed to find differences based on race or rurality for the disorders studied. It has been suggested that conclusions about psychiatric disorders in these populations are inaccurate and related to the poor representation of the samples of rural populations included in them and in the ECA study, as well as the insensitivity of measures used.

There is some evidence for differences in the prevalence of certain mental illness among the rural elderly. General estimates for the prevalence of mental illness among the rural elderly range from 23–25% (Scheidt & Windle, 1982; Rosen et al., 1981), compared with 15–25% in the general elderly population (Weber, 1990). The suicide rate is also high among rural elderly; however, the prevalence of depression is the same if not lower than among urban elderly (US Congress, Office of Technology Assessment, 1990). The suicide rate among the general elderly population is 19.8 per 100 000, compared with 12.6 for the general population. Little is known about the dynamics of suicide among rural elderly or the consistent rise in suicide among African-American elderly.

Many nursing and adult homes exist in rural areas. Between 60 and 90% of the residents of these institutions have been diagnosed as having a mental illness. Many of these homes are not licensed, are poorly staffed, maintain inadequate records, and do not provide adequate programs for their residents.

Taken as a whole, these epidemiological studies do not provide compelling evidence for major differences in the incidence and prevalence of mental disorders between urban and rural populations. Admittedly there are specific social and cultural issues peculiar to rural communities that must be taken into consideration in the design of intervention programs. A key question is how rural persons conceptualize their symptoms, and whether or not they access services. How rural persons interpret physical illness symptoms, seek confirmation of the presence and meaning of symptoms, and make decisions about where to go for help is not well understood. Even less well understood is the experience and meaning of symptoms of psychiatric disorders among rural minority and poor persons. To understand help-seeking for mental health problems among these individuals, issues surrounding availability, accessibility, and acceptability of care must be examined (Blank, Fox, Hargrove, & Turner, 1995).

10.11.5 MENTAL HEALTH SERVICES

10.11.5.1 Healthcare Utilization

Despite claims that the disparity between rural and urban health service availability is narrowing (Freeman et al., 1987) and that differences in access to healthcare in rural and urban areas are less, patterns of utilization still reflect tremendous inequity (Gesler & Ricketts, 1992). Although rural residents are more likely to suffer from chronic health problems and limited functional status, they are more likely to be without a regular source of health care (Robert Wood Johnson Foundation, 1987). They are also less likely to see a physician, and those without Medicaid or private insurance are the least likely to access health services.

Inequities in health service utilization are further exacerbated among cultural and ethnic minorities in rural areas. In the USA, rural African-Americans are twice as likely as Whites to be without a regular source of healthcare (Davis et al., 1987). Further, service access and utilization for poor rural African-Americans in the south continue to lag even further behind service access in other geographical regions. Some have suggested that lack of insurance and social isolation among these rural poor minorities contribute substantially to the absence of a regular source of care (Lewin-Epstein, 1991). Given these circumstances, it is even more important to design interventions that take into account the barriers to care, community residents' beliefs about illness, and help-seeking patterns.

10.11.5.2 Specialty Mental Health Services

In the USA most inpatient mental health care (43%) is provided by general hospitals, with only 35% provided by state and county hospitals (Narrow et al., 1993). Compared with several decades ago, the total number of mental health facilities has increased but the number of inpatient beds has decreased. Thus the average facility has downsized while the overall number of facilities has increased.

Over the same period of time, downsizing and closing of state and county hospitals has been a well-documented change in the specialty mental health system. Inpatient, outpatient, and partial care services have declined in the public sector while the availability of private services has increased dramatically. There has also been a parallel increase in the number of private psychiatric hospitals and psychiatric units in general hospitals. The number of staff available to these facilities has also increased dramatically (Redick et al., 1992). Unfortunately, these changes have not substantially affected the mental health care of rural persons, since these facilities are most frequently located in urban areas, or in close proximity to urban hubs.

A major concern for healthcare planners is the distribution of mental health services across different regions of North America and specifically within rural areas. It has been estimated that 50% of rural persons with mental disorders do not seek any help (Lee & Bowles, 1974). No doubt, numerous factors contribute to this reluctance to seek assistance, but the fact is that there are 1682 counties in the USA without any psychiatrists, psychologists, or social workers. All of these counties are rural. Inpatient, outpatient, and partial hospitalization programs are much less likely to be located in rural than urban areas. For example, only 13% of nonmetropolitan counties have psychiatric inpatient units (Wagenfeld et al., 1988). Many poor rural residents do not qualify for Medicaid because they own land (the "landed poor") and they are more likely to be uninsured. It is unlikely that a market for private psychiatric services will develop in rural communities in the near future. The evidence that rural persons are more likely to be admitted to public mental hospitals probably reflects the absence of alternative mental health services in rural areas.

In the USA, specialty mental health service organizations have expanded rapidly since 1980. Documented increases in service delivery would indicate that these agencies are providing important services to individuals with mental disorders. Unfortunately, rural areas most frequently do not have access to adequate mental health services or service providers. Therefore, rural individuals with mental disorders are most likely to go without appropriate care. If they do access care, they do so later in the course of the illness, which results in increased cost and length of treatment. Also, because of the shortage of specialty mental health providers in rural areas, they are more likely to access care provided by poorly trained or more entry-level professionals. Further, rural residents are more likely to access care at a great distance from their home community which can result in loss of work and a severing of community ties (National Association for Rural Mental Health, 1993).

10.11.5.3 Public Policy

Rural mental health is a field that has been historically neglected both by researchers and policy makers, rendering the development of coordinated and empirically based services even more difficult (Fox, Blank, Kans, & Hargrove, 1994). The economic realities of providing public rural mental health services also serves as an obstacle to implementing theory-driven service delivery systems. For example, despite frequent claims of the cost effectiveness of model prevention and treatment programs, there are declining allocations for new research in rural mental health. Further, most of the funding of public services for community-dwelling mentally ill persons currently flows from entitlement programs such as Medicaid which are administered at the state level. This shift in the locus of authority from a federal to state operation of mental health services reduces the opportunities both for national initiatives as well as for more carefully tailored local efforts in rural systems development (Hargrove & Melton, 1987). What is needed is an empirical base and the development of sound theoretical models of health and illness in rural areas, which can then develop into the deliberate development and testing of interventions designed to fit within a rural social ecology.

Continuing healthcare reform efforts have emphasized a lack of health and mental health services for rural poor and minority persons. This lack of services can be conceptualized as including problems of availability, accessibility, acceptability, and accountability (Blank et al., 1995). Service providers and health policy analysts are beginning to address how mental healthcare needs are identified among rural poor and minority persons, and how healthcare providers in existing rural healthcare sites address these needs. The impact of inadequate diagnosis and ineffective treatment of mental disorders on utilization patterns and costs of other types of healthcare for rural minority and poor persons needs further research.

Most rural persons with mental illness receive services in the general medical sector of the healthcare system and through other nonspecialty providers including social support networks rather than through formal mental health specialist services. This commonly existing loose and fragmented collection of mental health services has been described as the "*de facto* mental health service system." The *de facto* system includes specialty mental health services, general medical services including primary care and nursing homes, other human service providers such as ministers and counselors who are not principally mental health specialists, and voluntary services including self-help groups, families, and friends.

Healthcare reform efforts have been directed toward extending access to health services for previously uninsured and undeserved persons while simultaneously controlling overall costs for care. Rowland and Lyons (1989) demonstrated that a large number of rural, minority, and poor persons are included in the underserved and uninsured population. In order for public policy to change to improve efficacy and cost containment a better understanding of mental health needs, as well as current modes of service access and utilization, are imperative.

10.11.5.4 Empirical and Theoretical Basis for Planning Services

Rural mental health service delivery is frequently described as costly, inefficient, and/or ineffective (Aviram, 1990), although there is a paucity of data regarding cost, effectiveness, or outcomes. There is no doubt that the "boundarylessness" (Bachrach, 1983) of mental health service delivery in rural areas care not only requires management of psychiatric symptoms, but also frequently requires attention to physical health and to long-term needs including housing, transportation, and safety (Bigelow, McFarland, & Olson, 1991).

Presently, public care for rural mentally ill consumers is unable to provide consistent and reliable service focused on the complex requirements of effective community care. The lack of data regarding the distribution of providers and the characteristics, needs, and outcomes of rural dwellers with regard to mental health services makes planning for policy dependent on idiosyncratic beliefs of powerful decision makers. In rural areas, the increasing dependency upon local authority makes public mental health policy even more dependent upon a few individuals who may or may not be well informed (Blank et al., 1995). As a result, rural service delivery systems are more vulnerable to changing political forces (Fox et al., 1994).

In order to provide better service delivery systems in rural areas and evaluate them, more consistent theoretical perspectives and more uniform standards of care are needed. Social isolation and greater geographic distances in rural environments contribute to the variability and inconsistency of service systems. Because of the lack of attention to rural areas by the scientific community as well as policy makers, there is relatively little to guide practice in this area. The emerging literature of rural mental health care is influenced by assumptions about the nature of human service delivery in rural contexts which are frequently contradictory (Murray & Keller, 1991).

The importance of understanding the influence of informal sources of care in rural areas cannot be overemphasized. Fox et al. (1994) have proposed a model for linkage of formal and informal care-givers for mental health service provision among seriously mentally ill consumers in rural areas. This model is based on the Balance Theory of Coordination developed by Litwak and Meyer (1966) and is applied to service delivery systems in rural areas. Critical features of this model are the formation of linkages between formal and informal care providers which are characterized by neither too much social distance nor overly enmeshed relationships, and the fit of task to structure. By testing the applicability of such a model to rural case management services, it may be possible to ascertain the factors necessary to provide optimal care for seriously mentally ill persons who live in rural areas.

10.11.5.5 Healthcare Reform

Rural persons are disadvantaged by services that are almost exclusively conceptualized as facility-based. Given the characteristics of rural populations and rural areas, the mental health of rural communities may be better served by outreach treatment modalities and the development of in-home services. That is, services cannot and should not be limited to the confines of a particular place, and need to utilize existing community structures better, and expand upon informal systems of care. Ironically, more community-responsive models of service such as home-based services and smaller population-specific clinics are emerging in urban areas (clinics specifically for women, homosexuals, minorities, etc.). However, perhaps owing to more severe financial constraints in rural areas, parallel specialty services are not being developed in rural areas. In fact, Mermelstein and Sundet (1988) found that rural community mental health centers were less likely to create new and innovative services during the rural crisis in the 1980s.

Another important feature in planning rural mental health service delivery systems is that frequently the entry points into the mental health system are existing rural organizations. An increasingly frequent example of this is the use of churches in collaboration with mental health professionals in providing for their congregations (Pargament et al., 1991). Churches provide naturally occurring, convenient gathering places for the surrounding community, and through true collaboration and mutual help, congregations can perceive ownership of innovative programs which can reduce suspiciousness, fear, and stigma, and increase participation.

Rural mental health services can also learn from work in developing countries. Susser, Schanzer, Varma, and Gittelman (1996) note that in these countries the family often plays a central role in the care of patients with mental illness. It has been known that despite the lack of availability of hospital care, mental patients in developing countries have been found to suffer from less impairment and disability than those in developed countries (Jablensky et al., 1992). Susser et al. (1996) suggest that this apparent advantage is due to the involvement of the family who are encouraged to understand the mental health problem and to develop ways of coping with the patient's needs and demands. With such a shortage of hospital care in rural areas, the potential involvement of the family in patient care offers much promise.

10.11.5.6 Primary Care

In both urban and rural settings most individuals with mental health problems only receive care in the general medical care system. The National Co-morbidity Survey reported that of the 42% of people with psychiatric problems who received professional help, only 26% obtained help from mental health specialists (Rich, 1994). An overwhelming majority of people with psychiatric problems are being managed through the general health sector. Furthermore, persons with mental health problems make about twice as many visits to primary care providers as do primary care patients without mental health problems (Cleary, 1987). Approximately 22% of persons utilizing primary care suffer from a mental health problem (Narrow et al., 1993). Despite considerable concern about the co-occurrence of mental illnesses or emotional dysfunction and physical illnesses in primary care populations, there has been little consideration of the impact of the separate health and mental healthcare services for individuals accessing primary care (Coulehan et al., 1990).

Lack of integration of general medical and mental health services is an often cited barrier to more effective referral from primary care to mental health specialists (Kamerow, Pincus, & MacDonald, 1986). Widespread concern has been expressed about primary care providers' lack of recognition, and treatment or referral of patients with mental disorders (Jones et al., 1987). Approximately one-third of primary care patients with psychiatric disorders remain unidentified and untreated and almost 40% of persons receiving treatment for mental disorders receive all their treatment through general medical services (Jones et al.).

According to Morlock (1989), primary care physicians record a primary or secondary psychiatric diagnosis for only about 4.4% of patient visits despite a significantly higher prevalence of mental disorders in the primary care patient population. In a study of 1000 primary care patients, Spitzer et al. (1994) found that 26% of those primary care patients met full diagnostic criteria for mental disorder with an additional 13% meeting conditions for subthreshold diagnosis. However, approximately half of those patients (48%) had not been recognized by their physicians as having a diagnosis. It is alarming that despite healthcare reform efforts, no reports have been published documenting the capacity of the general medical sector to identify, treat, or refer minority or poor persons for mental disorders.

Limited attention to mental health training of primary care providers, negative provider and patient attitudes about mental illness, and practice constraints have been highlighted as barriers to more effective mental health treatment and referral in primary care practice. Numerous investigators and clinicians have proposed that psychiatric diagnostic instruments and psychiatric epidemiological research instruments (the American Psychiatric Association's *Diagnostic and statistical manual of mental disorders* Diagnostic Interview Schedule) are not appropriate for use in primary care sites and there is a need for development of sensitive and specific mental health screening instruments for general healthcare sites (Spitzer et al., 1993). Other investigators highlight resistance of care providers and patients in primary care sites to refer to or comply with recommended treatment of mental health problems identified through screening. Little is known about which mental health approaches may be more or less culturally acceptable and thus promote compliance in primary care patients needing mental health services.

There are few studies on the management of psychiatric conditions in primary care practices, factors that influence care providers' decisions about mental health interventions, and how and why these decisions differ for patients of various cultural and ethnic backgrounds and geographic regions. Service systems have historically been resistant to providing integrated health and mental health services. The stigma associated with mental illness and treatment of mental disorders has also been blamed for underdevelopment of mental health screening and intervention in primary healthcare settings. Additionally, little is known about the delivery of standard effective mental health treatments in different types of primary care sites or how these treatments are related to health outcomes. The absence of research on outcomes of mental health treatment in primary care contributes to general healthcare providers' reluctance to incorporate mental health screening and treatment more rigorously in primary care encounters (Davenport, Goldberg, & Millar, 1987).

In view of the greater availability of primary care physicians than specialists in rural areas (Dor & Holahan, 1990), they have potentially an even more important role than their urban counterparts to play in the care of patients with mental health problems. Greater cooperation between psychologists and primary care physicians will ensure a more accessible service for people with mental health problems.

10.11.5.7 Telemedicine

Interest in telemedicine and communications technologies to improve health and mental healthcare in rural areas has increased dramatically since 1985. The introduction of telemedicine offers great potential to enable the patient/client to overcome the physical/geographical barriers to accessing specialist healthcare and to enable the health professional to continue his or her education (Preston, Brown, & Hartley, 1992).

Zelman (1995) has described a typology for innovative technologies using POTS (Plain Old Telephone Service) and PANS (Pretty Amazing New Stuff). The PANS consist of two-way interactive televideo systems which typically utilize high-speed dedicated access (such as T1, ISDN, or switched-56 lines), and are dependent upon sophisticated (and expensive) equipment. The US Office of Rural Health Policy has funded over a dozen demonstration projects for telemedicine since 1992, many of which include mental health treatment as part of their goal. To date, there have been no mental health services research studies concerning the cost, effectiveness, or attitudes of consumers and providers toward innovative technologies. One study did examine the reliability of assessments using this technology for persons with obsessive-compulsive disorder (OCD; Baer et al., 1995). These researchers concluded that standardized assessments for OCD could be administered reliably using interactive televideo systems.

Mental health service delivery seems particularly well suited for dissemination using two-way interactive televideo systems. Unlike many of the medical specialties, mental health services need to be delivered in real time. Further, most assessments and treatments rely on the type of face-to-face interaction that is supported by these systems. Given that most of the diagnostic information typically relied upon is visual and verbal, these systems hold great promise for extending our reach into underserved rural areas.

There are several public policy pitfalls awaiting telemedicine. Perhaps most obvious is the question of whether services delivered through these media will be eligible for third party reimbursement. It seems clear that health services research will need to be conducted to determine the quality and effectiveness of specific procedures such as diagnosis, other assessment, and treatments delivered at a distance through new technologies. Another difficult policy issue concerns licensure of health professionals. Typically, licenses to practice are issued by states, yet these televideo transmissions may frequently cross state lines. Recognition of state licensure in other jurisdictions presents a number of legal and administrative problems. There are also concerns about practice liability and confidentiality of video transmissions.

10.11.6 PSYCHOLOGY AND RURAL MENTAL HEALTH

10.11.6.1 Historical Background

The discipline and profession of psychology has played a variable role in the history of mental health services in the rural areas of the North America. As a part of the community mental health centers movement in the USA in the early 1960s, psychology was by mandate integrally involved in the planning, development, and implementation of services in the catchment areas. But a further, more refined focus on rural services within that movement was left to various multidisciplinary groups and psychology as a profession took little interest in rural communities or the rural context of the practice of psychology. As Keller and Prutsman (1982) pointed out:

> Psychology has traditionally been an urban profession. Most psychologists are trained in, and subsequently remain in, large metropolitan areas or atypical university communities. Consequently, psychologists have largely failed to consider the special mental health needs of more than one-quarter of the nation's population. (p. 190)

Professional groups such as the Rural Social Work Caucus and the National Association for Rural Mental Health were active in the 1960s and 1970s, typically as a part of the community mental health center movement. The American Psychological Association (APA) demonstrated interest in the late 1980s with the appointment of a Rural Task Force to address the issues of psychologists practicing in rural communities. While psychologists had been involved in the rural mental health movement for a number of years, this was the first time that organized psychology devoted resources and gave recognition to an important issue for many of its members.

As one of the four core professions designated by the National Institutes of Mental Health (NIMH), psychologists were typically well represented in the early mental health centers and continued until the system experienced major structural changes in most states in the early 1980s. Prior to the development of these centers, mental health services were typically not available to rural residents, who had to rely on whatever types of assistance may have been available in communities from other agencies or professionals or travel to the nearest urban centers.

10.11.6.2 Roles of Psychologists in Rural Communities

The roles of psychologists in rural mental health programs have included provider of clinical services, program and agency administrator, program evaluator, clinical supervisor, and program and service planner. From the number and diversity of roles that psychologists play in mental health agencies in rural settings, it is clear that psychologists must be able to perform a wide range in a number of different aspects of the service delivery system. Berry and Davis (1978) pointed out that "rural mental health workers must be a practitioner–generalist, able to handle a variety of problems because the rural community cannot afford a large selection of specialists or referral resources" (p. 677).

Keller and Prutsman (1982) argue that rural psychologists "must be flexible generalists who comfortably serve a wide range of human needs." They added:

> In a time when much of psychology is becoming highly specialized, the rural psychologists will need to fulfill a broad range of functions partially because there exists a lack of specialists and persons from other disciplines who are available to meet unusual needs. (p. 1992)

Hargrove and Howe (1981) identified the generalist style as an objective of clinical psychology training for rural service delivery. Hargrove (1983) further refined the concept of generalist for psychologists and identified the various components of that style of practice in the light of professional identity.

When the role of generalist is interpreted within the clinical domain of practice, the psychologist must be able to call upon a broad range of assessment and intervention strategies. A doctoral-level psychologist may be required to conduct assessments for school systems, courts, law enforcement agencies, social service agencies, as well as for the mental health system. In addition to these uniquely psychological functions, the psychologist is also likely to be expected to do case management and other programmatic and clinical functions as needed.

It has been noted that doctoral-level psychologists are likely to rise rapidly in the administrative structure of programs and agencies. It was not infrequent in the early days of community mental health centers for doctoral-level psychologists to become directors of centers with responsibilities for recruitment, personnel management, systems development, fiscal operations, management information systems, contract negotiation, and board administration in addition to the clinical and programmatic operations.

The generalist concept, then, reached far beyond serving a broad range of clients with a wide range of problems. It included involvement in the internal administrative operations of the agency, clinical and program management, and community linkages. Few psychologists were trained to assume such a broad range of responsibilities at such significant levels in the organizations.

10.11.6.3 Training Psychologists for Rural Practice

Psychology training has largely taken place in urban settings. The greatest contextual influence on training, then, has been an urban one. This created problems for psychologists who wished to work in rural settings because they did not have appropriate conceptual frameworks or experiences to successfully work there.

As this urban domination of training programs and models became known, the NIMH in the 1980s began its focus on prioritized rural populations, among others, for special attention in the funding of training programs in psychology, psychiatry, social work, and nursing for rural practice. Several university and free-standing programs for psychological training for rural practice developed in conjunction with this initiative.

An important recent initiative has been taken by the APA to develop a common training program for psychologists, social workers, and nurses working in rural mental health. The development of the common curriculum (APA Office of Rural Health, 1994) not only signaled the increasing awareness of the need for training materials for those working in this area but of the necessity for collaboration in training. Unlike urban practitioners, rural health workers in general find that there is less value in maintaining strict lines of professional demarcation and more need for interprofessional collaboration to overcome the inadequacy of resources and the breadth of mental health problems.

This common curriculum emphasized the need for rural psychologists to consider: (i) the social, economic, political, and religious influences affecting rural communities; (ii) the importance of ethnic and cultural influences in rural communities and the importance of oral tradition; and (iii) the uniqueness of each region and community. This report also refers to the reluctance of rural residents to seek professional support, often turning instead to the clergy and family members in times of distress. Further, the report reminds the psychologists to be reflexive in their practice and to recognize the impact of their own culture on the delivery of care and on their sensitivity to the client.

Several other issues are important for professional psychology's rural training agenda. First is training for personal and family adaptation to the rural environment. Frequently it is difficult to assist in the personal preparation of professional persons in academic settings because of the limited scope of traditional activities. Second is whether doctoral-level psychologists are necessary for rural service delivery or whether persons with masters degrees are adequate for this work. Jerrell and Herring (1983) studied psychologists in 20 rural Pennsylvania counties and found that there was little difference in job function between doctoral- and masters-level providers. Doctoral persons were slightly more likely to assume administrative roles. The entry-level credentials have been and continue to be a controversial topic for organized professional psychology.

Training for personal adaptation is a difficult task under any circumstances; much less in an academic context. Personal adaptation to the rural environment involves the individual and intimate choices that are made by persons and families, including choices of living environments, and the associations with friends. They also include the preferences and needs for certain types of resources. The unexpected characteristics and demands of the rural environment, particularly when the new recruits are not accustomed to rural lifestyles, can be devastating to individuals and families who are not able to anticipate them. Even students who have grown up in rural areas had difficulties assuming the role of a professional person while adapting to the lifestyle in the small community. Personal and family adaptation to the rural community is essential if the psychologist is to be successful. Training for this adaptation is typically lacking in psychology training programs. Further, Murray (1990) recommends that "rural recruiters [should] seek people who really understand rural life and who value its virtues and are not just intent on escaping urban irritants" (p. 18).

The second important training issue for psychologists is the level of training. Typically, in North America, the doctoral degree is the entry credential. However, many states and several Canadian provinces license persons with masters degrees. Indeed, persons with masters degrees in psychology have begun to demand parity with doctoral providers both in public agency service as well as in independent practice. Strong positions have been taken on both sides and the issue is far from settled.

The importance for the rural area is that most human resource distribution studies show that doctoral providers are not practicing in rural communities. Several investigators (e.g., Sladen & Mozdzierz, 1989) have studied various aspects of the distribution of psychologists in different parts of the country and typically found a lack of doctoral providers.

10.11.7 TYPES OF INTERVENTION

10.11.7.1 Fitting the Intervention to the Context

The focus of the practice of psychology and other mental health professions in rural communities has been on the alleviation of the suffering of individuals and families who live in relatively remote areas, removed from the traditional resources associated with mental health services. Since no consistent types of psychopathology have been reported to characterize rural people or rural environments, there are also no consistently recommended types of interventions that are especially designed for people in rural settings. While there have been attempts to identify "ruralness" as a trait of individuals who live in rural environments (Flax, Wagenfeld, Ivens, & Weiss, 1979; Melton, 1983), and consistent perceptions of the environment among rural and urban people (Melton & Hargrove, 1987), no reliable support for such constructs has been found.

It has been argued, however, that since peoples' values determine how they interpret their experience, values also influence how they define problems in mental health terms. This definition has an impact on their choice of whether and how individuals choose to seek help for problems (Wagenfeld & Wagenfeld, 1981). Mazer (1976) adds that the values and definitions influence the expectations that people have when they seek assistance for problems. The rural context is characterized by certain attitudes that mitigate against seeking assistance for psychological problems (Bachrach, 1977; Kenkel, 1986). An awareness of these characteristics and of the broader changing social context within which people live and work is essential for the effective delivery of psychological services.

The manner in which the intervention is implemented also depends on the context in which it occurs. Espousing the behavioral-ecological perspective, Jeger and Slotnick (1982) point out that:

> individual-level community mental health interventions should aim to provide learning opportunities to consumers that will increase their ability to influence their environments (i.e., promote competence). Behavioral training to facilitate coping with stress, developing social skills, and improving general problem-solving capacities are compatible with this value. (p. 11)

They document Rappaport's caution that:

> competence should not become a substitute label for psychotherapy, which maintains a hierarchical doctor–patient relation. Furthermore, experts should not offer canned behavioral packages to teach specific skills under the guise of competence training. Instead, the broader community context within which competence training takes place must be considered, since the community provides the meaning system and values of what constitutes adaptive behavior.

The person suffering from schizophrenia who has supportive family members in the immediate vicinity will be treated quite differently from the transient person who appears in town from unknown places. While the technology of the therapeutic intervention may not differ substantially between rural and urban environments, the choices and application of interventions are heavily influenced by the contexts in which they are applied. The rural psychologist must be aware of the changing family, social, and working life of rural communities and especially attuned to the impact of ongoing social crises. The person who loses his farm that has been in his family for generations and that provides a livelihood for an extended family needs to be approached differently from a person who loses his job in a context of expanding urban opportunity.

10.11.7.2 The Rural Psychologist as a Generalist

Psychologists, like most mental health workers, must function as generalists within the rural context (Hargrove, 1983, Keller & Prutsman, 1982). The demand of the generalist role counters the tendency toward specialization that characterizes the training and development of professional psychologists. Generalist practice requires the psychologist to be skillful in a broad range of psychological functions with an even broader range of potential clients.

The mental health system in the rural context is characterized by few professionally trained practitioners who are separated from one another by either long distances or natural barriers, or both (Hargrove, 1982). There are fewer potential clients in the community and they will probably reside and work at great distances from the providers. In most cases, the public delivery system, whether an outpost of a larger community mental health program or a specialized mental health unit of a health department, is responsible for the delivery of care. There are relatively few doctoral psychologists who practice privately in rural areas. Furthermore, there are relatively few practitioners in other mental health or mental health-related professions in rural areas.

The result of this scarcity is that those providers who are available in the rural community must be able to respond to the mental health needs that present themselves. Since there are no data to indicate that rural environments are exempt from the broad range of mental disorders, it is reasonable to assume that rural mental health providers will probably encounter most, if not all, of the major mental disorders at one time or another. It is not likely, on the other hand, that they will encounter them in great numbers.

This characteristic has several consequences. First, the mental health providers in rural areas must be prepared to respond to the broad range of mental disorders without a significant amount of collateral professional resources and support. Second, these providers must respond to needs without the benefit of being able to aggregate the clientele in either clinically or economically beneficial ways. Finally, providers must be at least familiar with a broad range of mental, emotional, and behavioral disabilities to be responsive to the needs of the population that they serve.

10.11.7.3 The Concept of Community and Psychological Intervention

It has been suggested that the best psychological interventions are not in the clinic, but in the community. The concept of "community" is deeply embedded in the sense of ruralness both in definitional as well as experiential terms. Virtually all definitions of rural contain references to small communities of people that are some distance from other people. The idea of ruralness is not limited to the population base of small communities, but is applicable to the experience of small communities with their limited populations and greater knowledge of each other's affairs (see Section 10.11.4.3).

Bell and Newby's (1972) use of Tonnies' concepts of *Gemeinschaft* and *Gesellschaft* provides a model for a general understanding of the rural community. *Gemeinschaft* is described in terms of the intimacy of relationships, kinship, and one's place in the social and community structure. The terms "blood," "kinship," and "friendship" are used to characterize this concept of community. *Gesellschaft*, on the other hand, represents large, depersonalized communities in which relationships might best be categorized as contractual. *Gemeinschaft* is closer to the traditional rural community in which the rural mental health worker may be located.

Heyman (1982), noting the lack of models for rural service delivery and the dominance of urban models for training and service, suggested that there was some freedom in the lack of constraints of rural practice:

> Every rural worker must deal with the absence of a "general" model by developing situation-specific models. There may be similarities in the implementation of these models, but the dissimilarities, in response to the varying situations, are likely to be critical to their actual functioning. The absence of a model provides a freedom and flexibility that complements the unique nature of each community. (p. 36)

Heyman points out the opportunities for rural service that are grounded in the *Gemeinschaft* orientation to community. They include visibility within the community and access to various dimensions of the community, including those in which power is embedded.

Psychological and social intervention are conducted within these contexts of social intimacy and knowledge. They are also carried out within the context of a high level of visibility and access. Clearly, there are both positive and negative consequences of these features. First, the results of one's work is available and known throughout the community. Clinical failures as well as successes may well be common knowledge and may be topics of discussion in both personal and professional circles. Second, the mental health worker may well have access to people and resources to bring to bear healing forces that otherwise may be unavailable. Third, common knowledge of people, families, and groups within communities may be useful in programmatic and clinical activities.

While Heyman (1982) certainly advocates intense involvement of the rural mental health worker in the community in which he or she lives and/or practices, he acknowledges that this involvement must be a cautious one. He calls upon the participant–observer model as one that would be satisfactory. Precaution must be taken to be involved in a broad, flexible way, active but not over involved and certainly not in a polarizing manner.

Psychologists and other mental health workers who work in rural settings do not have the luxury of limiting their perspectives of intervention to face-to-face contact between clients and clinicians. Some of the characteristics of rural environments preclude reliance on clinical service delivery as the only means of providing mental health care to the population. Distances, for example, prevent people from being able to meet at frequent intervals. The infrequency of the occurrence of similar types of psychopathology, sometimes the criterion for grouping consumers into group-oriented treatment programs, prevents the use of these types of intervention strategies.

As a result of these characteristics, rural mental health service providers, researchers, and administrators have utilized strategies of prevention and collaboration with other agencies and indigenous groups to enhance the quality of care available in the rural environments. D'Augelli and Vallance (1981) reported on the Community Helpers Project in which local residents were trained in basic helping skills who, in turn, trained others to provide informal help to persons in crisis. Libertoff (1980) presented a case study in which the informal system of care of a small New England community was utilized in developing youth and family services. Bergstrom (1982) summarized the research and made recommendations for collaboration with natural helpers for rural mental health service delivery.

A number of programs that utilize paraprofessionals have been described (e.g., Connors & Gabel, 1983; D'Augelli, 1982; D'Augelli & Vallance, 1981; Echterling, 1981; Heyman, 1982; Sundberg, 1986) These programs typically involve mental health professionals training paraprofessionals, collateral workers, and indigenous persons to be responsible to the mental health needs of people in rural areas and small towns.

An example of an initiative in community mental health service delivery was the Community Support Program (CSP) developed by the NIMH in the USA (Turner & TenHoor, 1978). The CSP, which has been successfully applied in rural settings, has a number of components including building social support for the client. A similar program developed by the New York State Office of Mental Health (Baker & Intagliata, 1984) also placed emphasis on developing opportunities for work and social interaction, competency skills training, social clusters, evening, and outreach programs, and so on.

Comprehensive psychological intervention requires going beyond the traditional clinical treatment approach to consider prevention and rehabilitation. In the rural context this requires that the psychologist not only be prepared for crisis intervention in the face of both personal and social crises but also to intervene to prepare and enhance people's resources to deal with and to combat such assaults on their way of life (see Trainor, Pope, & Pomeroy, 1997).

10.11.7.4 Ethical Dilemmas in Rural Practice

When the expectations of professional helpers encounter the intimacy and complexity of relationships that customarily exist in a rural community, the fabric of professional practice is strained. This is particularly true in the ethical guidelines that govern the conduct of practice of most mental health providers. The emerging literature on ethical complexities in rural mental health practice (Hargrove, 1986) has identified three problematic areas. These are dual relationships, limits of competence, and confidentiality.

Small communities have a finite number of people and potential relationships. Further, people relate to one another on various levels and in various domains of the community. For example, the physician may be an elder in the church, on the school board, and a director on the local bank's board. This places the psychologist in a special relationship to other members of the church, the minister and family, teachers and administrators of the school system, and employees and customers of the bank. These relationships give the character of the therapist–client relationship a special personal quality that can potentially be compromised if considerable caution is not taken.

Many people play many roles in rural communities. Therefore many people are involved with several, different aspects of each others' lives. The prohibition against dual relationships contained in the ethical codes of mental health professionals presents potentially difficult constraints on the professional and personal lives of rural practitioners.

The second problematic area consists of limits of competence. The mental health professional is in a difficult situation when he or she is the only practitioner in a community and does not have requisite skills to handle certain clinical problems. Many problems of course are so far outside the practitioner's competence that there is no question but that a referral must be made. The need for neuropsychological assessment or rehabilitation is clearly outside the competence of the average, clinically trained psychologist. But, as specialties develop and techniques are refined, it is frequently difficult for the general practitioner to know whether the practice is within the limits of competence.

Third, confidentiality may be problematic because of the high level of visibility and intimacy that is characteristic of rural communities. Certain professional relationships may carry the expectation of information exchange regardless of whether releases of information have been executed. The physician, for example, who refers a patient to the mental health center may expect a report from the center on the progress of the patient. The release of information, a necessary formality, may not be important to this physician because of the history of practice and involvement with people in the community. If the release is not signed and the mental health professional refuses to report to the physician, the political and community consequences could be quite problematic.

The high levels of visibility and access of mental health professionals in the rural community require certain precautions and preventive measures to avoid unnecessary ethical conflicts. Typically, frank and open discussion with clients in the clinical setting about boundaries and suggested courses of action if and when awkward situations develop is sufficient to avoid difficult situations.

10.11.8 FUTURE DIRECTIONS

Rural America is changing, and for a large number of its residents the future is not bright. There is an urgent need for the careful development of mental health services to address the many problems faced by rural people. The discipline of psychology is also changing, embracing a broader range of activities but also continuing toward increased specialization.

Three areas appear to characterize the immediate future in the profession and discipline of psychology as it might appear in rural America. First, the tendencies toward behavioral health and, in some venues, becoming a primary care provider have expanded the roles of psychologists beyond that of mental health provider. The development of the family psychology specialty and the harmonious relationships with family physicians have given psychologists new perspectives of research, training, and practice.

Second, the development of collaborative relationships with other professionals and with nonprofessionals and indigenous workers characterizes the work of psychologists in rural settings. Collaboration is a relative newcomer to the psychology lexicon, but the complexity of the contexts in which psychologists practice requires functional reciprocity. Fox et al. (1994) have provided a theoretical framework for coordinating rural mental health services based on Litwak's Balance Theory of Coordination and have provided guidelines for collaboration with at least one population of providers.

Finally, in the USA managed care is oozing into rural areas at a slower pace than it has flowed into urban and suburban. There appear to be several reasons for this. First, there are fewer providers in rural areas. Second, the market is considerably smaller. Third, provision of adequate health and mental health services is considerably more difficult in rural areas. It is not clear how managed care companies will respond to the health and mental health problems of rural environments.

10.11.9 SUMMARY

Rural society represents a large, although neglected, part of North American society. It is extremely diverse in its makeup. However, one consistent pattern is poverty and aging. Admittedly, there are certain pockets of wealth, but overall rural society is deprived with reference to urban society. The character of rural society is changing from one of full employment based on exploitation of natural resources to one of underemployment and greater employment in service and manufacturing industries. As a consequence, social and working life in rural America is undergoing dramatic change. Formerly it was a cohesive and supportive society but now there is less evidence of social cohesion.

In view of the diversity and changing character of rural society it is not surprising that it is difficult to identify some consistent patterns of health. However, it is apparent that there is a considerably lower degree of provision of health, including mental health, services. This lowered degree of availability is coupled with difficulties in accessibility. There have been some limited initiatives in community mental health services but there is a need not only for more resources but also for careful planning and evaluation of service provision.

Psychologists have had a lengthy but checkered involvement in rural mental health work. Even today, few doctoral-level psychologists practice in rural areas. There is greater need for advanced training in rural practice. Several recent initiatives have developed interdisciplinary training programs. In particular, the psychologist needs to be trained to become more involved in primary care and in collaborating with primary care physicians and other health professionals so as to provide integrated mental health services. Further, a psychologist working in a rural setting will confront many personal problems and ethical dilemmas. The rural psychologist should be aware of these issues and how best to deal with them.

Working in a rural setting offers many opportunities for a psychologist to treat a variety of mental health problems. For this reason the prychologist's orientation must be that of a generalist. In addition, rural psychologists need to consider the full spectrum of psychological services from health promotion through crisis intervention to long-term care of the chronically mentally ill. Further, intervention must be matched to the context to be effective. In this respect rural psychologists need to be aware of the sociocultural patterns of rural life and of the many changes rural society is currently experiencing.

10.11.10 REFERENCES

Albrecht, D. E., & Murdock, S. H. (1988). The structural characteristics of US agriculture: Historical patterns and precursors of producers' adaptations to crisis. In S. H. Murdock and F. L. Leistritz (Eds.), *The farm financial crisis: Socioeconomic dimensions and implications for producers and rural areas.* Boulder, CO: Westview.

American Psychological Association Office of Rural Health (1994). *Caring for the rural community: An interdisciplinary curriculum.* Washington, DC: American Psychological Association.

Armstrong, P. S., & Schulman, M. (1990). Financial strain and depression among farm operators: the role of perceived economic hardship and personal control. *Rural Sociology, 55,* 475–493.

Aviram, U. (1990). Community care of the seriously mentally ill: Continuing problems and current issues. *Community Mental Health Journal, 26,* 69–88.

Bachrach, L. L. (1977). Deinstitutionalization of mental health services in rural areas. *Hospital and Community Psychiatry, 28,* 669–672.

Bachrach, L. L. (1983). Psychiatric services in rural areas: a sociological overview. *Hospital and Community Psychiatry, 34,* 215–226.

Baer, L., Cukor, P., Jenike, M. A., Leahy, L., O'Laughlen, J., & Coyle, J. T. (1995). Pilot studies of telemedicine for patients with obsessive-compulsive disorder. *American Journal of Psychiatry, 152,* 1383–1385.

Baker, F., & Intagliata, J. (1984). Rural community support services for the chronically mentally ill. *Journal of Rural Community Psychology, 5,* 3–14.

Bealer, R. C., Willis, F. K., & Kuvlesky, W. (1965). The meaning of rurality in American society: some implications of alternative definitions. *Rural Sociology, 30,* 255–266.

Bell, C., & Newby, H. (1972). *Community studies: An introduction to the sociology of the local community.* New York: Praeger.

Belyea, M. J., & Labao, L. M. (1990). Psychosocial consequences of agricultural transformation: The farm crisis and depression. *Rural Sociology, 55,* 58–75.

Bender, L., Green, B., Hady, T., Kuehn, J., Nelson, M., Perkinson, L., & Ross, P. (1985). *The diverse social and economic structure of nonmetropolitan America* (Rural Development Research Report No. 49). Washington, DC: US Government Printing Office.

Bergstrom, D. A. (1981) Collaborating with natural helpers for delivery of rural mental health services. *Journal of Rural Community Psychology, 3*(2), 26.

Berry, B., & Davis, A. E. (1978). Community mental health ideology: A problematic model for rural areas. *American Journal of Orthopsychiatry, 48,* 673–675.

Bigbee, J. L. (1990). Stressful life events and illness occurrence in rural versus urban women. *Journal of Community Health Nursing, 7,* 105–113.

Bigelow, D. A., McFarland, B. H., & Olson, M. M. (1991). Quality of life of community mental health program clients: Validating a measure. *Community Mental Health Journal, 27*(1), 43–57.

Blank, M. B., Fox, J. C., Hargrove, D. S., & Turner, J. T. (1995). Critical issues in reforming rural mental health service delivery. *Community Mental Health Journal, 31*(6), 511–524.

Bluestone, H., & Daberkow, S. G. (1986). Employment growth in non-metro America: Trends and prospects to 1990. *Rural Development Perspective, 20,* 34–37.

Bolaria, B. S., Dickinson, H. D., & Wotherspoon, T. (1991). Rural issues and problems. In B. S. Bolaria (Ed.), *Social issues and contradictions in Canadian society* (pp. 393–416). Toronto, Canada: Harcourt Brace Jovanovich.

Brody, H. (1973). *Inishkillane: Change and decline in the West of Ireland.* London; Faber and Faber.

Bollman, R. D., & Smith, P. (1988). Integration of Canadian farm and off-farm markets and the off-farm work of farm women, men, and children. In G. S. Basran & D. A. Hay (Eds.), *The political economy of agriculture in Western Canada* (pp. 85–202). Toronto: Garamand Press.

Bosack, J., & Perlman, B. (1982). A review of the definition of rural. *Journal of Rural Community Psychology, 3,* 3–34.

Brooks, N. L., Stucker, T. A., & Bailey, J. A. (1986). Income and well-being of farmers and the farm financial crisis. *Rural Sociology, 51,* 391–405.

Bruhn, J. G., & Wolf, S. (1979). *The Roseto story: An anatomy of health.* Norman, OK: University of Oklahoma Press.

Burawoy, M. (1976). The functions and reproduction of migrant labor: comparative material from Southern Africa and the United States. *American Journal of Sociology, 81,* 1050–1087.

Bushy, A. (1993). Rural women: Lifestyle and health status. *Nursing Clinics of North America, 28,* 187–197.

Cleary P. D. (1987). Gender differences in stress related outcomes. In R. Barnett, L. Biener, & G. Baruch (Eds.), *Women and stress* (pp. 39–74). New York: Free Press.

Cochrane, R. (1983). *The social creation of mental illness.* London: Longman.

Connors, G. J., & Gabel, H. (1983). Effect of paraprofessional contacts in rural parent group recruitment. *Journal of Rural Community Psychology, 4*(1), 35–42.

Cordes, S. M. (1989). The changing rural environment and the relationship between health services and rural development. *Health Services Research, 23,* 757–784.

Cordes, S. M. (1990). Come on in, the water's just fine. *Academic Medicine, 65,* S1–S9.

Coulehan, J.L., Schulberg, H. C., Block, M. R., et al. (1990). Depressive symptomatology and medical comorbidity in a primary care clinic. *International Journal of Psychiatry in Medicine, 20*(4), 335–347.

Coward, R. T., & Jackson, R. W. (1983). Environmental Stress: the rural family. In H. I. McCubbins & C. R. Tigley (Eds.), *Stress and the family. vol. 1: Coping with normative transitions* (pp. 188–200). New York: Brunner/Mazel.

D'Augelli, A. R. (1982). Future directions for paraprofessionals in rural mental health, or how to avoid giving indigenous helpers civil service ratings. In P. A. Keller & J. D. Murray (Eds.), *Handbook of rural community mental health* (pp. 210–222). New York: Human Sciences Press.

D'Augelli, A. R., & Vallance, T. R. (1981). The helping community: Promoting mental health in rural areas through informal helping. *Journal of Rural Community Psychology, 2*(1), 3–16.

Davenport, S., Goldberg, D., & Millar, T. (1987). How psychiatric disorders are missed during medical consultations. *Lancet, 2*(8556), 439–441.

Davidson, O. G. (1989). *Broken heartland: the rise of America's rural ghetto.* New York: Free Press.

Davis, K., Lillie-Blanton, M., Lyons, B., et al. (1987). Health care for black Americans: The public sector role. *The Milbank Quarterly, 65*(1), 213–247.

DeLeon, P. H., Wakefield, M., Schultz, A. J., Williams, J., & VandenBos, G. R. (1989). Rural America: Unique opportunities for health care delivery and health services research. *American Psychologist, 44,* 1298–1306.

Dengerink, H., & Cross, H. (Eds.) (1982). *Training professionals for rural mental health.* Lincoln, NE: University of Nebraska Press.

Dor, A., & Holahan, J. (1990). Urban–rural differences in medicare physician expenditures. *Inquiry, 27,* 301–318.

Echterling, L. G. (1981). A rural program for enhancing prevention and intervention skills. *Journal of Rural Community Psychology, 2*(1), 32–38.

Egolf, B., Lasker, J., Wolf, S., & Potvin, L. (1992). The Roseto effect: A 50-year comparison of mortality rates. *American Journal of Public Health, 82,* 1089–1092.

Fitchen, J. M. (1991). *Endangered spaces, enduring places: Change, identity, and survival in rural America.* Boulder, CO: Westview.

Flax, J. W., Wagenfeld, M. O., Ivens, R. E., & Weis, R. J. (1979). Mental health and rural America: An overview and annotated bibliography (DHEW Publication No. ADM 78-753). Washington, DC: US Government Printing Office.

Fox, J. C., Blank, M. B., Kane, C. F., & Hargrove, D. S. (1994). Balance theory as a model for coordinating delivery of rural mental health services. *Applied and Preventive Psychology, 3*(1), 121–129.

Freeman, H., Blendon, R., Aiken, L., Sudman, S., Mullinix, C. F., & Corey, C. R. (1987). Americans report on their access to health care. *Health Affairs, 6,* 6–17.

Gesler, W. M., & Ricketts T. C. (Eds.) (1992). *Health in rural North America: The geography of health care services and delivery.* New York: Rutgers University Press.

Harding, L., & Sewel, J. (1992). Psychological health and employment status in an island community. *Journal of Occupational and Organizational Psychology, 65,* 269–275.

Hargrove, D. S. (1982). An overview of professional considerations in the rural community. In P. A. Keller & J. D. Murray (Eds.), *Handbook of rural community mental health* (pp. 169–189). New York: Human Sciences Press.

Hargrove, D. S. (1983). The rural psychologist as generalist: A challenge for professional identity. *Professional Psychology, 13*(2), 302–308.

Hargrove, D. S. (1986). Ethical issues in rural mental health practice. *Professional Psychology: Research and Practice, 17,* 20–23.

Hargrove, D. S., & Howe, H. E. (1981). Training in rural mental health delivery: a response to prioritized needs. *Professional Psychology, 12,* 722–731.

Hargrove, D. S., & Melton, G. B. (1987). Block grants and rural mental health services. *Journal of Rural Community Psychology, 8,* 4–11.

Herzlich, C. (1974). *Health and illness: A social psychological analysis.* London: Academic Press.

Heyman, S. R. (1982). Capitalizing on unique assets of rural areas for community interventions. *Journal of Rural Community Psychology, 3*(1), 35–48.

Hoyt, D. R., O'Donnell, D., & Mack, K. Y. (1995). Psychological distress and size of place: The epidemiology of rural economic distress. *Rural Sociology, 60,* 707–720.

Human, J., & Wasem, C. (1991). Rural mental health in America. *American Psychologist, 46,* 232–239.

Jablensky, A., Sartorius, N., Ernberg, G., et al. (1992). Schizophrenia: manifestation, incidence, and course in different cultures: A World Health Organization ten country study. *Psychological Medicine Supplement, 20,* 97.

Jahoda, M. (1972). *Employment and unemployment: A social psychological analysis.* Cambridge, UK: Cambridge University Press.

Jeger, A. M., & Slotnick, R. S. (1982). Community mental health: Toward a behavioral-ecological perspective. In A. M. Jeger and R. S. Slotnick (Eds.), *Community mental health and behavioral-ecology: A handbook of theory, research, and practice* (pp. 7–26). New York: Plenum.

Jensen, L., & Tienda, M. (1989). Nonmetropolitan minority families in the United States: Trends in racial and ethnic economic stratification, 1959–1986. *Rural Sociology, 54,* 509–532.

Jerrell, J., & Herring, J. (1983). The role of psychologists in rural community mental health facilities. *Journal of Rural Community Psychology, 4*(2), 3–17.

Johnson, K. M., & Beale, C. L. (1992). Natural population decrease in the United States. *Rural Development Perspectives, 8,* 20–27.

Jones, L. R., Badger, L. W., Ficken, R. P., et al. (1987). Inside the hidden mental health network examining mental healthcare delivery of primary care physicians. *General Hospital Psychiatry, 9,* 287–293.

Kamerow, D. B., Pincus, H. A., & MacDonald, D. I. (1986). Alcohol abuse, other drug abuse and mental disorders in medical practice: Prevalence, costs, recognition, and treatment. *Journal of the American Medical Association, 255* (15), 2054–2057.

Keating, N. C. (1987). Reducing stress of farm men and women. *Family Relations, 36,* 358–363.

Keller, P. A., & Prutsman, T. D. (1982). Training for professional psychology in the rural community. In P. A. Keller & J. D. Murray (Eds.), *Handbook of rural community mental health.* New York: Human Sciences Press.

Kenkel, M. B. (1986). Stress-coping-support in rural communities: A model for primary prevention. *American Journal of Community Psychology, 14*(5), 457–478.

Kessler, R. C., McGonagle, C. A., Zhao, S. et al. (1994) Lifetime and 12-month prevalence of DSM-III-R psychiatric disorders in the United States: Results from the National Comorbidity Survey. *Archives of General Psychiatry, 51,* 8–19.

Kropotkin, P. (1939). *Mutual aid.* Harmondsworth, UK: Penguin.

Labao, L. (1996). A sociology of the periphery versus a peripheral sociology: Rural sociology and the dimension of space. *Rural Sociology, 61,* 77–102.

Lee, A. S., & Bowles, G. K. (1974). *Policy implications of the movement of blacks out of the rural south.* Washington, DC: Economic Research Service, National Science Foundation.

Lewin-Epstein, N. (1991). Determinants of regular source of health care in black, Mexican, Puerto Rican, and non-Hispanic white populations. *Medical Care, 29*(6), 543–557.

Li, P. S., & MacLean, B. D. (1989). Changes in the rural elderly population and their effects on the small town economy: The case of Saskatchewan 1971–1986. *Rural Sociology, 54,* 213–226.

Libertoff, K. (1980). Natural helping networks in rural youth and family services. *Journal of Rural Community Psychology, 1*(1), 4–17.

Lichter, D. T. (1989). Race, unemployment hardship, and inequality in the American nonmetropolitan south. *American Sociological Review, 54,* 436–446.

Litwak, E., & Meyer, H. J. (1966). A balance theory of coordination between bureaucratic organizations and community primary groups. *Administrative Science Quarterly, 2*(1), 31–58.

Mansfield, P., Preston, D., & Crawford, C. (1988). Rural–urban differences in women's well-being. *Health Care for Women International, 9,* 289–304.

Mazer, M. (1976). *People and predicaments: Of life and distress on Martha's Vineyard.* Cambridge, MA: Harvard University Press.

Melton, G. B. (1983). Ruralness as a psychological construct. In A. W. Childs & G. B. Melton (Eds.), *Rural psychology.* New York: Plenum.

Melton, G. B., & Hargrove, D. S. (1987). Perceptions of urban and rural communities. *Journal of Rural Community Psychology, 8,* 3–13.

Mermelstein, J., & Sundet, P. (1988). Factors influencing the decision to innovate: The future of community responsive programming. *Journal of Rural Community Psychology, 9,* 61–75.

Miller, M. K., Farmer, F. L., & Clarke, L. L. (1994). Rural populations and their health. In J. E. Beaulieu & D. E. Berry (Eds.), *Rural health services: A management persepective.* Ann Arbor, MN: Alpha Press/Health Administration Press.

Morlock, L. L. (1989). Recognition and treatment of mental health problems in the general health sector. In C. A. Taube, D. Mechanic, & A. A. Hohmann (Eds.), *The future of mental health services research* (pp. 39–61). Rockville, MD: National Institute of Mental Health.

Murray, J. D. (1990). Professional survival and success in the rural community. *The Clinical Psychologist, 10,* 16–21.

Murray, J. D., & Keller, P. A. (1991). Psychology and rural America: Current status and future directions. *American Psychologist, 46,* 220–231.

Murray, J. D., & Kupinsky, S. (1982). In P. A. Keller & J. D. Murray (Eds.), *Handbook of rural community mental health* (pp. 62–73). New York: Human Sciences Press.

Murray, M., & Dolomount, M. (1995). *Accidents in the inshore.* Report submitted to the Occupational Health and Safety Branch, Department of Employment and Labour Relations, Government of Newfoundland and Labrador.

Naples, N. A. (1994). Contradictions in agrarian ideology: Restructuring gender, race-ethnicity, and class. *Rural Sociology, 59,* 150–165.

Narrow, W., Regier, D., Rae, D., et al. (1993). Use of services by persons with mental and addictive disorders. *Archives of General Psychiatry, 50,* 95–107.

National Association for Rural Mental Health (1993). *Where we stand: Health care reform, rural mental health.* Washington, DC: Authors.

National Farmers' Union (1989). *Statement on the subject of the foreclosure of farm land in the prairie region.* Saskatoon, Canada: Authors.

Neff, J. A. (1983). Urbanicity and depression reconsidered. *Journal of Nervous and Mental Disease, 171,* 546–552.

Olson, K. R., & Schellenberg, R. P. (1986). Farm stressors. *American Journal of Community Psychology, 14,* 555–569.

Ortega, S. T., Johnson, D. R., Beeson, P. G., & Craft, B. J. (1994). The farm crisis and mental health: A longitudinal study of the 1980s. *Rural Sociology, 59,* 598–619.

Pargament, K., Falgout, K., Ensing, D. S., Reilly, B., et al. (1991). The Congregation Development Program: Data-based consultation with churches and synagogues. *Professional Psychology Research and Practice, 22*(5), 393–404.

Preston, J., Brown, F. W., & Hartley, B. (1992). Using telemedicine to improve health care in distant areas. *Hospital and Community Psychiatry, 43,* 25–32.

Redick, R. W., Witkin, J. J., Atay, J. E., et al. (1992). Specialty mental health system characteristics. In Center for Mental Health Services and National Institute of Mental Health, R. W. Manderscheid & M. A. Sonnenschein (Eds.), *Mental health, United States.* DHHS Pub. No. (SMA) 92-1942. Washington, DC: Supt. of Docs., US Government Printing Office.

Regier, D. A., Goldberg, I. D., & Taube, C. A. (1978). The *de facto* US mental health services system: A public health perspective. *Archives of General Psychiatry, 35,* 685–693.

Rich, S. (1994). Study: Half of US adults have had mental illness. *Washington Post,* January 14, p. 2.

Robert Wood Johnson Foundation (1987). *Access to health care in the United States: Results of a 1986 Survey,* No. 2. Princeton, NJ: Authors.

Robins, L. N., & Regier, D. A. (1991). *Psychiatric disorders in America: The epidemiologic catchment area study.* New York: Free Press.

Rosemann, M. R., & Delworth, U. (1990). Clinical and community perspectives on the farm crisis. *The Clinical Psychologist, 10,* 10–16.

Rosenblatt, P. C., & Keller, L. O. (1983). Economic vulnerability and economic stress in farm couples. *Family Relations, 32,* 567–573.

Rowland, D., & Lyons, B. (1989). Triple jeopardy: Rural, poor, and uninsured. *Health Services Research, 23*(6).

Sanderson, G. (1974). The sweatshop legacy: still with us in 1974. *The Labour Gazette, 74,* 400–417.

Scheidt, R. J. (1985). The mental health of the aged in rural environments. In R. T. Coward & G. R. Lee (Eds.), *The elderly in rural society.* New York: Springer.

Scheidt, R. J., & Windle, P. G. (1982). Well-being profiles of small town elderly in differing rural contexts. *Community Mental Health Journal, 18,* 257–267.

Short, J. (1991). *Imagined country.* London: Routledge.

Sladen, B. J., & Mozdzierz, G. J. (1989). Distribution of psychologists in underserved areas: Changes over time, 1970–1981. *Professional Psychology, 20,* 244–247.

Snipp, C. M. (1996). Understanding race and ethnicity in rural America. *Rural Sociology, 61,* 125–142.

Schroeder, E. H., Fliegel, F. L., VanEs, J. C. (1985). Measurement of the lifestyle dimensions of farming for small-scale farmers. *Rural Sociology, 50,* 305–322.

Spitzer, R. L., Williams, J. B. W., Kroenke, K., Linzer, M., de Gruy, F. V., Hahn, S. R., Brody, D., Johnson, I. G.

(1994). Utility of a new procedure for diagnosing mental disorders in primary care: The PRIME-MD 100 study. *Journal of American Medical Association, 272,* 1749.

Srole, L. (1972). Urbanization and mental health: A reformulation. *Psychiatric Quarterly, 44,* 449–461.

Statistics Canada (1993). *1991 Census of Canada: profile of urban and rural areas, Part A: Canada, Provinces and Territories.* Ottawa: Industry, Science and Technology Canada.

Statistics Canada (1996). *Trends and highlights of Canadian agriculture and its people (Cat. 96-303E).* Ottawa: Industry, Science and Technology Canada.

Sundberg, N. D. (1986). Prevention and promotion—mental health in rural and small town settings. *Journal of Rural Community Psychology, 7*(2), 3–6.

Susser, E., Schanzer, B., Varma, V. K., & Gittelman, M. (1996). Topics for our times: Can we learn from the acre of persons with mental illness in developing countries? *American Journal of Public Health, 86,* 926–927.

Swanson, L., & Butler, M. (1987). Human resource base of rural economies. In Department of Agriculture, Economic Research service. *Rural economic development in the 1980s: preparing for the future.* Washington, DC: US Government Printing Service.

Task Force on Incomes and Adjustment in the Atlantic Fishery (1993). *Charting a new course: Towards the fishery of the future.* Cat. No. Fs 23–243/1993. Ottawa, Canada: Minister of Supply and Services.

Tolbert, C. M., & Lyson, T. A. (1992). Earnings inequality in the nonmetropolitan United States: 1967–1990. *Rural Sociology, 57,* 494–511.

Trainor, J., Pope, B., & Pomeroy, E. (1997). Critical challenges for Canadian mental health policy. *Canadian Review of Social Policy/Revue Canadienne de Politique Sociale, 39,* 55–64.

Turner, J. C., & TenHoor, W. J. (1978). The NIMH community support program: Pilot approach to a needed social reform. *Schizophrenia Bulletin, 4,* 319–348.

US Congress, Office of Technology Assessment (1990). *Health care in rural America* (OTA-H-434). Washington, DC: Government Printing Office.

US Department of Agriculture (1985). The current financial conditions of farmers and farm lenders. *Economic Research Service, Agriculture Information Bulletin, No. 490.* Washington, DC: Author.

Wagenfeld, M. O., & Wagenfeld, J. K. (1981). Values, culture, and the delivery of mental health services in rural areas. In M. O. Wagenfeld (Ed.), *Perspectives on rural mental health* (New Directions for Mental Health Services Series, No. 9). San Francisco: Jossey-Bass.

Wagenfeld, M. O., Goldsmith, H. F., Stiles D., et al. (1988). Inpatient mental health services in metropolitan and non-metropolitan counties. *Journal of Rural Community Psychology, 9*(2), 13–28.

Walker, L. S., & Walker, J. L. (1987). Stressors and symptoms predictive of distress in farmers. *Family Relations, 36,* 374–378.

Weber, S. (1990). Mental health and rural aging. *The Rural Elderly Networker, 2*(2), 1–5.

Wilkinson, R. (1996). *Unhealthy societies: The Afflictions of inequality.* London: Routledge.

Zahner, G. E. P., Jacobs, J. H., Freeman, D. H., & Trainor, K. F. (1993). Rural–urban child psychopathology in a northeastern US state: 1986–1989. *Journal of the American Academy of Child and Adolescent Psychiatry, 32,* 378–387.

Zelman, M. R. (1995). Telemedicine, POTS and PANS technology and rural health care in Texas. *Texas Journal of Rural Health, 14*(2), 1–4.

10.12 Objective Personality Assessment: Computer-based Minnesota Multiphasic Personality Inventory-2 Interpretation in International Clinical Settings

JAMES N. BUTCHER
University of Minnesota, Minneapolis, MN, USA
ELLEN BERAH
Monash Medical Centre, Clayton, Vic, Australia
BJORN ELLERTSEN
University of Bergen, Norway
PATRICIA MIACH
Monash Medical Centre, Clayton, Vic, Australia
JEEYOUNG LIM
Samsung Group, Jeongdun-Maul, Sungnam-City, South Korea
ELAHE NEZAMI
USC/IPR, Los Angeles, CA, USA
PAOLO PANCHERI
5a Cattedra di Clinica Psichiatrica, Rome, Italy
JAN DERKSEN
University of Nijmegen, The Netherlands
and

MOSHE ALMAGOR
University of Haifa, Israel

10.12.1 INTRODUCTION 278
10.12.1.1 Cultural Factors in Mental Health Assessment 279
10.12.1.2 Application of Psychological Tests Across Cultural Boundaries 279
10.12.1.3 Development of Automated Interpretive Strategies for Objective Personality Tests 280
10.12.2 EVALUATION OF COMPUTER-BASED MMPI-2 REPORTS IN INTERNATIONAL CONTEXTS: RESULTS FROM AUSTRALIA, FRANCE, NORWAY, AND THE USA 280
10.12.2.1 The Research Protocol 280
10.12.2.2 General Testing Procedures 280
10.12.2.3 Clinical Rating Procedures 281
10.12.2.4 The Test Sites 281
10.12.2.4.1 Australian clinical sample 281
10.12.2.4.2 French clinical sample 281
10.12.2.4.3 Norwegian clinical sample 282
10.12.2.4.4 US clinical sample 282
10.12.2.5 Results of the Studies 282
10.12.2.5.1 Validity considerations 282
10.12.2.5.2 Symptomatic pattern 283
10.12.2.5.3 Interpersonal relations 283
10.12.2.5.4 Diagnostic considerations 288
10.12.2.5.5 Treatment considerations 288
10.12.2.5.6 Overall accuracy 289
10.12.2.6 Discussion of Overall Accuracy 289
10.12.2.7 Limitations of this Research 290
10.12.3 CASES 290
10.12.3.1 Nijmegen, The Netherlands: The Case of Susan 290
10.12.3.1.1 The Minnesota Report on Susan 292
10.12.3.1.2 Comment 294
10.12.3.1.3 DSM-IV classification 294
10.12.3.1.4 Treatment 294
10.12.3.2 Rome, Italy: The Case of Mario P. 294
10.12.3.2.1 The Minnesota Report on Mario P. 295
10.12.3.2.2 Comment 298
10.12.3.2.3 Treatment 298
10.12.3.3 Iran, United States: The Case of Ms. B. 298
10.12.3.3.1 The Minnesota Report on Ms. B. 300
10.12.3.3.2 Diagnostic impression 302
10.12.3.3.3 Treatment 302
10.12.3.4 Seoul, Korea: The Case of Kim 302
10.12.3.4.1 Family history 303
10.12.3.4.2 Behavioral observations 303
10.12.3.4.3 Symptomatic behavior 303
10.12.3.4.4 The Minnesota Report on Kim 303
10.12.3.4.5 Diagnosis 306
10.12.3.5 Haifa, Israel: The Case of Yuri Z. 306
10.12.3.5.1 The Minnesota Report on Yuri Z. 307
10.12.3.5.2 Treatment 310
10.12.3.6 Cross-national Generality of Psychopathology: What We Have Learned from the Cases 310
10.12.4 FUTURE DIRECTIONS 310
10.12.5 SUMMARY 311
10.12.6 REFERENCES 311

10.12.1 INTRODUCTION

The use of psychological testing in clinical assessment situations has been expanding from its origins within Europe and the USA to numerous other countries around the world. The rapidly increasing use of Western-derived clinical tests results from several factors including: the expansion of available mental health services in many countries since the mid-1980s, the growth in the number of assessment-trained psychologists in other countries, an increased recognition that psychological assessment can provide valuable information in mental health contacts, and as a result of increased professional communication through international congresses. Many psychologists have become aware of the effectiveness of psychological tests in countries like the USA and have adapted these procedures for use in their own countries.

Can psychological assessment and clinical diagnostic procedures developed in one language and culture be readily adapted and applied in another? Do stimuli employed in objective personality tests, such as the items in the most widely used clinical measure, the Minnesota Multiphasic Personality Inventory (MMPI-2), transcend the gulf of language and culture and apply effectively in different cultural contexts? Do psychological tests that are translated into other languages require special test development methods? Can norms from one culture be "transplanted" to another? These questions have been addressed extensively in the cross-cultural testing literature and are briefly summarized below (Butcher, 1996; Kazarian & Evans, in press; Lonner & Berry, 1986).

10.12.1.1 Cultural Factors in Mental Health Assessment

Although language and customs, as reflected in familial and social practices, vary between countries, there are also many common features. Psychological disorders appear to be generally comparable across different cultures and, although there have reportedly been some "exotic" or culture-specific conditions (Yap, 1951), many commonalities exist with similar symptoms and common manifestations across diverse groups. For example, schizophrenia appears to occur in all known cultures and societies through history (where records permit comparison) although the symptoms may vary somewhat and rates may differ (Butcher, Narikiyo, & Bemis-Vitousek, 1992).

Commonalities across cultures in mental disorder have allowed for the development of the international classification of mental disorders (World Health Organization, 1992) referred to as ICD-10 (the most up-to-date version). The ICD-10 diagnostic system parallels the diagnostic system developed in the USA, the *Diagnostic and statistical manual of mental disorders* (4th ed.; *DSM-IV*), which is also in wide use in several other countries. Many psychiatrists employ *DSM-IV* instead of ICD-10. The very existence of a common language for describing these psychological disorders and their apparent relevance around the world suggests that the elements of mental disorders, that is, the symptoms, features, established course, and so forth, are relatively stable if not universal across cultures.

10.12.1.2 Application of Psychological Tests Across Cultural Boundaries

The use of clinical personality tests across cultures has a history dating back to the 1920s. There were several early studies devoted to exploring the generalizability of psychoanalytic test constructs across cultures by administering the Rorschach test to individuals from different cultural backgrounds and comparing their responses to those of Westerners (see Adcock & Richie, 1958). The use of the Rorschach in anthropological research was, however, replete with problems and this approach had pretty well run its course by the late 1950s. Lindzey (1958) discussed the problems of the projective method in cross-cultural research and summarized these difficulties.

The overall use of psychological tests across cultural boundaries was, however, not decreased by any means. In fact, the practical use of translated and adapted personality tests was only beginning. The 1950s and 1960s witnessed a number of projects to translate and adapt objective personality instruments across cultures, not for the purposes of anthropological study, but for the emphatically practical aim of making clinical decisions in a more objective manner than was currently available.

One of the most widely employed and internationally adapted personality inventories used in clinical assessment has been the MMPI, which was subjected to a number of early translations, including Italian (Reda, (1948), Japanese (Abe, (1955), and German (Sundberg, 1956). In the years that followed, over 150 translations of the MMPI were developed and the inventory came to be widely employed in over 46 countries (see Cheung & Song, 1989; Cheung, Song, & Butcher, 1991; Cheung, Zhao, & Wu, 1992; Kim, 1988; Risetti, Himmel, Maltes, & Gonzalez, 1989; Strassberg, Clutton, & Korboot, 1991; Strassberg, Tilley, Bristone, & Tian, 1992; Zou & Zhao, 1992). In 1976, Butcher and Pancheri published an international handbook on using the MMPI across cultures that described model translation projects, provided substantial psychometric equivalence data, and illustrated clinical validation efforts in international contexts.

With the redevelopment of the MMPI and the publication of MMPI-2 in 1989, a new wave of test translation projects was initiated. A number of recent studies have explored the use of the MMPI-2 in other cultures and a broad collection of clinical researchers, from several different countries, have described their translation and adaptation research efforts and highlighted clinical usage in a compendium of papers (Butcher, 1996). This international handbook includes three chapters on test translation methods and recommended procedures for evaluating translation equivalence. Central to using the MMPI-2 in cross-national settings is the establishment of sound translation of the items into the target language and culture and demonstration of test equivalence, but the core of the volume is 56 contributions from psychologists and psychiatrists from around the world.

10.12.1.3 Development of Automated Interpretive Strategies for Objective Personality Tests

Progress in civilization has often involved the evolution of labor-saving techniques or inventions that free human beings from routine or laborious tasks. Assessment psychologists have long been interested in the use of automated or mechanical methods for assisting in the routine and often onerous task of scoring and processing responses to psychological tests. Mechanical test-scoring devices have been employed in psychology since the 1940s, and in the 1950s, mainframe computers were first used to process large batches of test protocols quickly and accurately.

Paralleling this technical effort to develop more efficient data-processing techniques came conceptual progress into methods of making clinical decisions more objective. With several publications by Meehl (1954, 1956) and his followers (Gilberstadt & Duker, 1965; Halbower, 1955; Marks, Seeman, & Haller, 1974) the automatic interpretation of one test, the MMPI by mechanically combining established test correlates, received broad attention. The MMPI, being an instrument that was developed according to an empirical scale-validation approach, had acquired by 1960 a very substantial research base supporting the interpretation of scales and combinations of scales (profile codetypes). In the 1960s psychologists began to experiment with the actual interpretation of psychological test scores using computers. The first of these approaches, an MMPI computer interpretation program developed at the Mayo Clinic in Rochester, Minnesota, demonstrated the effectiveness and accuracy of objective interpretation with the computer (Rome et al., 1962). Computer test interpretation programs have evolved substantially over the succeeding decades and have become an accepted strategy for interpreting psychological tests in the USA (American Psychological Association [APA] 1986; Butcher, 1987; Eyde, Kowal, & Fishburne, 1991; Fowler, 1969; Ziskin, 1981).

With computerized test interpretation programs for the MMPI/MMPI-2 becoming widely available for clinical use in the USA (Butcher, 1995), psychologists in other countries also began to explore computer-derived personality assessments (Fowler & Butcher, 1987; Gillet et al., 1996; Pancheri & Biondi, 1987; Pancheri, Sirigatti, & Biondi, 1996). An early study of the utility of a computer-based report (Roche Psychiatric Service Institute) on the original version of the MMPI in Australia produced promising results (Fowler, 1978). More recently, research has confirmed that computer-based MMPI-2 reports provided accurate and useful information when applied with Australian psychiatric patients (Berah et al., 1993; Berah, Miach, & Butcher, 1995).

In this chapter we explore the objective use of psychological tests in cross-cultural settings in two ways. We describe an empirical evaluation of the generalizability and accuracy of computer-derived MMPI-2 reports describing the symptoms and behavior of patients in four countries—Australia, France, Norway, and the USA. This discussion will be followed by several case examples from other countries.

10.12.2 EVALUATION OF COMPUTER-BASED MMPI-2 REPORTS IN INTERNATIONAL CONTEXTS: RESULTS FROM AUSTRALIA, FRANCE, NORWAY, AND THE USA

10.12.2.1 The Research Protocol

The research design for this project was similar in all four countries. Clinicians who were evaluating their patients administered the MMPI-2 to each client using a booklet format. The appropriate language version was used in each country. A broad range of clients were tested in a variety of settings: inpatient, outpatient, court-ordered, neuropsychological, and gender reassignment assessment. No effort was made to obtain homogeneous research groups but to simply evaluate any available patients being assessed in an ongoing process, so that the psychologist would have sufficient information about the patient to be able to rate the adequacy of the computer-based report.

10.12.2.2 General Testing Procedures

The MMPI-2 testing was conducted by psychologists who were seeing the patients for clinical evaluations or psychological treatment.

Following an explanation to the patient of the reasons for the assessment, testing took place in individual sessions using standardized test instructions. Softcover booklet format was used, with patients completing the test at a private table under supervision in the psychologist's office. The MMPI-2 was usually administered in one long session but, depending on the needs of the particular patients, it was occasionally administered in two or three shorter sessions. When there was any doubt about a patient's reading ability, a test to help determine reading comprehension was usually first administered. The completed MMPI-2 answer sheets and relevant demographic information were sent to James Butcher in Minneapolis, Minnesota for scoring and data processing. The item responses of each patient were key-entered or optically scanned to a computer disk and scored by personal computer. The Minnesota Report, a computer-based narrative interpretation program (Butcher, 1993), was generated by microcomputer. (It is important to note that the American norms were used in all of the countries to compare the cases.) The computer report printout was sent back to the test location for the next phase of the project: the ratings of report adequacy.

10.12.2.3 Clinical Rating Procedures

Ratings were completed by the same psychologists who were seeing the patients in the context of psychological evaluation or therapy at the time of the study. The Rating Form required the following information on each report: Patient Information (gender, age, education, marital status, clinical setting, and clinician's hours spent with the patient); Rater Information (degree, profession, years of experience); Report Rating (the validity considerations, symptomatic pattern, interpersonal relations, diagnostic considerations, and treatment considerations sections of each report were each rated as providing "insufficient," "some," "adequate," "more than adequate" or "extensive" information. Raters also indicated the percentage of statements in the report they considered to be accurate descriptions of the patient, using the categories of less than 20, 20–39, 40–59, 60–79, or 80–100%). Finally, open-ended questions were asked for symptomatic and diagnostic information, and for ways in which the report could have been improved.

The raters participating in the evaluation program were clinicians who were seeing the patient in the professional diagnostic context or for therapy at the time of the study. Each rater was given a copy of the computer report output and asked to evaluate the adequacy and accuracy of the narrative report in describing the behavior and symptoms of the client and to complete the Rating Form.

10.12.2.4 The Test Sites

10.12.2.4.1 Australian clinical sample

The Australian patients were clients in the Adult Psychiatry Service of Monash Medical Centre, Melbourne, Australia, a 700-bed general hospital affiliated to Monash University. The Adult Psychiatry Service provides treatment for patients from its local and regional communities, from other services of the hospital and, for its specialist programs, from the wider community. It has a 36-bed inpatient unit which admits informal and involuntary patients, several community clinics, a mobile community treatment team, and extensive consultation–liaison services to the divisions of obstetrics and gynecology, medicine and surgery. Specialist inpatient and outpatient assessment and treatment programs are provided through the eating disorders and the mothers and babies clinics. A specialist gender dysphoria clinic, the only such clinic in Australia, accepts referrals from the whole country for assessment of gender dysphoria and admission to the program for sexual reassignment surgery. The Adult Psychiatry Service works on a multidisciplinary basis with a staff of 11 clinical psychologists.

Patients were referred to the Adult Psychology Section by their consultant psychiatrist for psychological assessment to help in differential diagnosis and treatment planning in the early stage of admission or outpatient presentation. The two exceptions to this were patients from the eating disorders and the gender dysphoria clinics who are routinely administered the MMPI-2. The patients ($N = 167$) included 67 men and 100 women with an age range of 16 to 75; 94 were being evaluated as outpatients, 69 were inpatients, and four were from other settings. The clinical diagnoses of the patients covered a broad range of problems. The amount of time the clinician-raters spent with patients is an important consideration in the study. Nearly all patients (97%) had been seen by the psychologist for three or more hours and half had been seen for five or more hours. The amount of contact between raters and patients, in all likelihood, provided raters with sufficient knowledge of the patients' problems and symptoms to be an appropriate source of external information about the patients.

10.12.2.4.2 French clinical sample

The French clinical study involved testing 100 patients (54 inpatients and 46 outpatients) in two specialized psychiatric departments in Paris: the Clinique des Maladies Mentales et de l'Encéphale (CMMD), which is part of the Hôpital Sainte Anne, and the Hôpital International de l'Université de Paris (see Gillet et al., 1996). The test was administered using the French language MMPI-2 booklet. A total of 22 mental health specialists, all of them psychiatrists, evaluated the 100 computerized reports. Their clinical experience varied as follows: 33 reports were analyzed by five practitioners with 4–6 years of experience in psychiatry, 33 reports were analyzed by 10 practitioners with 7–10 years' experience, and 33 reports were analyzed by 10 practitioners with more than 10 years' experience. The time spent with each patient varied from two to six hours (or more). Demographic data for the population studied include the following: four patients were between the ages of 18 and 19 years; 71 patients were between the ages of 20 and 40 years; 22 patients were between the age of 41 and 60 years; and three patients were older than 60 years. The number of years of schooling for the sample was as follows: 21 patients had less than 10 years; 26 patients had between 10 and 12 years; 23 patients had between 13 and 14 years; and 30 patients had 15 years or more.

10.12.2.4.3 Norwegian clinical sample

The Norwegian study involved 99 valid patient protocols. Among these, 60 patients were in psychotherapy (outpatients), eight were psychiatric inpatients, 10 were medical (neurology) inpatients, nine were substance abuse inpatients and 10 were in counseling settings. A total of 10 clinicians with PhDs, situated in different counties covering all parts of Norway, evaluated the protocols. Nine of these clinicians evaluated 10 protocols whereas one evaluated nine protocols. Among the clinicians, nine had more than four years of clinical experience whereas one had three years. The time spent with the patients being evaluated was more than six hours in 75% of the cases, five or six hours in 10%, three or four hours in 8% and two hours in 7%. The clinical sample consisted of 56 males (mean age 35, range 10–62) and 43 females (mean age 35, range 18–58).

10.12.2.4.4 US clinical sample

The patients included in the US study were 263 people who were being evaluated using the Minnesota Report in the Minnesota Psychotherapy Project (Butcher, 1996). A total of 44 psychotherapists from several states and from diverse clinical settings (including independent practice, mental health clinics, hospital practice, court setting, and so forth) were asked to rate their patients on a number of personality and symptom variables. They were also provided with a copy of the Minnesota Report derived from the patient's responses to the MMPI-2. The therapists had a broad range of backgrounds, although the majority had PhDs (46%) or PsyDs (20.5%) or MAs (23%) in psychology; 50% of these were trained in clinical and 23% in counseling psychology, and 2.3% were trained in social work. Finally, 63.6% considered themselves cognitive-behavioral; 11.4% were behavioral; 31.8% were psychodynamic; and 6.5% were client-centered. The mean number of years the therapists had been conducting a practice in psychotherapy was 11.5 years.

10.12.2.5 Results of the Studies

The results of the four projects will be reported for each section of the Minnesota Report. For example, under the heading "Validity considerations" the findings from each country will be presented. In addition, the results from the four countries will be shown in graphic form to give the reader a visual comparison of the summaries of the clinicians' ratings in each country.

10.12.2.5.1 Validity considerations

(i) Australia

Valid, interpretable profiles were produced by 95% of the sample ($N = 59$). While the validity considerations sections of the computerized reports were provided and rated for all patients, the remaining sections of the reports were unavailable for patients with invalid profiles. Over 90% of the computer-based reports were rated as providing adequate-to-extensive information in their appraisal of patients' approach to the testing (Figure 1); fewer than 5% of the reports were considered to have insufficient information about protocol validity.

(ii) France

Of the 100 MMPI-2s completed, only 17 profiles were found to be invalid and were not included in the study. Of these 17 invalid MMPI-2 inventories, 11 of the patients had been diagnosed as psychotic, three had personality disorders, one was suffering from an eating disorder, another from an affective disorder, and the last from a mixed disorder (Axis I and Axis II on the *DSM-III-R*). The raters evaluated 83 profiles, from 25 males and 58 females. Only 13.3% of the cases were thought to provide insufficient information; 61.3% were viewed as adequate, more than adequate, or as providing extensive information (Gillet et al., 1996; Figure 2).

(iii) Norway

All of the Norwegian sample produced valid, interpretable profiles. Clinicians evaluating the assessment adequacy of the Minnesota Report validity in appraising their patient's approach to the testing rated the reports as providing adequate-to-extensive information (82.8%). Only 4% of the reports rated were considered to have insufficient information about the patient (Figure 3).

(iv) USA

Fewer than 1% of the reports were considered to provide insufficient information, and 92% of the reports were considered to provide adequate (50.2%), more than adequate (27.2%), or extensive information (14.8%) (Figure 4).

10.12.2.5.2 Symptomatic pattern

(i) Australia

The description of patients' symptom patterns provided by the computerized reports was considered by the clinician-raters to provide adequate, more than adequate, or extensive information in 77% of cases (Figure 1). Information was rated as insufficient in 8% of reports.

(ii) France

According to Gillet et al. (1996), the clinicians' opinions of the quality of descriptions in the symptomatic pattern section were favorable in 59% of the cases, if the categories "extensive," "adequate," and "more than adequate" and more than sufficient information were pooled (Figure 2).

(iii) Norway

In terms of symptom pattern exhibited by the patients in the Norwegian study, 78.9% of the Minnesota Reports were rated as providing adequate, more than adequate, or extensive information, and only 2.0% of the narrative reports were considered insufficient by the judges (Figure 3).

(iv) USA

Only 1.5% of the Minnesota Reports were considered to provide insufficient information on the symptomatic pattern section of the report. On the other hand, 89.5% of the Minnesota Reports were rated as having adequate (39.7%), more than adequate (31%) or extensive information (17.6%) (Figure 4).

These findings are consistent with the results of other studies of the generalizability of MMPI-2 descriptors to patients in other countries (Butcher & Pancheri, 1976; Manos, 1984; Savasir & Erol, 1990) and provide support for the general clinical impression reported by the raters that the MMPI-2 correlates can be confidently applied to patients in other countries.

10.12.2.5.3 Interpersonal relations

(i) Australia

Of the reports, 78% were considered to provide adequate, more than adequate, or extensive information on patients' interpersonal relationships, while 6% were rated as providing insufficient information (Figure 1).

(ii) France

The clinicians' ratings of the interpersonal relations section of the 83 patient reports were favorable in 70% of the cases when the categories "extensive," "adequate," and "more than adequate" information were pooled (Gillet et al. 1996) (Figure 2).

(iii) Norway

The MMPI-2 report also provided substantial information about the interpersonal behavior of clients, according to practitioner ratings. Only 4% of the reports were judged to provide insufficient information on this variable; however, 76% of the narrative reports were considered adequate, more than adequate, or extensive in information provided (Figure 3) and 21% of the raters stated that the reports provided some information.

(iv) USA

In the US sample, only 2.7% of the patient reports were considered to provide insufficient information (Figure 4) while 85.4% were considered to be adequate (39.2%), more than adequate (29.2%), or to provide extensive information (16.9%).

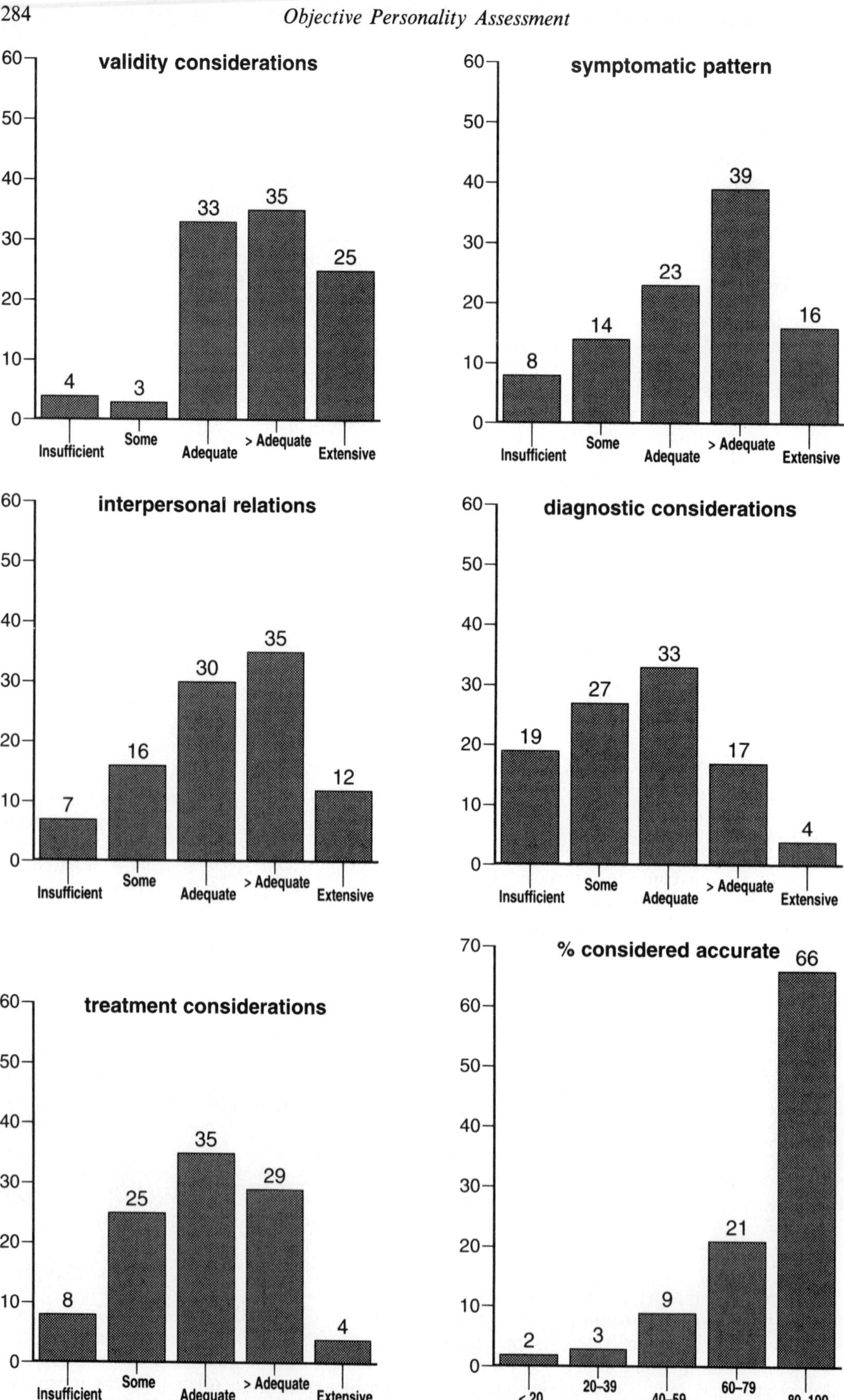

Figure 1 Evaluations of computer-based MMPI-2 reports: Australian sample.

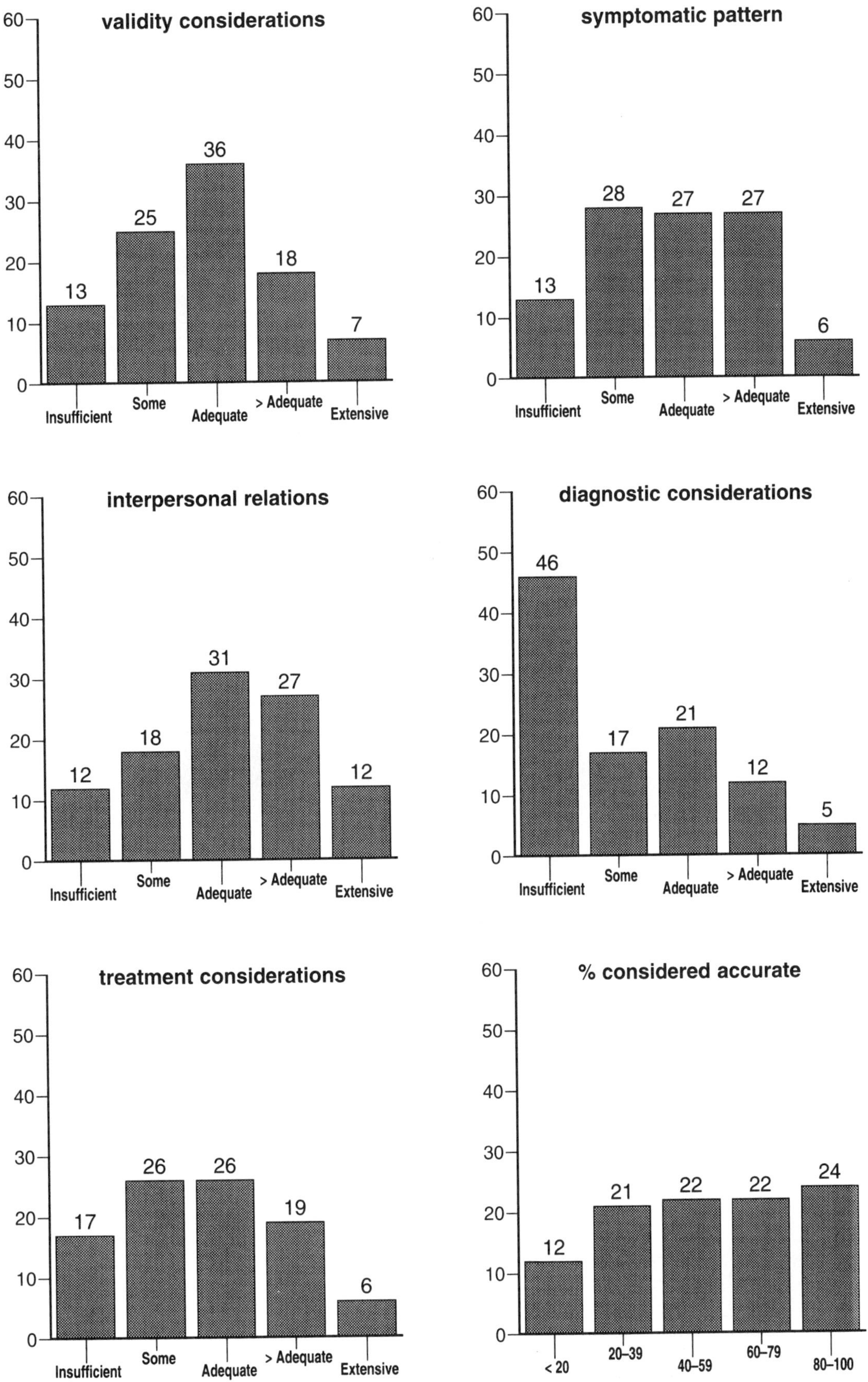

Figure 2 Evaluations of computer-based MMPI-2 reports: French sample.

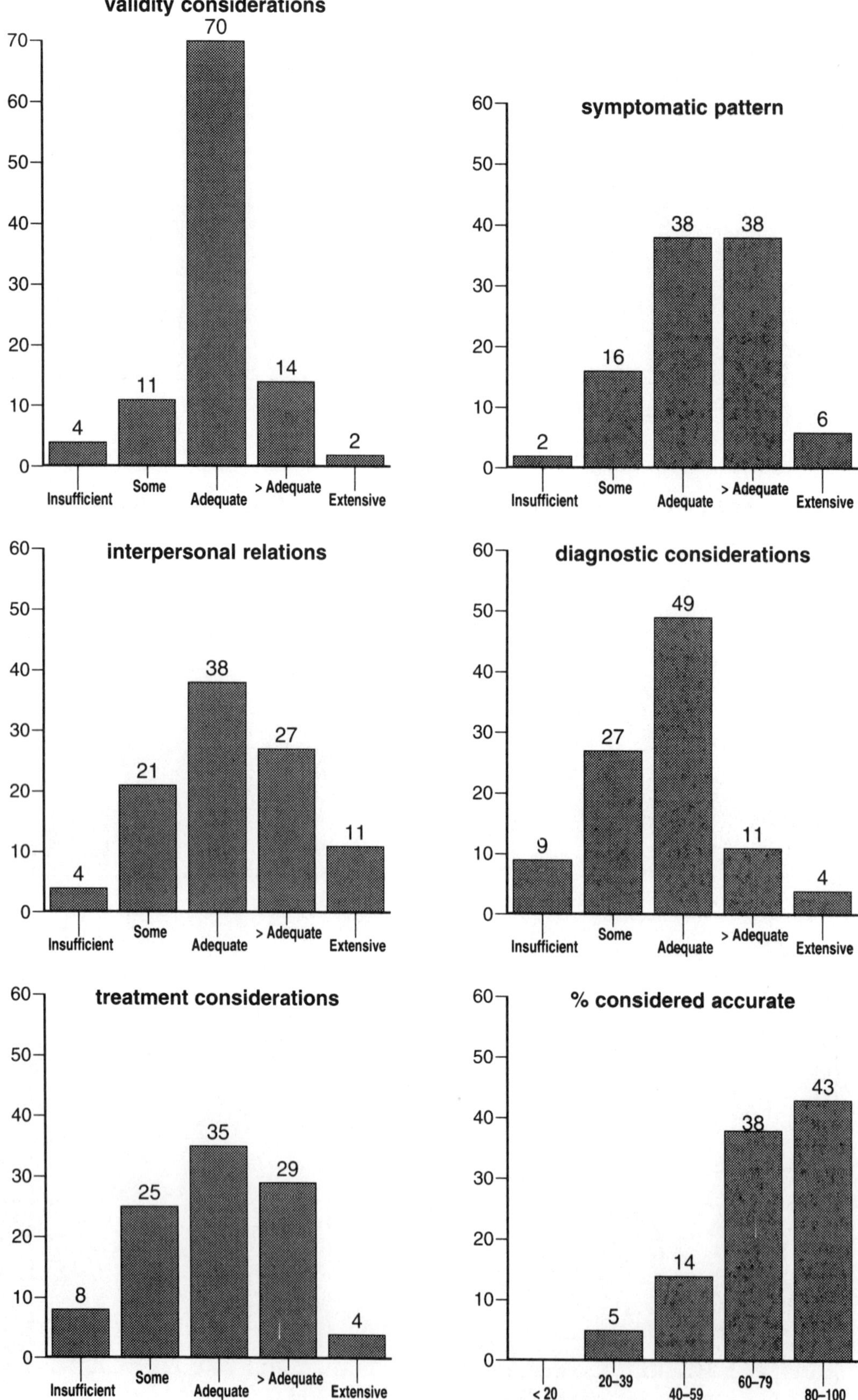

Figure 3 Evaluations of computer-based MMPI-2 reports: Norwegian sample.

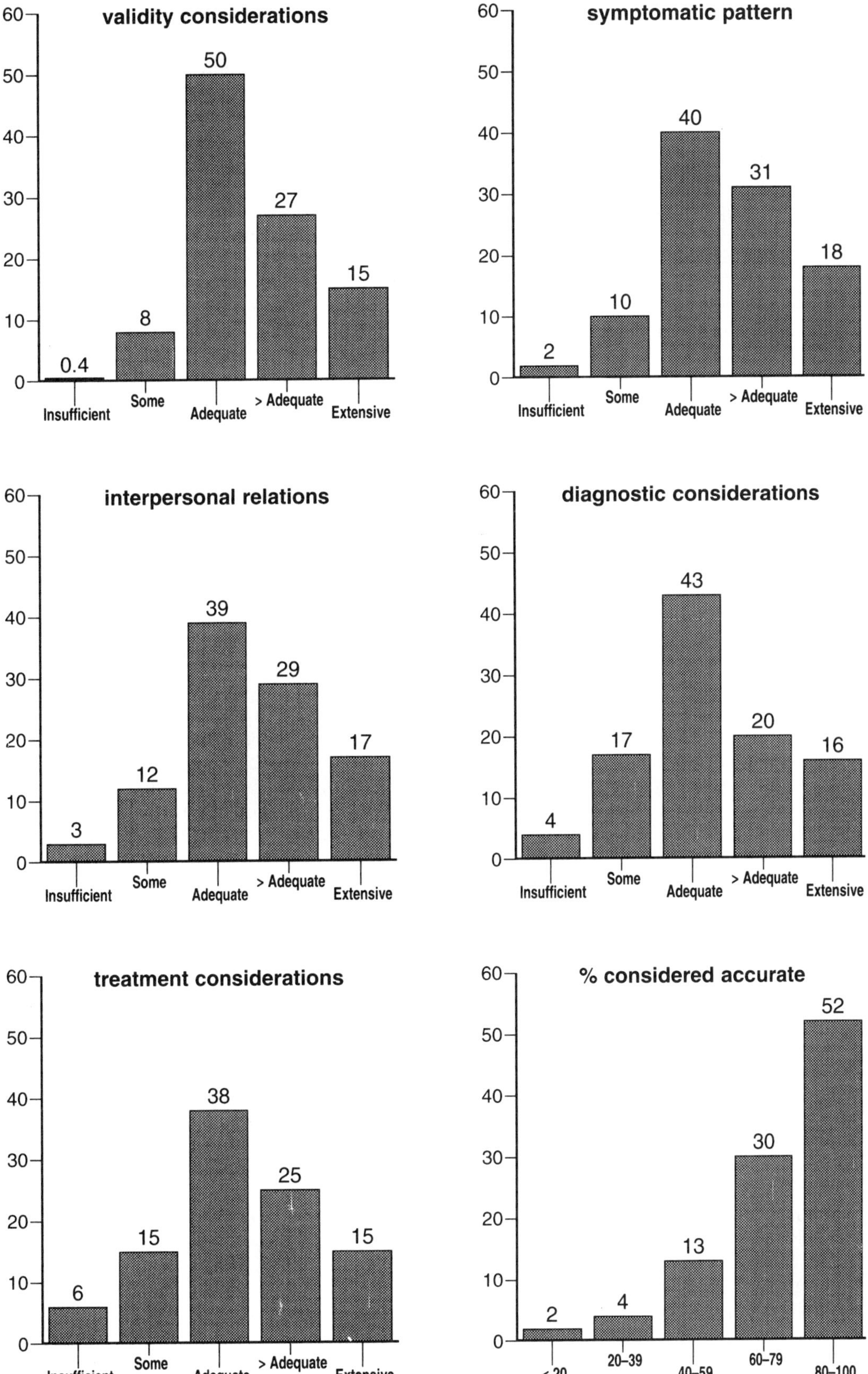

Figure 4 Evaluations of computer-based MMPI-2 reports: US sample.

Thus reports from all four countries were thought to provide substantial information about, the interpersonal behavior, of patients.

10.12.2.5.4 Diagnostic considerations

(i) Australia

This section of the computerized reports was considered by raters to be less adequate than the above sections. Even here, however, over half (55%) of the narrative reports were rated as containing at least adequate information on diagnosis, while 18% were thought to provide insufficient information (Figure 1).

(ii) France

According to Gillet et al. (1996), the clinicians' views of the diagnostic considerations section of the 83 reports were favorable in 38% of the cases when the categories "extensive," "adequate," and "more than adequate" and more than sufficient information were pooled (Figure 2). This finding of less relevant diagnostic information in the ratings probably results from the reliance upon a different diagnostic system in France than in the USA.

(iii) Norway

The diagnostic sections of the computer report were considered by raters to be slightly less comprehensive than other sections of the report (Figure 3). Nevertheless, over 60% of the narrative reports were judged to contain adequate, more than adequate, or extensive diagnostic information about their clients. Only 8.1% of the protocols were considered to provide insufficient information in the area of clinical diagnosis.

(iv) USA

The clinicians from the USA considered 4.2% of the reports as providing insufficient diagnostic information. However, 78.9% of the reports were thought to contain adequate (42.5%), more than adequate (20.1%) or extensive information (16.2%) (Figure 4).

Several factors may account for the variation in results in the rating of clinical diagnosis:

(i) Clinical diagnosis is a task that usually requires more information than is available through an objective self-report questionnaire. Practitioners usually need to obtain a detailed history and behavioral descriptions in order to obtain a clinical diagnosis.

(ii) The diagnostic procedures differed somewhat between countries with *DSM-IV* being used in the USA, Australia, and Norway and the ICD-10 in France.

(iii) Another difference to consider in the cross-cultural comparisons is that in France the ratings were completed by psychiatrists and in the other countries psychologists were the predominant professional performing the ratings.

The above differences aside, the majority of raters in all four countries considered the reports to have adequate, more than adequate, or extensive information available for the task of clinical diagnosis from the MMPI-2.

10.12.2.5.5 Treatment considerations

(i) Australia

As with diagnosis, 8% of reports were deemed to provide insufficient information regarding treatment planning. Two-thirds (68%) were considered to provide adequate, more than adequate or extensive information (Figure 1).

(ii) France

The clinicians' ratings of the treatment considerations section of the 83 reports were favorable in 51% of the cases when the categories "extensive," "adequate," and "more than adequate" and more than sufficient information were pooled (Figure 2). The lower agreement found between the clinicians and the computer-based reports, compared with other countries, probably resulted from different treatment orientations and practices in France.

(iii) Norway

Similarly to diagnosis, the treatment considerations section of the Minnesota Report was rated as providing valuable information on clients. Over 64% of the patient MMPI-2 reports were considered to provide adequate-to-extensive information for treatment planning (Figure 3). Only 8% of the patient reports were thought to provide insufficient information for treatment planning. The relatively high rate of positive evaluations of the treatment considerations section of the report suggests that treatment planning in Norway and the USA may rely upon similar types of clinical information, much of which is available through the MMPI-2.

(iv) USA

The therapists rating the American patients considered the reports to be helpful in treatment planning. Only 5.8% considered the reports to provide insufficient information while 78.9%

thought the reports provided adequate (38.1%), more than adequate (25.4%), or extensive information (15.4%).

In general, as with clinical diagnosis, therapists like to have extensive information for treatment planning, and test-based information is not the sole source of data required. However, in all four countries the majority of the clinicians rated the reports as adequate or better in their evaluations.

10.12.2.5.6 Overall accuracy

(i) Australia

In addition to rating the adequacy of the information provided in the narrative reports, raters estimated the percentage of statements they considered to be accurate descriptions of their patients (Figure 1). Two-thirds (66%) of reports on Australian patients were rated as having 80–100% accuracy, while 87% were rated as having more than 60% accuracy. Only 2% were rated as having less than 20% accuracy. As noted above, a large number of patients in the study (46) were gender-dysphoric clients undergoing evaluation for possible gender reassignment surgery. It might be hypothesized that their inclusion may have lowered the overall adequacy and accuracy ratings because of possible attempts by these patients to present themselves in an overly positive manner. This was not the case. There was no significant difference between the ratings of gender-dysphoric and other patients on the symptomatic pattern ($t(157) = -0.53$), the interpersonal relations ($t(157) = 1.14$), the diagnostic considerations ($t(156) = 1.79$) and the treatment considerations ($t(154) = 0.46$) sections of the reports. With respect to the two other ratings, the reports on the gender-dysphoric patients were actually rated more positively than those of the other patients (validity considerations, $t(165) = -2.84$, $p < 0.01$; overall accuracy, t for unequal variances $(110) = -2.15$, $p < 0.05$).

(ii) France

The overall relevance of the report to French clinicians was considered high when categories D and E were met and 67.5% if we consider categories C, D, and E.

(iii) Norway

In addition to the question of the thoroughness of the information provided by the narratives, the study addressed the accuracy of computer-generated personality descriptions at describing patients. As shown in Figure 3, the clinician ratings provided strong support for using the MMPI-2 in clinical assessment in Norway. Overall, 92.9% of the reports were rated in the adequate, more than adequate, or extensive information categories . Over 42.4% of the patient reports were classified as being in the 80–100% range of accuracy and 38.4% were judged to possess between 60 and 79% accuracy. Interestingly, only 5% of the narrative reports were considered low in accuracy. Overall, the accuracy at describing clinical behavior and symptoms in a diverse clinical sample was considered to be high.

(iv) USA

In terms of overall accuracy, the American clinicians rated the reports as being quite accurate. Only 1.9% were considered to be inaccurate while 81.6% were considered to be over 60% accurate with over half (52.1%) being rated in the highest category (Figure 4).

10.12.2.6 Discussion of Overall Accuracy

The results of these studies are generally consistent with the impressions of practitioners using computerized reports in other countries, namely that the automated MMPI-2 interpretations generalize well to other locations and that the descriptors about patients apply well in countries other than the USA. These results support the conclusion that computer-based reports of the MMPI-2 can be a valuable aid in clinical assessment in other countries.

Although the overall acceptability of the Minnesota Report in France was good, the ratings provided by French mental health professionals on the utility of the reports were somewhat lower than those obtained by their counterparts in Australia (Berah et al., 1993), Norway, and the USA. These findings might reflect differences in clinical practice in different countries, different attitudes toward computers, or genuine personality differences between the French and patients from other countries. Further research will be needed to clarify this finding.

Relatively few of the practitioners in any of the four countries studied found the reports inappropriate or inaccurate. The sections for which most of the reports were considered as valuable and to provide in-depth information were the validity considerations, the symptomatic patterns, and the interpersonal relations sections and, to a lesser degree, the diagnostic and the treatment considerations sections.

10.12.2.7 Limitations of this Research

The limited information that was available on each patient from the clinicians prevented a fuller exploration of the descriptive power of the MMPI-2. As with any field study conducted in service-oriented clinics or hospitals, the amount of extra work that can be asked of clinicians is limited. While more extensive ratings would have been desirable, the cooperation of clinicians may well have been sacrificed if the task was seen as overly burdensome.

Second, it should be kept in mind that the study employed US norms for the computer-derived interpretations. It is possible that the use of country-specific norms, particularly in France, might have added a higher degree of accuracy to the reports and greater congruence in the ratings. French norms are now available for the MMPI-2. Future research might be developed with country-specific norms, which gives different results.

Finally, we were not able, in this study, to provide an estimate of inter-rater reliability. It would have been desirable to have had a number of cases rated by at least two clinicians, so that interrater reliability could have been assessed. It is not known whether use of a different group of clinicians in completing the ratings would have produced similar results leading to the present conclusions. Future research might be directed toward obtaining a broader base of information.

Because of these limitations the results of this study can be taken as only suggestive; it is felt, nonetheless, that the data indicate that the computer-based Minnesota Report can be a useful aid to assessment in other countries to aid clinicians in interpreting MMPI-2 results. Even with these limitations, the results of the present study were very informative and encouraging with respect to the use of computer-based MMPI-2 reports in other countries. Overall, the reports were considered to provide a considerable amount of valuable information.

We turn next to illustrations of the use of the computer-based report in clinical settings from several other countries. We provide clinical case material from several other countries along with the MMPI-2 computerized report to provide the reader with an example of the kinds of information available in the report and its relevance for other countries.

10.12.3 CASES

10.12.3.1 Nijmegen, The Netherlands: The Case of Susan

In our outpatient psychological practice, patients with many types of complaints are treated, usually on a short-term basis. The mental health facility is integrated into the primary health care system and wide-ranging referrals are accepted. Patients usually come in for an assessment initially and treatment starts immediately. The mean number of sessions (including assessment) is 16 and the complaints include: anxiety disorders, mood disorders, somatoform disorders, adjustment disorders, family problems, and personality disorders. A group of eight clinical psychologists and two psychological assistants staff the facility. The practice is in a rural area near two cities, Nijmegen and Arnhem, and we work closely with 15 family practice physicians for referrals. Every week about six new patients are referred to the clinic. The treatment orientation is eclectic: we do behavioral therapy, rational emotive therapy, family therapy, short-term psychodynamic therapy, group therapy, and assertiveness training.

The case described here is a 23-year-old woman named Susan who came to our practice on referral from her physician. Initial impressions suggested an attractive young woman, a bit shy, but pleasant in the interpersonal sphere. Her chief complaints were obsessive ruminations and a feeling of uncertainty about what she wants to do and can do with her life. She expressed feelings of depression and feelings of inferiority which she connects with her negative self-image. A direct reason for asking for help could be found in her suicidal thoughts that made her panic and feel ashamed. She sleeps well, has no weight loss, and does not complain about fatigue. Besides the symptoms mentioned earlier, she has had an eating disorder and problems with the acceptance of her body which she considers too fat. Although she is slightly overweight at present, this is only to a minor degree.

The initial assessment did not result in a diagnosis of major depressive disorder and psychotic symptoms were lacking. She does show elements of dysthymia. Her personality organization, in terms of Kernberg criteria, is neurotic.

Susan was born in the eastern part of The Netherlands and about six months before she came for treatment she had moved to a rural area near the practice. This happened at the time that her boyfriend took over his father's business, a nursery for growing roses. Susan and her boyfriend started living together at that time and she began working in this family enterprise. Her chief complaints started when, in summer, they had a lot of work to do and lots of responsibilities; amongst other things she had to manage the staff. Especially when alone, she began to feel unhappy. She responded by trying to avoid these feelings as long as possible and then by binge eating. In addition she often had crying spells. She connected the binge eating with a need to pamper herself.

During the assessment phase her boyfriend was invited for a session and he explained that Susan had chosen to live with him but was not eager to work in the rose nursery. He himself has worked in this business since he was 16 years old and is aware that the work is demanding and stressful at times. He would like her to enjoy this work because he wants to share everything with her. The possibility of Susan choosing a different career path is felt by him as a threat.

Susan is the youngest in a family with two daughters. She reports some positive early childhood memories. She experienced her family as very well attached; many family activities were shared together. Her mother was, like Susan, rather introverted and also reports problems with accepting her body and difficulties with bodily contact. Susan never felt secure with her mother. She described her father as a warm and sensitive but somewhat prudish man. He works for an insurance company and was always busy and stayed away from home a lot. Her father used to call Susan the "sunshine in the house." Her mother was responsible for the children's upbringing and stopped working as a typist when she gave birth to the oldest. It is striking that, in the interview, when Susan made a critical comment about her parents she immediately covered it up with a positive one.

During puberty she had difficulties with the development of female secondary sex characteristics because she really wanted to be a boy. There were some precursors for this in the family because her father often treated her as though she was a boy. She was always quiet, introverted, well-adapted, nice, and sensitive but she never knew what to do with her life. Her sister, who is two years older, however, always manifested herself in a rebellious manner, refused to accept societal and family norms and values, and was extreme in her dress, for example she often dressed as a "punk." Her parents devoted a lot of attention to her older sister. Susan solved her problems herself and asked little from her parents.

During her adolescence, her mother criticized her quite often because of her weight and her tendency to be introverted. This criticism resulted in her developing some irritation and resentment. Her mother thought she was stubborn if Susan did not do what she asked her to do. During adolescence Susan always felt inferior to her sister and thought that her mother preferred her sister. When she was 16 she had a brief relationship with her first boyfriend; however, she refused sexual intercourse with him. Prior to this relationship her interest in boys was purely nonsexual and she was afraid that boys might take advantage of her. The relationship with her first boyfriend ended because he felt that she could not express any feelings toward him. She always wanted to be strong and tough but the end of the relationship was difficult for her and she never really worked through her feelings about it.

After school Susan attended a lower professional school (training as a hospital orderly) but stopped in the second year of her education because she was unable to maintain good interpersonal contact with co-workers and the patients. During this period, when she was 19 years old, she met her present boyfriend who is also her employer. She characterizes him as also being introverted. After he had known her for one-and-a-half months he asked her whether she would like to work in the rose nursery and she accepted his offer. She believed that their relationship would have ended if she had rejected his offer. Their relationship started very cautiously and the sexual part of it has been problematic from the beginning.

From the earliest days of their relationship she did not stand up for her needs and wants. In addition, because she was afraid of losing him, she demanded perfection from herself. She feels that she must be steady and very adaptable to the demands of her boyfriend's family. She also feels quite stressed over the great demands placed on her by the work in the nursery. Part of her difficulty comes from the dual relationship she has with her employer. Her boyfriend is also her boss and he often makes administrative decisions about, for instance, when she can have a day off. She often becomes emotional when this complex relationship is discussed and she tends to protect him immediately indicating that "he is so patient with her."

Her binge eating usually becomes manifest when she is alone. She often stores candies and then eats them all at once. She feels ashamed over her behavior and was especially guilty when her boyfriend discovered her problem. One major cause of hurt for her was when her boyfriend once told her that he was not primarily attracted to her body but rather her character. She told her mother, her best friend and her sister about her problems and was surprised that they were so supportive of her.

During the evaluation and also later in therapy she impressed the psychologist as playing the role of a victim in the mixed relationships in which she was involved with her boyfriend and her own family. Everyone seems to know what was best for her and she had borne these burdens but was feeling unhappy now. She seemed unable to assert herself with others and to express her own anger in a productive way.

The following psychological tests were administered as well as the MMPI-2. On the Wechsler Adult Intelligence Scale she had a verbal IQ of 103 and a performance IQ of 104 which is in agreement with her school education. On the "house–tree–person" test she drew a person with only a head. It seems as if her thinking is most important and she likes to control things rationally. Several other projective techniques were administered, such as the Thematic Apperception Test and the Sentence Completion Test. Themes that appeared prominent were her sexual problems, hidden aggression in relation to her parents, idealized pictures of other people, not knowing where to go in life, and a lack of perseverance.

10.12.3.1.1 The Minnesota Report on Susan

On the MMPI-2 she produced the profiles shown in Figures 5 and 6 and the following interpretation.

Profile validity

This is a valid MMPI profile. The client's attitude toward the testing was appropriate. She responded to the items in a frank and open manner, freely admitting to some psychological problems, which are described below.

Symptomatic patterns

The behavioral correlates included in the narrative report are likely to provide a good description of the client's current personality functioning. The clinical scale prototype used in the report, which incorporates correlates of D and Pt, is based on scores with high profile definition. The client's MMPI-2 clinical profile reflects much psychological distress at this time. She has major problems with anxiety and depression. She tends to be high-strung and insecure, and she may also be having somatic problems. She is probably experiencing loss of sleep and appetite and a slowness in personal tempo.

Individuals with this profile often have high standards and a strong need to achieve, but they feel that they fall short of their expectations and then blame themselves harshly. This client feels quite insecure and pessimistic about the future.

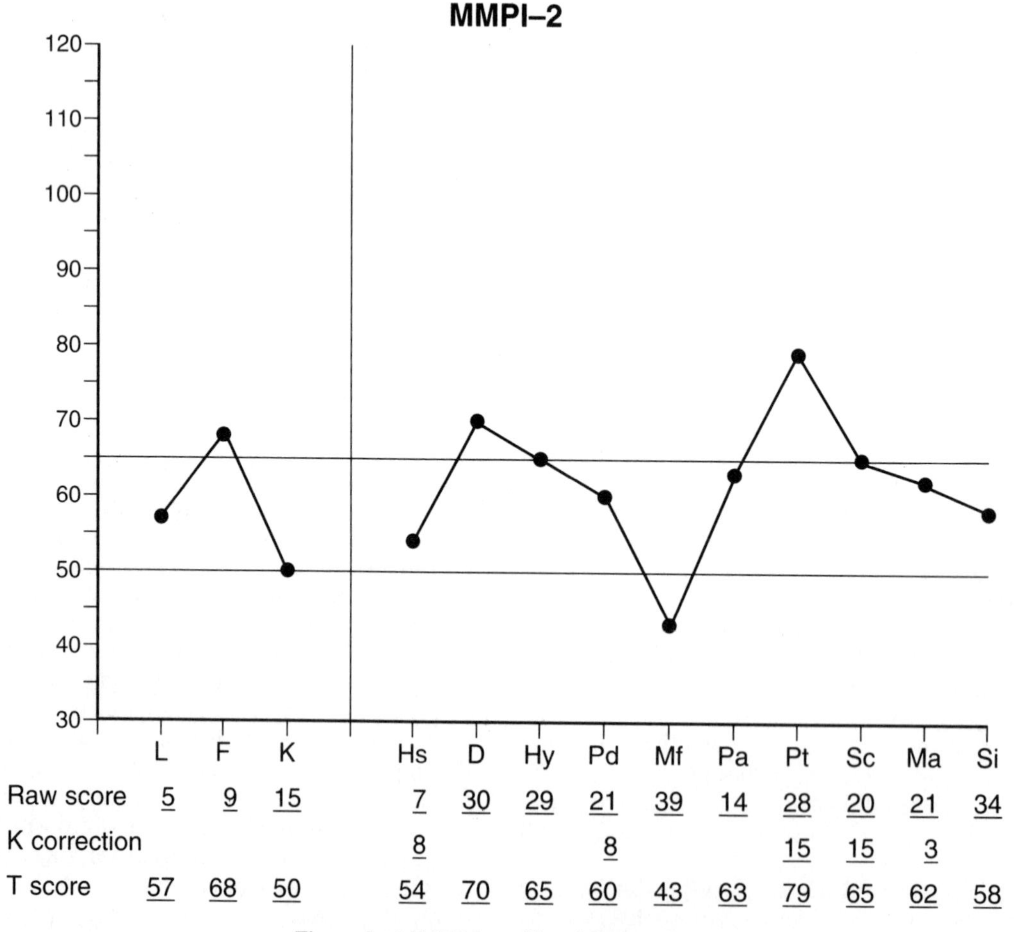

Figure 5 MMPI-2 profile of Susan (1).

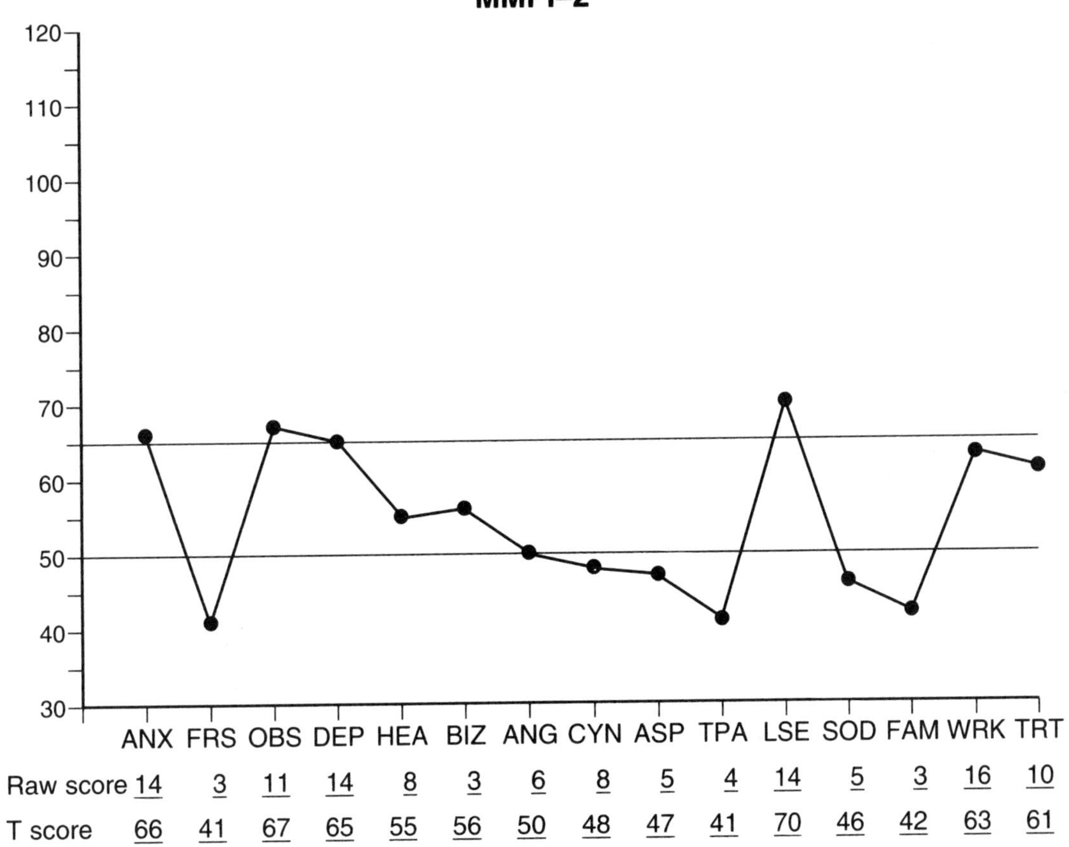

Figure 6 MMPI-2 profile of Susan (2).

She also feels quite inferior, has little self-confidence, and does not feel capable of solving her problems.

In addition, the following description is suggested by the content of the client's item responses. She has endorsed a number of items suggesting that she is experiencing low morale and a depressed mood. She reports a preoccupation with feeling guilty and unworthy. She feels that she deserves to be punished for wrongs she has committed. She feels regretful and unhappy about life, and she seems plagued by anxiety and worry about the future. She feels hopelessness at times and feels that she is a condemned person. She views her physical health as failing and reports numerous somatic concerns. She feels that life is no longer worthwhile and that she is losing control of her thought processes.

According to her response content, there is a strong possibility that she has seriously contemplated suicide. The client's recent thinking is likely to be characterized by obsessiveness and indecision.

Profile frequency

It is usually valuable in MMPI-2 clinical profile interpretation to consider the relative frequency of a given profile pattern in various settings. The client's MMPI-2 high-point clinical scale score (Pt) is found in only 5.1% of the MMPI-2 normative sample of women. Only 2.1% of the women have Pt as the peak score at or above a T score of 65, and less than 1% have well-defined Pt spikes. This high MMPI-2 profile configuration (2–7/7–2) is very rare in samples of normals, occurring in 1.2% of the MMPI-2 normative sample of women.

Her MMPI-2 high-point score is relatively uncommon in various outpatient settings. In the National Computer Systems (NCS) outpatient sample, only 6.4% of the females have this MMPI-2 high-point clinical scale score (Pt). Moreover, only 5.3% of the female outpatients have the Pt scale spike at or above a T score of 65, and only 2.1% have well-defined Pt peaks. Her elevated MMPI-2 profile configuration (2–7/7–2) is found in 7.4% of the women in the NCS outpatient sample. This is the second most frequent elevated two-point code in the sample.

Profile stability

The relative scale elevation of the highest scales in her clinical profile reflects high profile definition. If she is retested at a later date, the peak scores on this test are likely to retain their relative salience in her retest profile pattern. Her high-point score on Pt is likely to remain stable over time. Short-term test–retest studies have shown a correlation of 0.88 for this high-point score.

Interpersonal relations

She appears to be quite passive and dependent in interpersonal relationships and does not speak up for herself even when others take advantage of her. She avoids confrontation and seeks nurturance from others, often at the price of her own independence. She forms deep emotional attachments and tends to be quite vulnerable to being hurt. She also tends to blame herself for interpersonal problems. Individuals with this profile are often experiencing psychological distress in response to stressful events. The intense feelings may diminish over time or with treatment.

Diagnostic considerations

Individuals with this profile tend to be considered neurotic and receive diagnoses such as Dysthymic Disorder or Anxiety Disorder. They may also receive Axis II diagnosis of Dependent or Compulsive Personality Disorder

Treatment considerations

Individuals with this MMPI-2 pattern are usually feeling a great deal of discomfort and tend to want help for their psychological problems. The client's self-esteem is low and she tends to blame herself too much for her difficulties. Although she worries a great deal about her problems, she seems to have little energy left over for action to resolve them.

Symptomatic relief for her depression may be provided by antidepressant medication. Psychotherapy, particularly cognitive behavioral treatment, may also be beneficial.

The passive, unassertive personality style that seems to underlie this disorder might be a focus of behavior change. Individuals with these problems may learn to deal with others more effectively through assertiveness training.

If psychological treatment is being considered, it may be profitable for the therapist to explore the client's treatment motivation early in therapy. The item content she endorsed includes some feelings and attitudes that could be unproductive in psychological treatment and in implementing change.

Note. This MMPI-2 interpretation can serve as a useful source of hypotheses about clients. This report is based on objectively derived scale indices and scale interpretations that have been developed in diverse groups of patients. The personality descriptions, inferences, recommendations contained herein need to be verified by other sources of clinical information because individual clients may not fully match the prototype. The information in this report should most appropriately be used by a trained, qualified test interpreter. The information contained in this report should be considered confidential.

10.12.3.1.2 Comment

Susan produced a valid profile. The higest scale is scale 7 (79), followed by scale 2 (70), and 3 (65). The profile is essentially a neurotic one; she seems to be controlling feelings by way of rationalizing and ruminating. Her subjective suffering is clearly present (scale 2). Scale 7 assesses abnormal fears, self-criticism, difficulties in concentration and guilt feelings. Further, the item content reflects a characterologic basis for a wide variety of psychasthenic symptoms. Anxiety is a persistent trait. This seems in agreement with her complaints and attitudes. On the content scales her highest scale score was on Low Self Esteem (70) and her second highest was Obsessions (67) and then Anxiety (66). Depression is 65 and Problems in Relation to Work 63.

10.12.3.1.3 DSM-IV classification

This was as follows:

Axis I: 313.82 Identity Problem

307.50 Eating Disorder Not Otherwise Specified

Axis II: 301.60 Traits of the Dependent and Obsessive-Compulsive Personality Disorder.

10.12.3.1.4 Treatment

Individual insight-oriented sessions were initiated with Susan to give her the opportunity to explore her needs and wishes in relation to her work, study, sexual behavior, and partner choice. Although her intelligence is only average, she is well motivated to work things out for herself. An attempt has been made to focus on her conflicts between dependency and autonomy. The aim is to facilitate the process of individualization and to provide her with the opportunity to discover her feelings of anger that she holds toward others close to her.

Treatment progress has thus far been effective. During the course of her treatment she has gradually discovered better her own needs and preferences. She has started to understand her ambivalent feelings towards her parents and also towards her boyfriend. At the present time in therapy she is exploring her fantasies of leaving him and starting a different life. Her characterologic basis for psychasthenic traits, indicated by the MMPI-2, has appeared very strong and difficult to influence so far.

10.12.3.2 Rome, Italy: The Case of Mario P.

Mr. P. is a 36-year-old male from a low socioeconomic background and educational level. At the age of 21 he married an 18-year-old woman and they now have two children aged 14 and six. He was referred to our outpatient psychiatry service by an otolaryngologist whom he consulted for a "lump in his throat" when his physician could find no organic basis to his symptoms. He has a family history of depression: his mother suffered from depression in the past and one of his three sisters is presently depressed. His wife, who recently left her job to dedicate herself to housekeeping, had suffered in the past from what seems to be somatic complaints of depression.

Until recently the patient was working as a manual laborer until 2.00 a.m. every night because he held two jobs. However, he had to give up one of his jobs three months ago, just prior his first visit to the clinic, because he developed nervousness, apathy, tension, and irritability. At this visit he reported poor sleep quality, reduced appetite, and excessive increase in cigarette smoking. He lacked a drive for living; he could not face life either at home or at work and saw no "way-out." He felt guilty about not being able to care for his children, he seemed discouraged and "switched-off." His impulse control is poor; he reported several acts of violence (having beaten his children). Fearing the consequences of his impulsive behavior and being afraid of his lack of control over his acts, he often leaves his home for hours, walking with no precise destination, seeking isolation to escape from difficulties. He was prescribed 1.5 mg/die oral desmethyldiazepam and took this medication for some time but had to reduce it to 0.5 mg/die due to the development of marked sedation that impaired his daytime performance.

During the interview, the patient spoke spontaneously, with a monotonous, low voice. Speech content and form were normal, however, and he expressed guilt, pessimism, and inadequacy. He showed no evidence of free-floating anxiety. His mood was markedly depressed and he frequently sighed aloud. He appeared to have good insight with respect to his psychopathological problems and was willing to accept treatment.

10.12.3.2.1 The Minnesota Report on Mario P.

The patient completed the MMPI-2 at the end of his first visit to the clinic producing the profiles shown in Figures 7 and 8 and the following narrative report.

Profile validity

The client responded to the MMPI-2 items in an unusual manner. He claimed an unrealistic amount of virtue while also endorsing a great number of psychological difficulties. This infrequent response pattern reflects some unconventional and possibly bizarre beliefs.

Careful evaluation of the individual's response attitudes should be undertaken to explain this unusual validity scale pattern. The following hypotheses might be explored. He may have consciously distorted the test responses to create a particular impression, or he may be generally unsophisticated. The resulting clinical pattern should be interpreted with caution.

The client's responses to items in the latter portion of the MMPI-2 were somewhat exaggerated in comparison to his responses to earlier items. There is some possibility that he became more careless in responding to these later items, thereby raising questions about that portion of the test. Although the standard validity and clinical scales are scored from items in the first two-thirds of the test, caution should be taken in interpreting the MMPI-2 Content Scales and supplementary scales, which include items found throughout the entire pool.

Symptomatic patterns

This report was developed using the D, Pt, and Sc scales as the prototype. A pattern of chronic psychological maladjustment characterizes individuals with this MMPI-2 clinical profile. The client is overwhelmed by anxiety, tension, and depression. He feels helpless and alone, inadequate and insecure, and he believes that life is hopeless and that nothing is working out right. He attempts to control his worries through intellectualization and unproductive self-analysis, but he has difficulty concentrating and making decisions. This is a rather chronic behavior pattern. Individuals with this profile typically live a disorganized and pervasively unhappy existence. They may have episodes of more intense and disturbed behavior resulting from an elevated stress level.

He is functioning at a lower level of efficiency. He tends to overreact to even minor stress, and he may show rapid behavioral deterioration. He also tends to blame himself for his problems. His lifestyle is chaotic and disorganized, and he has a history of poor work and achievement. He may be preoccupied with obscure religious ideas.

The client seems to have a rather limited range of cultural interests and tends to prefer stereotyped masculine activities to literary and artistic pursuits or introspective experiences. Interpersonally, he may be somewhat intolerant and insensitive.

Profile frequency

It is usually valuable in MMPI-2 clinical profile interpretation to consider the relative frequency of a given profile pattern in various settings. The client's MMPI-2 high-point clinical scale score (Pt) is found in only 4.9% of the MMPI-2 normative sample for men. Only 3.1% of the sample have Pt as the peak score at or above a T score of 65, and only 1.6% have well-defined Pt spikes. This

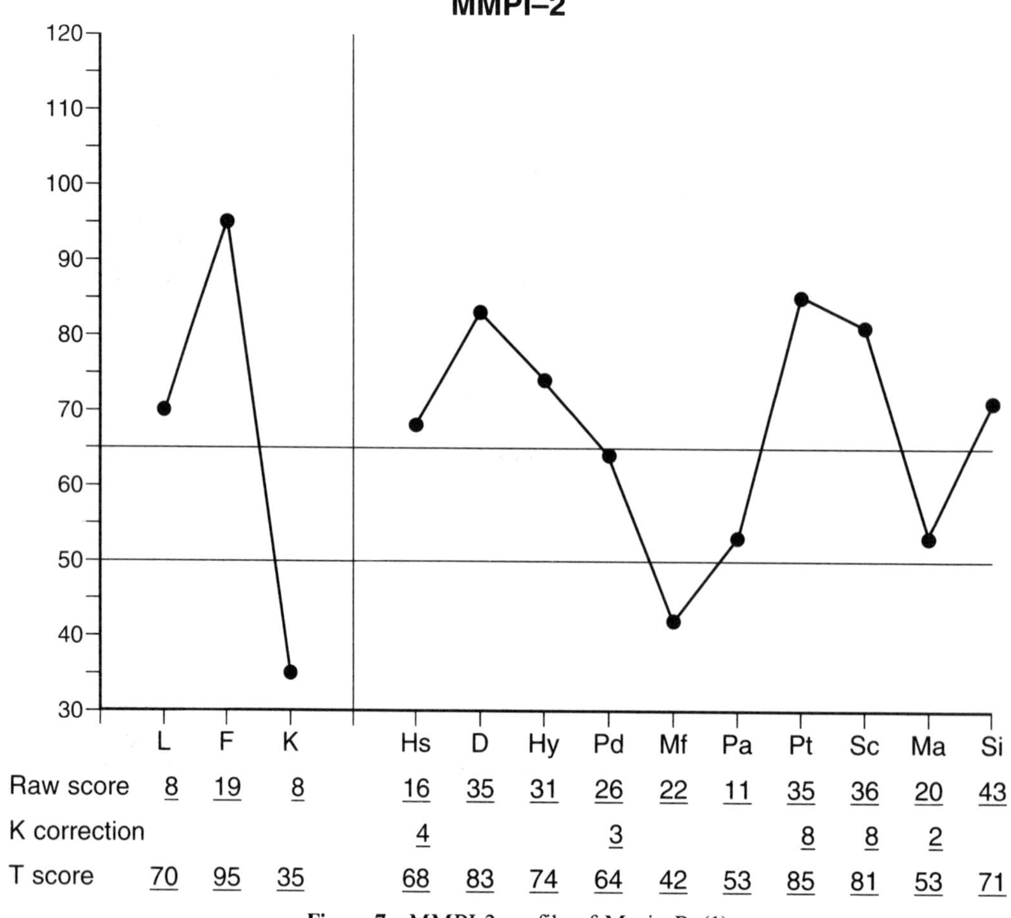

Figure 7 MMPI-2 profile of Mario P. (1).

elevated MMPI-2 profile configuration (2–7/7–2) is very rare in samples of normals, occurring in less than 1% of the MMPI-2 normative sample of men.

The relative frequency of this MMPI-2 high-point score is informative. In the NCS outpatient sample, 7.7% of the males have this MMPI-2 high-point clinical scale score (Pt). Moreover, 6.5% of the male outpatients have the Pt scale spike at or above a T score of 65, and 3.3% have well-defined Pt spike scores in that range. His elevated MMPI-2 profile configuration (2–7/7–2) is relatively common in outpatient men. It occurs in 4.8% of the men in the NCS outpatient sample. The 2–7 profile code is the second most frequent two-point code in outpatient men when both scales are at or above a T score of 65.

He scored relatively high on MAC-R, suggesting the possibility of a drug or alcohol abuse problem. The base rate data on his profile type among residents in alcohol and drug programs should also be evaluated. His MMPI-2 profile code, including D and Pt, is the second most frequent two-point code among men in alcohol- and drug-abusing populations. Over 13% of the men in substance-abuse programs have this pattern (McKenna & Butcher, 1987).

Profile stability

The relative scale elevation of the highest scales in his clinical profile reflects high profile definition. If he is retested at a later date, the peak scores on this test are likely to retain their relative salience in his retest profile pattern. His high-point score on Pt is likely to show high stability over time. Short-term test–retest studies have shown a correlation of 0.89 for this high-point score. Spiro, Butcher, Levenson, Aldwin, and Bosse (1993) reported a test–retest stability index of 0.65 in a large study of normals over a five-year test–retest period.

Interpersonal relations

Problematic personal relationships are also characteristic of such clients. He seems to lack basic social skills and is behaviorally withdrawn. He may relate to others ambivalently, never fully trusting or loving anyone. Many individuals with this profile never establish lasting, intimate relationships. His marital situation is likely to be unrewarding and impoverished. He seems to feel inadequate and insecure in his marriage.

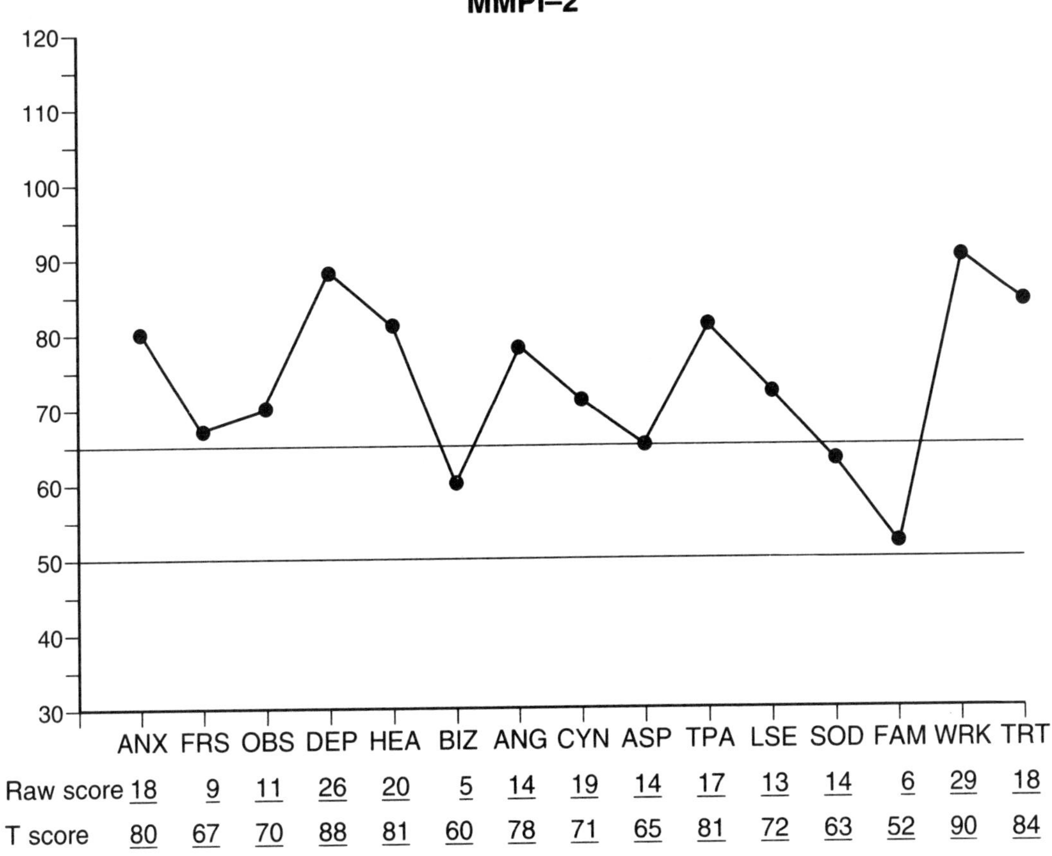

	ANX	FRS	OBS	DEP	HEA	BIZ	ANG	CYN	ASP	TPA	LSE	SOD	FAM	WRK	TRT
Raw score	18	9	11	26	20	5	14	19	14	17	13	14	6	29	18
T score	80	67	70	88	81	60	78	71	65	81	72	63	52	90	84

Figure 8 MMPI-2 profile of Mario P. (2).

He is a very introverted person who has difficulty meeting and interacting with other people. He is shy and emotionally distant. He tends to be very uneasy, rigid, and overcontrolled in social situations. His shyness is probably symptomatic of a broader pattern of social withdrawal. Personality characteristics related to social introversion tend to be stable over time. His generally reclusive behavior, introverted lifestyle, and tendency toward interpersonal avoidance may be prominent in any future test results.

His very high score on the Marital Distress Scale suggests that his marital situation is quite problematic.

Diagnostic considerations

Individuals with this profile have a severe psychological disorder and would probably be diagnosed as severely neurotic with an Anxiety Disorder or Dysthymic Disorder in a Schizoid Personality. The possibility of a more severe psychotic disorder, such as Schizophrenic Disorder, should also be considered, however.

His extremely high scores on the addiction proneness indicators suggest the possible development of an addictive disorder. Further evaluation of substance use or abuse problems is strongly recommended.

Treatment considerations

Individuals with this MMPI-2 clinical profile often receive psychotropic medications for their depressed mood or intense anxiety. Many individuals with this profile seek and require psychological treatment for their problems along with any medication that is given. Because many of their problems tend to be chronic, an intensive therapeutic effort might be required in order to bring about any significant change. Patients with this profile typically have many psychological and situational concerns; consequently, it is often difficult to maintain a focus in treatment.

He probably needs a great deal of emotional support at this time. His low self-esteem and feelings of inadequacy make it difficult for him to get energized toward therapeutic action. His expectation for positive change in therapy may be low. Instilling a positive, treatment-expectant attitude is important for him if treatment is to be successful.

Individuals with this profile tend to be over-ideational and given to unproductive rumination.

They tend not to do well in unstructured, insight-oriented therapy and may actually deteriorate in functioning if they are asked to be introspective. He might respond more to supportive treatment of a directive, goal-oriented type. Individuals with this profile present a clear suicide risk; precautions should be taken.

Note. This MMPI-2 interpretation can serve as a useful source of hypotheses about clients. This report is based on objectively derived scale indices and scale interpretations that have been developed in diverse groups of patients. The personality descriptions, inferences, recommendations contained herein need to be verified by other sources of clinical information because individual clients may not fully match the prototype. The information in this report should most appropriately be used by a trained, qualified test interpreter. The information contained in this report should be considered confidential.

10.12.3.2.2 Comment

Mario P. obtained high scores on the D scale, compatible with a depressive state, high scores on the Pt and Sc scales, compatible with the symptoms of irritability, anxiety, avoidance, and tension, and marginally high social introversion that can explain his pursuit of isolation. His scores on the Pd scale reflect his violent acts and impulsiveness. Higher than average scores on the Hs and Hy scales are consistent with the presence of the lump in the patient's throat (globus hystericus) and with the tendency to use bodily symptoms to resolve his conflicts. The mood axis is oriented towards depression. The presence of an 8–7–2 codetype reflects his pessimism, weakness and fatigue, lack of initiative, perception of loneliness, poor description of his own emotional state, self-blame, worthlessness, and impulsiveness. The personality profile, with the T scores of all neurotic scales being over 65, was compatible with the presence of a neurotic disorder, and the diagnosis was made of severe, single episode major depression.

10.12.3.2.3 Treatment

The patient was started on oral chlomipramine, 100 mg/die, titrated upwards. This drug is marketed in Europe as an antidepressant; it is also used for obsessive-compulsive disorder and other disorders of the obsessive-compulsive spectrum, including those where impulsive behavior predominates. The patient returned regularly every 2–4 weeks for his follow-up visits. At the second visit, the patient was switched to slow-release chlomipramine, 150 mg/die, titrated upwards to 187.5 mg/die. Sodium valproate, 1 mg/die, was added to control impulsiveness. He reported outbursts of aggression and impulsiveness, with mood swings during the day, but overall, he felt slightly better. By the third visit, one month after the beginning of drug treatment, the patient started to report better control of his impulses and satisfactory mood improvement. He further improved with time, returning to work after three months of therapy. By this time, the quality of sleep had improved and his appetite had increased, especially for carbohydrates. Impulsiveness and dysthymic mood were no longer reported.

He developed a fine tremor that subsided the next month. After four months of treatment, his mood was stabilized and the patient was more active. He returned to work but still felt the presence of a lump in his throat, although only occasionally. About this time he developed hypersomnia. He tried to suspend treatment for a week or so, but his symptoms worsened. He had his chlomipramine reduced to 112.5 mg/die and valproate to 500 mg. Improvement continued and after seven months the patient seems to have completely recovered and is maintained on the above drug combination.

10.12.3.3 Iran, United States: The Case of Ms. B.

The patient is a 30-year-old female Iranian, who is currently separated. She has an AA degree in fine arts and is currently unemployed. She was self-referred for therapy. Ms. B.'s initial complaints included a wide range of psychosomatic problems including headaches, dizziness, weakness, sore throat, pressure in the chest cavity, and upset stomach. She added that she felt sad, anxious, and angry and worried that she might lose her mind. Ms. B. indicated that no one understands or accepts her. This feeling generates a tremendously high level of stress, sadness, and anger. As a result of the lack of understanding, she feels lonely and tries to justify herself and goes through lengthy explanations to prove that she really is a good woman and worthy of love. This urge to prove her virtues is dated back to the time that her family found out about her sexual intimacy with an older man when she was 16 years old. The patient got herpes from this two-year relationship. Ms. B. considers herself a victim of rape in this relationship and believes that the trauma and the consequent problems continue to have an impact on her present life.

Ms. B. stated that her parents had a turbulent marriage. According to the patient her mother married her father because of coercion, not love.

She added that her mother was depressed when she was pregnant with the patient. During her childhood she witnessed family discord and conflicts with repeated discussions of divorce. According to the patient her father used to beat her mother. Consequently, the patient would stay home to provide some sort of protection for her mother. Her parents were separated for a couple of years but never got divorced. Her mother repeatedly told her that she did not get a divorce because of her and blamed the patient for her unhappiness.

The patient's emotional status has deteriorated following early separation after a short-lived marriage a couple of months before the present testing session. Ms. B. has been experiencing more problems, including depression and frustration, following her separation.

The patient denied a history of previous psychiatric problems, but later mentioned that she had received short-term counseling in the past. The patient has been diagnosed with herpes since the age of 16. No other medical problems are indicated. Ms. B. denies a history of substance abuse.

The patient is an Iranian and the oldest of three children. One of her younger brothers has been diagnosed with schizophrenia. The patient denied any history of other psychiatric problems in her family. She also denied any history of alcohol or substance abuse in her family. However, during therapy the presence of personality problems and antisocial characteristics among the family members was detected. As a child, she reported being emotionally abused. Her parents, especially her mother, blamed her for their unhappy marriage and she witnessed repeated family fights as she was growing up. Her mother repeatedly told her that she was an unwanted child.

The patient reported having sex with an older man at age 16. She remained intimate with this man for a couple of years. When her family found out about her relationship they severely chastised her and told her that she was not suitable for marriage any longer. She has always had difficulty in maintaining relationships with men, particularly when there was a hint that it might become serious. At age 29, the patient was married for a very short period of time. This

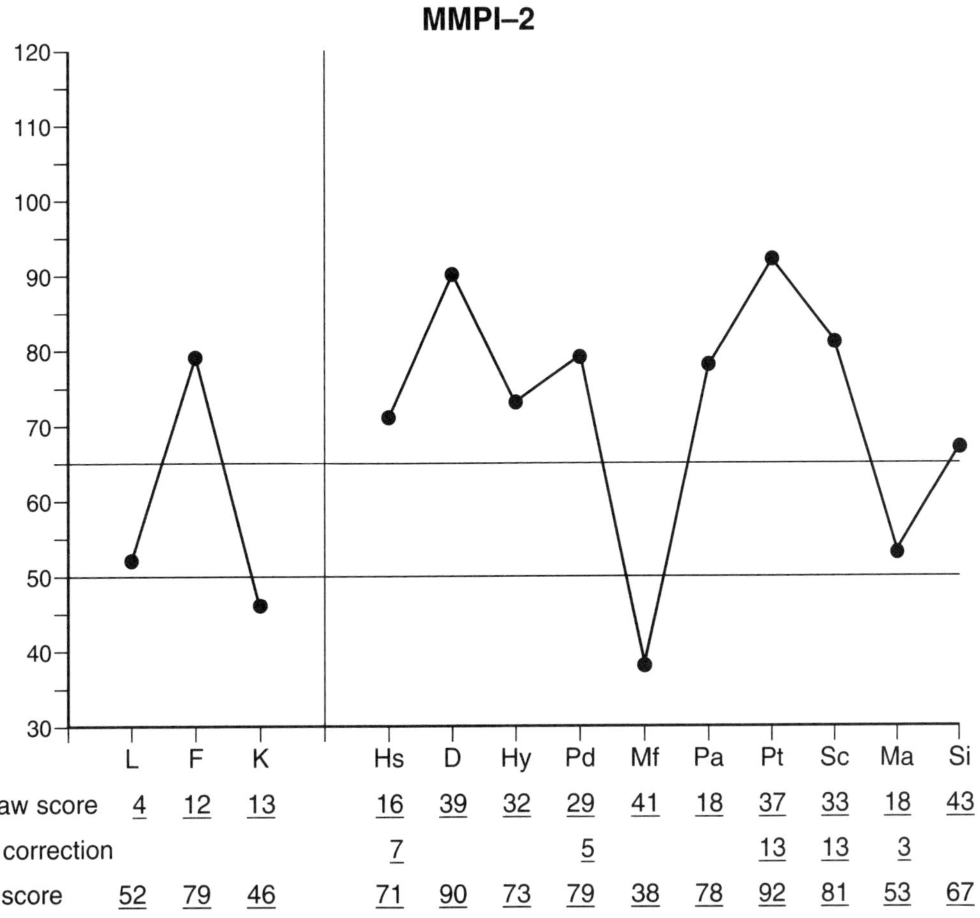

Figure 9 MMPI-2 profile of Ms. B. (1).

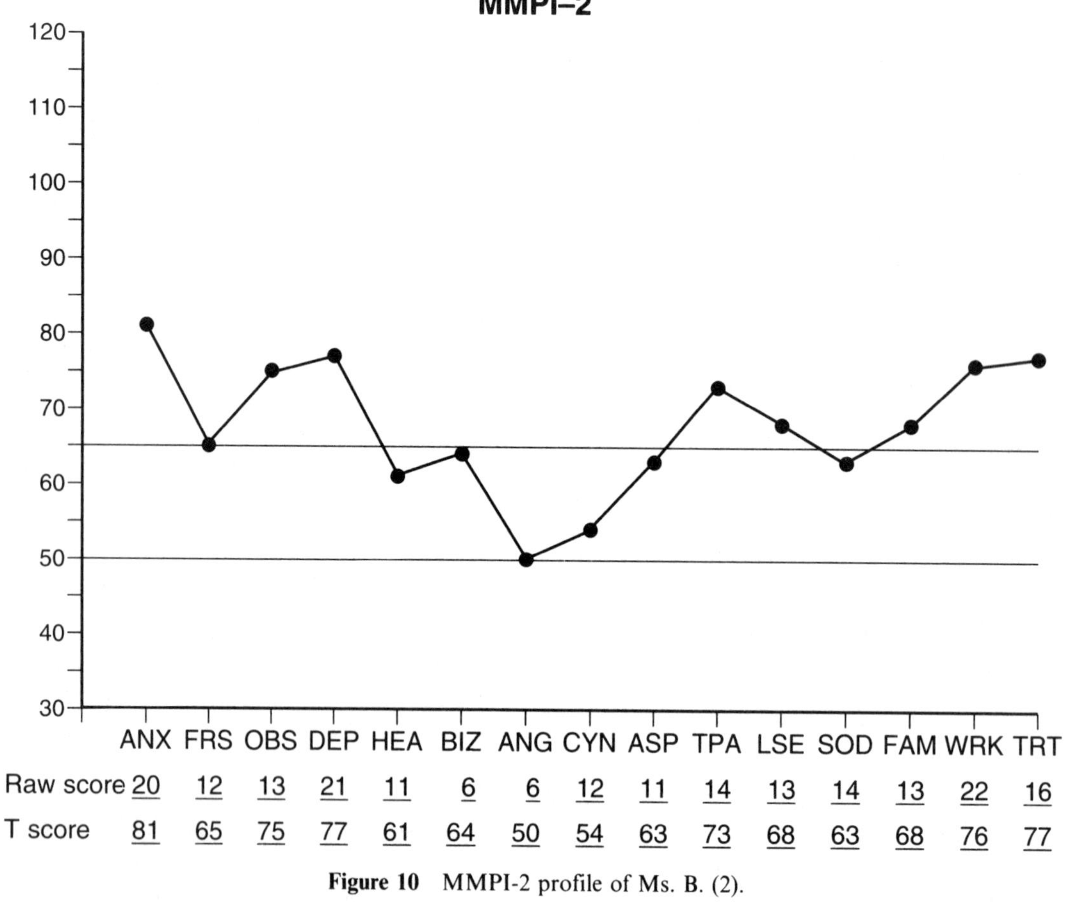

Figure 10 MMPI-2 profile of Ms. B. (2).

short marriage was marked by mistrust, ambivalence, verbal abuse, and recurrent arguments, resulting in a separation.

The assessment was conducted in an outpatient setting. At the time of testing, Ms. B. presented as well-groomed and fashionably dressed. She was oriented and her speech was fluent and intelligible. No suicidal or homicidal thoughts were indicated. She denied having any hallucinations and no delusions were noted. Remote memory and immediate memory for recall were intact.

10.12.3.3.1 The Minnesota Report on Ms. B.

When the MMPI-2 was administered, Ms. B. produced the profiles shown in Figures 9 and 10 and the following narrative report.

Profile validity

This client has endorsed a number of psychological problems, suggesting that she is experiencing a high degree of stress. Although the MMPI-2 clinical scale profile is probably valid, it may show some exaggeration of symptoms.

She endorsed the items at the end of the booklet in an extreme or exaggerated manner, producing a high score on F(B). This elevated score could result from a number of conditions such as confusion, exaggerated symptom checking, or consistently misrecording her responses on the answer sheet. The scores on the MMPI-2 Content Scales, supplementary scales, and content component scales could be influenced by this tendency.

Symptomatic patterns

This report was developed using the D, Pt, and Sc scales as the prototype. A pattern of chronic psychological maladjustment characterizes individuals with this MMPI-2 clinical profile. The client is overwhelmed by anxiety, tension, and depression. She feels helpless and alone, inadequate and insecure, and she believes that life is hopeless and that nothing is working out right. She attempts to control her worries through intellectualization and unproductive self-analysis, but she has difficulty concentrating and making decisions. This is a rather chronic behavioral pattern. Individuals with this profile typically live a disorganized and pervasively unhappy existence. They may have episodes of more intense and disturbed behavior resulting from an elevated stress level.

She is functioning at a very low level of efficiency. She tends to overreact to even minor stress, and she may show rapid behavioral deterioration. She also tends to blame herself for her problems. Her lifestyle is chaotic and disorganized, and she has a history of poor work and achievement. She may be preoccupied with obscure religious ideas.

The client does not report great concerns about her sex-role identity. However, the extent to which her rather "traditionally feminine" feelings and attitudes are integrated into her life at this point may need to be evaluated further.

In addition, the following description is suggested by the content of the client's item responses. She has endorsed a number of items suggesting that she is experiencing low morale and a depressed mood. She reports a preoccupation with feeling guilty and unworthy. She feels that she deserves to be punished for wrongs she has committed. She feels regretful and unhappy about life, and she seems plagued by anxiety and worry about the future. She feels hopeless at times and feels that she is a condemned person. She endorsed response content that reflects low self-esteem and long-standing beliefs about her inadequacy. She views her physical health as failing and reports numerous somatic concerns. She feels that life is no longer worthwhile and that she is losing control of her thought processes.

According to her response content, there is a strong possibility that she has seriously contemplated suicide. The client's recent thinking is likely to be characterized by obsessiveness and indecision. She feels somewhat self-alienated and expresses some personal misgivings or a vague sense of remorse about past acts. She feels that life is unrewarding and dull, and she finds it hard to settle down. She views the world as a threatening place, sees herself as having been unjustly blamed for others' problems, and feels that she is getting a raw deal out of life. She is rather high-strung and believes that she feels things more, or more intensely, than others do. She feels quite lonely and misunderstood at times. The client attests to having more fears than most people do. Her high endorsement of general anxiety content is likely to be important to understanding her clinical picture.

Profile frequency

It is usually valuable in MMPI-2 clinical profile interpretation to consider the relative frequency of a given profile pattern in various settings. The client's MMPI-2 high-point clinical scale score (Pt) is found in only 5.1% of the MMPI-2 normative sample of women. Only 2.1% of the women have Pt as the peak score at or above a T score of 65, and less than 1% have well-defined Pt spikes. This high profile configuration (2–7/7–2) is very rare in samples of normals, occurring in 1.2% of the MMPI-2 normative sample of women.

Her MMPI-2 high-point score is relatively uncommon in various outpatient settings. In the NCS outpatient sample, only 6.4% of the females have this MMPI-2 high-point clinical scale score (Pt). Moreover, only 5.3% of the female outpatients have the Pt scale spike at or above a T score of 65, and only 2.1% have well-defined Pt peaks. Her elevated MMPI-2 profile configuration (2–7/7–2) is found in 7.4% of the women in the NCS outpatient sample. This is the second most frequent elevated two-point code in the sample.

Profile stability

The relative elevation of her clinical scale scores suggests that her profile is not as well defined as many other profiles. That is, her highest scale or scales are very close to her next scale score elevations. There could be some shifting of the most prominent scale elevations in the profile code if she is retested at a later date. The difference between the profile type used to develop the present report and the next highest scale in the profile code was 2 points. So, for example, if the client is tested at a later date, her profile might involve more behavioral elements related to elevations on Pd. If so, then on retesting, acting-out, aggressive, and irresponsible behavior might become more pre-eminent.

Interpersonal relationships

Problematic personal relationships are also characteristic of such clients. She seems to lack basic social skills and is behaviorally withdrawn. She may relate to others ambivalently, never fully trusting or loving anyone. Many individuals with this profile never establish lasting, intimate relationships.

She is quite shy and inhibited in social situations, and she may avoid others for fear of being hurt. She is emotionally alienated from others. She is likely to have very few friends and to be considered by others as distant and hard to get to know. She is quiet and submissive and lacks self-confidence in dealing with other people. Individuals with this passive and withdrawing lifestyle are unable to assert themselves appropriately and are frequently taken advantage of by others. Personality characteristics related to social introversion tend to be stable over time. Her generally reclusive behavior, introverted lifestyle, and tendency toward interpersonal avoidance may be prominent in any future test results.

Her very high score on the Marital Distress Scale suggests that her marital situation is quite problematic at this time. She has reported a number of problems with her marriage that are possibly important to understanding her current psychological symptoms.

Diagnostic considerations

Individuals with this profile have a severe psychological disorder and would probably be diagnosed as severely neurotic with an Anxiety Disorder or Dysthymic Disorder in a Schizoid Personality. The possibility of a more severe psychotic disorder, such as Schizophrenic Disorder, should also be considered, however. Her self-reported tendency toward experiencing a depressed mood should be taken into consideration in any diagnostic formulation.

Treatment considerations

Individuals with this MMPI-2 clinical profile often receive psychotropic medications for their depressed mood or intense anxiety. Many individuals with this profile seek and require psychological treatment for their problems along with any medication that is given. Because many of their problems tend to be chronic, an intensive therapeutic effort might be required in order to bring about any significant change. Patients with this profile typically have many psychological and situational concerns; consequently, it is often difficult to maintain a focus in treatment.

She probably needs a great deal of emotional support at this time. Her low self-esteem and feelings of inadequacy make it difficult for her to get energized toward therapeutic action. Her expectation for positive change in therapy may be low. Instilling a positive, treatment-expectant attitude is important for her if treatment is to be successful.

Individuals with this profile tend to be overideational and given to unproductive rumination. They tend not to do well in unstructured, insight-oriented therapy and may actually deteriorate in functioning if they are asked to be introspective. She might respond more to supportive treatment of a directive, goal-oriented type. Individuals with this profile present a clear suicide risk; precautions should be taken.

The client endorsed item content that seems to indicate low potential for change. She may feel that her problems are not addressable through therapy and that she is not likely to benefit much from psychological treatment at this time. Her apparently negative treatment attitudes may need to be explored early in therapy if treatment is to be successful.

Her item content suggests some family conflicts that are causing her considerable concern at this time. She feels unhappy about her life and resents having an unpleasant home life. Psychological intervention could profitably focus, in part, on clarifying her feelings about her family.

In any intervention or psychological evaluation program involving occupational adjustment, her negative work attitudes could become an important problem to overcome. She has a number of attitudes and feelings that could interfere with work adjustment.

Note. This MMPI-2 interpretation can serve as a useful source of hypotheses about clients. This report is based on objectively derived scale indices and scale interpretations that have been developed in diverse groups of patients. The personality descriptions, inferences, recommendations contained herein need to be verified by other sources of clinical information because individual clients may not fully match the prototype. The information in this report should most appropriately be used by a trained, qualified test interpreter. The information contained in this report should be considered confidential.

Ms. B. presents with a long-lasting discontent with her life accompanied by mild depression which has worsened following her separation. She reports numerous physical complaints which might indicate somatization in the face of stress or health concerns in accordance with a high level of general anxiety and the belief that nothing is working for her. While depressed the patient has low self-esteem and feels hopeless. According to the patient, she was emotionally abused as a child and sexually abused at the age of 16. She feels tremendous guilt and a need to explain the past. There is a strong need for approval and unconditional love. She blames herself for her parents' unhappiness in addition to bringing shame on her family. While blaming herself for everything that has gone wrong in her parents' life as well as her own, she feels helpless and insecure in the face of any challenges or problems. Following her separation, she reports that life is full of difficulties and devoid of any happiness or reinforcers.

10.12.3.3.2 Diagnostic impression

According to the psychiatrist, Ms. B.'s clinical diagnosis, at least for insurance purposes, was considered to be major depression.
Axis I: Major Depression
Axis II: Mixed Personality (borderline, passive-aggressive, narcissistic, antisocial, histrionic, and dependent)
Axis III: Herpes.

10.12.3.3.3 Treatment

Ms. B. was in therapy for a total of three years. She was prescribed Prozac, 40 mg, which was later reduced to 20 mg. Her treatment plan consisted of weekly individual therapy sessions to address current stress due to her separation and divorce proceedings. Supportive therapy in a safe environment was provided to allow her to discuss issues related to her childhood trauma and acceptance of the past. According to the therapist, Ms. B. was always demanding and never satisfied with anything including therapy.

10.12.3.4 Seoul, Korea: The Case of Kim

Kim is a 36-year-old unemployed, unmarried Korean man with two years of college education. Kim has been obsessed with suicidal ideas (disembowelment) since 1992. He feels extremely guilty and depressed. Kim feels that he has to die, but he doesn't know what to blame for his problems.

In 1987, at the age of 27, Kim went to Australia for his college education. In 1990, he stopped taking regular courses because of language difficulties and came back to Korea. In 1992, he went to Australia again to continue his studies, but had a lot of difficulty in getting along with people, because he felt that people didn't like him and spoke ill of him behind his back. Kim decided to go to a psychiatric clinic but tried to jump off the roof of the hospital because he felt that some racists had followed him to the hospital to kill him. A month later (in September, 1992), Kim came back to Korea and was extremely anxious because he thought the Mafia would kill him and his family. A few weeks later, Kim tried to cut his wrist and was brought to a psychiatric hospital in Korea. He was hospitalized with the diagnosis of schizophrenia, and remained at the hospital until January, 1993.

After being released from the hospital, he stayed home in a relatively isolated state, receiving outpatient treatment for a year. Kim moved from job to job until the summer of 1995. In November, 1995, Kim's brother suggested to him that they start a small construction company together. Kim was supposed to do the jobs after his brother had made the business arrangements. However, three days before starting work, Kim began to feel extremely anxious about the new business and suddenly told his family that he would kill himself. Kim was then brought to the hospital by his family and was hospitalized.

10.12.3.4.1 Family history

Kim's father is 80 years of age and owns a lot of land in the southern part of Korea. However, he is extremely stressed about money and exists on only minimal living expenses. He had considerable trouble with his wife and children because he was very stubborn, mean with money, and did not listen to anybody. He does not get along well with people around him and is very indifferent to his children. Kim's mother, who died in 1994, had received only six years of elementary school education. She was very introverted and passive, and had much trouble with her husband who was verbally and physically abusive toward her. She relied on her children and often told them how her husband abused her. Her children were always on their mother's side. Kim has one sister (age 54) who is a pharmacist who worked at this occupation and helped support her siblings until she got married. Kim has a brother who is a 47-year-old obstetrician. He got married when he was in medical school and has a daughter. He was divorced after a few years, because he got a girlfriend whom he married. He also has troubles with his new wife. Kim's brother also had some psychiatric problems when he was a high school student. At that time, he was worried that he would die of lung cancer even though he had no health problems. He was also very afraid that the roof might fall down. Since then, he has not had any mental problems. Kim also has a second brother, age 33, who runs a construction company and who is very close to the patient.

10.12.3.4.2 Behavioral observations

Kim does not talk easily with people and prefers to keep a distance from others. He always worries about what other people think of him or are saying about him, and is afraid that he might make a mistake in front of people. Kim spends most of the time staring at the wall or lying in his bed. At times, he can be heard talking to himself in a very loud voice.

10.12.3.4.3 Symptomatic behavior

Kim's symptoms and behavior reflect severe psychopathology as is shown below.

(i) *Thought control.* He feels as though his thoughts are being controlled by others, and that somebody is telling him to jump off a mountain or a building. He feels as though other people are controlling his thinking processes through the television or through birds.

(ii) *Thought broadcasting or leaking.* Kim feels that other people know what he thinks even though he says nothing to them. He feels that, in spite of precautions, what he thinks just leaks out and he can not control it.

(iii) *Idea of reference and paranoid ideas.* Kim feels that someone overhears his talking on the phone, and he suspects people around him are trying to do him harm. He thinks that all Koreans know that he has committed grave offenses and are backbiting him.

(iv) *Feels guilty and depressed.* He says that he feels depressed whenever he thinks about all of his faults. He also reported that he feels more depressed since he failed to kill himself. Kim is worried now about how to kill himself.

10.12.3.4.4 The Minnesota Report on Kim

The problems of Kim's psychopathology are clearly described in the MMPI-2 profiles of Figures 11 and 12 and the following narrative report.

Profile validity

This MMPI-2 profile should be interpreted with caution. There is some possibility that the clinical report is an exaggerated picture of the client's

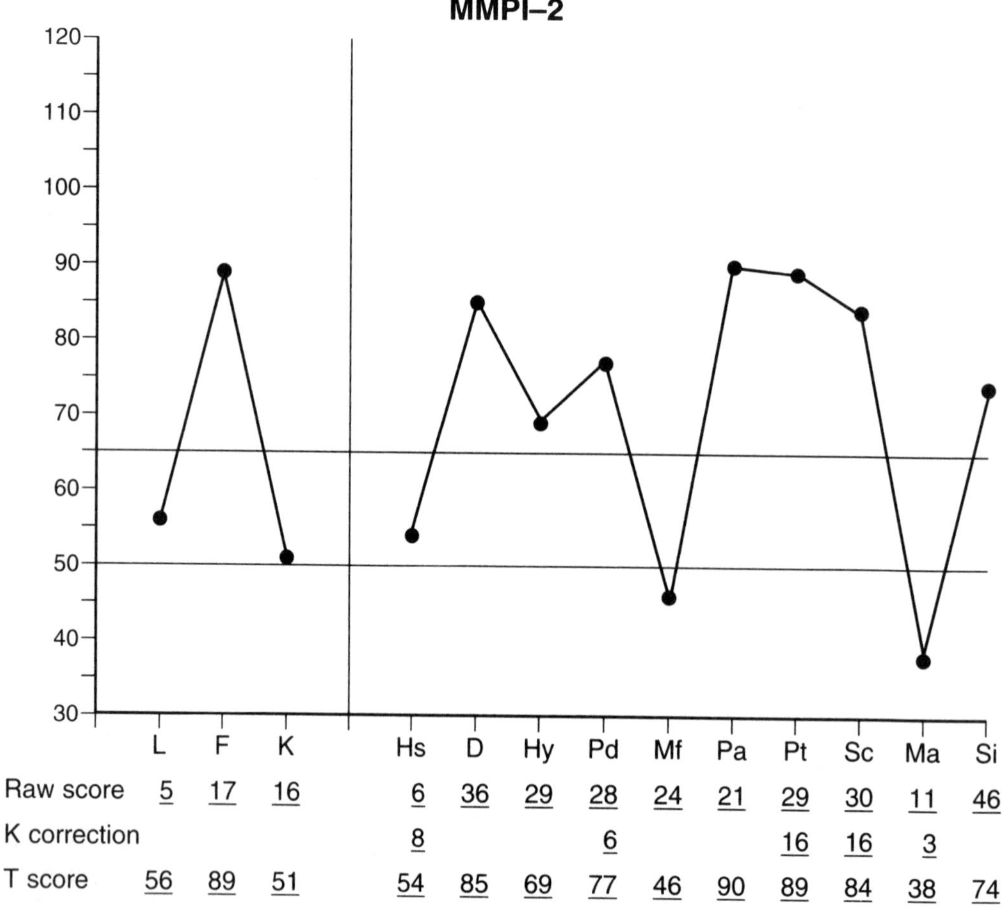

Figure 11 MMPI-2 profile of Kim (1).

present situation and problems. He is presenting an unusual number of psychological symptoms. This response set could result from poor reading ability, confusion, disorientation, stress, or a need to seek a great deal of attention for his problems.

His test-taking attitudes should be evaluated for the possibility that he has produced an invalid profile. He may be showing a lack of cooperation with the testing or he may be malingering by attempting to present a false claim of mental illness. Determining the sources of his confusion, whether conscious distortion or personality deterioration, is important because immediate attention may be required. Clinical patients with this validity profile are often confused and distractible and have memory problems. Evidence of delusions and thought disorder may be present. He may be exhibiting a high degree of distress and personality deterioration.

The client's responses to items in the latter portion of the MMPI-2 were somewhat exaggerated in comparison to his responses to earlier items. There is some possibility that he became more careless in responding to these later items, thereby raising questions about that portion of the test. Although the standard validity and clinical scales are scored from items in the first two-thirds of the test, caution should be taken in interpreting the MMPI-2 Content Scales and supplementary scales, which include items found throughout the entire item pool

Symptomatic patterns

This report was developed using the Pa and Pt scales as the prototype. The client's MMPI-2 clinical profile suggests that he is experiencing many psychological problems at this time. He appears to ruminate a great deal and may manifest obsessional or compulsive behavior. He holds beliefs that others are not likely to accept and tends to obsess about them to the point of alienating others. He appears to be quite intense, anxious, and distressed. Individuals with this profile may be overreacting to environmental situations with intense anxiety, suspicion, and concern. He feels insecure and inadequate when dealing with his problems. He may feel very angry with himself and others, and he may feel very guilty about his fantasies or beliefs. Often rather rigid, he may have problems controlling and directly expressing his anger.

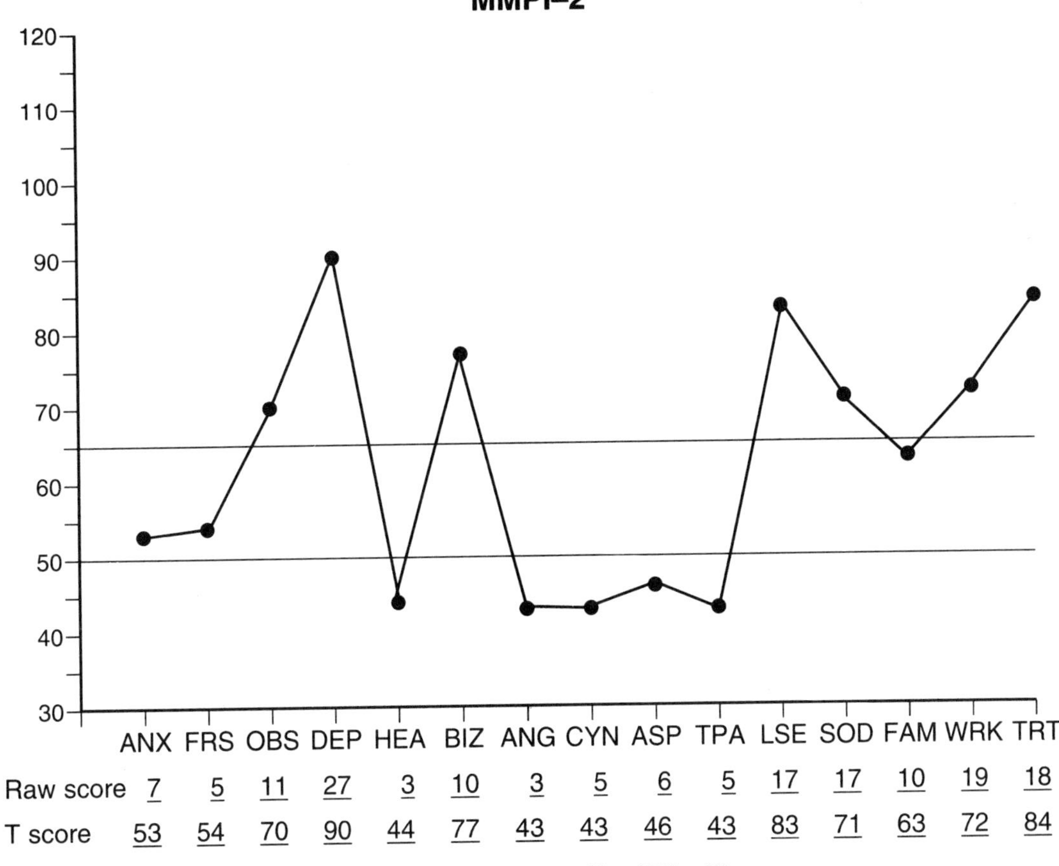

Figure 12 MMPI-2 profile of Kim (2).

Profile frequency

Profile interpretation can be greatly facilitated by examining the relative frequency of clinical scale patterns in various settings. The client's high-point clinical scale score (Pa) occurs in 9.6% of the MMPI-2 normative sample of men. However, only 3% of the sample have Pa as the peak score at or above a T score of 65, and only 2.2% have well-defined Pa spikes. This elevated MMPI-2 pattern (6–7/7–6) is very rare in samples of normals, occurring in less than 1% of the MMPI-2 normative sample of men.

The frequency of this MMPI-2 high-point Pa score is relatively high in various inpatient settings. In the Graham and Butcher (1988) sample of psychiatric inpatients, this profile peak is the second most frequent peak score (15.7%) for males, with 12.6% of the cases scoring in the clinically significant range (8.2% are well defined). In the large NCS inpatient sample, this high-point clinical scale score (Pa) is the third most frequent peak score, occurring in 14.3% of the men. Moreover, 12.1% of the males in the inpatient sample have this high-point scale spike at over a T score of 65, and 7.5% are well defined in that range. Male inpatients in a Veterans Administration setting (Arbisi & Ben-Porath, 1993) produce this high-point peak score with 10.1% frequency; 9.1% of the cases have Pa elevated above a T score of 65, and 6.1% of the cases are well defined.

This elevated MMPI-2 pattern (6–7/7–6) is found in less than 1% of the males in the Graham and Butcher (1988) sample, in 2.6% of the males in the NCS inpatient sample, and in 1.7% of the men in a Veterans Administration inpatient sample (Arbisi & Ben-Porath, 1993).

Profile stability

The relative scale elevation of his highest clinical scale scores suggests some lack of clarity in profile definition. Although his most elevated clinical scales are likely to be present in his profile pattern if he is retested at a later date, there could be some shifting of the most prominent scale elevations in the profile code. The difference between the profile type used to develop the present report and the next highest scale in the profile code was 4 points. So for example, if the client is tested at a later date, his profile might involve more behavioral elements related to elevations on D. If so, then on retesting, pronounced complaints of depressed mood and low morale might become more prominent.

Interpersonal relations

Individuals with this profile tend to be experiencing some interpersonal distress. The client seems somewhat shy and may have excessively high moral standards by which he judges others. His inflexibility in interpersonal situations may place a great strain on close relationships because he seems to test other people to reassure himself. He appears to be rather touchy or hostile interpersonally, and he may brood over what he imagines others have done to him. He tends to feel insecure in personal relationships, is hypersensitive to rejection, and may become jealous at times. He tends to need a great deal of reassurance.

He is a very introverted person who has difficulty meeting and interacting with other people. He is shy and emotionally distant. He tends to be very uneasy, rigid, and overcontrolled in social situations. His shyness is probably symptomatic of a broader pattern of social withdrawal. Personality characteristics related to social introversion tend to be stable over time. His generally reclusive behavior, introverted lifestyle, and tendency toward interpersonal avoidance may be prominent in any future test results.

Diagnostic considerations

His excessive anxiety and obsessive behavior should be taken into consideration in the final diagnosis. In addition, the possibility of a Paranoid Disorder or Paranoid Personality should be evaluated.

Treatment considerations

Inpatients with this MMPI-2 clinical profile usually have severe psychological problems as well as physical health concerns. Psychiatric treatment should focus on the client's anxiety and self-doubts. The use of medication to relieve his intense tension should be considered. The possibility that he has suspicious or paranoid ideas should be kept in mind when considering psychological treatment options. He may have difficulty forming a therapeutic relationship. He is quite rigid and intellectualizes a great deal; therapeutic progress is likely to be slow. Individuals with this MMPI-2 Clinical profile tend to have unrealistic expectations of themselves and perfectionistic ideals that may require some challenging if their personal vulnerability is to be diminished. A therapeutic approach such as rational-emotive therapy might enable him to acquire more self-acceptance.

Note: this MMPI-2 interpretation can serve as a useful source of hypotheses about clients. This report is based on objectively derived scale indices and scale interpretations that have been developed in diverse groups of patients. The personality descriptions, inferences, recommendations contained herein need to be verified by other sources of clinical information because individual clients may not fully match the prototype. The information in this report should most appropriately be used by a trained, qualified test interpreter. The information contained in this report should be considered confidential.

10.12.3.4.5 Diagnosis

Possibly schizophrenia or delusional disorder. Rule out depression with psychotic feature.

10.12.3.5 Haifa, Israel: The Case of Yuri Z.

The patient, Yuri Z., is a 30-year-old male who was born in Israel of Polish immigrant parents. He is married and he and his wife are expecting their second child. He has completed 13 years of education and at present he is a student in a large university and works part-time as a security guard. He was referred by the student counseling center of the university for psychological evaluation and possible treatment.

Yuri came to the clinic following a brief course of couple therapy where he and his wife were treated for severe marital problems. Following this family therapy Yuri decided to seek further individual therapy even though he still sees that separation from his wife is a possibility because their problems, though lessened, are still present.

Yuri is the youngest child in a family of four siblings. His older sister is doing her residency in psychiatry at Harvard. He initially described his family home life as "loving, encouraging, and wonderful' but later in the session changed this interpretation to more rigid, Spartan, encouraging to "hold on," and generally a "struggle" much of the time. Yuri's parents are Holocaust survivors and the father is described as saying that he is not a victim of the Holocaust but a victor of the Holocaust. The father has tried to cut himself and his children off from the terrible family history. The daughter, unlike Yuri, felt that the father did not allow her to grow and develop her own identity and she disconnected from the father a long time ago. Yuri sees his father as emotional, kind, and highly protective. He described his mother as a model mother, a wonderful person. His mother is a nurse who works with babies and who has always devoted herself to helping others. Later in the session he described his mother as distant, cold, and "frozen."

Yuri is a very bright person who had been an excellent student all through his earlier school years. However, he had school behavior problems all the time. Yuri considers himself to have been an undiagnosed and untreated hyperactive child. Due to behavior problems he was suspended from junior high school for a month (this was very unusual in the school he was attending). The reason for the suspension, after several reprimands, was his unexcused absences from school. After a period of time he was allowed to return to school. However, he lost his motivation to attend the regular school system and he transferred to another school. But when he learned about the possibility of going to a new kibbutz, he was excited, and left home despite his parents' objections, especially those of his mother who was afraid he wouldn't complete school. Yuri describes his years at the kibbutz as the best time in his life. He felt as though he had gained freedom, and enjoyed the open land and young peers.

He enlisted in the army, in a unit that consisted mainly of persons who wished to live on a kibbutz. He served in an elite unit in that corps. His mother died the day that he enlisted in the army. He served in the army for five years in what was described as a rigorous and very hard duty, mostly in the field and in the front line, because "I had nothing waiting for me outside the army." He saw many of his friends die or be wounded and he participated in several killings of enemy terrorists. Images of scenes from that period still recur in his dreams. He was a superb soldier in the army, but even there he had disciplinary problems because of his irresponsible behavior at times. His underlying personality problems persisted.

10.12.3.5.1 The Minnesota Report on Yuri Z.

Yuri Z's personality problems are illustrated in the MMPI-2 profiles of Figures 13 and 14 and the following narrative report.

Profile validity

This MMPI-2 profile should be interpreted with caution. There is some possibility that the clinical report is an exaggerated picture of the client's present situation and problems. He is presenting an unusual number of psychological symptoms. This response set could result from poor reading ability, confusion, disorientation, stress, or a need to seek a great deal of attention for his problems.

His test-taking attitudes should be evaluated for the possibility that he has produced an invalid profile. He may be showing a lack of cooperation with the testing or he may be malingering by attempting to present a false claim of mental illness. Determining the sources of his confusion, whether conscious distortion or personality deterioration, is important because immediate attention may be required. Clinical patients with this validity profile are often confused and distractible and have memory problems. Evidence of delusions and thought disorder may be present. He may be exhibiting a high degree of distress and personality deterioration.

Symptomatic patterns

This report was developed using the Pd and Sc scales as the prototype. A somewhat mixed symptom picture is reflected in this profile. Individuals with this MMPI-2 clinical scale configuration tend to show a pattern of chronic psychological maladjustment. The client appears to be unconventional and nonconforming, tending to act impulsively without regard for the consequences. Apparently he is emotionally troubled, and his behavior is unpredictable. He may be aloof and withdrawn. He may also appear hedonistic and may engage in dangerous or deviant behavior for the thrill of it. He may have a history of unreliable and irresponsible actions, for which he often blames others. He tends to have low self-esteem, a history of underachievement, and problems with authority. Excessive alcohol or drug use is often found among individuals with this clinical pattern.

In addition, the following description is suggested by the content of the client's item responses. He had endorsed a number of items suggesting that he is experiencing low morale and a depressed mood. Although he may be socially assertive and may project a positive image to others, his response content indicates a rather negative self-image. He reports some antisocial beliefs and attitudes, admits to rule violations, and acknowledges antisocial behavior in the past.

Profile frequency

Profile interpretation can be greatly facilitated by examining the relative frequency of clinical scale patterns in various settings. The client's high-point clinical scale score (Pd) occurs in 9.1% of the MMPI-2 normative sample of men. However, only 3.3% of the normative men have Pd as the peak score equal to or greater than a T score of 65, and only 1.0% have well-defined Pd spikes. This elevated MMPI-2 profile configuration (4–8/8–4) is very rare in samples of normals, occurring in less than 1% of the MMPI-2 normative samples of men. A high-point Pd scale score occurs in 10.3% of the sample of military men (Butcher, Jeffrey, et al., 1990). However, only 3% of the sample have Pd equal to or greater than a T score of 65. Only 2% of these high-point peaks are well defined at that level of elevation.

He scored relatively high on AAS, suggesting the possibility of a drug- or alcohol-abuse problem. The base rate data on his profile type among residents in alcohol and drug programs should also be evaluated. This MMPI-2 profile configuration contains the most frequent high point, the Pd score, among alcohol- and drug-abusing populations. Over 24% of the men in substance-abuse treatment programs have this pattern (McKenna & Butcher, 1987).

Profile stability

The relative scale elevation of the highest scales in his clinical profile reflects high profile definition. If he is retested at a later date, the peak scores on

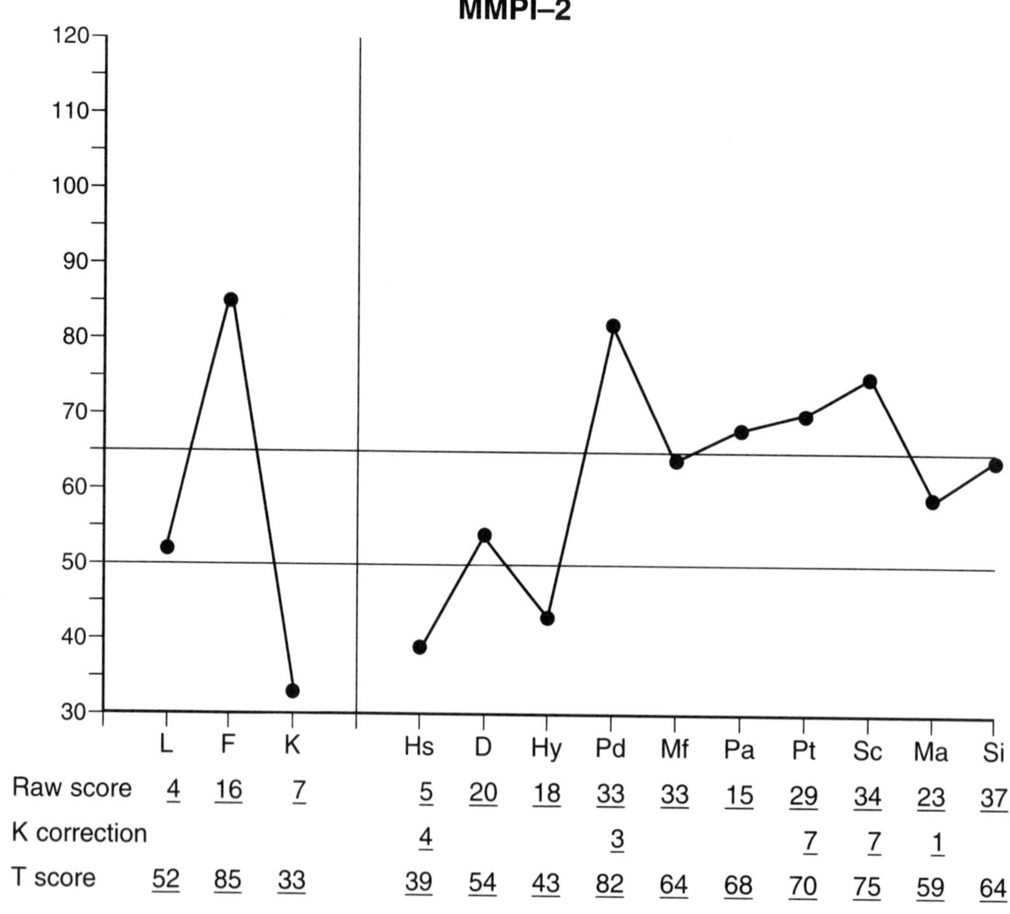

Figure 13 MMPI-2 profile of Yuri Z. (1).

this test are likely to retain their relative salience in his retest profile pattern. His high-point score on Pd is likely to remain stable over time. Short-term test–retest studies have shown a correlation of 0.81 for this high-point score. Spiro, Butcher, Levenson, Aldwin, and Bosse (1993) reported a moderate test–retest stability index of 0.62 in a large study of normals over a five-year test–retest period.

Interpersonal relations

Although his behavior is frequently seen as manipulative, he apparently lacks social skills. Often misunderstanding the motives of others and overly sensitive to rejection, he may appear aloof and feel insecure in close personal relationships. He may also greatly distrust others. He is probably behaving in unpredictable and erratic ways that may produce a great deal of marital strain. Many individuals with this profile have serious marital problems that require marriage counseling.

He is somewhat shy, with some social concerns and inhibitions. He is a bit hypersensitive about what others think of him and is occasionally concerned about his relationships with others. He appears to be somewhat inhibited in personal relationships and social situations, and he may have some difficulty expressing his feelings towards others.

His very high score on the Marital Distress Scale suggests that his marital situation is quite problematic at this time. He has reported a number of problems with his marriage that are possibly important to understanding his current psychological symptoms.

The content of this client's MMPI-2 responses suggests the following additional information concerning his interpersonal relations. He views his home situation as unpleasant and lacking in love and understanding. He feels like leaving home to escape a quarrelsome, critical situation and to be free of family domination.

Diagnostic considerations

Individuals with this profile usually receive a diagnosis of Personality Disorder. His response content is consistent with the antisocial features in his history. These factors should be taken into consideration in arriving at a clinical diagnosis. His self-reported tendency toward experiencing a depressed mood should be taken into consideration in any diagnostic formulation.

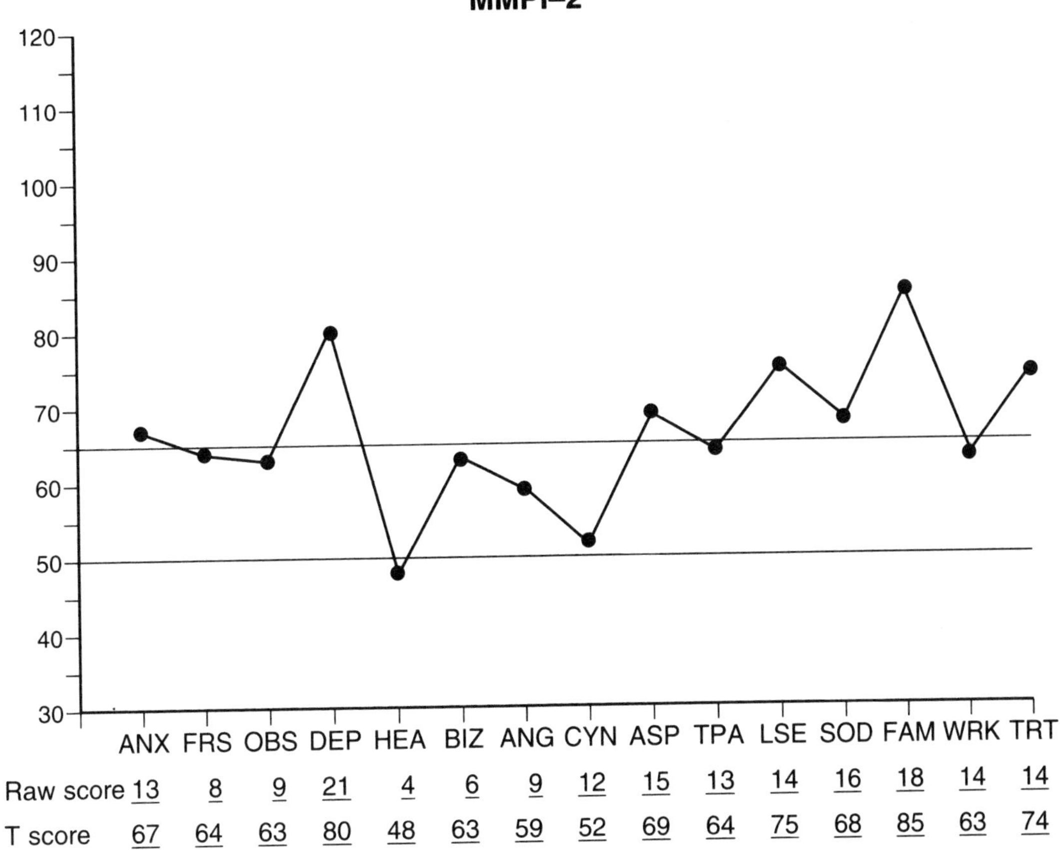

Figure 14 MMPI-2 profile of Yuri Z. (2).

He has a number of personality characteristics that are associated with a substance-use or abuse disorder. The client's scores on the addiction proneness indicators, along with the personality characteristics reflected in the profile, suggests that he resembles some individuals who develop addictive disorders. A substance-abuse evaluation should explore this possibility through a careful review of his personality traits and typical behaviors. In his responses to the MMPI-2, he has acknowledged some problems with excessive use or abuse of addictive substances.

Treatment considerations

Individuals with this profile often live stressful and crisis-filled lives and may need psychological treatment to enable them to structure their lives better. They typically have a number of reality-based problems that complicate treatment on an outpatient basis. Although they may seek temporary symptom relief or may be referred for psychological treatment by another person or agency, their long-standing personality problems make it unlikely that they would profit much from individual, insight-oriented psychotherapy. They are evidently not very reflective or introspective and would also have difficulty establishing a treatment relationship because they mistrust other people. The client is so emotionally and socially alienated that it would be difficult for a therapist to gain his confidence. Such individuals also tend to act out problems rather than attempting to understand and solve them.

Behavioral treatment that focuses on life management may be of value in teaching them more adaptive social functioning. Regardless of the treatment programs offered, their behavior may change quite slowly and there may be many crises during the course of therapy.

Note This MMPI-2 interpretation can serve as a useful source of hypotheses about clients. This report is based on objectively derived scale indices and scale interpretations that have been developed in diverse groups of patients. The personality descriptions, inferences, recommendations contained herein need to be verified by other sources of clinical information because individual clients may not fully match the prototype. The information in this report should most appropriately be used by a trained, qualified test interpreter. The information contained in this report should be considered confidential.

After his discharge from the army he felt very empty and depressed. He locked himself in at home for three months and was using drugs extensively at this time. Afterwards he was admitted to a technical program at the university. Later in that year his father died. A year later he went on a trip, a "root searching' tour to Poland. He described his parents' death as the beginning of his crisis. He feels that he has never really processed or coped with their deaths.

10.12.3.5.2 Treatment

Yuri was admitted to the clinic's outpatient program for individual psychodynamically oriented therapy. He comes quite regularly to sessions and has been in therapy for the last eight months.

10.12.3.6 Cross-national Generality of Psychopathology: What We Have Learned from the Cases

The case studies presented in this chapter illustrate clearly the generalizability of the MMPI-2 across diverse cultures. As one can see by reading the personality descriptions and problem situations described in the clinical cases from different countries, the MMPI-2 variables are what one would expect to find if the patients were American patients assessed in the USA. Moreover, these MMPI-2 profiles appear to be close matches with the cases, in spite of the fact that the profiles were generated on US norms. In addition, the computer-derived narratives, which were developed on research conducted in the USA, show close matches when the reports are applied in other countries.

How can an instrument developed in one language and culture show such robustness when applied to patients in other cultures who responded to translated versions of the items? Several factors account for this correspondence of patient description across cultures. Research in cross-cultural psychopathology has shown that mental disorders and diagnostic systems are comprised of similar symptom patterns in different cultures—a schizophrenic is a schizophrenic regardless of culture. Many similar disorders show common patterns of symptoms across cultural boundaries.

Similarly, the MMPI-2 items sample a broad range of symptoms and problems constituting the abnormal syndromes. Given a well translated item set, resulting in an equivalent form, the symptoms are found to describe well the disorders in each culture. Patients who are depressed, for example, tend to respond to the same types of items in the cultures studied here, producing familiar personality profile patterns. This is not to say that cultural factors are irrelevant to the manifestation of psychopathology. It has been shown that, for example, child-rearing patterns in Italy might result in a "dramatization of symptoms" (Butcher & Pancheri, 1976; Zola, 1966) that is not noted in other cultures. However, such differences do not greatly alter the main symptoms of disorder, thereby resulting in some commonality for disorders across cultures.

These case studies also provide an important example with respect to objective personality assessment. The study on computer-based assessment across Norway, France, Australia, and the USA shows that the empirical description of MMPI-2 patterns has broad generalizability whether interpreted by clinicians or by the computer.

10.12.4 FUTURE DIRECTIONS

Each year more foreign language translations of the MMPI-2 become available, providing clinicians and researchers in other countries the means of assessing clients in ways comparable to those in the USA. The availability of objective parallel methods of assessing psychological problems make it possible for joint international research programs to examine psychopathology cross-culturally. The MMPI-2 has shown considerable adaptability across international boundaries. When careful translation and adaptation procedures are followed to develop a sound translation, the MMPI-2 can be usefully employed in clinical assessment in other languages and cultures. Moreover, the translated version of the MMPI-2 appears to have a high degree of accuracy in characterizing personality and patient problems even with clients being assessed in very diverse settings. What can one conclude from this body of research?

The research reported here supporting the questionnaire approach to psychopathology should assure psychologists from other countries about the transportability of the MMPI-2. The utility of the instrument in making clinical decisions has been amply demonstrated through several international projects, and MMPI-2 profiles can add a salient dimension to clinical decision making in other countries. Psychologists and psychiatrists in other countries who are interested in studying psychopathology across different cultures or national groups might consider employing an objective measuring instrument, like the MMPI-2, to assess symptoms of disorder.

The accuracy of automated test interpretation has been demonstrated in the research reported here, and should provide researchers with an objective tool for cross-cultural research in psychopathology. When a computer-based interpretation, developed on normals and patients in the USA, is applied in international contexts, the resulting reports characterize well the patients in other countries. This finding has great implications for cross-cultural research on psychopathology in that subjectivity in interpretation in cross-cultural psychopathology comparisons can be substantially reduced.

10.12.5 SUMMARY

Psychologists have explored the use of computers to interpret psychological tests for many years. The first psychological test to be fully interpreted by computer was the Minnesota Multiphasic Personality Inventory in 1961 at the Mayo Clinic, Rochester, Minnesota. Since then a number of computer interpretation systems have become available in the USA. Previous studies on computer assessment for the original MMPI and MMPI-2 in Australia have shown it to be a promising interpretive approach. This chapter describes an empirical evaluation of computer-based MMPI-2 reports on Australian, French, Norwegian, and American patients. The patients were administered the MMPI-2 and computerized Minnesota Reports were generated. Clinicians familiar with the patients rated the reports in terms of adequacy of information and accuracy of descriptions and predictions. The computer-based reports were considered to provide valuable information, with two-thirds (66%) judged to be 80–100% accurate and 87% considered to be over 60% accurate in the information provided. The clinical application of computer-based reports was illustrated through case examples from several countries, including The Netherlands, Italy, Korea, Iran/United States, and Israel.

ACKNOWLEDGMENTS

We would like to express our appreciation to Joe Bolza, Shelly Colman, Pam McAsey, and Louise Sellenger from Australia for their cooperation in gathering the data for the study. We would especially like to thank Linda Fresquez for her tireless and efficient processing of test information and Steven Rouse and Russ Morfitt for their able assistance in the data processing.

10.12.6 REFERENCES

Abe, M. (1955). On the personality inventory. *Bulletin of Tohoku Institute of Correctional Science, 1,* 161–162.

Adcock, C. J., & Richie, J. E. (1958). Intercultural use of Rorschach. *American Anthropologist, 60,* 881–892.

American Psychological Association (1986). *American Psychological Association guidelines for computer-based tests and intepretations.* Washington, DC: Author.

Arbisi, P., & Ben-Porath, Y. S. (1993, March). *Interpreting the F scales of inpatients: Moving from art to science.* Paper presented at the 28th Annual symposium on Recent Developments in the Use of MMPI/MMPI-2/MMPI-A. St. Petersburg Beach, FL.

Berah, E., Butcher, J., Miach, P., Bolza, J., Colman, S. & McAsey, P. (1993, October). *Computer-based interpretation of the MMPI-2: An Australian evaluation of the Minnesota Report.* Poster presented at the 28th Annual Conference of the Australian Psychological Association, Gold Coast.

Berah, E., Miach, P., & Butcher, J. N. (1995, June). *The MMPI-2 downunder: Validation of computer-based interpretive reports in Australia.* Paper given at the 15th International Conference on Personality Assessment., Haifa, Israel.

Butcher, J. N. (Ed.) (1987). *Computerized psychological assessment.* New York: Basic Books.

Butcher, J. N. (1993). *User's guide for the MMPI-2 Minnesota Report: Adult clinical system.* Minneapolis, MN: National Computer Systems.

Butcher, J. N. (1995). How to use computer-based personality test reports. In J. N. Butcher (Ed.), *Clinical personality assessment: Practical approaches* (pp. 78–94). New York: Oxford University Press.

Butcher, J. N. (1996). *International adaptations of the MMPI-2: Research and clinical applications.* Minneapolis, MN: University of Minnesota Press.

Butcher, J. N., Jeffrey, T., Cayton, T. G., Colligan, S., DeVore, J., & Minnegawa, R. (1990). A study of active duty military personnel with the MMPI-2. *Military Psychology, 2,* 47–61.

Butcher, J. N., Narikiyo, T., & Bemis-Vitousek, K. (1992). Understanding abnormal behavior in cultural context. In H. Adams & P. Sutker (Eds.), *Comprehensive handbook of psychopathology,* (2nd ed., pp. 83–105). New York: Plenum.

Butcher, J. N., & Pancheri, P. (1976). *A handbook of cross-national MMPI research.* Minneapolis, MN: University of Minnesota Press.

Cheung, F. M., & Song, W. (1989). A review on the clinical applications of the Chinese MMPI. *Psychological Assessment, 1,* 230–237.

Cheung, F. M., Song, W., & Butcher, J. N. (1991). An infrequency scale for the Chinese MMPI. *Psychological Assessment, 3,* 648–653.

Cheung, F. M., Zhao, J., & Wu, C. (1992). Chinese MMPI profiles among neurotic patients. *Psychological Assessment, 4,* 214–218.

Eyde, L., Kowal, D., & Fishburne, F. J. (1991). In T. B. Gutkin & S. L. Wise (Eds.), *The computer and the decision making process* (pp. 75–123). Hillsdale, NJ: Erlbaum.

Fowler, R. D. (1969). Automated interpretation of psychological test data. In J. N. Butcher (Ed.) *MMPI: Research developments and clinical applications* (pp. 105–126). New York: McGraw-Hill.

Fowler, R. D. (1978). *Computer interpretation of the MMPI in Australia.* Unpublished manuscript.

Fowler, R. D., & Butcher, J. N. (1987). International applications of computer based testing and interpretation. *Applied Psychology: An International Review, 36,* 419–429.

Gilberstadt, H., & Duker, J. (1965). *A handbook for clinical and actuarial MMPI interpretation.* Philadelphia: Saunders.

Gillet, I., Simon, M., Guelfi, J., Baun, A., Monier, C. Seunevei, F., & Svarna, L. (1996). The MMPI-2 in France. In J. N. Butcher (Ed.) *International adaptations of the MMPI-2: A handbook of research and clinical applications* (pp. 395–415). Minneapolis, MN University of Minnesota Press.

Graham, J. R. & Butcher, J. N. (1988, March) *Differentiating schizophrenic and major affective disorders with the revised form of the MMPI.* Paper presented at the 23rd Annual Meeting of the Symposium on Recent Developments in the Use of the MMPI. St. Petersburg, FI.

Halbower, C. C. (1955). *A comparison of actuarial versus clinical prediction to classes discriminated by MMPI.* Doctoral dissertation, University of Minnesota.

Kazarian, S., & Evans, D. R. (in press). *Cross cultural clinical psychology.* New York: Oxford University Press.

Kim, A. S. (1988). *MMPI—The clinical interpretation.* Seoul, South Korea: National University Press.

Lindzey, G. (1958). *Projective techniques in cross cultural research.* New York: Appleton-Century-Crofts.

Lonner, W., & Berry, J. (1986). *Field methods in cross cultural research.* Beverly Hills, CA: Sage.

Marks, P. A., & Seeman, W. (1963).

Marks, P. A., Seeman, W., & Haller, D. L. (1974). *The actuarial use of the MMPI with adolescents and adults.* Baltimore: William and Wilkins.

Manos, N. (1984). Adaptation of the MMPI in Greece: Translation, standardization, and cross-cultural comparison. In J. N. Butcher & C. D. Spielberger (Eds.), *Advances in personality assessment* (Vol. 4, pp. 159–208). Hillsdale, NJ: Erlbaum.

McKenna, T., & Butcher, J. N. (1987). *Continuity of the MMPI with alcoholics.* Paper presented at the 23rd Annual Symposium on Recent Developments in the Use of the MMPI. Seattle, WA.

Meehl, P. E. (1954). *Clinical versus statistical prediction: A theoretical analysis and a review of the evidence.* Minneapolis, MN: University of Minnesota Press.

Meehl, P. E. (1956). Wanted—a good cookbook. *American Psychologist, 11,* 263–272.

Pancheri, P., & Biondi, M. (1987). Computerized psychological assessment in Italy. In J. N. Butcher (Ed.), *Computerized psychological assessment: A practitioner's guide* (pp. 236–260). New York: Basic Books.

Pancheri, P., Sirigatti, S., & Biondi, M. (1996). The MMPI-2 in Italy. In J. N. Butcher (Ed.), *International adaptations of the MMPI-2: A handbook of research and clinical applications* (pp. 416–441). Minneapolis, MN: University of Minnesota Press.

Reda, G. (1948). Unpublished translation. University of Rome, Italy.

Risetti, F. J., Himmel, E., Maltes, S., & Gonzalez, H. A. (1989). Estandarizacion del Inventario Multifasico de Personalidad de Minnesota (MMPI), en poblacion adulta Chilena [Standardization of the Minnesota Multiphasic Personality Inventory (MMPI) in the adult Chilean population]. *Revista Chilena de Psicologia, 10,* 41–62.

Rome, H. P., Swenson, W. M., Mataya, P., McCarthy, C. E., Pearson, J. S., Keating, F. R., & Hathaway, S. R. (1962). Symposium on automation techniques in personality assessment. *Proceedings of the Staff Meetings of the Mayo Clinic, 37,* 61–82.

Savasir, I., & Erol, N. (1990). The Turkish MMPI: Translation, adaptation, and validation. In J. N. Butcher & C. D. Spielberger (Eds.), *Advances in personality assessment* (Vol. 8, pp. 49–62). Hillsdale, NJ: Erlbaun.

Spiro, R., Butcher, J. N., Levenson, M., Aldwin, C., & Bosse, R. (1993, August). *Personality change over five years: The MMPI-2 in older men.* Paper at the Annual Meeting of the American Psychological Association, Toronto, Canada

Strassberg, D. S., Clutton, S., & Korboot, P. (1991). A descriptive and validity study of the Minnesota Multiphasic Personality Inventory-2 (MMPI-2) in an elderly Australian sample. *Journal of Psychopathology and Behavioral Assessment, 13,* 301–311.

Strassberg, D. S., Tilley, D., Bristone, S., & Tian, P. S. (1992). The MMPI and chronic pain: A cross-cultural view. *Psychological Assessment, 4,* 493–497.

Sundberg, N. (1956). The use of the MMPI for cross-cultural personality study: A preliminary report on the German translation. *Journal of Abnormal and Social Psychology, 58,* 281–283.

World Health Organization (1992). *ICD-10 classification of mental and behavioral disorder: Clinical description and diagnostic procedures.* Geneva, Switzerland: Author.

Yap, P. M. (1951). Mental diseases peculiar to certain cultures: A survey of comparative psychiatry. *Journal of Mental Science, 97,* 313–327.

Ziskin, J. (1981). The use of the MMPI in forensic settings. In J. N. Butcher, W. G. Dahlstrom, M. D. Gynther, & W. Schofield (Eds.), *Clinical notes on the MMPI* (whole #9). Nutley, NJ: Hoffman-LaRoche Laboratories/NCS.

Zola, I. K. (1966). Culture and symptoms—an analysis of patients' presenting complaints. *American Sociological Review, 31,* 615–630.

Zou, Y., & Zhao, C. (1992). The validity of the MMPI in the clinical diagnosis of 1422 Chinese subjects. *Chinese Mental Health Journal, 6,* 211–213.

10.13
Mental Health in the Arab World

MARWAN DWAIRY
Nova Southeastern University, Oakland Park, FL, USA

10.13.1 INTRODUCTION	313
10.13.2 ARAB SOCIOCULTURAL HISTORY AND POPULATION	313
10.13.3 PSYCHOCULTURAL FEATURES OF ARABS	314
10.13.4 CLINICAL ASSESSMENT CONSIDERATIONS	315
10.13.4.1 Manifestations of Psychosocial Disorders	315
10.13.4.2 Psychometric Characteristics	316
10.13.5 HELP-SEEKING BEHAVIOR	316
10.13.5.1 Traditional Arab Theory of Psychotherapy	318
10.13.6 EPIDEMIOLOGY OF CLINICAL PROBLEMS	318
10.13.6.1 Psychiatric Morbidity	318
10.13.6.2 Distribution of the Disorders	319
10.13.7 HEALTH SERVICE DELIVERY SYSTEM	320
10.13.8 FUTURE DIRECTIONS	321
10.13.9 SUMMARY	322
10.13.10 REFERENCES	323

10.13.1 INTRODUCTION

Compared to most Western societies, Arab societies are more collectivist and authoritarian, and Arab individuals thus adhere more closely to social values and norms. The relationship of the Arab individual to the family is characterized by interdependence, resulting in people who are less individuated than the typical Westerner. How do these sociocultural factors affect the Arabs" personality characteristics? How does the Arabic culture influence the epidemiology and manifestations of psychological disorders? How do Arabs perform on psychological tests? Given the individualistic background of psychotherapy, how do Arabs regard psychotherapy, and how do they deal with their psychological disorders? What kind of mental health system exists in Arabic countries? These points are addressed in this chapter, and suggestions are offered to psychotherapists for tailoring their therapies to the Arab client.

10.13.2 ARAB SOCIOCULTURAL HISTORY AND POPULATION

Arabs are currently living in 21 countries to the east and south of the Mediterranean sea, and in the Arabian peninsula. The vast majority are Muslims; however, a minority of Christians reside in Syria, Lebanon, Palestine, Jordan, and Egypt, and a minority of Druze in Syria, Lebanon, and Palestine. Despite the sociocultural diversity among Arabs, all share a historical experience that has shaped certain sociocultural features of contemporary Arab life.

Before the birth of Islam in 622, Arabs had lived in the Arabian peninsula, Syria, and Iraq, in a tribal social system characterized by collectivism and authoritarianism. From the beginning of Islam until the fifteenth century, Arabs experienced the glory period of the Arab-Islamic empire, in which they were the rulers of a state that expanded from Iran in the east, through North Africa, to Spain in the west. In this period, Arabs combined their tribal cultural heritage with the new values of Islam. Between the sixteenth and nineteenth centuries there was a stagnation period, in which they were governed by other Muslim states such as the Mamlukes and Ottomans (Turks). In the last two centuries, two important processes have taken place in the Arab world: a massive exposure to the democratic, more individualistic values of the West, and the establishment of separate independent states (Fattal & Sokari, 1988; Mansfield, 1991).

Four main historical periods can be identified, each noteworthy for a different collective experience: tribal, rulers, ruled, and westernization, successively. New periods added new layers of values that interacted with the former ones, such that each period is represented in contemporary Arab culture. In this way, the contemporary values of the Arab-Muslim people vary along two main dimensions: (i) collectivism–individualism, the first stemming from the tribal heritage and the second from exposure to the West; and (ii) ruler–ruled, the first with roots in the Arab-Muslim empire and the second from the period of stagnation (Dwairy, 1997b, 1998).

These two-dimensional value structures help to explain the cultural diversity among Arabs today. For example, the first cultural dimension would show that the majority of Arabs have adopted a traditional collectivistic way of life, in which the family is the primary social unit. The identity of the individual is derived from the family (Dwairy & Van Sickle, 1996; Meleis & La Fever, 1984), and family interests take priority over individual ones (Timimi, 1995). Family affairs are kept within the family, away from external intrusion (Meleis & La Fever, 1984). Familial affiliation is central for the majority of Arabs, as it meets the basic needs of the individual in exchange for the individual's adherence to family values and norms (Dwairy, 1997b, 1998). The development of an independent identity is not encouraged (Gorkin, Masalha, & Yatziv, 1985; Timimi, 1995). In addition to the collectivistic majority, there is a portion of Arabs that has to some degree assimilated into the Western individualistic culture, or has adopted a bicultural way of life (Dwairy, 1997b, 1998).

The second cultural dimension, ruler–ruled, helps to explain the hierarchy of authority in most Arabic societies, in which men and elders have exerted power over women and children (Budman, Lipson, & Meleis, 1992). Children are typically expected to obey the rules of the family and to modify their own desires for education, a job, and marriage, to meet family expectations. Females are expected to maintain the family's honor by chaste behavior, marrying through the family's arrangement or approval, and producing male children (Budman et al., 1992). In many Arab families, boys are regarded as an asset, whereas girls are a liability (Sharabi, 1977).

Socioeconomic styles of life explain much of the variance within the two cultural dimensions. Three major socioeconomic groups are found among Arabs: Bedouin (nomadic), rural, and urban. There has been a tremendous urbanization process since the late 1980s. Although the majority of Arabs have lived rural or Bedouin lives for centuries, endorsing a collective lifestyle, by the end of the twentieth century, 70% of Arabs will live in cities. Although living in a city is generally associated with less dependence on the family and less social control, collectivistic values are still esteemed. In fact, most Arabic cities do not meet all of the basic human needs; many urban citizens continue to work in agriculture and to maintain cohesive family relationships (Barakat, 1993; Fattal & Sokari, 1988). Thus, most urban, as well as rural and Bedouin families continue to endorse a traditional collectivistic way of living (Dwairy, 1997b, 1998).

10.13.3 PSYCHOCULTURAL FEATURES OF ARABS

Certain psychological features of Arabic culture are derived from the collectivistic and authoritarian structures in Arabic societies and are typified as follows:

(i) *External locus of control.* As a result of the actual helplessness of the individual who lives in a collective authoritarian society, he or she learns to believe that life events are determined by external powers—family, social leaders, or God. Religious people believe that their destiny is *maktoob* (written). Therefore, they do not feel responsible for their behavior or the events in which they have been involved (Al Khani, Bebbington, Watson, & House, 1986; Bazzoui, 1970).

(ii) *Interpersonal rather than intrapsychic sources of distress.* Arab individuals are conditioned through external threats of sanctions, making external controls more significant than internal (superego) ones. Therefore, shame rather than guilt dominates (Gorkin et al., 1985; Sharabi, 1975, 1977), and interpersonal coping strategies become more effective than intrapsychic defense mechanisms (Dwairy & Van Sickle, 1996).

(iii) *Indirect expression of emotions.* In Arabic socities, people tend to avoid expressing negative emotions such as anger and jealousy towards family members (West, 1987). Individuals are expected to exhibit emotions congruent to societal norms (*mosaiara*), and to hide authentic expressions. Other emotions are expressed through acting out behaviors away from the attention of others (*isligaba*) or through body language (Dwairy, 1997b, 1998; Sharabi, 1975).

(iv) *Unindividuated self.* The psychological autonomy and individuation that many Western psychosocial theories describe bear only limited relevance to the common pattern of psychosocial development in Arabic cultures (Dwairy & Van Sickle, 1996; Gorkin et al., 1985; Timimi, 1995). An Arab's identity is derived from the family, self-concept is enmeshed in the family concept, and an individual's needs, attitudes, and values stem from those of the family.

10.13.4 CLINICAL ASSESSMENT CONSIDERATIONS

Unfamiliarity with the Arabic culture may cause the clinician to misinterpret or pathologize certain cultural behaviors. Overdependence on the family, overprotective parents, avoidance of touching the opposite sex, passivity, ambivalence, reluctance to reveal family matters, hesitation in making personal decisions, and time-related problems are culturally normal and should not be considered as signs of immaturity or resistance (Budman et al., 1992). An Arab male inpatient's reluctance to make his bed or to clean his room is probably not resistance or regression; rather, it may well be his normal way of living (Meleis & La Fever, 1984).

10.13.4.1 Manifestations of Psychosocial Disorders

Because of the sociocultural background of Arabic patients, the manifestations of some psychological disorders may vary from those described in the *Diagnostic and statistical manual of mental disorders* (4th ed.) (*DSM-IV*, American Psychiatric Association, 1994). Due to the holistic cultural attitude toward mind and body adopted by Arabs, conflicts and distress, in general, are expressed in somatic terms (Dwairy, 1997c). This is the legitimate way of expressing personal problems (Budman et al., 1992; Racy, 1980). Sometimes somatic complaints are, indeed, the only expression of psychological distress.

Bazzoui (1970), for example, has identified certain characteristics of depression among patients in Iraq that are different from what is common in the West. Iraqi depressed patients show milder (and sometimes an absence of) mood changes. Mood changes were found in only 34% of depressed cases, and only 37% of manic cases displayed an elated mood. Feelings of guilt and worthlessness were almost absent among the depressed (only 13.8%). Suicidal thoughts and attempts were rare. Physical symptoms and hysterical behavior were the most outstanding features of depression, found in 65.5% of the cases. Fear of breaking the rules or shaming themselves and their families was much more dominant than feelings of individual responsibility and guilt (Bazzoui, 1970). Similar findings were reported for Sudanese depressed patients (Baasher, 1962).

Paranoid ideation, projection of responsibility, aggression, and "noisiness" were prevalent (47.5%) among hypomanic cases, and less common (27.6%) among depressed cases in Iraq. Interestingly, about one-quarter of the depressed population in the Iraqi study expressed a desire to run out of their homes into the wilderness, but this impulse was acted upon in only a few cases (Bazzoui, 1970). Bazzoui attributes these differences to the lack of individuated ego that is necessary to experience worthlessness. She suggests, moreover, that clinicians can diagnose Arab patients with depression even without the presence of miserable feelings (a hallmark feature for depression in the West), and with mania even when elated mood is absent.

According to Okasha and his colleagues, the obsessive-compulsive disorder (OCD) manifestations in Egypt are colored by Islamic religious rituals and beliefs that make the differential diagnosis difficult. Interestingly and in contrast to one of the *DSM-IV* criteria for OCD, most OCD subjects in the Egyptian study did not recognize the absurdity of their symptoms (Okasha, Saad, Khalil, Seif El Dawla, & Yehia, 1994).

Okasha and his colleagues also studied the manifestations of psychosis in Egypt. Delusions, depression, excitement, hallucinations, worrying, delayed sleep, and irritability were the most common presenting symptoms of Egyptian psychotic patients. The onset of acute psychosis occurred within five days in 68% of the cases. A stressor preceded the onset of psychotic symptoms in 74% of the Egyptian cases, and correlated positively with a favorable prognosis at the one year follow-up. During this same follow-up period, 64% of the cases had fully remitted. The social and clinical outcomes of the cases were not correlated with family psychiatric history (Okasha, Seif El Dawla, Khalil, & Saad, 1993).

The results of Okasha and colleagues agree with other studies that show similar psychotic syndromes among other non-Western cultures (Cooper, Jablensky, & Sartorius, 1990), and validate the presence of a special psychotic diagnostic category. This kind of psychosis is normally precipitated by stress, has an acute onset, and most patients recover rapidly. Associated symptoms are rather polymorphic, and include schizophrenic, affective, and neurotic symptoms.

El-Islam (1979) reported that Arab schizophrenics belonging to extended families had less malevolent manifestations, and were found to be less prone to deterioration into affectively blunted and withdrawn states than nuclear families.

Some delusional cultural beliefs, such as the devil, *Jinn*, sorcery, and the evil eye, may mislead the therapist who is not familiar with these beliefs (El-Islam, 1982). Much bizarre behavior which seems to be psychotic may occur: unacceptable wishes, feelings, and acts are liable to be projected onto the devil and appear as *wiswas*, or *jinn* possession. *Wiswas* is a rumination involving aggressive or sexual impulses that are attributed to the devil, enabling people to avoid responsibility and guilty feelings. *Jinn* possession permits acting out of forbidden drives, while claiming to be unaware of and not responsible for these acts (El-Islam, 1982).

Thin lines differentiate pathological delusions from cultural ones. Sometimes hallucinations may lose their perceptual quality and their contents are regarded as devil-induced thoughts. El-Islam (1982) noted that paranoid delusions may become normalized into ideas which are in keeping with beliefs about the evil eye or sorcery.

10.13.4.2 Psychometric Characteristics

Few studies have addressed psychometric aspects among Arabs. Ibrahim (1977, 1979, 1982) found some psychometric features among Egyptians. He found Egyptian students to be more dogmatic than Western students (Ibrahim, 1977), and less extraverted than Americans and British (Ibrahim, 1979). He found that cultural features such as oversensitiveness, superstition, and concern for socially sanctioned behavior and social desirability were more important personality factors among Egyptians than the neuroticism, psychoticism, and extraversion which are more common cultural features in the West (Ibrahim, 1982). The latter three factors do also apply in Arab societies, however (Farrag, 1987).

Based on clinical experience and field research, the present author has found the following psychometric characteristics of Palestinians" performance on some well-known (Western-developed) psychological tests:

(i) *Wechsler Intelligence Scale for Children-Revised* (*WISC-R*). Compared to Jewish students, Arab elementary school students in Israel had significantly lower IQ scores. The most common difficulties were in the similarities and comprehension subtests. The only subtest on which Arab students outperformed Jewish students was information. These differences may be at least partially explained by the culturally alien test items given to Arab students. In addition, these scores reflect the Arabic educational climate that encourages rote learning and discourages analytical thinking and the decision-making process.

(ii) *Bender-Gestalt and draw-a-person.* In both tests, performance of Arab students is similar to that of Americans until age seven, then the Arab scores show a comparative decline. At age 10–11, the performance of Arabs is equivalent to eight-year-old American children. This lag may be explained by the lack of encouragement for graphic activity by Arab parents and educators.

(iii) *Rorschach.* The performance of 50 Arab students, age 16, was compared to a similar age group of Westerners (reported by Levitt & Truumaa, 1972). Only slight differences were found. Arab students showed lower R (17.2 vs. 20.8), higher W (35% vs. 21.9%), lower P (4.5 vs. 5.3), and higher shading scores. All other scores were equivalent.

10.13.5 HELP-SEEKING BEHAVIOR

Generally speaking, Arabs tolerate their psychological distresses for a long time before seeking help. Among the Palestinian clients who sought help in the author's clinic in Nazareth, Israel, 44.2% came to therapy after years of hesitating, and another 44.2% came after months. Only 11% of the clients came after a couple of weeks, and 0.6% came without any delay (Dwairy, 1997b, 1998).

Arabs consider engaging in psychotherapy to be an admission of being crazy. Therefore, distressed people avoid this stigma by avoiding therapy. Furthermore, Arabs believe that physicians, native healers, religious figures, or family members are the proper alleviators of illnesses and distress. Seeing a psychiatrist or psychologist is a last resort (Okasha et al., 1994; Timimi, 1995).

Traditional and religious healers play a major role in primary psychiatric care in Arab countries. They use religious and group psychotherapies, and devices such as amulets and incantations. An estimated 60% of outpatients at the university clinic of Cairo, which serves patients of low socioeconomic levels, have sought treatment from traditional healers before coming to a psychiatrist (Okasha, 1993; Okasha, Kamel, & Hassan, 1968).

Arab families discourage long-term hospitalization or institutionalization for their patients. They feel they have the right and responsibility to be the caretakers of the unfortunate members of their family. Okasha (1993) reported that caring for an elderly demented person outside of the family is considered shameful; Egyptians, therefore, prefer to assimilate chronic mental patients. The parents of retarded or hyperactive children also feel a primary responsibility towards them rather than relinquishing them to institutionalized care (Okasha, 1993). Similar attitudes seem to exist in Qatar (El-Islam, 1982).

During hospitalization, Arab families do not discontinue their supportive role; on the contrary, family members and friends volunteer to attend to the patient. Groups of them stay with the patient for hours in the hospital, comforting him or her, bringing food from home, and offering their help. This cultural system of support seems unusual for the Western practitioner and may be considered intrusive. Meleis and La Fever (1984) reported that nurses and doctors in the USA often label Arab family members "anxious" and "intrusive," consider Arab patients "unpopular" or "chronic," and give them less time and personalized attention.

Males are currently approaching psychotherapy more than females. Among the clients of the author's clinic, 65.3% were males. Similarly, more males than females were represented in outpatient clinics in Cairo (Okasha et al., 1994). It seems that women may be more vulnerable to the stigma of psychotherapy. For example, the family does its best to hide, and manage at home, psychological disorders of females. They may even consider some disorders normal—such as anxiety and phobias. Males, on the other hand, are less vulnerable and could not be hidden at home. They are therefore referred more easily (El-Islam, 1969, 1982). It seems that psychiatric assistance is expedited for women only in severe cases, when the decision is finally made by the family. Therefore, women seem to be referred to hospitals more than men. The ratio between women and men in Saudi psychiatric hospitals was 1.6:1 (Rufaie & Mediny, 1991).

Arab clients typically are unaware of their mood and emotions. Initially, they present very supportive family relationships, and present their complaints in somatic terms, using metaphoric styles, such as "my heart feels like a dark room," or "my heart is dead" (Bazzoui, 1970; Timimi, 1995). Based on the belief that life, as well as the future, is "in the hands of Allah (God)," clients do not assume responsibility for their pathological actions (West, 1987). They place the responsibility for change on the therapist. They often appear silent, expecting the therapist to do all of the work. Because they regard comprehensive assessment as intrusive, they become uncommunicative when asked probing questions, and endeavor to absolve the family from responsibility for the illness. Their answers are often vague and unspecific because they question the relevance of this personal information to their health (Meleis, 1981; Meleis & La Fever, 1984). The concept of working to improve the self is generally nonexistent in Arab cultures (West, 1987). All these culture-bound behaviors are frequently misinterpreted by Western clinicians as resistance or lack of maturity (Dwairy, 1997a, 1998).

Typically, Arab patients expect an instant cure and assume that medication by intrusive methods (injections rather than pills) is most effective (Meleis & La Fever, 1984). They do not believe that talk therapy is worth paying for, unless it is direct advice. Long-term and non-directive therapy may confuse and frustrate the patient (Dwairy & Van Sickle, 1996; Gorkin et al., 1985; West, 1987).

Despite the above, psychotherapists are considered an authority in Arab societies. Influenced by sexist attitudes, however, Arab clients prefer and respect male rather than female therapists. Female therapists experience greater difficulties. Racy (1980) reported that even Saudi Arabian women preferred a male therapist.

He also described in detail the behavior of Saudi female patients. He reported that typically they would come to the clinic veiled and accompanied by a male member or several members of the family. They would limp in, leaning on the arms of a male relative. Dropping heavily into a chair, they may remain quiet and veiled until spoken to. Their demeanor reflects passivity to an extreme. Initially, they may say nothing and refer the question to the accompanying relative. Shoulders are frequently shrugged and "I don't know" is a common answer. They will answer only when pressed. Interpersonal and psychological difficulties are usually denied, and the therapist is assured that all is well and everyone is happy. Anger is transformed into sadness, disappointment, and/or self-blame, particularly when the object of anger is present. The patient may express her problem in somatic terms that prevent her from attending to her household duties and force her to spend much time resting. She does not assume responsibility for her illness nor does she accuse anyone else. She expects to be examined and prescribed a medication. Injections and large, colored pills are preferred (Racy, 1980).

In other Arab countries, especially in urban populations, the behavior of Arab clients may be very different from that of the Saudi example. Racy (1977) reported that among urbanized Arabs, the behavior of depressive patients is approaching that in the West. Among the Palestinian clients of the author's clinic, 29.6% came without informing their families, and 12.9% came in spite of family opposition (Dwairy, 1997b, 1998).

It is difficult to maintain professional relationships and boundaries with Arab clients. They often prefer to discuss problems in a social visit to their homes rather than in a formal session at the clinic. They may come late to the session or appear on the wrong date, or they may invite the therapist to the family home, or to a meal with the family. The therapist's negative response to such behavior is likely to be seen as insulting.

Although many clinicians have reported the difficulties of Arab clients in long-term therapy, no information has been reported about the attrition rate. In the author's clinic, only 15% remained in therapy for more than 10 sessions, and 49% dropped out after they achieved initial relief during 5–10 sessions. The rest were referred to other kinds of treatment (hospitals or psychiatrists) after the intake session or after reaching an impasse (Dwairy, 1997b, 1998).

10.13.5.1 Traditional Arab Theory of Psychotherapy

Germ theory and the evil eye have long provided explanations for illness (Meleis, 1981). Traditional Arabic beliefs about the origin of psychological problems frequently have linked them to supernatural causes: God, sorcery, or the evil eye. Many Arabs believe that evil thoughts could be transferred to another person through witchcraft or directly through the eye. The Arabic word for madness is *Junoon*, derived from the word *Jinn*, meaning evil spirit (Timimi, 1995). "Bad nerves" or "failure to eat" are other common explanations (Budman et al., 1992).

To undo the effects of *Jinn*, sorcery, or the evil eye, some rituals may be performed. Examples are antisorcery and antienvy rituals, including the use of amulets containing verses of the *Qura'an* (Muslim holy book), fumigation with incense, visits to the tombs of religious sheikhs, and purification rituals that involve drinking or washing in water that has been washed off *Qura'anic* verses written on a plate (El-Islam, 1982).

Another common ritual is the *Zar* ceremony. In this ceremony, participants experience states of trance under the influence of drumming, chanting, and dancing, during which they express worries and wishes that are otherwise socially prohibited. Each song is directed by the *Zar* healer to a particular spirit which, if present in the body of a member of the audience, will speak through him. It is to the spirit that strange wishes are attributed. Such wishes must be answered, for example, by sacrifices to placate the spirit and to persuade it to leave the possessed body. Birds, rams, and lambs are often slaughtered as sacrifices, and parts of them are then eaten by the person to be exorcized. Blue beads or figures involving the number five, such as hand symbols, are frequently used to protect people from the evil eye, sorcery, and *Jinn* (El-Islam, 1982).

In adddition to the aforementioned treatment types, marriage is often regarded as "the cure" for Arab patients. Schizoid, retarded, and depressed individuals may be forced into marriage by family elders on the assumption that marriage will take them out of their seclusion and improve their health, an assumption which is often disproved when they experience psychotic episodes soon after marriage (El-Islam & El-Deeb, 1968).

10.13.6 EPIDEMIOLOGY OF CLINICAL PROBLEMS

Epidemiological psychiatric studies are limited or localized in Arab countries, which makes it difficult to reach comprehensive conclusions without the risk of inappropriate generalizations. The main findings currently available are outlined below.

10.13.6.1 Psychiatric Morbidity

Based on Western measures, many studies have reported higher psychiatric morbidity among Arabs than Westerners. Ibrahim and Ibrahim (1993) reported higher neuroticism and lower extraversion scores among Egyptians compared to Americans and British. They also reported higher social anxiety and shyness among Libyan students than a comparable Western cultural group. The high level of anxiety and the tendency to develop neurotic disorders under stress were attributed to the social constraints imposed on individuals in Arabic societies (Ibrahim, 1979; Ibrahim & Ibrahim, 1993).

Based on the clinical interview schedule, the point prevalence rate of psychiatric morbidity among patients of a primary health care center in the United Arab Emirates was 27.6% (El-Rufaie & Absood, 1993). A high prevalence (26%) was also found in Saudi Arabia (El-Rufaie, Albar, & A-Dabar, 1988) and Dubai (22.7%) (Ghobash & Bibbington, 1994; Ghobash, Hamdi, & Bibbington, 1992). These rates were higher than those found in four other developing countries (Colombia, India, Sudan [an Arabic country], and the Philippines), in which the prevalence was between 10.6 and 17.7% (average 13.9%) (Harding et al., 1980). Some studies have indicated that the high morbidity in Saudi Arabia and the Gulf states is associated with sociocultural changes (Ibrahim & Al-Nafie, 1990).

In Dubai, psychiatric morbidity was found to be increased among women when their attitude and behavior departed considerably from each other. For example, psychiatric morbidity was particularly high for women harboring traditional beliefs but behaving less conventionally (Ghobash & Bibbington, 1994; Ghobash et al., 1992).

Conflicts between the traditional collectivistic authoritarian values and the individualistic liberal ones contribute heavily to the distress of Arabs. According to El-Islam (1979, 1982), intergenerational conflicts precipitated 50% of suicide attempts, 20% of neuroses, and 17% of schizophrenic illness among young Arab patients. Among the clients of the author's clinic, 18.1% of them exhibited client–family conflict by bringing it into therapy at the beginning, and 47.6% brought it during the course of therapy. Only in 34.3% of the cases had this familial conflict not emerged at all in therapy (Dwairy, 1997b, 1998).

Women and children were found to be more vulnerable to psychiatric illness than other social groups. Although men approached clinical help easier than women, studies indicate higher morbidity among women in the United Arab Emirates (31.9% female vs. 20.3% male) (El-Rufaie & Absood, 1993). Women reported more symptoms of anxiety and depression (Ibrahim, 1991), and neuroticism (Khalik & Eysenck, 1983). Although the general morbidity in Saudi Arabia was higher among men than women (El-Rufaie et al., 1988), more women were represented among hospitalized patients in Saudi Arabia (Rufaie & Mediny, 1991), suggesting the existence of covert morbidity among Saudi women. The unmarried, widowed, separated, polygamously married, and childless women were at high risk for psychiatric morbidity in Dubai (Ghobash et al., 1992), and for somatization disorder in Saudi Arabia (El-Islam, 1982).

It seems that in less traditional Arabic societies than Saudi Arabia, men rather than women tend to express their complaints in somatic terms. Among the Palestinian clients of the author's clinic, for example, men were more likely to express their distress by physical symptoms, whereas women tended to express their feelings of anxiety, fear, and depression directly. Expressions of anxiety, fear, and depression are normally considered signs of weakness in Arab societies. Therefore, it is more accepted among females, but detracts from the manhood of the Arab male, so somatic complaints may be more legitimate and less "damaging" for him (Dwairy, 1997b, 1998).

Children are also a higher risk group. Children represent 65% of outpatient visits in Saudi Arabia; almost 35% of them showed psychiatric disturbances that warranted intensive care (Ibrahim & Ibrahim, 1993; Tuma, 1989). Children in Sudanese nuclear families had more conduct, emotional, and sleep problems, and were more likely to be over-dependent than those living in extended families (Al-Awad & Sonuga-Barke, 1992).

Many areas in the Middle East such as Lebanon, Palestine, Iraq, Kuwait, and Sudan, have been fraught with extreme and continuous stressors in the last decade, because of war and occupation. Many studies have indicated a high prevalence of psychological disorders in those area—especially among children. Of Lebanese children, 20–30% have exhibited at least one of the following types of behavioral problem: hyperactivity, overdependence, aggression, depression, or social misbehavior, and 58% have exhibited psychosomatic problems (Chimienti & Abu-Nasr, 1992–93; Nassar, 1991). A high prevalence of psychological disorders has been reported in Palestine (Baker, 1990), Sudan, and Iraq (Raundalen & Melton, 1994).

10.13.6.2 Distribution of the Disorders

A significant number of studies have shown that somatization is the main form of psychological complaint, and therefore the most common diagnosis, in Iraq (Al-Issa & Al-Issa, 1969), Egypt (Isaui, 1994), Kuwait (Parhad, 1965), Palestine (Dwairy, 1997b, 1998; Gorkin et al., 1985), and Saudi Arabia (El-Islam, 1982; Racy, 1980; West, 1987).

The most common diagnoses encountered in the United Arab Emirates have been neurotic depression (55% of the cases), anxiety-depressive disorders (13.3%), and anxiety disorders (11.7%). Anxiety-depressive disorders have been more common in females. Neurotic depression and anxiety-depression disorders were most prevalent in the middle-aged group (35–54 years), while anxiety disorders were most common in the young age group (15–34 years) (El-Rufaie & Absood, 1993).

Depressive and related symptoms were common among Saudi university students (Ibrahim & Al-Nafie, 1991). Among these symptoms were self-blame (64% of the students), inability to concentrate well (54%), shyness (53%), shivering and shaking in response to interpersonal distress (42%), and academic problems (33%). A similar epidemiological study in Dubai showed that the prevalence of depression (13.7%) was higher than anxiety (7%) or mania and psychotic disorders (1.9%). Depressed mood was present in two-thirds of the anxiety cases, and autonomic anxiety was present in over half the cases of depression (Ghobash & Bibbington, 1994; Ghobash et al., 1992).

In Egypt, Okasha (1993) reviewed the diagnoses given to 800 patients admitted to the psychiatric center in Ain Shams in 1991 and revealed the following rates of disorders: mood disorders (18.3%); schizophrenia (16.1%); somatoform disorders (9.5%); substance-use disorders (8.5%); disorders of infancy, childhood, and adolescence (8.2%); and anxiety disorders (7.9%) (Okasha, 1993). The most frequent diagnosis among the psychotic Egyptian patients was brief reactive psychosis, with polymorphic acute symptoms precipitated by stress, and with rapid recovery (Okasha et al., 1993).

In contrast to the above, Bazzoui (1970) reported low rates of depression (1.3% depressive and 2.9% manic patients) among 1120 patients admitted to a psychiatric hospital in Iraq. These contradictory results may be attributed to demographic differences in the population, to the methodology, or to changes that have occured since Bazzoui's 1970 report, when only severe cases were sent to psychiatric hospitals. Among the Palestinian clients of the author's clinic, 60% complained of anxiety, phobias, somatoform disorders, and obsessive-compulsive disorders, compared to 32.6% complaining of depression (Dwairy, 1997b, 1998).

Eating disorders (anorexia and bulimia) in Arabic societies have been rare or absent in the past (Al-Issa, 1966; El-Sarrag, 1968); however, since the late 1980s these disorders have seemed to be on the increase—especially among Arabs in social transition. Nasser (1986) found that 12% of the female Arab undergraduate students attending London universities were bulimic, but found no anorexia or bulimia cases in a similar female Arab student group in Cairo. The absence of anorexia may be related to the Arabic cultural attitude towards food. Arabs also associate plumpness with attractiveness and health (Timimi, 1995).

Sexual dysfunction has been rarely studied in Arabic societies. Okasha and Demerdash (1975) reported on 68 male Arabs (Kuwaitis, Palestinians, and Egyptians) who had suffered erectile disorders and/or premature ejaculation. Of these, 45% reported a past history of homosexuality. When asked about their own evaluation of their disorder, most of these patients attributed it to undersized or diseased genitalia. Few of them blamed supernatural causes or masturbation. Many of the patients had accompanying somatic complaints, mostly backache.

Among the clients of the author's clinic, 18% of the women, but only 7% of the men, complained of sex-related anxiety. This difference may be attributed to the sexual oppression of Arab women or to the difficulties of the Arab man in admitting his sexual problems (Dwairy, 1997b, 1998).

10.13.7 HEALTH SERVICE DELIVERY SYSTEM

The first mental hospitals in the world were built in Arab countries: first in Baghdad, Iraq, in 705 AD, followed by hospitals in Cairo (800 AD) and Damascus (1270 AD) (Okasha, 1993). Although Arabs were the first to develop psychiatric institutions, their psychiatric problems today are often referred either to native (usually religious) healers (Timimi, 1995), or to medical doctors, due to the somatic manifestations of their distress. When they do reach psychiatrists, they are provided with medications or other medical treatments rather than psychotherapy (Gorkin et al., 1985; Ibrahim & Ibrahim, 1993; West, 1987). Psychiatric treatment then typically occurs in one of two settings: the traditional mental hospital or an outpatient setting. Private psychiatric clinics are also an option for some. A few private corporations, universities, and religious organizations own and operate some health services that also provide psychiatric services (Ibrahim & Ibrahim, 1993); however, in most of these institutions psychotherapy *per se* is not represented. Variations of counseling, behavior therapy, and family therapy are sometimes employed.

Obviously, the mental health system in the Arab world barely reaches a small portion of the population that needs psychological attention. Marital counseling, parent counseling, vocational guidance, crisis intervention, crisis support groups, school psychology, and other mental health services are rare or absent in most Arab countries. Psychologists who are trained in any form of psychotherapy are rare, making the need for research on mental health in general, and training programs in particular, imperative (Ibrahim & Ibrahim, 1993).

In general, there has been a paucity of information about mental health services in Arab countries. An exception is Okasha's (1993) detailed report about the mental health system in Egypt, considered one of the most developed Arab countries. According to this report, only 450 psychiatrists serve 57 000 000 citizens of Egypt (1 per 127 000 citizens). There are about 8000 psychiatric beds (1 bed per 7000 people), 5750 of them in Cairo. Only 250 clinical psychologists were reported to be practicing in Egypt, with hundreds of general psychologists working in fields unrelated to mental health services. There are many social workers practicing in psychiatric facilities, but they are not trained in psychiatric social work (Okasha, 1993).

Out of 24 governorates of Egypt, 19 have some kind of psychiatric clinic and outpatient unit, while five have no psychiatric services. Community care in the form of hostels, day centers, and rehabilitation centers is available only in Egypt's big cities. In the rural areas, community care is implemented without health care workers. Chronic and mild psychiatric patients are "rehabilitated" through cultivating and planting the countryside, under the supervision of family members. The programs for community care in big cities take the form of outpatient clinics, hostels for the elderly, institutions for the mentally retarded, centers for drug abuse, and school and university mental health. In Egypt, there are 13 medical schools, that for 35 years have offered school master's and doctoral programs in psychiatry (Okasha, 1993).

The denial of the role of emotions in physical health is common not only among patients, but among physicians, as well. That somatic symptoms could be of psychological origin is beyond the imagination of the average Arab patient and beyond the knowledge of many medical practitioners. Both physicians and patients are somatically oriented. When doctors fail to locate disease in the body, they typically make the diagnosis of "general physical weakness" and prescribe vitamins and rest (El-Islam, 1982).

Fortunately, some countries are witnessing the nascent growth and dissemination of information bringing to the awareness of practitioners the psychological and social contributors to illness. The psychiatric center in Ain Shams, for example, emphasizes a biopsychosocial approach to outpatient care. In addition, they are encouraging intensive psychiatric outpatient programs in all general hospitals (Okasha, 1993).

The Palestinians in the Gaza strip and the West Bank, as well as inside Israel, have made significant progress in developing mental health services during the last few years. In the Gaza strip (an area of 800 000 citizens), one psychiatric hospital and one community mental health program direct three local clinics. Programs utilize a multidisciplinary approach that employs psychiatrists, psychologists, social workers, nurses, and other specialists. In the West Bank (1 500 000 citizens) there is one large psychiatric hospital (320 beds) and three related local clinics. In 1995, the Palestinian authority initiated professional development courses for physicians to increase their awareness of mental health issues. In addition, a mental health plan was initiated to meet the needs of schools and families adversely affected by the 29 years of Israeli occupation (Palestinian Authority Report, 1994–1995). Among the Palestinians who live in Israel (800 000 citizens), there has been significantly more progress in the psychological services provided to schools. At least 24 centers for psychological services are now providing mental health services to the Palestinian Arab schools in Israel (Israeli Ministry of Education Report, 1997).

Despite limited mental health services and the lack of information about psychotherapy among Arab populations, the number of Arabs seeking psychotherapy has been steadily increasing (Dwairy, 1997b, 1998; Gorkin et al., 1985; Okasha, 1993).

10.13.8 FUTURE DIRECTIONS

Compared to most people living in more individualistic, liberal, Western societies, Arabs are more dependent on their families, their personalities are less individuated, and they do not welcome autonomy or self-actualization. Therefore, an individual's repression is maintained by external factors rather than intrapsychic constructs such as an ego or superego. Implementing psychodynamic or other nondirective therapies, which are designed to deal with intrapsychic processes and to motivate the patient towards self-actualization, may result in serious problems. First, they miss the main source of repression, which is external rather than internal; and second, they activate repressed emotions that may not be allowed to be expressed in the Arabic society, such as sexual drives or aggression towards family members. Therefore, "successful" treatment that makes the unconscious conscious converts the intrapsychic conflict into a conflict between the client and his or her family, and may leave the client with an untreated wound (Dwairy, 1997a; Dwairy & Van Sickle, 1996).

To avoid these problems, therapists are encouraged to be flexible, tailoring the therapy to the client, rather than fitting the client into their favorite treatment approach. Therapists need to be able to alter their personal therapeutic style, and be open and willing to learn new approaches to treatment (Budman et al., 1992). An understanding of the client's cultural identity and family relationships is essential evaluative information in directing the therapist's choice and trajectory of treatment. For Westernized Arabs, such as some of the more educated peoples of major urban areas, a therapist may consider insight-oriented therapies, whereas for traditional Arabs, behavioral, directive, goal-oriented, and short-term therapies are recommended. With traditional clients, psychotherapy may include counseling and academic and career assistance (West, 1987). The client's ego strength is another important factor to evaluate. Before implementing any type of insight therapy that may evoke culturally forbidden needs and emotions, the therapist should be reasonably sure that the client is strong enough to participate meaningfully in the conflicts that will emerge between the client and family.

Because Arab patients have many misunderstandings about psychotherapy, West (1987) suggested that issues of trust, the therapist–patient relationship, and status differentials need to be discussed openly in the early stages of therapy. Orientation to psychotherapeutic processes prior to commencing treatment may facilitate the effectiveness of the treatment, as well (Dwairy & Van Sickle, 1996). After careful consideration of the above factors, a therapist may begin treatment in a directive mode and later shift gradually to a nondirective and insight-oriented made (Gorkin et al., 1985).

When a traditional Arab client is not individuated from his/her family, parental authority is never to be challenged or criticized (West, 1987). Joining the authority of the family and gaining its trust is crucial at the beginning, especially when the client is a woman (Dwairy & Van Sickle, 1996; Racy, 1980). Without the collaboration of the family, therapy may well be sabotaged. A supportive personal approach that acknowledges cultural norms may enhance the trust.

Egalitarian family therapy that focuses on encouraging the direct expression of feeling is frustrating, if not impossible, with traditional families. Such therapy may threaten the authoritatian structure of the Arab family, and terminate treatment. Promotion of separation from the family is considered disrespectful (Budman et al., 1992).

Therapists should learn about the culture (values, norms, prohibitions, taboos, etc.) from the client, without imposing his or her own values on the client. Therapists may enlist parts of the Arabic culture to accomplish therapeutic changes (Dwairy, 1998; Dwairy & Van Sickle, 1996). West (1987) suggested cooperating with folk healers to broaden therapists" repertoire of treatment modalities that have been proven effective in Arab societies.

The therapist should find a way to help the client within the limitations and specifications of the client's culture. Their culture should be considered an immutable, but important, piece of the therapeutic process. Racy (1980) suggested that the therapist avoid both of two extremes: the temptation to be so respectful of tradition that one becomes paralyzed, and the tendency to become a social reformer. A combination of warmth, authority, diplomacy, and verbal facility can go far toward establishing an effective alliance.

Based on the sociocultural background of Arabs, characterized by the somatization of psychosocial distresses, and person–family interdependence, the flexible implementation of a biopsychosocial approach to treatment, involving the client's family, may be promising for the majority of Arab clients (Dwairy, 1997c).

10.13.9 SUMMARY

The Arabic culture is characterized by authoritarian and collective values rather than liberal and individualistic ones. The interpersonal relationship is both supportive and distressing. The locus of control is external, and the expression of emotions is indirect. An individual's self and identity are enmeshed in the collective identity.

Unfamiliarity with Arabic culture may lead to misinterpreting and pathologizing the normal behavior of Arabs. The manifestation of psychological disorders among Arabs is different from that in the West. Depression is characterized by somatic rather than mood changes. Guilt feelings, worthlessness, and suicidal thoughts and attempts among Arab depressive patients are rare or absent.

Obsessive-compulsive symptoms are influenced by and integrated with Islamic religious rituals. Delusional cultural beliefs such as the devil, sorcery, and the evil eye may overshadow the pathological delusions. Many psychotic Arab patients have psychogenic disorders that were precipitated by stress, have an acute onset, and, in most cases, show rapid recovery.

A few psychometric characteristics have been reported. Egyptians have been shown to be less extraverted, and more oversensitive, superstitious, and concerned for socially approved behavior. Due to sociocultural factors, Palestinian children in Israel have performed lower on WISC-R IQ tests compared to Jewish children. They also lag behind American children on graphic tests such as the Bender-Gestalt and Draw-a-person tests.

Arabs consider that there is a stigma attached to approaching psychotherapy. They seek psychotherapy after years of delay or after seeking help from traditional healers or physicians. It seems that men approach outpatient clinics more than women, who are often "helped" at home until they have severely deteriorated and are referred to hospitals.

Arab patients are typically unaware of their mood, do not feel responsible for their situation, and are reluctant to reveal family matters. They expect direct advice or medication. They attribute their symptoms to supernatural powers, germs, or the lack of food or rest.

High morbidity has been reported in Arab countries, especially in the areas of dramatic social transition. Women and children are at high risk. The mental health system in Arab countries barely reaches a small portion of the population. In rural areas it is almost absent. Somatic complaints are the most common presentation, and medication is the most common treatment offered. Psychotherapy is offered by only a few mental health facilities.

Insight and nondirective therapies, that emerged in the more individualistic West, encounter cultural barriers. Cultural discouragement of individuation and autonomy and the expression of emotions make psychotherapies that encourage emotional expression and self-actualization difficult. The cultural identity of the client and his or her family, as well as ego strength, are important factors that may help the therapist to tailor the therapy to the case. Collaboration with the family is vital for successful therapy. Learning the cultural background and the client's expectations is important to the therapeutic contract. Orientation to psychotherapy helps to make the client more engaged in the therapeutic process. Flexible, integrative approaches seem to be suited to the majority of Arab clients.

10.13.10 REFERENCES

Al-Awad, A. M. E., & Sonuga-Barke, E. J. S. (1992). Childhood problems in a Sudanese city. A comparison of extended and nuclear families. *Child Development, 63,* 906–914.

Al-Issa, I. (1966). Psychiatry in Iraq. *British Journal of Psychiatry, 112,* 827–832.

Al-Issa, I., & Al-Issa, B. (1969). Psychiatric problems in a developing country: Iraq. *International Journal of Social Psychiatry, 16,* 15–22.

Al-Khani, M. A. F., Bebbington, P. E., Watson, J. P., & House, F. (1986). Life events and schizophrenia: A Saudi Arabian study. *British Journal of Psychiatry, 148,* 12–22.

American Psychiatric Association (1994). *Diagnostic and statistical manual of mental disorders* (4th ed.). Washington, DC: Author.

Baasher, T. (1962). Some aspects of the history of the treatment of mental disorders in the Sudan. *Sudan Medical Journal, 1,* 44.

Baker, A. M. (1990). The psychological impact of the intifada on Palestinian children in the occupied West Bank and Gaza: An exploratory study. *American Journal of Orthopsychiatry, 60,* 496–505.

Barakat, H. (1993). *The Arab world: society, culture, and state.* Berkeley, CA: University of California Press.

Bazzoui, W. (1970). Affective disorders in Iraq. *British Journal of Psychiatry, 117,* 195–203.

Budman, C. L., Lipson, J. G., & Meleis, A. I. (1992). The cultural consultant in mental health care: The case of an Arab adolescent. *American Journal of Orthopsychiatry, 62*(3), 359–370.

Chimienti, G., & Abu-Nasr, J. (1992–93). Children's reactions to war-related stress. II. The influence of gender, age, and the mother's reaction. *International Journal of Mental Health, 21*(4), 72–86.

Cooper, J. E., Jablensky, A., & Sartorius, N. (1990). WHO collaborative studies on acute psychosis using the SCAAPS schedule. In C. N. Stefanis (Ed.), *Psychiatry: A world-wide perspective.* New York: Elsevier.

Dwairy, M. (1997a). Addressing the repressed needs of the Arabic client. *Cultural Diversity and Mental Health, 3*(1), 1–12.

Dwairy, M. (1997b). *Personality, culture, and Arabic society.* Jersusalem: Alnoor [Arabic.]

Dwairy, M. (1997c). A big psychosocial model of metaphor therapy with holistic cultures. *Clinical Psychology Review, 17*(7), 719–732.

Dwairy, M. (1998). *Cross-cultural counseling: The Arab-Palestinian Case.* New York: Haworth Press.

Dwairy, M., & Van Sickle, T. (1996). Western psychotherapy in traditional Arabic society. *Clinical Psychology Review, 16*(3), 231–249.

El-Islam, M. F. (1969). The educational and occupational correlates of psychiatric disorder. *International Journal of Social Psychiatry, 15,* 288.

El-Islam, M. F. (1979). A better outlook for schizophrenics living in extended families. *British Journal of Psychiatry, 135,* 343.

El-Islam, M. F. (1982). Arabic cultural psychiatry. *Transcultural Psychiatric Research Review, 19,* 5–24.

El-Islam, M. F., & El-Deeb, H. A. (1968). Marriage and fertility of psychotics. *Social Psychiatry, 3,* 24.

El-Rufaie, O. E., & Absood, G. H. (1993). Minor psychiatric morbidity in primary health care: Prevalence, nature and severity. *International Journal of Social Psychiatry, 39*(3), 159–166.

El-Rufaie, O. E., Albar, A. A., & A-Dabal, B. K. (1988). Identifying anxiety and depressive disorder among primary care patients: A pilot study. *Acta Psychiatrica Scandinavica, 77,* 280–282.

El-Sarrag, M. E. (1968). Psychiatry in the Northern Sudan:

A study in comparative psychiatry. *British Journal of Psychiatry, 114,* 946–948.

Farrag, M. F. (1987). Dimensions of personality in Saudi Arabia. *Personality and Individual Differences, 8*(6), 951–953.

Fattal, H., & Sokari, R. (1988). *Contemporary Arab history* Beirut, Lebanon: Gros Bryce. [Arabic].

Ghobash, E. H., & Bibbington, P. (1994). The Dubai community psychiatric survey: Acculturation and the prevalence of psychiatric disorder. *Psychological Medicine, 24,* 121–131.

Ghobash, E. H., Hamdi, E., & Bibbington, P. (1992). The Dubai community psychiatric survey: I. Prevalence and sociodemographic correlates. *Social Psychiatry and Psychiatric Epidemiology, 27,* 53–61.

Gorkin, M., Masalha, S., & Yatziv, G. (1985). Psychotherapy of Israeli-Arab patients: Some cultural considerations. *Journal of Psychoanalytic Anthropology, 8*(4), 215–230.

Harding, T. W., De-Arango, M. V., Baltazar, J., Climent, C. E., Ibrahim, H. H. A., Ignacio, L. L., Murthy, R. S., & Wig, N. N. (1980). Mental disorders in primary health care: A study of their frequency and diagnosis in four developing countries. *Psychological Medicine, 10,* 231–241.

Ibrahim, A. S. (1977). Dogmatism and related personality factors among Egyptian university students. *Journal of Psychology, 95,* 213–215.

Ibrahim, A. S. (1979). Extraversion and neuroticism across cultures. *Psychological Reports, 44,* 799–803.

Ibrahim, A. S. (1982). The factorial structure of the Eysenck personality questionnaire among Egyptian students. *Journal of Psychology, 112,* 221–226.

Ibrahim, A. S., & Al-Nafie, A. (1991). Perception and concern about sociocultural change and psychopathology in Saudi Arabia. *Journal of Social Psychology, 13,* 179–186.

Ibrahim, A. S., & Ibrahim, R. M. (1993). Is psychotherapy really needed in nonwestern cultures? The case of Arab countries. *Psychological Reports, 72,* 881–882.

Ibrahim, R. M. (1991). Sociodemographic aspects of depressive symptomatology: Cross-cultural comparisons. *Dissertation Abstracts International, 51*(12).

Isaui, A. (1994). *Psychosomatic disorders.* Beirut, Lebanon: Dar El-Nahda Al-Arabia. [Arabic].

Israeli Ministry of Education Report. Psychological services department (1997).

Khalik, A. M., & Eysenck, S. B. G. (1983). A cross-cultural study of personality: Egypt and England. *Research in Behavior and Personality, 3,* 215–226.

Levitt, E. E., & Truumaa, A. (1972). *The Rorschach technique with children and adolescents: Application and norms.* New York: Grune & Stratton.

Mansfield, P. (1991). *A history of the Middle East.* New York: Penguin.

Meleis, A. I. (1981, June). The Arab American in the health care system. *American Journal of Nursing,* 1180–1183.

Meleis, A. I., & La Fever, C. W. (1984). The Arab American and psychiatric care. *Perspectives in Psychiatric Care, 22*(2), 72–86.

Nassar, C. (1991). *The reality of war and its reflections on the child.* Tarablus, Lebanon: Gros Bryce. [Arabic].

Nasser, M. (1986). Comparative study of prevalence of abnormal eating attitudes among Arab female students of both London and Cairo universities. *Psychological Medicine, 16,* 621–625.

Okasha, A. (1993). Psychiatry in Egypt. *Psychiatric Bulletin, 17,* 548–551.

Okasha, A., & Demerdash, A. (1975). Arabic study of cases of functional sexual inadequacy. *British Journal of Psychiatry, 126,* 446–448.

Okasha, A., Kamel, M., & Hassan, A. (1968). Preliminary psychiatric observations in Egypt. *British Journal of Psychiatry, 114,* 494.

Okasha, A., Saad, A., Khalil, A. H., Seif El Dawla, A., & Yehia, N. (1994). Phenomenology of obsessive-compulsive disorder: A transcultural study. *Comprehensive Psychiatry, 35*(3), 191–197.

Okasha, A., Seif El Dawla, A., Khalil, A. H., & Saad, A. (1993). Presentation of acute psychosis in an Egyptian sample: A transcultural comparison. *Comprehensive Psychiatry, 34*(1), 4–9.

Palestinian Authority Report. Ministry of Health (1994–1995).

Parhad, L. (1965). The cultural–social conditions of treatment in psychiatric out-patient department in Kuwait. *International Journal of Social Psychiatry, 11,* 14–19.

Racy, J. (1977). Psychiatry in Arab East. In C. L. Brown & N. Itzkowitz (Eds.), *Psychological dimensions of Near Eastern studies (pp. 279–329).* Princeton, NJ: Darwin.

Racy, J. (1980). Somatization in Saudi women: A therapeutic challenge. *British Journal of Psychiatry, 137,* 212–216.

Raundalen, M., & Melton, G. B. (1994). Children in war and its aftermath: Mental health issues in the development of international law. *Behavioral Science and the Law, 12*(1), 21–34.

Rufaie, O. E. F., & Mediny, M. S. (1991). Psychiatric inpatients in a general teaching hospital: An experience from Saudi Arabia. *Arab Journal of Psychiatry, 2,* 138–145.

Sharabi, H. (1975). *Introductions to studying Arabic Society.* Jerusalem: Salah Eldeen. [Arabic.]

Sharabi, H. (1977). Impact of class and culture on social behavior: The feudal bourgeois family in Arab society. In L. C. Brown and N. Itzkowitz (Eds.), *Psychological dimensions of Near Eastern studies.* Princeton, NJ: Darwin.

Timimi, S. B. (1995). Adolescence in immigrant Arab families. *Psychotherapy, 32,* 141–149.

Tuma, J. M. (1989). Mental health services for children: The state of the art. *American Psychologist, 44,* 188–199.

West, J. (1987). Psychotherapy in the eastern province of Saudi Arabia. *Psychotherapy, 24*(1), 8–10.

10.14
Perspectives from Lithuania

DANUTĖ GAILIENĖ
University of Vilnius, Lithuania

10.14.1 INTRODUCTION 325
10.14.2 THE BEGINNINGS OF PROFESSIONAL PSYCHOLOGY 326
10.14.3 THE SITUATION OF PSYCHOLOGY UNDER SOVIET OCCUPATION 327
10.14.4 THE BEGINNINGS OF CLINICAL PSYCHOLOGY 328
10.14.5 REGAINING INDEPENDENCE 331
10.14.6 PRESENT SITUATION AND PROBLEMS 332
10.14.7 REFERENCES 334

10.14.1 INTRODUCTION

The situation and development of clinical psychology in Lithuania is inextricably related to the sociopolitical situation of the country and its rather dramatic history. This chapter is an attempt to show that all the historical and political changes have directly influenced clinical psychology in Lithuania.

Lithuania is situated near the Baltic Sea; it presently has a population of approximately 3.7 million. Around 3000 BC the first wave of Indo-Europeans appeared in these places, and the group of Baltic peoples formed. The Balts included Lithuanians, Latvians, and Prussians. The latter were destroyed by the German Order of the Knights of the Cross or assimilated by them a few centuries ago. Lithuanians now live in the neighborhood of Finno-Ugrians (Estonians, Finns) and Slavs (Russians, Poles). Lithuanians were the only Balt people to found a powerful state of their own in the middle ages, the Grand Duchy of Lithuania. This state survived up to the late eighteenth century. As it grew weaker, it was annexed to the Czarist Russian Empire. The following centuries demanded from Lithuanians a determined resistance to different occupations, threatened assimilation, and dissolution.

Let us consider what was happening in Lithuania at the time when clinical psychology appeared in the West, that is when Lightner Witmer founded a "psychological clinic" at Pennsylvania University, Emil Kraepelin began experimental psychological study in a psychiatric clinic, and Sigmund Freud was working out his theory and practice of psychoanalysis. At that time Lithuania constituted part of the Czarist Russian Empire. The only Lithuanian university, which was actually the oldest in Eastern Europe, founded in 1579 (Bumblauskas, 1994), had been closed for almost a century. This had been the reaction of the Czarist government to the uprising of 1831 against the imperial regime. After an even more powerful Lithuanian and Polish uprising in 1863, the reaction was still grimmer: the Lithuanian press was prohibited, Lithuanian schools were closed, even the Latin characters used in Lithuanian writing were prohibited; only the Cyrillic (Russian) script was allowed. Hundreds of people were murdered or deported to long years of exile in Siberia. The others resisted with determination the threatened national annihilation, until the press ban was abolished in 1904. This was the period of the "book-hawkers," the smugglers who secretly carried over the border Lithuanian periodicals and books published in East Prussia or elsewhere in the West. The so-called "hardship schools" appeared at this time, where country women would secretly teach children to read and write in Lithuanian.

10.14.2 THE BEGINNINGS OF PROFESSIONAL PSYCHOLOGY

It was only after the First World War that Lithuania was re-established as an independent state. The country witnessed a vivid development in all spheres of life: economic, cultural, and scientific. Since the capital city, Vilnius, was occupied by Poland in 1919, the University of Lithuania was founded in the temporary capital of Kaunas. There had been no professional psychologists in Lithuania up to that time, only students of psychology or representatives of other professions, such as physicians, biologists, and the clergy, who showed interest in the field (e.g., M. Reinys, J. Steponavičius, J. Vabalas Gudaitis, V. Lazersonas). The reason was that:

> The Lithuanian intelligentsia were not able to get jobs in Lithuania; most often they had to work in Russia. Only priests and representatives of the free professions—physicians and lawyers—could stay in Lithuania. Therefore Lithuanian intelligentsia would usually choose these professions. (Šapoka, 1989, p. 523)

The new university also had a department of pedagogy and psychology. Some specialists, for example, one of the most prominent pioneers of professional psychology in Lithuania, Alfonsas Gučas, having completed their studies here, went abroad to enrich their qualifications with the leading specialists of the time. In this way the first generation of professional psychologists came into existence. They taught psychology and organized practical and research institutions, created the system of teaching psychology, started experimental studies, actively participated in the press, and published and translated books on psychology. There also appeared what could be called the rudiments of clinical psychology.

In 1931 the Lithuanian Society of Psychotechnics and Vocational Guidance was founded, including a consulting department headed by the psychiatrist, Juozas Blažys (Gučas, 1937).

Some psychiatrists were interested in psychology and psychotherapy, and would apply methods of suggestion, hypnosis, and rational psychotherapy in their practice; they also took an interest in the newest trends and theories of psychotherapy. They applied their efforts to spreading and providing a critical evaluation of the new ideas, theories, and methods of clinical psychology, as well as towards educating society with regard to the prophylaxis of mental disease and to nurturing general psychic health.

As early as 1921 Blažys, who was the first professor of psychiatry in Lithuania and the author of the first Lithuanian psychiatry textbook (*Introduction to psychiatry*; Blažys, 1935), published an article entitled "Psychoanalysis and psychotherapy" in the journal *Medicina* (Blažys, 1921). It was a conceptual, exhaustive study, appearing in the early stages of the development of the new Lithuanian state and its medicine. The author stressed the necessity of psychotherapy, presented in sufficient detail the psychoanalytic theory of Freud and his methods, and maintained that "the time has passed for being content with mere bromides," and that psychological theory and practice concerning mental disorders are indispensable. Psychoanalysis occupied the central place in the treatment of neuroses, being a method based upon the psychogenic theory of the origins of neuroses and the principle of causality. Comparing psychoanalysis to other prominent methods of psychotherapy, the author asserted that in psychoanalysis, as in the rational psychotherapy of Dubois, explaining their situation to the patient is related to persuasion, and the therapeutic effect depends on the moral influence the doctor exerts upon the patient. Even though Blažys was a representative of biological psychiatry, in the *Introduction to psychiatry* he presented not only the biological aspects of psychic diseases, but also the latest tendencies of psychotherapy and clinical psychology: he discussed Freud's psychoanalysis and Adler's individual psychology, pointing out that these developments had illuminated the hitherto unpenetrated "secret" depths of the human mind. They had also demonstrated that not only in psychopathological disorders, but also in normal psychic life a very important role was played by the deeper psychic layers, and human feelings and drives. The author also introduced behaviorist views, at the same time pointing out their limitations: the analysis of psychopathology cannot ignore the subjective factors. As already mentioned, Blažys aligned himself with the neurological trend; however, he criticized physicians for their "medical materialism," and invited them to take a new look at man, to be aware of and seek new ideas, and also encouraged them to take up philanthropy. Eventually, the same author published a book entitled *Tolerance as a cultural principle* (Blažys, 1936), which was to be banned in Lithuania throughout the years of Soviet occupation for its strictly negative evaluation of totalitarian regimes, such as fascism and bolshevism.

Other methods of psychotherapy were also discussed, both in the specialist and popular press: autogenic training, hypnosis, and rational psychotherapy, as well as Jung's system of psychotherapy. Most publications could be characterized as adhering to the pragmatic view that no single theory can explain all of psychopathology, while each may be useful in a certain aspect. The questions widely discussed comprised the training of professional psychotherapists, problems of pediatric psychology, and the task of prophylaxis of mental disorder.

During the 20 years of independence the first professional psychologists were trained in Lithuania, and the period saw what could be called the beginnings of clinical psychology. The treatment of mental disorders did not comprise only biological methods but included psychotherapy as well; Lithuanian society was being informed and its psychological background enriched. Psychological knowledge was spread by people of various vocations—psychologists, medical specialists, Catholic priests and bishops.

All these achievements were doubtless very modest. But the span of time was also brief: 20 years is not very long in the life of a state, especially one which has started from nothing. However, the goal of building a state of their own mobilized enormously the activity and initiative of the people. With amazing determination they sought knowledge, high culture, and a more profound education. Even though the economic situation was difficult, young people studied foreign languages and made efforts to go to the best universities abroad, and upon returning they embarked on the task of creating a scholarship and culture of their own. Obstacles and hardships would foster character and a constant readiness to accomplish something which seemed impossible. Even though short, the period of the independent state helped an entire generation to cherish initiative, feelings of their own value, and responsibility for the state. A rather interesting point was made by the historian Danys in 1986. Writing about the emigrants from Eastern Europe escaping from the horrors of the Second World War, nazism, and communism, she notes that Lithuanians and emigrants from other independent states of the period differed greatly from the Soviet people who had lived for the same span under totalitarian regimes. The former generally had more initiative, and were more responsible and braver people since, in the author's view, they already possessed the experience of building their own state.

All these factors were also important in surviving another disaster that befell the country, that is the 50-year-long Soviet occupation. But even under the conditions of occupation, clinical psychology did gradually develop in Lithuania.

10.14.3 THE SITUATION OF PSYCHOLOGY UNDER SOVIET OCCUPATION

The existence of the independent state was again interrupted by subsequent occupations, first by the Soviets in 1940, then by the Nazis, and once again by the Soviets after the Second World War.

This had detrimental effects for the state in every way, and certainly interfered with the development of psychology; the humanities, as compared to the sciences, were especially strictly restrained. At the beginning of the Soviet period, the specialty of psychology still existed at Vilnius University; there was a department of psychology, and later a joint department of pedagogics and psychology, but these were soon closed, and the specialty abolished. A course for teachers of psychology, logics, and the Lithuanian language still existed for a time at the Vilnius Pedagogical Institute, but from 1956 even this training was stopped.

Soviet reality established itself firmly. A kind of Orwellian world crystallized, of which one of the strictest requirements was that of ideological purity and loyalty. All the humanitarian disciplines—philosophy, history, psychology, literary scholarship—had to be based not upon "idealist conceptions," but upon the foundations of dialectic materialism, whereas the "doctrines alien to our view" had to be abandoned. As in Orwell's world, a special language developed that for an outsider would sometime be very difficult to grasp. "Bourgeois ideology and idealist conceptions" were Western, non-Marxist creations; "obsequiousness before the West" and "views alien and unacceptable to us" were crimes that would not only draw criticism but could also possibly lead to imprisonment, Siberian exile, or even death. Such a perspective also confronted psychologists, and other specialists who contributed to the psychological culture of the country. Some perished, others were deported to Siberia, while some had managed to emigrate to the West before the "Iron Curtain" closed. The psychologists remaining in Lithuanian had to be extremely cautious, like all people working in the humanities. Most often psychological work would be restricted to comparatively "innocent" topics, remote from ideology, such as investigations of perception, psychophysiological measurements, and so on. Psychology was impoverished. It was "sovietized," which means that it was affected by the bureaucratization, ideologization and centralization of learning and teaching (Bagdonas, 1991).

From the beginning of the 1950s, when Nikita Khrushchev became leader of the Soviet Union, a period of "warming" began. First of all, this meant a more or less freer cultural climate.

Thanks to the initiative of Professor Alfonsas Gučas, a psychologist of the prewar period, the specialty of psychology was reopened at Vilnius University, and the department of psychology was refounded within the faculty of history. Officially the department was expected to train specialists in "engineering and work psychology." It soon emerged that under the conditions of a planned economy, the work of psychologists in various enterprises was hardly possible and altogether senseless. Where everything is decided "from above"; where "some pretend to be working while others pretend to be paying them"; where there is no place for practically any initiative; where the principle of equalization is applied everywhere; when it is not so much the quantity, quality, and realization of the produced goods that are important, but rather prestated plans "accomplished and overfulfilled" in papers and reports, as well as the "freely adopted" obligations of "socialist competition"; where the universal and most important aim of everyone's efforts is to cheat Moscow and to "draw" from it as much as possible—then simple, sound common sense and cynical socialist resourcefulness is quite enough. Professional psychologists have nothing to do in these areas.

However, these matters were merely the usual obstacles and absurdities that one would constantly face. Undoubtedly, the re-establishment of the psychology department at Vilnius University was of immense importance to Lithuanian psychology and clinical psychology. The head of the department, Professor Gučas, and its teachers, his former students, were anything but adepts of Marxist psychology and ideology. A positive element was also the fact that Lithuania had been incorporated into the Soviet Union considerably later than other countries. Being closer to the West and of a more European orientation, the country resisted Soviet indoctrination more persistently. The department existed in a rather liberal atmosphere. The teachers sought to present modern psychology and its history objectively, to foster a critical view of all the trends and fashions in psychology. Among the first graduates of the department, a few began to take an interest in clinical psychology (including the present author). The department's attitude was positive toward this, even though, as already mentioned, clinical psychology was not officially included among the spheres of study. Since higher education was strictly centralized, that is, the whole curriculum was compiled by the central Ministry of Higher Education in Moscow, to which all Soviet institutions of higher education were subordinated, the department was not allowed to introduce teaching courses or to plan studies on its own. The only liberty afforded the department was the "special courses" that constituted a very small part of the curriculum. The first course of psychotherapy for students of psychology was introduced in the form of such a special course. It was entitled "Methods of psychocorrection," since "psychotherapy," that is, healing, was a prerogative of physicians alone, and the fact that this type of healing meant "treatment by psychological means" did not interest the term-jugglers. Generally, according to the principle of economy, it was often more worthwhile to evade obviously absurd requirements and prohibitions than to try to prove their absurdity.

10.14.4 THE BEGINNINGS OF CLINICAL PSYCHOLOGY

Those starting to work in the field of clinical psychology had to make efforts to attain the appropriate education and at the same time to achieve professional recognition. Clinical psychology was taught and developed at two centers in the USSR, Moscow and Leningrad.

Incidentally, the term "clinical psychology" was not accepted, for ideological reasons. Everything went under the title "medical psychology," while in Moscow the term "pathopsychology" was also used, defined as being the application of psychological skills in a mental clinic.

> The psychologist assists the psychiatrist in the different stages of the investigation, treatment and examination of the patient, as well as participating in the preparation of sociopsychological recommendations for the integration of the patients into society. The main form of the pathopsychologist's work is the experimental psychological examination of psychiatric patients. (p. 5)

In thus such a complicated way was the psychologist's work defined in an instruction published in Moscow in 1975, *On the work of the pathopsychologist in a mental clinic* (Zuhar, Rubinštein, Poperečnaja, & Portnov, 1975), which was approved by the head of the Chief Coordinating Board for Research Institutes and Research, and which was addressed to "the chief specialists of psychiatric institutions, in order to lead and coordinate the pathopsychologists' work, and to psychologists as methodical instructions for practical work." As can be observed from the quoted passage, these instructions did not mention psychotherapy, since the treatment of mental disorders was supposed to be the prerogative of the medical specialists, and the latter in their turn would treat only by medication and other medical procedures. Incidentally, the "experimental psychological examination" mentioned here is a very characteristic example of the imprecise usage of terms. In this situation, empirical data is usually accumulated at the clinic by means of psychodiagnostic techniques, whereas the instruction presents this process, quite inadequately, as "experimental," attaching to it the title of an investigative strategy (Rimkutė, 1986).

In Moscow the dominating approach was Pavlovian, and altogether unfavorable with regard to psychotherapy. At Moscow University, however, research was carried out concerning the cognitive aspects of mental diseases and the psychological aspects of various somatic diseases.

The attitudes at Leningrad University and the Bekhterev Institute of Psychoneurology were rather more liberal; there, both psychodiagnostics and psychotherapy were developed. Psychological tests and techniques of examination worked out in the West were also applied there.

Thus, those Lithuanian psychologists who wished to work in the field of clinical psychology used to go to the universities and institutes of Leningrad or Moscow to continue their studies or to do postgraduate work. On the whole those who started to work as clinical psychologists would at the same time have to work independently and to seek opportunities to develop their skills. On the one hand, one had to strive for professional recognition, to seek good contacts with medical specialists, to prove that clinical psychology and psychotherapy offered much to medical practice. On the other hand, the information and literature available were insufficient, for Soviet literature, usually in Russian, was as a rule one-sided, while new literature from the West was very hard to obtain. Also there was no chance of breaking through the Iron Curtain and going abroad to study. Other ways and means had to be sought.

Comparatively good psychological literature was available from neighboring Poland, where the situation was more favorable than in Lithuania. Poland was not a Soviet republic, but only a satellite to the Soviet Union, and ideological restraints were not so severe there. Numerous valuable books were translated into Polish, and therefore quite easily obtainable; one had only to learn Polish.

Another possible way of developing skills was through contacts with colleagues in East Germany. In this country, otherwise most strictly socialist, the psychodynamic trend in clinical psychology was not banned. At the end of the 1970s Dr. Kurt Höck, a psychotherapist from East Berlin, began to organize yearly seminars in psychodynamic group psychotherapy for East German psychologists and psychotherapists. One small group in this seminar was international and included German-speaking colleagues from Poland, Hungary, Czechoslovakia and other East European countries. The two participants from Lithuania were the present author and the psychotherapist A. Alekseičikas. Of course, these visits were only a private initiative, unsupported by any institutions, at one's own expense and during one's vacation. But once an invitation "to visit acquaintances" was received, it was relatively simple to get leave to attend.

Participation in this seminar offered not merely the possibility of learning group psychotherapy; it was in a sense an aid to Lithuanian clinical psychology at large. The international group comprised active and creative people from the East European countries. Even after the several years' seminar program had been completed, the group continued to meet in different countries: East Germany, Poland, Lithuania, Hungary. All in all, this communication continued for 15 years. It offered opportunities to learn and to exchange experience, and the possibility of creating joint projects. We did our best to communicate the knowledge and new skills acquired during these sessions to our Lithuanian colleagues, as well as to mediate their new contacts with East European specialists.

This was a very special experience which unified the East European psychologists and psychotherapists, all deprived and isolated to a greater or lesser degree, and exerting immense efforts in order to achieve professional skills. The dramatic political events in East Europe were also experienced together—starting with the Solidarity movement in Poland and the first visit by Pope John Paul II there, the birth of the liberation movements in these countries, and finally, the destruction of the Berlin Wall.

This seminar program directly inspired the yearly seminars for psychotherapists, clinical psychologists and psychiatrists which we began to organize in the Vilnius Psychoneurological Hospital. The first seminar took place in spring 1978. Soon the initiative was taken over by the section of Clinical Psychology, the most active one in the Lithuanian branch of the Society of Psychologists of the USSR. (According to the already mentioned principle of centralization, the Soviet Republics had no right to form professional organizations of their own, only to have so-called branches of the central organizations.) The seminars would include reports on urgent subjects, as well as practical sessions. They were positively valued by most colleagues, and soon became well known throughout the whole of the Soviet Union as the "Vilnius spring seminars." They used to attract specialists from Estonia, Latvia, Georgia, the Ukraine, Russia, and even from Siberia and the Far East. The time came when all those wishing to attend could not possibly be received, so the participants had to be selected. On the whole, in the 1980s, the practical clinical psychology and psychotherapy of Lithuania were considered to be the most developed among Soviet republics. Lithuanians were often invited to other republics to conduct various training courses.

These seminars took place yearly for more than a decade and constituted an important contribution to the professional skills and consciousness of clinical psychologists and psychotherapists. Understandably, with time, the huge common undertaking began to fail to answer the needs of evermore differentiated professional interests and growing specializations. It was necessary to look for other forms also and various more specialized professional associations began to appear.

The pioneers of clinical psychology also received considerable assistance from the clinical psychologists of the Lithuanian emigration. In 1976 Vytautas Bieliauskas, Professor of Clinical Psychology at Xavier University (Cincinnati, Ohio) came to Lithuania for the first time. Since then he has been a frequent visitor and offers much help in training specialists in clinical psychology and raising their qualifications. In the 1990s his son Linas Bieliauskas, Professor of Neuropsychology at the University of Michigan, has also established contacts with Lithuanian psychologists and offers real assistance. During his first visits, Vytautas Bieliauskas delivered cycles of lectures on various questions of clinical psychology, to local clinical psychologists, psychotherapists, psychiatrists, and other medical specialists. This was of great importance not only because of the valuable information content, but also because it helped psychologists to spread psychological knowledge in the sphere of medicine, and contributed to the professional establishment of clinical psychologists. During further visits Vytautas Bieliauskas also conducted special training courses for psychologists and psychotherapists in the theory and practice of family therapy, as well as in clinical psychodiagnostics, presenting in detail the projective personality test of house–tree–person drawings.

For his first stay in Lithuania, Vytautas Bieliauskas had received a scientist's exchange grant from the National Institutes of Health, and visited the USSR as a health service representative. Thus he had an opportunity to also visit Leningrad and Moscow. He described his impressions from this trip in the journal *American Psychologist* (1977). Writing of the situation of clinical psychology and psychotherapy in the USSR and Lithuania, he pointed out that these were young professions in those countries. People working in them were young, enthusiastic, and hopeful. However, "everything requires time and a great deal of patience in the USSR" (p. 379). He also noted the dominating centralization and ideologization of science and learning. "My audience," wrote Professor Bieliauskas of his lectures in Vilnius, "showed a great deal of familiarity with our literature and with the literature of the West in general" (p. 378). He also stated that in Lithuania a wide interest in research and new trends of healing could be encountered, and the local psychiatric service was a little more developed than in other Soviet republics.

There were also occasions for learning from other prominent specialists. Carl Rogers visited Moscow and led seminars there, as did the creator of logotherapy, Viktor Frankl. (It was then that we started investigations of the "feeling of purpose in life" in Lithuania, as well as the adaptation of the Crumbaugh and Maholic purpose in Life test.) Virginia Satir also led family therapy seminars in Vilnius.

The first Lithuanian clinical psychologists began to work at state psychiatric hospitals (there was no other type at the time). Throughout the Soviet Union, psychology, and applied psychology in particular, was regarded rather suspiciously and only mental hospitals were allowed to introduce psychologists into their staff, but not other health institutions.

In Lithuania there were already some more progressive psychiatrists who were interested in psychology and psychotherapy, and applied psychotherapeutic techniques in their work. They included N. Indrašius, A. Alekseičikas, A. Dembinskas, L. Radavičius, and A. Vinkšna. Some of them had already acquired degrees in medical psychology in Leningrad. They were both the first teachers and our first colleagues. Alekseičikas was perhaps the only psychiatrist in Lithuania specifically practicing psychotherapy. The doctor of medical psychology Goštautas had already founded, at Kaunas Cardiology Institute, a laboratory of medical psychology which carried out research and the adaptation of psychodiagnostic methods. Dembinskas and Goštautas formed psychology and psychotherapy sections for medical students in the frame of students' research societies, in Vilnius and Kaunas respectively. Students of psychology joined them later. In this way circles of people were formed who sought to extend psychiatric aid in Lithuania beyond the biological approach, and to make psychotherapy available for patients too.

The pioneer clinical psychologists worked in the field of psychodiagnostics and to an even greater extent occupied themselves with psychotherapeutic work.

One must say that clinical psychology developed rather successfully in Lithuania, insofar as it was possible under the prevailing political conditions. Professional recognition was achieved in psychiatry. The mere fact that quite soon psychologists were working in all Lithuanian mental hospitals was proof of this (given that it was up to the hospitals to decide whether they needed such specialists), and some hospitals even developed departments of psychology, the so-called "psychology laboratories." Even some psychiatrists, having taken special courses, started working in clinical psychology (Juozaitytė, Dembinskienė, etc.).

In spite of various restrictions, the psychology graduates of Vilnius University made efforts to progress in diverse spheres of clinical psychology. This always required considerable initiative, commitment, and dedication. Much depended on the first specialist in a particular field. The prestige of psychology would be enhanced by personalities able to demonstrate competence and the value of psychology, as well as to establish good contacts and collaborate with other professionals; they would prepare the way for other colleagues in that field. Some of these pioneers should be mentioned. Rasa Bieliauskaitė started the development of child clinical psychology in Lithuania; Rūta Sargautytė was the first psychologist in a psychosomatic clinic; Gražina Gudaitė, a pioneer in Lithuania of Jung's analytic psychology, headed a department of a large mental clinic; Kristina Ona Polukordienė began work in the psychotherapy of adolescents, youth, and patients with stutters; Rimantas Kočiūnas and Aleksandras Kučinskas pioneered the humanist psychology and psychotherapy which won great popularity in Lithuania; and Laima Bulotaitė was the first to investigate the psychological aspects of alcoholism and drug addiction.

Alongside practical work, most psychologists took up research; they usually prepared and presented their doctoral theses in the universities of Moscow and Leningrad. In their dissertations they analyzed the cognitive peculiarities of schizophrenic patients (Gailienė), the personal peculiarities of children with a long history of illness (Bieliauskaitė), the effectiveness of group psychotherapy with young stuttering patients (Polukordienė), the possibilities of youth group psychotherapy (Želvys), the psychological problems of alcoholic patients (Bulotaitė), and psychological problems in cardiology (Rugevičius, Palujanskienė).

Clinical psychologists and psychotherapists also took up teaching; they gave various courses in clinical and medical psychology, clinical psychodiagnostics, and psychotherapy courses for students of medicine and psychology, as well as for physicians. They also wrote several textbooks (Dembinskas et al., 1981; Gailienė, 1989; Sargautytė & Želvys, 1988).

The work of popularizing psychology and psychotherapy, and informing the public was also very important. Psychologists wrote popular articles, spoke on radio and television and gave public lectures. In this way the popularity and authority of psychology grew, and psychological help become available to ever wider circles of society.

10.14.5 REGAINING INDEPENDENCE

In the late 1980s perestroika emerged in the Soviet Union, which meant the beginning of the crash of the totalitarian system. In Lithuania all the ties of exaggerated dependence were rapidly torn. Professional organizations were the first to free themselves from enforced centralization, and psychologists were among the very first. In November 1988 the Lithuanian branch of the Society of Psychologists of the USSR held a conference which adopted the decision to close the branch. The constituent conference of January 1989 founded an independent organization, the Lithuanian Union of Psychologists, confirmed its statute, and elected its council and president. An address to the Society of Psychologists of the USSR was adopted which was subsequently read at the Eighth Conference of the Society on January 30, 1989, which was "as usual, pervaded by chaos. We were only observers there" (Bagdonas, 1991, p. 62). The newly formed Lithuanian Union of Psychologists included 410 members. Moreover, clinical psychologists and psychotherapists made haste to enjoy the emerging opportunities and freedom, and created specialized associations. Thus the Lithuanian Association for Application of Psychoanalysis was founded, followed by the Lithuanian Association of Group Psychotherapy, and the Lithuanian Association for Humanistic Psychology, also uniting mainly clinical psychologists, and so on. It was then that the first private psychotherapy consultations appeared.

The same year witnessed radical reforms at Vilnius University. It was the first among the Soviet universities to declare the so-called ideological "sciences" to be pseudosciences, and to dissolve the departments of scientific communism, scientific atheism, and history of the Communist Party. Other Soviet universities followed this example. The oldest faculty of Vilnius University, the Faculty of philosophy, was re-established, including studies in philosophy, sociology, and psychology. Instead of one department of psychology, two were created—the department of clinical and social psychology and that of general and pedagogical psychology.

On March 11, Lithuania proclaimed its Act of Independence, which meant that Lithuania was to be freed from the Soviet empire and was to seek, by persistent peaceful means, *de facto* independence. In the summer of 1991, after the abortive putsch in Moscow, the independent state of Lithuania was recognized by the world.

On June 12, 1990 the Supreme Council of Lithuania confirmed the new Statute of Vilnius University, establishing the autonomy of the university. The university re-established the stages of study that had already been adopted in 1579: the bachelorship, mastership and doctorate. This had positive effects upon the training of clinical psychologists. The department of clinical and social psychology prepared master's and doctorate programs in clinical psychology. The first doctorate theses worked on at Vilnius University and written in Lithuanian have already been presented. (During the Soviet period, particularly in the 1970s and 1980s, an anticonstitutional requirement had been passed that dissertations should be presented only in Russian.) The teachers of the department have written textbooks to be used in these studies (Gudaitė, in press; Kočiūnas, 1995).

10.14.6 PRESENT SITUATION AND PROBLEMS

On the one hand the present situation is characterized by numerous positive changes in various ways. The public attitude towards psychology has changed. It is no longer "some kind of strange and funny profession," but an undoubtedly necessary and respected one. This is proved by the number of applicants each year to the specialties of psychology, the popularity of psychological literature, and the willingness of people in other professions to cooperate with psychologists. Of course, these changes greatly facilitate the work of psychologists. On the other hand, clinical psychologists maintain that fear of stigmatization is still too strong; people still hesitate too much before seeking the help of a psychologist.

For clinical psychologists the present situation opens up countless possibilities for learning. Contacts with other countries have become easier; many new professional contacts are being made. Psychologists go to European countries and the USA to study and to gain experience. Specialists in various trends come to Lithuania with lectures and seminars at the invitation of professional organizations and universities.

Vilnius University trains the clinical psychologists of Lithuania. Psychologists who have a master's degree in clinical psychology are allowed to practice and psychologists with a doctorate may teach students.

The postgraduate training of clinical psychologists and psychotherapists is mainly the business of professional associations. In the mid-1990s there are over 10 professional psychologists' organizations in Lithuania, and almost all of them encompass clinical psychologists and psychotherapists. Most of these organizations have already become members of corresponding international organizations.

The Lithuanian Psychotherapeutical Society is a member of the International Federation for Psychotherapy and the European Association of Psychotherapy. Its aim is that our schemes of teaching psychotherapy and our certification procedures should correspond to European requirements.

The Lithuanian Association for Application of Psychoanalysis maintains close contacts with the psychoanalytic associations of other countries. The Finnish Association organized full instruction for six colleagues from Lithuania. At present, in 1997, they have finished the course, received the status of associate members and are beginning to get back to work in Lithuania. Other members of the Association are participating in long-term programs for teaching psychoanalysis which have been worked out together with the Dutch and German psychoanalytic societies.

The field of group analysis, the concern of the Lithuanian Association of Group Psychotherapy also has long-term teaching programs. This association is a member of the International Association of Group Psychotherapy. It not only seeks study opportunities for its members but also organizes training courses in which colleagues both from Lithuania and neighboring countries willingly participate.

The Lithuanian Association for Humanistic Psychology also pays great attention to training, and has gone so far as to found the Institute of Humanistic and Existential Psychology (headed by Dr. R. Kočiūnas). Training courses are also organized by the Lithuanian Association of Hypnosis and the Lithuanian Society of Jungian Analytical Psychology.

Of the professional associations, the Lithuanian Suicidological Association, which is a member of the International Association for Suicide Prevention, is probably the most interdisciplinary, like suicidology itself. The problem of suicides in Lithuania has grown dramatically during the 1990s, and the specialists in this area are the first to be alarmed. They in their turn are trying to draw the attention of both society and of governmental institutions to the problem, to inform the public, conduct investigations, and create suicide prevention programs (Gailienė, 1996).

At present psychologists and psychotherapists work in all Lithuanian mental hospitals and in the psychiatric departments of various clinics and general hospitals. Both professions are practicing psychotherapy. Even though the formal position of the hospitals has not changed—they are all state mental health hospitals—some shifts have taken place in attitudes to patients and their treatment. The inpatient departments of mental hospitals have often introduced the principles of the therapeutic community, and have opened day-patient departments. Treatment is mostly combined medication and psychotherapy. Three mental hospitals already have inpatient psychotherapeutic departments where the main method of treatment is psychotherapy, while medication is used to a minimal extent. Mental hospitals most often apply group psychotherapy, client-centered psychotherapy, psychodynamic therapy, cognitive-behavioral therapy, and Gestalt therapy.

Certainly it would be an exaggeration to speak of an unproblematic integration of psychiatry and clinical psychology. There are problems and tensions enough, but there is also progress.

The Clinical Psychotherapy Center has been opened in Vilnius, offering specifically psychotherapeutic help. The Center includes inpatient departments for adults and children, an outpatient department, a psychotherapy and rehabilitation department for torture victims, and a department for the prevention of mental disorder in adolescents and young people. The Center is subordinated to the health department of Vilnius municipality, but receives patients from the whole republic, for there are practically no such institutions to be found in other cities. The financial situation of the center is rather typical of the present Lithuanian health service which has not yet turned into a health insurance-based system. Psychotherapeutic help here is paid for, but children, adolescents, invalids, and others needing social support receive free help. The prices are established by the Minister of Health, and are low.

Thanks to the work of Dr. K. O. Polukordienė, the Youth Psychological Aid Center (YPAC) has been opened in Vilnius. This is a nonprofit, nongovernmental organization which gives free psychological help to young people. Psychologists and psychotherapists work there, as well as over one hundred specially selected and trained volunteers. The Center provides the "Youth Line," a voluntary anonymous phone help service from other young people; professional psychological and psychotherapeutic aid; various clubs and groups (e.g., the Stuttering Problems Club), a youth discussion club, an art studio, and so on. The YPAC is a member of the International Federation of Telephonic Emergency Services and maintains close cooperation with Befrienders International, the international volunteer organization of the UK. The Center also assists all the new psychological help services being founded in Lithuania and employs both professionals and volunteers.

As a result of the persistent efforts of the child psychiatrist Dr. D. Pūras, the University Center for Children with Developmental Disorders began in Vilnius in 1991. Children with especially complicated psychosocial problems were, for the first time, treated not only biologically and by means of medication, but also by receiving far wider psychosocial help which was offered to them and their families by clinical psychologists, child psychiatrists, and social workers working as a team. Students of medicine, psychology, and social work are also trained at the Center, and, postgraduate courses are offered to specialists in these fields. The Center cooperates intensively with corresponding institutions in various foreign countries. The Center has created two models of service for children with developmental disorders which are being introduced in all the municipalities. The first is early intervention for children up to four years old with risk factors and for their families. It is carried out by physicians, clinical psychologists, social workers, physiotherapists, and speech therapists working as a team. The second model is that of child psychiatric help which also first involves planning various psychosocial interventions.

Help for alcoholic patients and those with addictive diseases has also broken out of the narrow medical framework. Although the number of institutions providing assistance to these patients is far from sufficient, in those that already exist, psychotherapy and psychosocial interventions are widely applied, and specialists of various professions cooperate.

Clinical psychologists also work in the field of health psychology: they investigate the risk factors for different disorders, organize teaching, write books (Gailenė, Bulotaitė, & Sturlienė, 1996; Lepeškienė, 1996) and edit the magazine *Psychology for You* (Dr. G. Chomentauskas).

However, qualified psychological and psychotherapeutic help is only available to the population of the few largest cities so far. In smaller settlements it is still lacking. Psychology has been introduced only to a small extent into other spheres of medicine beside psychiatry. This is conditioned by different factors. The economic situation of Lithuania is still rather unsteady. In the health service system even the most elementary needs of the patients are sometimes scarcely answered, so a more sophisticated kind of help, such as psychological aid, seems to be an unaffordable luxury. Moreover, the reform of the health service is proceeding very slowly. As already mentioned, there is no insurance-based medical system. Therefore as yet there is almost no private psychotherapy practice, since in this situation each payable service means that the client pays a double fee: once with his obligatory state taxes, and also when paying for the particular service.

Other acute problems also arise from the economic situation. For example, on account of the extremely poor salaries paid to specialists doing research or academic work, some capable people, especially the young, have to abandon these areas.

Bureaucratic reforms are also taking a long time. The legal status of the specialty of psychotherapy remains problematic. The certifying commission at the ministry decides upon the qualifications of psychologists and psychotherapists, assigning qualification categories according to which the salaries of these workers at governmental institutions are established. Previously this was a prerogative of the certifying commission for neurologists and psychiatrists which was far less competent, for that matter, than the present one. But probably in the future the task of certification of specialists will be taken over by professional organizations. For example, a licensing commission has already been formed at the Lithuanian Society of Psychologists which is working upon the licensing regulations for practicing psychologists.

Briefly speaking, the present situation of Lithuanian clinical psychology is more or less hopeful. One can expect that as the general situation of the country normalizes, the position of clinical psychology will improve as well, since the need for psychological help in this society is very great indeed.

10.14.7 REFERENCES

Bagdonas, A. (1991). Lietuvos psichologijos raida [The development of Lithuanian psychology]. *Mokslas ir Lietuva* [Science, arts and Lithuania], *2*, 55–63. (In Lithuanian)

Bieliauskas, V. J. (1977). Mental health care in the USSR. *American Psychologist*, *5*, 376–379.

Blažys, J. (1921). Psichoanalizė ir psichoterapija [Psychoanalysis and psychotherapy]. *Medicina*, *2*, 35–42. (In Lithuanian)

Blažys, J. (1935). *Į vadas į psichiatriją* [Introduction to psychiatry]. Kaunas, Lithuania: Vytauto Didžiojo universiteto Medicinos fakultetas. (In Lithuanian)

Blažys, J. (1936). *Tolerancija kaip kultūros principas* [Tolerance as a cultural principle]. Kaunas, Lithuania: Spaudos fondas. (In Lithuanian)

Bumblauskas, A. (1994). Vilniaus universitetas: politinės ir istoriografinės kolizijos [Vilnius University: political and historiographical collisions]. In *Vilniaus universiteto istorija 1579–1994* [History of Vilnius University 1579–1994] (pp. 7–17). Vilnius, Lithuania: Valstybinis leidybos centras. (In Lithuanian)

Danys, M. (1986). *Lithuanian immigration to Canada after the Second World War*. Toronto, ON: Multicultural History Society of Ontario.

Dembinskas, A., Alekseičikas, A., Gailienė, D., Goštautas, A., Grizickas, A., Pūras, A., & Radavičius, A. (1981). *Psichologija medicinoje* [Psychology in medicine]. Vilnius, Lithuania: Mokslas. (In Lithuanian)

Gailienė, D. (1989). *H. Roršacho metodika asmenybei tirti* [The Rorschach method of personality diagnosis]. Vilnius, Lithuania: Vilniaus universitetas. (In Lithuanian)

Gailienė, D. (1996). *Savižudybė? Ne!* [Suicide? No!]. Vilnius, Lithuania: ia Lietuvos suicidologijos asociacija. (In Lithuanian)

Gailienė, D., Bulotaitė, L., & Sturlienė, N. (1996). *Ašmyliu kiekvieną vaiką. Apie vaikų psichologinio atsparumo ugdymą* [In love each child. On training children's psychological resistance]. Vilnius, Luthiania: Valstybinis leidybos centras. (In Lithuanian)

Gučas, A. (1937). *Pašaukimas ir darbas* [Vocation and work]. Kaunas, Lithuania: Lietuvos psichotechnikos ir profesinės orientacijos draugija. (In Lithuanian)

Gudaitė, G. (in press). *Įvadas į analitinę psichologiją* [Introduction to analytical psychology]. (In Lithuanian)

Kočiūnas, R. (1995). *Psichologinis konsultavimas* [Psychological counseling]. Vilnius, Lithuania: Lumen. (In Lithuanian)

Lepeškienė, V. (1996). *Humanistinis ugdymas mokykloje* [Humanistic training at school]. Vilnius, Lithuania: Valstybinis leidybos centras. (In Lithuanian)

Rimkutė, E. (1986). Psichologijos tyrimo metodai [Methods of psychological investigation]. In A. Gučas (Ed.), *Bendroji psichologija* [General psychology] (pp. 24–36). Vilnius, Lithuania: Mokslas. (In Lithuanian)

Šapoka, A. (Ed.) (1989). *Lietuvos istorija* [History of Lithuania]. Vilnius, Lithuania: Mokslas. (In Lithuanian)

Sargautytė, R., & Želvys, R. (1988). *Medicininės psichologijos pagrindai* [Elements of medical psychology]. Vilnius, Lithuania: Lietuvos TSR aukštojo ir specialiojo vidurinio mokslo ministerija. (In Lithuanian)

Zuhar, V. P., Rubinštein, S. J., Poperečnaja, L. N., & Portnov, A. A. (1975). *O rabote patopsichologa v psichiatričeskoj bolnice* [On the work of the pathopsychologist in a mental hospital]. Moscow: Ministerstvo zdravoohranenija RSFSR. (In Russian)

10.15
From a Monocultural Identity to Diversity Identity: A Psychological Model for Diversity Management in South African Organizations

KEDIBONE LETLAKA-RENNERT
Johannesburg, South Africa
and
WOLFGANG P. RENNERT
University of the Witwatersrand, Johannesburg, South Africa

10.15.1 INTRODUCTION 335
10.15.2 PSYCHOLOGY IN SOUTH AFRICA: A HISTORICAL PERSPECTIVE 336
10.15.3 INDIVIDUAL AND CHANGE 336
10.15.4 A SOUTH AFRICAN MODEL FOR ORGANIZATIONAL DIVERSITY 337
10.15.5 MONOCULTURAL IDENTITY 338
10.15.5.1 Maintaining Monocultural Identity Through Restrictive Affirmative Action 339
10.15.5.2 Moving Towards an Identity of Awareness Through Restorative Affirmative Action 339
10.15.5.2.1 Role of the organizational psychologist: constructive affirmative action 340
10.15.6 IDENTITY OF MULTICULTURAL AWARENESS 340
10.15.6.1 From the Identity of Awareness to Diversity Identity Through Diversity Management Training 340
10.15.7 DIVERSITY IDENTITY: OUTLOOK FOR THE FUTURE 341
10.15.8 SUMMARY AND CONCLUSION 342
10.15.9 REFERENCES 342

10.15.1 INTRODUCTION

The urban traveler in the South Africa of today is frequently confronted with a sight unknown to his counterpart from older days: white homelessness. Street corners are occupied by weary looking men and women, sunburnt from hours of standing outside, holding up signs asking for food or for any job. The emphasis is on "any." The days of job preservation for whites are clearly over, and with a new political era comes the pressure for individuals as well as institutions and organizations to adapt to what bishop Desmond Tutu has named the "rainbow nation."

Identification as a rainbow nation demonstrates South Africa's will to survive change. Adopting the rainbow nation as a construct, although political and economic in nature, is also understandable psychologically. It is an inclusive construct that provides space for everybody to join a multicultural society. It enables the forging of a new identity, as members of a new nation. Simply stated, diversity has four components in South Africa. It is a unifying mechanism, it provides a preventative strategy, it creates a basis for proactive intervention, and lastly it is a compelling vision. If the nation's entrenched divisions were not to be permitted to run rampant and deepen, some sustainable way forward had to be found. Healing had to take place simultaneously with growing as a new nation. To varying degrees both the private and the public sectors have reacted to the implications of the new dispensation.

10.15.2 PSYCHOLOGY IN SOUTH AFRICA: A HISTORICAL PERSPECTIVE

Psychologists have been involved in the creation of apartheid from the outset and are becoming instrumental in overcoming it today. In 1928 a team of psychologists, sociologists, and educators were sent to South Africa by the Carnegie Commission to study the problems of poor whiteism. Their extensive report (Wilcocks, 1932) stated with great concern that the:

> Long continued economic equality of poor whites and the great mass of non-Europeans and propinquity of their dwellings tend to bring them to social equality. This impairs the tradition which counteracts miscegenation, and the social colour divisions are noticeably weakening. (p. 33)

Wilcocks continued to recommend the creation of employment categories reserved for whites and called for "legislation which inflicts severe penalties on sexual intercourse between the races" (p. 33).

Fellow psychologist and later prime minister H.F. Verwoerd used Wilcocks' recommendations and combined them with his own ideas of racial supremacy. Verwoerd became one of the architects of apartheid and focused particularly on "Bantu education" as a means with which to deprive the indigenous African population of any access to knowledge. He believed that:

> The school must equip the Bantu to meet the demands which the economic life of South Africa will impose on him . . . there is no place for him in the European community above the level of certain forms of labour . . . What is the use of teaching a Bantu child mathematics when it cannot use it in practice? . . . That is absurd. (Harrison, 1981, p. 194)

As late as 1986 South African psychologists applauded the Carnegie Investigation for its "usefulness in the solution of social problems" (Louw, 1986). Many professionals stood on the sidelines of the struggle for liberation and claimed that their disciplines were apolitical in nature, forbidding them to examine scientifically the consequences of racial and economic oppression, while benefitting themselves materially and in the progression of their careers from that very oppression (Biesheuvel, 1958). Few psychologists dared to speak out for a politicization of psychology, and went as far as to suggest that apartheid policies and the dehumanization of the vast majority of the population might actually be detrimental to the mental well-being of the community (Dawes, 1985).

For a while, the struggle became the focus of research for mostly white academic psychologists, who saw the writing on the wall and tried to jump ship before they might lose influence and privilege. Studies on torture, violence, and colonialism filled the journals authored by psychologists, who did not dare to venture out into the townships where their subjects lived, and who kept black professionals out of their own academic units (Letlaka-Rennert, 1991).

Psychologists of color, often against the resistance of their white colleagues, struggled to create an academic discourse of diversity, introducing African writers and theorists into the psychological mainstream (Bulhan, 1990; Manganyi & du Toit, 1990; Nicholas, 1993). It became obvious that the real liberation from apartheid required the transformation of the whole society including all institutions, organizations, and structures of political, social, and economic life. Clinical psychologists understand today that the transformation of the individual has to be accompanied by the transformation of institutions and organizations. It is here that psychologists contribute to the development of a new society, a rainbow nation. Therefore, the authors choose to use the field of organizational psychology and the area of organizational transformation in their discussion of diversity development and psychology in South Africa.

10.15.3 INDIVIDUAL AND CHANGE

In South African organizational psychology today, professionals are as much concerned with the psychological well-being of individuals within organizations as with the organizations themselves. It is not surprising that clinical psychologists find themselves working in institutions and organizations and that there is a demand for clinical skills from organizational psychologists.

What is at play when looking at the individual and change, from a clinical perspective? In order to tackle resistance and assist people seeking personal transformation in the context of diversity, one has to focus on the obstacles and problems related to change. It is one thing to consider the theoretical background of societal transformation. It is another to examine the foreground of personal interactions and behaviors as it presents itself in workshops and training sessions with employees and staff members.

The clinical psychologist working with diversity is confronted with reactions of people under threat. As coping with conflict, vulnerability, and exposure are called upon, issues of safety come to the fore. There is a risk of possible repercussions at the workplace connected to making disclosure in diversity management workshops after the encouraging and supporting psychologists have long gone. We also underestimate the resilience and power of stereotypes working against disclosure. Whites might fail to disclose because of their feeling that blacks are not good enough or sufficiently like them to appreciate them, warts and all. Similarly, blacks fail to disclose because of their feeling that whites cannot be trusted to operate on a basis of equality. Thus, when under pressure and scrutiny, the defense mechanisms of one's choice flare up (Duckitt, 1992). The challenge remains to enable individuals to disclose and to promote self-confidence, such that people cannot only take the risks of change in the workshop, but have the courage to try what they have discovered outside in the real world.

10.15.4 A SOUTH AFRICAN MODEL FOR ORGANIZATIONAL DIVERSITY

Companies and institutions looking for help in facilitating a process of adaptation are still hindered by the resistance of established power structures, prejudice, and a culture of exclusion. Psychologists and human resource strategists in South Africa have no indigenous models to help them conceptualize the state of an organization's cultural identity and to meaningfully assist in the implementation of strategies to facilitate collective and organizational identity development (Table 1). Although models have been developed in the western world, none has been derived from and designed for the specific conditions of Africa in general and South Africa in particular. Typically, models and conceptualizations borrowed from the USA are used to help understand what manifests here and unfortunately, occurances are not sufficiently contextualized (Cross, Katz, Miller, & Seashore, 1994; Thomas, 1996).

This chapter explains why it is in South African organizations' self-interest to become involved in diversity work, in its broadest sense, from merely promoting multiculturalism and pluralism to direct behavioral and mental health interventions. Thus, a model is presented for diversity development that is reflective of the specific historic and economic texture of South Africa. It tries to provide a conceptualization of a possible development from the monocultural philosophy of racial exclusion and oppression, as it was prevalent in the apartheid years, to a multicultural philosophy that acknowledges and respects difference and can provide the basis for the progression of the rainbow nation (Steyn & Motshabi, 1996).

The model is psychological in nature and explains how organizations reflect the cultural state of the society in which they operate. Historically, working environments in the South Africa of the apartheid era were structured and organized to care exclusively for the needs of the white minority. The organizational identity was monocultural. In many institutions and organizations this identity still prevails and will have to be transformed and developed. Changes have to be promoted and facilitated on a level of personal identity management for members of the organization, as well as on a collective level for the organization as a whole.

The initial process will be largely one of awareness building. In a society where, for generations, a small minority has succeeded in keeping a large indigenous population under conditions of total deprivation, psychological strategies of denial, rationalization, and displacement are widely prevalent cognitive processes and learned behaviors. Interventions will have to utilize internal measures of awareness building, together with external measures of reinforcement and control in order to overcome prejudice, ambivalence, and resistance. Once an organization and its members have reached a level of awareness that provides the background for active diversity seeking, an identity of multicultural awareness will have been reached.

From here onwards diversity becomes an integral part of the organization's strategies. External control measures will become redundant and diversity will become organizational policy until a state of diversity identity has been reached. Now that diversity is no longer an objective, it has become part of the organization's fiber. The following sections

Table 1 Concepts of South African organizational identity.

Monocultural identity	*Multicultural identity*	*Diversity identity*
Restrictive affirmative action External control measures External regulation	Restorative affirmative action Awakening internal control measures Practicing internal regulation	Affirmed environment Internalized control measures Internalized regulation, both individual and organizational
Racial superiority Entitlement Power	Multicultural awareness Appreciation of difference Sharing of power	Multicultural advancement and promotion Equality
Defensiveness Fear Sense of doom	Curiosity Openness Engagement	Deriving benefits for all from diversity management Confidence
Prejudice Cultural ignorance	Open-mindedness Culture of exploration, both internal and external	Integrationist orientation Culture of inclusion
Employee composition white Organization monocultural	Employee composition in transition Introduction of different cultures, multiculturalism	Employee composition diverse and integrated

explain the stages of the diversity management model in more detail and make reference to the specific South African context, from which it is derived.

10.15.5 MONOCULTURAL IDENTITY

In the South Africa of the 1940s to the 1980s the institutional and industrial culture was monocultural. In a country of 30 million people, only 4 million of European decent mattered. The indigenous population and, to a lesser degree, Asian immigrants and people of mixed racial origin, were used as industrial cannon fodder in a process that was exclusively geared to the promotion and development of the white minority (Davenport, 1987).

This process required a maximum level of external regulation and control, and promoted on the inside a mentality of racial and intellectual superiority, entitlement, and power, but also one of defensiveness, fear, and a sense of doom. The most powerful army on the African continent focused its patrols on the townships rather than the borders. The enemy was within the society, not outside it. White South Africans who had access to foreign passports were in a permanent state of preparedness to leave, while reaping the benefits of their privileged position as long as possible. White gun ownership far exceeded the statistics published in the USA, commonly known as the "armed society," and the illegal transfer of assets and money offshore totalled billions of rands. On the outside, physical terror and abuse were combined with a system of dehumanization, together with the slow implementation of a slave mentality (Fanon, 1967).

Organizations and institutions were a reflection of the minority rather than integrated into the society as a whole. Group thinking dominated industrial and political strategies, and promotional efforts were limited to members of the white group. At one stage, the mining industry management, down to the levels of foremen on the shaft floors, became so aloof from the black labor force that a new language—Funigalo—was invented, in order to maintain a minimum of communication between foremen and laborers.

Today, one still finds organizational thinking stuck in the same paralyzing framework of prejudice and cultural ignorance. A culture of exclusion has been sustained for decades through schools, universities, families, and the information industry. The basic fibre of organizational thinking has had to be loosened and rewoven into a culture of inclusion. It was interesting to note that, after the first democratic elections in 1994, conservative white circles immediately called for a white homeland, a move destined to maintain on a small scale, what had to be given up on the whole, namely apartheid, or the maintenance of a culture of exclusion. Somewhat more liberal elements, around the former president F. W. deKlerk, called for the inclusion of minority rights into the new constitution, and a white popular movement rallied around the few Afrikaans language schools trying to preserve a pocket of white cultural exclusivity. It was the enforced introduction of the same Afrikaans into the syllabus of black schools in 1976 that had led to township riots, scores of lost lives, and a whole generation of youngsters who refused to acquire even a minimal education. In the South Africa of today a culture of inclusivity rather than exclusivity has to be learned from scratch.

10.15.5.1 Maintaining Monocultural Identity Through Restrictive Affirmative Action

The instrument with which to maintain an institutional culture of exclusivity was what we would call "restrictive affirmative action." The development of a minority was furthered by the restriction of the majority. Pass laws were imposed on black laborers, controlling their influx into the industrial centres. Wages for blacks were kept at a level prohibitive to the support of a family, in order to keep women in rural farm labor. Black children were subjected to Bantu education, designed to restrict knowledge to the following of simple orders. Where, despite institutional disadvancement, black labor met with white labor in a potentially competitive situation, labor laws were designed to preserve certain jobs and job categories for whites. Mine workers handling explosives had to be white, not in the least in order to prevent a potentially dangerous skill transfer. The postal services and other government agencies became a haven for whites who could not otherwise secure employment. Apartheid laws enforcing segregated residential areas (Group Areas Act) and the prohibition of interracial relationships (Immorality Act, Mixed Marriages Act) cemented cultural exclusivity (Davenport, 1987; Mandela, 1994).

It is interesting to observe today, that those parts of society who have benefited from affirmative action then, are the most outspoken critics of affirmative action now. They fear more than anything the competition of well-educated blacks who are competing for jobs that whites have been occupying simply because they were white. Inevitably there will be a shift away from employment on racial grounds only, towards an employment strategy that aims at racial equality on the grounds of equal qualification and competency. More whites holding up signs at street corners will bear witness to the fact that being white alone no longer guarantees advancement.

10.15.5.2 Moving Towards an Identity of Awareness Through Restorative Affirmative Action

The predominant sentiment in the established white institutional and business community today is one of fear and insecurity. Although the new national leadership has made it very clear that it intends to include all communities in the process of national unification, there is an atmosphere of mistrust, partially because many whites fear the maintenance of cultural domination—black culture this time—and partially because there may be deeply rooted feelings, that the acquired privileges were achieved through oppression and violence and are therefore undeserved. The predominant discussion in the public domain today is about crime, about the redistribution of white wealth through black criminals. The call for punishment ranges from castration to the reintroduction of the death penalty, scrapped from the legal instrumentarium by the current government of national unity (Duckitt, 1992).

At this stage, the main need is one of awareness building, and the overcoming of resistance. Many institutions and organizations are hesitant, fearful, or simply ignorant about how to honestly and more fully open themselves to the needs and challenges of a multicultural society. Many companies lack diversity in their employee composition and have still to discover large parts of the population as customers and clients, struggling with the need to modify products and designs to accommodate different tastes (Gordon, 1991; Lau & Shani, 1992).

Here, affirmative action of a different kind, namely restorative affirmative action, is required to facilitate the achievement of an identity of awareness. Resistance and ambivalence can only be overcome with the help of external control measures, this time however, not with the intention of enforcing a system of injustice, but rather with the aim of setting in motion a dynamic of learning that will render the tool redundant in the end. Government legislation as well as organizational and institutional policies need to be set in place to provide the basis for the opening of organizational culture. Enhanced education of disadvantaged students through scholarships and improved educational strategies in the townships should be combined with provisions for improved on-the-job training for employees of color. Labor laws are being revised to abolish job preservation for whites and to guarantee equal opportunity employment and remuneration. Government tenders are becoming linked to affirmative action goals within the companies competing for the job (Jones, 1991; Witt, 1990).

The Truth and Reconciliation Commission is another unique South African initiative attempting to combine awareness of past injustices with reconciliation and a positive outlook on future cooperation between diverse racial and political groups. Despite being criticized by whites for being vindictive and by blacks for letting perpetrators of racial oppression off the hook, the commission has already achieved, long before its conclusion, the initiation of dialogue between the races and the creation of an atmosphere of reflection on the limitations of monoculturalism.

10.15.5.2.1 Role of the organizational psychologist: constructive affirmative action

On an intraorganizational level, companies are seeking help from organizational psychologists to further an atmosphere of awareness of difference and its advantages for obtaining business objectives. Companies are slowly understanding that diverse perspectives will provide greater flexibility, increased creativity and improved problem-solving strategies. What they lack is a system to facilitate communication and to understand different perspectives. Here South African human resource specialists such as psychologists can provide indigenous systems that help to bridge the gap between different cultural backgrounds. The aim is to acquire awareness of difference as something nonthreatening and potentially beneficial to the progression of the organization. There is a shift from a more external restorative affirmative action to a more internally motivate constructive affirmative action (Trompenaars, 1993).

A program has been designed for institutions and organizations to facilitate this process. A multitude of intervention programs, workshop designs, and strategies are marketed by various organizations and companies, none of which take into consideration the specific conditions of the South African context. The legacy of the past and the demands of the future pose unique challenges and obstacles that require an approach that is indigenous and sensitive to the multicultural background of the rainbow nation.

The program has two modules, the first of which is designed to facilitate the progression of an organizational identity from one of monoculturalism to one of cultural awareness. Exercises are introduced to value difference, to understand affirmative action, and to develop concepts for the management of diversity. Personal attitudes, assumptions, prejudices, and behaviors have to be analyzed and modified. The predominant organizational culture is investigated and put into a societal context. On a practical basis, intercultural communication skills are provided, dealing with stereotypes and myths, and methods useful in the overcoming of resistance are practiced. On a further level, personal diversity skills are integrated into an organizational diversity management framework. Teamwork, interpersonal understanding, relationship building, empowerment, and organizational commitment are introduced as competencies that comprise the pillars of diversity management.

A member of the South African Zulu people greets another with the word *sawubona*, (I see you). The reply is *sikhona* (I am here). Essentially, this greeting means "I exist because you see me." To see a person as what they are, rather than as what one's preconceptions of them are, is the aim of intervention programs at this stage. In addition, individuals finding out about and treating colleagues in ways that are meaningful to them, and not only in the way prescribed by the old corporate culture, is another fundamental objective of the program (Letlaka-Rennert, 1996).

10.15.6 IDENTITY OF MULTICULTURAL AWARENESS

The intermediate phase of organizational identity finds companies and institutions in a state of raised awareness and residual ambivalence, but with a positive attitude towards change. Staff members that have joined the company through affirmative action programs become appreciated as valuable additions to the team. There is less fear of retribution and reverse racism, but ambivalence and prejudice may still inhibit processes of further diversification. However, at this stage, institutional leaders and industrial managers will be able to set goals and create visions of complete diversity identity. They will have understood that, for an institution to thrive in a society, it has to become a reflection of that society, in its goals as well as in its composition (Trompenaars, 1993).

10.15.6.1 From the Identity of Awareness to Diversity Identity Through Diversity Management Training

Human resource strategies at this level will rely much less on externally controlled affirmative action programs. Now organizational psychologists will provide organizations with the tools to internally develop their identity towards diversity. Diversity management may affect marketing strategies, the expansion or alteration of product portfolios, the composition of management teams, modifications of managerial and production styles, and communication styles within the company and between the company and the society in general.

The second module of the diversity management program is designed to facilitate this transition. Managers learn how to create environments that allow diverse individuals within the organization to reach their full potential in pursuit of corporate objectives. The impact of multiculturalism on market forces, competition, customer composition, recruiting, decision making, competency, performance management, and conflict resolution within the company are discussed. Crisis management in relation to issues around diversity is exercised, self-awareness is practiced and different management styles are introduced and analyzed. The projection of positive self-fulfilling prophecies is demonstrated. Recruiting, hiring, and promoting staff is discussed in the diversity management context. Performance management, compensation and rewards, communication, training, and education are all discussed as part of integrated and successful diversity management. Finally, the process of diversity management itself is analyzed and reviewed from planning to intervention, monitoring, analysis, and evaluation (Boon, 1996).

Management styles may change from a hierarchical form emphasizing individual power within a set structure, to a communal form, emphasizing consent in decision-making processes. African management styles premised on the philosophy of *ubuntu* ("personhood" in the Xhosa language) are examined as an addition to the available repertoire of management styles. The Southern African principle of *ubuntu* sets the individual in their communal context. *Ubuntu ngumuntu ngabantu* means "a person is a person through other human beings." Consensus building, cooperation, and mutual supportiveness form the basis for personal management that brings all members of the organization together for the benefit of the whole organization. Once the individuals that shape the organization have been included into the process of moving the organization forward through mutual trust and cooperation, they will be able to share the vision of the organization and contribute fruitfully (Boon, 1996).

10.15.7 DIVERSITY IDENTITY: OUTLOOK FOR THE FUTURE

At a level of diversity identity the achievement of diversity is no longer a managerial goal. Diversity has become integral to the fiber of the organization. Difference is appreciated as enriching, and as furthering creativity. Valuing difference has to do with flexibility and conflict resolution, and capitalizing on it leads to market responsiveness and general productivity. Employees are appreciated for their job performance and judged in relation to achievement rather than background. The difference now is the openness of corporate culture to different approaches used to achieve the greater company good. An organization with a strong diversity identity does not try to become a melting pot in which all differences are amalgamated into a new singular identity. It becomes, rather, a salad bowl in which differences are maintained and appreciated but freed from discrimination. Interaction is possible with all aspects of society as they are represented within all structures of the organization (Letlaka-Rennert, 1996).

Diversity identity is the end result of a progression from prejudice in monocultural identity, through openmindedness in multicultural identity to an integrationist orientation. The culture has moved from one of exclusion and ignorance to one of exploration and ultimately one of inclusion and integration. Characteristics of the monocultural identity consist of racial superiority, elitism, entitlement, dominance, defensiveness, fear, aggression, and a siege mentality. Characteristics of the multicultural identity are openness, curiosity, discovery, engagement, and risk-taking. Characteristics of the diversity identity are appreciation of others, self-respect, differentiation, innovation, maturity, clarifying interactions, and ongoing dialogue.

Typically, in the South African monocultural context, the corporate or institutional employee composition was predominantly white. In the multicultural context of today, the employee composition is being addressed or redressed. Race and gender are at the forefront of the diversity drive, more so than sexual orientation or age. Skill shortages and the need for training and staff development are hindrances that have to be addressed. Organized labor is demanding to be included in the process. So far, diversity has not been achieved but it is becoming an organizational goal. In the South Africa of tomorrow, organizations will have a multicultural integrated work force representing diversity in race, gender, sexual orientation, disability, socioeconomic status, lifestyle, and family composition.

Both individuals and organizations will have evolved from the awakening internal control measures and their practice to a naturally internalized regulation. Multiracial advancement and promotion will be optimized for gaining a competitive edge. Organizational diversity will translate into organizational growth. President Nelson Mandela stated that

South Africa's greatest resource is its people. By empowering them to know how to work together in a conducive environment with an accommodating and permissive culture is the best reason to give diversity a chance.

10.15.8 SUMMARY AND CONCLUSION

The history of South Africa is one of racism, exploitation, and oppression. On every level of personal, organizational, and societal life individuals and institutions are faced with overcoming psychological and institutional barriers against change. Clinical and organizational psychologists are asked to help in facilitating a process of societal transformation that allows individuals as well as organizations and institutions to change their culture. Coming from a background of cultural exclusion, moving towards an awareness and appreciation of difference requires disclosure, vulnerability, and the tolerance of conflict. Prejudices and stereotypes have to be overcome and ingrained power structures have to be questioned and loosened.

In the South Africa of today we have a long way to go before our institutions—any of our institutions and organizations—can claim to have reached the diversity identity state. We are dealing with setbacks at every step of the way, we are hindered by old prejudices as much as by a sense of entitlement within the new elites, some of whom forget their constituencies once they have reached positions of influence and power. Corruption is a problem, as it is in every society today. But who would have predicted in 1989 or 1992 that a process of societal transformation could be achieved peacefully and with the full commitment of the vast majority of the people of this country. The road is still long, but South Africans are on the way, and we are determined to arrive together—a rainbow nation.

10.15.9 REFERENCES

Biesheuvel, S. (1958), Objectives and methods of South African psychological research. *Journal of Social Psychology, 47,* 161–168.

Boon, M. (1996). *The African way: The power of interactive leadership.* Johannesburg, South Africa: Zebra Press.

Bulhan, H. A. (1990) Afro-centric psychology: Perspective and practice. In L. J. Nicholas & S. Cooper (Eds.), *Psychology and apartheid* (pp. 66–78). Johannesburg, South Africa: Modiba Publications..

Cross, E. Y., Katz, J. H., Miller, F. A., & Seashore. E. W. (1994). *The promise of diversity.* New York: Irvin.

Davenport, T. R. H. (1987). *South Africa: A modern history.* Johannesburg, South Africa: Macmillan.

Dawes, A. (1985). Politics and mental health: The position of clinical psychology in South Africa. *South African Journal of Psychology, 15,* 55–61.

Duckitt, J. (1992). *The social psychology of prejudice.* Westport, CT: Praeger.

Fanon, F. (1967) *The wretched of the earth.* Harmondsworth, UK: Penguin.

Gordon, J. R. (1991). *Organizational behavior.* Boston: Allyn and Bacon.

Harrison, D. (1981). *The white tribe of Africa.* Los Angeles: University of California Press.

Jones, A. J. (1991). *Affirmative talk, affirmative action: A comparative study of the politics of affirmative action.* Westport, CT: Praeger.

Lau, J. B., & Shani, A. B. (1992). *Behavior in organizations: An experiential approach.* Chicago: Irvin.

Letlaka-Rennert, K. T. (1991). Ambivalence. *Agenda: A Journal about Women and Gender, 9,* 9–10.

Letlaka-Rennert, K. T. (1996). *The relationships among racial and gender identity models and locus of control and self-efficacy with black South African university students.* Unpublished doctoral dissertation, George Washington University, Washington, DC.

Louw, J. (1986). White poverty and psychology in South Africa: The poor white investigation of the Carnegie Commission. *Psychology in Society, 6,* 47–62.

Mandela, N. (1994). *Long walk to freedom: The autobiography of Nelson Mandela.* Randburg, South Africa: Macdonald Purnell.

Manganyi, C., & du Toit, A. (1990). *Political violence and the struggle in South Africa.* Halfway House, South Africa: Southern Book Publishers.

Nicholas, L. J. (1993). *Psychology and oppression: Critiques and proposals.* Johannesburg, South Africa: Skotavi.

Steyn, M. E., & Motshabi, K. (1996). *Cultural synergy in South Africa: Weaving strands of Africa and Europe.* Randburg, South Africa: Knowledge Resources.

Thomas, R. R. Jr. (1996). *Redefining diversity.* New York: AMACOM.

Trompenaars, F. (1993). *Riding the waves of culture: Understanding cultural diversity in business.* London: The Economist Books.

Wilcocks, R. W. (1932). *The poor white problem in South Africa: The report of the Carnegie Commission.* Stellenbosch, South Africa: Pro Ecclesia Drukkery.

Witt, S. L. (1990). *The pursuit of race and gender equity in American academe.* Westport, CT: Praeger.

10.16
Clinical Psychology in Asia: A Taiwanese Perspective

SUE-HUEI CHEN
National Taiwan University, Taipei, Taiwan
and
EUGENE K. EMORY
Emory University, Atlanta, GA, USA

10.16.1 INTRODUCTION 343
10.16.2 MANIFESTATION OF PSYCHOPATHOLOGY 344
10.16.2.1 Social Orientation and Collectivism as a Potential Cause 344
10.16.2.2 Social Orientation and Collectivism as a Buffer 345
10.16.3 DEVELOPMENT OF THE PROFESSION OF CLINICAL PSYCHOLOGY IN TAIWAN 346
10.16.4 CHOICE OF TREATMENT FOR PSYCHOLOGICAL DISORDERS 346
10.16.4.1 Treatment Choices 346
10.16.4.2 Therapy Models 347
10.16.5 CONCLUSIONS 347
10.16.6 REFERENCES 348

10.16.1 INTRODUCTION

Contrary to some Western conceptions, Asian people, such as those of Chinese descent, comprise a very heterogeneous group. The impact of Western culture on Chinese societies, in particular, Taiwanese people, may have positive and negative effects. One important feature of Westernization in Taiwan is the role it plays in the manifestation of psychological disorders. Cultural factors are imminently important in the identification and interpretation of clinical symptoms, and in the efficacy of certain forms of therapy. The emergence of doctoral level training of Taiwanese, from abroad and in the country itself, will have a profound influence on the future of clinical psychology in this Chinese island nation.

Asian people from different parts of the world are considered by most Westerners as a homogenous group. This tendency to homogenize distinctly heterogenous subcultures can lead to flawed concepts about these people. For example, many Westerners assume that people who live on the China mainland, in Hong Kong, and in Taiwan represent one ethnic group. While there are some obvious cultural and anthropologic similarities, including religious practices and physical features, these groups have markedly different social customs. They include dietary, religious, and even language differences. People in Hong Kong, for example, speak Cantonese, whereas Taiwan uses Mandarin Chinese. These are quite different dialects to what is spoken in various parts of mainland China. Moreover, vastly different ideologies and governmental policies exist. Thus, while similarities within Asian populations may appear obvious to outsiders, they are mostly superficial. Historical, geographic, and political segregation have made Chinese in Taiwan different from Chinese in other parts of the world, such as mainland China.

The transformation of the political system in Taiwan and the remarkably rapid economic changes and influences from the Western culture have altered the beliefs, value systems, and lifestyle of Taiwanese people. Therefore, the main sociocultural theme in Taiwan is a mixture of traditional Chinese culture and contemporary Western ideology. To what extent can one apply a traditional "Chinese" or Western psychological perspective to the people of Taiwan?

In a rapidly changing society, people may face heightened social and political stress. Economic competition and the standard of living have increased, but political conflicts between Taiwan and mainland China are persistent and apparent. Taiwanese people are experiencing higher levels of uncertainty about lifestyle and future well-being than they were in the past. In contrast, the traditional emphasis on family structure and collective social orientation is weakening (Yang, 1985, 1993, 1995). In societies where traditional norms and values change rapidly, new and effective coping strategies are needed. These sociopolitical conditions are associated with increasing psychopathology (Wallace, 1956). The lifestyle in Taiwan exhibits pervasive Western influences that are at variance with traditional Chinese values. The social impact appears to be a greater level of emotional distress. As a result, the manifestation of stress-related psychopathology represents itself in a changing pattern unique to this island. Could the pattern be depicted as a "Westernized" psychopathology?

In addressing the research and professional issues related to clinical psychology in Taiwan, it is appropriate to examine similarities and differences in the manifestation of psychopathology, development of clinical psychology, and choices of treatment for psychological disorders, in comparison to those in mainstream European and American society. There is a paucity of empirical and theoretical literature focusing on clinical psychology from a Taiwanese perspective, due in no small part to the limited number of Taiwanese clinical psychologists.

The goal of this chapter is to clarify a Taiwanese perspective on clinical psychology issues. It is hoped that the perspective from a rapidly changing society—Taiwan—may serve to provoke further discussions and deeper understanding of how such changes can alter social structures in an established society where social collectivism and group identity attempts to co-exist with increasing individualistic ideals. The impact of this change can be measured in psychological terms. There is still not enough empirical evidence to clarify these relationships. One outcome unfortunately may be a rise in the diagnosis of major psychological disorders. Our understanding of these outcomes may shed light on the universe of human psychopathology, not just the depiction of psychopathology and the emergence of clinical psychology in Taiwan.

10.16.2 MANIFESTATION OF PSYCHOPATHOLOGY

Traditionally familial rather than individual goals have been the measures of social success in Taiwan. According to K. S. Yang, a leading theorist of indigenous social and personality psychology, people in Taiwan have been influenced greatly by familial collectivism (Yang, 1972, 1995). On that account, social-oriented cultural features in Taiwan may very likely be seen as both a potential cause, as well as a buffer, of psychopathology. In fact, these concepts are not much different from the social dynamics that exist in the West.

10.16.2.1 Social Orientation and Collectivism as a Potential Cause

Traditionally Taiwanese people have a stronger social–collective rather than individual orientation. That is, the individual was inclined to subordinate her or his personal goals and choices for the sake of the family. More specifically, while dealing with family affairs, one tended to be primarily influenced by family's decision, regardless of one's individuality (Yang, 1972, 1995).

Such social oriented or collectivist attributes may be manifested in the symptoms of psychopathology. For example, concerns or problems about family conflicts outnumbered other psychological problems concerning individual issues in a Taiwanese sample who sought local spiritual help or professional counseling (Yee, 1985). Another interesting example is found in the delusional content of schizophrenics. Spirit possession phenomena (SPP) was noted in about 25% of first-onset schizophrenic patients. Of the variety of symptoms, there was a disproportionate number related to being possessed by ancestors or alive family members, rather than spiritual agents or demons (Wen, Lin, Chen, Chou, & Huang, 1992). Thus, as is the case in other societies, the content of delusional thought may be culturally balanced.

10.16.2.2 Social Orientation and Collectivism as a Buffer

Similar to the influence of social orientation on the manifestations of psychopathology, a family orientation may buffer individuals against psychological distress and thus decrease the frequency and type of psychological disorder. The different prevalence rates of major depression in Taiwanese and Americans patients may also reflect different distributions of psychopathology under the influences of collectivism or individualism, respectively. Several studies of Chinese samples carried out in Taiwan (Cheng, 1989; Compton et al., 1991; Lin, 1953; Lin, Rin, Yeh, Hsu, & Chu, 1969) and in the US (Weissman et al., 1992; Yamamoto, Yeh, Loya, Slawson, & Hurwicz, 1985) have found that the prevalence rate of major depression is lower among Chinese patients in Taiwan than American patients, ranging from 0.07 to 1.1% and from 5.2 to 17.1%, respectively. Furthermore, as reported in several studies, Chinese depressives manifest more somatic symptoms (e.g., Lin, 1982; Kleinman, 1982). This somatization tendency may thus contribute to the possibility of under-reporting or under diagnosing clinical depression in Chinese patients (Kleinman, 1982). What tends to be overlooked by these studies, however, is that somatization may play a role in the illness process. Maintaining the mixed anxiety-depressive state may in turn prevent the less depressed patients from becoming the hopeless depressive (Chen, 1995).

In Taiwan, the whole family tends to take responsibility for a psychological problem in order to protect the individual from being singled out. This buffering and shared responsibility may affect the revelation of a psychological disorder in the Western context. Taiwanese tend to express personal or social distress via somatization, which has been defined by Kleinman and Kleinman (1985) as the expression of personal and social distress in an idiom of physical complaints and medical help-seeking behaviors. Somatization may also be considered a reflection of basic cultural traits that discern Chinese society with a predominantly oral-hypochondriacal quality (Lin, 1982). In addition to this psychosomatic conception of "disorder," the social system shaped by collectivism has played a role in the expression of emotional distress.

Note that within the traditionally social-oriented collectivist Chinese society, the individual is not the unit of social structure. The individual's private emotions may be largely considered as a reflection of family matters. Public expression and discussing one's emotions, especially the negative emotions, may cause more social consequences and conflicts in the social milieu, thereby bringing more shame and guilt feelings to oneself and one's family or relatives. In reality these emotions may be more likely to result from an interpersonal conflict, but expression of depression or negative affect is culturally discouraged (Lin, 1982; Tseng & Hsu, 1969). Thus a more stoic demeanor is generally adopted.

Within the social-oriented system, somatization tends to have positive social consequences to the extent that both care-givers and receivers obtain affirmative evaluations in the helping process. Since psychological complaints did not have the same social efficacy that somatization had in generating support and care (Kleinman, 1982), it is thus more likely to find the somatic expression of depression in Chinese society. In the past, somatization had been commonly seen as an expression of psychological distress in Western society until psychological experience and its rationalization into discrete labels were regarded as one index of modernization. Psychologization, rather than somatization, consequently may have become the way of perceiving and expressing one's own distress in modern Western society (Kleinman & Kleinman, 1985). Could the declining trend of social orientation in Westernized human societies account for the fact that major depression rates are increasing both in Taiwan and in several Western countries?

Another factor that affects the manifestation of psychopathology may be the availability and acceptability of emotional expression. Taking depression as an index, Taiwan is in a progressive Westernization mode, and its rate of major depression is increasingly approaching statistics in the West. However, there has been a dearth of adequate "words" to express "depression" in Taiwan. In Chinese culture people were not used to expressing depression literally or verbally in colloquial speech. Instead, it was much easier to somatize (Tseng & Hsu, 1969), or to refer to those specific psycholinguistic expressions which have been shaped by the more somatic-toned culture (Cheng, 1989). Hence, it is not surprising that an enormous number of Chinese cases of depression have sought physical, rather than psychological and psychiatric, treatment for their illness (Sue & Sue, 1990). Younger people, however, seem to be conflicted between traditional values and contemporary Westernized culture. Again along with the declining trend of social orientation and collectivism among younger generations, one might associate this trend with the earlier onset of major depression in younger cohorts, both in Taiwan and in several Western countries.

10.16.3 DEVELOPMENT OF THE PROFESSION OF CLINICAL PSYCHOLOGY IN TAIWAN

As of 1996, the number of clinical psychologists remained very low in Taiwan. According to the author's own informal surveys, the estimated number is about 200. There are about 10 clinical psychologists who have a Ph.D. in clinical psychology. Among those doctorates, there are three US-trained clinical psychologists (including the first author) and one US-trained clinical neuropsychologist. The remainder received their degrees from the same local clinical psychology program, National Taiwan University. All of them currently hold a faculty position in clinical psychology programs at various universities and are carrying out part time clinical services at their affiliated medical centers. In addition, about a quarter have obtained a master's degree. The remainder hold a bachelor degree in psychology. There is no formal licensure for clinical psychologists in Taiwan.

In terms of subspecialties within Taiwanese clinical psychology, there are various programs established over the years, as is the case in many Western universities. At National Taiwan University, for example, there are traditional clinical psychology and child clinical psychology, health psychology, and clinical neuropsychology, which provide training associated with the application in psychiatric settings, family medicine settings, and neurology departments, respectively. Consistent with the Western trend, health psychology and neuropsychology have received more attention in recent decades. We note that there is only one health psychology program to date, but it has quickly developed and encountered less resistance in Taiwan, thanks, we suspect, greatly to the somatic-toned culture.

Although the first clinical psychology program started about 25 years ago, the number of Taiwanese clinical psychologists grew very slowly. This small number is due solely to the fact that clinical psychology is a recently developing profession in this transitional society, where psychological services were discouraged by traditional values. Although subtle resistance for the development of clinical psychology existed, the number of students now being trained is growing. Equally important, the percentage of master or doctorate level recipients has shown a rapid increase in recent years. This increase may mean that more, albeit still less than enough, research in Taiwanese clinical psychology may be generated by local or international psychologists in the foreseeable future, and more qualified and/or experienced clinical psychologists may be available to serve in both academic and clinical settings.

With regard to psychological assessment, there obviously exists a dearth of adequate tests during this beginning stage in the development of clinical psychology in Taiwan. Two attempts can be employed to "soothe the pang": to develop culturally sensitive tests or to conduct cross-cultural translation of those well-established Western tests. It seems more feasible to adopt and translate well-established clinical tests during this burgeoning period. In fact, some research concerning cross-cultural translation of Western tests such as Beck Depression Inventory (BDI) and Children's Depression Inventory (CDI) has been conducted. Several well-validated personality inventories have been used in Taiwan, such as Ko's Mental Health Questionnaire (Ko, 1977, 1995) and the Health–Personality–Habit Scale (Ko, 1996).

Efforts need to proceed with caution when conducting cross-cultural translation of Western tests. It was reported that Asian-Americans at UCLA tended to endorse more items on the MMPI-2 than their American counterparts (Dr. Hsieh, personal communication 1996). The authors shared similar observations while using the English form of the MMPI-2 with Taiwanese students at Emory University. Those students may not have presented a clear picture of distress at the interview, whereas they endorsed more items on some negative distress scales. A question thus arises as to whether the validity of assessment will be biased by test formats, such as self-report scales or interpersonal interview, across various groups from different cultural backgrounds. Still, such questions need to be answered.

10.16.4 CHOICE OF TREATMENT FOR PSYCHOLOGICAL DISORDERS

The behavioral patterns of people with a collectivism or social orientation may vary greatly from those who possess more individual-oriented characteristics. The same holds true in the manifestation of symptoms and their attribution of causes for psychopathology, and in turn, affects their choices related to treatment. Another factor affecting their choice of treatment models may be the limited number of clinical psychologists in the country.

10.16.4.1 Treatment Choices

We hypothesize that the choice of treatment for psychological disorders varies across social and economic status in Taiwan. The severity and types of the disorders may also affect the choice (Tseng, 1972; Tseng & McDermott, 1975; Wen, Lin, & Chen, 1993; Yee, 1985). Specifically, people with higher socioeconomic status (SES) tend to seek professional help from Western models of treatment including psychiatric medicine and psychotherapy for their mental illnesses and counseling for maladjustment problems. People with median SES have pluralistic help-seeking patterns. That is, they tend to utilize Western models for more severe mental disorders but Chinese medicine or folk therapy for psychosomatic-like disorders, as well as problems related to daily life. However, people with lower SES seldom access the services of Western treatment models. Rather, they tend to visit spirit mediums, fortune-tellers, shaman, and so forth (Yee, 1985). To date, this may suggest both a lack of knowledge of possible causes as well as a scarcity of available professional psychology services. One can see parallels in the utilization of psychological services as it relates to SES in both Taiwanese and American culture.

10.16.4.2 Therapy Models

Given that the availability of psychological services is limited in Taiwan, and the number of clinical psychologists is small, it comes as no surprise that theoretical orientation of clinical psychologists in the country appears relatively homogenous. According to the authors' anecdotal surveys, the cognitive-behavioral approach is the most popular model employed by clinical psychologists in Taiwan in both research and clinical settings. The phenomenological-humanistic approaches are second, followed by psychodynamic or psychoanalytic approaches.

Several factors presumably contribute to this pattern of theoretical orientation. The primary ingredient has been the lack of programs, as stated earlier, that recruit and train enough clinical psychologists to provide for varied theoretical orientations. Moreover, most mainstream clinical psychologists in Taiwan rarely stray from their mentors' orientation. Second, the authoritarian orientation of Chinese culture contributes to the preference for a particular orientation. Chinese tend to respect structure and formality in interpersonal relationships. The same holds true in therapeutic relationships. Yang (1995) pointed out, "as long as the Chinese see authorities as trustworthy and 'almighty,' they will be completely dependent upon those authorities." Respect for authority may take the form of agreeing readily to what the therapist does and proposes. The cognitive-behavioral approach offers relatively more formality and authoritarianism. Perhaps the very acceptability of formality and authoritarian aspects of psychotherapy in Taiwanese is likely to be consistent with the cognitive-behavioral approach. Unfortunately, there is a lack of empirical evidence making comparisons among various approaches applied to Taiwanese patients and clients.

To be sure, there are some commonalities among Asian populations with respect to psychological services. Atkinson, Maruyama, and Matsui (1978) revealed that, while treating Asian-Americans, the therapist may have to be more directive and active than they might otherwise be, given the preference of many Asian-Americans for a structured approach over an unstructured one. As proposed earlier, the younger cohorts have been dropping their social orientation and/or authoritarian attitude and becoming Westernized. Accordingly, what may be informative is whether or not the younger cohorts show an increase in their preference for less-structured therapies. Much research remains to be done with respect to how clinical psychology can be most appropriately applied in non-Western, especially Asian, culture.

10.16.5 CONCLUSIONS

As stated previously, the goal of this chapter is to provoke thought and further discussion on the topic of clinical psychology in Taiwan, and more generally, Asian cultures. Will the development of clinical psychology in Taiwan have similar trends to the US or other non-Western nations, or will its development be unique? Clinical psychology in Taiwan has developed from a circumstance in which scientific psychology has already developed itself as a mature science, whereas clinical psychology in Western countries, such as the US, seems to parallel the entire history of psychology. In some ways the development of clinical psychology in Taiwan seems to be a microcosm of the 100 years of Western clinical psychology. However, there are vast differences between the East and the West. It will be interesting and exciting to observe whether the development of clinical psychology in Taiwan, and Asia more generally, will continue the trend towards the West, or branch off into an entirely new direction.

The following factors will affect the future development of clinical psychology in Taiwan:

(i) diversity of training programs throughout the country;

(ii) the number of clinical psychologists trained locally and abroad;

(iii) the amount of empirical research conducted;

(iv) sociopolitical changes.

These factors, and perhaps others not mentioned here, will influence significantly the course of clinical psychology in Taiwan. Productive cross-cultural collaboration as well as indigenous research will undoubtedly contribute to the success of Taiwanese psychology.

10.16.6 REFERENCES

Atkinson, D. R., Maruyama, M., & Matsui, S. (1978). Effects of counselor race and counseling approach on Asian Americans' perceptions of counselor credibility and utility. *Journal of Counseling Psychology, 25*(1), 76–83.

Chen, S. H. (1995). *The role of certainty of helplessness in comorbidity of anxiety and depression: A prospective study of Chinese patients.* Unpublished doctoral dissertation, Emory University, Atlanta, GA.

Cheng, T. A. (1989). Symptomatology of minor psychiatric morbidity: A cross-cultural comparison. *Psychological Medicine, 19,* 697–708.

Compton W. M., III, Helzer, J. E., Hwu, H. G., Yeh, E. K., McEvoy, L., Tipp, J. E., & Spitznagel, E. L. (1991). New methods in cross-cultural psychiatry: Psychiatric illness in Taiwan and the United States. *American Journal of Psychiatry, 148*(12), 1697–1704.

Kleinman, A. (1982). Neurasthenia and depression: A study of somatization and culture in China. *Culture, Medicine, and Psychiatry, 6,* 117–190.

Kleinman, A., & Kleinman, J. (1985). Somatization: The interconnections in Chinese society among culture, depressive experiences, and the meanings of pain. In A. Kleinman & B. Good (Eds.), *Culture and depression: Studies in the anthropology and cross-cultural psychiatry of affect and disease* (pp. 429–490). Los Angeles: University of California Press.

Ko, Y. H. (1977). *Ko-Shi-Shin-Ger-Leong-Beau-Sou-Tzer (Manual of Ko's Mental Health Questionnaire)* [in Chinese]. Taipei, Taiwan: Chinese Behavioral Sciences Press.

Ko, Y. H. (1995). *Ko-Shi-Shin-Ger-Leong-Beau-Shou-Din-Yen-Gio (Validation Study of Ko's Mental Health Questionnaire)* [in Chinese]. Taipei, Taiwan: Ministry of Education.

Ko, Y. H. (1996). *Gen-Kon-Shin-Ger-See-Guong-Leong-Beau-Sou-Tzer (Manual of Health, Personality, Habit Scale)* [in Chinese]. Taipei, Taiwan: Testing Press.

Lin, T. Y. (1953). A study of the incidence of mental disorders in Chinese and other cultures. *Psychiatry, 16,* 313–336.

Lin, T. Y. (1982). Culture and psychiatry: A Chinese perspective. *Australian and New Zealand Journal of Psychiatry, 16,* 235–245.

Lin, T. Y., Rin, H., Yeh, E. K., Hsu, C. C., & Chu, H. M. (1969). Mental disorders in Taiwan fifteen years later. In W. Caudill & T. Y. Lin (Eds.), *Mental health research in Asia and the Pacific.* Honolulu, HI: East-West Center Press.

Shieh, B. L., & Sue, S. (1996). Deciphering psychopathology from cultural response sets: Asians and MMPI-2 performance. Abstract presented at the Annual Meeting of Chinese Psychological Association, Taipei, Taiwan.

Sue, D. W., & Sue, D. (1990). Counseling Asian Americans. In D. W. Sue & D. Sue (Eds.), *Counseling the culturally different: Theory and practices* (pp. 189–208). New York: Wiley.

Tseng, W. S. (1972). Psychiatric study of shamanism in Taiwan. *Archives of General Psychiatry, 26*(6), 561–565.

Tseng, W. S., & Hsu, J. (1969). Chinese culture, personality formation and mental illness. *International Journal of Social Psychology, 16,* 5–14.

Tseng, W. S., & McDermott J. F., Jr. (1975). Psychotherapy: Historical roots, universal elements, and cultural variations. *American Journal of Psychiatry, 132*(4), 378–384.

Wallace, A. F. C. (1956). Revitalization movements. *American Anthropologist, 58,* 264–281.

Weissman, M. M., & Cross-National Collaborative Group (1992). The changing rate of major depression. *Journal of American Medical Association, 268*(21), 3098–3105.

Wen, J. K., Lin, S. L., Chen, C. C., Chou, W. G., & Huang, H. L. (1992). Lin-Huang-Fu-Shen-Sheng-Seong: Tai-Wan-Ben-Tu-Der-Ea-Li-Ing-Eng-Shin-Wei (Spirit possession phenomena: Stress-Coping Behavior in Taiwan) [in Chinese]. In *Proceedings of Institute of Ethnology* (Vol. 73, pp. 1–32). Taipei, Taiwan: Institute of Ethnology, Academia Sinica.

Wen, J. K., Lin, S. L., & Chen, Y. P. (1993). Lin-Hung-Fu-Shen-Sheng-Seong-Gin-Shen-Gee-Bin-Yu-Shin-Li-Sher-Hui-Win-Hwa-Ing-Shu (Spirit possession phenomena, mental illnesses, and Psycho-socio-cultural factors) [in Chinese]. In K. S. Yang (Ed.), *Culture, psychological disorders and treatments.* Taipei, Taiwan: Indigenous Psychological Research Center Press.

Yamamoto, J., Yeh, E. K., Loya, F., Slawson, P., & Hurwicz, M. L. (1985). Are American Psychiatric outpatients more depressed than Chinese outpatients? *American Journal of Psychiatry, 142*(11), 1347–1351.

Yang, K. S. (1972). Expressed values of Chinese college students [in Chinese]. In Y. Y. Li & K. S. Yang (Eds.), *Symposium on the character of the Chinese: An interdisciplinary* (pp. 257–312). Taipei, Taiwan: Institute of Ethnology, Academia Sinica.

Yang, K. S. (1985). "The change of personality and behavior among the Chinese people in Taiwan" [in Chinese]. In *Proceedings of the Conference on Modernization and Its Problems in Taiwan* (pp. 75–100). Taipei, Taiwan: Institute of Three People's Principles, Academia Sinica.

Yang, K. S. (1993). Can traditional and modern values coexist? [in Chinese]. In K. S. Yang (Ed.), *Chinese values: A social science viewpoint* (pp. 65–120). Taipei, Taiwan: Kwai Kuan.

Yang, K. S. (1995). Chinese social orientation: An integrative analysis. In T. Y. Lin, W. S. Tseng, & Y. K. Yeh (Eds.), *Chinese societies & mental health* (pp. 19–39). Hong Kong: Oxford University Press.

Yee, D. H. (1985). *Tai-Wan-Min-Shu-Chin-Li-Fu-Dau (Folk counseling in Taiwan)* [in Chinese]. Taipei, Taiwan: Teacher Chang Publisher.

10.17 Clinical Psychology in Aotearoa/ New Zealand: Indigenous Perspectives

TAIMA M. MOEKE-PICKERING, MAHALIA K. PAEWAI, AMELIA TURANGI-JOSEPH, and AVERIL M. L. HERBERT
University of Waikato, Hamilton, New Zealand

10.17.1 INTRODUCTION 349

10.17.2 A BRIEF HISTORY 350

10.17.2.1 Maori Identity 350
10.17.2.2 The Treaty of Waitangi 350

10.17.3 PSYCHOLOGY IN AOTEAROA 350

10.17.3.1 Historical Context 350
10.17.3.2 The State of Maori Mental Health 351

10.17.4 DEVELOPING A BICULTURAL MODEL IN AOTEAROA 351

10.17.4.1 The Need for Change 351
10.17.4.2 A New Approach to Maori Mental Health 351

10.17.5 PSYCHOLOGY IN A BICULTURAL SETTING 351

10.17.5.1 The Changing Face of Psychology 351
10.17.5.2 Training in Psychology 352
10.17.5.3 National Standing Committee on Bicultural Issues 352

10.17.6 MAORI AND PSYCHOLOGY 352

10.17.6.1 Research, Training, and Teaching 352
10.17.6.2 Cultural Safety 353
10.17.6.3 Cultural Safety and Clinical Practice 353
10.17.6.4 Maori Psychological Initiatives 353

10.17.7 CONCLUSION 354

10.17.8 REFERENCES 354

10.17.1 INTRODUCTION

This chapter provides an indigenous perspective of psychology in Aotearoa (the Maori name for New Zealand) by examining bicultural developments in the fields of teaching, research, theory, and practice. The key issue for Maori (the indigenous people of Aotearoa) as psychology has evolved from early British to later American influences is the relevance of Western based psychological theory and practice. This raised questions about the need to develop indigenous paradigms in Aotearoa. The Treaty of Waitangi provided a unique basis for a bicultural model to be developed. Bicultural and Maori initiatives have played a significant role in psychology training programs. In particular, the development of Maori-initiated psychological programs demonstrate an increased acceptance of cultural dimensions in psychology.

10.17.2 A BRIEF HISTORY

10.17.2.1 Maori Identity

To understand the development of psychology in Aotearoa as well as its responsiveness to the needs of Maori, the historical and cultural context in which the discipline has developed must be considered. The dominant ethnic group in Aotearoa are Pakeha (mainly New Zealanders of predominantly European–British descent). Like the experience of many indigenous peoples from other settler colonies, Maori continue to strive for self-determination in an environment of Pakeha dominance (Hamerton, Nikora, Robertson, & Thomas, 1995; Jackson, 1988; Walker, 1990).

Prior to Pakeha contact, Maori identified themselves primarily from the strata of their tribal structures, these being *whanau* (extended family), *hapu* (subtribe), *iwi* (tribe), and *waka* (ancestral canoe linking *iwi* and the peoples of the Pacific). Tribal structure and organization were based on descent from a common Maori ancestor (Buck, 1949). Identity was derived from kinship and learning within these tribal structures (Moeke-Pickering, 1996).

Cultural practices were based on a shared system of understanding by a tribal group that were deemed to be important and meaningful to them (Moeke-Pickering, 1996). Language, customs, spirituality, respect for the land, kinship obligations, and traditions were fundamental to the socialization of Maori identities. In essence historical references, cultural practices, kinship structures, and the land served as charters for Maori identities (Ritchie, 1992).

10.17.2.2 The Treaty of Waitangi

During the period of early contact with Pakeha, the sovereign status of Maori was internationally recognized in the Declaration of Independence in 1836. Maori were involved in international trade and were both thriving and flourishing economically. The lawlessness of many early Pakeha settlers, however, was causing concern among Maori leaders. They resolved to enter into a constitutional arrangement with the British Crown which would allow the British to control the unruly behavior of its citizens resident in Aotearoa (Orange, 1987). The vehicle for this was to be the Treaty of Waitangi which was signed on the February 6, 1840 and marked the beginning of a new era for Maori. The treaty prescribed a proposed constitutional relationship between the Crown and Maori that outlined the duties and obligations of both parties. In delegating limited authority to the Crown, the Treaty of Waitangi guaranteed Maori sovereignty or chieftainship over their lands, their settlements, and all other property (Jackson, 1988). Written in both the Maori and English language, ambiguities in interpretation between both texts have caused much debate until the late 1990s (Jackson, 1988; Orange, 1987; Renwick, 1990).

In the intervening 156 years, the principles of the Treaty of Waitangi have been breached repeatedly through Pakeha hegemony and the ethnocentric attitudes that underpin it (Ballara, 1986). Maori have faced the trauma of loss of land, language, and dignity, as well as absolute control over their ability to maintain a separate culture and identity (Vasil, 1988). As a result they suffered cultural alienation, poverty, unemployment, and hardship which ultimately led to further entrenchment and subordination to dominant Pakeha cultural ways (Awatere, 1984; Lawson-Te Aho, 1984; Walker, 1990).

Clearly, both Maori and Pakeha ethnic identities have developed, out of a binary opposition between the two people with Pakeha becoming the dominant ethnic group (Walker, 1989). Today Maori people comprise 12% of the population, control less than 5% of the land, and continue to struggle to maintain a positive cultural identity.

10.17.3 PSYCHOLOGY IN AOTEAROA

10.17.3.1 Historical Context

Psychology modeled on the British system developed as a discipline within Aotearoa (Hamerton et al., 1995). The introduction of psychology was part of the imposition of a colonial knowledge system that systematically undermined Maori ways of knowing in favor of a Western world view. Evidence of this was clear in the way that the Western psychological paradigm was hierarchically positioned over and above Maori epistemology. Psychology had a status as a scientific discipline at a time when Maori knowledge was perceived as an inferior theoretical framework (Lawson-Te Aho, 1984; Stewart, 1995).

At that time, the application of a psychological paradigm foreign to Maori experiences became accepted practice by psychologists and was deemed to be appropriate despite obvious ethnocentric biases inherent within this framework. An example was the use of intelligence tests to stream Maori school children used in the

1950s and 1960s. Predictably, these tests were demonstrated to be both culturally biased and an unfair means of assessing the ability of Maori due to the culturally bound nature of the constructs used (Thomas, 1988).

10.17.3.2 The State of Maori Mental Health

During the 1990s it became clear that although Maori were becoming mentally ill at a similar rate to Pakeha, poorer outcomes were being experienced by Maori during the post-admission phases of treatment (Bridgman, 1993). Drug and alcohol related problems as well as other psychoses were the main categories underpinning Maori admissions. Although the actual statistics need careful examination, the overall trend highlighted the fact that the fastest growth area in terms of hospitalization was the readmission of Maori with serious psychotic illness (Awatere, 1984; Bridgman, 1993). Bridgman (1993) also suggested that psychiatric diagnoses for Maori presented a distorted picture with inaccurate assessments and ineffective hospitalization. Psychiatric statistics for Maori were less indicative of the levels of psychopathology in the population and more an indication of the inability of health providers to understand the social, educational, and economic realities faced by many Maori. Furthermore, attitudes in service agencies had failed to recognize or accommodate cultural differences (Spoonley, 1988).

10.17.4 DEVELOPING A BICULTURAL MODEL IN AOTEAROA

10.17.4.1 The Need for Change

The inability of the health sector to respond appropriately to many Maori clients became increasingly obvious to many health professionals and community workers and led to an examination of different approaches to Maori health (Durie, 1994). While Durie (1994) was able to identify earlier Maori health professionals who had established appropriate cultural practices, there was no widespread recognition for such contributions until the mid-1970s.

At this time the government finally addressed over a century of injustices with the passing of the Treaty of Waitangi Act 1975. This provided for the first time a recognized forum for Maori to air grievances and to advocate Treaty obligations in a bicultural milieu (Kawharu, 1989). This led to Maori people being legally recognized as "tangata whenua" or indigenous people of the land, with rights under the Treaty to their own language and cultural self-determination (Abbot & Durie, 1987). The passing of the 1975 Act and the Treaty itself gave impetus to claims by Maori that health policies and initiatives should reflect their rights to development and self-determination.

10.17.4.2 A New Approach to Maori Mental Health

By the 1980s, challenges to the discipline of psychology to recognize the significance of cultural issues further increased. A bicultural approach which served the health needs of Maori needed to be developed based on increased recognition of cultural differences between Maori and Pakeha. In practice, biculturalism as an approach to Maori health initially attempted to include a Maori perspective into existing health systems.

With the increasing awareness of a range of culturally determined behaviors, some professionals suggested that Maori were misdiagnosed as psychotic and inappropriately referred to psychiatric services. Of particular significance within the health field were Maori assertions that a bicultural model should provide equitably for both Treaty partners. Furthermore, provisions already existed in the articles of the Treaty of Waitangi to justify these claims. Durie (1994) noted that by 1985 the Standing Committee on Maori Health had recommended that the Treaty of Waitangi be regarded as the foundation for good health.

In the mental health setting, the application of a bicultural model in the 1980s relied upon good faith and agreed-upon-goals rather than formal conventions (Durie, 1994). As a result, the parameters of the bicultural model were not clearly defined and the rights and responsibilities of Maori and Pakeha were poorly understood. Some programs gave recognition, but little else, to the cultural traditions of Maori (Mulgan, 1989a) while others favored a redistribution of resources to Maori (Jackson, 1988). At one level there was an implied inclusion of Maori values in mainstream institutions, at another the development of specific Maori institutions to provide for Maori needs (Sharp, 1995). Regardless of these difficulties, the bicultural model served as a framework for other institutions, agencies, and social services to extend upon.

10.17.5 PSYCHOLOGY IN A BICULTURAL SETTING

10.17.5.1 The Changing Face of Psychology

Awatere (1981), a noted Maori psychologist, raised the notion that certain psychological techniques and practices used the privilege of power to further oppress Maori cultural processes. She expanded on this by asserting that:

> My job as a psychologist is to facilitate the process of understanding, confronting and changing; to use psychological techniques to help the powerless gain power instead of what psychologists have always done, which is to help maintain their power. (p. 202)

Waldegrave (1985), in developing therapies for Maori and Samoan families, found that the predominantly monocultural and monoclass approach was inadequate due to the existence of broader social and political issues which impacted on these cultural groups. He pointed out that psychologists were not required to demonstrate any knowledge of Maori culture at all, and that psychological knowledge, including family therapy, was considered sufficient to address the problems of both Maori and Pakeha families.

10.17.5.2 Training in Psychology

In the United States, Yutrzenka (1995) noted that until the 1970s there was little inclusion of cross-cultural material, as well as limited diversity in the client populations with whom trainees received their clinical service training. Increasing awareness in the 1980s and 1990s saw a change towards including more cross-cultural theory and practices in psychology training programs. Many professional psychologists were aware of this need to prepare for a multicultural, multiracial, and multiethnic environment, but as Yutrzenka (1995) commented, the commitment and implementation of cross-cultural understanding was highly variable across these programs.

To some extent this overseas trend was also being reflected in Aotearoa. For example, in 1987, a survey of the nine postgraduate training programs in clinical, educational, and community psychology in Aotearoa was completed (Abbot & Durie, 1987). The findings of this survey confirmed that few programs incorporated "taha Maori" (a Maori dimension). The monocultural training of psychologists compared unfavorably with social work and medical training. Both Abbot and Durie and later Brady (1992) questioned the credibility of the discipline and challenged it to: (i) increase the number of trained Maori psychologists; (ii) develop an increased awareness of entrenched attitudes; and (iii) invest more energy into making changes at all levels of training including format, assessment methods, texts, and ethics.

In 1990, a study conducted by Sawrey (1990) further illustrated the need to include "taha Maori" into training programs and to develop a Maori psychology as well as include Maori psychology programs within mainstream education. In this study of 163 clinical psychologists of whom only one was Maori, over 85% of the sample supported the notion that psychologists' knowledge of Maori culture was an important factor in good psychotherapeutic outcomes with Maori clients. Interestingly, 75% of the sample felt they had inadequate Maori knowledge to effectively work with Maori, while 85% believed that their psychological training had not equipped them sufficiently to effectively work with Maori clients.

10.17.5.3 National Standing Committee on Bicultural Issues

The report of Abbot and Durie (1987) presented a damning critique of psychological training. The report served as the catalyst for change in psychological training and two years later the National Standing Committee on Bicultural Issues (NSCBI) was established under the auspices of the New Zealand Psychological Society.

The NSCBI was formed to monitor the development of bicultural activities, organize symposia, disseminate information on issues relevant to indigenous development, and to develop and encourage policies and practices that reflected New Zealand's cultural diversity (Hamerton et al., 1995). The Committee's broad aims were to initiate social changes that supported recognition and development of Maori psychology, to assist the New Zealand Psychological Society to honor its obligations under the Treaty of Waitangi, and to assist psychologists to develop appropriate teaching, research, and practice (NSCBI, 1994a). These activities have been effective in instituting cultural agendas at both the national and regional levels.

10.17.6 MAORI AND PSYCHOLOGY

10.17.6.1 Research, Training, and Teaching

By 1996 most university psychology departments and psychological service providers have either considered, or put in place, initiatives aimed at supporting Maori students and practitioners. While bicultural initiatives in Aotearoa have served to increase acceptance of cultural issues in psychology, it had also become apparent that there was a need to develop a body of research relevant to Maori and psychology. There has been a considerable amount of research and literature relating to Maori and psychology which is now having some impact on both professional training and mental health services (Awatere, 1981; Durie, 1994; Lawson-Te Aho, 1984; McFarlane-Nathan, 1996; NSCBI, 1994b, 1995; Paterson, 1992; Ritchie & Ritchie, 1978; Stewart, 1995; Thomas & Nikora, 1992). In addition, the experiences of other colonized indigenous people overseas have relevance for Maori by serving to direct attention on similar issues within the context of Aotearoa (McFarlane-Nathan, 1996).

There are two universities in Aotearoa that currently offer courses which focus on Maori topics relating to psychology. In addition, two other universities have made an explicit commitment to developing course material and/or structures relevant to Maori in psychology (Stewart, 1995). These courses have had the effect of increasing Maori participation in psychology. An increase in the number of Maori enrolling in psychology training programs coupled with increased retention of Maori both within the discipline and as practitioners have resulted in a larger pool of Maori with relevant research and practical expertise. With increasing numbers both in practice and research, Maori are better placed to develop more appropriate theoretical frameworks.

The frameworks referred to above contribute to a psychology that services the needs of Maori in a way that is relevant to their needs and consistent with their world view. It has been necessary to develop a Maori resource base from which an understanding and awareness of cultural knowledge, skills, and competence can be drawn. Students are encouraged to read literature describing colonization, Maori history, Maori traditions, as well as tribal and cultural knowledge to gain background information pertaining to Maori people. Durie (1994), Ritchie (1992), and Walker (1990) provide comprehensive information on biculturalism, the impact of colonization, the development of bicultural policies, tribal development and identity, and Maori health.

Current research in the areas of cross-cultural psychology (Thomas, Nikora, & Moeke-Pickering, 1996), identity issues (Durie et al., 1995; Heperi, 1996; Hingston, 1993; Moecke-Pickering, 1996; Nikora, 1995b; Thomas & Nikora, 1996), and cultural practice issues (Paewai, 1996) have helped to shape alternative practices and strategies for working with Maori and provide insights into Maori conceptualizations.

10.17.6.2 Cultural Safety

While psychological literature contributes to a more informed trainee and practitioner, cultural approaches within other disciplines have assisted psychology training to provide strategies to improve cultural care, meaning, and sensitivity when working with Maori. One such approach is that of "cultural safety" which is described as

> ... actions which recognise, respect and nurture the unique cultural identity of tangata whenua, and safely meet their needs, expectations and rights. A culturally unsafe practice is (are) any actions which diminish, demean or disempower the cultural identity and well-being of an individual. (Ramsden, 1991, pp. 7–8)

Cultural safety was initiated by Maori nurses and later developed by the New Zealand Council of Nursing (Ramsden, 1991). As an approach, cultural safety has increased understanding of the different ways that helping professions might develop working guidelines. The focus of these guidelines is to enhance good teaching practices and strategies when educating health professionals. Cultural safety is now generally accepted in professional practice and training programs, including psychology.

10.17.6.3 Cultural Safety and Clinical Practice

Cultural safety incorporates two principles inherent in the Treaty of Waitangi. First, active protection of Maori Treaty rights, and second, recognition of all cultures in Aotearoa. A study by Paewai (1996) described various cultural safety strategies being employed by six Maori clinical psychologists working in Aotearoa. A significant finding in Paewai's study was that psychotherapeutic outcomes were improved if the clinician acknowledged the cultural identity of the client in assessment and treatment procedures.

To this end, some training programs are developing a curriculum that monitors, teaches, and evaluates cultural safety and competence. For example, at Waikato University, courses in cross-cultural psychology, community psychology, and Maori development and psychology highlight cultural safety concepts and approaches. These programs have been developed to assist psychology students to increase their cultural analysis by providing informed consideration of issues of culture, with the intent of avoiding ignorant rejection or violation of cultural norms (Nikora, 1995c).

10.17.6.4 Maori Psychological Initiatives

Three agency-based programs (one hospital-based and two in the Justice Department) developed specifically for working with Maori are presented in this section. The support of local tribes, Maori healers, and resource people have been essential (McFarlane-Nathan, 1996) to the success of these programs.

Whaiora is a ward based at a psychiatric hospital at Tokanui in the central North Island. It emerged from an increasing awareness among Maori nursing staff at Tokanui Hospital that the therapy strategies employed were culturally biased. They often alienated Maori clients (Durie, 1994). The successful development of a parallel Maori cultural therapy unit in 1986 was a direct attempt to redress the spiritual and psychological imbalance prevalent among Maori clients by implementing a more appropriate, holistic approach to mental health (Rankin, 1986). This approach encompassed many elements critical to Maori health and necessitated that a balance be maintained between each dimension for adequate well-being. One of these approaches is the Maori health model that incorporates the *tinana* (physical body), *hinengaro* (thoughts and aspects of the mind), *whatumanawa* (feelings and deep emotions), and *whanau* (extended family). The model provides a framework that assists in the understanding of Maori processes and people. In addition, Whaiora seeks to restore and enhance self-esteem, self-worth, and self-confidence by encouraging and promoting a sense of being and pride in the client's own cultural heritage (Rankin, 1986). The unit places strong emphasis on *whanau* involvement and community support networks which are fundamental to a smoother transition for Maori clients returning to the community and decreasing readmission rates.

Te Piriti Special Treatment Unit is a relapse prevention program for sex offenders based in Auckland. The main goal of the program is to reduce sexual reoffending and assist offenders and *whanau*/support people through the initial rehabilitation process. This organization has a Maori "cultural consultant" who is involved at both the assessment and intervention stage of the treatment. The assessment procedure begins with building trust then moving gradually into Maori identity issues such as place of origin, *whanau*, *hapu*, and *iwi*. Whakapapa (genealogy) is discussed, along with *tikanga* (beliefs and traditions) and *te reo* Maori (Maori language). All of these variables are fundamental to Maori identity and hence, play a key role in treatment procedures.

The Bicultural Therapy Model is also being currently piloted through the office of Psychological Services in Auckland. The Bicultural Therapy Model draws many elements from the work of Renfrey (1992) which recognizes the stressors caused by acculturation and/or deculturation. Cultural supervision of the clinician ensures that the necessary knowledge base is being maintained to enable satisfactory assessment of Maori clients. Clinicians require training which focuses on the cultural context within which Maori operate (McFarlane-Nathan, 1994). They must also develop an awareness of their own limitations for dealing with Maori clients. At the initial assessment stage, the trained clinician is encouraged to consider the possibility of deculturation and/or acculturation stressors in the assessment of etiology. The Bicultural Therapy Model recognizes that cognitive behavior therapy as a therapeutic approach provides a framework for the culturally-competent clinician to investigate the social and behavioral context of the client. The client's level of bicultural competence is also assessed to establish the "degree to which clients possess sufficient cultural resources to enable them to develop successfully as indigenous people in Western society" (McFarlane-Nathan, 1996).

10.17.7 CONCLUSION

Bicultural and Maori initiatives in psychology have contributed to an evolving understanding of cultural variables when working with Maori people. Contributions made by Maori psychologists, Maori students, and Maori-initiated programs have helped to refine a resource base where theory, research, and skills relevant to Maori development and psychology can be developed. As Maori are appointed to senior positions in health agencies and universities, there will be increasing opportunities for Maori initiatives in research and the development and application of indigenous psychological paradigms as well as Maori control of services for Maori.

10.17.8 REFERENCES

Abbot, M. W., & Durie, M. H. (1987). A whiter shade of pale: Taha Maori and professional psychology training. *New Zealand Journal of Psychology, 16*, 58–71.

Awatere, D. (1981). Maori counselling. In F. Donnnelly (Ed.), *A time to talk: Counsellor and counselled* (pp. 198–202). Sydney, Australia: Allen & Unwin.

Awatere, D. (1984). *Maori sovereignty*. Auckland, New Zealand: Broadsheet.

Ballara, A. (1986). *Proud to be white: A survey of Pakeha prejudice in New Zealand.* Auckland, New Zealand: Heinemann.

Brady, E. C. (1992). Cross-cultural issues in clinical psychology training programs. *New Zealand Journal of Psychology, 21*, 56–61.

Bridgman, G. (1993). *Nga ia o te oranga hinengaro Maori: Trends in Maori mental health—a discussion document.* Wellingon, New Zealand: Te Puni Kokiri Ministry of Maori Development.

Buck, P. T. (1949). *The coming of the Maori.* Wellington,

New Zealand: Maori Purposes Fund Board and Whitcombe & Tombs.

Durie, M. H. (1994). *Whaiora: Maori health development.* Auckland, New Zealand: Oxford University Press.

Durie, M. H., Black, T. E., Christensen, I. S., Durie, A. E., Taiapa, U. K., Potaka, U. K. J., & Fitzgerald, E. (1995, October). Te hoe nuku roa framework—A Maori identity measure. *ASSR NEWS* (Published Monthly by the Association of Social Science Researchers) 1–6.

Hamerton, H., Nikora, L. W., Robertson, N., & Thomas, D. (1995). Community psychology in Aotearoa/New Zealand. *The Community Psychologist* (Published by The Society for Community Research and Action) *28*(3), 21–23.

Heperi, L. (1996). *Awhi atu, awhi mai—Help seeking and Maori.* Unpublished master's thesis. Hamilton, New Zealand: University of Waikato.

Hingston, O. M. (1993). *Ethnicity and oppression: The perceptions of seven Maori individuals.* Unpublished master's thesis. Hamilton, New Zealand: University of Waikato.

Jackson, M. (1988). *The Maori and the criminal justice system: He whaipaanga hou—A new perspective (Part 2).* Wellington, New Zealand: Department of Justice, Policy and Research Division.

Kawharu, I. H. (1989). Introduction. In I. H. Kawharu (Ed.), *Waitangi: Maori and Pakeha perspectives of the Treaty of Waitangi* (pp. x–xxiv). Auckland, New Zealand: Oxford University Press.

Lawson-Te Aho, K. (1984). *The masters tools: Maori development inside Pakeha psychology.* Unpublished master's thesis. University of Waikato, Hamilton, New Zealand.

McFarlane-Nathan, G. (1994). *Cognitive behaviour therapy and the Maori client.* Unpublished paper. Department of Justice, Psychological Services Division, Auckland, New Zealand.

McFarlane-Nathan, G. (1996). *The bicultural therapy project.* Unpublished paper. Department of Corrections, Psychological Service, Auckland, New Zealand.

Moeke-Pickering, T. M. (1996). *Maori identity within whanau.* Unpublished master's thesis. University of Waikato, Hamilton, New Zealand.

Mulgan, R. (1989a). *Maori, Pakeha and democracy.* Auckland, New Zealand: Oxford University Press.

National Standing Committee on Bicultural Issues (NSCBI) (1994a). The New Zealand Psychological Society and the Treaty of Waitangi: Proposed implementation plan. *New Zealand Psychological Society Bulletin, 82,* 13–17.

National Standing Committee on Bicultural Issues (NSCBI) (1994b). An interview with Linda Waimarie Nikora, out-going convenor of the NSCBI. *New Zealand Psychological Society Bulletin, 83,* 6–8.

National Standing Committee on Bicultural Issues (NSCBI) (March). How does the Treaty of Waitangi (1840) relate to a science that developed after 1890? *New Zealand Psychological Society Bulletin, 84,* 8–11.

Nikora, L. W. (1995b). *The maintenance of Maori tribal identities in Aotearoa: Rationale and overview of working papers.* Unpublished paper. Waikato University, Hamilton, New Zealand.

Nikora, L. W. (1995c). *Cultural safety.* Unpublished paper. University of Waikato, Hamilton, New Zealand.

Orange, C. (1987). *The Treaty of Waitangi.* Wellington, New Zealand: Allen & Unwin.

Paewai, M. K. (1996). *Cultural safety within clinical psychology—A Maori perspective.* Unpublished paper. Waikato University, Hamilton, New Zealand.

Paterson, K. (1992). *Wahine maia, me te ngawari hoki: Maori women and periodic detention in Kirikiriroa: Their life difficulties and the system.* Unpublished master's thesis. University of Waikato, Hamilton, New Zealand.

Ramsden, I. M. (1991). *Kawa whakaruruhau: Cultural safety in nursing education in Aotearoa (New Zealand).* Wellington, New Zealand: New Zealand Council of Nursing.

Rankin, J. F. A. (1986). Whaiora: A Maori cultural therapy unit. *Community Mental Health in New Zealand, 2,* 38–47.

Renfrey, G. (1992). Cognitive behavior therapy and the Native American client. *Behavior Therapy, 23*(3), 321–340.

Renwick, W. (1990). *The Treaty now.* Wellington, New Zealand: GP Books.

Ritchie, J. (1992). *Becoming bicultural.* Wellington, New Zealand: Huia/Brasell.

Ritchie, J., & Ritchie, J. (1978). *Growing up in New Zealand.* Auckland, New Zealand: Allen & Unwin.

Sawrey, R. (1990). *A survey of psychologists' opinions and behavior on aspects of Maori mental health.* Unpublished master's thesis. Victoria University, Wellington, New Zealand.

Sharp, A. (1995). Why be bicultural? In M. Wilson & A. Yeatman (Eds.), *Justice and identity: Antipodean practices* (pp. 116–133). Wellington, New Zealand: Williams Books.

Spoonley, P. (1988). *Racism and ethnicity.* Auckland, New Zealand: Oxford University Press.

Stewart, T. R. (1995). *Ka pu te ruha, ka hao te rangatahi: Contributions to indigenous psychology in Aotearoa/New Zealand.* Unpublished master's thesis. University of Auckland, Auckland, New Zealand.

Thomas, D. R. (1988). Development of a test of Maori knowledge. *New Zealand Journal of Psychology, 17,* 59–67.

Thomas, D. R., & Nikora, L. W. (1992). From assimilation to biculturalism: Changing patterns in Maori-Pakeha relationship. In D. R. Thomas & A. Veno (Eds.), *Psychology and social change: Australian and New Zealand perspectives* (pp. 231–256). Palmerston North, New Zealand: Dunmore Press.

Thomas, D. R., & Nikora, L. W. (1996). Maori, Pakeha and New Zealander: Ethnic and national identity among New Zealand students. *Journal of Intercultural Studies, 17,* 29–40.

Thomas, D. R., Nikora, L. W. & Moeke-Pickering, T. M. (1996). *Readings in culture and ethnicity.* Department of Psychology, University of Waikato, Hamilton, New Zealand.

Waldegrave, C. (1985). Mono-cultural, mono-class and so called non-political family therapy. *Australia and New Zealand Journal of Family Therapy, 6,* 197–200.

Walker, R. (1989). Maori identity. In Novitz and Willmott (Eds.), *Culture and identity in New Zealand* (pp. 35–52). Wellington, New Zealand: Government Printer.

Walker, R. (1990). *Ka whawhai tonu matou: Struggle without end.* Auckland, New Zealand: Penguin.

Vasil, R. (1988). *Biculturalism: Reconciling Aotearoa with New Zealand.* Wellington, New Zealand: Victoria University Press.

Yutrzenka, B. A. (1995). Making a case for training in ethnic and cultural diversity in increasing treatment efficacy. *Journal of Consulting and Clinical Psychology, 63*(2), 197–206.

10.18
Perspectives from Sub-Sahara Africa

PIUS K. ESSANDOH
Jersey City State College, NJ, USA

10.18.1 MISCONCEPTIONS ABOUT AFRICA	357
10.18.2 SOCIOCULTURAL BELIEFS	358
10.18.2.1 Spirituality	358
10.18.2.2 Collective Responsibility and Cooperation	359
10.18.2.3 Kinship	359
10.18.2.4 Gender Roles	360
10.18.3 OTHER THEORETICAL ISSUES	360
10.18.4 TRADITIONAL COMMUNITIES AND PSYCHOPATHOLOGY	360
10.18.5 THE THERAPEUTIC PROCESS	362
10.18.5.1 Assessment/Diagnosis	362
10.18.5.2 Prognosis	362
10.18.5.3 Treatment/Cure	363
10.18.6 TRAINING IMPLICATIONS	363
10.18.7 CONCLUSION	363
10.18.8 REFERENCES	364

10.18.1 MISCONCEPTIONS ABOUT AFRICA

Despite its size and the role it has played in both ancient and modern civilization, Africa continues to be relatively unknown to the Western world. The little that has been written about Africa in general, and African psychology in particular, is full of myths and misconceptions. For example, it was widely believed that depression, suicide, and affective disorders were either nonexistent or less prevalent in African communities and that in general, Africans experienced fewer psychological problems than peoples from other cultures. Although such myopic views have been challenged by several authors, who point to as many psychological disturbances in Africa as in other cultures (Binitie, 1981; German, 1987; Leighton, Lambo, & Hughes, 1963), there has not been a consistent body of research on the theory of psychopathology and treatment issues.

The primary focus of this chapter is to discuss the sociocultural factors in psychological health in sub-Sahara Africa, bearing in mind that any good definition of mental health and the delivery of mental health services in Africa must take these factors into account. The chapter also discusses issues of diversity (e.g., gender) as they affect the delivery of psychological services. It should be pointed out that psychological therapy, as practiced in the West, is almost nonexistent in most parts of Africa and as such, for many people it is not an option for the resolution of interpersonal conflicts and other psychological problems. It is also important to point out that sub-Sahara Africa is so massive in size and rich in cultural diversity that to attempt to write about Africa as if it contained one homogeneous group would be the greatest act of disservice. Most of the generalizations made in this chapter about Africans or Africa are more impressionistic than empirical and are drawn primarily from my own experiences as an African and my work with African college students in the USA, and also from the works of other indigenous African researchers.

A suggestion frequently made is that African traditional life and culture are primarily variants of folk culture that existed throughout the rest of the world in the preindustrial revolution era and are therefore not relevant for the postindustrial revolution era. This is in spite of the fact that most Western nations are desperately seeking some aspects of traditional life and culture as vital to national and individual well-being and as needed additions to industrial and economic development. It is commendable that despite the fact that sub-Sahara Africa is witnessing major political and economic changes typical of postindustrial revolution, most of the urban communities remain traditional and they continue to have a more stable and homogeneous cultural tradition. Writing about traditional healing in Africa and its implication for cross-cultural counseling, Vontress (1991) pointed out that even when they are outside of their countries, most African students in the USA retain their traditional beliefs; this presumably slows down the process of acculturation. It is reasonable to suggest then that when they are in Africa, urbanized Africans, in spite of some changes in their world views, may continue to hold a culturally pluralistic view of mental health and psychological well-being. Inherent in this cultural pluralism is group identity, collective responsibility, cooperation, interdependence, certain values and beliefs about etiological causes of mental illness, attribution of disturbances, and spirituality. These values are for the most part retained or revisited when individuals have to respond to some psychological symptoms of stress and alienation that industrialization and urbanization present. In most instances, urbanized Africans utilize both systems of care—traditional and Western—sequentially, if not simultaneously. They see these two systems not as contradictory but as reinforcing each other (Onyioha, 1977). The implications for psychological development and services have probably only been inferred or assumed at this time but clinical psychologists must understand some aspects of these sociocultural beliefs before they are able to work with clients from this culture.

10.18.2 SOCIOCULTURAL BELIEFS

African etiological theory of mental illness and psychological disorders is still profoundly rooted in sociocultural and spiritual foundations (Danquah, 1982; Essandoh, 1995; Wyllie, 1983). Enemies use witchcraft and other magical means to afflict their victims with mental illness. Binitie (1991) has indicated that it is the belief of some Africans that witches "can do harm from a distance without being in physical contact with their victims ... They terrorize the victims through their capacity to cause illness, misfortune, childlessness, poverty, and death" (p. 5); thus, presenting problems that traditional healers as well as clinical psychologists have to deal with. The gods and ancestors can afflict individuals with mental illness as well as provide cure and grant success and well-being. As agents of healing power and knowledge, they influence to a very large extent the moral development of individuals as well as the social changes that take place in the community. Binitie (1991) has pointed out further that witches are viewed as "judicial agents" and also as "agents of socialization" who help "to equilibrate society by preventing social greed and unscrupulous behavior" (p. 5). Individuals and communities become aware of the possible social consequences of their behavior and thus they show deep respect for customs and traditions and also work on improving interpersonal, family, and social relationships, very critical components of good mental health. When there are any lapses that lead to mental health or physical problems, traditional healers who serve as intermediaries between the spirit world and the physical world intercede with sacrifices and provide treatment. Traditional healers also serve as interpreters and teachers of social values and beliefs.

10.18.2.1 Spirituality

African traditional beliefs emphasize the importance of spirituality and external supernatural sources of help. There is a sense of reliance and dependence on a supreme being and on nature. People must either be subjugated to nature or live in harmony with it and submit to the authority of God or a deity to whom everybody is accountable. Faith in the supernatural influences most, if not all, healing. Thus, traditional healers and religious/spiritual healers become particularly powerful, not only because they share these same beliefs as their clients, but also because only they have the skills to lock up evil spirits as well as invoke the help of good spirits through prayer, sacrifices, and concoctions.

There is also the belief in reincarnation. This is expressed in ceremonies concerning life and death. For example, a new-born child is named after a dead ancestor and is sometimes believed to be this dead ancestor who has reincarnated. The link between the metaphysical and the physical must remain unbroken and the new-born is expected to develop such altruistic attributes of sharing and interdependence that characterized the life of the deceased relative. For living relatives, it is a great honor to have a new-born baby named after them. This is a testimony of their moral character and the respect enjoyed between the family and community. Young ones learn early in life that if they do good, they can reap the benefit in this current life or the life thereafter.

10.18.2.2 Collective Responsibility and Cooperation

Traditional African families derive their strength from cooperation and mutual helpfulness. Individual growth and development must be seen in the context of family growth and development. This collateral relationship which emphasizes self as part of a group, and people as more important than possessions, is different from other world views where individualism and task productivity are more important than relationships. The African is brought up with values that encourage mutual support in times of good fortune as well as in times of adversity, ill-health, and failure. The only contribution in life which significantly influences development is to cooperate with the family and group. Individual happiness means interdependence (not independence); there is no other means of meaningful life. Interdependence is a life-long virtue and a yardstick for measuring the "good life." Too much independence is interpreted as pride and a haughty attitude, and one is often punished by the gods for this kind of attitude. Within this culturally defined belief system that exalts interdependence above independence, the development of mental illness (and to some extent physical illness) depends on the disturbed person's interpersonal relationship; recognizing the importance of interdependence can ensure good psychological health, but not recognizing this important aspect of human development can lead to poor psychological health.

Collective responsibility and mutual cooperation also demand that parents (including the extended family of uncles, aunts, etc.) provide for the welfare and security of children who in turn will ensure the security of parents in their old age. This view is nicely summarized by a Ghanaian proverb (Akan) which, when literally translated into the English language, states that if you depend on people during infancy when you are growing your teeth, you reciprocate this gesture by helping these individuals during old age when they lose their teeth. This kind of reciprocal expectation, when not properly resolved, could lead to anxiety over one's inability to be a good provider for one's children or parents. For the African parent, this relationship could lead to good mental health and respectability in the community, as well as provide social security during old age. For the African child, failure to live up to this filial obligation has very serious social and mental health consequences.

Even on the international scene, African leaders have often recognized the importance of collateral relationships. For example, Nkrumah of Ghana articulated very strongly and clearly the notion that Ghana's independence (and by extension, development) was meaningless unless it was tied to the total emancipation and development of all Africa. Nkrumah's new republic was not ready for competitive nationalism. Instead, he was ready to cooperate in a harmonious relationship with the rest of Africa for its political as well as economic development. Thus, the African value of interdependence and collective responsibility is clearly demonstrated not only at the individual/family level but also at community, national, and continental levels.

10.18.2.3 Kinship

One of the most distinctive features of traditional African communities is the importance of kinship ties and communal style of living. All activities of social life—economic, political, and religious—are based on such kinship relations. Such ties bring people together for very important family activities like farming and harvesting (e.g., the Ndoboa system among the Akans of Ghana where families help each other in cultivating the land and in harvesting the produce), the birth of a child, puberty rites, and marriage and funeral ceremonies. Feeling closely related to kin offers security in all aspects of family life—economic, social, and psychological—and it gives expression to the sense of interdependence and cooperation. A strong social support network, very instrumental in preventing some psychological problems (e.g., stress, depression, uncomplicated bereavement), develops. Practitioners must recognize and utilize this network in the delivery of psychological services.

10.18.2.4 Gender Roles

A number of researchers have estimated that the ratio of African males to females in terms of psychiatric hospitalization is two to one (Dawson, 1964; Lamptey, 1977; Orley, 1972). Yet, despite this difference in the rate of hospitalization, it appears that African women present with higher incidence of depression and other psychosomatic disorders than their male counterparts. Kisekka (1990) has speculated that the low hospitalization rate among women may well be due to the fact that women use alternative forms of treatment (such as spiritual healing and traditional healing); or that because men are over-represented in the formal employment sector, they have access to free medical care; and that men are over-represented in cases of mandated admission from law enforcement agencies, particularly the police. Kisekka has further hypothesized that gender-role stressful situations such as a "barrenness, failure to have the desired number and sex of children, unwanted pregnancies, divorces, matrifocality, and early and forced marriages" (p. 10) may impact women more significantly than they do men. The etiology and nature of these emotional disturbances in Africa seem to point to sociocultural factors rather than intrapsychic factors. If this assertion is accurate, it will be imperative for psychologists and other mental health professionals to consider sociocultural factors in psychopathology and treatment as an integral part of competent professional practice.

10.18.3 OTHER THEORETICAL ISSUES

Although it is clear from the discussion of the sociocultural beliefs that differences exist between sub-Sahara Africa and the Euro-American culture, it is important to point out that differences exist also in terms of the psychological characteristics of individuals from these different cultures. There is evidence of variation in the definition of some psychological constructs. Traditional psychological theories have often defined development from a Eurocentric world view. This world view is middle class, male, white, and with Protestant values in orientation. Development is conceptualized in terms of self-actualization, separation, differentiation, independence, respect for personal boundaries, and self-development. All this takes precedence over group and community interests. But even in the West, feminist critics and multicultural experts have challenged such Eurocentric developmental theories (Asante, 1987; Atkinson, Morten, & Sue, 1993; Cross, 1971; Gilligan, 1982; Jackson, 1975; Miller, 1976) and they have pointed out that women, as well as the culturally different way of knowing and developing, are somehow different from the stages proposed by these Euro-American theories.

Most developmental theories in psychology and education follow a stage-wise, linear, predictable, and hierarchical progression. They measure development in stages across life-span and this life-span is divided into prenatal, infancy, early childhood, late childhood, adolescence, young adulthood, middle age, old age, and death. To most Africans, life-span development has very few stages—prenatal, childhood, adulthood, and old age. The kind of identity confusion that faces Western children as they make the transition from late childhood to adolescence simply may not exist for the African child, who becomes an adult overnight after certain rites of passage ceremonies have been performed. In a similar vein, using Eurocentric theories to measure constructs like self-esteem, self-actualization, autonomy, doubt, initiative, and guilt do not make sense. Development from an African frame of reference, including even life-span, is cyclical, nonlinear, multigenerational, as well as transgenerational and it measures constructs such as collaboration, communal values, and spirituality. In Africa, development in any facet must include character training (similar to Kohlberg's moral development) and only this is seen as beneficial to society. It is important to understand that if these theoretical constructs have different meaning for the African, then a transcultural description of psychopathology may not be possible after all and that the development of a common psychological language for communication between sub-Saharan African mental health professionals and their Euro-American counterparts is a long way from happening. This has important implications for training, research, and practice.

10.18.4 TRADITIONAL COMMUNITIES AND PSYCHOPATHOLOGY

The suggestion that traditional African life and culture are not relevant for the post-industrial revolution era raises a number of important questions. Should modernization—technological, industrial, and economical—always be at the expense of the social, spiritual, and communal values that have sustained the African continent for hundreds of years? Does the African culture help lay a foundation for a psychologically healthy personality strong enough to withstand the pressures of industrialization and urbanization? Answers to these questions may help explain how psychopathology develops in the sub-Sahara African context. If one adopts the unipolar way of thinking that folk culture is not relevant for development in the postindustrial revolution era, one will fail to recognize that the modern world, when alienated from social, spiritual, and communal values, experiences a breakdown in moral values that leads to the disintegration of families in particular and society in general. The argument for the retention of traditional cultural beliefs and practices also presupposes that Africans will enjoy an improved psychological health if they retain these beliefs. The truth, however, is that there are many aspects of traditional life that could either initiate psychological problems or exacerbate them.

The role of sociocultural factors in the development of psychopathology has not received any serious research consideration in sub-Sahara Africa. While cultural factors could be the source of cohesion, identity, and strength, and be instrumental in the development of good psychological health and the prevention of some serious psychological disorders, in some instances these same factors could be the source of psychopathology. For example, it is often believed that the extended family/kinship system provides personal and social security. However, literature is often silent on the fact that such deep commitment to the extended family could lead to stress, anger, intergenerational conflict, feelings of betrayal and shame, marital problems, and a host of other problems. Writing about bereavement and stress in career women in Nigeria. Kalu (1990) has indicated that friends and relatives take over "the care of children, household chores, and errands connected with funeral announcement and arrangement" (p. 79). This arrangement could prevent "depression and low morale as the result of major life events" (p. 75). She also indicates, however, that the contemporary Nigerian widow "is under stress not so much from the loss of the spouse but from the demands of a large and sometimes unwieldy group of significant others who participate in the funeral process" (p. 81). Is the source of this strain, discordance, and strife clinical or is it a conflict over the ways of achieving social values?

Another area where cultural factors become a source of stress, anxiety, and depression revolves around generativity and the expectation to have children to continue the cycle of life. The African society is family focused and it values child bearing and child rearing. In most instances, singleness and childlessness are not options, especially for the African woman. Kisekka (1990) notes the excessive stigma attached to barrenness and goes on to point out that "both traditional and modern folklore, literature and popular music are replete with depictions of barren women as lonely, malicious, [and] cruel to children" (p. 6). It appears that the feelings of isolation, loneliness, and even depression are the expressions of the problems of living in this culture and are culturally induced rather than being intrapsychically induced.

Although cultural factors could exacerbate and even initiate psychopathology, urbanized Africans may experience psychopathology because of the degree of their alienation from these traditional and cultural values. For example, Africans have become enslaved to the corrupting influences of individualism (the "me first" attitude), and they have made social and cultural adaptations from kin-bound societies and kinship ties that provided the much needed solidarity for physical as well as mental growth. The extent to which these individuals want to assimilate the West culture creates an identity confusion. The Western culture is very different from the African culture and as Taft (1977) has suggested, when the size of the gap between a familiar culture and an unfamiliar culture is very big, it is difficult for individuals to adjust and cope with the changes that they need to make. Thus, caught between retaining most of the traditional African values and beliefs that are incompatible with the values of a competitive, impersonal, and technologically oriented value system, and the desire to be accepted by the West; the social, spiritual, and communal values of Africans become very adulterated and compromised. As Some (1993) has observed, the "sweeping industrial imperialism" (p. 36) brought on Africans puts the African in two worlds: the traditional and the corporate. He further argues that:

> the corporate world dims the light of the traditional world by exerting a powerful magnetic shadow-like pull on the psyche of the individual. Thus the individual feels compelled to respond. But as he or she tries to respond, the individual begins to realize that the source of the pull is elusive. (p. 36)

To maintain a sense of self, there is the need to remain somewhat linked to "essential traditionalism" (Some, 1993). If this does not happen, the development of a healthy personality is affected. The African becomes marginalized and this creates some stressful conditions that may very well be misdiagnosed. When misdiagnosed these stressful conditions may not respond to traditional treatment.

10.18.5 THE THERAPEUTIC PROCESS

10.18.5.1 Assessment/Diagnosis

The issue of lack of trained mental health professionals in sub-Sahara Africa has been well documented (Danquah, 1982; Lamb, 1983; Okpaku, 1991). Thus, the variety of assessment methods described here are ones used primarily by traditional healers. However, it is important to recognize parallels between what traditional healers do and what Western-trained mental health professionals do or should do when working with sub-Sahara African clients. This has implication for training since the use of any assessment methods requires cultural knowledge on the part of practitioners. Recognizing parallels will also encourage cooperation between the two systems of helping.

Assessment in traditional healing often begins with the healer attempting to establish credibility and genuineness. Among some Nigerian tribes, for example, traditional healers initiate the session by offering cola nuts. The belief is that "he who brings cola, brings life" and as Onyioha (1977) further explains, cola suggests that "one is bound to be faithful to a man with whom one has eaten cola—you must not lie against him, you must not plan evil against him" (p. 214). Healers pledge to be faithful and truthful and they expect forthrightness from their clients. When this mutual pledge for truth and respect is established, clients are asked in a life-history or autobiographical approach (biographical approach if a client is not competent or capable of doing so) to tell their story to the healer. Although the African culture does not encourage self-disclosure outside of the family, the client now is ready to talk about everything that the healer is ready to listen to and the healer does not impose any constraint on what should be included in the story. The content of the story provides the data for diagnosis as well as for treatment planning. Traditional healers, therefore, listen very attentively asking very few questions. Essandoh (1995) has suggested that this life-history narrative sometimes includes multigenerational historical accounts and he has compared this to the use of genogram by family therapists in the West. It is amazing that with no recording devices, traditional healers are able to remember many of the details of what clients disclose to them; evidence of their effective listening skills.

The use of divination in diagnosis and treatment provides a link between therapeutic methods and the spiritual and ceremonial life of the African culture. If culture is truly a shared world view, the healer's use of divination respects this world view, in which ancestral spirits and supernatural powers play an important role both in the origin and treatment of diseases. Divination, religion, sorcery, and witchcraft all serve very important psychological and metaphysical functions in this context. The divination system includes the use of beads, amulets, rings, and other paraphernalia needed for the ritual and magical treatment as well as to provide protective charm for the client.

Other assessment techniques include behavior observational techniques by the healer, who will either move in and live with the family or ask the client and sometimes family members to move in and live with them (Vontress, 1991). Again, like the life-history approach, healers have no specific behaviors to observe. Instead they allow a more naturalistic observation to proceed but as difficulties in interpersonal relationship or other conflicts unfold, healers use this diagnostic information to their advantage. Yalom (1995) describes most forms of psychopathology as difficulties in interpersonal relationships, and psychotherapy (especially group psychotherapy) as an exercise to improve or repair interpersonal relationship. This is consistent with what most traditional healers do when they use this naturalistic observation technique.

10.18.5.2 Prognosis

Traditional healers may use any of the diagnostic assessment methods described above or several others to determine the prognosis for a client. In some instances they may use herbs or perform some initial rituals. If the disorder does not respond to these treatments, there is a rediagnosis, and other assessment methods are considered. Essandoh (1995) has described this practice as similar to the use of decision trees and differential diagnosis in clinical practice in the West and has suggested that when traditional healers rule in or rule out causes of disorders, there is the implication that something else (often supernatural) is causing the disease. Danquah (1982) has suggested that some disorders do not respond to initial treatment because traditional healers give instructions that are impossible to follow leading to a high "patient relapse rate" (p. 8) which benefits the healer. Rediagnosis, according to Danquah; involves giving the client "a few simple post-treatment instructions to enable him to carry them out daily with success, and less anxiety" (p. 8). In most instances, significant alleviation of symptoms happens, albeit temporarily leading both the client and the healer to believe that the prognosis is good.

10.18.5.3 Treatment/Cure

Traditional healers use a variety of techniques that have been empirically proven effective in Western psychotherapy. One of their many strengths is their ability to engender faith and hope in the therapeutic process (Frank, 1978; Yalom, 1995). Especially for spiritual healing, it is important for the client to have faith and hope in the process. Doubt and the lack of faith do not lead to significant therapeutic gains. In fact, psychotherapy and medical treatment in all societies benefit from faith and hope long before the other therapeutic factors kick in. Thus, the ability of traditional healers to mobilize their clients" hope becomes an important variable in the therapeutic process.

Traditional healers are also holistic in their approach. Treatment usually combines the physical, social, and spiritual in an effort to restore harmony to the client. Herbal treatment is employed where necessary and social and spiritual interventions are made as appropriate. Whenever necessary (although very infrequently) referral is made to another healer. In all instances, family and close neighbors participate in the treatment, making it easy for the healer to employ all available resources for support and effective treatment. What is good for the client is decided by all of them within the context of the plural medical systems; choosing to use the systems concurrently or simultaneously.

Treatment techniques also include traditional music and dancing, therapeutic rituals and sacrifices, suggestions, hypnosis, and other techniques similar to cognitive-behavioral approaches. The important thing throughout all counseling is the attention given to interpersonal relationships, significant others, and contextual issues.

10.18.6 TRAINING IMPLICATIONS

The preceding paragraphs should have placed issues in their proper perspective not only for clinical recognition by psychologists and mental health professionals in sub-Sahara Africa but also for training and empirical research. The lack of mental health resources—human and infrastructural—makes access to Western-type mental health services very limited. In spite of industrialization and urbanization, sub-Sahara Africans seem to be on a journey to reinvent the traditional African culture. Any training of mental health professionals should recognize this journey by not assuming that mental health problems associated with industrialization will be manifested in sub-Sahara Africa the same way as they are in the West.

One of the first implications is that sub-Sahara Africa must develop its own graduate programs in psychology and mental health to prevent its mental health professionals from receiving graduate training almost exclusively in Europe and North America. Training programs should incorporate traditional medicine and healing into their curriculum in order to be responsive to the needs of a large segment of the population that continues to retain the traditional culture. Courses should be organized around themes that emphasize world views and the sociopolitical nature of differences in the region. Students who choose to train in Europe or North America must be encouraged to consider practicum and internship experiences in Africa supervised either by indigenous clinicians in Africa or culturally competent and sensitive non-Africans. This will increase self-knowledge and understanding of other sociocultural factors in mental health. Graduate programs in Europe and North America where most African governments send their citizens to train must develop multicultural competencies that take traditional healing methods into account. More culture-specific strategies must be taught to sub-Sahara African students who will go back to work within this cultural context.

In terms of assessment measures, sociocultural factors should influence their development very significantly. Assessment should also look at the importance of sociodemograhpic variables as they predict psychopathology. This will help in classification systems that will facilitate communication between sub-Sahara African mental health professionals and their counterparts overseas.

Both faculty and students must be encouraged to consider research into traditional healing methods and also sociocultural factors and psychopathology. Such research should utilize both the empirical and experiential approaches in order to capture the totality of the African reality.

10.18.7 CONCLUSION

The influence of the world view on how counseling is delivered and/or accepted in a given society cannot be overemphasized. If such differences in the world view are important considerations in clinical psychology, then more empirical research is needed to define clearly what mental health means in sub-Sahara Africa. A diversified society in which people hold culturally pluralistic views requires a mental health system that is pluralistic, not monocultural. This is a social reality, the recognition of which will facilitate cooperation between

Western trained providers of mental-health services and traditional healers. More than ever, clinicians and researchers must redouble their efforts to reaffirm their belief in the importance of sociocultural factors in psychotherapy as well as the effectiveness of indigenous modes of helping. Cultural competence requires this kind of collaboration between the different forms of traditional psychotherapy and these indigenous modes of treatment.

10.18.8 REFERENCES

Asante, M. K. (1987). *The Afrocentric idea.* Philadelphia: Temple University Press.

Atkinson, D. R., Morten, G., & Sue, D. W. (1993). *Counseling American minorities: A cross-cultural perspective.* Dubuque, IA: Brown.

Binitie, A. (1981). The clinical manifestation of depression in Africans. In T. A. Ban, R. Gonzales, A. S. Jablensky, N. A. Sartorius, & F. E. Vartanian (Eds.), *The prevention and treatment of depression.* Baltimore: Johns Hopkins University Press.

Binitie, A. (1991). The mentally ill in modern and traditional African societies. In S. O. Okpaku (Ed.), *Mental health in Africa and the Americas today: A book of conference proceedings.* Nashville, TN: Chrisolith.

Cross, W. E., Jr. (1971). Negro-to-Black conversion experience: Toward a psychology of black liberation. *Black World, 20*(9), 13–27.

Danquah, S. A. (1982). The practice of behavior therapy in West Africa: The case of Ghana. *Journal of Behavioral Therapy and Experimental Psychiatry, 13*(1), 5–13.

Dawson, J. (1964). Urbanization and mental health in a West African community. In A. Kiev (Ed.), *Magic, Faith and Healing.* New York: Free Press.

Essandoh, P. K. (1995). Counseling issues with African college students in US colleges and universities. *The Counseling Psychologist, 23*(2), 348–360.

Frank, J. D. (1978). *Psychotherapy and the human predicament.* New York: Schocken.

German, G. A. (1987). Mental health in Africa: I. The extent of mental health problems in Africa today: An update of epidemiological knowledge. *British Journal of Psychiatry, 151, 435–439.*

Gilligan, C. (1982). *In a different voice: Psychological theory and women's development.* Cambridge, MA: Harvard University Press.

Jackson, B. (1975). Black identity development. *Journal of Educational Diversity and Innovation, 2, 19–25.*

Kalu, W. (1990). Bereavement and stress in career women. *Women and Therapy, 10*(3), 75–87.

Kisekka, M. N. (1990). Gender and mental health in Africa. *Women and Therapy, 10*(3), 1–13.

Lamb, D. (1983). *The Africans.* New York: Vintage.

Lamptey, J. J. (1977). Patterns of psychiatric consultation at the Accra Psychiatric Hospital. *African Journal of Psychiatry, 3, 123–127.*

Leighton, A. H., Lambo, T. A., & Hughes, C. C. (1963). *Psychiatric disorders among the Yoruba.* Ithaca, NY: Cornell University Press.

Miller, J. B. (1976). *Toward a new psychology of women.* Boston: Beacon Press.

Okpaku, S. O. (1991). *Mental health in Africa and the Americas today: A book of conference proceedings.* Nashville, TN: Chrisolith.

Onyioha, K. O. K. (1977). The metaphysical background to traditional healing in Nigeria. In P. Singer (Ed.), *Traditional healing: New science or new colonialism.* New York: Conch Magazine.

Orley, J. (1972). A prospective study of 372 consecutive admissions to Butabika Hospital, Kampala. *East African Medical Journal, 49, 16–26.*

Some, M. P. (1993). *Ritual: Power, healing and community.* Portland, OR: Swan/Raven.

Taft, R. (1977). Coping with unfamiliar cultures. In N. Warren (Ed.), *Studies in cross-cultural psychology* (Vol. 1). New York: Academic Press.

Vontress, C. E. (1991). Traditional healing in Africa: Implications for cross-cultural counseling. *Journal of Counseling and Development, 70, 242–249.*

Wyllie, R. W. (1983). Ghanaian spiritual and traditional healers' explanation of illness: A preliminary survey. *Journal of Religion in Africa, 14, 46–57.*

Yalom, I. D. (1995). *Theory and practice of group psychotherapy.* New York: Basic Books.

Subject Index

Every effort has been made to index as comprehensively as possible, and to standardize the terms used in the index in line with the following standards:

Thesaurus of Psychological Index Terms, APA, Eighth Edition, for the selection of psychological terms.

Thesaurus of ERIC Descriptors, ERIC, Twelfth Edition, for the selection of education terms not covered by the above.

EMTREE Thesaurus for the selection of medical terms not covered by the above.

IUPAC Recommendations for the nomenclature of chemical terms, with trivial names being employed where normal usage dictates.

In general, the index follows the recommendations laid down in BS ISO 999:1996.

In view of the diverse nature of the terminology employed by the different authors, the reader is advised to search for related entries under the appropriate headings.

The index entries are presented in word-by-word alphabetical sequence. Chemical terms are filed under substituent prefixes, where appropriate, rather than under the parent compound name; this is in line with the presentation given in the *Thesaurus of Psychological Index Terms.*

The index is arranged in set-out style, with a maximum of three levels of heading. Location references refer to page number; major coverage of a subject is indicated by bold, elided page numbers; for example,

professional licensing, oral examinations **1234–55**
  and public accountability 266

See cross-references direct the user to the preferred term; for example, character *see* personality

See also cross-references provide the user with guideposts to terms of related interest, from the broader term to the narrower term, and appear at the end of the main heading to which they refer; for example

credentialing
  see also professional certification; professional licensing; recredentialing

ability
  cultural bias 60
  see also quantitative ability; spatial ability; verbal ability
aboriginal populations, communication style 99
ABP *see* Association of Black Psychologists (ABP)
ACA *see* American Counseling Association (ACA)
academic achievement, cross-cultural differences 186
acculturation *see* cultural assimilation
achievement
  cross-cultural differences 186
  tests, content bias 66
  see also academic achievement
AD (autistic disorder) *see* autism
ADHD *see* attention-deficit hyperactivity disorder (ADHD)
adherence (treatment) *see* treatment compliance
Adler, Alfred (1870–1937), individual psychology 326
adolescent pregnancy
  cross-cultural differences 187
  prevalence 187
adolescents
  conflicts 189
  drug abuse, cross-cultural studies 199
  families of 184
  family therapy 199
  group identity 185
  homosexuality 225
  identity development 115
  identity problems, cross-cultural differences 360
  racial and ethnic identity 156
  self-concept 185
  sexual activity 199
  sexual orientation, awareness 215
ADRESSING, in family therapy 201
adult children *see* adult offspring
adult offspring, home leaving, cross-cultural differences 187
adultery, cross-cultural differences 180
affective disorders *see* affective disturbances
affective disturbances
  Africa 357
  assessment, culture loading 61
affirmative action
  constructive, South Africa 340
  restorative, South Africa 339
  restrictive, South Africa 339
Africa
  affective disturbances 357
  collateral relationships 359
  collectivism 7
  cultural regions 21
  folk culture 358
  psychology, misconceptions 357
  traditional life 358
  see also South Africa; sub-Saharan Africa
African-Americans *see* Blacks
Africans
  childlessness, social stigma 361
  childrearing attitudes 361
  communal values 361
  cooperation 359
  cultural beliefs 358
  development perspectives 360
  developmental psychology, life span perspectives 360
  emotional trauma, sociocultural factors 360
  ethnic values 359
  filial obligations 359
  identity confusion 361
  infertility, and stress 360
  interdependence 359
  kinship 359
  multiculturalism 358
  psychiatric hospitalization, human sex differences 360
  rites of passage 360
  self-concept 361
  sex roles 360
  spirituality 358

supernatural beliefs 358
urbanization 358
and psychopathology 361
witchcraft 358
see also Blacks
Afrikaans (language), in schools 338
afterlife, cultural significance 178
aged
autobiographical memory, problems 190
definitions 190
cultural differences 190
family therapy 200
independence 190
issues 190
life experiences 189
racial and ethnic identity 189, 191
see also older adults
aged (attitudes toward)
clothing, traditional 190
cross-cultural differences 190
and cultural identity 190
aggressive behavior
human sex differences 163
and stress management 167
aging, of rural population 257
agricultural occupations
and depression (emotion) 259, 261
stress 259
agricultural workers
dispossessed 260
in rural environments 257
AIM *see* American-Indian Movement (AIM)
Akans (Ghana), Ndoboa system 359
AMCD *see* Association for Multicultural Counseling and Development (AMCD)
AMEG *see* Association for Measurement and Evaluation in Guidance (AMEG) (US)
America
family, definitions 175
individualism 6
see also Latin America; North America
American Counseling Association (ACA) 97, 112
American-Indian Movement (AIM) 145
American-Indians
aged, independence issues 190
attitudes, to therapists 201
cross-cultural studies 21
demography 128
family, definitions 176
family therapy
goal-setting 195
interdependence 197
intervention 196
treatment termination 193
interviews, language problems 104
posture 102
racial and ethnic identity 184, 191
therapist preferences 107
treatment outcomes, research 108
American Personnel and Guidance Association (APGA) 58
resolutions 58
American Psychiatric Association (APA)
Diagnostic and statistical manual of mental disorders (DSM-II),
neurasthenic neurosis 39
Diagnostic and statistical manual of mental disorders (DSM-III), cultural issues 36
Diagnostic and statistical manual of mental disorders (DSM-IV)
cultural issues 36
development 279
in family therapy 194
glossary of cultural terms 37
homosexuality 208
religious problems 245
policies, on religion 236
American Psychological Association (APA)
Committee on Lesbian, Gay and Bisexual Concerns (CLGBC) 208
bias studies 209
guidelines 208
cultural test bias studies 58
Ethical Principles of Psychologists and Code of Conduct (1992) 128
ethnicity 112
program design 138
religion 236
guidelines
for ethical practice 193
multicultural counseling 97
homosexuality
conversion therapy 220
policies 208
Office of Rural Health 268
Americans, childrearing practices 181
Amish
family life cycles 177
marriage
age factors 179
roles 180
sexual attitudes 187
amok, definition 37
analysis of variance (ANOVA)
in cross-cultural studies 15
limitations 66
test bias studies 66
ancestors
and family structure 175
multiracial 152
and witchcraft 358, 362
Anglo-Americans, attachment behavior 182
Anglocentrism, and intelligence measures 55
anomie, theories 145
anorexia nervosa
Arabs 320
as culture-bound syndrome 38
see also bulimia nervosa
ANOVA *see* analysis of variance (ANOVA)
antidepressant drugs, studies, placebo 242
anxiety
Arabs 318
attitudes 319
cross-cultural studies 9
construct validity 12
human sex differences 163
and *koro* 38
anxiety disorders, human sex differences 163
anxiety neurosis *see* anxiety disorders
Aotearoa *see* New Zealand
APA *see* American Psychiatric Association (APA); American Psychological Association (APA)
apartheid
development 336
laws 339
role of psychologists in 336
APGA *see* American Personnel and Guidance Association (APGA)
appetite disorders *see* eating disorders
aptitude *see* ability
Arab nations
authoritarianism 314, 319
characteristics 313
psychological 314
collectivism 314, 319
cross-cultural differences 314
epidemiological studies 318
family role 314
health care delivery 320
mental health 313
future trends 321
services 321
psychiatric hospitals 320
psychotherapists 321
human sex differences 317
socioeconomic groups 314
urbanization 314
war, effects on children 319
see also Iran; Iraq; Kuwait; Saudi Arabia; United Arab Emirates
Arabs
anxiety 318
attitudes toward 319
arranged marriage 179
attempted suicide 319
client attitudes 318
clinical assessment, issues 315
depression (emotion) 315, 320
distress 314
eating disorders 320
expressed emotion 315
faith healing 316
family relations 317
family therapy 322
help-seeking behavior 316
hospitalization 317
institutionalization 317
internal–external locus of control 314
IQ studies 316
irrational beliefs 316, 318
mental disorders 315
children 319
mental illness (attitudes toward) 316
morbidity 318
human sex differences 319
neurosis 319
neuroticism 318
obsessive-compulsive neurosis 315
parental attitudes, to adolescents 185
population, distribution 313
professional–client relationship 322
psychometrics 316
psychotherapist attitudes to 317
psychotherapy
attrition rate 318
human sex differences 317
schizophrenia 316, 319
self-actualization 323
self-concept 315

sexual function disturbances 320
sociocultural history 313
periods 314
somatization 315, 317, 321, 322
prevalence 319
superstitions 316
treatment
expectations 317
traditional 316, 320
armed conflict *see* war
arranged marriage, cross-cultural differences 179
Asia
clinical psychology, Taiwanese perspective 343
collectivism 7
Asian American Movement 145
Asian Americans *see* Asians
Asians
aged, independence issues 190
communication style 99
cross-cultural differences 23
studies 44
cross-cultural studies 21
exogamous marriage 181
family, definitions 175
family therapy
goal-setting 195
intervention 196
treatment termination 193
interracial marriage 181
mental health services 347
psychotherapy, language problems 104
therapist preferences 105
see also Chinese; Japanese; Taiwanese; Vietnamese
assessment
clinical, Arabs 315
cultural sensitivity in 135
definitions 135
multicultural 193
see also psychological assessment
Association of Black Psychologists (ABP) 58
Committee on Testing 59
Association for Measurement and Evaluation in Guidance (AMEG) (US) 58
Association for Multicultural Counseling and Development (AMCD), standards 97
asylums *see* psychiatric hospitals
atherosclerosis, estrogen protectivity 166
attachment behavior, cross-cultural differences 182
attempted suicide, Arabs 319
attention-deficit hyperactivity disorder (ADHD), ethnicity factors 64
Australia
Minnesota Multiphasic Personality Inventory-II studies 281
accuracy 289
diagnostic considerations 288
interpersonal relations 283
statistical validity 282
symptomatic patterns 283
treatment considerations 288
authoritarianism
Arab nations 314, 319
cross-cultural differences 186
autism, ethnicity factors 64
autistic disorder (AD) *see* autism
autobiographical memory, aged, problems 190
autobiography, in folk medicine 362
autonomy (personality) *see* independence (personality)
awareness, multiculturalism, South Africa 337, 339, 340

baby boomers
biracial 142, 143, 151
United States 141
Balance Theory of Coordination 265, 272
Bantu education, Verwoerd's theories 336
baptism, in Roman Catholicism 177
bar mitzvah, cultural significance 177
BDI *see* Beck Depression Inventory (BDI)
Beck Depression Inventory (BDI), studies, Taiwan 346
Bedouins, lifestyle 314
behavior
antecedents
distal 95
proximal 95
cross-cultural differences 4
observations, in folk medicine 362
vocational 114
see also aggressive behavior; attachment behavior; child behavior; coping behavior; help-seeking behavior; illness behavior; psychosexual behavior
behavior disorders, human sex differences 162
behavior modification, cross-cultural training 29
behavioral health *see* health care psychology
behavioral medicine *see* health care psychology
belief in God, prevalence 234
Bender–Gestalt Test
Arabs 316, 323
cultural bias test studies, internal-consistency estimates 76
BET *see* bicultural effectiveness training (BET)
biphobia, use of term 220
bias
in construct validity 72
in content validity 65
definitions 54
heterosexist, in psychological services 226
in predictive validity 77
in psychometrics, issues 54
and socioeconomic status 63
sources of 59
see also cultural test bias; test bias
bicultural effectiveness training (BET), applications 200
Bicultural Therapy Model (New Zealand), goals 354
biculturalism
advantages 21
and cultural assimilation 20
definitions 3
and psychology, Maori 351
theories 145
Bieliauskas, Vytautas
links
with Lithuania 330
with Russia 330
bilingualism
and professional–client relationship 104
in translation processes 18
Bill of Rights (US) 144
Binet, Alfred (1857–1911), intelligence measurement studies 54
Binet–Simon scale, translations 85
biomedical approach, in health care 161
biopsychosocial approach, in health care 161, 170
biraciality, use of term 115
birth
cross-cultural differences 181
cultural significance 177
bisexuality
attitudes toward 220
conceptualization 207
definitions 209
Blacks
adolescent pregnancy 187
Afrocentric pride 183
aged
autobiographical memory problems 190
independence issues 190
childrearing practices 181
cross-cultural counseling 105
cross-cultural studies 21
cultural beliefs 358
demography 128
exogamous marriage 181
extended family, childrearing practices 182
family
definitions 175
parental child 176
family therapy
genograms in 194
goal-setting 195
intervention 196
problem-solving 196
treatment termination 193
help-seeking behavior 192
intelligence measures 54
kinship 175
lesbianism
community attitudes 189
studies 212
life expectancy 190
marriage rites 178
mental health services, access 263
mental illness, diagnosis 63
parental caretakers 189
personality disorders 144
personality traits 23
population, rural–urban differences 257
racial and ethnic identity 22, 145
and rootwork 177
self-concept 24
sexual behavior 187
slaves, mental health 262
therapist choice, age differences 188
therapist preferences 106
treatment outcomes, research 108
see also Africans
blame, individual differences 96

Blažys, Juozas
  Introduction to psychiatry (1935) 326
  Tolerance as a cultural principle (1936) 326
blood pressure, and stress, human sex differences 166, 168
"born again" beliefs 234
Bosnians, refugees, family therapy 194
brain, structure, and male homosexuality 214
brain function, and sexual orientation 214
brainwashing, delusions of, case studies 303
Britain *see* United Kingdom (UK)
bulimia nervosa
  Arabs 320
  see also anorexia nervosa
Bureau of the Census (US) 151
  definitions 256
burials *see* death rites

California Achievement Test (CAT), predictions 82
California Test of Mental Maturity (CTMM), prediction 83
Cambodians, treatment outcomes, research 108
Canada
  agricultural occupations, stress studies 259
  agricultural workers, dispossessed 260
  farms, numbers 260
  rural environments, population 256
caregivers, cross-cultural differences 181, 190
Carnegie Commission, studies, in South Africa 336
case studies
  clinical psychology, and religion 251
  Minnesota Multiphasic Personality Inventory-II 290
CAT *see* California Achievement Test (CAT)
Cattell culture fair intelligence test *see* culture fair intelligence tests
Caucasians *see* Whites
CBS *see* culture-bound syndromes (CBS)
CDI *see* Children's Depression Inventory (CDI)
Census Bureau (US) *see* Bureau of the Census (US)
chaperons, in social dating 186
character disorders *see* personality disorders
Chicano Movement 145
Chicanos, cross-cultural studies 28
child abuse, human sex differences 163
child behavior, and cultural context 184
child maltreatment *see* child abuse
childbearing, issues 181
childbirth *see* birth
childhood development, coping behavior 184
childlessness, social stigma 361
childrearing attitudes, Africans 361
childrearing practices
  cross-cultural differences 181
  and family structure 181
  and family therapy 198
  issues 181
  and socioeconomic status 182
children
  family assessment 198
  gender identity, atypical 214
  as interpreters 199
  labeling 63
  launching, cross-cultural differences 187
  parental 176
  psychological problems, Arabs 319
  sex role studies 165
  sexual orientation self-disclosure to 225
  socialization, cultural context 198
Children's Depression Inventory (CDI), studies, Taiwan 346
China
  cross-cultural differences 343
  depression (emotion), studies 43
  neurasthenic neurosis
    historical background 40
    studies 40
    use of term 39
  somatization
    prevalence 41
    studies 47
Chinese
  aged, and cultural identity 190
  arranged marriage 179
  communication style 99
  death rites 178
  family, definitions 175
  help-seeking behavior 43
  intelligence measures, studies 74
  interpersonal interaction 347
  marriage rites 178
  Minnesota Multiphasic Personality Inventory studies 46
  parental caretakers 189
  psychological problems, coping strategies 42
  sexual attitudes 187
  somatization 345
  therapist preferences 106
Chinese Americans *see* Chinese
Chinese Personality Assessment Inventory (CPAI), Chinese Tradition factor 47
Chinese traditional medicine, and somatization 42
chlorimipramine *see* clomipramine
Christianity, fundamentalist, homosexuality (attitudes toward) 219
chronic illness, human sex differences 162
chronic schizophrenia *see* schizophrenia
churches, as community mental health centers 265
circumcision, in Judaism 177
CIS *see* Clinical Interview Schedule (CIS)
civil rights movement, United States 144
clergy, referrals 247
CLGBC *see* American Psychological Association (APA), Committee on Lesbian, Gay and Bisexual Concerns (CLGBC)
client attitudes, Arabs 318
client behavior, Arabs, human sex differences 317
client–psychologist relationship *see* professional–client relationship
clients
  cross-cultural differences 23
    and clinicians 24
  preferences, ethnic factors 105
  religiosity 246
clinical case conceptualization *see* functional analysis
clinical intervention
  cross-cultural 93
    assessment techniques 114
    future trends 111
  cultural capacity in 136
  processes 97
  terminology, issues 111
Clinical Interview Schedule (CIS), Arab studies 319
clinical psychologists
  cultural competence 133
  decentralization 127
  and diversity issues 337
  empathic decentering 136
  ethnic background 36
  preparedness 138
  religiosity 235, 246
  roles, South Africa 336
clinical psychology
  Asia, Taiwanese perspective 343
  assess–treat–refer model 250
  cultural competence training in 127
  culture-bound assumptions 36
  development, Taiwan 346
  diversity 1
    issues 234
  education, religious diversity 249
  ethnocentric approach 36
  and forgiveness 248
  Lithuania 325
    historical background 328
  and morality 239
  as postpositivistic science 240
  practice, and cultural safety 353
  and religion 233
    case studies 251
    empirical research 245
    future trends 250
  vs. religious beliefs 240
  sex issues 161
  and spirituality 233
  sub-Saharan Africa 357
  world views 6
Clinical Psychotherapy Centre (Vilnius), establishment 333
clinical training, and racial and ethnic identity 23
clinicians, and client cross-cultural differences 24
clomipramine, applications, case studies 298
clothing, traditional, and aged 190
CMHCs *see* community mental health centers (CMHCs)
code switching, and foreign language translation 103
codes of conduct *see* professional ethics
cognition
  shared, in cross-cultural studies 16
  see also social cognition
cohabitation, West Indians 180
collaboration *see* cooperation

collectivism
  Arab nations 314, 319
  concept of 6, 7
  cross-cultural differences 95, 150
  Taiwan 344
college students, racial and ethnic identity, studies 188
colonialism
  impact 145
  and racial and ethnic attitudes 142
    historical background 143
coming out (disclosure) *see* self-disclosure
commitment, religious, dimensions of 243
communication skills, development 183
communication style
  cross-cultural differences 99
  definitions 98
communities
  concept of, and psychological intervention 270
  religious 238
  traditional, and psychopathology 360
  see also rural environments
community attitudes, lesbianism 189
Community Helpers Project 271
community mental health centers (CMHCs), rural 265
Community Support Program (US) 271
competence
  bicultural 184
  multicultural 112
  in rural practice 272
  see also cultural competence
computer applications, test scoring 280
concepts, culturally-specific 135
confidentiality, in rural practice 272
Constitution (US) 144
construct validity
  bias in 72
  cross-cultural studies 12
  factor analysis 72
constructionism *see* constructivism
constructivism
  in cross-cultural studies 13
  models 137
  see also social constructivism
content analysis, in cross-cultural studies 17
content validity, bias in 65
control (locus of) *see* internal–external locus of control
cooperation
  Africans 359
  in extended family 359
  in rural environments 271
coping behavior
  acquisition 41
  childhood development 184
  hazardous 163
coronary artery disease, human sex differences 162, 166
corporal punishment *see* punishment
counseling
  bilingual 104
  cross-cultural 358
    ambiguities 100
    empathy 113
    research hypotheses 113
  and cultural assimilation 113
  and culture (anthropological) 44
  generic characteristics 99
  see also cross-cultural counseling; multicultural counseling and therapy (MCT)
counselors
  culturally-sensitive 97
    perspectives 98
  racial preference 105
  religious beliefs, disclosure 247
county asylums *see* psychiatric hospitals
couples
  heterosexual, marriage contracts 180
  see also homosexual couples; marriage
CPAI *see* Chinese Personality Assessment Inventory (CPAI)
credentialing, psychologists 269
credibility, therapists 96
Creoles, cultural assimilation 184
cross-cultural communication, style 98
Cross-cultural Competence Inventory 98
cross-cultural counseling
  barriers to 99
  definitions 97
  factors affecting 105
  paralinguistics 103
  see also multicultural counseling and therapy (MCT)
cross-cultural differences
  academic achievement 186
  achievement 186
  adolescents
    identity problems 360
    pregnancy 187
  adult offspring, home leaving 187
  adultery 180
  aged
    attitudes toward 190
    definitions 190
  apparent 9
  Arab nations 314
  arranged marriage 179
  attachment behavior 182
  attitudes, toward mental health services 192
  authoritarianism 186
  behavior 4
  birth 181
  caregivers 181, 190
  childrearing practices 181
  China 343
  clients 23
  collectivism 95, 150
  communication style 99
  death rites 178
  depression (emotion) 144
  divorce 180
  effects on professional–client relationship 97
  employment status 24
  exogamous marriage 181
  eye contact 101
  eye fixation 101
  facial expressions 102
  family, rites 177
  family structure 175
  family therapy, treatment termination 193
  femininity 95
  fidelity 180
  future research 30
  gestures 101
  group identity vs. individualism 99
  head movements 102
  health risks 170
  help-seeking behavior 43, 192
  home leaving 187
  and human sex differences 165
  individualism 95, 150
  individualist vs. collectivist 27
  interactional arrhythmia 103
  interpersonal communication 195
  interracial marriage 181
  kinesics 101
  life expectancy 190
  marital relations 197
  marriage contracts 180
  marriage rites 178
  marriage roles 180
  masculinity 95
  mental health assessment 279
  mental health interventions 266
  nonverbal communication 100
  paralinguistics 103
  parent–child relations 182
  parental illness and death 189
  personality traits 360
  polygamy 180
  posture 102
  and professional–client relationship 249
    training 25
  proxemics 100
  psychosexual behavior 187
  punishment 182, 192
  schizophrenia 144
  school performance 186
  self-concept development 182
  separation–individuation 199
  sex roles 186, 210
  sexual attitudes 186
  sexual orientation 189
    self-disclosure 216
  sexuality 186
  social dating 186
  social rules 182
  stress 144
  sub-Saharan Africa 357
  training, behavior modification 29
  treatment outcomes, research 107
  verbal communication 100
  Western culture vs. African culture 361
  see also racial and ethnic differences
cross-cultural studies
  adolescents, drug abuse 199
  assessment
    dynamic 114
    techniques 114
  bias
    androcentric 19
    ethnocentric 19
  blacks 21
  construct validity 12
  constructivism in 13
  criteria 20
  differentiation 10
  emics 12, 110
  epistemology 111
  ethical acceptability 11
  ethical issues 112
  etics 12, 110

European-Americans 21
evaluation 9
focus groups 15
future trends 112
hypothesis testing 18
informed consent in 19
instrumentation 110
interpretation 11
limitations 10
meaning issues 11
measurement equivalence 12
methodologies 109
recommendations 110
motivation 10
multimethod measurements 15, 17
multiple choice tests 10
operant methods 17
personal narratives in 111
professional ethics 19
professional issues 112
pseudoetics 13
psychology 352
psychopathology 35
qualitative research 111
quantitative research 111
reality
constructionism 13
convergence 13
reliability 109
research agendas 113
respondent methods 17
response sets 11
risk analysis 19
rival hypotheses 9
elimination 12
sampling 11
sex roles 166
social distance 14
statistical validity 109
strategies 11
terminology, issues 111
tests 16
Thurstone scales in 14
translation in 18, 85
values 95
cross-cultural treatment
clinical intervention 93
future trends 111
see also multicultural counseling and therapy (MCT)
crowding, and intimacy 101
CTMM *see* California Test of Mental Maturity (CTMM)
Cuban Americans *see* Cubans
Cubans
family therapy, language problems 198
racial and ethnic identity 185
social dating, chaperons 186
Cuento therapy, Puerto Ricans 108
culturagrams, in family therapy 194
cultural assimilation
accommodation 20
and aged immigrants 190
assimilator programs 26
general 29
and counseling 113
definitions 3
vs. ethnic affirmation 20
factors affecting 20
learning, methods 24
marginalization 20
mechanisms 184
professional–client relationship
training 26
and social identity 21
studies 20
cultural beliefs
Africans 358
blacks 358
genital disorders, retraction 38
India 5
and industrialization 361
sub-Saharan Africa 358
cultural blindness, concept of 131
cultural capacity
in assessment 135
in clinical intervention 136
concept of 131
continuum 131
dimensions 133
future trends 139
levels of 131
evaluation 133
in research 137
cultural competence
characterization 132
concept of 127
and cultural reference groups 130
definitions 129
and emics 127
in family therapy 195
features 129
as good science and practice 128
and reference groups 133
training
in clinical psychology 127
psychologist attitudes to 139
sub-Saharan Africa 363
value-added capability 130
cultural complexity, concept of 6
cultural context
and child behavior 184
and family therapy 174, 202
and personality disorders 144
cultural destructiveness, concept of 131
cultural differences *see* cross-cultural differences
cultural distance, concept of 4
cultural factors *see* sociocultural factors
cultural identity
and aged 190
development 183
organizations, South Africa 337, 340
respect for 202
cultural incapacity, concept of 131
cultural nuances, in clinical psychology 132
cultural pluralism *see* multiculturalism
cultural proficiency
attitudes 138
characterization 133
concept of 127
in research 137
and social action research 128
cultural psychiatry *see* transcultural psychiatry
cultural responsiveness, concept of 130
cultural safety
and clinical psychology practice 353
concept of 353
cultural sensitivity
characterization 131
concept of 129
definitions 98
models 98
therapists 97, 191
cultural syndromes
ascription–achievement 8
definitions 3
diffuseness–specificity 8
Dionysian vs. Apollonian 9
honor 8
and human nature 8
instrumental–expressive 8
interrelationships 9
time orientations 8
universalism–particularism 8
world views 6
cultural test bias
definitions 64
early studies 53
future research 85
hypothesis, issues 56
intelligence measures 53
research strategies 65
and labeling effects 62
personality measures 53
culture (anthropological)
active–passive syndrome 7
collectivist 4
complex, roles 6
concept of 130
and counseling 44
definitions 2, 94, 112, 174, 175
epiphenomenal perspectives 36
and family life cycles 173
high contact vs. low contact 9
horizontality 7
looseness 6
and psychopathology 44
rejection 183
risk factors 161
tightness 6
verticality 7
culture-bound syndromes (CBS) 35
alternative views 38
as culture-related syndromes 39
definitions 38
emic–etic diversity 39
studies 37
terminology 37
culture fair intelligence tests 61
development 61
culture loading
affective disturbance assessment 61
definitions 61
culture shock
definitions 4
therapists 24

DAP *see* Draw-A-Person (DAP)
dating *see* social dating
de Klerk, Frederik Willem (1936–) 338
death rites, cross-cultural differences 178
decentering
empathic 136
advanced 137
theoretical 137
delusions, case studies 303
dementia praecox *see* schizophrenia
demographic characteristics
racial and ethnic differences 151
sexual orientation 210
United States 256
deontology *see* professional ethics

dependence, cross-cultural differences 182
depersonalization, and *koro* 38
depression (emotion)
  and agricultural occupations 259, 261
  Arabs 315, 320
  core syndromes 46
  cross-cultural differences 144
  cross-cultural studies 46
  human sex differences 163
    Africans 360
    Arabs 319
  prevalence, rural environments 262
  Taiwan 345
  theories, learned helplessness 168
  see also major depression
descendants, and family structure 175
desegregation, schools 144
desmethyldiazepam, applications, case studies 295
Detroit Test of Learning Aptitude-3 (DTLA-3), test bias studies 68
developed countries, sex roles 166
developing countries
  mental health care 265
  sex roles 166
development
  African perspectives 360
  life span, Africans 360
  see also childhood development; psychosocial development
developmental psychology, life span perspectives, Africans 360
diagnosis
  category fallacies 41
  differential, in folk medicine 362
  instruments, in primary health care 266
  psychiatric 41
  and religion 247
DIF *see* differential item functioning (DIF)
differential item functioning (DIF), detection 67
differentiation (racial) 145
  constructive 146, 148
  destructive 146, 147
  negative 146, 147
  see also racial and ethnic differences
disclosure (self) *see* self-disclosure
discrimination, childhood coping behavior 184
disease
  and illness compared 41
  see also illness
distal variables
  definition 95
  sociocultural factors 96
  studies 96
distress
  Arabs 314
  manifestations 41
diversity
  and clinical psychology 337
  definition 2
  identity 337
    future trends 341
  and multiculturalism 337
  types of 2
diversity management
  effects, on organizations 340
  programs 340
  psychological models
    development 337
    facilitation 341
    South African organizations 335
    stages 338
    training 340
diversity training, development 202
divination, in folk medicine 362
divorce
  cross-cultural differences 180
  rites, cross-cultural differences 178
domestic service personnel, racial and ethnic relations 144
domestic violence *see* family violence
dominance, and stress management 168
domination *see* authoritarianism
Draw-A-Person (DAP), Arabs 316, 323
drug abuse, adolescents, cross-cultural studies 199
DSM-II see American Psychiatric Association (APA), *Diagnostic and statistical manual of mental disorders* (*DSM-II*)
DSM-III see American Psychiatric Association (APA), *Diagnostic and statistical manual of mental disorders* (*DSM-III*)
DSM-IV see American Psychiatric Association (APA), *Diagnostic and statistical manual of mental disorders* (*DSM-IV*)
DTLA-3 *see* Detroit Test of Learning Aptitude-3 (DTLA-3)
dualism, in psychopathology 36
Dubai
  depression (emotion), studies 320
  morbidity studies 319
Dutch, marriage roles 180
dysfunctional family, conceptual problems 176
dysphoria *see* major depression

early intervention, in family therapy 199
East Europe, clinical psychology 329
East Germany (former), clinical psychology 329
East Indians, racial and ethnic identity 184
eating disorders
  Arabs 320
  case studies 291
  Minnesota Multiphasic Personality Inventory-II studies 281
  see also anorexia nervosa; bulimia nervosa
ECA *see* National Institute of Mental Health (NIMH) (US), Epidemiological Catchment Area (ECA)
ecology
  definitions 4
  rural environments 256
economic crisis, farms 260, 261
economics, effects on rural environments 260
educable mentally retarded (EMR), placement, bias studies 63
educational field trips, professional–client relationship training 26
educational level, rural population 257
egalitarian fallacy, use of term 61
egalitarianism, concept of 7
egocentrism, in psychopathology 36
Egypt
  mental disorders, studies 320
  mental health services 321
  obsessive-compulsive neurosis, studies 315
  psychosis, studies 315
  somatization, prevalence 319
Egyptians
  psychometrics 316
  treatment, traditional 316
elderly *see* older adults
emics
  in cross-cultural studies 12, 14, 38, 48, 110
  and cultural competence 127
  definitions 5
  and etics 5, 48, 111
emotional expressiveness *see* emotionality (personality)
emotional trauma, sociocultural factors, Africans 360
emotionality (personality), human sex differences 169, 171
employment *see* employment status
employment status, cross-cultural differences 24
empty nest, syndrome 187
EMR *see* educable mentally retarded (EMR)
Epidemiological Catchment Area (ECA) *see* National Institute of Mental Health (NIMH) (US), Epidemiological Catchment Area (ECA)
epidemiology
  gender–health relationship 162
  research instruments, in primary health care 266
epistemology, in cross-cultural studies 111
ESCAPE model, in family therapy 195
Espiritismo therapy 115
essentialism, theories, of sexual orientation 210
estrogen, and health 166
ethics
  and religion 237
  see also professional ethics; religious beliefs
ethnic affirmation, vs. cultural assimilation 20
ethnic differences *see* racial and ethnic differences
ethnic discrimination *see* racial and ethnic discrimination
ethnic groups
  diversity 132
  membership factors 143
  needs 128
  poverty, rural–urban differences 257
  research
    criticisms 109
    methodologies 110
  superior vs. inferior 145
ethnic identity *see* racial and ethnic identity
ethnic issues *see* racial and ethnic issues
ethnic values

Africans 359
aged, and professional–client relationship 192
psychotherapist attitudes 191
studies 95
ethnicity
bias 64
definitions 94, 111, 141
and race compared 142
United States 141
ethnocentrism
and cultural destructiveness 131
in cultural perspectives 6
definitions 4
ethnogenesis, processes 150
ethnography, cross-cultural studies 15
etics
criticisms 13
in cross-cultural studies 12, 14, 48, 110
definitions 5
and emics 5, 48, 111
etiology, psychosocial 161
Eurocentrism
criticisms 360
perspectives 136
European-Americans
cross-cultural differences 23
cross-cultural studies 21
help-seeking behavior 192
evil eye, Arab beliefs 318
exclusivism, and religion 236, 241
exogamous marriage
cross-cultural differences 181
prevalence 198
experiences (life) *see* life experiences
experimental methods, in cross-cultural studies 16
expressed emotion
Arabs 315
Taiwanese 345
extended family
childrearing practices 181
cooperation in 359
cross-generational subsystems 176
psychological problems 361
eye contact, cross-cultural differences 101
eye fixation, cross-cultural differences 101

face validity, in intelligence measures 70
facial expressions, cross-cultural differences 102
factor analysis
construct validity studies 72
in cross-cultural studies 12
factor invariance 73
factor similarity 73
human figures drawing 75
religion 236
faith healing 239
Arabs 316
and folk medicine 363
see also witchcraft
family
adaptation, to rural environments 268
assessment
characteristics 202
culturally-sensitive 191
caretaking patterns 199
changing nature of 202
definitions 175
dynamics, and racial and ethnic identity 156
dysfunctional, conceptual problems 176
ethnic values 191
function, normal vs. abnormal 176
interventions, culturally-sensitive 191
rites, cross-cultural differences 177
see also dysfunctional family; extended family; nuclear family
family caregivers *see* caregivers
family counseling *see* family therapy
family life cycles
adolescents 184
concept of 177
cultural perspectives 173
and immigration 178
later life 189, 200
and marriage 179
and migration 177, 178
new parents 181
culturally-sensitive assessment 198
and rites 177
separation–individuation 185
and sex roles 189
stages 174, 177, 179
family relations
Arabs 317
lesbian, gay, and bisexual persons 222
rural environments 259
family role
Arab nations 314
Taiwan 345
family structure
and childrearing practices 181
complexity 6
cross-cultural differences 175
and family theory 176
and life experiences 189
Taiwan 344
triangulation 176
family systems therapy *see* family therapy
family theory
concept of 174
and family structure 176
family therapy
adolescents 199
aged, assessment 200
Arabs 322
assessment 194
culture-free 195
future research 201
goal-setting 195
methods 195
problem definition 195
and childrearing practices 198
communication styles 198
concept of 174
culturagrams in 194
in cultural competence 195
and cultural context 174, 202
early intervention 199
empowerment 196
and ethnic values 191
conflicts 192
modification 192
family of origin approach 200
future trends 201
genograms in 194
help-seeking behavior 192
intervention 195, 200
misdiagnoses 201
multigenerational perspectives 200
older adults
assessments 200
intervention 201
problem-solving, strategies 196
psychotherapist attitudes in 194, 196
psychotherapist credibility 194
role models 197
and sex roles 200
strategies 193
techniques, culturally-sensitive 197
therapist characteristics 193
treatment termination, cross-cultural differences 193
working alliance 194, 196
family violence, prevalence 198
farm laborers *see* agricultural workers
farmers *see* agricultural workers
farms
economic crisis
impact 261
and support services 260
economic viability 260
fatigue, and neurasthenic neurosis 40
feedback, in programmed instruction 27
females *see* human females
feminine gender role stress (FGRS) model 167
scores 168
femininity
characteristics 162
cross-cultural differences 95
measures 209
feminism
and gender research 164
historical background 163
political agendas 163
FGRS *see* feminine gender role stress (FGRS)
fidelity, cross-cultural differences 180
field trips *see* educational field trips
figure drawing *see* human figures drawing
filial obligations, Africans 359
financial status, and marriage 179
firearms, ownership, South Africa 338
fishermen, income level 258
fluoxetine, applications, case studies 302
folk culture
Africa 358
and industrialization 361
folk medicine
autobiography in 362
multigenerational accounts 362
behavior observation in 362
diagnosis methods 362
differential diagnoses 362
and faith healing 363
holistic approach 363
Nigeria 362
prognosis methods 362
sub-Saharan Africa 358, 362
therapeutic processes 363
treatment 363
folk psychology, benefits 358
foreign language translation

and back-translation 18
in cross-cultural studies 18, 85
techniques 18
in psychotherapy 103
of tests, validity issues 56
forgiveness, and clinical psychology 248
France
Minnesota Multiphasic Personality Inventory-II studies 281
accuracy 289
diagnostic considerations 288
interpersonal relations 283
statistical validity 282
symptomatic patterns 283
treatment considerations 288
Freud, Sigmund (1856–1939)
homosexuality theories 213
theories 326
functional analysis, religion 236, 247
funerals *see* death rites
Funigalo (language), development 338

GATB *see* General Aptitude Test Battery (GATB)
gay couples *see* homosexual couples
gay males *see* male homosexuality
gay parents *see* homosexual parents
gazing *see* eye fixation
geisha, concepts of 14
Gemeinschaft, concept of 270
gender
markers 145
schemas
and coping responses 167
studies 165
use of term 162
see also sex
gender differences *see* human sex differences
gender identity
atypical, children 214
development 145
gender issues *see* sex issues
gender roles *see* sex roles
General Aptitude Test Battery (GATB) 83
general practitioners (GPs), roles, in mental health 43
generalists
psychologists as 267
in rural environments 270
genital disorders, retraction, cultural beliefs 38
genocide, and racial and ethnic attitudes 142
genograms
in family therapy 194
and folk medicine autobiography compared 362
geographic regions *see* geography
geography, and racial and ethnic identity 155
Germans
aged, independence issues 190
parental caretakers 189
Gesellschaft, concept of 270
gestures
conversational 102
cross-cultural differences 101
Ghana
farming, cooperation 359
independence 359
girls *see* human females
Global Assessment Scale (GAS) 105
globus hystericus, case studies 295
Goodenough–Harris Human Figure Drawing Test, factor analysis 75
GPs *see* general practitioners (GPs)
Graduate Record Examination (GRE), cultural test bias studies 67
GRE *see* Graduate Record Examination (GRE)
Great Britain *see* United Kingdom (UK)
Greece, social distance, studies 14
Greeks, parental caretakers 189
Group Areas Act (South Africa) 339
group identity
adolescents 185
vs. individuality, cross-cultural differences 99
group psychotherapy, in rural environments 271
group therapy *see* group psychotherapy
guilt, individualism vs. collectivism 47
guns *see* firearms

Haitians, childrearing practices 181
Hannon, PASE v. 54
hardiness, and homosexuality 217
head movements, cross-cultural differences 102
healing *see* treatment
health
rural environments, issues 261
see also mental health
health care
models
biomedical 161
biopsychosocial 161, 170
see also mental health care; primary health care
health care delivery, Arab nations 320
health care psychology
in rural environments 272
Taiwan 346
health care reform, rural environments 265
health care services
interaction, human sex differences 162
see also health care utilization
health care utilization, and masculinity 162
health psychology *see* health care psychology
help-seeking behavior
Arabs 316
cross-cultural differences 43, 192
family therapy 192
human sex differences 168, 170
heterosexuality
conceptualization 207
and homosexuality (attitudes toward) 221
Hinduism, death rites 178
Hispanics
aged
attitudes toward 190
independence issues 190
attitudes, to therapists 201
communication style 99
cross-cultural differences 23
cross-cultural studies 13
demography 128
family, definitions 175
family life cycles 177
family therapy
and childrearing practices 198
goal-setting 195
intervention 196
treatment termination 193
help-seeking behavior 192
response sets 11
simpatia cultural script 5
treatment outcomes, research 108
see also Cubans; Mexicans; Puerto Ricans
holistic approaches, folk medicine 363
Holocaust survivors, family therapy 194
home leaving
cross-cultural differences 187
single young adults 188, 200
homelessness, whites, South Africa 335
homophobia *see* homosexuality (attitudes toward)
homosexual couples
issues 223
relationship duration 224
sex roles 224
stereotyped attitudes 224
homosexual parents, issues 224
homosexuality
adolescents 225
conversion therapy, issues 219
definitions 209
diagnostic criteria 208
early studies 208
ego dystonic 208
etiology, Freud's theories 213
family issues 222
and hardiness 217
measures 209
myths 210
and psychotherapeutic neutrality 222
psychotherapy, errors 221
stigma 208
treatment, issues 219
see also lesbianism; male homosexuality
homosexuality (attitudes toward)
fundamentalist Christianity 219
and heterosexuality 221
historical background 208
negative, internalized 217
psychotherapists 221
in psychotherapy 209
Hong Kong
cross-cultural studies 16
help-seeking behavior 43
languages 343
neurasthenic neurosis, studies 40
honor, as cultural syndrome 8
hormones
heart disease protectivity 166
see also estrogen; sex hormones
hospitalization
Arabs 317
see also psychiatric hospitalization
House-Tree-Person (HTP), training 330
housing, rural–urban differences 258
Hoyt's formula 76

HTP *see* House-Tree-Person (HTP)
human females
  health problems 162
  roles
    changing 44
    cross-cultural differences 189
  in rural environments 259
  self-disclosure 169
human figures drawing, factor analysis 75
human males
  expressiveness in 165
  health problems 162
  personality disorders, antisocial 162
human nature, and cultural syndromes 8
Human Relations Area Files, applications 17
human rights, homosexuality 208
human sex differences
  aggressive behavior 163
  anxiety 163
  anxiety disorders 163
  behavior disorders 162
  child abuse 163
  chronic illness 162
  coronary artery disease 162, 166
  and cross-cultural differences 165
  depression (emotion) 163
  emotionality 169, 171
  health
    future research 170
    and hormones 166
  health problems, and marriage 162
  help-seeking behavior 168, 170
  historical background 163
  interaction with health care services 162
  learned helplessness 168
  lifestyle, risk factors 162
  lung cancer 162
  mental health problems 171
  morbidity, Arabs 319
  partner abuse 163
  personality disorders 162
  physical abuse 162
  power 170
  premature death 162
  psychiatric hospitalization, Africans 360
  psychological stress 166
  psychosocial factors 162
  psychotherapy, Arabs 317
  quantitative ability 163
  racial and ethnic identity 156
  self-disclosure 168
    sexual orientation 216, 225
  self-fulfilling prophecies 165
  sexual abuse 162
  sexual deviations 163
  sexual function disturbances, Arabs 320
  social support 169
  spatial ability 163, 164
  stress management 162
  studies, meta-analysis 164
  suicide, attempt to completion ratio 168
  theories
    biological perspectives 164
    cross-cultural perspectives 165
    evolutionary 164
    interactional perspectives 164
    overview 164
    social psychological perspectives 165
  verbal ability 163
humans, common attributes 3
Hungarians, marriage roles 180
husband–wife relations *see* marital relations
hypodescent, use of term 143
hypothesis testing, cross-cultural studies 18
ICD-10 see International classification of diseases (ICD-10)

identity
  development, sexual orientation 216
  see also cultural identity; gender identity; racial and ethnic identity; self-identity; social identity
identity (personal) *see* self-concept
Illinois, cross-cultural studies 16
Illinois Test of Psycholinguistic Abilities, factor analysis 75
illness
  and disease compared 41
  see also disease
illness behavior, acquisition 41
immigrants *see* immigration
immigration
  adolescents, and cultural assimilation 199
  aged, and cultural assimilation 190
  and family life cycles 178
  stages 178
  see also migration
Immorality Act (South Africa) 339
immune function
  human sex differences 166
  and self-disclosure 169
inclusivism, and religion 241
income level, rural–urban differences 258
independence (personality)
  aged 190
  young adults 188
India
  cultural beliefs 5
  social distance 14
Indian Drug Prevention Program (IDPP) 199
individual differences, blame 96
individual–system blame continuum 96
individualism
  American perspective 6
  concept of 6, 7
  cross-cultural differences 95, 150
individuality, vs. group identity, cross-cultural differences 99
industrial psychology
  South Africa 336
    roles 340
industrialization, and folk culture 361
infertility, and stress, Africans 360
informed consent, in cross-cultural studies 19
inhibition (personality), and learning theory 57
insight, in psychotherapy, cultural differences 99
institutionalization
  Arabs 317
  and religion 238
intellectual assessment *see* intelligence measures
intelligence
  assessment 57
  definitions 73
  minority groups, issues 144
intelligence measures
  cultural test bias 53
    expert judgments 68
    future research 85
    research strategies 65
  face validity 70
  fairness in 70
  issues 53
  racial and ethnic differences 54
  see also culture fair intelligence tests; intelligence quotient (IQ); Stanford–Binet Intelligence Scale; Wechsler Intelligence Scale for Children-Revised (WISC-R)
intelligence quotient (IQ)
  Arabs 316
  Jews 316
intelligence tests *see* intelligence measures
intelligentsia, Lithuania 326
interactional arrhythmia, cross-cultural differences 103
interdependence
  Africans 359
  cross-cultural differences 182
intergenerational relations, extended family, problems 361
intermarriage *see* exogamous marriage
internal–external locus of control
  Arabs 314
  concept of 95
International Association of Cross-Cultural Psychology 112
International classification of diseases (ICD-10)
  development 279
  neurasthenic neurosis 39
  sociocultural lexicon 36
interpersonal communication, cross-cultural differences 195
interpersonal interaction, Chinese 347
interpersonal relations, and mental disorders 359
interracial marriage
  cross-cultural differences 181
  and family life cycle 181
  increases 151
interracial offspring, increase 151
interracial persons
  issues 143
  life experiences 152, 156
intervention
  behavioral–ecological perspective 269
  family therapy 195
  multicultural 193
  psychological, and communities 270
  types of, in rural environments 269
  see also clinical intervention; early intervention
interviewing
  in cross-cultural studies 16
  distal variables 97
  older adults 201
  proximal variables 97

interviews
  bilingual 104
  clinical, and religion 244
intimacy
  and crowding 101
  emotional, human sex differences 169
IQ *see* intelligence quotient (IQ)
Iran, Minnesota Multiphasic Personality Inventory-II case studies 298
Iranians
  adult offspring, launching 188
  marriage
    age factors 179
    rites 178
Iraq
  depression (emotion) studies 315
  mental disorders, studies 320
  somatization, prevalence 319
Irish
  death rites 178
  stress management, strategies 197
Irish Americans *see* Irish
irrational beliefs, Arabs 316, 318
IRT *see* item response theory (IRT)
Islam
  arranged marriage 179
  death rites 178
  establishment 314
Israel
  mental health services 321
  Minnesota Multiphasic Personality Inventory-II case studies 306
Italians
  adult offspring, launching 188
  family therapy, strategies 197
  histrionic behavior 197
  parental attitudes, to adolescents 185
  parental caretakers 189
  sexual attitudes 187
Italy, Minnesota Multiphasic Personality Inventory-II case studies 294
item bias *see* test bias
item response theory (IRT)
  in cross-cultural studies 12
  in test bias studies 67

Jamaicans
  children, punishment 192
  marriage, age factors 179
  twin households 180
James, William (1842–1910), on religious diversity 234, 238
Japan
  culture (anthropological) 7
  emics 5
  neurasthenic neurosis 39
Japanese
  aged, autobiographical memory problems 190
  communication style 99
  intelligence measures, studies 74
  interracial marriage 181
  marriage roles 180
  parental attitudes, to adolescents 185
  therapist preferences 106
Japanese Americans *see* Japanese
Jensen, Arthur R.
  culture-bound fallacy 62
  egalitarian fallacy 61
  on intelligence measures 56
  test bias studies 54
Jews
  aged
    autobiographical memory problems 190
    independence issues 190
  family therapy 197
  IQ 316
  parental caretakers 189
  see also Holocaust survivors; Judaism
jinn, Arab beliefs 316, 318
job applicant screening, cultural test bias studies 78
Joint Technical Standards for Educational and Psychological Tests and Manuals 60
Judaism
  circumcision 177
  death rites 178
  divorce rites 178
  marriage
    age factors 179
    contracts 180
  rites 177
jumping the broom, cultural significance 178
Jung, Carl Gustav (1875–1961), psychotherapy system 327

K-ABC *see* Kaufman Assessment Battery for Children (K-ABC)
Kaufman Assessment Battery for Children (K-ABC)
  predictive validity 84
  racial and ethnic differences 54
  test bias studies 67
kinesics, cross-cultural differences 101
kinship
  Africans 359
  blacks 175
knowledge level, development, and religion 250
Koraan, religious practices 318
Korea, Minnesota Multiphasic Personality Inventory-II case studies 302
Koreans
  cross-cultural studies 21
  interracial marriage 181
koro
  definition 38
  etiology 38
  prevalence 38
Kuwait, somatization, prevalence 319

La Raza *see* Chicano Movement
labeling
  children 63
  and cultural test bias 62
  and racial and ethnic identity 142, 147
laborers (farm) *see* agricultural workers
language
  and professional–client relationship 100
  see also foreign language translation
language identity, development 184
Laotians, treatment outcomes, research 108
Larry, v. Riles 54
latah, definition 37
late life *see* aged; older adults
Latin America, collectivism 7
Latinos *see* Hispanics
learned helplessness, human sex differences 168
learning theory
  issues 57
  and sexual orientation 214
leaving home *see* home leaving
Lebanon, war, effects on children 319
Leningrad University, clinical psychology 329
lesbian couples *see* homosexual couples
lesbian parents *see* homosexual parents
lesbianism
  adolescents 225
  blacks, studies 212
  community attitudes 189
  conceptualization 207
  definitions 209
  etiology 214
    genetic factors 214
  family issues 222
  human rights 208
  and mental health service utilization 218
  prevalence, United States 210
  self-disclosure 216
  see also male homosexuality
LGB sexual orientation *see* sexual orientation, lesbian, gay and bisexual
life change *see* life experiences
life cycle *see* life span
life expectancy, cultural differences 190
life experiences
  aged 189
  and family structure 189
  interracial persons 152, 156
life history *see* autobiography
life span, development, Africans 360
life span (duration) *see* life expectancy
lifestyle
  Bedouins 314
  hazardous 162
  and religion 238
  risk factors, human sex differences 162
  rural, personal adjustment 268
  rural–urban differences 258
  Taiwan 344
LISREL Structural Equations Program, in factor analysis 73
literalism, vs. symbolism 237
Lithuania
  Act of Independence 332
  "book-hawkers" 325
  clinical psychology 325
    access 334
    current issues 332
    historical background 328
    recognition 334
  and Czarist Russia 325
  historical background 325
  independence 331
  intelligentsia 326
  perestroika 331
  professional organizations 331, 332
  psychiatric hospitals 333

psychiatry, historical background 326
psychology, development 326
Soviet occupation, effects on psychology 327
Lithuanian Association for Application of Psychoanalysis, activities 332
Lithuanian Association of Group Psychotherapy, activities 332
Lithuanian Association for Humanistic Psychology, activities 332
Lithuanian Association of Hypnosis, activities 332
Lithuanian Psychotherapeutical Society, activities 332
Lithuanian Society of C. G. Jung Analytical Psychology, activities 332
Lithuanian Society of Psychotechnics and Vocational Guidance, establishment 326
Lithuanian Suicidological Association, activities 333
Lithuanian Union of Psychologists, establishment 331
living standards, rural–urban differences 258
locus of control *see* internal–external locus of control
longevity *see* life expectancy
lunatic asylums *see* psychiatric hospitals
lung cancer, human sex differences 162

machismo, in marriage 180
madhouses *see* psychiatric hospitals
major depression
case studies 295, 302
Minnesota Multiphasic Personality Inventory-II studies 281
prevalence, Taiwan 345
see also depression (emotion)
male homosexuality
adolescents 225
and brain structure 214
conceptualization 207
etiology, genetic factors 214
human rights 208
and mental health service utilization 218
prevalence, United States 210
self-disclosure 216
see also lesbianism
males *see* human males
managed care, in rural environments 272
management styles, African 341
Mandela, Nelson (1918–) 341
Maori
cultural safety 353
Declaration of Independence (1836) 350
family therapy 352
health model 354
identity 350
mental health 351
new approaches 351
psychological perspectives 349
psychology
and biculturalism 351
future trends 354
initiatives 353
research 352
self-determination 350
tribal structures 350
marginality, theories 145
marital relations
behavior theories 165
cross-cultural differences 197
cross-cultural studies 16
physical abuse 198
marital violence *see* family violence
marriage
common-law 180
cross-cultural age differences 179
cultural significance 177
and family life cycles 179
and financial status 179
health problems, human sex differences 162
as rite of passage 180
roles, cross-cultural differences 180
as status 180
see also arranged marriage; exogamous marriage; interracial marriage
marriage contracts, cross-cultural differences 180
marriage rites, cross-cultural differences 178
masculine gender role stress (MGRS), model 167
masculine gender role stress scale (MGRSS), applications 168
masculinity
characteristics 162
cross-cultural differences 95
and health care utilization 162
measures 209
mass media, images, of lesbian, gay and bisexual orientations 217
MAT *see* Metropolitan Achievement Test (MAT)
McCarthy Scales of Children's Abilities
factor analysis 75
predictive validity 83
MCT *see* multicultural counseling and therapy (MCT)
mean score differences, as test bias 60
Medicaid (US)
administration 264
rural population 263
meditation
and relaxation therapy 248
techniques 248
melancholia *see* major depression
men *see* human males
mental disorders
Arabs 315
Blacks, diagnosis 63
cultural explanations 45
natural 45
physical–medical 45
sociopsychological 45
supernatural 45
cultural invariance 45
etiology, Africans 358
and interpersonal relations 359
rural–urban differences 262
treatment, Taiwan 346
mental health
Arab nations 313
future trends 321
assessment
cultural factors 279
sub-Saharan Africa 362
effects of religion on 234
interventions, cross-cultural differences 266
Maori 351
prayer in 248
problems, human sex differences 171
and psychology, rural environments 267
and religion 234, 245
in rural environments 255
historical background 267
and witchcraft 358
mental health care
planning 263
training, for primary health care providers 266
mental health services
Arab nations 321
Asians 347
attitudes toward, cross-cultural differences 192
inconsistency 264
rural environments 263
access 264, 272
future trends 272
planning 264
public policy 264
specialty 263
utilization
lesbians 218
male homosexuals 218
minority groups 109, 263
refugees 178
rural environments 263
variability 264
mental hospitals *see* psychiatric hospitals
mental illness *see* mental disorders
mental illness (attitudes toward), Arabs 316
mental institutions *see* psychiatric hospitals
Mental Measurements Yearbook 58
mental stress *see* psychological stress
mestizo, use of term 149
meta-analysis, human sex difference studies 164
Metropolitan Achievement Test (MAT)
advantages 83
performance prediction 79
Metropolitan Readiness Test (MRT)
factor analysis 75
predictive validity 83
structure 75
Mexicans
childrearing practices 181
marriage roles, machismo 180
therapist preferences 106
MGRS *see* masculine gender role stress (MGRS)
MGRSS *see* masculine gender role stress scale (MGRSS)
migrant farm workers, North America 260
migration
and family life cycles 177, 178
see also immigration; rural to urban migration
mind–body *see* dualism

mining industry, South Africa 338
Minnesota Multiphasic Personality Inventories (MMPI)
  in cross-cultural studies 46
  cultural test bias studies 76
  translations 279
Minnesota Multiphasic Personality Inventory-II (MMPI-II)
  applications
    in international clinical settings 277
    multicultural 279
  clinical ratings, procedures 281
  computer-based report studies 280
    accuracy 289
    case studies 290
    diagnostic considerations 288
    interpersonal relations 283
    limitations 290
    statistical validity 282
    symptomatic patterns 283
    treatment considerations 288
  cross-cultural studies 279
  cultural test bias studies 76
  future research 310
  interpretation, automatic 280
  profiles 292
  studies, Asians 346
  test equivalence 279
Minnesota Psychotherapy Project 282
Minnesota Report, studies 281
minority, definitions 94
minority groups
  children, intelligence issues 144
  development, South Africa 339
  future research 114
  help-seeking behavior 192
  identity model 148, 150
  mental health service utilization 109, 263
  older adults, clinical intervention 201
  psychometrics, criticisms 59
  in psychotherapy research 112
  and religion 245
  treatment compliance 193
  vocational issues 115
  see also subcultural groups
Mixed Marriages Act (South Africa) 339
MMPI *see* Minnesota Multiphasic Personality Inventories (MMPI)
MMPI-II *see* Minnesota Multiphasic Personality Inventory-II (MMPI-II)
moderator variables 136
monoculturalism
  characteristics 341
  and organizations 337
  South Africa 338, 341
    maintenance strategies 339
mood disorders *see* affective disturbances
morality
  and clinical psychology 239
  and religion 237
  see also religious beliefs
morbidity, Arabs 318
mores *see* values
Morita therapy 115
Mormons, marital relations, cross-cultural studies 16
Moscow University, clinical psychology 329
MRT *see* Metropolitan Readiness Test (MRT)
Multicultural Awareness–Knowledge–Skills Survey 98
Multicultural Counseling Awareness Scale 98
Multicultural Counseling Inventory 98
multicultural counseling and therapy (MCT)
  historical background 94
  theories 94
    future research 114
  use of term 94
  see also cross-cultural treatment
multicultural psychology, education 363
multiculturalism
  Africans 358
  awareness, South Africa 337, 339, 340
  and counseling 44
  and diversity 337
  and religion 241, 249
  see also biculturalism; monoculturalism
multiple choice (testing method)
  cross-cultural studies 10
  test bias studies 67
muscle relaxation therapy *see* relaxation therapy
Muslims *see* Islam
mysticism, vs. religion 239
myths
  homosexuality 210
  and religion 237

NAACP *see* National Association for the Advancement of Colored People (NAACP) (US)
NAESP *see* National Association of Elementary School Principals (NAESP) (US)
Naikan therapy 115
NARTH *see* National Association for Research and Therapy of Homosexuality (NARTH)
National Association for the Advancement of Colored People (NAACP) (US) 58
  resolutions 58
National Association of Elementary School Principals (NAESP) (US) 58
National Association for Research and Therapy of Homosexuality (NARTH), activities 219
National Association for Rural Mental Health (US) 267
National Comorbidity Survey (NCS) 262, 265
National Education Association (NEA) (US) 58
National Institute of Mental Health (NIMH) (US) 267
  education programs 268
  Epidemiological Catchment Area (ECA), studies 262
National Institutes of Health (NIH) (US) 112
National Standing Committee on Bicultural Issues (NSCBI) (New Zealand) 352
nationalism, competitive 359
Native Americans *see* American Indians
native healing *see* treatment, traditional
Navajos, marital relations, cross-cultural studies 16
NCS *see* National Comorbidity Survey (NCS)
Ndoboa system 359
NEA *see* National Education Association (NEA) (US)
negative affectivity *see* affective disturbances
Netherlands, The, Minnesota Multiphasic Personality Inventory-II case studies 290
neurasthenic neurosis
  characterization 39
  as culture-related syndrome 39
  treatment, folk medicine 39
  use of term 40, 43
neurolinguistic programming (NLP), cross-cultural studies 102
neurophysiology, theories, Pavlovian 40
neuropsychology, Taiwan 346
neurosis
  Arabs 319
  see also anxiety disorders; neurasthenic neurosis; obsessive–compulsive neurosis
neuroticism
  Arabs 318
    human sex differences 319
neutrality (psychotherapeutic) *see* psychotherapeutic neutrality
New York State Office of Mental Health 271
New Zealand
  bicultural model development 351
  historical background 350
  psychology in
    historical background 350
    indigenous perspectives 349
  universities, Maori psychology courses 353
New Zealand Council of Nursing 353
New Zealand Psychological Society, National Standing Committee on Bicultural Issues (NSCBI) 352
Nigeria
  folk medicine 362
  human females, studies 361
Nigerians, widowhood, and stress 361
NIH *see* National Institutes of Health (NIH) (US)
NIMH *see* National Institute of Mental Health (NIMH) (US)
NLP *see* neurolinguistic programming (NLP)
nonverbal communication, cross-cultural differences 100
North America
  mental health, in rural environments 256
  migrant farm workers 260
  psychologists, credentialing 269
  rural environments, diversity 257
  rural to urban migration 256

social change 259
see also Canada; United States (US)
Norway
Minnesota Multiphasic Personality Inventory-II studies 282
accuracy 289
diagnostic considerations 288
interpersonal relations 283
statistical validity 283
symptomatic patterns 283
treatment considerations 288
nuclear family
and Hispanics 175
triangulation 176
nursing homes, in rural environments 262

obesity, as culture-bound syndrome 38
obsessions, case studies 302
obsessive–compulsive disorder (OCD) *see* obsessive–compulsive neurosis
obsessive–compulsive neurosis
Arabs 315
treatment, telemedicine 266
obsessive neurosis *see* obsessive–compulsive neurosis
occupations
classification 6
crisis, United States 258
rural environments 256, 259
rural population 257
see also agricultural occupations
OCD *see* obsessive–compulsive neurosis
Office of Rural Health Policy, telemedicine studies 266
old age *see* aged
older adults
definitions 190
family therapy 200
independence 190
racial and ethnic identity 189, 191
religious coping 234
rural environments, mental health 262
see also aged
oppression, and racial and ethnic attitudes 142
optimism, and religion 235
organizational psychology *see* industrial psychology
organizations
cultural identity, South Africa 337, 340
culture (anthropological) 129
diversity management psychological models, South Africa 335
and monoculturalism 337
see also professional organizations
outcomes research
cross-cultural 107
problems 108
overweight *see* obesity

Pacific Islanders, demography 128
Pakeha
breaches of Treaty of Waitangi 350
cultural identity 350
Palestine
mental disorders, studies 320
mental health services 321
somatization, prevalence 319
Palestinians
psychometrics 316
somatization 319
treatment studies 316
panic disorder, and *koro* 38
PANS *see* Pretty Amazing New Stuff (PANS)
paralinguistics, cross-cultural differences 103
paranoia, case studies 303
paraphilias *see* sexual deviations
paraprofessional personnel, in rural environments 269, 271
parent–child relations, cross-cultural differences 182
parental attitudes, to adolescents 185
parents
death, cross-cultural differences 189
illness, cross-cultural differences 189
new, family life cycles 181
see also homosexual parents; single parents
partner abuse, human sex differences 163
PASE, v. Hannon 54
path analysis, predictive validity bias studies 84
pathogenesis *see* etiology
patient attitudes *see* client attitudes
PD *see* panic disorder
Peabody Picture Vocabulary Test-Revised (PPVT-R)
cultural test bias studies 67
internal-consistency estimates 76
peer relations, cross-cultural differences 186
perestroika, effects, on Lithuania 331
personal accounts *see* autobiography
personal adjustment, to rural environments, education 268
personal narratives, in cross-cultural studies 111
personal space, use of term 100
personality
and psychosexual behavior 215
see also emotionality (personality); independence (personality); inhibition (personality)
personality assessment *see* personality measures
personality disorders
blacks 144
and cultural context 144
human sex differences 162
see also obsessive–compulsive neurosis; paranoia; schizophrenia
personality factors *see* personality traits
personality measures
applications, cross-cultural 279
computer-assisted 280
cultural test bias 53
future research 85
interpretation, automated 280
objective 277
see also Chinese Personality Assessment Inventory (CPAI); Minnesota Multiphasic Personality Inventories (MMPI); Minnesota Multiphasic Personality Inventory-II (MMPI-II)
personality traits
cross-cultural differences 360
factors affecting 103
and racial and ethnic identity 152
"ruralness" 269
personnel screening *see* job applicant screening
phenotypes, race 143
physical abuse
human sex differences 162
marital relations 198
pibloktoq, definition 37
placebo, antidepressant drug studies 242
Plain Old Telephone Service (POTS) 266
pluralism
definitions 94
in folk medicine 363
James on 234
and religion 241
Poland, clinical psychology 329
Poles, racial and ethnic identity 185
political divisions *see* geography
polygamy, cross-cultural differences 180
poor whites, South Africa 336
population
distribution, historical background 256
rural environments 256
see also aboriginal populations; rural population
population characteristics *see* demographic characteristics
Portuguese, sexual attitudes 187
posture, cross-cultural differences 102
POTS *see* Plain Old Telephone Service (POTS)
power, human sex differences 170
PPVT-R *see* Peabody Picture Vocabulary Test-Revised (PPVT-R)
prayer, in mental health 248
prediction, bias in 77
predictive validity
bias in 77
path analysis 84
prejudice, definitions 5
premarital intercourse, prevalence 187
premature death, human sex differences 162
Pretty Amazing New Stuff (PANS) 266
preventive medicine, human sex differences 162
primary health care
providers, mental health training 266
rural environments 265
problem-solving, strategies, in family therapy 196
problems, culture-related 44
professional–client relationship
with aged, and ethnic values 192
Arabs 322
and bilingualism 104
counselor–client similarity 106
cross-cultural differences 249
cultural issues 97, 193
ethnic matching 104
human sex differences 170
and language 100

and religion 241, 247
training
culture-general vs. culture specific 25
experiential 26
field trips 26
local culture exposure 26
programmed instruction 27
self-insight 26
professional ethics, cross-cultural studies 19
professional organizations, Lithuania 331, 332
progesterone, and health 166
programmed instruction
cultural assimilation 26
construction 28
professional–client relationship training 27
proxemics, cross-cultural differences 100
proximal variables
definition 95
studies 95
Prozac *see* fluoxetine
pseudoetics, in cross-cultural studies 13
psychiatric disorders *see* mental disorders
psychiatric hospitalization, human sex differences, Africans 360
psychiatric hospitals
Arab nations 320
Lithuania 333
private 263
psychiatry, sociocultural lexicon 36
psychological assessment, Taiwan 346
psychological disorders *see* mental disorders
psychological models, diversity management, South African organizations 335
psychological processes
definitions 4
testing, and bias 57
psychological stress
and health risks 166
human sex differences 166
psychological testing *see* psychometrics
psychologist attitudes, to cultural competence training 139
psychologists
credentialing 269
culturally-sensitive 191
as generalists 267
in rural environments 270
religiosity 235
religious beliefs, disclosure 247
roles, in rural environments 267
see also clinical psychologists
psychology
cross-cultural studies 352
methodological studies 110
outcomes 108
evolutionary 164
global 115
Maori and 352
and mental health, rural environments 267
moral nature of 239
in New Zealand, indigenous perspectives 349
professional, Lithuania 326
religious nature of 239
research, heterosexist bias 227
services, heterosexist bias 226
in South Africa, historical background 336
see also clinical psychology; developmental psychology; health care psychology; industrial psychology; neuropsychology
psychology education
heterosexist bias 226
for rural environments 268
curriculum 268
sub-Saharan Africa 363
psychology practice, heterosexist bias 227
psychometrics
applications, multicultural 279
Arabs 316
bias, issues 54
development 278
labeling effects 62
minority groups, criticisms 59
and religion 243
see also tests
psychopathology
choice of, cultural factors 45
cross-cultural 45, 360
research 47
and cross-cultural differences 25
cross-cultural studies 35, 310
future research 48
population surveys 46
cultural dimensions 47
and culture (anthropological) 44
dualism in 36
egocentrism in 36
sociocultural factors 361
Taiwan 344
and traditional communities 360
universalism vs. relativism 45
and urbanization, Africans 361
psychosexual behavior
cross-cultural differences 187
and personality 215
psychosis, Egypt 315
psychosocial development, cultural factors 193
psychosocial factors, human sex differences 162
psychosomatic disorders
human sex differences, Africans 360
and *koro* 38
and neurasthenic neurosis 40
psychotherapeutic neutrality, with homosexual clients 222
psychotherapist attitudes
to Arab clients 317
ethnic values 191
in family therapy 194, 196
to homosexuality 221
psychotherapists
Arab nations 321
human sex differences, Arab nations 317
racial preference 105
religiosity 246
psychotherapy
foreign language translation in 103
generic characteristics 99
homosexuality (attitudes toward) 209
human sex differences, Arabs 317
indigenous 111
insight, cultural differences 99
lesbian, gay and bisexual persons 219
religion in 246
religious techniques 248
research, minority groups in 112
theories, Arab 318
value convergence 246
see also group psychotherapy
psychotic disorders *see* mental disorders
puberty, rites 359
Puerto Rican Americans *see* Puerto Ricans
Puerto Ricans
attachment behavior 182
childrearing practices 181
Cuento therapy 108
marriage roles 180
treatment outcomes, research 108
punishment, cross-cultural differences 182, 192

QOL *see* quality of life (QOL)
QT *see* Quick Test (QT)
qualitative research
cross-cultural studies 111
see also autobiography; ethnography
quality of life (QOL), and religion 234
quantitative ability, human sex differences 163
questionnaires, and religious variables 244
Quick Test (QT), predictive validity 83
quinceaneras, cultural significance 177

race
definitions 94, 111, 141
differentiation processes 145
and ethnicity compared 142
markers 145
phenotypes 143
societal anxiety 156
United States 141
race attitudes *see* racial and ethnic attitudes
race differences *see* racial and ethnic differences
race relations *see* racial and ethnic relations
racial discrimination *see* racial and ethnic discrimination
racial and ethnic attitudes
and colonialism 142
historical background 143
and genocide 142
and oppression 142
racial and ethnic differences
demographic characteristics 151
differentiation processes 145
identity issues 142
intelligence measures 54
self-disclosure 337
sexual orientation 211
United States 22
see also cross-cultural differences; differentiation (racial)
racial and ethnic discrimination, factors 142
racial and ethnic identity 141

adolescents 156
aged 189, 191
autonomy 22
blacks 22, 145
clinical implications 155
and clinical training 23
construction 145
contact 22
development 144, 145, 183, 185
communication style 183
disintegration 22
ethnic psychological captivity stage 147
factors affecting 151
and family dynamics 156
heritage 148
human sex differences 156
influences
geographical 155
inherited 152, 155
issues 142
and labeling 142, 147
marginalization 156
markers 143
models 149, 155
bicultural 149
comparisons 150
contemporary 152
ecological 152, 155
multicultural 148
multidimensional 149
nigrescence 147, 150
orthogonal 149
psychological 149
stage 147, 150
transitional 149
typology 147
older adults 189, 191
orthogonal cultural identification theory 149
and personality traits 152
political consciousness 146
positive 184
pseudo-independence 22
racial pride movements 148
reintegration 22
rejection 156
and self-esteem 185
social context 153
stigma 142
studies 183, 188
theories 142, 147
United States 22
whites 22, 148
racial and ethnic issues
authenticity 146, 150
future trends 157
identity 141
insider–outsider attitudes 145
marginality 142
regional differences 155
self-identity 143
solidarity 145
strategies 151
United States, historical background 144
racial and ethnic relations, domestic service personnel 144
racial identity *see* racial and ethnic identity
racial issues *see* racial and ethnic issues
racial segregation
demographic effects 257
South Africa 339
racism
definitions 4
paternalistic models 144
stereotyped attitudes 147
Raven's Progressive Matrices, cultural test bias studies 67, 76
RCMAS *see* Revised Children's Manifest Anxiety Scale (RCMAS)
reciprocity, in extended family 359
reductionism, and negative differentiation, racial and ethnic issues 146
reference groups
cultural 133
and cultural competence 133
primary 135
secondary 135
within-group variability 136
refugees
children, launching 188
family therapy, genograms in 194
mental health service utilization 178
psychotherapy, use of interpreters 104
regional differences, racial and ethnic issues 155
regression analysis *see* statistical regression
reincarnation, belief in 359
relativism
and counseling 44
cross-cultural psychopathology 45
criticisms 46
relaxation therapy, and meditation 248
reliability (statistical) *see* statistical reliability
religion
behavioral dimensions 244
and clinical interviews 244
and clinical psychology 233
case studies 251
empirical research 245
future trends 250
and clinical research 248
cognitive differences 237
and community 238
definitions 234
and diagnosis 247
diversity issues 234, 236
training 249
doctrines 237
effects, on mental health 234
and ethics 237
and exclusivism 236, 241
extrinsic 235, 246
factor analysis 236
faith development 244
functional analysis 236, 247
and inclusivism 241
and institutionalization 238
intrinsic 235, 246
and lifestyle 238
and mental health 234
and minority groups 245
and morality 237
and multiculturalism 241, 249
multidimensionality 236
vs. mysticism 239
and myths 237
and optimism 235
and pluralism 241
and professional–client relationship 241, 247
psychology of 234, 243
and psychometrics 243
in psychotherapy 246
and quality of life 234
roles 244
sacred texts 237
and spirituality 239
world views 237
see also spirituality
religiosity
of clients 246
of psychologists 235
of psychotherapists 246
see also spirituality
religious beliefs
vs. clinical psychology 240
diversity 236
psychologists, disclosure 247
United States 234
see also ethics; morality; spirituality; witchcraft
religious commitment, dimensions of 243
religious coping
older adults 234
and stress 234
religious experiences 238
religious groups
authoritarian 236
diversity, United States 250
as support resource 248
see also Hinduism; Islam; Jews
religious individuals, and mental health 245
religious practices
cross-cultural differences 177
diversity 237
Koraan 318
see also faith healing; meditation; prayer
religious variables
measurement 243
Allport's approach 243
quest approach 243
and questionnaires 244
research
clinical, and religion 248
cultural capacity in 137
cultural proficiency in 137
see also outcomes research; qualitative research; social action research
researchers
leadership 138
role models 138
resilience (psychological) *see* hardiness
response sets, in cross-cultural studies 11
responsibility, locus of 96
return to home *see* empty nest
Revised Children's Manifest Anxiety Scale (RCMAS), cultural test bias studies 76
Riles, Larry v. 54
risk analysis, cross-cultural studies 19
rites (nonreligious)
family, cross-cultural differences 177
and family life cycles 177
zar 318
rites of passage
adulthood 360

marriage as 180
rituals (nonreligious) *see* rites (nonreligious)
rituals (religion) *see* religious practices
Roman Catholicism, baptism 177
rootwork, and blacks 177
Rorschach Inkblot Test *see* Rorschach Test
Rorschach Test, Arabs 316
Roseto (US), social studies 262
rural, definitions 256
rural communities *see* rural environments
rural environments
changes 260
economic 261
community mental health centers 265
definitions 256
demographic change 256
diversity 257
family relations 259
group psychotherapy in 271
health care reform 265
health issues 261
human females in 259
intervention, types of 269
mental health in 255
historical background 267
and psychology 267
mental health services
access 263, 264, 272
future trends 272
planning 264
public policy 264
non-farm employment 257
nursing homes in 262
occupations 259
paraprofessional personnel in 271
poor, mental health service access 263
practice
competence 272
ethical issues 271
primary health care 265
psychologist roles in 267
psychology education for 268
sex roles in 259
social cohesion in 261
social life 258
social structure 261
social support in 261
stress in 261
structure 256
telemedicine in 266
rural population
age patterns 257
educational level 257
factors affecting 256
occupations 257
Rural Social Work Caucus (US) 267
rural societies *see* rural environments
rural–urban differences
age profiles 257
educational level 257
housing 258
income level 258
lifestyle 258
living standards 258
mental disorders 262
population, blacks 257
poverty, ethnic groups 257
studies 258
rural to urban migration, North America 256
"ruralness," as personality trait 269
Russian Empire, and Lithuania 325

Samoans, family therapy 352
sampling (experimental)
cross-cultural studies 11
sexual orientation studies, problems 211
Santoria therapy 115
SAT *see* Scholastic Aptitude Test (SAT)
Saudi Arabia
client behavior, human sex differences 317
depression (emotion), studies 320
morbidity
human sex differences 319
studies 319
Scandinavians
aged, independence issues 190
parental caretakers 189
schizophrenia
Arabs 316, 319
case studies 303
core syndromes 46
cross-cultural differences 144
cross-cultural studies 46
Taiwan 344
Scholastic Aptitude Test (SAT), predictive validity 79
school performance, cross-cultural differences 186
schools, desegregation 144
segregation (racial) *see* racial segregation
selection tests
bias studies 64
goals 64
equal opportunity 64
equality of outcome 64
representative equality 64
self *see* self-concept
self-actualization, Arabs 323
self-attribution *see* self-concept
self-concept
adolescents 185
Africans 361
Arabs 315
cross-cultural differences 24
definitions 3
development, cross-cultural differences 182
and differentiation 145
ideal 145
positive 183
self-disclosure
human females 169
human sex differences 168
and immune function 169
racial and ethnic differences 337
sexual orientation 211
benefits 216
to children 225
cross-cultural differences 216
definitions 215
human sex differences 216, 225
risks 221
stages 220
stress 216
and stereotyped attitudes 337
self-esteem
and racial and ethnic identity 185
studies 183
self-fulfilling prophecies, human sex differences 165
self-identity, racial and ethnic issues 143
self-sufficiency, in rural environments 259
senescence *see* aged
senior citizens *see* aged
sentence completion tests, case studies 292
separation–individuation
age-appropriate 197
cross-cultural differences 199
family life cycles 185
single young adults 188
sex
use of term 162
see also gender
sex differences *see* human sex differences
sex hormones, and health, human sex differences 166
sex issues, clinical psychology 161
sex roles
Africans 360
cross-cultural differences 186, 210
cross-cultural studies 166
and family life cycles 189
and family therapy 200
homosexual couples 224
ideology 166
in rural environments 259
and stress 165, 167
faulty gender-determined appraisals 167
and stress management 168
theories 165
sexual abuse, human sex differences 162
sexual activity, adolescents 199
sexual attitudes, cross-cultural differences 186
sexual behavior *see* psychosexual behavior
sexual deviations, human sex differences 163
sexual disorders (physiological) *see* genital disorders
sexual dysfunction *see* sexual function disturbances
sexual function disturbances, Arabs 320
sexual identity (gender) *see* gender identity
sexual orientation 207
assumptions 207
atypical, inhibition 210
awareness 215
adolescents 215
and brain function 214
concealment 220
conceptualization
historical background 207
issues 209
cross-cultural differences 189
definitions 207
issues 209
Western cultures 209
demographic characteristics 210
determination 221
future research 228
lesbian, gay and bisexual 207
acknowledgement 211

definitions 209
developmental problems 215
etiology 213
family issues 222
hardiness 217
identification problems 210
identity development 216
mass media images 217
mental health concerns 218
mental health service utilization 218
myths 210
pathology model 219
psychodynamic theories 213
psychological problems 215
psychotherapy 219
self-concept 210
self-disclosure 211
stigma 209
perspectives
essentialist 210
international 212
social constructivist 210
racial and ethnic differences 211
self-disclosure 211, 215
risks 221
studies
generalizations 212
sampling problems 211
see also gender identity; heterosexuality; homosexuality; lesbianism; male homosexuality
sexual selection, evolutionary factors 165
sexual stereotypes, studies 166
sexuality
cross-cultural differences 186
see also heterosexuality; homosexuality; male homosexuality
shenjing shuairuo, use of term 39
single parents, in rural environments 259
single persons, home leaving 188
skills *see* ability
Slosson Intelligence Test, predictive validity 83
Slosson Oral Reading Test, predictive validity 83
social action research, and cultural proficiency 128
social cognition, proximal variables 95
social cohesion, in rural environments 261
social constructivism, theories, of sexual orientation 210
social context, racial and ethnic identity 153
social dating
cross-cultural differences 186
interethnic 186, 189
interfaith 186, 189
interracial 186, 189
social identity, and cultural assimilation 21
social life, rural environments 258
social rules, cross-cultural differences 182
social structure, rural environments 261
social support
human sex differences 169
in rural environments 261
social support networks, and stress 169
sociocultural beliefs, sub-Saharan Africa 358
sociocultural factors
distal variables 96
emotional trauma, Africans 360
in psychopathology 361
rural environments 256
socioeconomic groups, Arab nations 314
socioeconomic status
and bias 63
and childrearing practices 182
sodium valproate, applications, case studies 298
somatization
Arabs 315, 317, 319, 321, 322
as category fallacy 41
Chinese 345
cultural assumptions 41
definitions 42
as idiom of distress 43
as illness experience 42
and neurasthenic neurosis 40
Palestinians 319
and suffering 42
Taiwanese 345
somatization disorders *see* psychosomatic disorders
somatoform disorders *see* psychosomatic disorders
South Africa
affirmative action
constructive 340
restorative 339
restrictive 339
Afrikaans (language), in schools 338
apartheid
historical background 336, 338
laws 339
psychological research 336
clinical psychologists, roles 336
diversity
aspects of 336
development 336
diversity management
programs 340
psychological models 335
training 340
employment strategies 339
firearm ownership 338
government of national unity 339
"homestead," demand for 338
industrial psychology 336
roles 340
lesbianism, studies 212
management styles 341
mining industry 338
minority rights 338
monoculturalism 338, 341
multiculturalism, awareness 337, 339, 340
organizations
cultural exclusion 338
cultural identity 337, 340
diversity management 335
poor whites 336
psychology, historical background 336
racial segregation 339
as "rainbow nation" 336
state control 338
Truth and Reconciliation Commission 340
ubuntu philosophy 341
whites, homelessness 335
Spanish Americans *see* Hispanics
spatial ability, human sex differences 163, 164
special education, placement recommendations, bias studies 63
spirit possession phenomena (SPP), Taiwan 344
spiritual healing *see* faith healing
spirituality
Africans 358
and clinical psychology 233
definitions 239
and religion 239
see also religion; religiosity; religious beliefs
spouse abuse *see* partner abuse
SPP *see* spirit possession phenomena (SPP)
Stanford–Binet Intelligence Scale
cultural test bias studies 68
regression analysis 82
translations 85
state hospitals *see* psychiatric hospitals
statistical regression, homogeneity 78
statistical reliability
cross-cultural studies 109
internal-consistency estimates 75
statistical validity
criterion-related 77
cross-cultural studies 109
differential 65
single-group 65
see also construct validity; content validity; face validity; predictive validity
stereotyped attitudes
concept of 131
homosexual couples 224
racism 147
and self-disclosure 337
stigma
homosexuality 208
racial and ethnic identity 142
Strayhorn, William Thomas ("Billy") (1915–67), sexual orientation studies 217
stress
agricultural occupations 259
appraisal 167
cross-cultural differences 144
culture-produced 44
early studies 166
extrafamilial 177
future research 170
and infertility, Africans 360
intrafamilial 177
and religious coping 234
in rural environments 261
and self-disclosure 216
and sex roles 165, 167
vulnerability
biological 166
cognitive 167
culture-inherited 45
and widowhood, Nigerians 361
see also psychological stress
stress management
and aggression 167
dysfunctional coping styles 168

human sex differences 162
and sex roles 168
sub-Saharan Africa
clinical psychology 357
cross-cultural differences 357
cultural competence training 363
folk medicine 358
mental health
assessment 362
education 363
research 363
sociocultural factors 357
psychology education
assessment measures 363
graduate programs 363
psychopathology, and traditional communities 360
sociocultural beliefs 358
subcultural groups
characteristics 131
and cultural competence 130
see also minority groups
substance abuse *see* drug abuse
Sudan, depression (emotion) studies 315
suicidal ideation, case studies 302
suicide
attempt to completion ratio, human sex differences 168
prevalence, rural environments 262
see also attempted suicide
Suoyang, definition 38
supernatural beliefs, Africans 358
superstitions, Arabs 316
support
religious groups as resource for 248
see also social support
support givers *see* caregivers
susto, definition 38
symbolism, vs. literalism 237
sympathetic nervous system, arousal, factors affecting 169
synergy, cross-cultural studies 21
taha Maori, in psychology training programs 352

Taiwan
clinical psychology 343
development 346
future trends 347
collectivism 344
depression (emotion) 345
family role 345
family structure 344
health care psychology 346
lifestyle 344
major depression, prevalence 345
mental disorders, treatment 346
neuropsychology 346
political change 344
psychological assessment 346
psychopathology 344
schizophrenia 344
spirit possession phenomena 344
treatment, models 347
values 344
Taiwanese
expressed emotion 345
somatization 345
Te Piriti Special Treatment Unit (New Zealand) 354
teenage pregnancy *see* adolescent pregnancy
telemedicine
policy issues 267
in rural environments 266
studies 266
temperament *see* personality
Terman, Lewis Madison (1877–1956), Stanford–Binet Intelligence Scale development 85
test bias
achievement tests 66
definitions 64, 65
issues 53
mean score differences as 60
Test of Memory and Learning (TOMAL), test bias studies 68
test scores, computerized 280
testosterone, and health 166
tests
in cross-cultural studies 16
foreign language translation of, validity issues 56
see also culture fair intelligence tests; psychometrics; selection tests; sentence completion tests
Texans, marital relations, cross-cultural studies 16
texts
sacred 237
absolute authority 242
Thailand, culture (anthropological) 7
theology *see* religion
therapeutic outcomes *see* treatment outcomes
therapeutic processes, in folk medicine 363
therapist characteristics, in family therapy 193
therapist effectiveness, and racial and ethnic identity 23
therapists
credibility 96
culturally-sensitive 97, 191
culture shock 24
see also psychotherapists
therapy *see* treatment
thought control *see* brainwashing
Thurstone scales, in cross-cultural studies 14
Tierra del Fuego, *mamihlapinatapei*, concept of 12
time
monochronic 103
polychronic 103
Tokanui Hospital (New Zealand), Maori mental health studies 354
TOMAL *see* Test of Memory and Learning (TOMAL)
traditional healing *see* folk medicine
transcultural psychiatry, development 36
translation (foreign language) *see* foreign language translation
trauma (emotional) *see* emotional trauma
treatment
in folk medicine 363
mental disorders, Taiwan 346
traditional 115
Arabs 316, 320
see also cross-cultural treatment; family therapy; group psychotherapy; psychotherapy; relaxation therapy
treatment adherence *see* treatment compliance
treatment compliance, minority groups 193
treatment dropouts, minority groups 193
treatment outcomes
definitions 107
and ethnicity 112
research 107
cross-cultural 107
studies, cross-cultural 108
treatment termination, family therapy, cross-cultural differences 193
Treaty of Waitangi (1840)
bicultural perspectives 349
breaches 350
historical background 350
Treaty of Waitangi Act (1975) 351
Truth and Reconciliation Commission (South Africa) 340
ubuntu, philosophy 341

Union of Soviet Socialist Republics (USSR) (former)
clinical psychology 329
occupation, of Lithuania 327
United Arab Emirates
anxiety 320
depression (emotion) 320
morbidity studies 319
United Kingdom (UK)
cross-cultural counseling 103
test bias, issues 53
United States (US)
baby boomers 141
Bill of Rights 144
blacks, cultural beliefs 358
Bureau of the Census 151
definitions 256
civil rights movement 144
Constitution 144
cross-cultural studies 11
cultural assimilation 184
cultural syndromes, studies 8
demographic change, and cultural competence 128
demographics 256
ethnicity 141
family, definitions 175
interracial marriage 181
lesbianism, prevalence 210
male homosexuality, prevalence 210
mental health care, rural environments 263
mental health services, specialty 263
Minnesota Multiphasic Personality Inventory-II studies 282
accuracy 289
case studies 298
diagnostic considerations 288
interpersonal relations 283
statistical validity 283
symptomatic patterns 283
treatment considerations 288
psychometrics, development 278
race 141
race and ethnic differences 22
racial and ethnic identity 22
racial and ethnic issues, historical background 144
religious beliefs 234

religious groups, diversity 250
rural environments
mental health care 263
population 256
social distance, studies 14
social solidarity, decline 262
test bias, issues 53
universalism
and counseling 44
cross-cultural psychopathology 45
criticisms 46
University Centre for Children with Developmental Disorders (Vilnius), establishment 333
urban environments
definitions 256
service provision 256
urban–rural differences *see* rural–urban differences
urbanization
Africans 358
Arab nations 314
and psychopathology, Africans 361

Vail Conference (1973) (US), cross-cultural counseling, ethics 112
validity *see* statistical validity
values
convergence, in psychotherapy 246
cross-cultural studies 95
structure 95
Taiwan 344
see also ethnic values
variables
culture-specific 95
universal 95
see also distal variables; moderator variables; proximal variables; religious variables
verbal ability, human sex differences 163
verbal communication, cross-cultural 100
Verwoerd, Hendrik Freusch (1901–66), apartheid development 336
Vietnamese
divorce 180
treatment outcomes, research 108
Vilnius Psychoneurological Hospital 329
Vilnius University 326
clinical psychology 328
graduates 331
Department of Psychology 328
reforms 332
Voodoo therapy 115

Waikato University (New Zealand), courses 353
war
children, Arab Nations 319
see also World War I; World War II
Wechsler Intelligence Scale for Children (WISC) 63
Arab studies 316
cultural test bias studies, factor analysis 73
Wechsler Intelligence Scale for Children-Revised (WISC-R)
Arab studies 323
cultural test bias studies 66, 68, 71
expert judgments 69
factor analysis 73
internal-consistency estimates 76
predictive validity 79
Wechsler Intelligence Scale for Children-Third Edition (WISC-III), cultural test bias studies 70
Wechsler Preschool and Primary Scale of Intelligence-Revised (WPPSI-R)
cultural test bias studies
expert judgments 68
factor analysis 75
weddings *see* marriage rites
West Indians
cohabitation 180
divorce 180
marriage, as status 180
whites
adult offspring, launching 188
childrearing practices 181
exogamous marriage 181
firearm ownership, South Africa 338
homelessness, South Africa 335
intelligence measures 54
racial and ethnic identity 22, 148
stages 22, 148
superiority 148
therapist preferences 106
see also poor whites
wholeness *see* holistic approaches
widowhood, and stress, Nigerians 361
WISC-R *see* Wechsler Intelligence Scale for Children-Revised (WISC-R)
wiswas, Arab beliefs 316
witchcraft
Africans 358
and ancestors 358, 362
see also faith healing; religious beliefs
women *see* human females
Wonderlic Personnel Test
cultural test bias studies 66, 68
expert judgment 69
internal-consistency estimates 76
World Health Organization (WHO), *International classification of diseases (ICD-10) see International classification of diseases (ICD-10)*
world views
clinical psychology 6
cultural perspectives 5
Eurocentric, criticisms 360
in folk medicine 362
methodologies 9
psychology education 363
religion 237
World War I, Lithuania, post-war development 326
World War II, Lithuania, emigrants 327
WPPSI-R *see* Wechsler Preschool and Primary Scale of Intelligence-Revised (WPPSI-R)

young adults
coaching 200
conflicts 189
independence 188
single, home leaving 188, 200
social dating 189
youth *see* adolescents
Youth Psychological Aid Centre (YPAC) (Vilnius), establishment 333
zar, rites (nonreligious) 318

Zulus, greetings 340